Understanding Sport Organizations

The Application of Organization Theory

Second Edition

Trevor Slack, PhD
University of Alberta

Milena M. Parent, PhD
University of Ottawa

Human Kinetics

Library of Congress Cataloging-in-Publication Data

Slack, Trevor, 1948-
  Understanding sport organizations : the application of organization
theory / Trevor Slack, Milena M. Parent.-- 2nd ed.
       p. cm.
  Includes bibliographical references and index.
  ISBN 0-7360-5639-4 (hard cover)
  1. Sports administration--Handbooks, manuals, etc. 2. Organizational
sociology--Handbooks, manuals, etc. I. Parent, Milena M. II. Title.
  GV713.S576 2006
  796'.06'9--dc22

                                    2005019202

ISBN: 978-0-7360-5639-7

The Web addresses cited in this text were current as of October, 2005, unless otherwise noted.

Acquisitions Editor: Myles Schrag; **Developmental Editor:** Maggie Schwarzentraub; **Assistant Editors:** Maureen Eckstein and Carla Zych; **Copyeditor:** Nancy Humes; **Proofreader:** Kathy Bennett; **Indexer:** Gerry Lynn Messner; **Permission Manager:** Dalene Reeder; **Graphic Designer:** Fred Starbird; **Graphic Artist:** Dawn Sills; **Photo Manager:** Sarah Ritz; **Cover Designer:** Jack W. Davis; **Photographer (interior):** © Human Kinetics, unless otherwise noted; **Art Manager:** Kelly Hendren; **Illustrator:** Craig Newsom; **Printer:** Total Printing Systems

Printed in the United States of America.   10

The paper in this book is certified under a sustainable forestry program.

Human Kinetics
Web site: www.HumanKinetics.com

United States: Human Kinetics
P.O. Box 5076
Champaign, IL 61825-5076
800-747-4457
e-mail: info@hkusa.com

Canada: Human Kinetics
475 Devonshire Road, Unit 100
Windsor, ON N8Y 2L5
800-465-7301 (in Canada only)
e-mail: info@hkcanada.com

Europe: Human Kinetics
107 Bradford Road
Stanningley
Leeds LS28 6AT, United Kingdom
+44 (0)113 255 5665
e-mail: hk@hkeurope.com

Australia: Human Kinetics
57A Price Avenue
Lower Mitcham, South Australia 5062
08 8372 0999
e-mail: info@hkaustralia.com

New Zealand: Human Kinetics
P.O. Box 80
Mitcham Shopping Centre, South Australia 5062
0800 222 062
e-mail: info@hknewzealand.com

E3343

Contents

Foreword

It is with great pleasure that I am writing this foreword to the second edition of Dr. Trevor Slack's book *Understanding Sport Organizations: The Application of Organizational Theory*. Dr. Slack is one of the most highly respected and prolific scholars in sport management internationally, and the previous edition of this book marked a seminal contribution to our field. The book was the first of its kind to apply organizational theory to sport management, filling a noticeable gap in our knowledge base by drawing on the vast and stimulating literature in management studies. Dr. Slack clearly demonstrated how the broader management literature could inform and advance our understanding of sport organizations, and at the same time he showed how they serve as useful illustrative examples for understanding and asking questions about complex concepts such as power and politics, organizational structure and culture, and organizational change.

Dr. Slack overcame considerable adversity to write this second edition along with Milena Parent. Those of us who know him admire his courage, strength, and tenacity and wish him all the best in his continued recovery from a very serious illness. We are most fortunate that Dr. Slack is once again able to contribute to the field that he is so passionate about. I feel privileged to be able to learn more from his considerable grasp of the broader management literature, the sport management research being produced internationally, and the contemporary examples and events shaping the world of sport through the reading of this book. Dr. Slack has served as the editor of the *Journal of Sport Management* and the *European Sport Management Quarterly* and authored dozens of articles and book chapters. He has been invited to be a keynote speaker at conferences in many countries around the world. His contributions have been acknowledged through numerous awards including the Earle F. Zeigler Award, the highest scholarly award presented by the North American Society for Sport Management (NASSM). Dr. Slack was also appointed as a Tier 1 Research Chair in Canada, the only sport management scholar to be so honored. Based on these and many other credentials, Dr. Slack is eminently qualified to be an author of this book.

I have used *Understanding Sport Organizations: The Application of Organizational Theory* as a textbook in a course I teach at the University of British Columbia. I welcome this updated edition that is sure to stimulate more vigorous discussion and intellectual debate in the classroom. Students have found that the material resonates with their own experiences as athletes, volunteers, or employees in sport organizations, and it encourages them to think about how they could do things better when they enter the workforce. Students find the learning objectives at the beginning of each chapter useful, the Time Out sections help them apply concepts, and the review questions at the end of each chapter encourage critical thinking. For those students interested in graduate studies, the book provides a foundation that connects theory, method, and practice in a number of important ways.

Dr. Slack is skilled at making complex theoretical material understandable, accessible, and applicable through the use of a variety of sport-related examples. Dr. Slack does not rely only on sport settings that we might be most familiar with, like professional sport, because his detailed and carefully researched examples span the public, nonprofit, and commercial sectors.

In this highly readable and informative second edition, Dr. Slack and Dr. Parent draw on new literature and provide several current illustrations from an array of sport organizations globally that make the subject matter come alive. Dr. Slack and Dr. Parent are careful to explain how organizational theory (OT) differs from but is related to organizational behavior (OB), and they provide readers with a number of convincing arguments as to how an in-depth understanding of organizational theory can help people become better sport managers.

The book covers a range of topics and the two new chapters are timely and important additions. Chapter 7 deals with strategic alliances, reflecting the reality that few sport organizations operate in isolation or survive with an internal focus. To pool resources and achieve mutually desired goals, sport managers are partnering with other organizations, presenting a number of challenges that must be carefully managed. In chapter 2,

Dr. Slack and Dr. Parent describe the research process and some of the issues tackled and techniques used by sport management researchers. The addition of this chapter provides readers with foundational information that they can use to understand research-based articles they are reading, to conduct research in their own organizations to improve organizational decision making, or to embark on research projects if they decide to pursue graduate studies.

Another key strength of the book is the bibliography that draws on classic and current research in organizational management as well as sport management. Dr. Slack and Dr. Parent encourage readers to read extensively and to go to the original sources for more information. They are also aware that women and other groups remain underrepresented in senior sport management positions, and they have made an effort to promote diversity through the examples and language he has used.

I highly recommend *Understanding Sport Organizations: The Application of Organizational Theory*. The book is a must-have for all sport management students, faculty members, and managers. The book charts new territory, opens up new ways of thinking about sport organizations, and highlights the potential that the sport management field holds.

Wendy Frisby, PhD
Chair, women's studies
Associate professor, human kinetics
The University of British Columbia

Preface

In the early 1980s, when I began my doctoral studies in the area of sport management, I started to read the books that were being written about this relatively new area of study. Although there were only a few sport management texts at this time, I became increasingly frustrated with those that did exist because, with very few exceptions, they failed to take account of the vast body of literature available in the broader field of management studies. Why, I wondered, did scholars in the field of sport management fail to utilize work from such areas as organizational theory, organizational behavior, strategic management, marketing, the sociology of organizations, finance, and accounting? Don't sport organizations have cultures? Are they not expected to formulate strategies? Are their operations not influenced by technological and contextual changes? And do they not exhibit the same political and decision-making processes as other types of organizations? The answer to each of these questions is, obviously, "Yes!"

Over the last 15 to 20 years, however, a number of researchers in our field *have* become increasingly aware of the contribution that the literature from the areas just cited can make to our understanding of the structure and operations of sport organizations. The formation of the North American Society of Sport Management and the creation of the *Journal of Sport Management* have helped tremendously in this regard. However, despite these advances, a significant amount of the literature in sport management still shows little evidence of being informed by work in the broader field of management studies. *Understanding Sport Organizations: The Application of Organizational Theory* is a modest attempt to correct this situation.

The first edition of this book was well received and thus indicates the need for sport managers to understand the concepts of organizational theory. Milena Parent came on board as a coauthor for the second edition of this text, which is similar in format to the first edition but includes a chapter on research in sport management (chapter 2) and a chapter on strategic alliances (chapter 7), a new form of organizing both outside and within the sport industry.

The book presents the seminal works on various topics relevant to sport management. Although these works can seem dated, they are in fact very relevant today. Current examples are presented to illustrate their relevance.

Chapter 1 deals with some of the basic concepts of organizational theory and, to a lesser degree, organizational behavior. There we describe some different ways of looking at organizations and how the view sport managers adopt will influence what they see. Chapter 2 gives a basic description of how to do research in sport management. Students are encouraged not to rely on this chapter but to look at good articles on the subject or to refer to the methods in books mentioned in the chapter. In chapter 3 the focus is on the concept of effectiveness, which in many ways is the central problem of the sport manager. We review the major theoretical approaches to understanding effectiveness and show how the concept of effectiveness is paradoxical. Chapters 4 and 5 are devoted to the issues of structure and design: different structural elements and, hence, different designs. Some designs are more effective for certain types of sport organizations than for others, so we describe how structural elements are patterned into the various design types available. Certain determinants, such as strategy, environment, and technology, greatly influence the choice of an organization's design, and those are the topics of chapters 6, 8, and 9. In chapter 10, we take a less deterministic approach and look at power and politics in sport organizations and the role each may play in shaping the structure and operation of a sport organization.

Chapters 11 through 13 focus on some of the processes that take place in sport organizations, including managing conflict, implementing change, and making decisions. Chapters 14 and 15 deal with issues of culture and leadership.

We've provided numerous examples throughout the book to illustrate the concepts and ideas being discussed. The examples are taken from the variety of organizations that collectively make up the sport industry. All examples are from real organizations; in just a few cases the names of the organization or individuals involved have been changed to maintain confidentiality. In addition each chapter contains tips for managers that draw on ideas contained in the chapter.

We've provided several elements in each chapter that will help students bring the theoretical information into the practical realm. In addition, instructors may also use the cases that appear at the end of each chapter for class discussion and may develop questions other than those that accompany the case studies. The utility of several of the cases as topics for discussion is not necessarily limited to the focus of the chapter in which they appear. For example, the case on the Athens Olympics appears at the end of chapter 3 to raise issues about the effectiveness of organizations, but it also draws attention to issues of power, politics, and culture, which are the topics of chapters 10 and 14, respectively. In addition to the cases, the Time Outs that appear throughout the chapters may be used for discussion about how the concepts in the chapters are used in the real world. The questions at the end of the chapters provide an opportunity for a self-check of your understanding of the material.

Understanding Sport Organization: The Application of Organization Theory, Second Edition, contains a very detailed bibliography that includes citations from articles from the field of sport management as well as references to the organizational and management literature. Citations include articles that have appeared in such major journals as *Organization Studies, Administrative Science Quarterly, Journal of Management Studies, Academy of Management Journal,* and *Academy of Management Review.* References to the seminal works in the field are outlined in each chapter, as are more recent articles of quality that have built on these

earlier concepts and frameworks. Students and faculty members interested in a particular topic are advised not to rely solely on the summaries found in this text. Return to the original works and search the journals cited and others for more information. The suggestions for further reading at the end of each chapter are merely illustrative and should by no means be considered a definitive listing. We've cited only material that would be available in any reasonably sized university library. We've included very few references to many unpublished theses that have focused on managerial issues in sport organizations because they are not readily accessible to students and instructors.

We have tried to be conscious of maintaining a gender balance. However, when citing quotes we retained the original pronouns. Where possible, we've used examples involving female managers; however, these are not as widely available as examples of male managers. That is something we hope the readers of this text will strive to rectify.

Sport management is an exciting, new, and rapidly growing area of study. It is our hope that the second edition of this text will assist with this growth and will spotlight for students and instructors the idea that if we are going to realize the potential our field holds, our work must be informed by the ideas and theories found in the broader field of management and organization studies. We welcome any comments on the appropriateness of this text in helping achieve this goal.

Acknowledgments

About three years ago I suffered an aneurysm. Consequently, those who have supported my writing this book have become very important to me.

I would like to acknowledge my therapy team: Dr. Tammy Hopper, Stuart Cleary, Debbie Steadward, and Dr. Henriëtte Groeneveld. Most of all I would like to acknowledge my wife, Janet, who has supported and loved me through this whole experience. Without Janet's help this book would never have been started, never mind completed.

My two daughters, Chelsea and Meghan, have given me support and strength by pursuing their own academic pursuits so successfully.

Finally, Milena Parent has not only been an excellent coauthor but also someone who has supported me unconditionally. She is a valued colleague.

Trevor Slack, PhD

For my part, I am indebted to my supervisor, sport management mentor and coauthor of this book, Dr. Trevor Slack, who has demonstrated to me the necessity of having strong theoretical foundations for any sport management research that I undertake.

As well, Dr. David Deephouse, the source of my knowledge in strategy, deserves an award for being so patient with my seemingly endless questions about strategy and the research process in management, all these from a person who came into the PhD business program as a rookie in the social sciences.

Last but most important, *mille fois merci* to my parents, Ingrid Tepesh Parent and Marc Parent, and to my brother, Louis-Martin Parent, for sharing the ups and downs of writing a textbook—and of the PhD program in general. Their faith in my abilities has meant the world to me, especially that provided from afar.

Milena M. Parent, PhD

Acknowledgments

About three years ago I suffered a concussion. Consequently, those who have supported my writing this book have become very important to me.

I would like to acknowledge my therapy from Dr. Fanny Hopper, Stuart Chaney, Debbie Stedward, and Dr. Henriette Groeneveld. Above all, I would like to acknowledge my... who supported and lived me through this whole... which is not an easy thing to do. I would also like to acknowledge my... My two children, Jade-a and Magh-in, have given me support and strength by pursuing their own academic pursuits so successfully.

Finally, Milena Parent has not only been an excellent coauthor but also someone who has supported me unconditionally. She is a valued colleague.

Trevor Slack, PhD

For my part, I am indebted to my supervisor, sport management mentor and coauthor of this book, Dr. Trevor Slack, who has demonstrated to me the necessity of having a solid theoretical foundations for any sport management research undertaking.

As well, Dr. David Whitson... the strategy...
...to progress with my research endeavors,
...about... and the...
development of... is a person who...
...the PhD business program as a rookie in the social sciences.

Last but most important, while first merit to my parents, Ingrid Papas, Parent and Max. Parent, and to my brother Louis Martin Parent, for sharing the ups and downs of writing a textbook — and of the PhD program in general. Their faith in my abilities has meant the world to me, especially that provided from afar.

Milena M. Parent, PhD

Chapter 1

Organization Theory and the Management of Sport Organizations

LEARNING OBJECTIVES

When you have read this chapter, you should be able to

1. explain why it is important for sport managers to understand organizations,

2. define what we mean when we talk about a sport organization,

3. explain the terms organizational structure, design, and context,

4. distinguish between organizational theory and organizational behavior,

5. explain the different ways of looking at sport organizations, and

6. discuss the types of research studies dominating the field of sport management.

THE NIKE STORY

Most of you have probably walked through your local sporting goods store and seen the variety of athletic shoes lining the shelves and display units—shoes for football, running, tennis, golf, basketball, aerobics, cycling, windsurfing, cheerleading, and a whole range of other sport activities. The shoes, each with its own distinctive logo, come in bright colors, with added high-tech attractions such as HydroFlow, gel, and the Energy Return System.

One of the major producers of athletic footwear, with 2002 sales of over $10 billion (U.S.), is a company called Nike, with corporate head-quarters in Beaverton, Oregon. *Forbes* magazine identified Nike's president, chairman, and chief executive officer, Philip Knight, as the 53rd-richest man in the world at a net worth $7.1 billion in 2004. But Nike has not always been a large multimillion-dollar organization. In fact, Knight started the company by selling shoes from the back of his station wagon at track meets.

In the late 1950s Philip Knight was a middle-distance runner on the University of Oregon track team, coached by Bill Bowerman. One of the top track coaches in the United States, Bowerman was also known for experimenting

(continued)

(continued)

Visitors to Niketown in Chicago will find a retail experience totally devoted to the Nike brand.

with the design of running shoes in an attempt to make them lighter and more shock-absorbent. After attending Oregon, Knight moved on to do graduate work at Stanford University; his MBA thesis was on marketing athletic shoes. Once he received his degree, Knight traveled to Japan to contact the Onitsuka Tiger Company, a manufacturer of athletic shoes. Knight convinced the company's officials of the potential for its product in the United States. In 1963 he received his first shipment of Tiger shoes, 200 pairs in total.

In 1964, Knight and Bowerman contributed $500 each to form Blue Ribbon Sports, the small company that later became Nike. In the first few years, Knight worked for an accounting firm and later as an assistant professor of business administration at Portland State University. He distributed shoes from his father's basement and out of his car at local and regional track meets. The first employees hired by Knight were former college athletes, mainly from the University of Oregon. The company did not have the money to hire "experts," and there was no established athletic footwear industry in North America from which to recruit those knowledgeable in the field. In its early years the organization operated in a freewheeling, unconventional manner that characterized its innovative and

entrepreneurial approach to the industry. Communication was informal; people discussed ideas and issues in the hallways, on a run, or over a beer. There was little task differentiation, and some people moved from one job in the organization to another; what coordination was required was done informally by the senior managers. There were no job descriptions, rigid reporting systems, or detailed rules and regulations. The team spirit and shared values that were developed as athletes on Bowerman's teams carried over and provided the basis for the collegial style of management that characterized the early years of Nike.

When in the late 1960s and 1970s running became fashionable, Oregon became the running capital of the world. As a result, Blue Ribbon Sports grew: Revenues increased from $8,000 in 1964 to nearly $300,000 in 1969 and $3.2 million in 1973. As the organization grew, its nature started to change. In 1965 its first full-time employee was hired; by 1969 it had 20 employees and several retail outlets. In 1971 it started to manufacture its own shoe line; the swoosh logo and new company name Nike were created. In 1972 Nike introduced the famous waffle sole, developed by Bowerman, who poured rubber into a kitchen waffle iron. During the 1970s manufacturing facilities were opened in the United States, Korea, and Taiwan; top athletes signed contracts to wear Nike products and the number of employees rose to nearly 3,000. By 1980, Nike controlled almost 50 percent of the athletic footwear market.

Today, Nike's structure and the way it operates are considerably different from the organization Knight originated from the back of his car and his father's basement. As the company grew and more people were hired, jobs became more specialized. The organization now has 37 units, 24 of which deal with footwear. With increased size and complexity, the informal style of operating was no longer efficient. More formalized management systems had to be introduced: Meetings at all levels of management were held with relative frequency, the coordinating roles of managers were more formally established, planning systems were used to integrate related job functions, and policies and procedures were introduced to standardize operating practices.

Not surprisingly, Nike lost some of the team spirit that characterized its early operations. Units became compartmentalized, and some managers expressed concern about the lack of communication among the different levels of the organization. Professionally trained man-

agers now head departments concerned with areas such as international marketing, sales, finance, and advertising and promotion. The company is no longer solely concerned with footwear; it has expanded into athletic apparel and accessories.

However, as with any large corporation, Nike is not immune to criticism. Notably, Nike's profit and success have come about at the expense of workers in developing countries, especially children and women. These workers are paid pennies for products that consumers buy at tens or hundreds of dollars. Workers are treated as machines. Nike, and other sport apparel companies, are fighting hard to distance themselves from the negative images of these sweatshops.

Based on information in Davies (1990), Timelines (mimeographed by Nike), Harvard Business School (1984), Magnet (1982), Eales (1986), Forbes.com (2003, 2004), and Bakan (2004).

What Philip Knight created was a sport organization. As the organization grew, he found that the original informal operating structure and style of management were no longer efficient for producing 300 models of athletic shoes in 900 different styles for a worldwide market. This kind of volume requires a different type of organizational design, one with specialized units, complex coordinating mechanisms, and a hierarchical management structure. The success that Knight has achieved is, in large part, a result of the changes made to the structure of Nike as it has grown and faced new and different contextual pressures. To be able to compete in the athletic footwear industry, Knight set up offshore manufacturing plants to ensure minimal production costs, hired specialist designers to keep ahead of changing trends, and established computerized warehouses to ensure that products are shipped on time to the right retail outlets.

Nike's situation is not unique. To operate effectively and efficiently, any sport organization needs to adapt its structure and management processes to meet the demands of its contextual situation. As we will show in this book, a knowledge of organization theory can help the sport manager in this task.

Why Sport Managers Need to Understand Organization Theory

In North America, Europe, and throughout many countries, sport is a rapidly growing and increasingly diverse industry. Increased amounts of discretionary income, a heightened awareness of the relationship between an active lifestyle and good health, and a greater number of opportunities to participate in sport have all contributed to this growth. In Great Britain, the journal *Retail Business* described the sport industry as "one of the most buoyant consumer markets of the 1980s" (Economic Intelligence Unit, 1990, p. 61) and predicted real-term growth into the 1990s. This prediction is also true for the 21st century. In the United States the magazine *Sports Inc.* predicted that the "gross national sport product" would be $85 billion in 1995, growing to $121 billion by the year 2000. In Canada it was estimated that Canadians spent close to $4.5 billion on sporting goods alone in 1989. Although it is difficult to measure the size of the sport industry, figure 1.1 provides some indication of its magnitude today.

1. In 2003, Americans spent an estimated $79.8 billion in sporting goods (National Sporting Goods Association, 2002).
2. In 2002, 98.1 percent of Canadian households reported spending money on recreation with an average spending of $3537 per household (Statistics Canada, 2004).
3. The 2004 Athens Summer Olympics had a projected budget of €1.962 billion (Athens2004, 2004).
4. In 2003, the NFL's Washington Redskins were worth $952 million (Ozanian, 2003).
5. Global broadcast revenues for the 2004 Athens Olympics were estimated at $1.498 billion (International Olympic Committee, 2004).
6. Over 80,000 buyers visit the annual Sporting Goods Manufacturers Association show (Ballard, 1989, p. 37).
7. Corporate sponsorship of the 2002 Winter Olympic Games in Salt Lake City, Utah, totalled $876 million (International Olympic Committee, 2005a).

Figure 1.1   *Indicators of the size of the sport industry.*

A large number of different types of organizations make up the sport industry, that wide array of public, private, and voluntary organizations involved in the provision of sport products and services. Some, like Brunswick Corporation, heavily involved in bowling centers and marine equipment, and the Forzani Group, a large sporting goods retailer, have sales in the millions of dollars and employ thousands of people. Others, such as the Derbyshire Skeet and Trap Club, a gun club operated by former Olympic skeet shooter Joe Neville, operate on a considerably smaller scale. A large number of the organizations we will look at in this book are designed to make a profit for their owners; others, such as Mountain Equipment Co-op (MEC) of Vancouver, operate on a cooperative basis and turn a large percentage of their profits back to their members—the people who buy their products. Many **sport organizations** operate as voluntary or nonprofit organizations; the funds they generate are used to further activities that benefit their membership or the communities where they are based. Some sport organizations, particularly those from the public sector, have as their primary function to aid and assist other organizations in the delivery of sport. For example, the Sport, Recreation, and Active Living Branch of the Government of New Brunswick's Culture and Sport Secretariat has as its mandate "to provide leadership and services to the community to increase opportunities for physical activity and the pursuit of excellence" (Culture and Sport Secretariat, 2004). Many sport organizations are linked to educational institutions and provide recreational and competitive sport opportunities as a part of the educational process. The sport industry also includes professional sport organizations, which contract with athletes and pay them to compete in their particular sport; the given event is then sold to live audiences and to TV networks for its entertainment value.

Organizations are, then, an integral and pervasive part of the sport industry. For those of you who hope to work in this industry, a knowledge of organization theory will help you to understand the organizations with which you will interact (and which may employ you) and why they are structured and operate in a particular way. For students specializing in sport management, presumably one of the reasons for studying organizations is that someday you hope to work for or eventually manage an organization. Knowledge of organization theory that has been systematically and scientifically derived can help you to better understand the problems you will face as a manager. It can help you design an appropriate structure, manage the changes that need to be made in your organization's structure as changes take place in its contextual situation, provide appropriate leadership, adopt appropriate technologies, resolve conflicts, manage human resources, and achieve the goals of your organization. *In short, it can help you become a better manager.*

Some Definitions

We have already seen that there are many different types of sport organizations. The terms structure, design, and context have been used to describe aspects of these organizations; and it has been suggested that organization theory can help in the task of managing these organizations. But what exactly is meant by these terms? In this section of the book some definitions are provided to help facilitate an understanding of these concepts; more detailed explanations can be found in later chapters. Although some management theorists (cf. March & Simon, 1958) suggest that definitions do not clearly delimit the object being examined, Hall (1982) argues that definitions provide a starting point for understanding the element of interest. While we acknowledge that sport organizations (and their context, structure, and design) are not unitary entities that can be exactly defined, but rather are complex processes and sets of socially and historically constituted relationships, the approach taken here is consistent with Hall's argument that defining concepts can provide a basis for their understanding.

What Is a Sport Organization?

While Nike and agencies like the Atlanta Falcons, the Canadian Olympic Committee, the Ladies Professional Golf Association, Creative Health Products, the British Columbia Lions Football Club, the Alberta Cricket Association, and Manchester United Soccer Club can all be classified as sport organizations, what is it that makes them sport organizations? Certainly it is not size (Creative Health Products makes a variety of fitness testing products, yet it has only seven employees). It is not the amount of money they make (a number of professional sport teams such as those in the Canadian Football League consistently lose money), nor is it the existence of employees (the Alberta Cricket Association has no paid staff). The definition of a sport organization used in this book is based on definitions of an organization provided by Daft (1989, 2004) and Robbins (1990) and is as follows: *A sport organization is a social entity involved in the sport industry; it is goal-directed, with a consciously structured activity system and a relatively identifiable boundary.*

There are five key elements in this definition and each warrants further explanation:

• **Social entity:** All sport organizations are composed of people or groups of people who interact with each other to perform those functions essential to the organization.

• **Involvement in the sport industry:** What differentiates sport organizations from other organizations, such as banks, pharmaceutical companies, and car dealerships, is the former's direct involvement in one or more aspects of the sport industry, for example, through the production of sport-related products or services. While agencies like banks, pharmaceutical companies, and car dealerships can be and have been involved in sport (primarily through sponsorship), they are not usually directly involved with the phenomenon and hence are not included in this book. The aim of the book is, however, to be inclusive rather than exclusive in explaining the nature of sport organizations. Hence, examples will be drawn from companies such as W.L. Gore & Associates, the manufacturer of Gore-Tex, a product used in a range of sportswear and equipment; the various national and state park recreation agencies that support many natural resources in which sport activities are often practiced; and organizations such as Yamaha and the Minnesota Mining and Manufacturing Corporation (3M), which, while they do not have sport products or services as their central focus, still have substantive involvement in the sport industry.

• **Goal-directed focus:** All sport organizations exist for a purpose, be it for making a profit, encouraging participation in a given sport, or winning Olympic medals. The goals of a sport organization are not usually as easily obtainable by an individual as they are by members working together. Sport organizations may have more than one goal, and individual members may have different goals from those of the organization.

• **Consciously structured activity system:** The interaction of people or groups of people in sport organizations does not occur through random chance; rather, there is a conscious structuring of activity systems such as marketing, product and service development, financial management, and human resource development. The main functions of the sport organization are broken down into smaller tasks or groups of tasks; the mechanisms used to coordinate and control these tasks help ensure that the goals of the sport organization are achieved.

• **Identifiable boundary:** Sport organizations need to have a relatively identifiable boundary that distinguishes members from nonmembers. Members of a sport organization usually have an explicit or implicit agreement with the organization through which they receive money, status, or some other benefit for their involvement. For some sport organizations, particularly those in the voluntary or nonprofit sector, the boundaries may not be as easily identified as in those sport organizations concerned with making a profit or those in the public sector. Nevertheless, every sport organization must have a boundary that helps distinguish members from nonmembers, but these boundaries are not fixed and may change over time.

The elements of our definition are evident in Nike, the sport organization that Philip Knight and Bill Bowerman created. The goals of the company are to produce athletic footwear and to sell it at a profit. As Nike has grown and more people have been hired, activity systems have been consciously structured to effectively and efficiently achieve the goals of the organization. The people hired identified themselves as employees and managers of Nike, which creates for them an identifiable boundary to differentiate their company from its competitors in the athletic footwear industry.

Organizational Structure of a Sport Organization

The term **organizational structure** is used here to define the manner in which the tasks of a sport organization are broken down and allocated to employees or volunteers, the reporting relationships among these role holders, and the coordinating and controlling mechanisms used within the sport organization. A typical organizational chart outlines, in part, the structure of an organization (see figure 1.2).

Identifying the dimensions that constitute the structure of any organization is, at best, a difficult exercise and one that has yielded inconsistency across studies. Yet organizational structure is an important concept to study because, as Miller (1987a) suggests, it "importantly influences the flow of interaction and the context and nature of human interactions. It channels collaboration, specifies modes of coordination, allocates power and responsibility, and prescribes levels of formality and complexity" (p. 7). Hall (1982), Miller and Dröge (1986), and Van de Ven (1976) all suggest that structure should be examined using three dimensions: complexity, formalization, and centralization. We look at each of these structural dimensions in more detail in chapter 4.

Organizational Design

The concept of **organizational design** refers to the patterning of the structural elements of an organization. All managers seek to produce a design that will enhance their ability to achieve the goals of their organization. Miller (1981) argued that organizations must be constructed to ensure that there is complementary alignment or fit among their structural variables. In what is probably the best-known attempt to identify organizational designs, Mintzberg (1979) proposes five design configurations: the simple structure, the machine bureaucracy, the divisionalized form, the professional bureaucracy, and the adhocracy. Sport organizations can be found in each of these categories; we discuss them more specifically in chapter 5.

Context of a Sport Organization

The structure of a sport organization is closely related to the particular *context* in which the organization operates. The term **organizational context** merely refers to "the organizational setting which influences the structural dimensions" (Daft, 1989, p. 17). We find variation in the structures of sport organizations mainly because they operate with different contextual situations. As was the case with organizational structure, different studies have identified different dimensions as characterizing an organization's context. Contextual dimensions are often referred to in the literature as determinants, imperatives, or, most frequently, contingencies. Supporters of this school of thought (i.e., contingency theory) argue that changes in an organization's structure are contingent on changes in its contextual situation. We look at the three main contextual factors identified as influencing structure—strategy, environment, and technology—in chapters 6, 8, and 9.

Organizational Theory

Organizational theory, a disciplinary area within the broader field of business/management studies, is concerned with the structure and design of organizations. Scholars in this field seek to identify commonly occurring patterns and regularities in organizations, and understand their causes and consequences. While organizational theorists are concerned with theoretical issues, that is, pushing back the frontiers of knowledge about organizations, sport management students should not be concerned that the subject area has no practical application. On the contrary, scholars in this area frequently work with the practicing manager (i.e., consulting work); the central focus of a large percentage of the research they undertake is to discover ways to help managers in their jobs. For

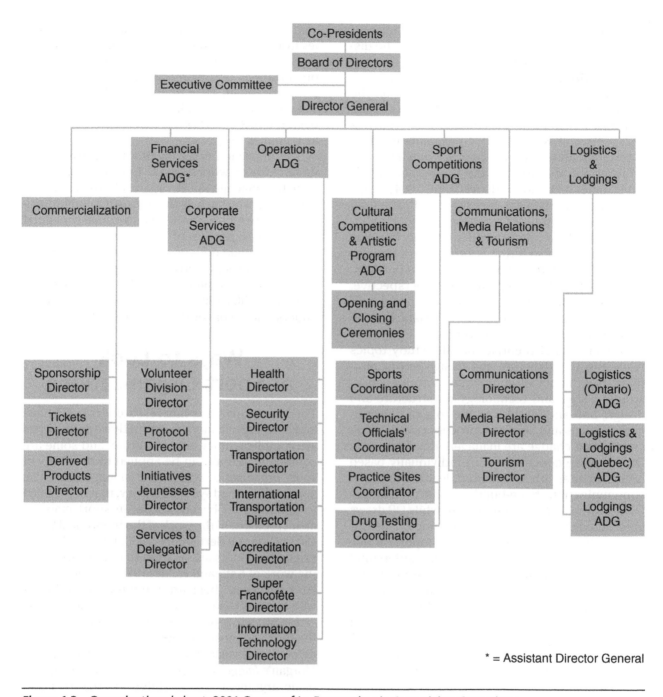

Figure 1.2   *Organizational chart: 2001 Games of La Francophonie Organizing Committee.*

Adapted, by permission, from Comité Organisateur des Jeux de la Francophonie - COJF, 2001, *Manuel d'événement rédigé à l'intention des délégations* (Ottawa, Canada: Comité Organisateur des Jeux de la Francophonie), 3.

sport managers, organizational theory can provide a better understanding of the way sport organizations are structured and designed, how they operate, and why some are effective when others are not. This understanding can help sport managers analyze and diagnose more effectively the problems they face, and enable them to respond with appropriate solutions.

Distinction Between Organizational Theory and Organizational Behavior

All organizations can be studied at different levels and in different ways; sport organizations are no exception. Within the field of sport management, students should understand what is often referred to as the *macro and micro distinction*, or the distinction between **organizational theory** (OT) and **organizational behavior** (OB). Organizational theory, the macro perspective, focuses on the organization (or its primary subunits) as its unit of analysis. To explain a sport organization from this perspective, it is necessary to examine its characteristics and composition (i.e., departments, groups) but also to examine the organization's environmental characteristics (Daft, 2004). Organizational theorists are concerned with the total organization's ability to achieve its goals effectively; thus, they must consider not only how it is structured but also how it is situated in a broader sociopolitical and economic context. In contrast, organizational behavior, the micro perspective, focuses on individuals and small groups within the organization, and the characteristics of the environment in which they work.

Organizational theorists usually study topics related to the structure and design of organizations; the impact of contextual factors such as strategy, size, and technology on structure and design; and such issues as the role of power in organizations and how such processes as decision making and change are managed. Researchers in OB are more concerned with individually based issues such as job satisfaction, leadership style, communication, team-building, and motivation. OT draws strongly from sociology, while OB draws predominantly from social psychology. This distinction between OT and OB is an important one for sport management students to understand because, with some exceptions, the dominant trend of the empirical work in our field has been concerned with OB topics, such as the level of job satisfaction, leadership, and motivation of sport managers.

The OT and OB distinction is certainly not a clear one; both approaches are important to a full understanding of sport management. For example, the lack of women in senior positions in management (and sport management in particular) has often been explained by looking at the individual and her motivation, leadership ability, and skills—an OB approach. While this approach can provide useful material to start to correct some of the inequalities we see in sport organizations, it fails to address the structural conditions that constrain women's progress in these organizations,

something an OT approach would consider. Studies from both perspectives would provide a fuller understanding of the gendered nature of sport organizations and many other important issues in management. (See Kanter [1977] for work of this nature and Hall, Cullen, and Slack [1989] for an overview of the gender and management literature as it applies to sport.)

The approach taken in this book draws predominantly on work from OT to help explain how to better manage sport organizations. However, some chapters, such as the one on leadership, utilize some work traditionally more closely aligned with the perspective of OB. Sport management students should not view OT and OB as opposing or conflicting perspectives. Rather, each perspective emphasizes different levels of analysis that should complement the other in providing a fuller understanding of sport management.

Ways to Look at Sport Organizations

There are many ways that researchers in OT have looked at organizations; some of these approaches are complementary, some overlap, and some are conflicting, but all can be applied to the study of sport organizations and their management. The approach, termed **systems theory,** that has tended to dominate OT-based studies in sport management, grew out of the work of the theoretical biologist Ludwig von Bertalanffy (1950, 1968) and is best exemplified in its application to organizations by the work of Katz and Kahn (1978). As we will see later, however, there are a number of problems with systems theory and a number of other equally viable ways to look at sport organizations. One of the best and most recent works to categorize the different ways of looking at organizations is Gareth Morgan's *Images of organization* (1986). Morgan's basic argument is that different "theories and explanations of organizational life are based on metaphors that lead us to see and understand organizations in distinctive yet partial ways" (p. 12). By looking at these different perspectives on organizations we come to better understand them and their management. These metaphors are explained in more detail in the passages to follow, and where available examples from the literature on sport organizations are provided.*

---

*Parts of this section were published in Slack, T. (1993). Morgan and the metaphors: Implication for sport management. *Journal of sport management, 7,* 189-193.

Organizations as Machines

One of the most pervasive images we have of organizations is as machines. Originating with the classical theorists, such as Henri Fayol and, in particular, Frederick Taylor with his notions of scientific management, organizations are seen from this perspective as a series of interrelated parts, each performing a narrowly defined set of activities to achieve a particular end product. Like a machine, the organization is expected to operate in a rigid, repetitive, and impersonal manner.

Although heavily criticized for their impersonal nature (cf. Braverman, 1974), ideas grounded in "Taylorism" still pervade the way in which many organizations, including some in the sport industry, operate. Sport organizations most likely to employ elements of this approach are those involved in the assembly-line production of commodities such as athletic shoes, baseball bats, hockey sticks, and

Manufacturers of sporting goods are among those companies that might use a mechanistic approach to organization.

bicycles. Mechanistic approaches to organization are also promoted in some elements of the sport management literature. Several textbooks in the area are constructed around Henri Fayol's concepts of planning, organizing, coordinating, commanding, and controlling. In addition, many public-sector documents on the management of sport, and some sport management texts (cf. Horine, 1985; VanderZwaag, 1984), stress the usefulness and importance of the more modern mechanistic approaches to management such as management by objectives (MBO) and planning, programming, budgeting systems (PPBS). Sport teams have also often been described as machine-like in their operation (cf. Castaing, 1970; Terkel, 1972; Fielding, Miller, & Brown, 1999).

Organizations as Organisms

In large part as a reaction to the technical emphasis of scientific management, scholars like Herzberg, Mausner, and Snyderman (1959), Maslow (1943), and McGregor (1960) started to focus on the "needs" of the individual, the group, and the organization. This focus, by necessity, drew attention to the environment in which the organization existed as a source of satisfaction for these needs. Thus, organizations were likened to organisms that come in a variety of different forms and rely on their environment in order to survive. Also, like organisms, organizations were seen to exhibit different systems (usually termed the input, throughput, and output systems) that interacted with each other and their environment. Figure 1.3 shows these systems as they would apply to a sport equipment manufacturer. In each of the three systems there is a reliance on the environment for certain organizational "needs." The systems theory approach to the study of organizations has frequently been used in sport management. Chelladurai, Szyszlo, and Haggerty (1987), for example, used a systems-based approach to examine the effectiveness of Canadian national sport organizations.

Within the broader field of management, a logical extension to systems theory and a more dominant approach to the study of organizations is contingency theory. In keeping with the metaphor of organizations as organisms, the structure of an organization is seen as being contingent on contextual factors (size, strategy, and so forth). Effectiveness is seen as being dependent on the proper fit between structure and context. For example, a large sport organization such as Rossignol, the

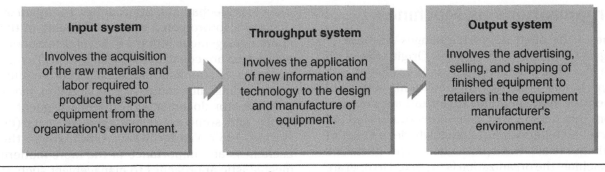

Figure 1.3 *Systems of a sport equipment manufacturer.*

ski manufacturer, will require a structure different from a small retail sporting goods store. The structure of each organization must fit with the demands that their size produces. While work on sport organizations has often implicitly acknowledged the importance of context to structure and effectiveness, there have been few studies specifically focused on these relationships. The idea that organizations are products of their context and the realization that these contexts vary gave rise to the notion of variation in organizational design. Like organisms, some organizational forms are more suited to certain contextual conditions than to others. This idea has led researchers to attempt to classify different types of organization and the conditions under which they will be most effective (cf. Mintzberg, 1979). In the field of sport management there have been attempts to use existing typologies to classify sport organizations (cf. Chelladurai, 1985). However, Kikulis, Slack, Hinings, and Zimmermann (1989) have taken the idea of classification further. Building on the ideas of scholars like Carper and Snizek (1980), McKelvey (1975, 1978, 1982), and Miller and Friesen (1984), they developed an empirical taxonomy of organizational design for voluntary sport organizations. The taxonomy illustrates the different types of organizational design with which these organizations can operate.

The biological metaphor of organizations as organisms has also been adopted by researchers who approach the study of organizations from what is termed the **life cycle perspective** (Kimberly & Miles, 1980). Here, organizations, like organisms, are seen to go through distinctive life stages, their management requirements reflecting the stage of their development. Yet a further extension of the biological metaphor has given rise to an approach to studying organizations termed **population ecology**. Unlike many other approaches, population ecology focuses not on individual organizations but on populations of organizations. The idea is that organizations are dependent on their environment to acquire the necessary resources to survive, just as living organisms in nature do. To do so, they must compete with other organizations because resources are scarce, resulting in a survival of the fittest (Morgan, 1986). By plotting birth-and-death rates and patterns of growth and decline in organizations, population ecologists have provided important insights into organizations and their management. Although this approach has not been used by sport management scholars to date, sport organizations that come and go very rapidly, such as fitness centers and sporting goods stores, would provide a highly appropriate population of organizations for this type of work.

Organizations as Brains

The image of organizations as brains draws attention to the information-processing capacity of organizations. While the mechanistic type of organizations advocated by Frederick Taylor may work well for performing regularized tasks in a stable environment, organizations operating under changing conditions have to be able to monitor these conditions, question the appropriateness of their actions, and, if necessary, make modifications. This necessity requires that organizations, like brains, have to exhibit information-processing capabilities and communication and decision-making systems. As such, they may also have to develop the capacity to learn in a brainlike way and eventually engage in self-management and self-organization.

This way of thinking about organizations owes much to Herbert Simon's (1945) work on decision making and his concept of bounded rationality (see chapter 13). For Simon, organizational members have limited information-processing capabilities that become institutionalized in the structure and ways of operating of organizations. Thus, organizations become understood "as kinds of institutionalized brains that fragment, routinize, and bound the decision process in order to make it manageable" (Morgan, 1986, p. 81). New ways of thinking about organizations and their design and operation have developed from this emphasis on decision making. Galbraith (1974, 1977) and Thompson (1967), for example, focused on the relationship between the information-processing capabilities of an organization and organizational design.

This interest in information processing has led organizational researchers to **cybernetics**, a field of study concerned with "the behavior, organization, and design of mechanisms, organisms, and organizations that receive, generate, and respond to information in order to attain a desired result" (Haggerty, 1988, pp. 54-55). Applied to organizations, the field of cybernetics has been concerned with designing systems that can learn, much like a brain learns, and thus can regulate themselves. A further extension of this approach is to view organizations as holographic systems, when each part of the organization has a picture of the whole, thus allowing learning and self-renewal. Given the rapid expansion of information processing in organizations, we may see cybernetic and holographic approaches, while still developing as ways to understand organizations, as providing the direction for future changes that will accompany these developments. In the field of sport management only Haggerty (1988) has completed work using this approach. Haggerty suggests that cybernetic strategies can be used for improving the control and information systems of sport organizations.

Organizations as Cultures

With the success of Japanese management and the globalization of many industries has come an increased interest in the relationship of culture to organizational life. While organizational theorists acknowledge that the culture of the society in which an organization exists will influence its modes of operation, there has been growing interest in what is often termed "corporate culture." Growing out of the idea that organizations are themselves mini societies, culture in this sense is concerned with the shared values and meanings that create the reality of organizational life. Scholars who study organizations as cultures are concerned with issues, such as the way these shared values and meanings are created and maintained, the role of leadership in this process, the existence of competing cultures, and the manifestation of an organization's culture in its design and operation.

Corporate culture reveals itself in such areas of the organization as its ceremonies, stories, myths, symbols, language, and physical layout. Sport organizations are rich in these areas. Ceremonies to initiate rookie football players, stories about coaches and managers, the symbols of athletic goods companies (the Nike swoosh, Adidas's three stripes), and the specialized language that characterizes many sports can all be examined to gain an understanding of the shared values and meanings that underpin the design and operation of sport organizations. Despite the potential of the culture approach to understanding sport organizations, there has been virtually no work of this nature in sport management. Many popular books on sport organizations (cf. Prouty, 1988; Williams, 1995) provide implicit accounts of the type of values that shape their operation, yet by their nature offer little or no scholarly analysis. Hall, Cullen, and Slack (1989) briefly examine the potential of a cultural approach to understanding gender issues in sport organizations but warn that it is frequently men's accounts of organizational reality, not women's, that dominate most analyses of an organization's culture. The work that comes closest to a systematic analysis of the culture of a sport organization and its effects on structure and design is Fine's (1987) work on Little League Baseball.

Organizations as Political Systems

All organizations are political. The image of organizations as political systems challenges the view that they are rational entities working for a common end. Rather, the view is one of individuals and groups loosely coupled together in order to more efficiently realize their own ambitions and self-interests. Scholars who work with this perspective are interested in the political activity that manifests itself in the power plays and conflicts pervading all organizations. Some would suggest this approach is particularly applicable to organizations concerned with sport!

Few studies in sport management have specifically examined sport organizations as **systems of political activity**. Stern's (1979) analysis of the development of the National Collegiate Athletic

Association (NCAA) and Sack and Staurowsky's (1998) critique of the NCAA's position on college athletes, as well as Lenskyj's (2000) analysis of the International Olympic Committee (IOC) and its Olympic Games are three of the best examples. However, there are other studies that, although it was not their primary focus, provide examples of the type of political struggles that shape sport organizations. Sack and Kidd (1985) and Kidd (1988) discussed the political struggles of athletes to gain representation in the sport organizations that control their athletic destinies. Macintosh and Whitson (1990) examined struggles between professional staff and volunteers to determine the program focus of national sport organizations in Canada. Much of the work on gender and organizations is about political struggles between men and women (cf. Hall, Cullen, & Slack, 1989; Hult, 1989; Lovett & Lowry, 1994; White & Brackenridge, 1985).

Organizations as Instruments of Domination

In describing organizations as **instruments of domination,** Morgan (1986) suggests that we are usually encouraged to think of organizations as positive entities created to benefit the interests of all who come in contact with them. Certainly sport organizations are often portrayed in this manner; however, Morgan challenges this perspective. Here organizations are seen as instruments designed to benefit the interests of a privileged few at the expense of the masses; sport organizations have not been immune from this criticism. From this more critical perspective, organizations (or more accurately their dominant coalitions) are seen as exploiting their workers, their host communities, and often the environment, for their own ends. Unions, work-related stresses, industrial accidents, drug and alcohol abuse, and alienation are all products of this exploitation. While researchers who see themselves as working primarily in the field of sport management have, for the most part, failed to deal with these issues, they are no less important than any others for a comprehensive understanding of sport organizations and their successful management. Kidd and Donnelly (2000) have examined sport and domination issues (human rights in their case).

While neglected by sport management scholars per se, this approach to organizations has been used by a number of writers from both the popular and academic literature on sport. Several authors have written in the popular press about the manner in which professional sport organizations (most notably football teams) and some colleges dominate and exploit their athletes (cf. Huizenga, 1994; Manley & Friend, 1992; Telander, 1989). Government organizations have also been seen as exploiting the talents of their international athletes to meet their own ideological and policy aims (cf. Harvey and Proulx, 1988; Kidd, 1988; Macintosh & Whitson, 1990), and strong arguments have been made for class-, race-, and gender-based exploitation in sport organizations (cf. Cashmore, 2000; Gruneau, 1983; Whitson & Macintosh, 1989). Finally, companies like Nike have been criticized for exploitative labor practices in their Third World production plants (Ballinger, 1993; Clifford, 1992).

State of the Art in Sport Management and Suggestions for Future Directions

As we have just seen, there are a number of ways we can look at sport organizations. The central premise of Morgan's approach to understanding organizations is that they cannot be adequately described, understood, or explained using just one approach. By looking at different images of organizations, we are better able to understand their complex and paradoxical nature, and thus become better managers. As the few previous examples illustrate, sport management scholars have tended to be relatively narrow in the way they look at sport organizations. The two dominant perspectives within the literature have been to look at organizations from a mechanistic point of view or to utilize the systems theory approach. While work of this nature is not without value, it is somewhat problematic in terms of its ability to provide a holistic understanding of sport organizations and their management. (A large number of studies in the field of sport management fail to use any type of theoretical framework; as such, while some of them provide useful descriptive material, they do little to enhance our overall understanding of sport organizations and their management.)

Mechanistic approaches to the study of sport organizations, as noted earlier, have generally focused on some variant of Henri Fayol's five basic managerial functions. A number of textbooks in our field have been constructed around these concepts. However, such approaches are problematic; because, as Mintzberg (1973a, p. 10) notes, "these words do not in fact describe the actual work of managers at all, they describe certain vague objectives of managerial work. As such they have long served to block our search for a deeper understanding of the work of the manager." Such an approach is also limited in that it fails to recognize the ability of organizations to change as their contextual situation changes. It can also be dehumanizing for employees. Because it promotes an image of workers as cheerful robots unquestioningly going about their daily tasks, it can promote bureaucratic pathologies such as goal displacement and alienation. Finally, this approach to organizations fails to recognize the importance of power and politics in creating the reality of organizational life.

While studies based on systems theory have been more useful in providing interesting and relevant information, this approach is also limited in its explanatory abilities. Studies based on systems theory tend to be overly deterministic, ignoring the role of strategic choice in the construction of organizations. That is to say, far too much emphasis is placed on context as a determinant of structure and design, and far too little attention is given to the creative actions of individuals within the organization. Such an emphasis also presents a view of organizations as functionally unified with all the component parts working together to a common end. Consequently, as with mechanistic approaches, issues of power and politics are ignored and conflict is dismissed as being "dysfunctional."

It is important that, as a sport management student, you realize the strengths and limitations of the dominant approaches to the study of sport organizations. While the findings that emanate from the most prevalent type of studies in our field are useful and informative, they frequently present only a partial view of sport organizations and their management. Studies based on the approaches of contingency theory and population ecology, for example, while not without their shortcomings, would certainly enhance our understanding of the impact of contextual pressures on the structure and design of sport organizations. It is also important to conduct studies to determine the nature and extent of variation in the design of sport organizations. As McKelvey (1975) has suggested, such classifications are in many ways one of the fundamental elements in the development of a comprehensive understanding of organizations.

The increasing importance of information processing and communication in organizations, and the interest generated by such popular literature as Peters and Waterman's (1982) *In Search of Excellence* and Kanter's (1983) *The Change Masters*, have respectively prompted an interest in cybernetics and **organizational culture**. Martin (2002), for example, has provided three perspectives to illustrate the numerous ways organizational culture can be conceptualized: integration, fragmentation, and differentiation. These approaches would provide useful insights if applied to sport organizations. Work that looks at sport organizations as "political systems" and "instruments of domination" would help free us from the highly functional view of these organizations that has long characterized our field. These approaches would also bring issues of power and politics, something that has been missing from previous studies, to a more central position in the study of sport management. Furthermore, sport management research must start looking not only on intraorganizational relationships (e.g., power and relationships studies) but also on interorganizational relationship. With an increasing number of organizations seeking opportunities in new and emerging markets, it becomes necessary to understand how these interorganizational relationships work. Chapter 7 is dedicated to these types of relationships—strategic alliances.

Still, the adoption of some of these perspectives will require us to employ different theoretical approaches from those currently found in the sport management literature. For example, not only have any of the approaches that comprise critical theory been absent from the study of sport organizations, but also their use has been implicitly if not explicitly frowned upon. For example, studies underpinned by Marxist theory in any of its variant forms are noticeably absent from our literature; yet organizational scholars such as Thompson and McHugh (1990) and Clegg (1989), to name but a few, have employed elements of Western Marxist thought to make a major contribution to our understanding of organizations and their management. Marx himself wrote considerably about one organization, the state, which in many Western liberal democratic countries has a considerable impact on the way sport is managed. More recently, Alvesson and Deetz (2000), and Alvesson and Willmot (2003), argue for a critical management perspective of organizations. Slack and Amis (2004) and Frisby (2005) have supported this call within sport management.

While feminist theory has been used more frequently in the sport management literature, most of the completed work in this area has adopted a liberal feminist approach that emphasizes how women need to change to better fit into the existing male-stream system. Such work does little to challenge or change the hegemonic conditions that have long constrained women's mobility in organizations, but a body of work is emerging in the organizational literature that critically analyzes the role of gender in organizations. This work (Burrell, 1984; Hearn & Parkin, 1983, 1987; Hearn, Sheppard, Tancred-Sheriff, & Burrell, 1989; Mills & Tancred, 1992), with its emphasis on sexuality, has considerable scope for work on sport organizations (cf. Hall, Cullen, & Slack, 1989).

The adoption of any of these approaches will, of course, require somewhat different research techniques from those previously found in sport management. As Olafson (1990) demonstrated, survey-type studies have dominated the sport management literature. While there is still considerable scope for this type of work, new and different theoretical approaches will require us to employ research designs and modes of analysis not commonly used to study sport organizations. Those who engage in quantitative studies will need to become more sophisticated in terms of the statistical procedures they employ and the manner in which their data are integrated into or used to extend existing theoretical frameworks. Qualitative approaches, which are still relatively rare in the academic sport management literature, will also have to be more frequently employed. Techniques such as participant observation, in-depth interviews, and semiotic analysis, when applied appropriately, can all yield new insights to help the sport manager.

The essential point here is not that one theoretical approach or research technique is better than another, but that different approaches explain different parts of the reality of organizational life. In sport management, we have tended to use only one or two perspectives and a limited range of research methodologies; consequently, our view of sport organizations is very narrow. As Morgan (1986) points out, organizations are complex and paradoxical; by using different approaches to understand their complex and paradoxical nature, we will be better able to design and manage them. Chapter 2 provides a first step in understanding the possible research designs in sport management.

It is impossible in one book to deal, even in a minor way, with all the approaches to sport organizations mentioned here. In fact, some of them are only in their infancy in the broader field of management. The point of discussing the state of the art in our field is to alert readers to the potential these approaches have to enhance our understanding of sport organizations and their management. This text has been written in an effort to tap some of this potential. By focusing on a number of the central ideas in organizational theory and their application to our field, it is hoped that the book will provide you with a better understanding of sport organizations, and that this increased understanding will ultimately make you a better manager. You should look at each chapter of this book as a stepping-stone for that highlighted aspect of organizations. If a particular aspect interests you, then the key researchers mentioned and further readings will help you delve deeper into your topic of interest.

Format of the Book

Like a successful sport organization, a good textbook needs an appropriate structure. The 15 chapters in this book are arranged to provide a logical progression to understanding the structure, context, and processes of sport organizations. As you have seen, chapter 1 explains what organization theory is and how it can help the sport manager to understand sport organizations. In chapter 2, we deal with the various aspects of doing research in sport management. In chapter 3, we discuss the central problem with which sport managers must be concerned: the issue of organizational effectiveness. Effectiveness is strongly linked to an appropriate organizational structure and design. Consequently, in chapter 4 we look at the different structural elements of sport organizations and how they are related. In chapter 5, we look at the patterning of structural variables and how they combine to produce particular organizational designs. We focus specifically on Mintzberg's five design configurations—simple structure, machine bureaucracy, divisionalized form, professional bureaucracy, and adhocracy, and show that we can find examples of each of these in the sport industry. Because of the importance attached to an appropriate organizational design, considerable attention is given to those factors seen as influencing this aspect of organization. Consequently, in chapters 6 through 9 we focus on strategy, strategic alliances, environment, and technology. In chapter 10 we move away from the contextual situation of the organization, and focus on the way in which dominant individuals and coalitions exercise power in an organization to create a design that will maximize their control. Finally, in chapters 11 through 15 we focus on some of the processes with which managers are involved, specifically conflict, the management of change, decision making, organizational culture, and leadership.

Format of Each Chapter

Although each chapter varies slightly depending on the topic being covered, the format throughout the book is fairly consistent: Each chapter begins with a vignette from an actual sport organization, illustrating the topic to be covered. The major theoretical ideas about the particular topic are then introduced and related specifically to sport organizations. Appropriate figures and tables are used to help explain the points being made. At several places in each chapter you will find a Time Out that illustrates the issues being discussed by providing accounts taken from actual situations concerning sport organizations or from research findings. A section outlining key issues for managers brings the research presented to the level of the sport manager. Each chapter has a summary and a list of the key concepts discussed. A set of review questions is provided to stimulate discussion about central issues in the chapter. A section containing suggestions for further readings at the end of each chapter includes readings from the general management literature and the sport management literature. Finally, each chapter (except chapter 1) has a Case for Analysis, taken from an actual situation in a sport organization (in some instances the names of the people and organizations involved have been changed for reasons of confidentiality). Questions about the case are provided for class discussion.

KEY CONCEPTS

cybernetics (p. 11)

instruments of domination (p. 12)

life cycle perspective (p. 10)

organizational behavior (p. 8)

organizational context (p. 6)

organizational culture (p. 13)

organizational design (p. 6)

organizational structure (p. 6)

organizational theory (p. 8)

population ecology (p. 10)

scientific management (p. 9)

sport organizations (p. 4)

systems of political activity (p. 11)

systems theory (p. 8)

REVIEW QUESTIONS

1. Is a group of friends playing basketball a sport organization? Why or why not?

2. Why is an understanding of organization theory important for the sport manager?

3. What factors do you feel have contributed to the growth of the sport industry?

4. Select a sport organization with which you are familiar. Briefly explain how each part of the definition of a sport organization applies to the organization you selected.

5. Compare organizational structure and organizational design.

6. Select a sport organization with which you are familiar. Explain the context in which it exists.

7. Contrast organizational theory with organizational behavior.

8. How can the approaches of OT and OB complement each other?

9. Pick a sport organization with which you are familiar and, using two or more of the ways to look at organizations described in the text, explain how your impression of this sport organization would vary depending on the perspective you picked.

10. Contrast the image of organizations as machines with the one that sees them as political systems.

11. What problems can you see in an approach to understanding sport organizations that likens them to organisms?

12. Select a research article on sport organizations. Which perspective on organizations do you think it uses?

13. Why do you think sport management scholars have not focused to any great extent on issues of power and politics in sport organizations?

14. With which of the ways of looking at sport organizations are you most comfortable? Why?

15. Using the vignette at the start of the chapter, explain how Nike's structure and context have changed over the years.

SUGGESTIONS FOR FURTHER READING

The first edition of the *Journal of Sport Management* (Vol. 1, No. 1) contains an interesting article by Zeigler (1987) about the past, present, and future status of sport management. Also noteworthy in this edition is Paton's (1987) article on the progress that has been made in sport management research. Olafson's (1990) article in the *Journal of Sport Management* (Vol. 4, No. 2) provides some interesting and relevant ideas on research needs in sport management. Slack's (1991a) work on future directions for our field (*Journal of Sport Management*, Vol. 5, No. 2) relates to some of the ideas found in this first chapter. Frisby's (2005) article in the *Journal of Sport Management* (Vol. 19, No. 1) adds to this discussion by providing a critical perspective on the sport management field.

Students are of course referred to Gareth Morgan's (1986) *Images of organization* as probably the best source of information about the different ways researchers have looked at organizations. Also see Slack's (1993) article "Morgan and the Metaphors: Implications for Sport Management,"

which appeared in the *Journal of Sport Management* (Vol. 7, No. 3). Alvesson and Deetz (2000) in their book *Doing Critical Management Research* and Alvesson and Willmot (2003) in their book *Studying Management Critically* provide a much-needed critical perspective on organizations. Slack and Amis (2004) use a critical perspective to examine sport sponsorship in their article "Money for Nothing and Your Cheques for Free? A Critical Perspective on Sport Sponsorship" in Slack's *The Commercialization of Sport*. Students are directed to read *The Corporation* by Joel Bakan (2004)—also the subject of a documentary film that features Nike—to see organizations, especially sport organizations and their management, in a critical light. Finally, although more sociologically than managerially oriented, students may also find useful ideas in Rob Beamish's (1985) "Sport Executives and Voluntary Associations: A Review of the Literature and Introduction to Some Theoretical Issues" in *Sociology of Sport Journal* (Vol. 2, No. 3, pp. 218-232).

Chapter 2

Doing Research in Sport Management

LEARNING OBJECTIVES

When you have read this chapter, you should be able to

1. explain the different steps of the research process,
2. provide examples of some common research designs,
3. provide examples of possible data collection and analysis techniques,
4. evaluate the quality of an article, and
5. provide examples of research write-up options.

QUALITY RESEARCH DOES EXIST IN SPORT MANAGEMENT

A typical research article will have a short abstract, an introduction, a review of the literature (or theoretical framework to be used in the research), a description of the research design, the presentation of the results, a discussion of those results, implications for researchers and managers stemming from the study's results, and a conclusion. An explanation of the limitations of the piece of research is often included.

Laurence Chalip is a well-known and respected researcher in the field of sport management. His 2003 article in the *Journal of Sport Management,* with Christine Green and Brad Hill, is an example of good sport management research. The article, "Effect of Sport Event Media on Destination Image and

Intention to Visit," has a title that echoes the topic, is supported by an abstract describing the topic, explains the source of the samples (since there was a comparison of regional differences in the study), and details the main findings. The authors then provide an introduction of events and their relationship to the marketing mix and local politics and how these two issues are related. This is followed by a **theoretical framework** describing the value of media to encourage attendance of sport events through the influence of movies and television. This allows the authors to point out key problems still unanswered in the literature; problems they want to address are stated as clear research questions at the end of this section. Next, the authors provide

(continued)

(continued)

a methods section that includes a description of the sample, the methods used, the variables examined and how they will be measured, and data analysis techniques. In the results section, the authors provide a description of every data analysis result used for each research question and whether these results are statistically significant or not (since data analysis is statistical in nature). The discussion section then critically looks at each result and discusses its significance in the context of the research; it analyzes the meaning of the numbers and their practical and theoretical implications. The discussion is therefore tied back to the theoretical framework. The authors conclude their article by summarizing what they believe are the key elements.

These are the authors' main findings of the study: Event telecast, event advertising, and destination (location of the event) advertising have an impact on different elements of the destination's image. They also found a wider range of effects in the United States sample than in the New Zealand sample. The authors conclude that if an event can be linked to the marketing strategy and communications mix of the local region, then the event is in a position to provide more value and be more viable.

Based on information in Chalip, Green, and Hill (2003).

The first thing to do when writing up research is to provide a good introduction that leads to the purpose of the paper. This will be discussed at length.

Throughout this textbook, we present a range of research to help explain various concepts related to the management of sport organizations. This chapter provides an introduction to the **research process** to explain how the research cited in this book was conducted. The small selection of published management research in the book should give any future sport manager or researcher an idea of how to evaluate the quality of a piece and conduct research. Even if you do not plan to be involved in academia, you will undertake some kind of research during your career (e.g., a survey of your company's customers) to help your organization become more successful in one way or another. If you become a consultant, you will do research for sport organizations in order to help your clients. If you hire a consultant, as a manager you will have to judge the quality of the consultant's final report.

A cursory search of university classes and books related to the research process reveals a wealth of possibilities. Examples of books include Miles and Huberman's (1994) *Qualitative Data Analysis, Second Edition;* Coffey and Atkinson's (1996) *Making Sense of Qualitative Data;* Crotty's (1998) *The Foundations of Social Research;* Denscombe's (1998) *The Good Research Guide for Small-Scale Social Research Projects;* Bauer and Gaskell's (2000) *Qualitative Researching With Text, Image, and Sound;* and Yin's (2003) *Case Study Research: Design and Methods, Third Edition.* As you can see, there is a book for virtually every aspect of the research process. Therefore, the goal of this chapter is not to go into great detail about the research process but to present the basics of doing research in a sport management context. You will then be better equipped to delve into areas of the research process that interest you, to evaluate current research, and to undertake research. We will look at the research process, the qualitative–quantitative debate, research design, data collection and analysis techniques, issues of quality, and the final write-up.

The Research Process

If you examine a good article, you will most likely find the following sections: an introduction of the topic, information about its theory, a description of its general method and specific techniques, an overview of the results, a discussion of the findings, and a conclusion often containing implications for theorists and managers. What do the preceding terms mean? What do they involve? How do you get to the point of writing an article?

Before starting the actual process, you need to understand some terms you may encounter in the chapter or other sources dealing with the research process. Research in the social sciences (sport management in our case) is both *theoretical* in nature, involving developing, exploring, testing, rejecting, or extending theories, and *empirical*, which requires observation and the measurement of a chosen setting (Trochim, 2001). A piece of research can be theoretical, empirical, or both.

Research is usually one of three types: exploratory, descriptive, or explanatory. **Exploratory research** uncovers facts about a certain subject or setting. The goal is to discover as much as possible about the general topic and then develop propositions or hypotheses that can be examined at a later date. A rationale for such a study could be phrased in the following qualitative way: "What can be learned from the study of local figure-skating clubs?" **Descriptive research**, as the name suggests, goes deeper into a specific topic to analyze it in greater detail. For example, if our exploratory study determined that management strategies, power structures, and volunteer commitment were the three main findings of the research, we may want to delve deeper into the management strategies. Finding this, we could decide to ask the following question: "What is the decision-making process for a volunteer board in a local figure-skating club?" Finally, **explanatory research** is causal in nature, meaning it studies the relationships of variables to explain and predict behavior. It is more about the cause-and-effect relationship. An example of an explanatory study for our local figure-skating club topic may be "What is the effect of the volunteer board members' past experience on the decision-making process?" (Trochim, 2001; Yin, 2003). Of course, the three types of research are not mutually exclusive. Depending on how you set up your research, it may be both exploratory and descriptive or descriptive and explanatory. Finally, regardless of the type of research you use, you will be doing *cross-sectional* (at one point in time) or *longitudinal* (over a period of time) research. Longitudinal research is better suited for examining changes of a variable over time or for examining different processes.

We can now go deeper into the research process. Most of the time, a study starts with a research topic that interests the researcher. For example, how are large-scale sporting-event organizing committees managed? The problem will usually be that the topic is too broad. In this case, what does "managed" mean? This broad topic must be narrowed down to a specific research question, the more specific the better. A good way to build a specific **research question** is to include who, what, where, or when elements in your question. In other words, who are we going to research, what variables are we interested in, and where or when will

this take place. In our example, we could pose the following research question: "What stakeholder issues must the 2010 Vancouver Winter Olympics organizing committee deal with?" At this point we know the who (stakeholders), the what (issues), and the where or when (2010 Vancouver Winter Olympics). The more focused your research question is, the easier it will be to actually do the study and evaluate the findings.

Once the research question is posed, the temptation is to jump into operationalizing your variables and gathering the data. Before beginning, however, you need a strong foundation in order to explore the right concepts in the right manner. This is done through the use of a *theoretical framework*. This theoretical framework is a description of the theory or theories (if you develop a framework to be tested) that will inform the research design.

The theoretical framework drives a study's *research design*, which can be described as the overall plan of action, strategy, or process that holds the choice of methods together and links that choice to the research's desired outcomes (Crotty, 1998). The *methods* mentioned are "the techniques or procedures used to gather and analyze data related to some research question or hypothesis" (Crotty, 1998, p. 3). Figure 2.1 provides a visual description of what the research process can be.

We will now provide you with a brief description of the theoretical framework in social sciences. Research design and methods will be reserved for the subsequent sections, followed by quality issues, a description of key elements of the write-up of an article, and practical issues for managers.

Theoretical Framework

Doing good research starts with a strong theoretical foundation. This foundation is usually a theoretical framework, which results from an overview of key concepts and current shortcomings of a chosen theory or theories. For proper theoretical frameworks, sport management researchers can look to the management literature, as we have done throughout this book (e.g., institutional theory, stakeholder theory, population ecology, and so forth).

While the theoretical framework reviews the key concepts, it is not a review of the literature. A review of literature is much broader in its treatment of a theory's key concepts. In fact, a review

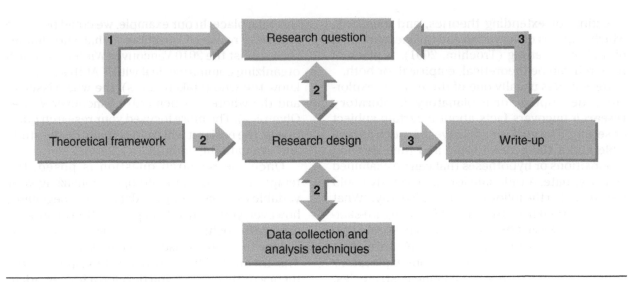

Figure 2.1 *The research process.*

of literature presents the "state of the research" in a particular area: all possible concepts, research findings, and remaining questions within that particular area of study. In contrast, the theoretical framework is focused solely on presenting the essential concepts and gaps in the literature that will help drive the research design and show the importance of the research.

Sometimes the theoretical framework simply provides the key concepts for the research, but it also can include a proposed outline (already found in a theory or developed by the researcher) that will be used as the guide for data collection and analysis. Regardless, it is important to know that, in terms of the number of concepts presented or length of the theoretical framework, more is not necessarily better. In other words, it is better to focus on those concepts that are essential for the development of the data collection and analysis methods.

The So-Called Debate on Qualitative-Quantitative Research

Before describing research designs and methods, we must make one important definitional note. We have, so far, been careful to use social sciences instead of qualitative research to describe research done in sport management, compared with the traditional natural, or "pure," sciences. This is an important point, and the title speaks to the debate currently going on to prove that good

research can be done with or without numbers. Many researchers still refer to the term qualitative to describe research done outside of the natural sciences—just look at the titles of references cited in this chapter. There is still a negative connotation to qualitative research in the sense that quantitative research is good research so qualitative research must be bad research. This is erroneous!

Research outside the natural sciences can be **quantitative** (uses numbers) in nature just as research in the natural sciences can use **qualitative** data (e.g., the smell or color of a chemical solution). Moreover, if a study relies on quantitative data, results must be interpreted to bring in a qualitative component. The main difference is how one looks at a phenomenon. What drives the type of data gathered is the research question. Therefore, social science research is more appropriate than qualitative research when describing the study's overall setting, and numerical and nonnumerical research is preferred to quantitative and qualitative research when describing the methods. Depending on the type of research done, it may be appropriate to use both qualitative and quantitative data. A researcher following this approach would be seen as using a mixed-methods research design (Creswell, 2003). The point is that the research question directs the approach.

Research Design

A **research design** is based not only on the theoretical framework but also on the research question,

TIME OUT   *Research Is Not Only Empirical; It Can Be Theoretical*

While we talk mostly about doing research in an empirical way—in other words, obtaining some type of result from a given research design—good research can also be purely theoretical. You can see it mostly in the form of a review of literature on the state of a research topic or as a development of a theoretical model. One example of theoretical research is Mark Rosentraub and David Swindell's (2002) article "Negotiating Games: Cities, Sports, and the Winner's Curse." The article examines how professional teams in North America present bargaining demands on their communities. Rosentraub and Swindell want to know if communities can avoid subsidizing sport

teams. The researchers first introduce the topic of cities bidding for teams and events. They then explain how bargaining and bidding are related to the state of information and the control of capital. These two elements join to construct a framework that large cities can follow to avoid the so-called winner's curse. This framework is based on external factors, such as league rules and the control over the supply and location of teams. It also depends on internal factors—cities' market characteristics, team owners' goals, related income potential, and public sector goals.

Based on information in Rosentraub and Swindell, (2002).

context, possibility of controlling events, and the desired outcomes. The key, however, is the research question. Getting the research question right makes the research process easier. We will now look at some of the more popular research designs.

Experiments and Quasi-Experiments

First, the research design most associated with the natural sciences is the *experiment*. An experiment seeks to answer how and why questions, so it is an explanatory type of research design. Using an experiment also requires the control of the study's events and, therefore, must be contemporary in nature (Yin, 2003), which means it is happening in real time. Pure experiments cannot truly be done in the social sciences. However, there are quasi-experiments. This research design approximates the experiment setting. It will often be used for psychological research, when subjects are asked to perform or be tested on a task. As such, it is a contemporary controlled setting.

The article by Chalip and colleagues (2003) presented in the vignette at the beginning of this chapter illustrates an experimental design with participants watching eight different videos. Kyle, Kerstetter, and Guadagnolo (2003) also use an experimental design to manipulate consumer price expectations of a 10K road race. Tarrant (1996) relied on a laboratory experiment as part

of a larger study to examine outdoor recreation experiences. Finally, Swearingen and Johnson's (1995) behavioral experiment examines the impact of uniformed park employees on visitors' off-trail hiking.

Surveys

A popular research design in sport management research is the *survey*. This is a popular strategy in sport management because it can answer who, what, when, where, and how many or how much—sometimes more than one question in the same study—without needing to control the setting (Yin, 2003). Because of this quality it can be used for exploratory, descriptive, or explanatory studies, depending on the exact question. Surveys are more accurate when done for contemporary events than for past events. Think of public opinion polls as the typical example of this strategy. The goal is to find out what people think on a certain topic. However, bigger does not mean better. More precisely, sample size must be carefully considered—it is as possible to get an equally good result with 200 participants as with 2,000, and it is cheaper and less time consuming when it comes to data entry and analysis.

An example of survey use is Chang and Chelladurai's (2003) study looking at differences in organizational commitment and citizenship behavior between part-time and full-time Korean sport organization employees. In turn, Funk, Ridinger, and Moorman (2003) show how the Sport Interest Inventory (SII) survey determines individual differences among women's professional sport consumers. Taylor (2003) relies on a national survey research design to examine the value and practice of diversity management of team-based community sport groups at sports' grassroots level.

Case Studies

A research design that is gaining popularity is the *case study*. Case studies are in-depth studies about a certain setting or event. This event can be historical or contemporary in nature. Case studies usually seek to answer *how* or *why* questions, but they can also answer *who, what, where,* or *when* questions for more exploratory or descriptive studies. Yin (2003) described case studies as an empirical inquiry investigating a real-life phenomenon whose boundaries and context are not clearly evident. Case studies have been criticized for lacking rigor, having little basis for generalization, taking too long, and resulting in too much information (and more variables than data points). However, there are steps a researcher can take to remedy these problems, such as using multiple sources of evidence, creating a case study database (database and investigator's report), and maintaining a chain of evidence among the case study questions, protocol, evidentiary sources, database, and report (Yin, 2003). In addition, within the case study research design, you may have one or more case studies, depending on your research question. For example, if you are interested in the challenges faced by volunteer sport groups at the grassroots level, you may conduct only a single case study of a typical sport group. However, if you are interested in the impact of culture on the challenges faced by volunteer sport groups at the grassroots level, then you would have to do a case study in various cultures and compare the results (e.g., Canada versus United Kingdom versus China versus Brazil).

There are quite a few examples of case studies conducted by sport management researchers in the literature. Gladwell, Anderson, and Sellers (2003) take a case study of North Carolina to examine fiscal trends in public parks and recreation between 1986 and 2001. Mason and Slack's (2003) case study of professional hockey explores the principal–agent relationship described in agency theory. Roche (1994) finds that a case study of the 1991 Sheffield Universiade Games illustrates how research on event production should use planning, political, and urban contextual processes as a framework.

Ethnographies

The *ethnography* is a popular research design with anthropology-based research. However, it is relatively unused in sport management research. An ethnography is similar to a case study in that it is a study about a given event or setting. Ethnographic methods use participant or close-up observations of the natural world and attempt to stay away from any prior theory commitment. Conversely, case studies can and do use theory to ground their research and narrow their focus as well as incorporate other methods (Yin, 2003). Ethnographic research is definitely field research, often requiring years of commitment.

For example, Tsang's (2000) ethnographic narrative explains her perspective on one part of her personal identity, her identity as a high-performance athlete. Silk and Amis (2000) collect ethnographic data to examine institutional pressures found in the production of televised sport for the 1998 Kuala Lumpur Commonwealth Games. Fourre (2001) incorporates sociological, psychological, and ethnographic viewpoints to examine the use of outdoor courses for business managers as professional training.

Grounded Theory

A related research design to ethnography is *grounded theory*. This research design originated with Glaser and Strauss (1967). It can actually be seen as a particular type of ethnographic inquiry with the purpose of building theory (Crotty, 1998). Specific steps are taken to have theory emerge from the data.

Jones (2002) takes a longitudinal grounded theory approach to look at the management implications in the development of voluntary community groups in urban parks, and finds that both the community and local council must be committed to the project to succeed. Schinke and da Costa (2001) turn to the principals of grounded theory to build a conceptual framework of elite athletes' explanations and behaviors in relation to support-staff behavior.

Action Research

A research design used for action-oriented studies is *action research*. As the name suggests, the focus is to perform research in an applied manner. Unlike the previous research designs, this strategy often originates with a protagonist, or "local" (organization, group, or individual), approaching a researcher for a specific purpose. The researcher and local outline a design for the field experiment. Findings are revealed to the protagonist as feedback and to set up the next step, if there is one (Miles & Huberman, 1994).

One of the best sport management action researchers is Wendy Frisby. In a 1997 article with Crawford and Dorer, she analyzes a participatory action research project done with low-income women to help them access local physical activity services. Frisby and her colleagues believe that action research can potentially "provide a new perspective by bringing those outside the physical activity system in contact with those who control service provision, policy development, and knowledge production in order to promote social and organizational change" (p. 9). The authors use a framework developed by Green et al. (1995) to evaluate an action research project. The framework includes elements related to participants and the nature of their involvement, the origin of the research question, the purpose of the research, its process and context, opportunities to address the issue of interest, and the nature of the research outcomes.

Frisby et al.'s (1997) research and its subsequent analysis shows that the local sport system can become more inclusive and the research can provide better understanding of, in this case, community involvement, collaborative decision making, resource control, power imbalances, nonhierarchical structures, and resistance to change. Green (1997) performs action research, to evaluate a soccer program as a child-centered alternative to traditional programs. Burden's (2000) work with action research examines community building and volunteering in Brisbane, Australia.

Data Collection Methods

Once the research design is chosen, the **data collection methods** and data analysis methods can be determined. But first, the unit of analysis must be selected. The *unit of analysis* is what you are studying. It is the focus of your research; it is the heart of your research. A unit of analysis can be an individual, a role, a group, an organization, a community, and so on. For example, if you are looking at volunteer commitment in a local sport club, your unit of analysis is the individual volunteer. In conjunction, the sampling procedure must be decided. Determining this and the unit of analysis is an important step because it helps to set boundaries on the research. You cannot research everything and everyone. These factors also place boundaries on the conclusions you can draw from your research and on the confidence in these conclusions (Miles & Huberman, 1994).

Sampling

Knowing the unit of analysis will help you determine your *sampling* strategy. If you are studying individuals, then your sample will be made up of individuals. If you are studying organizations (e.g., a case study of organizational performance), then you will be creating a sample of organizations. The key in sampling is to be representative of the population; size is *not* the most important factor. You can actually have a sample of one, whether one individual, group, or organization (e.g., a single case study). However, keep in mind sampling biases of noncoverage (missing key types of participants) and nonresponse (by having more than one planned participant per category) (Bauer & Aarts, 2000).

Gouldner's (1954) research had a profound influence on management studies. His longitudinal case study (done between 1948 and 1951) on the General Gypsum Company was one of the first to use a single case study in the management literature, and he showed how a single case study can have an impact on this body of literature.

Who you sample will depend on your research question, context, and desired outcome. For example, if you want to generalize, then you will want a more random sampling for as much representation of the population as possible. However, if you are doing an exploratory study and cannot determine your exact sample in advance or if you are interviewing elites—a finicky group—you may be able to access them only through a snowball sampling (i.e., start with one, get a referral to another, and so on). However, the final size of your sample is important, because it will determine whether, and to what extent, you can generalize your findings. If you are doing interviews, for example, and are unsure of how many to conduct, you will know it is time to stop when you reach saturation—the point when you aren't covering new ground because of the limited number of interpretations or versions of a reality.

Other examples of sampling strategies include maximum variation (units present the whole possible range of a characteristic, and patterns emerge), homogeneous (units are the same), theory-based (a fit emerges from your theoretical development), typical case (the average is exemplified), confirming or disconfirming cases (units support a pattern or variations), extreme or deviant case (examples represent extremes), random purposeful (a random sample examines a too-large population), stratified purposeful (subgroups of a population are examined, especially if comparisons are desired), criterion-based (units meet specific characteristics), opportunistic (unexpected or new lead is pursued), combination (sampling of multiple types), and convenience (time or money or effort saved) (Miles & Huberman, 1994).

Sport management research uses many of the sampling strategies, although often the sampling strategy is not explicitly stated; instead details of the sample are provided. Alexandris, Dimitriadis, and Kasiara (2001) apply a random purposeful sampling to examine behavioral consequences of perceived service quality in Greek fitness clubs. Boronico and Newbert (2001) combine a typical case, criterion-based, and convenience sampling in the study of Monmouth University to empirically examine mathematical modeling analysis of play-calling strategy in U.S. football.

Questionnaires

Once the unit of analysis and sampling procedures are determined, you must establish what type of data will uncover the answer to your research question. One of the most widely used data collection methods is the *questionnaire*. There are two advantages: You can potentially reach thousands of people quickly, and data analysis can be simplified if you set up closed response (fixed number of possible answers) questions with a statistical analysis software program such as SPSS. While it may seem simple to build a questionnaire, it is actually an art form. You have to consider question wording (it must be response-friendly), response categories (Likert scale, such as ranges of 1 to 7, 1 to 3, 1 to 4, 1 to 5, or 1 to 6 or numbers for salaries: "under $10,000, $10,000-$30,000," and so forth) versus raw data, the questionnaire length, how to raise potentially difficult or objectionable questions (e.g., respondent's Social Security number), the order of the questions (one shouldn't influence those that follow), and random respondent versus the identified respondent (name is on questionnaire)

(Poe et al., 1988; Dillman, Sinclair, & Clark, 1993; Kronberger & Wagner, 2000).

You also must decide how you will be presenting the questions: in person, by phone or mail, or through the Internet (either by e-mail or through a Web site). The way the questionnaire is distributed will affect your response rate: Mailed questionnaires typically have the lowest return rate. Another large consideration is the number of respondents: You can reach more people through e-mail than you can by visiting each person (although the quality of data through e-mail may be lower than that of a face-to-face encounter). Data analysis of questionnaires is dictated by your response categories. Closed questions typically are analyzed quantitatively (e.g., "30 percent of respondents made less than $10,000 a year") and usually with a statistical analysis software program such as SPSS. Open-ended questions are qualitatively analyzed for emerging response patterns, usually with a qualitative data analysis software program such as ATLAS.ti or NVivo.

Questionnaires can be designed as the sole element of a study, as in the case of Kang's (2002) questionnaire to develop a decision-making process framework for participant sport consumption, a framework integrating the participant's own image congruence, attitude, and intentions. But a questionnaire is also effective in combination with other methods (e.g., interviews), as in the case of Gladden and Funk's (2002) questionnaire following a focus group method to understand brand association in team sport.

Interviews

The *interview* is an effective data collection method preceding or following the questionnaire, or on its own. Whether the interview is done in conjunction with the questionnaire (or any other method) or by itself will depend on the type of research and desired result. For example, an exploratory study on large-scale sporting events may start with interviews to determine the issues involved in such a setting, and then move to observations and questionnaires as the study develops a descriptive and then explanatory focus.

Interviews can be done one-on-one or in groups (called focus groups), face to face, or on the phone. A single interviewer usually conducts 15 to 25 personal interviews, or six to eight group interviews. Another way of determining the number of interviews is to set a two-interviews-per-cell characteristic. In other words, you multiply the number of characteristics you want to study by

A successful interview requires trust and rapport between interviewer and interviewee.

two and end up with a rough estimate of your total sample size (Gaskell, 2000). Reaching saturation then indicates the end of your sampling. Of course, the number of interviews you do can depend on cost, time frame, and availability.

The purpose of interviews typically is to collect a range of opinions on the issue being studied. The interview is a joint effort between the interviewer and interviewee (Gaskell, 2000), and issues of trust and rapport can influence the depth of the interviewee's responses. These responses will also vary, depending on the type of interview guide (list of questions). The interview format may be structured (no deviation from question list; oftentimes a questionnaire), semistructured (questions are set, but others can be added), or unstructured (questions emerge as interview progresses) (Yin, 2003).

The strength of the interview is that it is highly revealing, even through perceived causal inferences, and has a clear focus (the research topic) (Yin, 2003). However, interviews do have limitations: language barriers (misinterpretations can result), omitted details (probe for more information), distorted views and response bias (compare responses to confirm veracity), reflexivity (the subject gives the response you want), bias from poorly constructed questions, and inadequate recall of the distant past (Gaskell, 2000; Yin, 2003).

The interview process can last from 20 minutes to more than two hours. However, interviews typically last 1 to 1 1/2 hours. The process starts with the interview guide, which should be tied to the theoretical frame. Once you meet your interviewee, introduce the topic of interest (purpose of the research), thank the subject for agreeing to the interview, ensure confidentiality, ask if there are questions related to the research or the process, and, if applicable, get permission to tape the interview so you are free to talk, not having to take notes. Depending on your questions you may not need a recorder. If your questions require short answers there is no need to record them, for example, if you ask the gender or the age of a participant. It is best to record involved answers (longer than a paragraph) to capture accurate responses. Regardless of the use of a tape-recorder, interview or field notes usually supplement answers. Start an interview with nonthreatening questions, and probe first responses for more information or clarification. At the end, thank the interviewee. Finally, give the subject time to relax after the interview is officially concluded; you may get some extra information (Gaskell, 2000).

Once the interview is over, transcribe the recording, including such details as the length of pauses between responses if you are doing a conversation analysis. In a basic analysis, emphasis is on what they said, not how they said it. Interview analysis typically involves reading and re-reading transcripts, constructing a matrix table for each issue studied, and looking for patterns of responses (cf. Miles & Huberman, 1994; Gaskell, 2000).

In research, interviews may be the only data source, as in the case of Chalip and Leyns' (2002) study on business leveraging in relation to a sport event. Higham and Hinch (2003) predominately use interviews in their study of sport, space, and time in relation to the effects of a New Zealand rugby team's influence on tourism. But interviews may be merged with other data sources, especially if you are doing a case study. For example, Mason and Slack (2003) combine interviews with archival material and documentation to examine principal–agent relationships in professional hockey.

Observations

The method of *observation* is often used in conjunction with other types of data gathering. Observation can be direct (you watch what is going on) or participant (you take part in and watch what is going on) in nature. Observation activities range from the formal protocol, which involves measuring the incidence of a particular issue over a particular time, to the more casual, for example if you simply need to see the environment in which your research is taking place. One strength of observation is its real-time and contextual nature (it provides context for a phenomenon going on at that actual time). Another strong point, especially for participant observation, is that it provides a description of interpersonal behavior and motive. However, observation methods can be time-consuming, costly, selective (you can't watch everything at once; you miss key elements), reflexive (individuals may modify their normal behavior or act as they think you expect they should—it's called the Hawthorne Effect), and biased, because the participant observer is manipulating the setting (Yin, 2003).

Participant observation typically is done in combination with other data collection techniques. Fairley (2003) uses participant observation in combination with interviews to answer the question of why some fans travel to follow professional sport teams. Silk, Slack, and Amis (2000) combine observations with interviews and document analysis to examine the production of televised sport.

Archival Material and Documentation

Interviews and observations are often supplemented by *archival material and documentation*

data collection methods. Types of data include documents such as memoranda, bulletins, agendas, minutes of meetings, letters, organizational charts, reports, proposals, announcements, formal evaluations, newspaper clippings, service records, maps, lists, and personal records. These data can be gathered from myriad places: the media, the Internet, archival organizations (including city hall), organizations, individuals, and so on. Collecting these types of data is best done first because they help clarify the research setting. Such data also supports findings from other sources (e.g., interviews) because they are stable (can be examined repeatedly), not obtrusive to possible participants, exact (e.g., accurately names board members of an organization), broad in possible coverage (over time, events, or settings), and precise (and often quantitative in nature). However, they may be hard to obtain, you may have access blocked (for political reasons or because of sensitive material such as health reports), they may be selective (you may be limited to particular information), and they can have a certain reporting bias from the author (Yin, 2003).

Archival material and documentation can be the single data source, as in the case of Pedersen, Whisenant, and Schneider's (2003) study on gendering of sport newspaper personnel and newspaper coverage. However, archival material and documentation often are combined with other data sources, especially to provide a better overview of the case at hand, as is the case with Mason and Slack's (2003) study or in the case of O'Brien and Slack's (2003) use of documents and interviews to examine organizational change in the English Rugby Union.

Other Types of Data

Other types of data that can be collected include physical artifacts, visual, electronic, and audio materials. Physical artifacts, such as instruments, tools, works of art, and high-tech gear, can provide a study with insight into either cultural features of a setting or technological operation (e.g., the quality of the production processes of a sporting goods manufacturer). However, their availability and selectivity can be a problem (Yin, 2003). Visual, electronic, and audio materials reveal various clues, such as a representation of the study participants or to discern the meaning of a phenomenon for a particular society or culture. Discerning meaning is usually done through the use of semiotics (the science of signs) by comparing the signifier (what you actually see and hear) with the signified (what the signifier refers to, a concept, an idea, a meaning) (Penn, 2000). For an example of semiotics, see Barthes' (1957) *Mythologies*. If you are using moving images or sound (e.g., a song, a sound byte), you need to transcribe what you see and hear. This can have drawbacks: It can be time consuming and selective (you can't transcribe everything you see and hear in a movie excerpt). Therefore, you must be selective in what you transcribe and that selection must be theory driven (Rose, 2000).

Sport management researchers are starting to use these other types of data in their studies. Pedersen, Whisenant, and Schneider's (2003) study is such an example, combining archival material and documentation with photographs as data sources. Higgs and Weiller (1994) analyze 60 hours of taped televised coverage of the 1992 Barcelona Summer Olympics to examine gender bias in television coverage.

Data Analysis Methods

Once you have your data, you have to manipulate it in one way or another in order to answer your research question. This is where **data analysis methods** enter. Data analysis must be tied not only to your collected data but also to your research question and theoretical framework so that you can obtain meaningful results. Complex analysis combined with poor data will lead only to poor results. Be sure to collect the right data and select the appropriate analysis.

Statistical Analyses

When dealing with quantitative (numerical) data of any sort, you will most likely use a *statistical analysis* technique. This is usually done with a software program such as SPSS. The first thing you must know is the type of data or score you have. Nominal variables have values that differ in quality only (e.g., gender). Ordinal variables have values ordered by quantity (e.g., social class). Interval variables are ordinal variables but with equally sized intervals between each. Ratio variables are interval variables but with a true zero point (e.g., test scores) (Evans, 1998; Babbie, 1999).

The next step is to determine the statistical analysis you want to do. You have three choices: descriptive, inferential, or correlational and predictive statistics. Descriptive statistics help you to summarize, present, or organize your data

set. They are mostly for clarification purposes. Descriptive statistics include the mean or average, median, mode, range, frequency, variance, and standard deviation of a particular score within a group of scores (Evans, 1998). Inferential statistics are used when you want to infer something about the population at large from the information provided by a sample of that population. Inferential statistics include chi square (to determine the probability that a discrepancy in the sample is due only to sampling error), t-test (for comparing two sample means), and ANOVAs (to determine the effect and interaction of two different treatments on a sample) (Evans, 1998; Babbie, 1999). If you have only nominal and ordinal variables, you would apply the chi square technique. If you have a nominal or ordinal and interval or ratio variables, then you would rely on the t-test or ANOVA techniques (Babbie, 1999). Finally, correlation and predictive statistics are used to describe a relationship between events (correlation) or to predict the outcome from one event to the next (predictive). Correlation however does not mean causation—you can correlate almost anything. Causation can only be done in an experimental design. Correlation statistics include the Pearson product-moment correlation (a reflection of how close two variables are to a linear relationship) and the Spearman rank-order correlation (correlation indicator for nominal or ordinal variables) (Evans, 1998; Trochim, 2001). The main predictive technique is regression analysis, which may be linear, multiple, partial, or curvilinear in nature (Babbie, 1999). The regression line is created by plotting the complete set of calculated predicted values of the dependent variable (y) for the set values of the independent variable (x) (Evans, 1998).

Many examples of statistical analysis are found in sport management research. Armstrong-Doherty (1996) used a Spearman rank-order correlation analysis to show that various stakeholders can have resource dependence-based (perceived) control over university athletic departments. Kent and Chelladurai's (2001) study found that both the Pearson product-moment correlation and regression analyses indicate that there was a correlation between transformational leadership and leader–member exchange quality, as well as to show that these two elements are related to organizational commitment and organizational citizenship behavior. McGehee, Yoon, and Cárdenas (2003) use a combination of descriptive statistics, Cronbach's alpha, and cluster analysis to study involvement and travel for recreational runners.

Two notes of caution for all these statistical analyses:

1. Used improperly, they can make bad data seem good.
2. The data set may give you a statistic as a finding but you must still interpret the end result to determine whether it is significant or not and what that number means in reference to your sample and population. Use the theoretical framework to do so.

Content Analysis

If you have qualitative (nonnumerical) data, then you may want to do a *content analysis*. This technique is a systematic classification involving the counting of sections or units of a text. The result of the content analysis is the dependent variable (i.e., what you are looking for). Content analysis designs can be descriptive, normative (comparison between sample and a given standard), cross-sectional (different contexts, for example), longitudinal (over time to look at changes), cultural indicator for a certain issue, or parallel (comparison of longitudinal studies) in nature (Bauer, 2000).

Content analysis involves coding, or the assigning of labels to sections of text. The coding frame (set of codes) can be theory driven or emerge out of the data. Consideration must be made for the coding frame, such as the nature of the categories, the types of code variables, the organizing principal of the coding frame, the coding process, and the coder training. The coding frame must be coherent, explicit (a code book helps), reliable, and valid.

Content analysis allows for the systematic and public analysis of textual material (whether this material be originally in written, verbal, physical, audio, video, or electronic form) to make generalizations to the collective level from individual texts. It can also help construct historical data. However, separating the units analyzed may create inaccuracies in interpretation because it tends to focus on the frequency, the recurrence of codes, thereby neglecting rare or absent elements that could have a potential impact on findings. The relationship between sections in the text that are coded differently can also be lost (Bauer, 2000). Silk (2001) provides a description of his inductive content analysis procedure for examining the importance of the nation in media representation during the 1998 Kuala Lumpur Commonwealth Games.

Coding

Coding means finding patterns and identifying themes. Coding is an intrinsic part of nonnumerical data analysis. It helps to link different segments of the data, it identifies relevant concepts or themes, it helps make the data set more manageable, and it helps expand and transform the data. Once concepts or themes are highlighted, examples of those phenomena can be retrieved within the data set, and an analysis of those segments can be done in order to find similarities, differences, patterns, and structures within the text to see the possible relationships between concepts (Coffey & Atkinson, 1996).

To help in comparing the different segments of interest, Miles and Huberman (1994) propose two methods: matrix and network. A matrix is a table showing the relationship between an independent variable and a dependent variable. It is useful for determining the flow, location, and connection of events, and to eyeball patterns. This technique is good for exploratory studies and for comparisons of studies. A network is a collection of points (nodes) connected by lines (links). This technique works for dealing with many variables at one time and when trying to draw relationships among the different variables. In this way, explanatory studies can benefit from this technique.

A good example of a content analysis coding method is O'Brien and Slack's (2003) article "An Analysis of Change in an Organizational Field: The Professionalization of English Rugby Union." In the article, O'Brien and Slack describe the types of data they gathered, their coding scheme, and their coding procedure. Other examples include articles such as Pedersen, Whisenant, and Schneider's (2003) study on gender in sport newspaper personnel and newspaper coverage, and Mason and Slack's (2003) principal–agent study in professional hockey.

Of course, coding is also found with numerical data analysis. However, it occurs in a different way. For example, a researcher may be interested in the popularity of sport as a marketing strategy. In this case, every time a sport reference is made in an advertisement, the researcher would code that instance, and then she would proceed to an appropriate statistical analysis.

Computer-Assisted Analysis

As alluded to earlier in this chapter, *computer-assisted analysis* is done to help with data analysis. Programs like NUD*IST, NVivo and ATLAS.ti are tools to mechanize tasks of ordering and archiving. They don't actually do data interpretation. Codes are used to highlight sections of text referring to a particular issue of interest. These codes can originate from theory, from common sense, or from the data itself if you are doing grounded theory. Creating subcategories of these codes or dimensions is called dimensionalization. Comparison and dimensionalization allow for deeper, more fine-tuned analyses than those done manually. It allows you to see co-occurrences, such as overlapping text segments, nesting segments within segments, proximity of two segments, and sequences of segments. However, it does not highlight the relationship between concepts—you have to do that. This allows you to see the relationship between different highlighted concepts, and helps you analyze your data. Of course, once analysis is done, you must return to the data to confirm or discount your findings.

Using computer-assisted analysis increases efficiency (you can increase your sample size and number, and decrease cost), increases accuracy (it is a more systematic and explicit research process), and increases creativity (you can play with the data to extract more results). However, it can also alienate the researcher from the data

because you focus on the codes and it can reify codes (Kelle, 2000).

While most articles do not go into detail on how to use computer-assisted analysis (it is understood that for any large amount of nonnumerical data, a computer program must be used to make data analysis simpler and less time-consuming) Cousens and Slack (1996) include a paragraph to explain that their data on sport sponsorship and the fast food industry was scanned for the occurrence of key words, which indicates their use of computer-assisted analysis.

Issues of Quality

How do you evaluate your research and other research? Two key terms that you may have heard are *validity* and *reliability*. **Validity** refers to the degree to which an instrument measures what it is supposed to measure, and **reliability** refers to consistency of measurement. If you look in different books dealing with validity, you may find differences in the number and names of validity types. However, here are the most widely used (cf. Gaskell & Bauer, 2000; Trochim, 2001; Yin, 2003):

TIME OUT   *Research in Book Form*

Usually, researchers will publish their research in leading academic journals. This is done in part to reach a target (academic) audience, as a job requirement for academics, and to get a certain prestige if you can publish in a top journal. Also, the 20-odd pages of a research article are usually enough to adequately present research findings. There are cases, although scarce, of sport management research being published in book format. This allows the authors to reach a potentially large audience and provide more details of their research, especially if they are using case studies or other qualitative methods.

One example is Burbank, Andranovich, and Heying's (2001) *Olympic Dreams: The Impact of Mega-Events on Local Politics*. The authors examine the impact of mega-events—specifically the Olympic Games—and the role

of local politics. Three case studies are used: Los Angeles, Atlanta, and Salt Lake City. They frame the studies in regime theory that follows the principle of division of state (government institutions controlled by publicly elected officials) and market (an economy that is driven by largely private enterprise). Collected data comes from multiple sources: interviews, archival material, documents, and poll survey results. The book is organized as follows: introduction and research design, theoretical framework, case studies, and conclusion. The major theme of the findings is that the symbolic value of the Olympics allows proponents to set the boundaries of public policy debates and is a vehicle for pushing development and infrastructure interests.

Based on information in Burbank, Andranovich, and Heying (2001).

- **Construct validity:** Is there adequate relationship between the test and the theoretical framework?
  - Content validity: Is the sample adequate for the concept you want to measure?
  - Face validity: Have you, on the surface, measured the concept you actually wanted to measure?
- **Criterion validity:** Can different elements within the test be differentiated if they are related in any way?
- **Internal validity:** Can readers have confidence in your findings through explicit telling of the coding frame?
- **External validity:** Can results be statistically (for numerical data) or analytically (linking results back to the theory; for nonnumerical data) generalizable?

Reliability has two forms: interrater and test–retest reliability. Interrater reliability is the main focus of qualitative research and refers to whether two different researchers get the same results with the same data set. The more detail that is provided during data collection and analysis, as well as the reporting of results, the higher the likelihood that interrater reliability will be high. Test–retest reliability is usually reserved for numerical data and refers to whether the same data set will provide the same findings when tested and retested using the same instrument (Gaskell & Bauer, 2000). Think of when you step on a scale to weigh yourself. If you weigh yourself once, step off the scale, then weigh yourself again. The scale should give you the same number. If it does, then it has high test–retest reliability.

The Write-Up

So you've set up your research, you've collected your data and analyzed it, now what do you do? As a practitioner, you would write a report and present your findings to your superiors or employer (if you are under contract). Unlike the academic process described below, writing a report is usually a shorter process because 1) you may have a specific deadline, 2) you do not need to go through the peer-review process, 3) you typically do not need to provide a theoretical framework or discuss validity and reliability, and 4) your superiors are more interested in the findings' bottom line. However, you still want to be as explicit—yet concise—

Submission requirements for various journals are usually posted on the journals' websites.

as possible in your writing so that your readers have confidence in your results and suggestions for actions, if any. The report would typically start with a title page followed by a table of contents. An executive summary (about one page) of the report and its findings would then be provided. This would be followed by a background section that can include an introduction, history, or context for the report, and a description of the methodology used. The results are then presented. A summary with recommendations typically ends the actual report. Appendices are included to provide additional information not essential to the basic understanding of the report but important to the process (e.g., details of respondents, action plan, and time lines). The exact format of the report should be agreed upon with your employer or supervisor at the beginning of the process.

Alternatively, you can publish the findings in a book or an article, or present your findings at a conference (although this alternative does not always require the writing of a full article). While a book can reach a broader range of readers, the article is the more popular format. The article's actual format can be traditional—title, abstract, introduction, theoretical framework, research design, results, discussion, conclusion—or instead use narratives (storylike) or modifications of the traditional format.

Writing an article is a long process. You have to determine what to include and be precise, but not exclude information pertinent to understanding the research process and findings. The key is to be as transparent as possible, especially if you are going to be collecting and analyzing qualitative data. Transparency means being as explicit as possible about your perspective, research design, data collection, and analysis techniques, and the range of results obtained. Your perspec-

tive is *not* simply a review of the literature—that would be like listing all possible works on a given topic. Instead, you must ensure that you build a theoretical framework, which guides your choice of research design (including data collection and analysis methods), results presentation, and discussion. In turn, the discussion is not a review of your results but a discussion of the results in relation to your theoretical framework.

Also be sure to check the required format and writing style before submitting to the journal you hope will publish your article. Select a journal based on its audience and the focus of your article (e.g., researcher versus practitioner, sport versus management journals). In other words, the same piece of research would be written differently if it were sent to the *Journal of Sport Management* (sport, researcher) versus the *Academy of Management Journal* (management, researcher) versus *SportBusiness International* (sport, practitioner).

The writing process does not end here because an article is typically peer-reviewed—usually three reviewers will evaluate the article in a blind review format (there is no name on the manuscript; only the editor knows the article's author). This process has one of three outcomes: accepted for publication, rejected, or returned for revisions and resubmission (with no guarantee of acceptance). Unless you are accepted for publication on the first try, which is rare, you will have to revise your article, probably more than once. From the time you begin to write to the point of acceptance for publication, you will go through many drafts—it is not unusual to have more than 10 drafts for one article—and it can take a year or more for this whole writing process. Table 2.1 provides an overview of the research process steps and their respective components.

Table 2.1 Components of the Research Process

Research designs	Data collection methods	Data analysis methods	Write-up
Experiment and quasi-experiment	Questionnaire	Statistical analysis	Article
	Interview	Content analysis	Report
Survey	Observation	Computer-assisted analysis	Conference proceeding
Case study	Archival material and documentation		Book
Ethnography	Physical artifacts		
Grounded theory	Visual, electronic, audio material		
Action research			

Based on information from Miles and Huberman (1994), Crotty (1998), Evans (1998), Babbie (1999), Bauer and Gaskell (2000), and Yin (2003).

KEY ISSUES FOR MANAGERS

As a sport manager, you may be asked to do some research to help your company's performance (e.g., customer satisfaction survey) or evaluate research to determine the best course of action (e.g., a new test is developed for detecting a performance-enhancing drug). As a consultant, you would be asked to do research to help the employer (the company hiring you) be more effective or efficient in a certain area. For these reasons, you must be aware of the relationship between the research question, the theoretical approach, research design, methods, findings, and data interpretation. A good piece of research will be clear about each step and flow logically from one to another. However, your employers or clients may not be as interested in your research design or require a detailed description of it. They are more interested in the summary of the findings and any suggestions for future action that stem from your research. Establish a writing tone consistent with your organization's vocabulary—it doesn't have to sound "scientific." The point is, be clear about the format of the report to be presented (i.e., ask your superior), but the presentation style should not have an impact on your actual research method.

SUMMARY AND CONCLUSIONS

Research can be exploratory, descriptive, or explanatory in nature. The research question, written properly, will dictate the appropriate theoretical framework and methods used to collect and analyze data.

Research design includes data collection and analysis techniques. Before collecting any data, you must determine your unit of analysis and sample size. Research designs include quasi-experiments, surveys, case studies, ethnographies, grounded theory, and action research. Data collection methods include questionnaires, interviews, observations, as well as the use of archival material and documentation, physical artifacts, visual, electronic, and audio material.

Data analysis methods can be statistical in nature. Statistical analyses can be descriptive, inferential, or correlational–predictive in nature. Qualitative data will often be dissected using content analysis. Software programs are of great help in content analysis. The coded data can be placed in a matrix or network for analysis.

Finally, the quality of the research can be determined according to the degree of validity and reliability. Validity types are internal, external, criterion, and construct (content and face), and refer to how well an instrument measures what it is supposed to measure. Reliability can be interrater or test–retest reliability, and refers to the degree of measurement consistency.

KEY CONCEPTS

data analysis methods (p. 27)
data collection methods (p. 23)
descriptive research (p. 19)
explanatory research (p. 19)
exploratory research (p. 19)
qualitative (p. 20)
quantitative (p. 20)

reliability (p. 29)
research design (p. 20)
research process (p. 18)
research question (p. 19)
theoretical framework (p. 17)
validity (p. 29)

REVIEW QUESTIONS

1. List the different steps of the research process.

2. What is the difference between exploratory, descriptive, and explanatory research?

3. What is the difference between a theoretical framework and a review of the literature?

4. Why is a theoretical framework essential in research?

5. What is the quantitative–qualitative research debate?

6. What are validity and reliability and why are they important in research?

7. Choose a recent article from an academic sport management journal and evaluate the research presented.

8. Choose a professional sport management report and evaluate the research presented.

9. Pick a topic from one of the chapters in this textbook. What research designs can be used to examine this topic and why?

10. You have been approached by the municipal parks and recreation department to do a study on the effectiveness of its organization. Describe the research process starting with the research question all the way to the write-up.

11. You are a researcher interested in the following research question: Is there a difference between the high school football fan and the professional football fan? If so, what are the differences? Explain how you would go about answering this question and how you would present your findings, providing a reason for each choice.

12. You are the manager of the local minor-league hockey association and are asked to remedy the problem of losing volunteers every year. Pose your research question and explain how you would go about answering the association's problem through an appropriate research process.

13. You have been named national minister of sport after your country experienced the worst Summer Olympic Games showing ever. How would you conduct a research project to analyze the national sport system's performance?

14. Skim through the recent issues of different sport management journals. What are some of the most important research questions in sport management today?

15. What sport management research questions would you like to see answered? Why? How?

SUGGESTIONS FOR FURTHER READING

A multitude of books and articles deal with the various steps of the research process (including concepts not dealt with here such as epistemology, ontology, and theoretical perspective), especially in the management and sociology literature. Some good examples that are also accessible for new researchers are Aiken and West's (1991) *Multiple Regression: Testing and Interpreting Interactions;* Bhaskar's (1989) *Reclaiming Reality: A Critical Introduction to Contemporary Philosophy;* Burrell and Morgan's (1979) *Sociological Paradigms and Organizational Analysis: Elements of the Sociology of Corporate Life;* Creswell's (2003) *Research design: Qualitative and Mixed Methods Approaches;* Denscombe's (1998) *The Good Research Guide for Small-Scale Social Research Projects;* Denzin and Lincoln's (2000) *Handbook of Qualitative Research, Second Edition;* Eisenhardt's (1989) "Building Theories From Case Study Research" in the *Academy of Management Review;* Evan's (1998) *Using Basic Statistics in the Social Sciences;* Guba's (1990) *The Paradigm Dialog;* Miles and Huberman's (1994) *Qualitative Data Analysis, Second Edition;* Morgan's (1983) *Beyond Method: Strategies for Social Research;* Strauss' (1987) *Qualitative Analysis for Social Scientists;* and Yin's (2003) *Case Study Research: Design and Methods, Third Edition.* There are also some good readings in sport literature, such as Brannigan's (1999) *The Sport Scientist: Research Adventures;* and Jackson and Burton's (1998) *Leisure Studies: Prospects for the 21st Century.*

CASE FOR ANALYSIS

A New Sport Policy for Canada

In May 2002, the Canadian government unveiled its new Canadian Sport Policy. The following is the process the government used.

In January 2000, a consultation process was launched by the federal secretary of state for amateur sport. Federal, provincial, and territorial governments worked together to ensure that major stakeholders at all levels of sport would be involved. These included more than a thousand individuals, such as athletes, coaches, parents, officials, volunteers, paid staff, representatives of municipal recreation departments, provincial and national sport organizations, local school boards, business people, and government officials.

These stakeholders were able to participate in six regional conferences to make their views known on the current state of sport in the country and their suggestions for the future. Working from discussion papers and the results of various surveys, the conference delegates provided their input on resources, ethics and values, leadership and partnership, participation, promotion, and development. Discussions were also held with the Aboriginal Sport Circle, Athletes CAN, sport officials, national single and multisport organizations, and the media. Discussions focused on the issues of inclusion and equity.

The conferences and discussion resulted in the following points for more effective Canadian sport policy:

- The recognition of the interrelationship between the various forms of sport;
- Sport has social and health benefits;
- Participation in sport at any level (entry level, recreational, or competitive) affects the other levels; and

- Development of sport is dependent on the effectiveness of school programs, the promotion of recreational activities, and the promotion of a healthy and active lifestyle for all Canadians.

In April 2001, the federal government released a discussion paper, *Towards a Canadian Sport Policy*, which formed the basis for the National Summit on Sport held later that month. The sport community's major stakeholders approved the paper's basic findings and recommendations.

The paper was then discussed at a conference that same month of federal, provincial, and territorial ministers responsible for sport, fitness, and recreation. The ministers agreed that a Canadian sport policy should be developed over the next 10 years with an aim to achieving a more effective and integrated Canadian sport system. An action plan by the federal government and complementary action plans by members of the sport community and each jurisdiction were then developed to determine how each stakeholder would contribute to the goals of the sport policy.

Based on information in *Sport Canada* (2002).

Questions

1. What were the research design, data collection, and data analysis methods used? If any, what additional information would you need to answer the question?

2. Evaluate the quality of this research, given the fact that this was a professional report and not an academic article.

3. Why is it important for the government to do a write-up of the findings?

4. How would you go about developing a complementary action plan for your jurisdiction?

Chapter 3

Organizational Goals and Effectiveness

LEARNING OBJECTIVES

When you have read this chapter, you should be able to

1. explain why goals are important in a sport organization,
2. identify the different types of goals that may be found in a sport organization,
3. explain the difference between organizational effectiveness and efficiency,
4. understand the different approaches that have been used to study organizational effectiveness, and
5. compare and contrast the benefits of each approach.

SWIMMING NATATION CANADA: AN EFFECTIVE ORGANIZATION?

At the 1978 British Commonwealth Games held in Edmonton, Alberta, Canadian swimmers won 15 gold medals. Graham Smith, the world record holder in the individual medley, won six of those gold medals. Members of the Canadian Amateur Swimming Association (now Swimming Natation Canada) were understandably elated and felt that there were even greater achievements to come. At their 1978 annual general meeting, delegates demonstrated their optimism about the future when they adopted as their organization's goal to be number one in the world rankings by the end of the 1980s. They even adopted a catchy motto, "Go for 1t," replacing the "I" in "It" with the numeral "1."

Canada, along with most Western nations, boycotted the 1980 Olympic Games in Moscow, but by the 1984 Olympics, Swimming Natation Canada appeared to be on the way to achieving its goal. Canadian swimmers won 10 medals, 4 of which were gold. Even the absence of Eastern Bloc athletes did little to detract from the Canadian performances; three of the four gold medals were won with world record times. During the 1980s, Canadian swimmers also won two world championship gold medals; athletes like Anne Ottenbrite, Peter Szmidt, Victor Davis, Alex Baumann, Tom Ponting, and Allison Higson produced world-class times.

(continued)

(continued)

One of the few successes of the Canadian swimming team in the 1990s and early 2000s was the gold medal won by the Canadian synchronized swimming team at the 1999 Pan American Games.

© Associated Press, AP

However, in 1988 in the Olympic Games in Seoul, Canadian swimmers won only two medals, one silver and one bronze; both were for relay events. Some members suggested that the organization had promoted its goal—to be number one—at the expense of other components of the national program. The organization was seen as lacking the infrastructure to meet the high performance requirements of the sport: It had no adequate talent identification system, coaching education was lagging behind other countries, and the needs of many grassroots members were not being met. As a result, in April 1989, a provincial executive directors' meeting proposed a new organiza-

Based on information in Stubbs (1989).

tional goal: "To provide the opportunity for every individual involved in the sport of swimming to reach his or her maximum potential in fitness and excellence."

While this grassroots approach may have worked well for the organization's membership, it hindered elite-level efforts. The goal had an impact on the Canadian swimming team's performance at the 2004 Athens Olympic Games: The team didn't win a single medal. Although there was public outcry and the national team's coach was fired, given the grassroots goal, the team's poor performance should not be a surprise to goal setters.

All organizations exist to achieve a particular goal or set of goals. For Swimming Natation Canada, that goal was to be number one in the world by 1990. Despite the successes of many individual athletes, the organization did not achieve its goal. Does this mean that Swimming Natation Canada was not an effective organization? Effectiveness, as we will see, is a difficult concept to define and measure. Researchers over the years have had considerable difficulty deciding exactly what the term means. In fact, some researchers (Goodman, Atkin, & Schoorman, 1983; Hannan &

Freeman, 1977a) have even suggested abandoning "effectiveness" as a scientific concept. In a similar vein, Connolly, Conlon, and Deutsch (1980, p. 211) criticized the research literature on effectiveness for being in a state of "conceptual disarray"; Nord (1983, p. 95) suggested the area is in a "chaotic state of affairs"; and Quinn and Cameron (1983) describe effectiveness as a paradoxical concept.

Robbins (1990) notes that a review of the organizational effectiveness studies that proliferated in the 1960s and 1970s identified 30 different criteria, all claiming to measure effectiveness (see

Campbell, 1977; Steers, 1975). Included were such concepts as productivity, profit, growth, goal consensus, and stability. In a study of effectiveness in intercollegiate athletic programs, Chelladurai, Haggerty, Campbell, and Wall (1981) identified 11 criteria of effectiveness:

- Achieved excellence
- Spectator interest
- Adequacy of facilities
- Career opportunities
- Student recruitment potential
- Competitive opportunities
- Sharing of costs by team
- Operating costs
- Activity as a life sport
- Satisfaction of athletes
- Sport characteristics (promotes fitness)

Despite the problems associated with the idea of organizational effectiveness, creating a successful organization is in many ways the central task of the sport manager. As Cameron (1986, p. 540) notes, "all theories of organization rely on some conception of the difference between high-quality (effective) performance and poor-quality (ineffective) performance. Hence, effectiveness is inherently tied to all *theory* on organizations" (emphasis in original). Benson (1977) similarly argues that whether explicit or not, organizational analysis deals with effectiveness.

In this chapter we examine the idea of goals and effectiveness. We look specifically at the importance of goals for a sport organization, the different types of goals a sport organization may have, the contrast between effectiveness and efficiency, and the different approaches used to study organizational effectiveness. The chapter also presents some of the concerns that have been expressed about the concepts of goals and effectiveness.

Importance of Understanding Organizational Goals and Effectiveness

Sport organizations are goal-seeking entities, structured to achieve a particular purpose (or purposes). The goals of a sport organization are extremely important for communicating its purpose and identity, to both employees and to external constituents. For some sport organizations, such as a professional hockey team or a college basketball team, it is often assumed that effectiveness is simply measured by the number of games the team wins. If this were the case, we may ask, why in 1988 did Edmonton Oilers' owner Peter Pocklington trade away the NHL's all-time leading goal scorer, Wayne Gretzky, at the height of his career? Did Mr. Pocklington want an effective organization? The answer is obviously yes! But, for a businessman like Mr. Pocklington, effectiveness was not measured solely by the number of games the Oilers won but also by the amount of money they made. More recently, soccer superstar David Beckham was transferred from Manchester United to Real Madrid in 2003 for the sum of €40 million (approximately U.S. $74 million) for the same reason.

For an organization such as the Commonwealth of Virginia's state Department of Conservation and Recreation, effectiveness may be determined by its ability to provide opportunities for participation in outdoor sport and recreation and, at the same time, conserve natural and recreational resources–two goals that at times may prove conflicting. For the many voluntary organizations involved in sport delivery, as new executive members are elected, goals may change. Some amateur sport organizations may in fact have conflicting goals: Some members may see its purpose as increasing the numbers participating in the sport, while others may see its most important goal as producing medal-winning athletes. The primary goal of some women's athletic programs at major universities may be to secure a more equitable share of resources so they can achieve other program goals.

As these brief examples illustrate, effectiveness is not a simple concept. Some organizational goals are not always readily apparent. Different constituents of a sport organization, for example, the athletes, coaches, owners, and spectators, may view effectiveness in different ways. Some sport organizations may have goals that conflict, and others may change their goals as their elected representatives change. In some sport organizations the achievement of financial goals may be necessary before other important goals can be attained. To manage this type of complexity, sport managers need a clear understanding of organizational goals and the relationship of these goals to measures of organizational effectiveness.

Organizational Goals

In this section, we look at the importance of goals for a sport organization, and examine the different types of goals a sport organization may set.

Importance of Organizational Goals

There are two main reasons goals are important in sport organizations. First, as pointed out in chapter 1, all sport organizations exist for a purpose; if a sport organization does not have a purpose then there is no need for it to exist. Goals are statements that summarize and articulate the purpose of a sport organization. Second, as outlined in more detail in this chapter, goals provide guidelines for managers and other employees in such areas as decision making, performance appraisal, the reduction of uncertainty, the direction and motivation of employees, and organizational legitimacy (Daft, 2004).

Decision Making

All sport managers are required to make decisions that influence the operation of their organization and its employees. Goals provide sport managers with an understanding of the direction to take the organization. With this understanding, sport managers can then more easily make decisions about such areas as structure, product expansion, and personnel recruitment, all of which move a sport organization toward achieving its goals. For example, in the fall of 1994, the chairman of the 1999 Pan American Games set forth the following mission statement:

> The 1999 Pan American Games will give all the communities in which the Games take place the opportunity to rekindle a sense of excitement, optimism and shared vision as we approach the 21st century. The Games provide the City of Winnipeg, the Province of Manitoba and Canada with a vehicle to promote new North and South economic and cultural relationships and, further, to showcase the city, the province and the country as attractive and dynamic communities. The Games will be a first class athletic event run for the benefit of athletes in a fiscally responsible manner. (PAGS, 1999, p. 10)

This mission statement guided not only the chairman's decisions but also the decisions of more than 25,000 volunteers and staff for the next five years, that is, until the end of the organization's existence in December 1999.

Performance Appraisal

At certain intervals, the performances of both individuals and subunits within a sport organization have to be assessed. The guidelines or criteria that provide a standard for this assessment are the goals of the organization. Those individuals or sub-

---

TIME OUT *At Eastern Michigan University Is Winning the Only Thing?*

A policy developed at Eastern Michigan University was designed to tie a coach's salary increases to the team's win and loss record, game attendance, and student grades. Kathleen D. Tinney, the director of information services and publications at Eastern Michigan, was quoted as saying the "goal is to provide an incentive for coaches to improve their programs to the level of those who consistently win." The formula for rewarding coaches was to be based on goals set before the season. Salary raises would be determined by whether or not the coach exceeded, met, or fell short of a set goal. Tinney noted that "It is an objective system but there is room for subjectivity."

Several athletic directors from other institutions criticized the system and suggested that it could lead to such abuses as cheating and coaches being pressured to play athletes with injuries. Charles McClendon, former Louisiana State football coach, commented, "I just hope the football coach gets to set his own schedule. A couple of toughies against someone out of your class could blow your raise for the entire season."

Based on information in Macnow (1985).

units seen as contributing the most to organizational goals are usually given the biggest rewards. Often in performance appraisals, suggestions are made as to how individuals or subunits can better contribute to organizational goals. In sport, we frequently base the performance appraisals of professional athletes on their contribution to the organizational goal of winning: The players who score the most goals or points are often given the highest salaries. For example, for the 2003 to 2004 season, Ottawa Senators star and team captain, Daniel Alfredsson, a consistent high scorer for the team, scored 32 goals and 48 assists, received a base salary of $5,050,000. In contrast, Shaun Van Allen, despite being a seasoned player, managed only 2 goals and 12 assists, and received a base remuneration of $450,000. However, in some types of sport organizations, such as those in the voluntary sector or a sporting goods store, it is not as easy to measure objectively an employee or subunit's performance.

Reducing Uncertainty

Uncertainty can be defined as "a lack of information about future events, so that alternatives and their outcomes are unpredictable" (Hickson, Hinings, Lee, Schneck, & Pennings, 1971, p. 219). Sport organizations, like all organizations, seek ways to reduce uncertainties; one of the ways to do this is through the setting of goals. The process of goal-setting is designed to allow the various constituents of a sport organization to discuss alternative goals, to reach consensus, and to decide on the goal(s) that are most important for the organization. Once goals are established, uncertainty within the organization is reduced. Goal-setting can be seen as a psychological way of decreasing uncertainty when stated goals are reached (Michael, 1973).

Directing and Motivating Employees

Goals describe a desired outcome or future state for a sport organization, and as such they give direction to employees. They can also motivate, if employees are a part of the process of goal-setting. For example, Ski Kananaskis, the company that operates Nakiska, the ski site of the 1988 Winter Olympic Games, sets its goals at a yearly meeting (traditionally away from the work site), at a location where employees also take part in recreational activities such as horseback riding and white-water canoeing. Mark Faubert, general manager at Nakiska, suggests that this type of involvement in goal setting helps the "team-build-ing process," and as a result employees become more committed to goals (personal communication, May 29, 1990).

Establishing Legitimacy

Sport organizations gain legitimacy through legal means such as incorporation or affiliation with an accredited body. However, they can also gain legitimacy through the goals they establish. Goals are a statement of the sport organization's purpose; they communicate what the organization stands for and provide a rationale for acceptance as a legitimate entity. Goals legitimize a sport organization to both its employees or members and to external constituents, such as funding bodies, alumni, and clients. Slack and Hinings (1992), for example, describe how Canadian national sport organizations who adopted the goal of producing high-performance athletes as their central focus increased their legitimacy in the eyes of the government funding agency, Sport Canada.

Types of Organizational Goals

Sport organizations usually have several different types of goals; each type performs a particular function within the organization. Some types of goals may overlap: For example, official goals are usually nonoperative, while short-term goals are usually operative. Table 3.1 summarizes those types of goals most frequently found in sport organizations, and provides an example of each as it could relate to a professional football team. Each type is then explained in more detail in the text that follows.

Official Goals

Charles Perrow (1961, p. 855) suggests that official goals are "the general purposes of the organization as put forth in the charter, annual reports, public statements by key executives, and other authoritative pronouncements." For example, the official goal (or mission statement, as it is often called) of Skate Canada is expressed as follows: "Skate Canada is an association dedicated to the principles of enabling every Canadian to participate in skating throughout their lifetime for fun, fitness, and/or achievement" (Skate Canada, 2004 p. 1). **Official goals,** often subjective and usually not measurable, express the values of the organization and give it legitimacy with external constituents. They describe the reason(s) for the organization's existence, and serve as a means for employees and members to identify with the organization.

Table 3.1 Classification of Goals: Examples From a U.S. Professional Football Team

Type of goal	Example
Official goal	To provide a high-quality football program to both entertain and benefit the community
Operative goal	To make money
Operational goal	To sell over 50,000 tickets for each home game
Nonoperational goal	To provide a fair return to shareholders
Short-term goal	To win two of the first three away games of the season
Long-term goal	To win the Super Bowl
Departmental or subunit goal	To generate at least 350 yards of offense at each game

TIME OUT *Intercollegiate Athletics Goals*

Trail and Chelladurai (2002) conducted a survey of students and faculty of a large Midwestern university to investigate the influence of personal values on the perceived importance of athletic goals. The authors distinguished between developmental and performance goals. Developmental goals included academic, health and fitness, social and moral, diversity, and career-related goals. Performance goals included university prestige and visibility, financial security, winning, entertainment, and national sport development.

The authors' findings present goals as mediating personal values and athletic processes. Interestingly, power values were found to be positively associated with the performance goals, while universalism values were found to be positively associated with developmental goals. These findings lead the authors to warn intercollegiate athletic directors to "link their emphases on specific processes and decisions to the relevant values" (p. 289) in order to get stakeholder support for those processes and decisions.

Based on information in Trail and Chelladurai (2002).

Operative Goals

While official goals exemplify what a sport organization says it wants to achieve, **operative goals** "designate the ends sought through the operating policies of the organization; they tell us what the organization actually is trying to do, regardless of what the official goals say are the aims" (Perrow, 1961, p. 855). An indication of the operative goals of an organization, which are usually not explicitly stated, may often be obtained by examining the way resources are allocated. The late owner of the Toronto Maple Leafs, Harold Ballard, gave a good indication of his operative goals for "the Leafs" when shareholders at the 1985 annual general meeting inquired about the team's dismal performance on the ice. He told them "our shares are all right and we're making money so what the hell do we care?" (Mills, 1991, p. 11). This financial concern happened to be the crux of the 2004 to 2005 National Hockey League (NHL) lockout situation. There was such a wide gap between NHL owners and players that the NHL announced the formal cancellation of the 2004 to 2005 season on February 16, 2005—the first time a professional sport league in North America has done so.

Operational Goals

Operational goals are goals that can be measured objectively; they may be official but are more likely to be operative. One of the main ways operating goals can be developed in sport organizations is through a process known as **Management by Objectives** (MBO). Growing out of the work of classical management theorists such as Fayol and Urwick, MBO is probably most often associated with the work of Peter Drucker (1954). Although it promotes the type of mechanistic approach to organizations that was outlined in chapter 1 and fails to consider many of the human and political aspects of organizations, MBO has frequently been suggested as a means of goal-setting for sport organizations (cf. Jensen, 1983; Kelly, 1991; VanderZwaag, 1984).

Nonoperational Goals

A **nonoperational goal** is one that cannot be measured objectively. Official goals, or mission statements, are usually nonoperational. For example, Huffy Corporation, one of the leading U.S. producers of bicycles, has the following as a part of its mission statement: 1) employee motivation to support organizational values and vision pursuit; 2) design, marketing, sales, and product and service distribution leader; 3) strong customer, supplier, and community relationships; 4) enhanced shareholder value through strong financial results; and 5) direction and management toward high retail customer and consumer asset value (Huffy Corporation, 2004). The statement is for the most part subjective and hence nonoperational.

Long-Term Goals

Long-term goals are those the sport organization would like to achieve over a relatively lengthy period of time—maybe a season or a period of years. For example, in its 2003 strategic plan, the North American Society for Sport Management (NASSM) set the following as long-term goals: Increase NASSM quality and enhance NASSM's position in the market. This is to be done by enhancing research quality, networks, and funding; enhancing teaching quality; and enhancing services to the sport management industry through networking, training, and consultancy (Chalip, Costa, Gibson, Inglis, Rascher, & Wolfe, 2003).

Short-Term Goals

Short-term goals are those set for a relatively brief period of time. For example, the general manager of a baseball team will often set short-term goals for the team, such as winning 50 percent of its games on the next road trip.

Department and Subunit Goals Versus Overall Goals

As we have seen, sport organizations formulate overall goals. They may be official or operative, operational or nonoperational, long term or short term. However, departments or subunits within a sport organization may also formulate their own goals. For example, the sales department of a company that produces sport equipment may set as a goal to sell a certain amount of their product, or the defensive unit of a college football team may set a goal to hold opponents to under a certain yardage. It is important that **department or subunit goals** do not work counter to overall organizational goals. Department and subunit goals should not be seen as ends in themselves but as a means of achieving the sport organization's desired end state.

Effectiveness or Efficiency

As Hannan and Freeman (1977a) point out, within the tradition that emphasizes the importance of organizational goals, an important distinction needs to be made between the concepts of organizational effectiveness and organizational efficiency. **Effectiveness** refers to the extent to which an organization achieves its goals. **Efficiency,** on the other hand, takes into account the amount of resources used to produce the desired output (cf. Pennings & Goodman, 1977; Sandefur, 1983). It is often measured in economic terms, usually the ratio of inputs to outputs. However, as Mintzberg (1982, p. 104) notes, "because economic costs can usually be more easily measured than social costs, efficiency often produces an escalation in social costs." Macintosh and Whitson (1990) illustrate the occurrence of such a situation in sport when they suggest that Sport Canada's push for international sporting success has been achieved at the expense of some of the other more socially oriented goals of sport such as gender equity and regional access.

While efficiency is a goal of all sport organizations, an efficient organization is not necessarily effective. For example, a sport organization may be efficient in the way that it makes its product but, like Puma athletic shoes in the mid-1980s (cf. Roth, 1987), if there is a reduction in the number of people buying the product, the organization will not be effective in meeting its goals. Likewise, an organization may be effective in that it achieves its goal(s) but it may not be efficient. For example, a professional soccer team that wins a championship but also spends large sums of money to buy established players would fall into this category.

Approaches to Studying Organizational Effectiveness

As would be expected, the varying opinions of what constitutes organizational effectiveness have led to several different approaches to studying the concept. Cameron (1980) identified four major approaches to evaluating effectiveness: the goal attainment approach, the systems resource approach, the internal process approach, and the strategic constituencies approach. We now look at each of these approaches, and the more recently developed competing values approach (Quinn & Rohrbaugh, 1981; 1983). The main principles of each approach are examined, and strengths and weaknesses discussed.

The Goal Attainment Approach

As we saw earlier in this chapter and in our definition in chapter 1, all sport organizations exist to achieve one or more goals. The **goal attainment approach** to organizational effectiveness is based on the identification of these goals, and how well the sport organization attains or makes progress toward them. Effectiveness is based on the achievement of ends, not means. The most important goals to focus on when using this approach to organizational effectiveness are operative goals (Hall & Clark, 1980; Price, 1972; Steers, 1975). For the goal attainment model to be workable, the sport organization being studied must have goals that are clearly identifiable, consensual, measurable, and time-bounded (Cameron, 1984). There must be general consensus or agreement on the goals and a small enough number of them to be manageable. Campbell (1977, p. 26) suggests that MBO "represents the ultimate in a goal-oriented model of effectiveness."

In studies of sport organizations the goal attainment approach has been the most frequently used method of evaluating effectiveness. The goals "most often measured in a sport context reflect an emphasis on performance outcomes and have been operationalized in terms of win/loss records or performance rankings in comparison to other teams" (Frisby, 1986a, p. 95). For example, Chelladurai, Szyszlo, and Haggerty (1987) in their study of national sport organizations used the number of medals won at major competitions and the number of victories at dual international events as indicators of effectiveness. They suggest that the goal model may be useful for evaluating the effectiveness of elite sport programs, but they reject the use of this approach for mass sport programs, since goal attainment is not as easily measured in the latter. Former Dallas Cowboy's owner H.R. "Bum" Bright shows how, in evaluating effectiveness, it is possible to reject one measure of goal effectiveness in favor of another. He noted "the actual success or failure of our investment in the Cowboys will not be measured by the profit/loss bottom line, but will be measured by their success in their competition on the football field" (Hampton, 1984, p. 24).

Despite its popularity, the goal attainment approach to organizational effectiveness has a number of problems. The first and, according to Hannan and Freeman (1977a), the most substantive of these problems arises because there is usually more than one organizational goal to achieve. While some sport organizations will have only one goal, others have more; the faculty of the physical education and recreation department at

---

TIME OUT · *Learning Versus Performance Goals*

Most goals are performance or end-state oriented. However, Seijts, Latham, Tasa, and Latham (2004) highlight the importance of learning goals. For example, the dean of a human kinetics faculty might set a learning goal for a new professor of developing five different teaching strategies the students enjoy instead of setting a performance goal of obtaining a mark of 4 out of 5 on teaching evaluations. Seijts et al. argue that in such situations (e.g., new hires or forays into new markets), learning goals are more successful than performance goals, because the individual is more likely to reach that goal even if it is a high standard.

Based on information in Seijts, Latham, Tasa, and Latham (2004).

the University of Alberta, for example, has goals that relate to teaching, research, and service. This multiplicity of goals is compounded in organizations when operative goals are added, and when subunits have their own goals, as is so often the case.

This multiplicity can also be problematic in that, as was pointed out earlier in the chapter, some goals may be competing or even incompatible. For example, Sport Canada has swung between promoting grassroots sport participation and funding elite-level sport for more than four decades. The limited budget usually provided to sport has been spread thinly and inconsistently across the system. The Canadian sport system has suffered because it lacked a clear long-term goal. Canadians are less active, and the Canadian Olympic team has never had an overall stellar performance. It has never been first in medal rankings. Therefore, the presence of multiple and conflicting goals means that effectiveness cannot be solely determined by one single indicator.

A second problem with the goal attainment approach is how to identify goals and actually measure the extent to which they have been achieved. As we pointed out earlier in the chapter, official goals are usually vague and operative goals are often not written down. While it is relatively easy to argue that for sport organizations like the Los Angeles Lakers and the Chicago White Sox the number of games won is a measure of goal effectiveness, it is harder to both identify and measure the goals of a high school physical education department. Likewise, profit-making sport organizations and professional sport teams may also have goals that relate to such areas as job satisfaction and player development. These goals can usually be measured only qualitatively and progress toward them is difficult to assess, further complicating the use of the goal attainment approach to effectiveness. Price (1972) suggests that one way to overcome the problem of goal clarity is to focus on the organizational decision makers, because their statements and actions regarding the organization's operations reveal its priorities. However, as Chelladurai (1985) points out, although Price's suggestion has merit, it tends to ignore the fact that there may not be consensus among decision makers as to what the sport organization's goals are; in addition, their goals may change inasmuch as their power to influence decisions changes.

A third problem with the goal attainment approach relates to the temporal dimension of goals. Hannan and Freeman (1977a) ask whether a short term, a long term, or both time frames should be considered. They suggest that most published empirical studies employing cross-sectional data focus on the short term but whether this focus is appropriate depends on "the nature of the goals' function for each organization" (p. 113). For organizations that stress a quick return on investment, as some profit-making sport organizations do, short-term goals should be considered. Organizations oriented toward continued production, however, such as a university producing physical education graduates, research, and so on, the focus should be over longer periods to minimize the importance of yearly fluctuations (Hannan & Freeman, 1977a). In addition, different sport organizations operating in the same environment and with the same structure may have similar goals but may place a different emphasis on their rate of return on investment.

A final problem with the goal attainment approach concerns whose goals count. Even within the senior management levels of a sport organization, there will be variation in beliefs about what are appropriate organizational goals. In some sport organizations, those with power may actually be outside the senior management levels. This condition is not uncommon in voluntary sport organizations, where individuals who may have held a power position (e.g., president) in the organization remain after their tenure as a member of the rank and file. Such individuals, despite not holding an official position, may still exert considerable influence on organizational goals. The goals usually attributed to the organization are actually those of the dominant coalition. It is also possible that the goals of an organization may be considerably influenced by the contextual situation in which the sport organization exists. Macintosh and Whitson (1990), for example, have suggested that Sport Canada strongly influenced the high-performance goals of Canadian national sport organizations.

Where then, we may ask, does all this leave us? How useful is the goal attainment approach to organizational effectiveness? While it is hard to question the fact that one of the main functions of sport organizations is to achieve their goals, the problems are identifying these goals, deciding which are important (or more important than others), and measuring whether or not they are achieved. Robbins (1990, p. 57) suggests five ways to increase the validity of the identified goals:

1. Ensure that input is received from all those having a major influence on formulating the official goals, even if they are not part of the senior management.
2. Include actual goals obtained by observing the behavior of organization members.
3. Recognize that organizations pursue both short- and long-term goals.
4. Insist on tangible, verifiable, and measurable goals rather than rely on vague statements that merely mirror societal expectations.
5. View goals as dynamic entities that change over time rather than as rigid or fixed statements of purpose.

Notwithstanding these suggestions and the fact that the goal attainment model of effectiveness has been used in several studies of sport organizations, those who choose to use this approach may be wise to consider Warriner's (1965, p. 140) caution, that goals should be thought of "as fiction produced by an organization to account for, explain, or rationalize its existence to particular audiences rather than as valid and reliable indications of purpose."

The Systems Resource Approach

While the goal attainment approach to effectiveness focuses on organizational outputs, the **systems resource approach** focuses on inputs. This particular approach to organizational effectiveness is based on open systems theory. Organizations are not closed to the outside. They develop exchange relationships with their environment in order to obtain resources. Consequently, effectiveness is defined as "the ability of the organization in either absolute or relative terms to exploit its environment in the acquisition of scarce and valued resources" (Yuchtman & Seashore, 1967, p. 898). The more effective organizations are those that can obtain more resources from their environments (Molnar & Rogers, 1976).

From a systems resource perspective, a sport organization like the New York Yankees would be considered effective on this criterion because it increased attendance every year between 2001 and 2004. Similarly, an organization like Hockey Canada, with more than 538,000 members, would, from a systems resource perspective, be considered more effective than the Canadian Weightlifting Federation, which has just over 1,200 members.

It is important, however, to note that resources are not limited to financial or physical objects, but can include intangibles such as reputation, influence (power), and knowledge of individuals, groups or the organization itself (cf. Gamson, 1966; Yuchtman & Seashore, 1967). Macintosh and Whitson (1990) exemplify the use of intangible resources when they point out that national sport organizations in Canada have actively sought out board members with "corporate credentials." Obviously, organizations who succeeded in placing senior management individuals on their board would, from a systems resource perspective, be seen as effective.

As Chelladurai (1985) points out, it may, at first, seem as though the goals model (focus on outputs) and the system resource approach (focus on inputs) are quite different. But as he goes on to point out, an organization can only secure inputs from its environment on a continuous basis if its outputs are perceived as acceptable by actors in the environment. Acquiring resources is based on the organization's attempt to achieve its goals (Hall, 1982). For example, when Virginia Tech's basketball team won the National Invitational Tournament in 1973, its president, T. Marshall Hahn, noted that considerable sums of money were pledged to the university. He also added that he felt alumni, corporations, and the state legislature would look more favorably on the university as a result of its success (Creamer, 1973). Clearly, here is a case where the output of the organization affected its sources of input. Frisby (1986a), in her study of Canadian national sport organizations, did in fact find significant correlations between measures of goal attainment and resource acquisition. Sack and Staurowsky (1998) found that NCAA members continue to value team wins as a means of getting more resources (especially financial) to the detriment of the student-athletes.

The strengths of the systems resource approach to effectiveness are threefold. First, unlike the goal attainment approach, which considers goals as cultural entities arising outside of the organization, the systems resource approach treats the organization itself as its frame of reference. Second, it takes into account the organization's relationship to its environment. Third, it can be used to compare organizations who have differing goals (Daft, 2004). For example, because all sport organizations have to obtain human, physical, and financial resources to survive (survival being the most basic measure of effectiveness), they can be compared on their ability to obtain these resources from their environment. The local baseball association able to attract a large number of members, for example, will probably be seen by the municipal council as more effective than a table tennis group with just a few members.

Despite its appealing qualities, the systems resource approach also exhibits several problems as a means of assessing effectiveness. First, and in many ways the foremost, of these problems is the fact that although this approach to organizational effectiveness is widely quoted in the management literature and even within the relatively sparse literature on the effectiveness of sport organizations, it has produced "no coherent line of research" (Goodman & Pennings, 1977, p. 4). A second problem is semantic; it concerns the question of what is an input and what is an output. By way of illustration, consider the example of attendance at New York Yankees games just cited; is this in fact one form of resource acquisition or is it actually a goal of the organization to increase attendance?

The systems resource approach is also problematic in its applicability to public-sector organizations concerned with sport, and to some voluntary sport organizations. The problem arises because often, for these types of organizations, a percentage of their funding is guaranteed, or at least highly certain, because it comes from a higher-level organization. For example, unlike the U.S. equivalents, many national sport organizations in Canada and Great Britain obtain a fairly large percentage of their financial resources from the government. So, using financial resources as an indicator of effectiveness is not particularly appropriate. It would, however, be legitimate to measure the effectiveness of these sport organizations by the amount of funding they obtain from other sources, such as membership fees or corporate sponsorship, because these funds are not guaranteed.

A final problem with the systems resource approach is that, as Cameron (1980) points out, organizations lacking a competitive advantage in their chosen market or unsuccessful in acquiring the best resources can still be effective. As an example, he uses the "no-name" Seattle Supersonics, who, in 1977 and 1978, were unable to obtain superstars for their basketball team—thereby losing a competitive advantage. Yet, with lower-quality resources (rookie coach and no superstar athletes), the team managed to reach the NBA finals in 1978 and then win in 1979. Conversely, the New York Rangers are infamous for having

the highest salary budget (they attract the biggest stars) in the NHL and for not being able to win the Stanley Cup.

The systems resource approach does present an alternative perspective to assessing organizational effectiveness. It is most applicable to understanding the following types of sport organizations: those whose outputs cannot be objectively measured; those that have a clear connection between the resources (inputs) obtained and what is produced (outputs) (cf. Cameron, 1980); and those whose supply of resources is not guaranteed by some formalized arrangement with another organization.

The Internal Process Approach

A third approach to determining organizational effectiveness is called the **internal process approach.** From this perspective, "effective organizations are those with an absence of internal strain, whose members are highly integrated into the system, whose internal functioning is smooth and typified by trust and benevolence toward individuals, where information flows smoothly both vertically and horizontally and so on" (Cameron, 1980, p. 67). While the goal attainment approach focuses on organizational outputs and the systems resource approach focuses on inputs, this approach focuses on the throughputs or transformation processes found in an organization. These relationships are illustrated in figure 3.1. Throughputs are the internal activities and processes of the organization by which inputs are converted into outputs.

The basis for this approach can be found in the work of writers such as Argyris (1964) and Likert (1967), who have all suggested that human resources practices are linked to organizational effectiveness. Daft (2004) suggests that, from this perspective, indicators of an effective organization would include such things as the supervisors' interest and concern for their workers; a feeling of team spirit, group loyalty, and teamwork; good communications; and a compensation system that rewards managers for performance growth, the development of subordinates, and the creation of an effective working group. In a study of national sport organizations, Chelladurai and Haggerty (1991) used items such as the meaningful organization of work, information sharing among members, and concern over employee welfare and happiness, as indicators of internal process effectiveness.

In contrast to an emphasis on human resources, some writers have suggested that economic efficiency should be the focus when evaluating the internal processes of an organization. Martindell (1962), for example, developed a management audit of organizations, which appraises performance on such criteria as health of earnings, fiscal policies, research and development, production efficiency, and sales. In a similar vein, Evan (1976) developed a quantitative method of looking at the economic efficiency of an organization. He suggested that it was possible to examine the inputs (I), outputs (O), and throughputs (T) of an organization; these variables could then be examined as ratios to evaluate the performance of the organization. Table 3.2 shows some of the ratios that could be used in a profit-making sport organization, a local basketball association, and a faculty of kinesiology. For example, if we use the ratio of throughput to input for the local basketball association or the faculty of kinesiology as an indicator of economic effectiveness, we could get three possible results. If the cost of operations is higher than the annual budget, the ratio would be X:1 where X > 1. In this situation the organization would probably be seen to be ineffective because it has gone over budget. If the cost of operations and the annual budget were the same, the ratio would be 1:1. If the costs of operations were less than the annual budget the ratio would be Y:1 where Y < 1. In these last two situations the organization would probably be seen as effective because it has stayed within its budget.

The major advantage of the internal process approach is that it can be used to compare organizations who have different outputs, different inputs, or little control over their environment. However, the first of a number of problems with

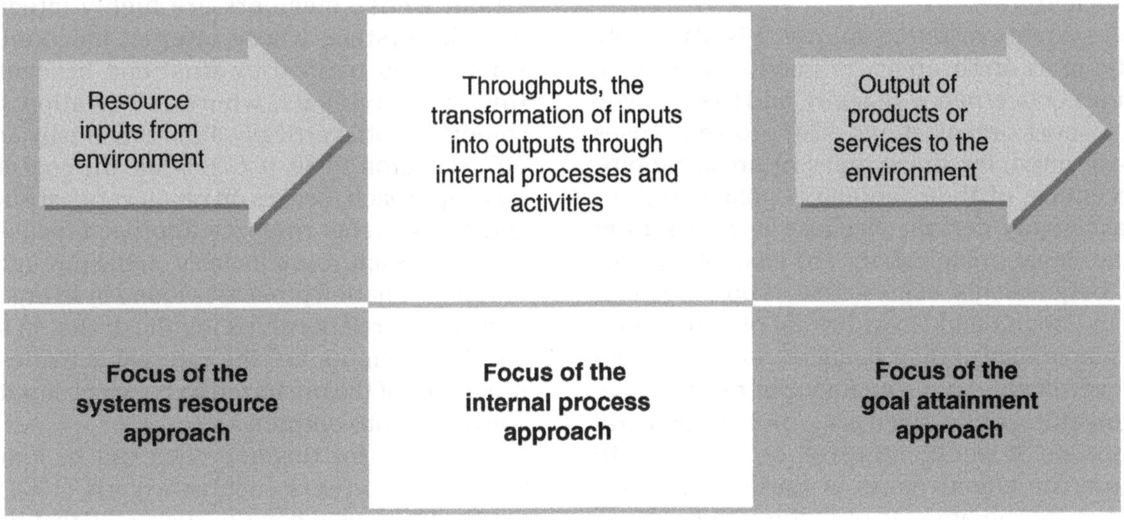

Figure 3.1 *Approaches to the measurement of organizational effectiveness.*

Table 3.2 Effectiveness Measures of Systems in Selected Sport Organizations

Systems variables	Profit-making sport organization	Local basketball association	Faculty of kinesiology
O/I	Return on investment	Number of games *played;* annual budget	Number of students *graduated;* annual budget
I/I	Change in working capital	Change in number of players	Change in number of students
T/I	Inventory turnover	*Cost of operations;* annual budget	*Cost of operations;* annual budget

O = Outputs; I =Inputs; T = Throughputs

Reprinted, by permission, from W.M. Evan, 1976, Organizational theory and organizational effectiveness: An exploratory analysis. In *Organizational effectiveness: Theory, research, utilization*, edited by S.L. Spray (Kent, Ohio: Kent State University Press), 22-23.

this approach relates to the measurement of human resource variables. For example, in their study of Canadian national sport organizations, Chelladurai, Szyszlo, and Haggerty (1987) used such throughput (transformation) variables as "morale among staff members and volunteers involved in community based programs" and "the working relationship between the NSGB [National Sport Governing Body] and its provincial branches on elite programs." While important aspects of the internal processes of these organizations, they are extremely difficult concepts to measure in any valid or reliable way.

Also, because it does not focus on organizational outputs or on an organization's relationship with its environment, the internal process approach offers only a very limited view of organizational effectiveness. As Das (1990) notes, an organization's success can be due to a unique combination of factors and conditions so that a change—whether major or minor—in these factors could result in a completely different outcome.

The internal process model also takes no account of the notion of equifinality—the ability of organizations to achieve similar ends through different means (Hrebiniak & Joyce, 1985). Two organizations with different internal processes may produce the same outputs, although two organizations with similar internal processes may produce different outputs (Das, 1990).

Finally, the internal process model is lacking in that an organization with internal problems, such as low morale, poor communication, and conflict, can still be successful. Cameron (1980, p. 69) provides a classic example—the New York Yankees of 1977 and 1978: "Lack of team discipline, fights among players and between players and coaches, threatened firings, turnover of key personnel, and lack of cohesion seemed to be the defining characteristics of that organization during the 1977 and 1978 baseball seasons. Yet the Yankees were the most effective team in baseball in terms of goal accomplishment; they won the World Series both years." The Yankees are still one of the most effective teams, even 20 years later.

The Strategic Constituencies Approach

A fourth, and more integrative, approach to organizational effectiveness is the **strategic constituencies approach,** which emanates from the work of Connolly, Conlon, and Deutsch (1980). It may also be beneficial to look at Keeley's (1978) treatment of effectiveness for information on the origins of this perspective. Fans, the media, sponsors, and owners are all examples of groups that could be considered the strategic constituents or stakeholders of a professional basketball organization. Each has a different interest in the performance of the organization and, in turn, the organization relies on these groups for resources and support. The extent to which the team is able to satisfy the criteria used by each group to evaluate it will determine its effectiveness. Table 3.3 provides examples of the type of effectiveness criteria that might be used by selected strategic constituents of a professional basketball organization. It is important to note that constituents may be internal (e.g., players) or external (e.g., sponsors) to the organization. We will look into internal and external constituents or stakeholders in future chapters.

Table 3.3   Effectiveness Criteria of Selected Strategic Constituents of a U.S. Professional Basketball Team

Constituency or stakeholder	Typical criteria of effectiveness
Owners	Profit; increased value of franchise
Players	Adequate salary and benefits; good working conditions
Fans	Entertaining games; reasonably priced tickets, concessions, and so on.
Community	Visibility through team activities; economic benefits for local businesses
Media	Newsworthy coaches and players
NBA	Compliance with rules; efforts to promote a positive image of the game
Sponsors	Media exposure; high attendance

The strategic constituencies approach is similar to the systems resource approach, yet with a different emphasis. While the systems resource approach is concerned with acquiring critical resources from the environment, the strategic constituencies approach is also concerned with the actions of its stakeholders. For example, a professional baseball team like the Toronto Blue Jays does not acquire resources from members of the print media, so from a systems resource perspective they would not be considered particularly important. However, the print media are stakeholders, in that they have an interest in the team and are able to exert considerable influence on its activities and success. Therefore, from a strategic constituencies perspective they are a significant group that can influence the team's effectiveness.

The strategic constituencies approach takes into account the fact that managers have to work toward several goals simultaneously. Typically, they have to satisfy the interests of a number of constituents who influence the organization's ability to achieve success. Consequently, the goals selected are not value-free; each favors one constituent over another. As a result, organizations are political; they have to respond to the vested interests of their various constituents. This is a very important point for sport managers, since much of the literature in our field has presented a view of sport organizations as apolitical (Slack, 1991a). Still, some researchers are showing the political nature of sport organizations, especially in relation to Olympic Games (see Lenskyj, 2000; Pound, 2004).

A strength of the strategic constituencies approach is that effectiveness is seen as a complex, multidimensional construct. It also considers factors internal and external to the organization. In addition, the issue of corporate social responsibility is taken into account (something not considered in any of the previous approaches), that is, what moral and ethical obligations the organization has to the community within which it operates. Another strength of this approach is that it forces sport managers to be cognizant of groups whose power could have an adverse effect on their operations. The Time Out sidebar about the athletic footwear industry provides a graphic example of the importance of this point. By knowing whose support it needs to maintain its operations, an organization can modify its goals to meet the demands of those particular constituents.

It is not always easy, however, to identify an organization's constituents and their relative importance. For example, in the case of the professional sport team, who is more important to success: the fans or the media? Another difficulty is that different people in the organization will see different constituents as being important; the finance officer of a university athletic department, for example, is unlikely to see the constituents of the organization in the same way as the head basketball coach. Also problematic is the fact that the relative importance of the different constituents will change over time. For example, in the founding stages of a fitness center, financial institutions will be important constituents; the center will need access to capital for startup costs and will look to these institutions to provide this money. In later years when the center is well established and has a reliable clientele, lending institutions will be less important as strategic constituents. Finally, even if the constituents can be identified, how do sport managers identify their expectations for the organization, and correctly measure this type of information?

Despite these difficulties, this approach to organizational effectiveness is gaining popularity (cf. Cameron, 1984; Kanter & Brinkerhoff, 1981). It offers a more holistic approach than previous models and, as mentioned earlier, emphasizes the political nature of organizations. Along with the competing values approach, which we will discuss next, it provides one of the better ways of determining organizational effectiveness.

The Competing Values Approach

Like the strategic constituencies perspective, the **competing values approach** is based on the premise that there is no single-best criterion of organizational effectiveness; rather, effectiveness is a subjective concept and the criteria used to assess it depend on the evaluator's value preferences. For example, in an athletic shoe manufacturing company such as Reebok, we would expect to find that the finance and accounting managers would define effectiveness in terms of profitability and a balanced budget; marketing managers would look at percentage of market share; production managers would be concerned with the number and quality of shoes manufactured. Finally, the city council in Stoughton, Massachusetts, where Reebok is headquartered, would define effectiveness in terms of the growth of the company's workforce.

TIME OUT *Responding to Strategic Constituents: The Athletic Footwear Industry*

Rudolf and Adolf Dassler first started making shoes in the German town of Herzogenaurach in 1920. Their business grew slowly; in 1936 they made the shoes in which Jessie Owens won four gold medals at the 1936 Olympic Games. However, in 1949 the brothers quarreled and each went his own way; Rudolf left and formed the Puma company, while Adolf, renaming the business Adidas, stayed on at the old factory. Throughout the 1950s, 1960s, and most of the 1970s, Adidas and Puma dominated the athletic footwear market. In the 1970s the industry started to change. Jogging became a major recreational activity, athletic shoes became fashion wear, and the

aerobics boom started to take off. Companies like Nike and Reebok started to cater to these changing customer demands by developing a broad range of brightly colored fashionable shoes. Adidas and Puma, slow to respond to these consumer demands, continued to make the type of shoes they had in the past; their market share dropped considerably, and the companies lost their preeminent position in the market. Adidas and Puma had failed to respond to the needs of one of their most important strategic constituents—their customers.

Based on information in Hartley (1989), Bruce (1985), and Roth (1987).

The competing values approach was developed by Quinn and Rohrbaugh (1981), who used a list of criteria that Campbell (1977) claimed were indicators of organizational effectiveness. The list was analyzed using multidimensional scaling. It produced three dimensions of organizational effectiveness seen as representing competing values. The first set of values involves organizational focus; these values range from those that emphasize the well-being and development of the people in the organization (an internal focus on the organization's socio-technical system) to a concern with the well-being and development of the organization itself (an external focus on its competitive position) (Quinn & Rohrbaugh, 1983). The second set of values concerns the structure of the organization, from a structure that emphasizes flexibility (i.e., a decentralized, differentiated structure with the ability to adapt, innovate, and change) to a structure that favors control (i.e., centralized, integrated and exhibiting stability, predictability, and order). The third set of values concerns means and ends. A focus on means stresses internal processes such as planning; a focus on ends emphasizes final outcomes such as profitability or win-and-loss record. As Quinn and Rohrbaugh (1981, p. 132) note, "these three sets

of competing values are recognized dilemmas in the organizational literature."*

The three sets of values can be combined, as shown in figure 3.2. The two axes—flexibility and control and internal and external focus—produce four quadrants. Quinn (1988) suggests that each one of the quadrants represents one of the four major models in organization theory—human relations, open systems, internal process, or rational goal. He goes on to suggest that the two sets of criteria in each of the quadrants relate to the implicit means or ends theory that is associated with each of the models. Thus, in the human relations model, a focus on means would see effectiveness being represented by a cohesive workforce with high morale; a focus on ends would emphasize human resources development. Table 3.4 shows the four models and how effectiveness would be defined in each, depending on whether the focus is on means or ends. It is important to note that each model has a polar opposite. As Quinn (1988, pp. 47-48) points out, "the human relations model, which emphasizes flexibility and internal focus, stands in stark contrast to the rational goal model, which stresses control and external focus. The open systems model, which is characterized by flexibility and external focus, runs counter to the internal

*For more information on the competing values approach refer to Vol. 5, No. 2 (June 1981) of *Public Productivity Review* that contains five articles (including Quinn & Rohrbaugh's work) focusing on this particular approach to organizational effectiveness.

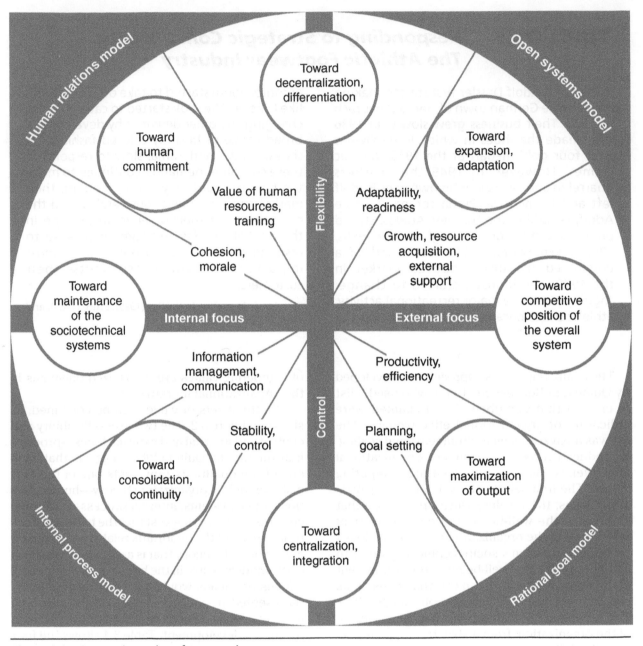

Figure 3.2 *Competing values framework.*

Beyond rational management: Mastering the paradoxes and competing demands of high performance, R.E. Quinn, Copyright ©1988. Reprinted by permission of John Wiley & Sons, Inc.

process model, which emphasizes control and internal focus."

Quinn goes on to point out parallels between the models. Both the human relations and open systems models emphasize flexibility; the open systems and rational goal models are focused on external issues, such as responding to change. Control is a value emphasized in the rational goal and internal process models; the human relations and internal process models both have an internal focus that emphasizes such things as the organization's human and technical systems. Managers are faced with decisions about which of these values will direct their organization.

The competing values perspective, unlike other approaches, takes into account the paradoxical nature of effectiveness. For example, the Indiana University basketball team formerly coached by Bobby Knight was generally seen as a very successful organization, at least in terms of its

Table 3.4 Criteria of Effectiveness for Competing Values Models

Model	Criteria of effectiveness
Human relations	
Means	A cohesive workforce where morale is high; employees work well together
Ends	An emphasis on the training and development of human resources to perform tasks in a proper manner
Open systems	
Means	A flexible workforce able to respond well to changes in external conditions and demands
Ends	A focus on growth and the ability to acquire external resources
Internal process	
Means	A focus on communication and information management; people being well informed about issues that influence their work
Ends	A focus on stability, order, and control; operations run smoothly
Rational goal	
Means	An emphasis on planning and the setting of identifiable goals
Ends	High productivity; efficiency in terms of outputs to inputs

win-and-loss record. Using the competing values perspective, most people would score the team high in terms of productivity (i.e., the rational goal model). However, as Feinstein (1986) indicated in his book on Knight and the Hoosiers basketball team, some of this success has been achieved at the expense of a concern with human resources. In 2001, Bobby Knight was finally fired by Indiana after a student blew the whistle on Knight's actions (see ESPN.com, 2001 for more information). The competing values approach does not suggest that these opposing values cannot mutually exist; rather, it helps us understand the trade-offs necessary in evaluating the effectiveness of an organization.

To operationalize the competing values approach, it is first necessary for a sport manager to identify those constituents seen as necessary for the organization's survival. The next step is to determine the importance those constituents place on the various values. This task can be done by the sport managers themselves, who have to try to determine what the various constituents value in the organization; alternatively, the constituents themselves may be surveyed.

Figure 3.3 provides an example of an instrument from a research project that used the competing values approach. The purpose of this project was to examine the outcomes of employee fitness and

health programs, which were valued in major corporations (cf. Wolfe, Slack, & Rose-Hearn, 1993). The instrument was administered to fitness and health professionals and to the corporation's senior management, to determine the type of outcomes they valued in an effective employee fitness and health program. By plotting the cumulative scores from an instrument like this, it is possible to get a picture of how different organizations, or different groups within an organization, determine effectiveness.

Figure 3.4 shows how two sport organizations could be plotted in terms of the four models of effectiveness (see also Quinn, 1988, chapter 9). Sport organization A could be a relatively large organization that has been in business for a number of years. It is quite likely to be structured along bureaucratic lines. Its primary emphasis is on productivity and efficiency. Planning and goal-setting are emphasized within this organization. There is little concern with flexibility, nor is there a great deal of concern with human resources development issues. In contrast, Sport organization B could be a relatively new organization seeking to establish itself in its particular market. Consequently, adaptability and the acquisition of external resources are highly valued in this organization. There is some concern with human resource issues and with productivity and planning, but there is

The following items relate to values you may attribute to your company's employee fitness and health program. Please use the following scale to indicate the extent to which each of the following is a value you attribute to this program.

Minor reason   1   2   3   4   5   6   7   Major reason

(Please write the appropriate number in the space provided.)

1. _____ To improve employee morale (HR)*
2. _____ To contribute to a more stable workforce (IP)
3. _____ To contribute to organizational profit (RG)
4. _____ To contribute to the organization's external competitiveness (OS)
5. _____ To improve employee cohesion (HR)
6. _____ To contribute to the continuity of the workforce (IP)
7. _____ To create a more flexible and adaptable workforce (OS)
8. _____ To contribute to achieving organizational goals (RG)
9. _____ To decrease employee conflict (HR)
10. _____ To increase cross-functional and cross-level interaction (IP)
11. _____ To contribute to organizational efficiency (RG)
12. _____ To ensure that our work force will be ready to meet its challenges (OS)
13. _____ To positively influence employee communication (IP)
14. _____ To contribute to individual productivity (RG)
15. _____ To positively affect the value of human resources (HR)
16. _____ To positively influence our external image (OS)

* The letters in parentheses indicate to which of the four models the statements relate. They were not included on the actual instrument.

Figure 3.3 *Measuring competing values: An example of employee fitness and health programs.*

little value placed on stability and information management.

The type of diagram shown in figure 3.4 can help determine the organization's effectiveness. If cumulative scores from the different constituents are used to plot the diagram, it tells managers in what particular areas they are strong and where they may improve. If plots are made for each of the constituent groups, the diagram shows the type of values each constituent expects from the organization. For example, in a company that produces some type of sport equipment the workers would probably see the organization as being effective if it emphasized values related to human resources development; shareholders' values would more likely relate to productivity. Plotting how the organization scores in these areas can help managers determine how effectively constituents believe it is performing its tasks. This information can then be used to determine the relative trade-offs that have to be made to maintain overall effectiveness.

It is important to note that different values may be emphasized at different stages of the organization's life cycle (cf. Cameron & Whetten, 1981; Quinn & Cameron, 1983). For example, in a relatively new organization like Sport organization B in figure 3.4, flexibility, creativity, and the ability to acquire resources from external sources are most likely to be the most valued as indicative of effectiveness. Later on in the life cycle, in what Quinn and Cameron (1983) call the formalization and control stage, the sport organization is more established, and constituents will likely value stability and productivity as measures of effectiveness.

The strength of the competing values approach is that it takes into account the paradoxical nature of organizational effectiveness. It also acknowledges that different constituents use different types of criteria in their assessment of an organization, that some of these criteria may be conflicting, and that some may change over time.

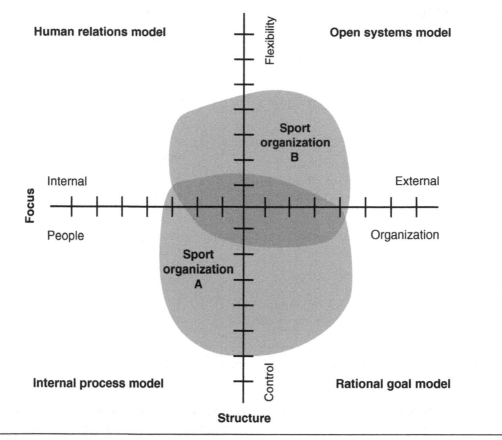

Figure 3.4 *Effectiveness values of two sport organizations.*
Based on information in J. Rohrbaugh (1981).

As a manager, you must be able to recognize, develop, and modify your organization's goals. As we have seen, there are different types of goals, some that overlap, and some that can be named differently (e.g., mission statement, purpose). These goals must fit with your organization's environment. If the organization has different departments, they may have goals different from the overall organization. However, these goals must not be contrary to the goals of other departments or the overall organization. Be careful when establishing goals, because they will affect all the organizational members' actions and, ultimately, the organization's performance (i.e., success). For example, setting hard-to-meet goals can actually lead to unethical behavior (Schweitzer, Ordóñez, & Douma, 2004).

You also must be able to determine your organization's effectiveness and efficiency if you want it to have a competitive advantage in the marketplace and acquire the necessary resources. As we have seen, both the strategic constituencies approach and the competing values approach recognize that organizational effectiveness is a multidimensional concept. Because of the paradoxical nature of the concept of effectiveness, the various approaches for determining organizational effectiveness presented in this chapter can be useful under different circumstances. Table 3.5 summarizes each of these approaches, how it defines effectiveness, and when it is most useful.

Table 3.5   A Comparison Among Major Models of Organizational Effectiveness

Model	Definition	When useful
	An organization is effective to the extent that . . .	*The model is preferred when . . .*
Goal attainment model	it accomplishes its stated goals.	goals are clear, time bound, and measurable.
Systems resource model	it acquires needed resources.	a clear connection exists between inputs and outputs.
Internal process model	it has an absence of internal strain with smooth internal functioning.	a clear connection exists between organizational processes and the primary task.
Strategic constituencies model	all strategic constituencies are at least minimally satisfied.	constituencies have powerful influence on the organization (as in times of little organizational slack), and it must respond to demands.
Competing values model	the emphasis of the organization in four major areas matches constituent preferences.	the organization is unclear about its own emphasis, or changes in criteria over time are of interest.

Reprinted from The effectiveness of ineffectiveness, K.S. Cameron. In *Research in organizational behavior: An annual series of analytical essays and critical reviews*, Vol. 6, edited by B.M. Straw and L.L. Cummings, p. 276. Copyright 1984, with permission from Elsevier.

The biggest problems with the competing values approach are determining which constituents are important to an organization, and then measuring the criteria they value and use in determining the effectiveness of their organization.

SUMMARY AND CONCLUSIONS

This chapter has examined the concepts of organizational goals and effectiveness. Goals serve a number of purposes in a sport organization: They provide a direction for the organization, guide managers in decision making and performance appraisal, reduce uncertainty, and help the sport organization establish legitimacy both with its own personnel and with external agencies. Sport organizations usually have several different types of goals; some are formally stated, others are more implicit in the activities of the organization; some are objective, others are purposely vague and general.

If a sport organization achieves its goals, it is often considered effective. However, as we saw, there are problems with this approach, and researchers have proposed several other methods of determining organizational effectiveness. As opposed to focusing on the organization's goals or outputs, the systems resource approach focuses on the organization's ability to obtain resources from its environment. The internal process approach focuses on internal climate and efficiency as the appropriate criteria for determining effectiveness. Two more contemporary approaches take a broader view of effectiveness. The strategic constituencies approach focuses on the extent to which an organization satisfies the requirements of its stakeholders. The competing values approach emphasizes that different constituents value different organizational outcomes. Effectiveness is determined by the extent to which an organization is able to meet these often differing value preferences.

Which of these approaches is the best? Each one in its own way is useful. Some writers have even suggested that effectiveness is better measured by integrating different approaches. Chelladurai (1987, p. 39), for example, suggests:

> When organizations are viewed as open systems inputs affect throughputs which affect outputs, which are exchanged with the environment for a return of inputs for

the organization. From this perspective of an organization the goals model, system resource model, and process model focus, respectively, on the output, input, and throughput sectors of an organization. The multiple constituencies approach emphasizes the organization's dependence on its environment represented by the various interest groups and the need to satisfy their expectations. Since all of the models deal with specific elements of the system . . . they are interrelated.

Hall (1982) extracts key elements from the systems resource and goal attainment approaches to produce what he calls a **contradiction model** of effectiveness. He argues that, because organizations have multiple and conflicting environmental constraints, goals, external and internal constituents, and time frames, no organization is effective. Rather, organizations are effective (or ineffective) to the extent to which they are able to reconcile these contradictions.

Effectiveness is therefore paradoxical in nature. As such, one of the best ways to summarize the various approaches that have been presented may be to suggest that each is useful under different circumstances. Table 3.5 summarizes each of the approaches presented.

KEY CONCEPTS

competing values approach (p. 48)

contradiction model (p. 55)

department and subunit goals (p. 41)

effectiveness (p. 41)

efficiency (p. 41)

goal attainment approach (p. 42)

internal process approach (p. 45)

long-term goals (p. 41)

management by objectives (p. 40)

nonoperational goals (p. 41)

official goals (p. 39)

operational goals (p. 40)

operative goals (p. 40)

short-term goals (p. 41)

strategic constituencies approach (p. 47)

systems resource approach (p. 44)

REVIEW QUESTIONS

1. How do an organization's goals influence managerial action?

2. Pick a sport organization with which you are familiar and find out what its official goals are. How do you think these might differ from its operative goals?

3. How do the operative goals of a high school football team differ from those of a professional football team?

4. Who should set the goals for a women's sport advocacy organization such as the Women's Sport Foundation or the Canadian Association for the Advancement of Women and Sport?

5. In the Time Out "At Eastern Michigan University Is Winning the Only Thing?" what approach to assessing effectiveness was being used? Why was it criticized?

6. Why is effectiveness such a difficult concept to measure?

7. What is the difference between effectiveness and efficiency? Can an organization be efficient without being effective and vice versa?

8. "For an organization that produces sport equipment or sport clothing the only measure of effectiveness is profit." Discuss.

9. You are the athletic director of a small junior college whose basketball team has just finished a season in which it won just under half of its games. Attendance at games was, however, the highest it has been for 10 seasons, and two players made the conference all-star team. How would you assess the team's effectiveness?

10. In what way are the systems resource model and the goal attainment model of effectiveness related?

11. Identify the strategic constituents of a community figure-skating club. How would your

answer differ if you examined the International Skating Union?

12. Select a sport organization you are familiar with and discuss how your assessment of its effectiveness would vary depending on the approach you used.

13. What are the major advantages and disadvantages of the internal process approach to organizational effectiveness?

14. Discuss the ways in which the competing values approach to organizational effectiveness differs from the goal attainment approach.

15. How will the stages of a sport organization's life cycle affect the way effectiveness is assessed?

SUGGESTIONS FOR FURTHER READING

The most significant work on the effectiveness of sport organizations is that of Chelladurai and his associates. Chelladurai's (1987) article in the *Journal of Sport Management* presents an interesting perspective on integrating approaches to effectiveness into a comprehensive framework. His work with Szyszlo and Haggerty (Chelladurai, Szyszlo, & Haggerty, 1987) produced a psychometric scale for determining effectiveness in national sport organizations; his work with Haggerty (1991) focuses primarily on differences between professionals and volunteers in their perceptions of process effectiveness.

In the broader field of management, the most comprehensive examinations of effectiveness are found in Goodman, Pennings, and Associates' edited book (1977) *New Perspectives on Organizational Effectiveness* and Kim Cameron and David Whetten's (1983b) *Organizational Effectiveness: A Comparison of Multiple Models*. Both are collections of essays containing interesting and useful analyses of effectiveness. In the Goodman and Pennings book, refer in particular to the chapter by Campbell (1977), which presents a major review of the different theories of effectiveness, and to the Hannan and Freeman (1977a) chapter, which presents a more critical examination of the concept and deals with some of the methodological problems in studying effectiveness. The Cameron and Whetten book is useful in that the various contributors, when presenting their approach to effectiveness, compare it to other perspectives. A useful and unique addition to this text is that each chapter concludes with nine questions—three related to theoretical issues, three to research issues, and three to practice. Each author addresses the questions in these areas from the perspective of his or her approach to studying effectiveness.

CASE FOR ANALYSIS

The 2004 Athens Olympic Games: Success or Failure?

On September 5, 1997, Athens was chosen to host the 2004 Summer Olympic Games. Athens had unsuccessfully bid for the 1996 games when it was the sentimental favorite because the first modern Olympics took place in Athens in 1896 and the ancient Olympics were held in Olympia, Greece. One reason for the unsuccessful bid was the International Olympic Committee's (IOC) concern related to Greece's reputation for red tape and inefficiency.

The Athens bid committee won on the slogan "Give us back our Games. Do it for little Alexis [aged 12] and his generation." The bid committee promised to prepare a "spectacular homecoming for the Olympics" by transforming Athens into a smog-free, leafy-green oasis with efficient transportation, and sleek, new venues (Peek, 2004, p. A14).

But from the moment it was named host, Athens was plagued with problems. First, such a large undertaking—301 events, 10,500 athletes, 3.7 billion television viewers—required strong leadership. The Athens Organizing Committee (AOC) did not seem to be able to hire and retain a strong leader, nor was any leader able to get projects going. Bureaucracy, lawsuits, and political infighting explained many of the delays.

By mid-2000, next to nothing had been done in preparation for the Olympics. The IOC started showing its impatience and anger, finally making

The goal of the Athens Organizing Committee, led by AOC president Gianna Angelopoulos-Daskalaki, was to have the city ready to host the 2004 Summer Olympic Games. Despite a slow start, the AOC met its goal; the games ran on schedule and were considered a success.

the Greeks stand and listen. Finally Gianna Angelopoulos-Daskalaki was hired as AOC president, having been president of the bid committee. She became the first woman to head an Olympic Games organizing committee.

At this same time, the new $3.8 billion international airport—situated an hour from Athens—was completed, but the road linking the airport to Athens was not. The Olympic Village was still a field, and no one yet knew where the soccer final would be held. There was also a serious lack of accommodations, 10,000 to be exact, by virtue of the moratorium on hotel growth since 1988. The AOC downscaled its plan to be ready by the opening ceremonies on August 13, 2004.

Red tape continued to plague the AOC and its preparations. In March 2002, a court injunction blocked the construction of one of the five media villages. Part of the building problem was simply the country's ancient history. It seemed like each time construction workers started site excavation they hit a new archeological layer.

Meanwhile, Athens worked on a new image. Part of the beautification efforts included rounding up stray dogs and cats, and banning prostitution in the city. All unwelcome guests would be escorted outside the city's boundaries. Athens also saw new cafés, restrooms, and hotels being built.

In February 2004, anti-Olympic activists co-opted the names of the games' mascots, Athena and Phevos, and then proceeded to firebomb two government vehicles. By the end of February, only 15 of the 39 venues were completed.

In March 2004, the 78-day torch relay began with the traditional ceremony at the site of Ancient Olympia. The torch traveled more than 48,000 miles around the world (a first) and passed through the hands of 11,000 torchbearers. At the same time, the AOC cancelled plans to install the roof over the main pool, to the great regret of FINA, the international swimming federation. AOC stated the deadlines were too tight.

With 18 weeks to go, the tram line was curtailed, the marathon route was changed, and the suburban rail project was in trouble, as was the main Olympic stadium. The government promised manpower would be doubled or tripled as needed to get the job done. On March 31, 2004, the country was hit with a nationwide general strike.

Teams of workers went 24 hours a day, seven days a week to achieve the stated goals. With less than a week to go, the main Olympic stadium was finally officially handed over to AOC with its roof completed but with details undone. Cranes and other construction equipment remained on the various sites. Downtown and Olympic-area roads were closed, except for one lane, which made it difficult for emergency vehicles to operate.

Throughout it all, Greek organizers promised they would be ready on time. Leonidas Chrysanthopoulos, Greece's ambassador to Canada, was quoted as saying: "I know my people and we do it our way. Our way always works out in the end. If it gives you a heart attack, that's your problem" (Cleary, 2002).

Despite these troubles, the 2004 Olympic Games did take place. On the evening of August 13, 2004, the Olympics started with a widely acclaimed opening ceremonies showing the history of Greece. Sporting events were held on time, Olympic transportation functioned, and there were enough rooms for all. In fact, there were still tickets and rooms available for late bookers. The Greek team had a stellar performance, except for two of its biggest stars who tested positive for drugs. The $1.4 billion security system worked well—no bombs or terrorist attempts came to light—during the first Summer Olympic Games since September 11. A record-breaking 3.9 billion people watched the games. At the closing ceremonies, the AOC president Angelopoulos-Daskalaki received the IOC's highest honor for her service to the Olympic movement. The IOC president praised Athens and the AOC for doing a great job.

The last estimate for the cost of the 2004 Summer Olympic Games was tallied at more than €13 billion (approximately U.S.$15 billion), largely incurred by the Greek government to get the facilities finished by the opening ceremonies. The cost, however, is shared by numerous European countries because Greece is part of the European Union.

Based on information in The Associated Press (2004), Athens2004 (2004), Bruni and Carassava (2002), Cleary (2002), Howden (2004), International Olympic Committee (2005), MacKinnon (2004, March 22), McShane (2004, August 10), Orkin (2002), Peek (2004), Quinn (2004).

Questions

1. How would you evaluate the effectiveness of the AOC?

2. How would your perception vary depending on which of the approaches you took to measure effectiveness?

3. What other type of information about the 2004 Summer Olympic Games would help you make a better assessment of the effectiveness of the organizing committee?

4. What elements of this case demonstrate the political nature of organizational effectiveness?

Chapter 4

Dimensions of Organizational Structure

LEARNING OBJECTIVES

When you have read this chapter you should be able to

1. explain the three most commonly cited elements of organizational structure,

2. describe the different ways in which a sport organization exhibits complexity,

3. discuss the advantages and disadvantages of formalization,

4. understand the factors that influence whether a sport organization is considered centralized or decentralized, and

5. explain the interrelationship of complexity, formalization, and centralization.

BRUNSWICK RESTRUCTURES

In the early 1980s Brunswick, one of the oldest companies in the United States involved in the sport industry, was a highly diversified organization with interests in bowling, billiards, recreational boats, defense, and medical equipment. Financial analysts were critical of the company and pessimistic about its future, suggesting that its only valuable asset was its medical equipment business. CEO Jack Reichert was annoyed by what he heard. Going against popular views he sold the medical equipment business, a subsidiary that had generated Brunswick approximately one-fifth of its net earnings, and set out to restructure the rest of his organization.

The steps Reichert took were drastic. Four hundred white-collar jobs and layers of middle management were eliminated. Corporate staff was reduced by nearly 60 percent and there were only five levels of management between Reichert and the lowest-paid employee. Two-thirds of the 600,000-square-foot company headquarters was subleased, saving the company $2 million. Computer systems were introduced, a just-in-time management program was created and staff was given incentive pay. Two of three corporate jets were sold and the executive dining room was eliminated. While the latter move did not save the company large amounts of money it was symbolic of Reichert's efforts to cut costs. Approximately $20 million was saved in salaries and other operating costs. Eleven divisions were consolidated into eight. Reichert was quoted as saying, "The pyramid was too tall." The company started to focus on what it did best—work in the sport indus-

(continued)

(continued)

try, with some involvement in aerospace and defense. Bowling alleys, which were spread throughout the country, were consolidated. At Brunswick's Mercury Marine Division, which produced outboard motors for boats, a product line structure and four divisions were changed to a functional structure.

Reichert's restructuring worked. In 1984 Brunswick's debt fell to 26.6 percent of capital as compared with 39.4 percent in 1981. By 1987 sales had risen from a 1982 figure of $1 billion to $3 billion. Managers at the operating level no longer had to go through numerous hierarchical levels to get approval for projects. The general managers of each division now reported directly to Reichert and the turnaround time for decisions was reduced from months to days or even hours. This restructuring continues to be successful, with 2003 net sales of more than $4.1 billion.

Based on information in *Business Week* (1984), Reichert (1988), Bettner (1988), and Brunswick (2003).

What Jack Reichert did at Brunswick was change the structure of the organization so it could more effectively achieve its goals. But what exactly do we mean when we talk about structure? For many people, organizational structure is something represented by the patterns of differentiation and the reporting relationships found on an organizational chart, and to a certain extent this view is correct. For Thompson (1967, p. 51), structure referred to the departments of an organization and the connections "established within and between departments." He suggested that structure was the means by which an organization was able to set limits and boundaries for efficient performance through controlling resources and defining responsibilities. The term structure has in fact been used by different theorists to encompass a wide variety of organizational dimensions and their interrelationships.

In this chapter we focus in detail on only the three most commonly used dimensions. However, we show how the terms complexity, formalization, and centralization may actually encompass some of the other terms used to describe organizational structure. We also look at the interrelationships among these three primary dimensions.

Complexity

Complexity is, in many ways, one of the most readily apparent features of any sport organization. Anytime we look at an organization we cannot help but be aware of such things as the different job titles, the way in which the organization is departmentalized or divided into subunits, and the hierarchy of authority. Even a cursory look at a sport organization such as a university's faculty of health, physical education, and recreation will verify this observation. Individuals have job titles such as dean, chair, professor, research associate, graduate student, and secretary. Faculties may also be divided into departments or subunits, with names such as leisure studies, health, and sport sciences. Even a sport organization such as a local judo club, which at first glance may appear relatively "noncomplex," will probably have job titles, a committee structure, and a simple hierarchy of authority. In some sport organizations the level of complexity may actually vary among departments that are perceived as equally important. A large sport equipment manufacturing company, for example, may have a research-and-development department with little in the way of a hierarchy of authority, no clearly defined **division of labor**, and a relatively wide span of control. In contrast, the production department is quite likely to have a clear chain of command, high levels of task differentiation, and a narrow span of control.

As we can see from these brief examples, complexity is concerned with the extent to which a sport organization is differentiated. This differentiation may occur in three ways: horizontally, vertically, or spatially (geographically).

Horizontal Differentiation

Horizontal differentiation occurs in two separate yet interrelated ways, specialization and departmentalization. *Specialization*, in many ways one of the central tenets of organizational theory, has its foundations in such works as Adam Smith's *The Wealth of Nations* (1776 and 1937) and Emile Durkheim's *The Division of Labor in Society* (1893 and 1933). There are two ways in which specialization occurs in sport organizations: first, through the division of an organization's work into simple and repetitive tasks, and second, through employ-

A local, independent sporting goods store might be viewed as having a relatively simple structure, yet complexity is evident in titles (e.g., owner, manager, assistant manager, sales clerk), a hierarchy of authority, and a division of labor.

ing trained specialists to perform a range of organizational activities. The more a sport organization is divided up in these ways, the more complex it becomes. Complexity occurs because **task differentiation** (or **functional specialization**, as it is often called), the dividing up of work into narrow routine tasks, means there are more jobs to manage and a need to establish relationships among these jobs. The specialization of individuals rather than their work, what Robbins (1990) calls **social specialization**, also increases organizational complexity. The different training and knowledge that specialists have, such as professionals (e.g., a sport lawyer) and craft workers (e.g., a custom-skate maker), create different approaches to work, and thus make the coordination of their activities more difficult. They may have different ideological positions, different goals for the organization, and even different terminology for the work they do. All of these differences make interaction among these people more complex. Slack and Hinings (1992), for example, report that as a result of their training and background, the professional staff of national sport organizations in Canada showed greater commitment to changes being brought about by a government-initiated rational planning system than did the volunteers who had traditionally operated these organizations.

The task differentiation that occurs when work is broken down into simple and repetitive tasks is most often found in sport organizations that produce large quantities of a commodity in the same way. For example, when Hillerich and Bradsby build one of their Power Bilt golf woods, the production process is broken down into 77 operations; an iron requires 36 operations. Since these processes are routine and uniform, this type of division of labor creates jobs that are relatively unskilled; hence, there is usually high substitutability in this type of work (management can usually replace workers easily). On the other hand, when the type of work to be performed is nonroutine and varied, specialization is usually based on education and training. Professionals or craft workers are employed because their skills cannot be easily routinized. In sport we find this type of specialization in organizations such as architectural firms specializing in sport facilities, custom-bike manufacturers, and university physical education departments. For example, Daniel F. Tully Associates, an architectural firm with a specialization in sport and recreation facility planning, not only utilizes a core project team but also has in-house professionals with such specialist titles as architect, engineer, designer, graphic artist, cost estimator, interior designer, and construction manager.

While specialization creates increased complexity within a sport organization that must be managed through processes of coordination and integration, there are several advantages to specialization. While these advantages pertain primarily to functional specialization, some are relevant to social specialization. Specialization means that the time required to learn a job is relatively short, the chances of making errors when learning the job are reduced, and (because the task is frequently repeated) the person becomes more skillful in its execution. Specialization also means that time is not lost switching from one task to another; the chance of developing techniques to improve the way the task is carried out is improved, and individual skills are used in the most efficient manner. The dehumanizing aspects of specialization (primarily functional specialization) have been well documented by human relations theorists such as Argyris (1964) and Likert (1967). In an attempt to counter these dehumanizing aspects, many organizations employ techniques such as job rotation, job enlargement, job enrichment, and (more recently) quality circles (Crocker, Chiu, & Charney, 1984; Lawler & Mohrman, 1985).

The specialization of individuals and their work gives rise to the second form of horizontal differentiation, that of departmentalization. **Departmentalization** refers to the way in which management groups differentiate activities into subunits (divisions, work groups, and so on) in order to achieve the organization's goals most effectively. As figure 4.1 shows, departmentalization may occur on the basis of product or service, function, or geographic location.

Reebok is departmentalized along product lines; Human Kinetics, the publisher of sport books (including this one) is departmentalized by function; and Canada Basketball is departmentalized by geographic location.

Researchers in both sport management and the broader field have defined these forms of horizontal complexity in different ways. Hage and Aiken (1967b) focused on levels of occupational specialization and professionalization. They suggested that complexity includes the number of occupa-

---

TIME OUT *Using Quality Circles in Intercollegiate Athletic Departments*

In recent years intercollegiate athletic departments have experienced considerable change. Pressure from shifting client attitudes and changing societal needs, and increased public and private competition have resulted in these organizations becoming more complex in terms of their structural arrangements. Such complexity can result in communication problems, employee feelings of inferiority, and loyalty to a subunit rather than a department. Hunnicutt suggests that, by introducing quality circles into athletic departments, these types of problems can be eased and team spirit can be created.

Quality circles, which originated in Japan but in recent years have been introduced into a number of North American businesses, are designed to bring small groups of employees together to solve problems relating to their work. Hunnicutt suggests three steps to making quality circles work in athletic departments. First, he suggests it is necessary to establish who participates in the circle. Membership should be voluntary and the size of the unit should be somewhere from 6 to 10 people. They meet approximately four times per month for about an hour, usually during business hours, to work on problems that they select. Problems discussed may range from issues such as academic advisement to facility maintenance. Second, the quality circle should have a facilitator who helps the members of the circle in case of difficulty and acts as a liaison with other circles. Finally, quality circle evaluation should be undertaken in a constructive manner. Hunnicutt believes that integrating participative management techniques, such as quality circles, can improve teamwork in an athletic department, increase productivity, and help solve the communication problems that may result from increasing complexity.

Based on information in Hunnicutt (1988).

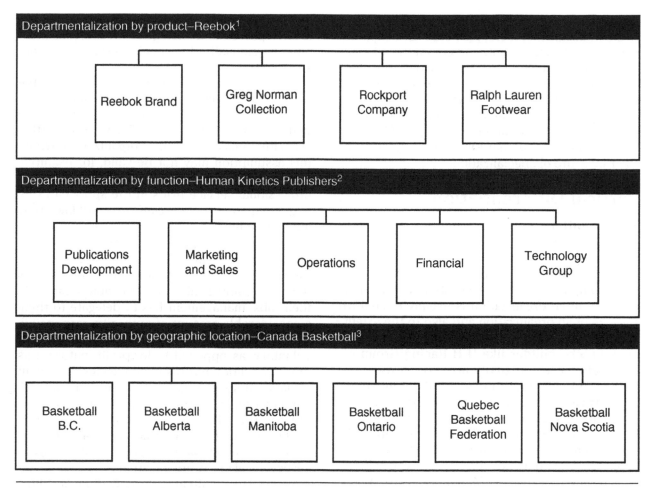

Figure 4.1 *Three types of departmentalization.*

[1]Based on Reebok 2002 Annual Report. [2]Based on material provided by Human Kinetics. [3]Based on information from Canada Basketball, www.basketball.ca.

tional specialties, professional activity, and professional training. They then classified individuals as to their occupational specialty (e.g., teacher, coach, athletic therapist) based on their major duties. Professional activity was measured by the number of professional associations in which an individual was a member, number of meetings attended, and so on, and the variable professional training was measured by the amount of education and other professional training an individual had experienced (Hage & Aiken, 1967a; Hage & Aiken, 1970). Basically, Hage and Aiken's (1967a) argument is that the more training people have in their different specialties, the more differentiated they are (greater degree of professional activity), and hence the greater the level of organizational complexity.

Peter Blau and his colleagues, in some of their work, adopt a somewhat different definition of horizontal differentiation. Blau and Schoenherr

(1971), for example, define horizontal differentiation as the number of major subdivisions in an organization and the number of sections per division. Hall, Haas, and Johnson (1967) and the Aston group (Pugh, Hickson, Hinings, & Turner, 1968) use similar measures to those of Blau. Hall et al. (1967) focus on the number of major divisions or departments in an organization and the way they are subdivided. The Aston group focuses on functional specialization and the extent to which there are specialized roles within these functions.

In the sport literature both Frisby (1986b) and Kikulis et al. (1989) have used aspects of the work of the Aston group to examine horizontal complexity. Frisby, in her study of the organizational structure and the effectiveness of voluntary sport organizations, used measures of professionalism and specialization. Professionalism was defined as the level of education attained by both volunteers and paid staff; specialization measures were based on the number of roles for board members, executive committee members, paid staff, and support staff, as well as the number of committees in the organization. Kikulis et al. (1989) used the concept of specialization in their work. It was a composite variable defined as "the extent and pattern of differentiated tasks, units, and roles allocated to different organizational segments" (p. 132). Table 4.1 shows the items that Kikulis et al. include in their measure of specialization.

Vertical Differentiation

Vertical differentiation refers to the number of levels in a sport organization. The more levels there are, the greater the problems of communication, coordination, and supervision, hence the more complex the sport organization. The number of levels in an organization is usually related to the size of an organization and also to the extent to which it is horizontally differentiated. A small custom-bike builder like H H Racing Group of Philadelphia has virtually no vertical differentiation and very little horizontal differentiation. In contrast, a large producer of sporting goods like Huffy has several vertical levels and shows a high level of horizontal differentiation. Although research findings vary, horizontal differentiation is generally seen as being related to vertical differentiation, because, as Mintzberg (1979, p. 72) notes, "when a job is highly specialized in the horizontal dimension, the worker's perspective is narrowed, making it difficult for him to relate his work to that of others. So control of the work is often passed to a manager. . . . Thus, jobs must often be specialized vertically because they are specialized horizontally."

The pattern of vertical differentiation is often assumed to represent the **hierarchy of authority** in an organization and, as Hall (1982) notes, in the vast majority of cases it does. There are, nevertheless, situations in some sport organizations where this assumption may not be valid, for example, when professionals work in bureaucracies. In professional service firms in the sport industry (e.g., companies that specialize in sport law, sport medicine clinics, and architectural companies that specialize in sport facilities), professionals, because of their specialist training, are central to the firm's operations. Because the professionals require a relatively high degree of autonomy to do their jobs, management has to delegate to them a considerable amount of authority, responsibility, and, subsequently, control. Heightened by a voluntary, as opposed to for-profit, nature, this type of situation has been increasingly prevalent in national sport organizations in Canada. Volunteers who have traditionally managed these organizations have in recent years lost much of their control to professionally trained sport managers who are actually positioned at a lower vertical level in the organization (cf. Macintosh & Whitson, 1990; Thibault, Slack, & Hinings, 1991). Thompson (1961) suggests that one way to deal with such a situation is to create a dual hierarchy. However, Schriesheim, Von Glinow, and Kerr

Table 4.1   Measures of Specialization in Voluntary Sport Organizations

Measure of specialization	Operationalization
Program specialization	The number of programs operated by the sport organization (e.g., national team, coaching certification)
Coaching specialization	The number of coaching roles within the sport organization (e.g., men's head coach, women's head coach, junior coach)
Specialization of professional staff	The number of professional staff roles (e.g., managing director, coach, technical director)
Specialization of volunteer administrative roles	The number of administrative roles held by volunteers on the sport organization's board of directors (e.g., vice president of administration, treasurer)
Specialization of volunteer technical roles	The number of technical roles held by volunteers on the sport organization's board of directors (e.g., vice president of coaching, director of officials)
Vertical differentiation	The number of levels in the sport organization's hierarchy

Based on information in L. Kikulis, T. Slack, C.R. Hinnings, and A. Zimmermann (1989).

(1977) raise a number of questions about the use of dual hierarchies. A more recent development to address this situation, and one used by a number of Canadian national sport organizations, is an organizational design known as the professional bureaucracy. Whereas the traditional bureaucracy "relies on authority of a hierarchical nature . . . the Professional Bureaucracy emphasizes authority of a professional nature—the power of expertise" (Mintzberg, 1979, p. 351). We examine this type of organizational design more fully in chapter 5.

As we have discussed, size influences the number of levels in an organization. It is nevertheless quite possible for two sport organizations with a similar number of nonmanagerial employees to have a different number of vertical levels. As figure 4.2 shows, some organizations like Organization A can have what is usually referred to as a **flat structure**. In contrast, Organization B has a relatively **tall structure**. The difference, as figure 4.3 shows, relates to what is termed the span of control (sometimes called the span of management). The **span of control** in an organization refers to the number of people directly supervised by a manager. In figure 4.3, although Organization X has just over 200 more first-level employees than Organization Y, it has a span of control of seven, and consequently fewer managers and a flatter structure. Organization Y, which has a span of control of three, has a tall structure and more managers.

Opinions vary as to what is an appropriate span of control. Classical theorists such as Urwick (1938, p. 8) suggest that "no superior can supervise directly the work of more than five or, at the most, six subordinates whose work interlocks." Human relations theorists favor a broader span of control that gives more autonomy to workers. A wider span of control can also enhance communication in an organization. As Simon (1945) notes, administrative efficiency increases when the number of organizational levels is minimized.

Employees may feel more secure in a taller structure because they are easily able to obtain help from a supervisor. However, tall structures with a narrow span of control may result in closer supervision than employees see as necessary. Cummings and Berger (1976) suggest that senior managers prefer tall structures whereas lower-level managers are more comfortable with a flatter structure. The nature of the work being performed also affects the size of the span of control. Some jobs require close supervision; others, particularly professional jobs, do not.

Spatial Differentiation

Spatial differentiation can occur as a form of either vertical or horizontal differentiation. That is to say, both levels of power and tasks can be separated geographically. For example in the province of Saskatchewan, the department responsible for sport, the Department of Culture, Youth, and Recreation, has a number of zone offices throughout the province that help facilitate the provision of opportunities for participation in sport. Power is differentiated between these zone offices and the central government offices in the provincial

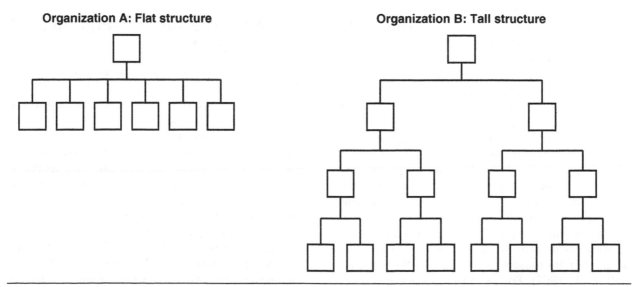

Organization A: Flat structure   **Organization B: Tall structure**

Figure 4.2 *Flat and tall structures.*

Organization X:

Span of control of 7

Organization Y:

Span of control of 3

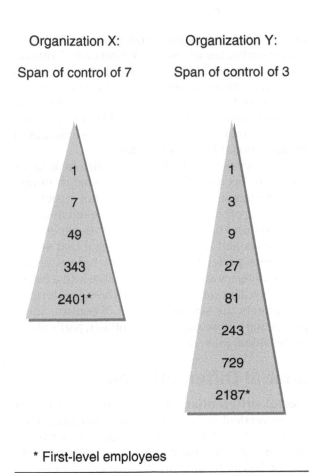

* First-level employees

Figure 4.3 *Comparing the span of control.*

capital, Regina. Because senior managers are housed in the provincial capital and lower-level zone managers are placed throughout the province, complexity is increased more than if they were all in one location.

Horizontally differentiated functions can also be dispersed spatially. Muddy Fox, a British-based mountain bike company, has offices and a warehouse just outside London, but buys Japanese components, has them assembled in Taiwan, and sells them through the approximately 600 approved Muddy Fox dealers dispersed throughout the United Kingdom (and a growing number in the United States) (Ferguson, 1988). The locations of the organization's central office, production source, and assembly plant in different parts of the world, and the use of 600 sales outlets, obviously increase organizational complexity.

The physical separation of an organization's operations increases its complexity, which can be further increased as a result of distance (cf. Hall et al., 1967). For example, a sporting goods company with several retail outlets throughout London would be considered less complex than the same type of company with a similar number of outlets dispersed throughout the United States.

Interrelationship Among Elements of Complexity

Although we have treated each of the three elements of complexity separately, you may be tempted to ask if there are interrelationships among the three. The most obvious interrelationships are in very big and very small sport organizations. Companies like CCM, a major manufacturer of hockey skates; Bally Manufacturing Corporation, a leading owner of health and fitness centers; and L.A. Gear, an athletic footwear manufacturer (and at one time one of North America's fastest-growing companies), all exhibit high levels of horizontal, vertical, and spatial differentiation. In contrast, companies such as Ed Milner Consulting Services, a small company that provides advice on sport surfaces and facilities; Yeti Cycles of Agoura Hills, California, a small custom-bike manufacturer; and the Double G Card Shop, a sport card store in Spruce Grove, Alberta, are low in all three areas.

Beyond these extremes of size it is hard to generalize. Universities, for example, often have high levels of horizontal differentiation in terms of the number of departments that exist, a relatively low level of vertical differentiation, and usually no spatial differentiation. Football teams have high horizontal differentiation, with roles such as running back, wide receiver, and linebacker, but usually only have two levels of vertical differentiation—coaches and players (Hall, 1982).

The Managerial Consequences of Complexity

As sport organizations grow, which most aim to do, they generally become more differentiated. People occupying different roles, working in different departments, and having different levels of training exhibit different attitudes and behaviors; they also have different goals and expectations for the organization. This complexity leads to problems of communication, coordination, and control. Consequently, as a sport organization becomes more complex increasing pressures are placed on managers to ensure that the organization progresses smoothly and efficiently toward achieving its goal(s). In short, managers have to manage complexity, so they introduce such things as committees, rules, procedures, and manage-

TIME OUT   *The Emergence of Elements of Complexity in a Voluntary Sport Organization*

The Alberta Section of the Swimming Natation Canada was founded in the 1920s by the members of three Edmonton swimming clubs. In its early years the organization operated with a relatively loose and informal structure; there was little in the way of any type of role specialization, as all members at various times had to assume the responsibilities of the coach, meet organizer, timer, starter, and so on. The members of the organization, with little in the way of any professional qualifications, attained their positions in the organization because of their enthusiasm, not through any type of special training or credentials.

As the organization grew, clubs from other parts of the province began to join the provincial association; hence, the organization became more geographically dispersed. Increased size also meant that members began to take on specialist roles; some concentrated on coaching, others focused on organizing meets or timekeeping. As clubs joined the association, zones were created, with the effect of introducing another level into the hierarchy of the organization, because these zones acted as links between the clubs in their area and the provincial association. Eventually, as the association grew relatively complex, one of the unstated qualifications for getting elected to the provincial executive was some type of professional qualification. It was felt that, by having people on the board with specialist training in areas such as accounting and business management, the association would run more effectively. Ultimately, the workload became so great that volunteers could no longer run the organization, so a staff person with a professional background in sport management was hired.

Based on information in Slack (1985).

ment information systems. The more complex the sport organization becomes, the more time and effort managers have to spend dealing with issues of communication, coordination, and control.

Hall (1982, p. 90) describes this phenomenon as "an interesting paradox in the analysis of organizations." He notes that, although complexity is increased to help organizations economically and to improve their efficiency, it also creates pressures to add managers to maintain communication, coordination, and control, and to reduce conflict. Consequently the economies and efficiencies realized by increased complexity have to be counterbalanced by the added burden placed on managers to keep the organization together.

Formalization

The second structural dimension is formalization, a key dimension because it strongly influences the way individuals are able to behave in an organization. Just as the rules of a sport limit the way an individual can behave in the playing area, formalization in organizations works to control the amount of discretion individuals or groups are allowed to exercise when performing their jobs.

As Hall (1982, p. 95) notes, the focus on the way formalization controls individual behavior does not mean a move away from "the organizational level of analysis. Formalization has important consequences for the organization and its subunits in terms of such processes as communication and innovation."

What Is Formalization?

Formalization refers to the extent to which mechanisms such as rules and regulations, job descriptions, and policies and procedures govern the operation of a sport organization. If a sport organization is highly formalized it will have lots of rules and regulations, comprehensive policies and procedures, and detailed job descriptions to guide its operations. In this type of sport organization, employees have little discretion over how and when they do their work. In sport organizations with low formalization, however, employees are given the freedom to exercise discretion about their work, and how and when it is carried out. In this sense, formalization is not only a structural component, but also a control mechanism that has political and ethical ramifications (cf. Braverman, 1974; Clegg & Dunkerley, 1980).

Different types of sport organizations exhibit different levels of formalization. W.L. Gore & Associates, the manufacturer of Gore-Tex, a product used in sport equipment such as rain gear, tents, and sleeping bags, prides itself on low levels of formalization. In contrast, other companies that mass-produce sport equipment usually have relatively large numbers of unskilled jobs, which are likely to be highly formalized. Even sport organizations that require employees to use some degree of discretion in their work will formalize aspects of their operations. U.S. Athletics, a specialty athletic footwear store, for example, has "compiled a 50-page training manual [for staff], which includes everything from store policies, to the anatomy of a shoe, to information about features and quality in athletic footwear" (Gill, 1987, p. 47). The more professionals there are in a sport organization, the less likely it will have high levels of formalization. Doctors who specialize in sport medicine, university professors who teach sport management, and architects who design sport facilities are all professionals in different aspects of sport organizations that demonstrate relatively low levels of formalization.

The extent of formalization differs not only from organization to organization but also among the hierarchical levels of an organization and among departments. At the higher levels of a sport organization, jobs are generally broad and nonrepetitive, and allow more discretion over how they are carried out than at the lower-level jobs; consequently, manager's jobs are less likely to have to follow formalized procedures than those they supervise. As we have already noted, production departments tend to be highly formalized; in contrast, a research-and-development department, because of the creative nature of the work and the fact that it is likely to be staffed by professionals, will not have high levels of formalization.

There is some question as to whether or not rules, procedures, and so on have to be stated in writing in order for an organization to be considered "formalized." Pugh et al. (1968) used the terms "formalization" and "standardization" in their work. The two concepts are in fact highly correlated. *Formalization* refers to "the extent to which rules, procedures, instructions, and communication are written" (Pugh et al., 1968, p. 75). In the research by Pugh et al. (1968) the concept was operationalized by measuring the extent to which an organization had such written documentation as policies and procedures, job descriptions, organizational charts, and employee handbooks. *Standardization*, on the other hand, refers to events that occurred regularly and were legitimated by the organization but not committed to written form. Pugh et al. (1968) rated activities such as taking inventory, ordering materials, and interviewing for their degree of standardization. Hage and Aiken (1970) used the term "formalization" to include both written and unwritten rules, by breaking formalization down into two elements: job codification (i.e., how many rules a worker is asked to follow) and rule observation (how closely workers must adhere to these rules). For their work they used both official documents and the perceptions of employees as measures of formalization. As Hall (1982) notes, the use of perceptual measures recognizes the existence of informal procedures in an organization, something that cannot be obtained from official records only. Despite the fact that both approaches purport to measure the same concept, they have been shown to produce different results (cf. Pennings, 1973; Walton, 1981).

Studies carried out on sport organizations have tended to focus on the existence of written documentation as an indicator of formalization. Frisby (1986b) in her study of organization structure and effectiveness used three indicators: publication formalization, the total number of publications produced by the sport organization; constitution formalization, an estimate of the number of words in the sport organization's constitution; and job description formalization, an estimate of the number of words in volunteer and paid staff job descriptions. Slack and Hinings (1987b) used the term "standardization" but note that standardized procedures are often committed to writing. Thibault et al. (1991), in their study of the impact that professional staff have on the structural arrangements of voluntary sport organizations, operationalize the concept "formalization" by measuring the existence of written documentation across a range of organizational activities such as personnel training, planning, marketing, and promotion.

Reasons for Formalization

Of the reasons for formalizing the operations of a sport organization, the most central are to replace direct supervision, which would be unduly expensive, and to provide a consistent way of dealing with recurring problems. In small organizations such as a local sport equipment store, a manager can supervise employees directly, because they are in close contact and there are few employees. In larger sport organizations this type of direct supervision is not possible. Although a narrow span of control can help supervision issues, it can be time-consuming if a problem has to go through several hierarchical levels before a decision can be made. Formalizing procedures so that recurring problems are handled in a consistent way can alleviate supervision problems.

Formalization also helps monitor employee behavior. In many sport organizations employees are required to submit reports about what they accomplish in their jobs on a weekly, monthly, or yearly basis. These reports help managers determine if employees are contributing to achieving the goals of the sport organization. Companies like Tottenham Hotspur Football Club, Reebok, and Huffy, because they are publicly held, all file formalized annual reports for their shareholders, who in essence own the company, to keep them informed of its accomplishments. Besides helping to monitor the behavior of employees, formalized procedures also help ensure employees understand procedure. For example, professors who teach sport management courses often receive guidelines about how to mark student papers and what to do if students miss assignments because of illness. Such procedures help ensure that all students are dealt with fairly and in the same manner.

Economic aspects of formalization are also important to consider. Formalizing jobs generally means that they require less discretion, and in turn

can be filled by less-qualified, and hence cheaper, workers. Formalization also promotes efficiencies, because organizations often spend considerable time, effort, and money to determine the best way to conduct a particular operation; once the best way is determined, formalizing the procedure induces other people who perform the operation to do so in the most cost-efficient manner.

Formalization clarifies job requirements. At Louisiana State University, student football managers are given an 87-page handbook that outlines their job responsibilities and how they should be performed (Equipment Handbook, 1988). Formalizing procedures is also beneficial to determine what the organization is supposed to do. For example, Sport Canada stresses that national sport organizations must write down organizational structures and processes if they want to receive funds.

No organization can develop formalized rules and procedures for every possible situation that can arise, but there are ways in which formalization can help. Many professional organizations develop a written code of ethics, which provides generally accepted principles based on professional values, and which can be followed when unfamiliar situations are encountered. Earle Zeigler proposed such a code of professional ethics for the North American Society for Sport Management (NASSM) (see Zeigler, 1989). Included in Zeigler's proposal are a commitment to a high level of professional practice and service, the availability of such services to clients of all ages and conditions, and professional conduct based

---

TIME OUT *Policies and Procedures Manuals: Making Life Easier for Athletic Department Administrators*

Milton E. Richards and George Edberg-Olson suggest that the management of college athletic departments has changed considerably during the last twenty years. In many ways athletic directors have become more like business people. In order to help athletic directors perform their jobs, Richards and Edberg-Olson suggest the development of a policies and procedures manual that formalizes many of the athletic department's operations. The format for this policies and procedures manual is based on an analysis of the manuals of 31 Division 1A schools. Figure

4.4 provides a sample outline of the areas Richards and Edberg-Olson suggest should be contained in the manual.

The authors acknowledge that it is not possible or maybe even desirable to cover all aspects of an athletic department's operations in a policies and procedures manual. However, they suggest that "for handling routine operations and normal, daily activities, many athletic administrators believe a manual of policies and procedures is an invaluable aid" (p. 40).

Based on information in Richards and Edberg-Olson (1987).

1. General preface or introduction
2. Purpose (and short history) of the department of intercollegiate athletics
3. Department personnel
   A. Organizational chart
   B. Job description and duties: relationships between department members as well as outside administration
   C. General policies and procedures
   D. Policy and professional organizations and meetings, scholarships, and publishing
4. Financial policies
   A. Budgeting
   B. Accounting and budget control
   C. Business office policies and procedures
   D. Athletic ticket priorities and privileges
   E. Funding, fund-raising, foundations, booster and pep clubs, cash donations, gifts, gifts-in-kind (trade outs)
5. Travel policies—team and individual
   A. Travel request policy
   B. Expense vouchers
   C. Accommodations: air travel, bus, personal automobiles, van, hotel, other
6. Purchasing
   A. General
   B. Equipment
   C. Capital expenditures

   D. Emergency requests
7. Facility operations
   A. Scheduling
   B. General maintenance
   C. Maintenance of records and files
   D. Events management
8. Scheduling/contracts
   A. Philosophy and mechanics of scheduling
   B. Revenue sports
   C. Non-revenue sports
9. Student-athletes
   A. Recruiting
   B. Admissions
   C. Financial aid
   D. Housing
   E. Academic advising (eligibility)
   F. Rules and regulations governing athletes
   G. Training and medical services
   H. Strength and fitness center
   I. Letter awards, academic honors, dean's list, etc.
   J. Sports banquets
10. Public affairs
   A. Sports information and publicity/media relations
   B. Marketing/promotions
11. Sports camps and clinics, lectures, and demonstrations
12. Miscellaneous

Figure 4.4 *A sample outline for a manual of policies and procedures.*

Reprinted, by permission, from M.E. Richards and G. Edberg-Olsen, 1987, "Policies and procedures manual: Making life easier for athletic department administrators," *Athletic Business* August: 38-40.

on sound management theory. NASSM adopted a code in 1992.

Finally, formalizing procedures provides an indication to employees as to the purpose of the organization, its overall goals, and what they as employees can expect from their involvement. Formalization can strengthen an employee's identification with the organization and provide a safeguard, because the organization's commitment to its employees is formally documented. Formalized commitments can help morale because employees have a tangible indication of their rights and responsibilities.

Methods of Formalization

There are a number of ways in which managers can formalize the operations of a sport organization. In this section we examine the methods most frequently used.

Hiring the Right Employee

As we saw earlier, sport organizations with high numbers of professionals tend to have relatively low formalized operations. The reason is that in many ways professional training is a surrogate for formalization, and may be considered a means of standardizing behavior prior to a job. Through their training, individuals not only learn technical skills, but also the standards, norms, and accepted modes of behavior of their profession. Consequently, in staffing, organizations face what Robbins (1990) calls "the make or buy decision": The organization can either control employee behavior directly through its own formalized rules and procedures, or control can be achieved indirectly by hiring trained professionals (Perrow, 1972).

Regardless of whether an organization is hiring professional staff or unskilled workers, candidates often deal with application forms, tests, reference letters, and interviews before employers hire the "right" person. The right person is someone who it is perceived will perform the job well and is willing to follow rules and regulations (cf. Hage and Aiken, 1970). Coaches often use this logic in team selection. Because they want players who are willing to conform to rules and show consistent behavior patterns, they do not always select talented players unless they "fit in" with the team. Selecting the right person is then a method of formalization; it helps ensure consistency in employee behavior.

On-the-Job Training

Even though they go to considerable lengths to hire the right people, some sport organizations still provide on-the-job training for their employees. Training activities may be influenced by a number of factors and can include such activities as workshops, films, lectures, demonstrations, and supervised practice sessions (cf. Slack, 1991b). The idea behind all of these methods is to instill in new employees the norms and accepted patterns of behavior of the organization. Mecca Leisure, a British organization involved with ice skating rinks and billiard and snooker halls, could not find the type of staff it needed from higher education, so it developed its own in-house training program (Brown, 1990). The organizing committee of the 2001 *Jeux de la Francophonie* (Games of La Francophonie) held in Ottawa-Gatineau, Ontario-Québec, Canada, developed a training program for volunteer employees. The program provided volunteers not only with information about the history, philosophy, and operation of the games, but also with some knowledge of the protocols that had to be followed when dealing with visiting dignitaries, members of competing teams, and spectators. Again, the idea behind the training was to standardize employee behavior.

Policies

Policies are general statements of organizational intent. They provide employees with a certain amount of discretion in making decisions in the areas covered by the policy. Policies may be internally focused; for example, Human Kinetics Publishers has policies that cover such areas as the advancement of employees and attendance at work. Policies may also be externally focused. A small sporting goods store, for example, may use them to cover situations such as returning merchandise and cashing personal checks. Policies are generally written to provide some leeway in their interpretation. The City of Winnipeg Parks and Recreation Department Sport Services policy (1990) states the following: "The Department will cooperate with other agencies and organizations to ensure a base level of sport programs and opportunities and encourage advanced levels of participation." The policy does not specifically state how the department will cooperate; consequently, staff is given the discretion to determine whether cooperation will merely mean endorsing a program or providing funding and other resources.

But policies can also conflict. With the return of the Olympic Games to Greece in 2004, the IOC promoted a policy of inclusion. It encouraged as many countries as possible to participate in the Olympic Marathon, which would follow the exact route Pheidippides ran on his way to Athens to tell of the victory of the battle of Marathon. However, the Canadian Olympic Committee (COC) set a seemingly conflicting policy of sending only top athletes who had a chance of winning a medal. Its very tough qualifying standards ultimately meant no Canadian marathoner was in the Olympic event.

Procedures

Procedures, developed for the **standardization** of particular organizational activities, are different from policies in that they are written instructions detailing how an employee should carry out an activity. These instructions, determined to be "the one best way" of operation, contribute to the efficiency of a sport organization by standardizing inputs and outputs, and abetting the optimal use of time and resources in the transformation process. While procedures can facilitate the smooth running of a sport organization, too many procedures, like other methods of formalization, can create difficulties for employees, customers, and clients. Good sport managers establish procedures only when they are necessary to help achieve organizational goals.

Rules

Rules are specific statements that tell employees what they may and may not do: "No smoking in the building"; "Employees are allowed an hour-long lunch break"; "All accidents must be reported immediately." Rules, unlike procedures, do not leave any leeway for employee discretion. Sport organizations will have rules for various aspects of the organization and its processes, products, and services, such as rules that apply to legal protection, public relations protocol, and employee work hours. Some sport organizations even have rules for clients as well as employees. Snow Valley Ski Club in Edmonton, Alberta, Canada, for example has the following rule: Place skis in rack when not in use (Snow Valley Ski Club, 1992). Rules such as these perform a public-relations function; they signal to people using the ski area that the management is concerned about public safety. They also serve a legal function in that they set limits on clients to reduce the chances of injury.

Job Descriptions

Each individual in a sport organization has a particular job to perform. Job descriptions provide written details of what a job entails. In this way they regulate employee behavior by making sure that job requirements are carried out and individuals do not impinge on other people's responsibilities. Job descriptions vary in terms of detail; some are very explicit as to responsibilities, while others are far more loosely defined. In general the farther up the organizational hierarchy one moves, the less specific the job description. Usually the job description outlines who the employee reports to and supervises, and the specific duties of the job. The job description for the manager of media relations, reporting to the director of communications of the COC, lists several such responsibilities:

- Develop and implement a national media relations plan and contribute to the development of corporate and games communications plans.

- Act as the day-to-day contact for sport and news media, and arrange interviews with COC representatives.
- Proactively identify and organize opportunities to increase corporate profile and exposure with national sport and news media.
- Identify emerging issues and prepare issue notes and key messages.
- Prepare news releases, backgrounders, press kits, speaking notes, and other communications materials.
- Lead organization of press conferences and other COC events (COC, 2005).

Committee Terms of Reference

Many sport organizations, particularly those that are volunteer-based, operate with a committee structure. Much as job descriptions provide individuals with direction to perform their job, so terms of reference provide committees with direction as to the areas for which they are responsible. For example, the executive committee of the COC has as part of its terms of reference the following responsibilities:

- Prepare the COC quadrennial budget and do all things necessary to ensure receipt of needed revenues and adequate control of projected expenditures.
- Receive reports from, and give direction to, the CEO and committees of the COC (Canadian Olympic Committee, 2003, p. 34).

The Dangers of Excessive Formalization

As we have seen, there can be considerable advantages to formalizing the operation of a sport organization. Nevertheless, excessive amounts of formalization can produce a number of dysfunctional consequences.

Goal Displacement

In some sport organizations adherence to rules and regulations becomes so important to members of the organization that the rules and regulations themselves become more important than the goals they were designed to help achieve. As Merton (1957) explains, instead of being seen as a means, adhering to the rules can become an end in itself. This condition results in what he calls **goal displacement.**

Minimal Adherence to Rules

The purpose of rules and regulations is to indicate to employees what is considered unacceptable behavior. But they can also be seen as the minimum level of employee performance required by the organization (Gouldner, 1954). Viewing the rules in this manner promotes a **minimal adherence to rules.** If employees are not motivated by their work, the existence of rules can encourage apathy; they come to define minimum standards of behavior rather than unacceptable behavior. When employees perform at the minimum acceptable level, management attempts to control behavior even more.

Bureaupathic Behavior

As a result of the growing gap between managers who have the right to make rules and regulations and the specialists (i.e., the skilled workers who operate at lower levels of the organization but have the ability to solve specialized problems), superiors come to depend on subordinates. This dependence creates anxieties and insecurities in superiors, who then react with excessive controls, overreliance on rules, and insistence on the rights of their position. This tendency to overemphasize rules and follow them for their own sake is what Thompson (1961) refers to as **bureaupathic behavior.**

TIME OUT   *John Tarrant, the Ghost Runner: The Tragic Consequences of Goal Displacement*

John Tarrant was born in London in 1932. Due to the death of his mother and his father being away in the army, John spent much of his early life in a children's home. In his last two years of school John developed an interest in running, but when he left school at age 15 to work as a plumber's mate, he found little interest in running in the town where he lived. He did, however, meet former RAF boxing champion Tom Burton, who was keen to promote boxing. Burton approached several local young men in the town to see if they would be interested in earning a little money in a boxing tournament. In 1950 Burton promoted his first tournament; 18-year-old John Tarrant fought four two-minute rounds, for which he was paid £1 (about $1.50 U.S.). In just under two years John fought eight bouts in unlicensed rings and won a total of £17 (about $25 U.S.), his largest "purse" being £4. In his eighth fight John was knocked out in 55 seconds; that convinced him that boxing wasn't his sport and he decided to return to his first love, running.

But when John applied to the Amateur Athletic Association (AAA) he was told that because he had boxed for money he would have to first be reinstated by the Amateur Boxing Association (ABA). John tried, but because he had broken the amateur rules he was turned down by the ABA. Despite repeated letters to both associations, John was unsuccessful in his efforts. But John's desire to run was not easily quashed; on August 12, 1956, he ran his first marathon as an unofficial competitor. Over the next year John gate-crashed several races, and in August 1957 actually received an invitation to gate-crash a 7 1/2 mile race. When he arrived at the race, instead of a number John was given a piece of cardboard with the word "GHOST" on it. John ran many races as the ghost runner. In 1958, after considerable pressure from the media and fellow runners, John was reinstated by the AAA, but under the rules of the International Amateur Athletic Federation (IAAF). The fact that John had broken amateur rules and boxed for money meant that he could not compete internationally for his country. Despite this ruling John continued to run in England and "ghosted" other races in different parts of the world. He set world records for the 40- and 100-mile distances, and won a number of marathons and many of the classic long-distance races. But because he had won £17 boxing, John had broken the rules; rigid adherence to those rules meant that he was never allowed to realize his ambition of competing for his country.

Based on information in Watman (1979).

Formalization and Complexity

A number of researchers have identified a strong positive correlation between formalization and complexity. In a study by Pugh et al. (1968), overall role specialization correlated highly with overall standardization (0.80) and with overall formalization (0.68). Other studies have produced similar findings (cf. Child, 1972a; Donaldson & Warner, 1974), but they apply primarily to situations when employees are performing simple and routine tasks in a repetitive manner. Here standardized rules are used to control employee behavior. In sport organizations this type of work situation is more frequent at a work site where a particular product, such as a hockey stick, is mass-produced.

In work situations that are less narrowly defined and use professionals or craft workers, the relationship does not hold true (cf. Hage, 1965), because, as we noted earlier, professional training is a surrogate for formalization. Consequently, in situations when relatively unskilled workers perform narrow and repetitive tasks, formalization will be high, but where professional or craft workers are used, formalization will generally be low. However, as the Time Out below shows, this general trend may not hold in some situations, such as this one involving voluntary sport organizations.

Centralization

All sport managers make decisions. The question is: Which managers get to make which decisions and how do they make them? For example, it is unlikely that Paul Fireman, the Chairman and CEO of Reebok, makes decisions about the purchase of paper clips and staples for his office staff; these decisions are delegated to lower-level managers. But in 1987 when Reebok acquired Avia, another athletic footwear company, Fireman and other members of the board of directors of Reebok were intimately involved in the acquisition decision. Questions about the authority to make decisions and how they are made are the issues addressed when we look at our third element of organizational structure, centralization.

What Is Centralization?

Of all three elements of organizational structure, **centralization** is by far the most difficult to explain. It is generally accepted that if decision making takes place at the top of the organization, it is centralized; when decisions are delegated to lower levels, the organization is **decentralized**. But consider the following:

TIME OUT *The Impact of Hiring Professional Staff on the Levels of Formalization in Voluntary Sport Organizations*

While the presence of professionally trained employees is usually associated with lower levels of formalization, Thibault et al. (1991) found in a study of voluntary sport organizations that when professionals were hired in these organizations, formalization increased. They provide two possible explanations for this unexpected phenomenon. First, when the professionals entered the organizations being studied, formalization was low; consequently the professionals created written rules, procedures, and guidelines to clarify their roles. A second explanation was that increased formalization was initiated by volunteers as a method of

retaining control of the organization. Because they were not willing to give up the power they had previously held to these newly hired professionals, the volunteers imposed formalized behavior controls on them. By instituting formalized policies and guidelines, the volunteer executives were able to ensure that the consistency they had established was maintained in the accomplishment of tasks, that standards were kept uniform throughout the organization, and (most important for them) that they maintained the control of the organization.

Based on information in Thibault, Slack, and Hinings (1991).

- In a large sport equipment manufacturing company the authority to make decisions has been delegated to department managers. However, the CEO of the company closely monitors these people; because she can considerably influence their career prospects, the department managers make their decisions based on what they think the CEO wants.

- In a chain of retail sporting goods stores managers have been told they "can run their own show." But policy manuals and frequent memos from the head office detail how inventory must be displayed, how sales people should deal with clients, and what type of sales promotions the store should be using. In addition, a computer information system provides corporate headquarters with up-to-the-minute information in areas such as staff costs, inventory, and sales figures.

- In a national sport organization the coach of the team has the authority to select the players he thinks are the best. However, final ratification of his decisions has to be undertaken by the members of the organization's board of directors, many of whom have never seen the players perform together.

- In a state high school athletic association Judy Smith served four terms as president; she then stepped down as president but still remains a member of the organization. Despite the fact that she is no longer on the board, many directors still consult Judy about the decisions they have to make.

These few hypothetical examples should serve to illustrate the difficulties of determining the extent to which a sport organization is centralized or decentralized. Researchers who have studied this aspect of organizational structure have had similar difficulties in their work and as a result have produced conflicting results; probably the most notable debate in the literature concerns the question of whether or not bureaucracies are centralized (cf. Aldrich, 1975; Blau & Schoenherr, 1971; Child, 1972a; Child, 1975a; Donaldson, 1975; Greenwood & Hinings, 1976; Holdaway et al., 1975; Pugh et al., 1968). Researchers have also defined the concept of centralization in a number of different ways. Pugh et al. (1968, p. 76) suggest that centralization has to do with the locus of authority to make decisions affecting the organization. This point in the hierarchy was ascertained by asking, "Who was the last person whose assent must be obtained before legitimate action is taken—even

TIME OUT *Centralized Functions at Synchro Canada*

In a study of Synchro Canada, Canada's governing body of synchronized swimming, Morrow and Chelladurai (1992) found that three primary organizational functions were centralized at the top of the organization's hierarchy with its board of directors. The three areas over which the board had ultimate control were budgeting, policy development, and personnel selection. The first stage in the preparation of the organization's budget was undertaken at the vice president level. The various vice presidents in the organization forwarded their budget request to the finance committee (a group consisting of the president, the vice president of finance, the treasurer, and the executive director). The finance committee was responsible for preparing an overall budget for revision and review. The final budget was approved by the board of directors, the highest level of the organizational hierarchy, and submitted to the annual general meeting for ratification.

Policy proposals were also ultimately approved or rejected by the board of directors. Although standing committees and professional staff could recommend and offer input into the policy process, the ultimate power for policy lay with the board. In terms of personnel decisions, a personnel committee was responsible for developing policy for employees. However, the hiring and firing of professional staff was the responsibility of an executive committee of the board of directors.

Based on information in Morrow and Chelladurai (1992).

if others have subsequently confirmed the decision?" This approach to centralization has been used in several studies of sport organizations (cf. Kikulis et al., 1989; Slack & Hinings, 1987a, 1987b; Thibault et al., 1991). Van de Ven and Ferry (1980) also use the locus of decision-making authority as a central premise of their definition. They suggest (p. 399) "when most decisions are made hierarchically, an organizational unit is considered to be centralized; a decentralized unit generally implies that the major source of decision making has been delegated by line managers to subordinate personnel." Van de Ven and Ferry further suggest that any consideration of centralization must take account of the substance of the decision. In a study of Canadian voluntary sport organizations Kikulis et al. (1995a) extend this idea and suggest that decisions of less strategic importance are more likely to be decentralized.

Mintzberg (1979) focuses his definition primarily on the issues of who has the power to make decisions and the extent to which this power is concentrated. He notes (p. 181) that "when all power for decision making rests at a single point in the organization—ultimately in the hands of a single individual—we shall call the structure centralized; to the extent that the power is dispersed among many individuals we shall call the structure decentralized." Hage and Aiken (1970, p. 38) propose a similar definition:

> Centralization refers to the way in which power is distributed in any organization. By power we mean the capacity of one actor to move another (or other) actors to action. The smaller the proportion of jobs and occupations that participate in decision making and the fewer the decision-

making areas in which they are involved, the more centralized the organization.

This approach was used by Frisby (1986b) in her study of the organizational structure and effectiveness of national sport governing bodies.

Brooke (1984) has examined the way the terms "centralization" and "decentralization" have been used in a number of empirical studies, and summarizes the differences in the connotations attached to the two concepts, as shown in table 4.2.

Issues of Centralization

The question of determining the extent to which an organization is centralized is complicated by several issues; some have already been alluded to in the examples in the preceding section of this chapter. In this section we explore these issues more fully.

What Role Do Policies and Procedures Play?

While many managers will delegate decisions to the lower levels of a sport organization, the amount of discretion an individual is allowed in making a decision may be severely constrained by the existence of policies and procedures. A sport manager can use them to limit the choices available to lower-level decision makers. Consequently, while the organization gives the appearance of being decentralized, decisions are actually programmed by the policies and procedures, and a high degree of centralization remains (Hall, 1982). For example, if a lifeguard at a swimming pool sees someone in the pool ignoring the established procedures, the person concerned may be asked to leave the pool. While it may appear that

Table 4.2 Characteristics of Centralized and Decentralized Structures

Centralized	Decentralized
Decisions made at the top of the organization	Decisions made at the lower levels of the organization
Limited participation by lower-level staff in decision making	Lower-level staff actively participate in decision making
Lower-level staff have restricted choice of decision-making alternatives	Lower-level staff given choices when making decisions
Top down decision making	Participative decision making
Senior managers control	Senior managers coordinate
Autocratic structure	Democratic structure

Based on information in M.Z. Brooke (1984).

the lifeguard is making the decision to remove this individual, the procedure and steps to follow in this situation have been established by management; consequently, the lifeguard has little choice in this situation.

What About Informal Authority?

As we saw in the preceding section the definitions of centralization used by both Pugh et al. (1968) and Van de Ven and Ferry (1980) focused on the authority to make decisions. While not explicit in their definitions, both are referring to the formal authority vested in managerial positions. But what about our example involving Judy Smith? Although Judy no longer had any formal authority, she was still able to influence the decision-making process of her state athletic association through informal channels. While most definitions of centralization focus only on formal authority, informal influences on the decision-making process should not be discounted.

Do Management Information Systems Help Maintain Control?

In many sport organizations advanced computer technology has become an accepted means by which managers obtain information about their organization's operations. Management information systems (MIS) are used to "collect, organize, and distribute data to managers for use in performing their management functions" (Daft, 1992, p. 288). Like policies and procedures, MIS act as a mechanism to control decision making. Even if decision making is delegated to the lower levels of the sport organization, using MIS allows managers to closely monitor these decisions. If lower-level managerial decisions are not in line with the expectations of senior managers, corrective action can quickly be taken. In these situations, although there is an appearance of decentralization, the sport organization remains centralized.

What Effects Do Professionals Have on Centralization?

The presence of professionally trained staff results in a more decentralized organization (Hage, 1980). The work of a professional is generally too complex to be supervised directly by a manager or to be standardized through the use of rules and procedures (Mintzberg, 1979). Consequently, professionals usually make many of the decisions concerning their work. In fact, Lincoln and Zeitz (1980) note that professionals seek participation in decision making, and as the number of professionals in an organization increases, all employees experience increased influence.

Centralized or Decentralized: Which Way Is Best?

The decision to centralize or decentralize the operations of a sport organization is a difficult one that involves a number of trade-offs. There are advantages and disadvantages to both types of structure; the advantages claimed for one approach are often the limitations attributed to the other.

The most commonly presented argument for a centralized structure is that it is the best means of achieving coordination and control in a sport organization. It is also argued that top managers should control decision making because they typically have the most experience. They may also own the sport organization or have a large amount of their own capital invested in it. From their position at the top of an organization, senior managers get a broader perspective on its operations and thus can make decisions based on the best interest of the entire organization. They can also see the relative balance between organizational activities, putting them in the best position to make decisions to maintain this balance.

A centralized structure is also economically advantageous. It avoids the duplication of effort or resources that can occur in decentralized organizations. Economic benefits are also realized by centralizing certain activities, such as planning, personnel, and finance, which are common to a number of organizational subunits. If responsibility for these activities were dispersed to subunits, it would be difficult for them to justify such costs from their own budgets.

Given all these advantages, why do organizations decentralize? First, it is often physically impossible for one person to understand all the issues to make the decisions necessary in a sport organization. How can the CEO of a chain of retail sporting goods stores with its corporate headquarters in Chicago make day-to-day decisions about store operations in California? Even with sophisticated computer technology, one person simply does not have the time or capacity to absorb all the necessary information to make informed decisions. By decentralizing operations, individuals who best understand the specifics of the situation are given the power to make decisions. Senior managers are then given more freedom to devote their time to broader policy issues that may have longer-term consequences for the sport organization.

Decentralization also allows an organization to respond quickly to changes in local conditions (Mintzberg, 1979). Information does not have to pass through the various hierarchical levels of a sport organization before a decision can be made. Those people closest to the changing situation, because they have more direct access to necessary information, can respond immediately.

A third argument for decentralization is that it can help motivate employees. Involving employees in decisions about their work can help them understand that what they are doing is important to overall organizational goals. This involvement is particularly important in sport organizations staffed by professionals but governed by volunteers. As we noted earlier, professionals expect to be involved in decision making. Only by allowing these people the power to make decisions about their own work can the sport organization expect to retain their services. A decentralized decision-making system can also motivate lower-level employees. By being involved in decisions about their work they come to understand the rationale behind decisions that affect them. Such involvement can also improve communication among the different hierarchical levels and engender a greater feeling of commitment to the organization. Filley, House, and Kerr (1976), in an examination of 38 studies on participative management, noted that such an approach to decision making is almost always related to improved employee satisfaction, productivity, or both. Miller and Monge (1986) report similar findings.

When a sport organization consists of relatively independent subunits, for example franchised retail sporting goods stores, decentralizing decision making to the managers of these units can result in a more effective system of control. The responsibilities of each subunit can be identified, input costs are readily determined, and the consequences of managerial action, as evidenced in performance outcomes, can be easily assessed. The use of profit centers and strategic business units are just two methods of decentralizing authority underpinned by this logic of control.

A final reason for decentralization is that it can act as an aid in management development. Involving lower-level managers in decision making can provide a good training ground for these people, if they wish to progress to the more senior levels of the sport organization.

Carlisle (1974, p. 15) identifies 13 factors of importance when "determining the need for a centralized or decentralized structure." These are listed below and followed by a brief explanation

1. **The basic purpose and goals of the organization.** Some organizations, for example a research-and-development company like Gore-Tex, because they seek to develop innovative new products, find it necessary to operate with a decentralized structure. In contrast, a football team requires the control that comes with centralized decision making.

2. **The knowledge and experience of top level managers.** If senior managers have more knowledge and experience than lower-level employees, the sport organization is likely to be centralized.

3. **The skill, knowledge, and attitudes of subordinates.** If lower-level employees have specialized skills and knowledge (i.e., they are professionally trained), and are seen as being committed to the goals of the sport organization, decision making is likely to be decentralized.

4. **The scale or size of the organizational structure.** As the size of a sport organization increases so does the number and complexity of decisions that have to be made. Consequently, there is a tendency to decentralize.

5. **The geographical dispersion of the structure.** The more geographically dispersed a sport organization, the harder it is to have a centralized structure.

6. **The scientific content or the technology of the tasks being performed.** As organizational tasks become more specialized and sophisticated, decision-making responsibility for these tasks is delegated to the specialists responsible for their execution. Therefore, the organization is decentralized.

7. **The time frame of the decisions to be made.** Decisions that need to be made quickly are usually decentralized.

8. **The significance of the decisions to be made.** Decisions that are of less strategic importance to a sport organization are more likely to be decentralized.

9. **The degree to which subordinates will accept, and are motivated by, the decisions to be made.** Involving subordinates in decision making has been shown to increase their acceptance of that decision. Consequently, when it is beneficial to get subordinates' acceptance of a decision because they will be responsible for its implementation, a decentralized system should be used.

10. **Status of the organization's planning and control systems.** If decision making is highly structured as a result of organizational planning and control systems, sport managers may decentralize because they are able to determine with relative accuracy what the outcome of a particular decision will be.

11. **The status of the organization's information systems.** Decisions are often decentralized if the sport organization has a good management information system, because errors can be quickly spotted and corrective action taken.

12. **The conformity and coordination required in the tasks of the organization.** Organizational tasks requiring precise integration are best accomplished using a centralized system.

13. **External factors.** If a sport organization deals with several external organizations it is best to centralize the point of contact for each organization.

As Carlisle (1974, p. 15) notes, not all factors are "present in all situations, and their significance will vary from situation to situation." He also stresses that it is the "composite interrelationships of the variables" that a manager must consider. All 13 factors will not necessarily always point to the same type of structure; they do, however, provide guidelines for managers in determining the need for a particular type of structure.

Centralization, Formalization, and Complexity

Several studies have examined the relationship of centralization to the other two structural variables. The findings of these studies are summarized here.

Centralization and Formalization

Research examining the relationship between centralization and formalization has produced conflicting results. Hage (1965, p. 297) in his "axiomatic theory" proposed that "the higher the centralization, the higher the formalization." The Aston group (Pugh et al., 1968), however, found no strong relationship between formalization and centralization; Hinings and Lee (1971) supported this conclusion. Child (1972a) replicated the Aston studies using a national sample rather than following the Aston approach of drawing a sample from just a single region of the country. He also focused on autonomous organizations, whereas the Aston studies included subsidiaries and branch units. Child found a strong negative correlation between formalization and centralization; that is, where

---

TIME OUT *Decentralizing Club Corporation of America*

Club Corporation of America is described as the world's largest manager of private clubs. It owns or manages more than 200 facilities, including a number of golf and racquet clubs. In 1988 Club Corp. had 400,000 members, an annual revenue of over $600 million, and a staff of 18,000. Much of the growth that Club Corp. has experienced has been attributed to a 1985 decision to decentralize its club operations. Management at Club Corp. determined that it could not realize the aggressive growth goals it had set for itself, nor continue to provide the necessary attention to employees and members, if it maintained its centralized power structure. Control of operations was concentrated at the top of a pyramid-shaped organization. President Bob Johnson felt that with this type of structure they were unable to keep in touch with what was going on at the club level. He felt the company could better serve its members by delegating responsibility for decision making down the organization and having those managers who dealt with customers on a daily basis involved in the management process. Consequently, as part of an overall restructuring, the company was divided into several smaller companies. The club operations were then divided into six regions, each staffed with experts in the areas of management, finance, food and beverage services, human resources, and recreation. Because these regional officers and managers were closer to their customers, they were better able to meet the demands of each club.

Based on information in Tobin (1989) and Symonds (1989).

formalization is high the organization will be decentralized. Donaldson (1975) reran the Aston data removing the nonautonomous organizations and concluded it made no difference to the original Aston correlations. Child (1975a) responded that it may be beneficial to look at the difference between the governmental and nongovernmental organizations in the Aston study. Aldrich (1975) then removed the government organizations from the Aston sample and also found that it made little difference to the original correlations. Holdaway et al., (1975) complicated the issue even more with their study of educational organizations, finding a positive relationship between centralization and formalization. In response to these differing results, Greenwood and Hinings (1976) looked at the Aston measures of centralization once again, and suggested that rather than treating centralization as a single scale, it should have been viewed as three subscales. In the most recent attempt to solve this problem, Grinyer and Yasai-Ardekani (1980) used a different set of organizations from the Aston study and found support for the relationship between formalization and decentralized decision making.

Within the sport management literature there has been no attempt to examine the relationship between formalization and centralization. Intuitively it would seem logical to suggest that in sport organizations such as an equipment manufacturing plant, where work is relatively narrowly defined and mainly filled by unskilled workers, we would find high levels of formalization and also centralized decision making. In sport organizations where there are a large number of professionals, such as a faculty of kinesiology, there would be decentralized decision making and little formalization, at least in those areas directly related to the professionals' work. However, as the Time Out "The Impact of Hiring Professional Staff on the Levels of Formalization in Voluntary Sport Organizations" (detailing the work of Thibault et al. 1991) shows, there are exceptions to this general trend. Given the diversity of organizations in the sport industry and the lack of research on this relationship in these organizations, it is hard to draw conclusions beyond general trends. As with many other aspects of organizational structure, there is considerable scope for work of this nature on sport organizations.

Centralization and Complexity

As with centralization and formalization, there have been no studies within the sport management literature explicitly examining the relationship between complexity and centralization. The literature from the broader field of management indicates a strong relationship between high complexity and decentralization of decision making (cf. Hage & Aiken, 1967b; Pugh et al., 1968). We could assume a similar relationship in sport organizations; that is, as the complexity of a sport organization increases either through the addition of professionals or the dividing up of work into more narrowly defined tasks, decision making ought to become decentralized. Once again, however, research on this relationship in a variety of sport organizations could move us beyond these intuitive suggestions.

KEY ISSUES FOR MANAGERS

In order to run your organization efficiently and effectively, you must have a good understanding of two aspects of your organization's structure:

- **Characteristics.** Examine its goals (purpose, mission), size, life-cycle stage (starting, growing, mature, or declining), number and type of organizational members, for-profit versus nonprofit, local versus national versus international scope.
- **Environment.** Examine the type of marketplace it's in and the characteristics of competitors. Changes in the environment such as changes in technology, politics, economies, or social structures can have a large impact on sport organizations (Theodoraki & Henry, 1994).

Once you determine these elements, you can begin to set up appropriate levels of complexity, formalization, and centralization. What is even more important is the interrelationship between the structural dimensions themselves and the organization's and the environment's characteristics.

SUMMARY AND CONCLUSIONS

In this chapter we looked at the three most common dimensions of organizational structure: complexity, formalization, and centralization.

Complexity describes the way in which an organization is differentiated. Three types of differentiation are found in a sport organization: horizontal, vertical, and spatial (geographic). Sport organizations are horizontally differentiated when work is broken down into narrow tasks, when professionals or craft workers are employed, and when the organization is departmentalized. Vertical differentiation refers to the number of levels in the organizational hierarchy. A sport organization is spatially differentiated when tasks are separated geographically. Spatial differentiation occurs vertically when different levels of the organization are dispersed geographically, and horizontally when the functions of the organization take place in different locations. The greater the horizontal, vertical, and spatial differentiation, the more complex the sport organization.

One of the ways used to manage complexity is formalization, the second dimension of organizational structure that we examined. Formalization refers to the existence of mechanisms, such as rules and procedures, that govern the operation of a sport organization. Formalization, whose purpose is to regulate employee behavior, takes place in two ways: through the existence of written documentation such as job descriptions, and through professional training. The former approach is most common when work is narrowly defined, the latter when jobs are broader and require greater discretion.

Centralization, the last dimension of structure and the most problematic of the three, is concerned with who makes decisions in a sport organization. When decisions are made at the top of an organization it is considered centralized; when decisions are made at the lower levels it is decentralized. However, several factors can complicate this general trend: the decisions to be made, the existence of policies and procedures, the use of a management information system, and the presence of professionals.

The structural elements of a sport organization provide a means of describing and comparing these types of organizations. They show how the work of the sport organization is broken down and the means used to integrate the different tasks. To manage a sport organization effectively and efficiently, it is essential that sport managers understand the various elements of structure and their interrelationships.

KEY CONCEPTS

bureaupathic behavior (p. 73)

centralization (p. 74)

complexity (p. 60)

decentralization (p. 74)

departmentalization (p. 62)

division of labor (p. 60)

flat structure (p. 65)

formalization (p. 67)

functional specialization (p. 61)

goal displacement (p. 72)

hierarchy of authority (p. 64)

horizontal differentiation (p. 60)

minimal adherence to rules (p. 73)

social specialization (p. 61)

span of control (p. 65)

spatial differentiation (p. 65)

standardization (p. 71)

tall structure (p. 65)

task differentiation (p. 61)

vertical differentiation (p. 64)

REVIEW QUESTIONS

1. How do levels of complexity vary within and among sport organizations?

2. Why has functional specialization been criticized as dehumanizing, and what steps can be taken to counter its dehumanizing qualities?

3. How does the span of control affect an organization?

4. Do employees prefer working in an organization with a tall or a flat structure?

5. Why does increasing complexity create a paradox for managers?

6. Select a sport organization with which you are familiar. How has it formalized its operations?

7. How does your training in sport management relate to formalization? Discuss.

8. What are the advantages and disadvantages of formalization for employees?

9. If you were studying a group of sport organizations, how would you measure formalization?

10. As the manager of several professionals, what areas of their work do you think it would be feasible to formalize?

11. What is it about centralization that makes it a difficult concept to study?

12. Select a sport organization with which you are familiar. How are decisions made in this organization? What influences the way they are made?

13. As the manager of a small racquet club, which decisions would you centralize and which would you decentralize?

14. What are the trade-offs involved in the decision to centralize or decentralize the operations of an organization?

15. How would you expect the relationship between centralization and formalization to vary among different types of sport organizations?

SUGGESTIONS FOR FURTHER READING

Much of the key work on organizational structure was carried out in the 1960s and early 1970s. Of particular importance are the works of Hage and Aiken (see especially Hage, 1965; Hage & Aiken, 1967b, 1970), the Aston group (Hinings & Lee, 1971; Pugh et al., 1968) and Child (1972a). Other related and important early works that shaped much of the future work on organizational structure are Lawrence and Lorsch's (1967) *Organization and Environment* and Thompson's (1967) *Organizations in Action*.

Given the nexus between writings on bureaucracy and organizational structure, it is useful for students to read Weber's writing on bureaucracy (Gerth & Mills, 1946, chapter 8). Also important is Richard Hall's work in this area (Hall, 1963, 1968; Hall & Tittle, 1966).

More recent works that deal with organizational structure are Henry Mintzberg's (1979) *The Structuring of Organizations*, particularly part II, and Richard Hall's (1982) *Organizations: Structure and Process*, chapters 3, 4, 5, and 6. Both provide a comprehensive treatment of the issues along with extensive referencing. Mintzberg's approach is managerial; Hall's is more sociologically informed.

Both Slack and Hinings (1987b) and Frisby (1985) have developed frameworks specific to sport, based on the Aston approach to organizational structure. Frisby (1986b) uses her framework to examine the relationship of structure to organizational effectiveness in Canadian national sport organizations.

Other sport management studies focusing on structure include Amis and Slack's (1996) look at the size structure relationship within voluntary sport organizations and Stotlar's (2000) study of the sport and entertainment industry's successful implementation of vertical integration.

CASE FOR ANALYSIS

Restructuring the United States Olympic Committee

In 1978, the United States government passed a law that became the United States Olympic Committee's (USOC) charter. Essentially, the USOC had control over all Olympic sports in the United States and it would hold all the rights to Olympic Games aspect (e.g., logo, name) in the country. It was governed by a 123-member board and a 20-member executive committee. On average, between 1999 and 2003, the USOC was spending 24 percent of its $127 million budget on overhead; other nonprofit organizations, like the American Red Cross, were spending only 10 percent.

In 2000, CEO Sandy Baldwin quit after she admitted falsifying her resume. This started a series of organizational problems for the USOC.

The structure of the United States Olympic Committee was recently reorganized; serving as chairman of the USOC is Peter Ueberroth. Ueberroth was head of the 1984 Los Angeles Summer Olympics.

Associated Press, AP

For example, a USOC scandal broke regarding bribes provided to IOC members by the Salt Lake City bid committee to help secure the city as the host of the 2002 Winter Olympic Games.

Baldwin's successor, Lloyd Ward, was soon plagued with a series of allegations concerning the awarding of contracts to his brother's company. The multiple calls for his resignation contending ethical and management transgressions finally resulted in an investigation. But the ethics committee was unable to discipline Ward, their boss. Multiple conflicts of interest had been found and the head of the panel investigating the matter was then accused of telling the ethics officer, Patrick Rodgers, to cover things up. This resulted in the resignation of the ethics officer, USOC president Marty Mankamyer, and three other ethics committee members, John Kuelbs, Edward Petry, and Stephen Potts. Ward finally quit on March 1, 2003.

Olympics sponsors, such as John Hancock—a financial services company with a $55 million IOC sponsorship deal, $10 million of which went to the USOC—called for audits and a USOC restructuring.

In the meantime, interim CEO Jim Scherr began serving as the fifth CEO since 2000, and the new president, Bill Martin, from the University of Michigan, was named the third president in a year.

The CEO of John Hancock and others outside of the USOC, including athletes, appeared in front of a U.S. Senate committee task force established to resolve the USOC's problems. The USOC also created a task force of its own. On October 18, 2003, the USOC approved a restructuring plan with the following changes. The 123-member board was reduced to 11 and the executive committee was eliminated. (Essentially, the members voted themselves out of power.) The restructuring program eventually passed a vote. It called for the new board to be composed of four independent members, three American International Olympic Committee members, and four members nominated by athletes and sport organizations. Most committees were eliminated, and more stringent ethics regulations were implemented.

Peter Ueberroth, former major league baseball commissioner and head of the 1984 Los Angeles Summer Olympics, became the new USOC board chairman on June 14, 2004. It is hoped his expertise and success with the 1984 Olympics will invigorate the USOC and move it forward to better things.

For its part, the Senate recently passed a bill similar to the USOC's reorganization but with two differences: The majority of the board must have no ties to the USOC, and the board is not to follow the International Olympic Committee's voting guidelines. The House has yet to approve this proposal. However, a house committee has approved a bill based on the USOC's internal task force recommendations.

Unfortunately, at this time, the USOC faces accusations of covering up and being lax with drug testing of U.S. track and field athletes.

Based on information in Borzilleri (2003), Carter (2003), CNN.com. (2003), Marshall (2003), Michaelis (2003), Rednova.com (2004), Singer (2004), Stupak (2004).

Questions

1. What made the USOC finally examine its structure?

2. What impact would cutting the board size and eliminating the executive committee have on the structure of the organization and its processes?

3. What problems do you think the half-USOC half-independent members' board will encounter? In what way should they be resolved?

4. What would you suggest to the USOC in its restructuring process if you were a consultant in this case?

Chapter 5

Design Options in Sport Organizations

LEARNING OBJECTIVES

When you have read this chapter you should be able to

1. understand the difference between a typology and a taxonomy,
2. explain the five parts of an organization,
3. describe each of the five basic design types,
4. explain the advantages and disadvantages of each design type, and
5. know under what conditions each design type would be found.

ORGANIZING COMMITTEES WITH A DIFFERENCE

The 1999 Pan American Games were held in Winnipeg, Manitoba. The games brought together 5,000 athletes from 42 countries to participate in 41 different sport events. They were organized by the Pan American Games Society (PAGS). This organizing committee was led by a volunteer board of directors, and its chairman envisioned the games as fully community led and prepared by volunteers. The objectives of the committee were to create excitement and pride in the community, foster international trade opportunities for the city and province, and create a first-rate event to be remembered by the participants, all of this in a fiscally responsible manner. Volunteer committees were established to deal with, notably, games operations, volunteers, sponsorship, marketing, communication, finances, and sport. A small staff was hired to help support the volunteers. Decision making was to be pushed down the hierarchy so that by the start of the games, venue teams composed of volunteer representatives from the various divisions would be fully in charge of running them. Two years out from the games, the volunteers realized that this project was much larger and more complex than they expected. A major restructuring occurred and more staff was hired. Staff took over the day-to-day operations and largely dealt with internal issues (as opposed to the volunteers, who handled mainly external issues). However, the venue-team concept remained. The games were run by a completely volunteer force of over 20,000 individuals. By the end of the games, the objectives were reached, with no major economic impact.

(continued)

(continued)

Team Canada at the opening ceremony of the IV Games of La Francophonie.

Photograph of the IV Games of La Francophonie, Department of Canadian Heritage, 2001. Reproduced with the permission of the Minister of Public Works and Government Services, 2001. Photographers: Dan Galbraith & Donavon Gaudette.

In contrast, the 2001 Jeux de la Francophonie (Games of La Francophonie) were held in Ottawa-Gatineau, Ontario-Québec, and brought together 3,000 athletes and artists from 51 countries to participate in eight sport and eight cultural events. The games were organized by the Comité Organisateur des Jeux de la Francophonie (Games of La Francophonie Organizing Committee, 2001) or COJF. This organizing committee was led by a volunteer board of directors, who hired an event management and sponsorship company to run the games. The company's owner became the executive director of the games, a paid position. He wanted the games to be "large and beautiful." Hired staff was divided into divisions to organize sponsorship, finances, corporate services, games operations, cultural competitions, sport competitions, logistics, communication, media relations, and promotions. Volunteers were recruited to assist the staff in running the games. A form of the venue-team management system was used but was run by staff, supported by more than 4,000 volunteers. By the end of the games, consensus was that they were a success. The events were large (the nation's capital region had never hosted an international competition of this magnitude before), the region beautifully decorated, and participants and visitors enjoyed themselves. Best of all, the games were reported to have made a profit of Can$2 million.

Based on information in PAGS (1999).

Despite the fact that both organizing committees had the same purpose—to host a major sport event—they were structured differently. In fact, no two organizations within the sport industry are exactly alike, even though they may operate within the same market. The Chicago Bulls management structure is different from that of the New York Knicks. Likewise, the athletic department at the University of Massachusetts runs differently than the one at the University of Tennessee.

Although no two sport organizations are exactly alike, they do have commonly occurring attributes that allow us to classify and compare them. Take, for example, Holland Cycle and the Double G Card shop; one makes bikes, the other buys and trades sport cards. But if we look closely at their structures we find they have at least two common features: Each is low in complexity and formalization. By identifying commonly occurring features of sport organizations we can classify them into what are termed design types or configurations. In many ways classification is one of the central tasks of organizational theorists (cf. McKelvey, 1982; Miller & Friesen, 1984; Mintzberg, 1979). Once commonalties are identified and sport organizations are classified, it is possible to use the resultant design types for the generation of hypotheses, models, and theories. As Mills and Margulies (1980, p. 255) point out, "Typologies play an important role in theory development because valid typologies provide a general set of principles for scientifically classifying things or events. What one attempts to do in such endeavors is to generate an analytical tool or instrument, not only as a way of reducing data, but more significantly to stimulate thinking." This point is further underscored by McKelvey (1975, p. 523):

> Organization science, and especially the application of its findings to the problems of organizations and managers, is not likely to emerge with viable laws and principles until substantial progress is made toward an acceptable taxonomy and classification of organizations. The basic inductive-deductive process of science does not work without the phenomena under investigation being divided into sufficiently homogeneous classes. Managers cannot use the fruits of science unless they first discover which of all the scientific findings apply to their situation.

In this chapter we look first of all at the methods used to classify organizations and produce design types. We then discuss the typology of organizational designs developed by Mintzberg (1979). We look in depth at each of Mintzberg's designs and show how examples of each can be found within the sport industry. We also explain the advantages and disadvantages of each design, and describe the conditions under which it is most likely to be found.

Typologies and Taxonomies

Two main approaches can be used to uncover design types (configurations). The first of these is the creation of typologies; the second is the development of taxonomies.

> Typologies are, in a sense, of an *a priori* nature; they are generated mentally, *not* by any replicable empirical analysis. Taxonomies are derived from multivariate analyses of empirical data on organizations. Typically organizations or aspects of their structure, strategies, environments, and processes are described along a number of variables. Attempts are then made to identify natural clusters in the data, and these clusters, rather than any *a priori* conceptions serve as the basis for the configurations (Miller & Friesen, 1984, pp. 31-32) (emphasis in original).

In the next few pages we look briefly at the main typologies and taxonomies found in the management literature, and those schema that have been developed for classifying sport organizations.

Typologies

The first attempt to classify organizations into types can be found in Weber's (1947) writings on social domination and the attendant patrimonial, feudal, and bureaucratic forms of organization. Weber demonstrated how each type of organization "could be characterized by a number of mutually complementary or at least simultaneously occurring attributes" (Miller & Friesen, 1984, p. 32). In the 1950s, Parsons (1956) followed Weber and created a **typology** based on the goals or functions of the organization. He identified organizations that had economic goals, political goals, integrative functions, or pattern maintenance functions. As Carper and Snizek (1980, p. 66) note "Parsons' approach represents an early and limited form of systems theory thinking in that it attempts to tie the organization to the environment through the activities that the former performs for the latter."

Burns and Stalker (1961) suggested two types of organizational design, organic and mechanistic. The *organic* type of organization was found in changing conditions where new and unfamiliar problems had to be dealt with; it contained no rigid control systems, and employees showed high levels of commitment to the organization. In contrast, *mechanistic* organizations were found in stable conditions; tasks were narrowly defined, and there was a clear hierarchy of control, insistence on loyalty to the organization, and obedience to superiors. This form of organization is very much like Weber's legal-rational bureaucracy. Organic and mechanistic types of design were viewed as polar opposites, with organizations described according to their position on a continuum between them. Shortly after Burns and Stalker, Blau and Scott (1962) produced a typology based on the principle of cui bono or "who benefits" from the organization. Four types of structure were identified: mutual benefit organizations, where the prime beneficiary is the membership; business concerns, where the prime beneficiary is the owner(s) of the business; service organizations, where the clients benefit; and commonweal organizations, whose prime beneficiary is the public at large. Chelladurai (1987) has suggested that the prime beneficiary approach could be used in conjunction with the strategic constituents approach to evaluate the effectiveness of sport organizations.

Several typologies have focused on the organization's technology as the criterion variable for classification. Woodward (1958, 1965) distinguished organizations as to whether they used unit or small batch, large batch or mass, or continuous-process types of technology. Perrow (1967, 1970) focused on whether technology was craft, routine, nonroutine, or engineering; Thompson (1967) used core technologies, which he described as either long-linked, mediated, or intensive, as his basis for classification (see chapter 9 for more details on the work of Woodward, Perrow, and Thompson).

Another typology is Gordon and Babchuk's (1959) tripartite classification: instrumental, expressive, instrumental-expressive. Specifically developed to classify voluntary organizations, it has been used to examine voluntary sport organizations. Instrumental organizations are designed "to maintain or create some normative condition or change" (Gordon & Babchuk, 1959, p. 25). Expressive organizations are designed to satisfy the interests of their members. Instrumental-expressive organizations show elements of both functions. In a study of the members of badminton and judo clubs, Jacoby (1965) found

a very high expressive and very low instrumental orientation.

The only attempts to create typologies specifically related to sport organizations are those developed by Chelladurai (1985, 1992). In his 1985 book *Sport Management: Macro Perspectives*, he proposes a 12-cell classification system for sport and physical activity organizations. As shown in figure 5.1 the classification was based on three dimensions: (1) whether the organization was profit-oriented or nonprofit; (2) whether it provided professional or consumer services; and (3) whether it was part of the public, private, or third sector. "Third sector" indicates an organization, for example, some universities, "partly or wholly funded by tax moneys and managed privately" (Chelladurai, 1992, p. 39).

Chelladurai (1985) makes no attempt to categorize sport organizations into the various cells of his model; some of the cells may actually describe few if any sport organizations. For example, it may be difficult to find public-sector sport organizations that explicitly aim to make a profit and offer consumer services. Public-sector organizations are generally not concerned with making a profit per se, and usually provide professional (not consumer) services. Notwithstanding these short-

	Consumer service		Professional service	
	Profit	Nonprofit	Profit	Nonprofit
Private sector				
Public sector				
Third sector				

Figure 5.1 *Framework for classifying sport organizations.*

Reprinted, by permission, from P. Chelladurai, 1985, *Sport management: Macro perspectives* (London, Ontario: Sports Dynamics).

comings, which Chelladurai (1985) acknowledges when he suggests his framework requires extensive research, this classification scheme does provide a useful starting point for further discussion.

In extending his work on classification, Chelladurai (1992) does not focus on sport organizations per se but on the services they provide. Using two dimensions, "the type and extent of employee involvement in the production of services" and "client motives for participation in sport and physical activity," he produces six classes of sport and physical activity services: consumer pleasure, consumer health and fitness, human skills, human excellence, human sustenance, and human curative. Chelladurai (1992) goes on to describe each of these classes and discuss their managerial implications.

We see, then, that we can classify organizations, including sport organizations, in a number of ways. Although fewer typologies have been created in the sport literature than in the general management literature, sport organizations can obviously be typed in many of the more general classification schema. We could, for example, categorize sport organizations on the organic or mechanistic continuum or on the basis of "who benefits."

Carper and Snizek (1980, p. 70) have criticized the large number of typologies produced, suggesting that "there are virtually as many different ways to classify organizations as there are people who want to classify them." They suggest that the diversity of conceptual schemas, which have been developed, indicates a lack of agreement as to which variables should be used in constructing a typology. Most existing typologies have limited explanatory power because they are based on only one or two variables. Miller and Friesen (1984) support the need to focus on a broad array of variables when constructing typologies. They argue (1984, p. 33) that narrowly focused typologies "are not sufficiently encompassing to serve as a basis for reliable prediction or prescription." One typology that uses a large number and wide range of variables is developed by Mintzberg (1979). Based on an extensive survey of the literature, Mintzberg's classification scheme attempts to synthesize many of the research findings of the past two decades to produce five design types (Miller and Friesen, 1984). We examine these design types in detail a little later in this chapter, and show how they apply to sport organizations.

Taxonomies

A **taxonomy** is an empirically constructed classification that identifies "clustering among organiza-

tional variables that is statistically significant and predictively useful and that reduces the variety of organizations to a small number of richly defined types" (Miller & Friesen, 1984, p. 34). McKelvey (1978, 1982) has advocated the development of taxonomies to understand a number of organizational phenomena such as environmental adaptation, structural design, and change. Nevertheless, there have been considerably fewer attempts to construct taxonomies than to construct typologies. The first empirical taxonomy of organizations was developed by Haas, Hall, and Johnson (1966). Using a sample of 75 organizations they produced 10 design types; the number of organizations found in each design type ranged from 2 to 30. Much of their work deals with the methods they used to generate their taxonomy; there is no attempt to elaborate on the nature of the design types they established, or to replicate their approach on a different set of organizations to see if the same type of designs emerge.

Pugh, Hickson, and Hinings, the Aston group, (1969) developed a taxonomy based on structural data obtained from 52 relatively large (over 250 employees) organizations. Their analysis produced seven different types of bureaucratic structure, which led them to conclude (1969, p. 115) that the Weberian notion of a single bureaucratic type "is no longer useful, since bureaucracy takes different forms in different settings."

The most sophisticated use of taxonomy is found in the work of Miller and Friesen (1984). Using a sample of 81 organizations described along 31 variables of strategy, structure, information processing, and environment, they produced 10 common organizational design types, or what they term "archetypes." Identifying six of these types as successful, four as unsuccessful, Miller and Friesen argue that the notion of taxonomy can be extended to study organizational transitions between these archetypes. Based on 24 variables that described changes in such areas as strategy-making, structure, and environment for each transition, nine "transition archetypes" were produced. Thus they argue that the taxonomic approach can identify common paths in organizational evolution.

Within the sport literature there have been only two instances of using a taxonomic approach to identify organizational design types. Both of these emanate from the work of Slack and Hinings and their students. Using data on the structural arrangements of 36 Canadian national-level sport organizations Hinings and Slack (1987) developed 11 scales that addressed three aspects of organizational structure: specialization, standardization, and centralization of decision making. After a factor analysis, two factors were produced: one concerned with the extent of professional structuring in these organizations, and the other with volunteer structuring. By dividing the scores of the 36 organizations at the mean on each factor, Hinings and Slack produced nine organizational design types, and were able to demonstrate the extent to which these national sport organizations exhibited characteristics of professional bureaucratic structuring. Sport Canada, the federal government agency that provided a large portion of the national sport organizations' funding, has been pushing them toward such a design.

In a somewhat similar study Kikulis et al. (1989) created a taxonomy using data from 59 provincial-level sport organizations. Using Ward's method of hierarchical agglomerative clustering, Kikulis et al. produced eight structural design types, ranging from sport organizations that were "implicitly structured" to those that, within this institutional sphere, showed high levels of professional bureaucratic structuring. Kikulis et al. argue the merits of their study in demonstrating the variation in structural design in these sport organizations and as a basis for understanding a

range of organizational phenomena. They note (1989, p. 148) that, once structural designs are identified, it is possible "to conduct in-depth studies of representative organizations and develop qualitative data bases to provide us with richer insights into the internal dynamics, formative processes, and performance implications of each structural design."

Mintzberg's Configurations

One of the most sophisticated and frequently used of all organizational typologies is the one developed by Henry Mintzberg (1979). Mintzberg uses "design parameters"—specialization, formalization of positions, training of members, and the nature of decentralization—along with contingency factors—age, size, and environment—to produce five design types, or what he terms configurations. They are: simple structure, machine bureaucracy, professional bureaucracy, divisionalized form, and adhocracy. Essentially, Mintzberg argues that there are five parts of an organization and five methods by which coordina-

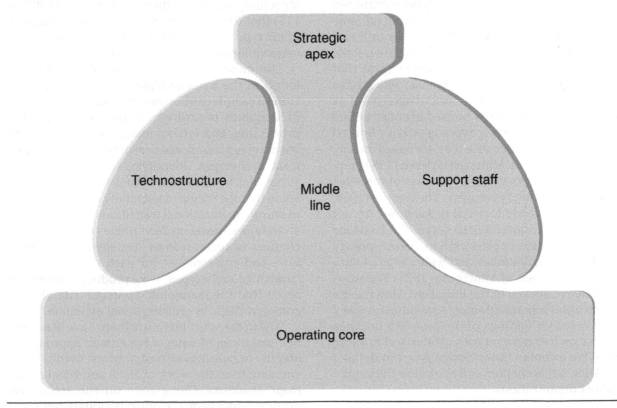

Figure 5.2 *Five basic parts of organizations.*

MINTZBERG, HENRY, STRUCTURING OF ORGANIZATIONS, 1ˢᵗ Edition, © 1979. Adapted by permission of Pearson Education, Inc., Upper Saddle River, NJ.

tion is achieved. The five parts of the organization are shown graphically in figure 5.2, and explained here.

Parts of the Organization

- **Operating core:** This is where we find those employees responsible for the basic work necessary for producing the organization's products or services. At Huffy this is where we find the people who are involved in assembling the bikes. In a sport medicine clinic, the doctors and physiotherapists who treat the patients constitute the operating core.

- **Strategic apex:** This is where we find the senior managers of the sport organization.

- **Middle line:** These are the managers who join the operating core to the strategic apex. In a government agency concerned with sport, for example, these people would be the middle managers who provide the link between staff and the senior bureaucrats.

- **Technostructure:** This is where we find the analysts responsible for designing the systems that standardize work processes and outputs in a sport organization. In an organization that produces sport equipment, the technostructure would be made up of people such as the industrial engineers, who standardize the work process, and the planners and accountants, who standardize the organization's output.

- **The support staff:** These are the people who provide support to the sport organization. For example, in a competitive gymnastics club, the support staff includes everyone from the athletic therapists and sport psychologists to the staff who take care of the equipment.

Methods of Coordination

Mintzberg (1979) describes the five ways in which coordination can be achieved in an organization—direct supervision, standardization of work processes, standardization of outputs, standardization of skills, and mutual adjustment. Each is explained here as they may apply to a sport organization.

- **Direct supervision:** Here one individual in the sport organization gives orders to the others, to coordinate their work.

- **Standardization of work processes:** This method is used when the way in which work is to be carried out is determined by someone else.

For example, the way ski jackets are produced in a company like Columbia is determined by the people who control the computerized design and pattern-making systems, not by the people who actually produce the jackets.

- **Standardization of outputs:** This method is used when the results of the work, that is the type of product or performance to be achieved, are specified. For example, output is standardized when the corporate headquarters of a sporting goods company specifies to its divisions that it wants them to increase sales by 10 percent in the upcoming year, but leaves the method of achieving this increase up to the divisional managers.

- **Standardization of skills:** Skills are standardized through programs designed to ensure the coordination and control of the work processes. Sport medicine clinics employ doctors just for this purpose. When an injured athlete enters the clinic, the doctor has been trained to deal with the situation and assess the injury and the treatment required.

- **Mutual adjustment:** Here the coordination of work is achieved through informal communication. A group of sport management professors who plan a training workshop for local entrepreneurs in the sport industry would probably adopt this approach to coordination.

Design Types

In each of the design types (configurations) one part of the organization and one method of coordination dominates. Table 5.1 provides an overview of Mintzberg's (1984) suggested organizational and coordination combination for each design type, as well as the major reason for each combination.

We find examples of each of these design types or configurations in the sport industry. Each has strengths and weaknesses and works best under certain conditions. In the remainder of this chapter we look in detail at each design type, discuss its advantages and disadvantages, and discuss when it is the most appropriate design for sport managers to use.

The Simple Structure

What do sport organizations such as a ski rental shop, the local water polo club, and a small voluntary group such as Luge Canada have in common? They all exhibit the characteristics of a simple structure.

As its name implies, the most evident characteristic of this design type is its simplicity. Typically the **simple structure** has little or no technostructure, few support staff, no real middle line (hence no lengthy managerial hierarchy), and a loose division of labor (Mintzberg, 1979). The organization has low levels of formalization and is unlikely to rely heavily on planning and training devices. As figure 5.3 shows, the most important parts of this organizational design are the strategic apex and the operating core. The structure is a relatively flat one and everyone reports to the strategic apex, which is usually one individual in whom power is concentrated. Coordination is achieved through direct supervision. Decision making is informal, with all important decisions being made by the CEO who, because of proximity to the operating core, is easily able to obtain any necessary information and act accordingly.

Advantages and Disadvantages

The main advantage of the simple structure is its flexibility. Because the person at the strategic apex is in direct contact with the operating core, communication is easily achieved. Information flows directly to the person in charge, so decisions can be made quickly. The goals of the sport organization are easily communicated to employees and they are able to see how their efforts contribute to achieving these goals. Since everyone reports to the strategic apex, lines of accountability are clear and straightforward. Also, decisions are made by the strategic apex with extensive knowl-

Table 5.1   Organizational and Coordination Tendencies in Mintzberg's Design Types

Design type	Part of the organization	Method of coordination	Reason
Simple structure	Strategic apex	Direct supervision	Strategic apex wants tight control
Machine bureaucracy	Technostructure	Standardization (especially work process)	Agrees to decentralize decisions to the technostructure
Professional bureaucracy	Operating core	Standardization of skills	Operating core wants autonomy
Divisionalized form	Middle line	Standardization of outputs	Middle line wants semiautonomy
Adhocracy	Support staff	Mutual adjustment	Support staff wants decentralization to increase group work (collaboration)

Based on information in Mintzberg (1984).

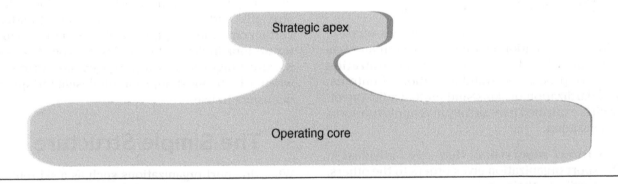

Figure 5.3 *The simple structure.*

edge of what is going on below (Mintzberg, 1979). Many people enjoy working in a simple structure because they are unencumbered by bureaucratic controls; a sense of mission often pervades this type of sport organization.

The main disadvantage of the simple structure is that it is useful only for smaller sport organizations. As a sport organization grows and its environment becomes more complex, the simple structure design type is no longer appropriate. The complexities of a large sport organization cannot be handled by a simple structure. There is also the possibility that the person who has the power to make changes, the CEO, may resist growth because it will mean increased formalization and possibly a reduction of this individual's power. The centralization of power at the top of the simple structure is in fact a double-edged sword. While it facilitates decision making, it can lead to the CEO's unwillingness to give up responsibility to others and resentment on the part of employees that one person "calls all the shots." Strategic issues may be pushed to the side if the CEO gets too involved with operational issues (Mintzberg, 1979). Finally, a simple structure is a risky design type in that, as Mintzberg (1979, p. 312) puts it, "one heart attack can literally wipe out the organization's prime coordinating mechanism."

TIME OUT   *The Running Room: From Simple Structure to International Success*

John Stanton started running in 1981 in an effort to get in shape. As he improved, he needed better running shoes. However, he would find that the staff who typically worked on commission in sporting goods stores, not only knew little about running shoes but also tried to sell the most expensive pair instead of the best pair. There was also a lack of quality shoes, even in large sporting goods stores, so Stanton decided to solve this problem.

In 1984, Stanton opened a one-room store in a renovated living room of an old house in Edmonton, Alberta. He called it The Running Room. Employees were called team members, and Stanton wanted the store to be run by runners for runners. The store became known for product innovation, quality service, quality products, and sport knowledge. Staff and customers are invited to give feedback about

Photo courtesy of Running Room.

John Stanton founded the Running Room in a one-room store; the business now has over 70 store locations. As a small sport organization experiences growth, the simple structure design type may no longer be appropriate.

the products, providing a "proven track record" for products sold. The Running Room created its own label to provide customers with products that were stylish and functional, composed of innovative fabric, and affordable.

By 2005, The Running Room had more than 75 locations in Canada and in the United States. The store offers clinics on walking, running, marathons, and personal training, and at least 400,000 individuals have graduated from these clinics to date. A Running Room Running Club—no membership fees required— allows club members to work out in a social context and have access to coaching to improve their techniques and training methods.

The concept has been so successful that Stanton has decided to open a similar store, The Walking Room, dedicated to gear for walkers.

Based on information in Running Room Ltd. (2003).

Where Do We Find the Simple Structure?

The most common place to find a simple structure is in a small sport organization, a sport organization in its formative years, or one that is entrepreneurial in nature. Simple structures are also used when a sport organization's environment is simple and dynamic, when larger sport organizations face a hostile environment, and when CEOs have a high need for power or power is thrust upon them.

In a small sport organization coordination is achieved through direct supervision. It is relatively easy for one person to oversee the organization's operations and to communicate informally with employees. Many different types of smaller organizations within the sport industry have adopted the simple structure for these reasons. Figure 5.4 shows the structure of Mike's Bike and Sport Store, a small retail sporting goods store that operates with a simple structure.

A sport organization's stage of development, as well as its size, can influence its design. Most organizations exhibit characteristics of a simple structure in their formative years, but some may maintain this design type beyond this stage of their development (Mintzberg, 1979). The Time Out earlier in this chapter illustrates how, in its early days, The Running Room operated with a simple structure.

Entrepreneurial organizations within the sport industry often adopt the simple structure design because it allows them to be aggressive and innovative within simple and dynamic environments. This mirrors the entrepreneur's tendency to have an autocratic and charismatic leadership style (Mintzberg, 1979). Successful entrepreneurial companies often do not maintain the simple structure type of design for any length of time; as they grow, the design is replaced with a different set of structural arrangements. Gould (1989) describes how successful entrepreneurial sport organizations such as the Fitness Group of Vancouver, Sun Ice, and Bloor Cycle all operated with a simple structure in their early years.

Even for other types of companies a simple and dynamic environment is best served by a simple structure. The simple environment is easily scanned by the person at the strategic apex, and the organic operating core found in a simple structure means a quick reaction to changes in the environment.

A crisis situation may force larger sport organizations to adopt the characteristics of a simple structure. When a sport organization's environment is hostile, the CEO may tend to centralize power and reduce bureaucratic controls to respond to the crisis. For example, in 1984 when Nike was experiencing financial problems and a serious challenge from Reebok, Philip Knight took back the presidency of Nike, which he had turned over to Bob Woodell about a year earlier.

Finally, the need for power may also precipitate the adoption of a simple structure. Given the concentration of power at the strategic apex and the lack of formalization or any type of technostruc-

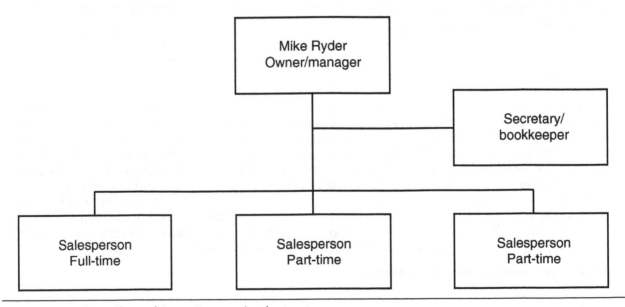

Figure 5.4 *Mike's Bike and Sport Store: a simple structure.*

ture, this type of design is ideal for those CEOs who seek to maintain power. Alternatively, this design may be found when CEOs do not necessarily seek power but members bestow it on them. Mintzberg (1979) refers respectively to these variants of the simple structure as autocratic and charismatic organizations.

The Machine Bureaucracy

When a sport organization produces a standard output such as a hockey stick, when there is a requirement for fairness and public accountability such as we find in a government agency, and when consistency is required in performing relatively simple tasks such as on a football team, the most appropriate structure to use is a machine bureaucracy. Like Weber's legal-rational bureaucracy, the **machine bureaucracy** is characterized by high levels of standardization, formalized communication procedures, the functional grouping of tasks, routine operating procedures, a clear delineation between line and staff relationships, and a centralized hierarchy of authority. Figure 5.5 shows

Mintzberg's depiction of a machine bureaucracy. In this type of design the technostructure is the key part of the organization, and contains the analysts, such as the quality control engineers, planners, and designers who standardize the work to be performed. Although their role is primarily advisory, they exercise considerable informal power because they structure everyone else's work (Mintzberg, 1979).

Advantages and Disadvantages

The main advantage of the machine bureaucracy is its efficiency, because it allows "simple, repetitive tasks [to] be performed precisely and consistently by human beings" (Mintzberg, 1979, p. 333). The grouping of specialist tasks in a machine bureaucracy results in certain economies of scale and less duplication of activities. In some cases, particularly those sport organizations involved in mass production, the high levels of standardization found in a machine bureaucracy mean less-qualified, and hence cheaper, employees can be used. In government agencies that use what Mintzberg (1979) calls a public machine bureau-

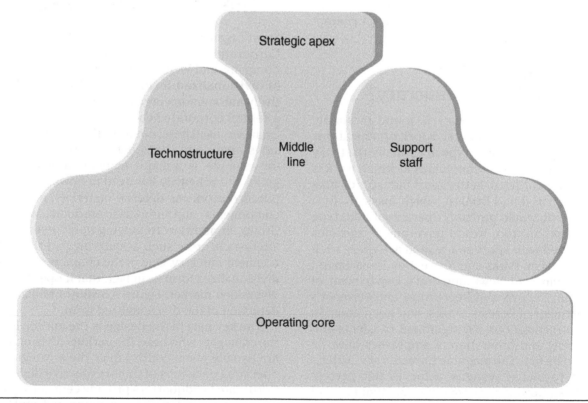

Figure 5.5 *The machine bureaucracy.*

cracy design, the use of low-cost labor is less pronounced. Because the lines of authority are clearly outlined in a machine bureaucracy, workers know their responsibilities. And, centralized control means that outside of the strategic apex, and to a certain extent the technostructure where the work is standardized, there is little need for creative thinking.

The three disadvantages of a machine bureaucracy identified by Mintzberg (1979) are human problems, coordinating problems, and adaptation problems at the strategic apex. Many of the human problems emanate from the narrow specialization of work found in this design type; often dehumanizing for employees, it stifles creative talents and produces feelings of alienation. Hence coordination is made difficult. Such divisions can also promote "empire building" within the functional areas, which in turn creates conflicts that impede communication and coordination.

Finally, while the machine bureaucracy works well in stable environments it does not respond well to change. As Mintzberg (1979) points out, change generates nonroutine problems. When these become frequent, there can be work overload at the strategic apex, because these problems are passed up the hierarchy. Quick responses are difficult since managers are not in direct contact with the problem areas.

Where Do We Find the Machine Bureaucracy?

The machine bureaucracy is found in simple and stable environments. Sport organizations that adopt this design type are usually relatively large, with routine technologies in which work is easily standardized. In the sport industry companies like Head and Dunlop, which mass-produce equipment, would probably operate with this type of design. So, too, would government agencies concerned with sport and related activities, such as the Oregon Parks and Recreation Department; the Province of Newfoundland's Department of Tourism, Culture, and Recreation; and Vermont's Department of Forests, Parks, and Recreation. In these organizations the treatment of clients and the hiring and promotion of employees must be seen to be fair. The machine bureaucracy, with its highly regulated systems, achieves this perception best. Guttmann (1978) suggests that many of the major governing bodies of sport such as the Marylebone Cricket Club (MCC), the International Association of Athletic Federations (IAAF), and the Federation Internationale de Football Association (FIFA) exhibit a number of the characteristics of a machine bureaucracy.

Even a baseball team or a football team may operate as machine bureaucracies. George Allen, the former general manager of the Washington Redskins, exemplified this type of thinking when he suggested this analogy:

> A football team is a lot like a machine. It's made up of parts. I like to think of it as a Cadillac. A Cadillac's a pretty good car. All the refined parts working together make the team. If one part doesn't work, one player pulling against you and not doing his job, the whole machine fails (Terkel, 1972, p. 508).

The owner of the team represents the strategic apex, the players the operating core, and the general manager the middle line. The support staff is made up of team doctors, athletic therapists, strength coaches, and equipment personnel. The technostructure consists of coaches, assistant coaches, and scouts who standardize the work processes of the players in the operating core.

The Divisionalized Form

Sport organizations such as Time Warner, Disney Corporation, Brunswick Corporation, Coleman Company, and Wembley Group all use some type of **divisionalized form**, essentially a set of relatively autonomous organizations coordinated by a central corporate headquarters. In some of the examples used here, not all of the company's divisions operate in the sport industry. Brunswick, for example, is a major manufacturer of power boats and is heavily involved in bowling centers, but also produces defense materials, aerospace components, and industrial products. Wembley Group, in addition to staging sport events, has interests in areas such as catering and the entertainment industry. One of the characteristics of a divisionalized form is, in fact, that it operates in a diversified market. Figure 5.6 shows Mintzberg's depiction of the divisionalized form.

The key part of the design is the middle line—the managers who head the various divisions and are usually given control over the strategic and operating decisions of their respective divisions. Corporate headquarters provide centralized support in areas such as finance, personnel, and legal matters. They also exercise some degree of control over divisions by monitoring and evaluating outcomes such as profit, market share, and

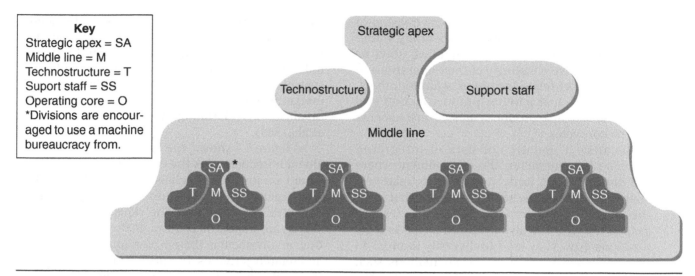

Key
Strategic apex = SA
Middle line = M
Technostructure = T
Suport staff = SS
Operating core = O
*Divisions are encouraged to use a machine bureaucracy from.

Figure 5.6 *The divisionalized form.*

MINTZBERG, HENRY, STRUCTURING OF ORGANIZATIONS, 1st Edition, © 1979. Adapted by permission of Pearson Education, Inc., Upper Saddle River, NJ.

sales growth. Essentially, division managers are allowed to operate as they see fit, provided they conform to corporate guidelines. The divisions that constitute the overall structure may exhibit a variety of designs. But the fact that corporate headquarters retains control by monitoring performance, a procedure that requires clearly defined standards, means that the divisionalized form is better suited to an organization that has machine bureaucracy-structured divisions (Mintzberg, 1979).

Advantages and Disadvantages

One of the main advantages of the divisionalized form is that its divisions are relatively autonomous. Their managers have operational and strategic control for markets falling under their responsibility (Mintzberg, 1979). This means that corporate staff does not concern itself with day-to-day operational issues and thus can pay more attention to long-term strategic planning for the entire organization. Using a divisionalized form means that corporate headquarters can allocate its financial resources more efficiently. If needed, capital can be extracted from one division and allocated to another. This type of structure also has been seen as a good training ground for senior managers. Division managers essentially run a business within a business, so they are able to gain experience in all areas. The divisionalized form is advantageous in that it allows a company to spread its risk (Mintzberg, 1979). Because it operates in diversified markets economic fluc-

tuations are dealt with more easily; if one part of the organization does not perform up to required expectations it can be closed down or sold off with relatively little impact on other operations.

As might be expected, the divisionalized form is not without its faults. Some of its main disadvantages revolve around the relationship among divisions and between divisions and corporate headquarters. Conflict may occur among divisions when they compete in similar product markets or when they vie for corporate resources. Conflict is also created when a division's goals run counter to corporate goals or when the constraints the corporation imposes on a division are seen as overly restrictive.

The existence of several divisions within the overall structure can lead to problems of coordination and control. Control in this type of design is usually achieved through quantitative performance measures, which can in turn lead to an emphasis on economic indicators and a tendency to ignore the social consequences of the division's operations.

Where Do We Find the Divisionalized Form?

The divisionalized form is most frequently found in organizations operating in diversified markets. As Mintzberg (1979, p. 393) points out, this type of structure "enables the organization to manage its strategic portfolio centrally, while giving each component of the portfolio the undivided attention of one unit." For our purposes it is important to note that in most cases not every division of the overall organization will be operating within the sport industry. Some companies, such as Brunswick, have a majority of their operations in sport and sport-related products, while for others, sport may be just another product market in a company that also produces musical instruments and motorcycles.

Because it usually consists of integrated machine bureaucracies, the environment where the divisionalized form works best is relatively simple and stable, the same conditions that favor the machine bureaucracy. Size and age are also associated with the divisionalized form. As organizations grow they tend to diversify in order to protect themselves from market fluctuations; such diversification leads to divisionalization. Likewise, with time, a company's existing product markets may face challenges from new competitors; thus they are forced to look for new markets. Success in these markets leads to an increased number of divisions.

The Professional Bureaucracy

The last three decades have seen the emergence of many new professions (Larson, 1977; Johnson, 1972). Sport, like other areas of social life, has not gone untouched by these developments (cf. Lawson, 1984; Macintosh & Whitson, 1990). Sport psychologists, athletic therapists, coaches, and sport managers have all laid claim to professional status. The rise of professionalism has led to the creation of a new organizational form. The **professional bureaucracy** combines the standardization of the machine bureaucracy with the decentral-

ization that results from a professional's need for autonomy. The professional bureaucracy is found in a number of different areas of the sport industry; faculties of kinesiology often adopt this type of design, as do sport medicine clinics, sport marketing companies, and some voluntary sport organizations (cf. Hinings and Slack, 1987; Kikulis et al., 1989).

As figure 5.7 shows, the key part of the professional bureaucracy is the operating core. This is where we find the specialists, the professionals who operate relatively autonomously in this decentralized structure. The skills of the professionals are standardized through their training and their involvement in their professional association and related activities, but discretion is granted in the application of skills. For example, in a sport marketing company an individual client services manager will be expected to have some standard skills in the different areas of marketing but at the same time will be given relative discretion as to how to go about obtaining accounts. Unlike the machine bureaucracy, where work standards are developed by analysts in the technostructure and enforced by managers, the standards of the professionals emanate from their training and their involvement in their professional association. In addition to the operating core, the only other part of the professional bureaucracy developed to any extent is the support staff who assists the professionals. Because work is too complex to be supervised by a manager or standardized by analysts, there is usually only a small strategic apex and middle line, for example, the senior partner of the sport marketing company and perhaps some managers who have a coordinating function. There is also little need for any type of technostructure.

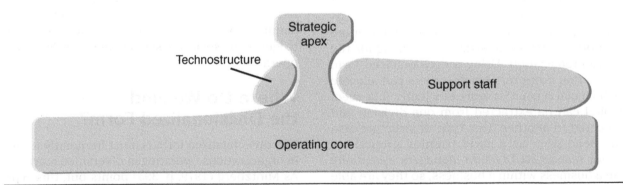

Figure 5.7 *The professional bureaucracy.*

Advantages and Disadvantages

In chapter 4 we saw how some elements of bureaucratic structuring, such as formalization and centralization, conflicted with professional values for autonomy. The advantage of the professional bureaucracy is that it minimizes these conflicts by combining the professional's need for autonomy with standardization. However, standardization is not achieved with detailed rules and procedures, but through training and other forms of professional practice (social specialization). The autonomy the professionals achieve is only acquired after lengthy education and often on-the-job training. So when an orthopedic surgeon working in a sports medicine clinic operates on the knee of an athlete, the athlete knows the chance of a mistake has been minimized—the surgeon was trained for the procedure in medical school, and watched and helped colleagues perform the surgery many times before attempting it.

The autonomy that a professionally trained person experiences from working in a professional bureaucracy is the major advantage of this type of design. It does, however, have disadvantages in that it can create coordination problems. Professionals, such as sport management professors, who work in a department that operates as a professional bureaucracy may have little in common with other departments, for example colleagues in exercise physiology. They have different training, different research agendas, and even a different terminology for their work. While each may prefer to be left alone "to do his own thing," it is necessary for each to get along with colleagues from other areas and coordinate their efforts to produce a well-balanced physical education and sport studies program.

A further disadvantage of this type of design is that, as Mintzberg (1979, p. 373) notes, it is "appropriate for professionals who are competent and conscientious. Unfortunately not all of them are, and the professional bureaucratic structure cannot easily deal with professionals who are either incompetent or unconscientious." This type of structure is also problematic in that allowing professionals a high level of autonomy can work against the development of any type of team approach to the problems and issues confronting the sport organization.

TIME OUT   *A Structural Taxonomy of Amateur Sport Organizations: The Professional Bureaucracy*

In a study of provincial-level sport organizations Kikulis et al. (1989) produced a structural taxonomy of organizational design types. Five of the organizations in the study—figure skating, ice hockey, soccer, swimming, and volleyball—exhibited the characteristics of a professional bureaucracy. These organizations had high levels of professional specialization and an extensive range of programs. Volunteer specialization, in both technical and administrative roles, was not as high as in many other organizations, indicating that program operation and management were in the hands of professionals assisted by volunteers. Coordination of programs and staff was achieved through a large number of meetings. There was, however, a relatively high level of standardization, a structural characteristic not usually found in professional bureaucracies but, for these organizations, a reflection of their strong ties to government.

Decision making was centralized at the volunteer board level. Although in an ideal professional bureaucracy the decision making is decentralized to the professional levels, Kikulis et al. point out that in voluntary sport organizations, the situation is somewhat more complex. In these types of organizations, decisions are actually made by professionals but ratified by the board. Although decisions must go to the board level for approval, the professionals in these organizations are able to structure the flow of information to the board in order to get the response they want. Consequently, while there is an appearance of board control, decision making is controlled by the professional staff, as we would expect in a professional bureaucracy.

Based on information in Kikulis, Slack, Hinings, and Zimmermann (1989).

Where Do We Find the Professional Bureaucracy?

We find professional bureaucracies in environments that are both complex and stable. Environmental complexity means that the skills to be learned require extensive periods of training but the stability of the environment means these skills can be well defined, in essence standardized. Age and size do not play a major role in influencing the choice of a professional bureaucratic design. We find small professional bureaucracies, for example, in a law firm that specializes in contract work for professional athletes, which may operate with three or four lawyers, an office manager, and support staff. We also find the professional bureaucratic design used in relatively new sport organizations. Unlike the machine bureaucracy, which often starts out as a simple structure, the professional bureaucracy requires little startup time.

The technology of the professional bureaucracy is important because it does not excessively regulate, it is not sophisticated, and it is not automated (Mintzberg, 1979). The presence of any of these characteristics in the organization's technology mitigates against the autonomy of professionals who requires discretion to carry out their work.

Adhocracy

Adhocracy is a highly flexible and responsive form of sport organization, what Burns and Stalker refer to as an organic structure. Used when a high level of innovation is required in the work processes, it may be a permanent or temporary design. The adhocracy has low levels of formalization, no structured hierarchy of authority, and high levels of horizontal differentiation, with specialists grouped into functional units for organizational purposes but often deployed to project teams to do their work. There are high levels of decentralization, little if anything in the way of standardized operating procedures, and coordination achieved through mutual adjustment, as teams containing managers, operators, and support staff work together to solve unique problems. In sport we find the adhocracy being used in television companies covering major sporting events, in research-and-development companies such as W.L. Gore & Associates, and in some university research labs.

As figure 5.8 shows, the adhocracy has little or no technostructure because its work cannot be standardized or formalized. The middle-line managers, the operating core, and the support staff are all professionals, so there is no clear demarcation between line and staff. Decisions are made by those who possess the expertise. The managers in the strategic apex spend their time monitoring projects, resolving the conflicts that inevitably arise in this type of free-flowing structure, and (probably most importantly) communicating with the external environment.

It is difficult to produce an organizational chart for an adhocracy because the internal structure of these organizations changes frequently as new

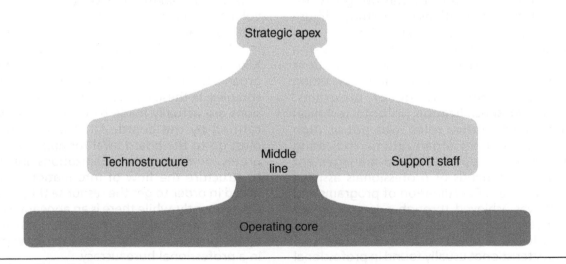

Figure 5.8   *The adhocracy*

problems require new project teams. Unlike the professional bureaucracy, the experts who work in adhocracies cannot rely on standardized skills to achieve coordination, as this would move away from innovation toward standardization (Mintzberg, 1979). Rather, in the adhocracy, groups of professionals combine their efforts to build on their existing knowledge and skills to produce innovative solutions to new and different problems. For example, in order to conduct research on the contribution that sport and other forms of physical activity make to increasing an individual's well-being, a department of health, physical education, and recreation may create a research unit that houses physiologists, psychologists, and sociologists. While these people do not normally work together, they could all combine their knowledge and skills to produce innovative solutions to

TIME OUT   *Televising the Olympic Games*

NBC paid $300 million for the American rights to televise the 1988 Summer Olympic Games from Seoul, South Korea. It's not an assignment that happens regularly at NBC. In fact, the last time the network televised an Olympics was the 1972 Games from Sapporo, Japan.

NBC spent three years planning the two-week extravaganza. What made the project uniquely challenging was its complexity. First, all preparations had to be made in addition to NBC's normal broadcasting operations. None of the planning effort for the Olympics could interfere with the day-to-day broadcasting of NBC's regular programs. If it was necessary to take people off their normal jobs to work on the Olympics, a replacement had to be found. Second, the project was immense. The physical distance of Seoul from NBC's New York headquarters, and language and cultural differences, made the job particularly challenging. A 60,000-square-foot broadcast center had to be erected in Seoul. At least $60 million in state-of-the-art technical equipment had to be shipped to South Korea and set up. More than 1,100 NBC employees—approximately 500 in engineering, 300 in production, and 300 in management and clerical positions—were needed to run the 100 monitor control rooms, 15 edit rooms, 150 tape machines, 100 NBC cameras, 17 mobile units, and to coordinate operations. Third, televising the Olympic Games demands high flexibility because unexpected, world-class performances can occur at almost any time. There were 220 events taking place at 23 different locations throughout Seoul. In many cases a half-dozen or more events were going on simultaneously, and NBC had to be able to switch from one site to another instantly if something noteworthy was occurring. Finally, NBC had a lot at stake in these games. It was competing against ABC's successful record of televising past summer and winter Olympics. Moreover, it had sold some 1,750 minutes of advertising time at an average of $660,000 per minute in prime time. Sponsors were expecting high ratings; if they didn't materialize there was the possibility that NBC would have to return part of the money to the advertisers. If ratings slacked, the estimated $50 to $75 million in profits that NBC was estimating from the Olympics could quickly turn to a loss. Of course, a successful performance in the ratings would have a positive effect, giving the network's fall schedule a strong boost.

How did NBC organize the task of broadcasting the games? They utilized an adhocracy. While NBC is essentially a machine bureaucracy, the structure used to plan and operate the Olympics had few formal rules and regulations. Decision making was decentralized, although carefully coordinated by NBC's executive producer for Olympic operations. The need to bring together more than a thousand technical specialists, who could apply their skills on a temporary project in a dynamic environment requiring the ability to respond rapidly to change, led NBC to use an adhocracy. Using any other design would have lessened the company's effectiveness in achieving its objectives.

Organization Theory: Structures, Designs, and Applications, by Robbins (1990). Reprinted, by permission, of Pearson Education.

this type of problem. A similar type of adhocratic structure may be created by a municipal council developing a plan to build a new multiuse sport facility; experts would be needed from departments concerned with land-use planning, sport programming, environment, transportation, and so on.

Advantages and Disadvantages

The main advantage of the adhocracy is that it can respond rapidly to change. It promotes creativity by bringing diverse groups of professionals together to work on specific projects. Adhocracies may be permanent structures, such as the lattice type of organizational design used at W.L. Gore & Associates (Rhodes, 1982), or they may be set up on a temporary basis. For example, in 2000 the government of Canada created a task force, which is a type of adhocracy, to investigate the structure of the Canadian sport system. The task force filed its report with the Minister of Canadian Heritage in May 2002 and was then disbanded. This type of temporary setup is not as easily achieved with other organizational design types.

The flexibility of the adhocracy is a weakness as well as a strength. High levels of flexibility mean that the adhocracy is the most politicized of the design types we have examined. There are no clear lines of authority and no formalized rules; consequently, employees may be involved in "political games" to achieve their goals, more than in other organizational designs. The political nature of the adhocracy means a potential for high levels of conflict, which can create stress for employees and for those who do not like rapid change and prefer consistency in their jobs. These stresses are compounded by the flexibility of the adhocracy.

Inefficiency is also a weakness of the adhocracy. The flexibility required in this structure means high levels of face-to-face communication, frequent discussions, and meetings, all costly in time and money. Another source of inefficiency is the unbalanced workloads—periods of high activity followed by periods of slower activity—for specialists (Mintzberg, 1979).

Where Do We Find the Adhocracy?

The innovative nature of the work performed in an adhocracy means that it is found in environments that are both dynamic and complex. As Mintzberg (1979, p. 449) notes, "in effect, innovative work,

being unpredictable, is associated with a dynamic environment; and the fact that the innovation must be sophisticated means that it is difficult to comprehend, in other words associated with a complex environment." For these reasons, research units such as those found in a faculty of physical education and sport studies may choose to adopt this organizational design. So, too, may the organizing committee for a temporary event such as a road race or a basketball tournament.

Technology will also influence the decision to structure as an adhocracy. An organization with a sophisticated technical system requires "specialists who have the knowledge, power, and flexible work arrangements to cope with it" (Mintzberg, 1979, p. 458). This requirement creates a decentralized structure and considerable integration of the analysts in the technostructure, the operators, and the support staff, an integration best achieved with an adhocracy.

Other factors influencing the choice of an adhocracy are age or, as Mintzberg notes, more specifically, youth and fashion. Youth is a factor because a number of young organizations seek to be innovative with new products and markets; adhocracy facilitates this quest for innovation. Fashion is a factor because much of the "pop culture management" literature has critiqued notions of hierarchy and centralization in organizations, and has suggested the need for more organic structures and innovations such as project teams and task forces. Again, the adhocracy is designed to meet these kinds of requirements.

Organizational Designs as Ideal Types

It is important to note that the five design types described here are, in fact, **ideal types**. As such, it is quite possible that no sport organization will be exactly like one of these designs. For example, when we look at a set of sport organizations we may find that a number of them may be in transition between designs. In the late 1950s Coleman, a major producer of equipment for outdoor sports, had been operating with a machine bureaucracy design; management, realizing it had grown too big and diverse for this type of structure, started a process of divisionalization. Such changes take time to achieve; anyone studying this organization in its transition period would not find a neatly laid-out design type as described here. Kikulis et al. (1989) show evidence of transitional designs.

TIME OUT   *W.L. Gore & Associates: The Lattice Organization*

W.L. Gore & Associates is a manufacturing and research company worth more than a billion dollars. Gore-Tex fabrics are used to make skiwear, running suits, golf gear, tents, and clothing for hunting and fishing. The company promotes innovation through a unique organizational design, the lattice, a type of adhocracy in which the guiding principle is described as "unmanagement." Within the lattice organization every "associate" (as employees are called) must deal with other associates one-on-one. There are no hierarchies, no job titles, no bosses, and no authoritative commands. When they join the organization, new associates are sponsored by an established associate. New associates pick the area to work in which they think they can make the best contribution. They are then challenged to do their best in this area. Associates are given the freedom to experiment with new ideas and to follow through on those that are potentially profitable. They must, however, consult with associates before taking any action that the company terms as being "below the waterline" and having the potential to cause serious damage to the organization.

Based on information in Simmons (1987).

In their research they found a number of amateur sport organizations that were moving toward a professional bureaucratic structure but, at the time of the study, had not reached this design; they called these organizations nascent professional bureaucracies.

In addition to finding organizations in transitional states, it is also possible that we will find a number exhibiting what is referred to as a **hybrid structure**. That is to say, they exhibit the characteristics of more than one design type. It may be, for example, that a company producing sport equipment and operating with a machine bureaucracy design may wish to develop new products and enter new markets; it may create a small adhocracy as an appendage to its existing machine bureaucracy design. Brunswick took this type of initiative when it established venture capital groups within its divisions in order to nurture new products.

What does all this mean, then? Does the fact that we may not find the exact type of organizational design we have described mean that they are not useful? Of course not. As we pointed out at the start of this chapter, scholars who study organizations of all types have long considered a means of classification as one of the basic requirements of the field. As table 5.2 shows, the five designs developed by Mintzberg enable us to compare and contrast sport organizations on a number of dimensions. They also provide us with a basis for studying a wide variety of other organizational phenomena. For example, how does a sport organization change from a simple structure to a machine bureaucracy to a divisionalized form? Do machine bureaucracies and professional bureaucracies formulate strategy in different ways? Are decisions made differently in a professional bureaucracy than in an adhocracy? And, how is power exercised in each of these different designs? All of these questions, and many more, are valid topics of investigation for sport management students. The design types outlined can provide a useful basis for investigation into these areas.

Notes on Organizational Size

In this chapter we have made the implicit assumption that an organization's design is dependent, in part, on its size. Organizational **size** can be defined in many ways: total assets, return on investment, market share, sales volume, number of clients, number of employees, number of members, net profits, and so on. Kimberly (1976) suggests a combination of four aspects as a more appropriate way to operationalize the size concept: physical capacity of the organization, personnel available to the organization (the most commonly used aspect), volume of input or output, and the discretionary resources available to the organization (e.g., organizational wealth and assets).

Table 5.2 Dimensions of the Five Organizational Design Types

Dimensions	Simple structure	Machine bureaucracy	Professional bureaucracy	Divisionalized form	Adhocracy
Horizontal complexity	Low	High-functional	High-social	High-functional	High-social
Vertical complexity	Low	High	Medium	High within divisions	Low
Formalization	Low	High	Low	High within divisions	Low
Centralization	High	High	Low	High within divisions	Low
Technology	Simple	Regulating, not automated, not sophisticated	Not regulating or sophisticated	Divisible like machine bureaucracy	Sophisticated and often automated
Size	Small	Large	Varies	Large	Varies
Environment	Simple and dynamic	Simple and stable	Complex and stable	Simple and stable diversified markets	Complex and dynamic
Strategy	Intuitive and opportunistic	To maintain performance in chosen markets	Developed by individuals controlled by professional association	Portfolio	Seeks new products and new markets

MINTZBERG, HENRY, STRUCTURING OF ORGANIZATIONS, 1st Edition, © 1979. Adapted by permission of Pearson Education, Inc., Upper Saddle River, NJ.

KEY ISSUES FOR MANAGERS

There are different ways to theoretically or empirically categorize organizations. Managers must be concerned with two major aspects:

- The parts of the organization: What types of employees work here, and what is the overall nature of the organization (i.e., its goals, size, structural aspects, type of coordination)?
- The type of environment: Is it stable or unstable, and what is the nature of the market?

Determining these aspects helps narrow the best type of organizational design to fit the organization's needs and desires. Remember that there can be a design within a design (as explained in the Time Out on NBC) and an organization can be transitional in nature. Practically speaking, while organizations will be similar to those in this chapter most will not fit the ideal types because there are too many factors in play at the same time.

The emerging design type in sport organizations, alliances, is gaining popularity in such areas as public-private partnerships or joint ventures (Babiak, 2003; and chapter 7). The point for a sport manager is that the best design type must be chosen, even if it is new or unpopular. In that way, the organization's goals can be best achieved.

An organization's size will determine the choice of organizational design type. For example, the local sporting goods store owner will most likely choose a simpler organizational structure than would Adidas. Any increase (or decrease) in size can dictate a necessary change in organizational design type in order to stay efficient.

Size can have an impact on the different elements of organizational structure. Notwithstanding the nature of the organization (e.g., entrepreneurial versus manufacturing), an increase in size often goes hand-in-hand with an increase in the complexity and formalization of the organization (cf. Miller, G., 1987; Rushing, 1980; Slack, 1985; Slack & Hining, 1992). The relationship between size and centralization, however, is somewhat more difficult. On one hand it would be logical to think that growth means decentralizing to avoid overloading senior managers (Child, 1973a). On the other hand, owners may be reluctant to give up their control. This can be especially true for professional sport team owners.

SUMMARY AND CONCLUSIONS

Although no two sport organizations are exactly alike, they do exhibit common features that form the basis for classifying them into design types, or configurations. Classification has been identified as one of the most important tasks for organizational theorists because it provides a basis for the generation of hypotheses, models, and theories. There are two main ways of classifying organizations: Conceptually based schema are called typologies; those that are empirically based are referred to as taxonomies.

One of the most common organizational typologies is the one developed by Mintzberg (1979), who identifies five parts of an organization. Depending on the part that dominates, we get one of five organizational designs: the simple structure, the machine bureaucracy, the divisionalized form, the professional bureaucracy, or the adhocracy. We can find sport organizations representative of each of these design types.

The simple structure, most often found in small sport organizations and those in the early stages of their development, usually shows low levels of specialization and formalization. The key part of a simple structure is the strategic apex, where we find the individual who runs the sport organization and with whom power is centralized. Simple structures work best in environments that are simple and dynamic.

The machine bureaucracy is usually found in sport organizations that produce a standard output, government agencies concerned with sport, and organizations that need relatively simple tasks performed in a consistent manner. Its main attribute is its efficiency. The key part of the machine bureaucracy is the technostructure that standardizes work. We find the machine bureaucracy in simple and stable environments.

The divisionalized form is actually a group of organizations, usually machine bureaucracies, coordinated by a central headquarters. The divisions, not all of which are always involved in sport, provide product and market diversity. The key part of this organization is the presence of middle-line managers, those individuals who control the divisions. The divisionalized form is found in large organizations that have either product or market diversity; it operates in simple and stable environments.

The professional bureaucracy caters to the needs of the professional by providing the standardization of the bureaucracy but at the same time allowing professionals control of their own work. Faculties of physical education and sport studies often operate with a professional bureaucratic structure, as do sport medicine clinics and architectural firms specializing in sport facilities. The key part of the professional bureaucracy is the operating core, which contains the professionals. We find this type of design in sport organizations with complex and stable environments.

The final design is the adhocracy. NBC used this form of organization when it televised the Seoul Olympics. We also find it in research units and specialized structures such as a task force. Its strength is its flexibility and, hence, its ability to respond to change. The key part of this sport organization is the support staff of experts, on which the organization is dependent. We find this type of structure in complex and dynamic environments.

Each of the designs discussed is an ideal type, so we seldom find sport organizations that fit the pattern exactly as described. Some sport organizations may approximate one of the main designs, some may be in transitional states between designs, and others may exhibit a hybrid structure that exhibits the characteristics of more than one design.

KEY CONCEPTS

adhocracy (p. 100)

divisionalized form (p. 96)

hybrid structure (p. 103)

ideal types (p. 102)

machine bureaucracy (p. 95)

middle line (p. 91)

operating core (p. 91)

professional bureaucracy (p. 98)

simple structure (p. 92)

size (p. 103)

strategic apex (p. 91)

support staff (p. 91)

taxonomy (p. 89)

technostructure (p. 91)

typology (p. 87)

REVIEW QUESTIONS

1. How does a typology differ from a taxonomy?

2. What does Mintzberg suggest are the five parts of an organization?

3. What type of organizational design would you expect a small entrepreneurial sport organization to use? Why?

4. Describe the characteristics of the machine bureaucracy. What are the advantages and disadvantages of this design?

5. Pick some familiar sport organizations. What type of design do they have?

6. What type of design would you expect to find in a faculty of physical education and sport studies?

7. Discuss how the method of coordination varies in each of the five designs.

8. Describe the divisionalized form and explain where you might find this type of organiza-

tion in the sport industry. What are its advantages and disadvantages?

9. What are the characteristics of an adhocracy? Where would you expect to find this type of design in the sport industry?

10. In what type of sport organizations would you expect to find the professional bureaucracy?

11. What type of design did Nike use in its early years (see chapter 1)? What type of design do you think it uses now?

12. How does an adhocracy differ from a professional bureaucracy?

13. Discuss how the role of the strategic apex varies in each of the five designs.

14. Adhocracies have been described as fashionable. Why do you think this is?

15. In which of the design types is formalization likely to be low? Why?

SUGGESTIONS FOR FURTHER READING

For further reading, students are obviously referred to Mintzberg's (1979) work on organizational design. The most comprehensive treatment is found in his book *The Structuring of Organizations*. While part 4 of his book deals specifically with design, the earlier chapters lay much of the foundation for his work in this area and should have relevance for students interested in this topic. More condensed versions of Mintzberg's (1981) work on design can be found in his chapter,

"A Typology of Organizational Structure," and his articles "Organizational Design: Fashion or Fit?" in *Harvard Business Review*, and (1980) "Structure in 5's: A Synthesis of the Research on Organizational Design" in *Management Science*. Information on typologies and taxonomies can be found in Miller and Friesen's (1984) *Organizations: A Quantum View*. While this is the most sophisticated work on these topics, some of it is difficult reading, particularly chapter 2, which deals with methods of developing taxonomies. You should also see Carper and Snizek's (1980) "The Nature and Types of Organizational Taxonomies: An Overview," in the *Academy of Management Review*.

Within the sport literature, Chelladurai's work (1985) on typologies in *Sport Management: Macro Perspectives* is a useful starting point for discussions on this topic. Also interesting is his 1992 article "A Classification of Sport and Physical Activity Services: Implications for Sport Management," in the *Journal of Sport Management*. In regard to taxonomies of organizations, students should see Hinings and Slack's (1987) chapter "The Dynamics of Quadrennial Plan Implementation in National Sport Organizations" in their (Slack & Hinings, 1987a) edited book *The Organization and Administration of Sport*. A more methodologically sophisticated taxonomy is developed and discussed in an extension of this work in Kikulis et al.'s (1989) article, "A Structural Taxonomy of Amateur Sport Organizations," in the *Journal of Sport Management*.

CASE FOR ANALYSIS

Reshaping National Sport Organizations

Sitting in her home in the suburbs of Toronto, Susan Collinson, the volunteer president of a small Canadian sport organization, reread the material she had just received from the federal government agency, Sport Canada.* Susan had been the president of her organization for two years and had frequently expressed her concern about the increased involvement the government was taking in its operation. The material she just received had Susan worried.

For the past 15 to 20 years Sport Canada had provided many of the national-level amateur sport organizations with funds to operate their programs. The funds were not large and they were given with few strings attached. Susan's organization had been fairly successful and had used their funds well, building a very strong volunteer base within the various clubs that existed throughout the country. Their provincial associations were also well organized. The national organization's board of directors was an enthusiastic group of volunteers, many of whom held managerial positions with local and national companies. Using the funds they received from Sport Canada, and other monies from membership fees and fund-raising ventures, this group of volunteers had established a wide range of developmental programs to encourage people to get involved in their sport. They had also been reasonably successful in international competition, because Jim Kramer, one of the top club coaches in the country, had worked with the national team as a volunteer coach.

The organization operated in a collegial manner. Although there were the occasional disputes, members worked well together. They had no detailed policies and procedures they had to follow; they basically "got on with the job." About three years ago the board had hired Katrina Torkildson, a former athlete who understood sports, to be their executive director. While she had no formal management training she was regarded as bright, enthusiastic, and well organized. Katrina worked for the board and essentially helped do the things they needed doing to make the organization run smoothly. As Susan read the material from the federal government, she wondered if all this was going to change.

Essentially, what the government was proposing was to increase significantly the amount of money they were providing to the national sport organizations. In large part their rationale was that this new funding would increase Canada's chances of doing well in the Olympic Games and other major international sporting events. Although no definitive figures were given, Susan roughly estimated that the funds her organization was receiving could quadruple.

However, there was a catch. To receive the funds, national sport organizations had to prepare a "plan." The plan should outline the type of changes the sport organization would make in order to operate in a more efficient and businesslike manner. This efficiency, Sport Canada felt, was what was needed to increase Canada's medal count at major games. The plan should also contain detailed policies and procedures that documented how the organization conducted its business. One of the other changes the government appeared to be promoting was the hiring of an increased number of professionally trained staff to run the affairs of the organization, enhance its

---

*Although the situation in this case is based on actual events the names are fictitious.

developmental programs, and coach its national teams. Funds were to be provided, up to 75 percent of their salary, to hire these people; Sport Canada would, however, have a voice in who was hired. Although it was not stated as such, implicit in the material Susan received was the idea that volunteers would play a considerably smaller role in the organization's operation, which would be turned over to the new professional staff. As Susan pondered the material, she wondered what impact all this would have on her organization and how she should deal with the information she had received.

Questions

1. What would you do if you were Susan and you had just received the material from the federal government?

2. What is the potential impact of the government's proposed initiatives on the design of this national sport organization?

3. How do you think Jim and Katrina will feel about the government's proposals?

4. Is there any way that Susan could take advantage of the increased funding offered by the government, yet at the same time maintain the type of organizational design that currently exists?

5. Fast-forward 15 years: Susan has followed the government's guidelines thinking it was better to do as the government said to get the money. However, the government of Canada now decides it cannot keep supporting the Canadian sport organizations given the tougher economic times. The government plans to cut its annual funding by half but still expects the same performance level from the organizations. Also, the guidelines are still in place. What would you do if you were Susan?

Strategy

ADIDAS REINVENTS ITSELF

Adolph "Adi" Dassler started out helping his family make house slippers from leftover military bags in a Germany devastated by World War I. His heart, however, was in athletics, especially soccer, so in 1920 he started making sport shoes. By 1928, Adidas* shoes were worn in the Olympics, and in the 1936 Berlin Olympics Jesse Owens wore Adidas shoes when he won four gold medals.

The popularity of the Adidas brand grew because Dassler was constantly innovating. He created cleats for soccer shoes and the spikes for track and field shoes. Adidas became the shoe of choice for professional athletes up until the end of the 1980s. During the 1990s, Nike and Reebok started outselling Adidas and eventually surpassed it.

To regain its foothold in the sport shoe industry, Adidas created a game plan: reinvention. This strategy had various components. First, Adidas reorganized to focus on products for three groups of consumers:

1. Sport performance gear for the running, football, basketball, tennis, and training athletes
2. Sport heritage for the lifestyle consumers who look for trendy street clothes with authentic origins
3. Sport style for the fashion-conscious consumers who desire stylish activewear

Designer Yohji Yamamoto was brought onboard in 2003 to spearhead collections

(continued)

---

*The company has chosen to use an all-lowercase presentation for its brand name and logo (adidas); here, however, the name of the company is presented as a proper noun (Adidas).

(continued)

© Sportschrome

Adidas' strategy to reach new markets included a prominent presence in Athens during the 2004 Olympic Games.

for the Sport style division. In 2004, fashion designer Stella McCartney entered into a partnership to create a collection of activewear for running, training, and swimming as part of the sport performance division.

Second, Adidas developed more specific strategies to boost its market share. It started associating itself with megastars such as David Beckham, Kobe Bryant, and Tracy McGrady. In fact, Beckham and McGrady now have lifetime deals with Adidas. The $161 million partnership with Beckham—one of the biggest sport stars in the world—allowed Adidas to penetrate the very large and lucrative Asian market. In 2001, Adidas increased its sales in Asia by 15 percent, to the tune of $878 million. Adidas' total sales that year rose to U.S.$2.7 billion.

In 2004, a joint lifestyle initiative between Adidas and Beckham was announced, consisting of 23 clothing items and seven accessory styles to be distributed in more than 20 countries.

Not only is Adidas creating alliances with the world's sport superstars, but it is also eyeing future stars. The company developed various youth sport projects, such as the Adidas America's ABCD camp for top high school basketball athletes. The hope is to attract these future stars into endorsement deals.

Having penetrated the Asian market, Adidas set its sights on major sport events, sponsoring soccer teams such as Real Madrid, AC Milan, and Bayern Munich. It was part of the 2003 FIFA Women's World Cup and the 2004 UEFA Championships. It was the official supplier of 18 National Olympic Committees for the 2004 Athens Olympic Games, and will be the official supplier, sponsor, and licensee of the 2006 FIFA World Cup and the 2008 Beijing Olympic Games.

Finally, following Nike's Niketown lead, Adidas launched its first megastore in Paris in 2001, on the heels of France's 1998 World Cup and 2000 Euro Cup championships. The hope is to spread the concept across Europe and North America.

Adidas is now the second largest sport brand in the world.

Based on information in Adidas-Salomon (2004a; 2004b), Haig (2004), India Sports Forum (2005), Manning-Schaffel (2002), and Sinofile.net (2004).

Adidas changed its strategy to respond to changes in its environment. It concentrated on being innovative and reaching new markets. A number of research studies (Miles, Snow, Meyer, & Coleman, 1978; Miller, 1987b) have suggested that, in order to be successful, organizations must respond to changes in their environment with appropriate strategies, which will in turn require structural changes. In fact, when organization theory first started to develop as a distinct area of study, there was a belief that strategy was the only variable to determine structure. To be effective there had to be an appropriate "fit" between an organization's strategy and its structure (Robbins, 1990).

Now we know that strategy is in fact just one variable that can influence the structure of an organization. In the next four chapters we look at these contingencies, determinants, imperatives, or contextual factors (as they are variously called). In this chapter we focus on the concept of organizational strategy. We look at what we mean when we talk about strategy and we discuss the differences between corporate-level strategies and business-level strategies. We also examine how strategy is formulated and implemented, and the relationship between strategy and structure. In the following chapter we look at an example of a type of strategy called strategic alliances. In chapters 8 and 9, we look at the influence of two contingencies, environment and technology, on organizational structure. In chapter 10, we look at how power, a noncontingent factor, can be used to influence structure.

What Is Organizational Strategy?

Das (1990, p. 294) likens an organization's strategy to the game plan developed by a sport team:

> [B]efore a team enters the field, an effective coach looks at the team's strengths and weaknesses and also those of its competitors. The coach carefully studies the two teams' past successes, failures, and behaviors on the field. The obvious objective is to win the game with minimal risk and personal injuries to the players. Thus, a coach may not use all the team's best players if it is not warranted (they may be kept in reserve for future games or to maintain an element of surprise). The key goal is to win the game, and the game plan itself might be modified to recognize the emerging realities.

Das goes on, however, to point out that while a football or volleyball team has a game plan for each game and each opponent, an organization's strategy is more long-term and must deal with a number of issues, internal and external to the organization. Alfred Chandler, one of the first to carry out research on organizational strategy, suggested (1962, p. 13) that "strategy can be defined as the determination of the basic long-term goals and objectives of an enterprise and the adoption of courses of action and the allocation of resources necessary for carrying out these goals." Mintzberg (1987) argues that strategy can be seen as a plan, a ploy, a pattern, a position, and a perspective. Sometimes the term "strategy" is used synonymously with the terms "goals" and "objectives." But, as both Chandler's and Mintzberg's explanations make clear, strategy is more than goals and objectives; it also involves the means by which goals are to be achieved.

All sport organizations formulate strategies; they may be deliberate or emergent. **Deliberate strategies** are intended courses of action that become realized. In contrast, **emergent strategies** are those that are realized but not necessarily intended (Mintzberg, 1978). The acquisition of Bauer, the leading manufacturer of hockey products, by Nike is an example of a deliberate strategy. Nike wanted to enter the hockey market—and enter it as number one. An example of a more emergent type of strategy was the one displayed by Wilson Sporting Goods. Originally in the meat business, Wilson diversified into sporting goods because gut, a by-product of the meat industry, was used in the strings of tennis rackets (Aris, 1990). In another case, Walvin (1975) describes how the strategy of some churches to use soccer as a means to combat urban degeneration among the working classes led to the formation of soccer clubs. Aston Villa, Birmingham City, Bolton Wanderers, and Fulham are all notable examples. It is, of course, possible that deliberate strategies, as they become realized, may become in part emergent, and emergent strategies in time get formalized as deliberate (Mintzberg, 1978).

In summary, strategy may then be planned and deliberate, it may emerge as a stream of significant decisions, or it may be some combination of both. In any of these situations organizational decision makers base their choice of strategy on their perceptions of the opportunities and threats in the environment, and the internal strengths and weaknesses of their organization. Then, as a result of the strategy they choose, they institute an appropriate organizational structure. This sequence is shown graphically in figure 6.1.

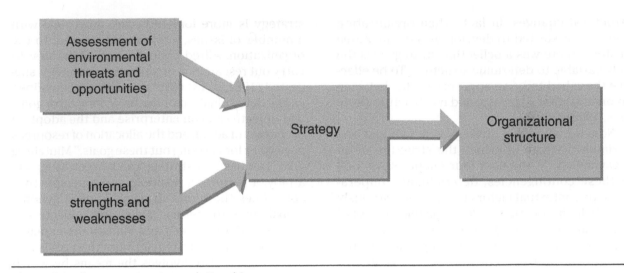

Figure 6.1 *Strategy–structure relationship.*

Levels of Strategy

Sport organizations can formulate strategies at two levels, the corporate level and the business level. **Corporate-level strategies**, which are followed by the organization as a whole, are required when a sport organization competes in a number of different industries. They answer the question "What businesses should we be involved in?" For example, Rogers Communications followed a corporate strategy that involved it not only in the communications industry but also in major league baseball, through its ownership of the Toronto Blue Jays. Obviously there are benefits, if corporate-level strategies involve "synergies among the business units and with the corporation" (Yavitz & Newman, 1982, p. 60). The Rogers and Blue Jays' relationship accomplished this synergy; ownership of the Blue Jays gave Rogers key sport programming content for its cable channels.

While some degree of synergy among the different businesses in a corporation can be beneficial, some organizations adopt a strategy of operating in diversified markets. We have previously mentioned Brunswick (powerboats and defense) and Wembley Group PLC (hosting sport events and catering). Other examples involving sport are Wight, Collins, Rutherford, and Scott, a major communications company in the United Kingdom. It had as part of its portfolio, until 1993, Alan Pascoe Associates (APA) a sport sponsorship company; Yamaha, which produces musical instruments, motorcycles, and sport and recreational goods; and Provigo, a consumer-goods distributor that until early 1994 owned Sports Experts, a sporting goods chain.

Business-level strategies address questions about how to compete within a particular industry; when a sport organization competes only in one industry, its business-level strategy and its corporate-level strategy will be the same. But for sport organizations competing in a number of industries, each division will formulate its own strategy. For example, a corporation like International Management Group (IMG) in all likelihood will formulate strategies for its figure-skating division (sport agents), its research division, its broadcasting division, its academies division (sport training centers), and its literary division. Figure 6.2 shows the relationship between corporate-level and business-level strategies.

A corporate strategy is usually the end result of a business-level analysis technique called **portfolio analysis** (Bates & Eldredge, 1984). We discuss this topic more fully in the next section of this chapter, where we examine corporate strategies in more detail.

Corporate-Level Strategies

There are four different types of corporate strategy in which an organization can engage. Hodge and Anthony (1991) term them growth strategies, stability strategies, defensive strategies, and combination strategies.

Growth Strategies

Almost all sport organizations seek growth as one of their goals. A growth strategy may be pursued in two major ways at the corporate level: diversification and integration. **Diversification** helps a company grow while at the same time

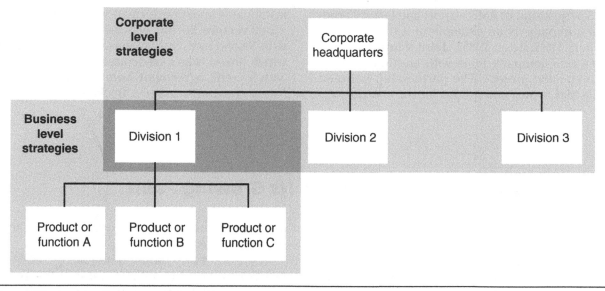

Figure 6.2 Levels of strategy.

spreading its risk. Diversification strategies may be related or unrelated. A related diversification strategy "calls for the acquired investment to have some relation to the existing businesses, such as technology, product group, managerial knowledge, or distribution channels. [It] permits a firm to spread its risk while at the same time capitalizing on its strengths" (Bates & Eldredge, 1984, p. 137). The acquisition of Bauer by Nike, mentioned earlier in this chapter, is an example of a related diversification. Both Nike and Bauer are in the sport industry, and Nike wanted to enter the hockey market dominated by Bauer. An unrelated diversification strategy means that a corporation is pursuing acquisitions in areas not necessarily related to its existing business units. The decisions of successful business people such as Mike Ilitch (Little Caesar's) and Jerry Jones (oil) to acquire professional sport franchises (respectively the Detroit Red Wings followed by the Detroit Tigers, and the Dallas Cowboys), are all examples of an unrelated diversification strategy; Ted Turner's involvement in the Atlanta Hawks and the Atlanta Braves, however, could be seen as a related diversification, since both teams provide programming for his TV station.

In addition to diversification, growth can also be achieved through *integration*. Integration may be achieved horizontally or vertically. **Horizontal integration** involves adding another product, often a competitor in the same business, by buying an organization. AstroTurf manufacturer Balsam's acquisition of smaller artificial turf producers such as All Pro, Omni Turf, and Super Turf is an example

of horizontal integration. **Vertical integration** occurs either when a sport organization acquires its distributors (forward integration) or its suppliers (backward integration). Vertical integration allows for more control over the production process, for potentially reduced costs by bringing the supplier in-house, and for potentially increasing higher sales margins by bringing the distributor in-house (Bates & Eldredge, 1984). An example of backward integration would be Nike purchasing Tetra Plastics, the company that produces the plastic film used in the production of Air Sole Cushioning, in 1991. In the early 1990s Nike also bought out many of its distribution operations, an example of forward integration ("Can Nike just do it?" 1994).

A sport organization can use a number of techniques when it adopts a growth strategy. For example, diversification may be achieved through mergers, acquisitions, takeovers, or joint ventures. A **merger** occurs when two or more companies combine to produce one. For example, in Canada in 1989, the Canadian Women's Field Hockey Association and the Canadian Field Hockey Association, previously two separate entities, merged to form Field Hockey Canada. An **acquisition** involves one company buying another and absorbing it into its operations. Such was the case in 1983 when Bally Manufacturing, best known for its association with slot machines, acquired Health & Tennis Corporation of America, the world's largest chain of health clubs. A **takeover** involves one company attempting to obtain control of another against the wishes of shareholders and management. Irwin L. Jacobs'

1985 acquisition of AMF, a sport and leisure products company, is an example of a takeover (cf. Ehrlich, 1985; Ross, 1985). **Joint ventures** occur when one company joins with another to work on a specific project. The partnership between Stella McCartney and Adidas for the creation of a fashionable sport performance line is essentially a joint venture. So, too, was Nike's 1980 agreement with Nissho Iwai, the Japanese trading company, which linked Nike's trademark license for Japan with a credit agreement from Nissho to finance Nike's growth (Strasser & Becklund, 1991). Such

TIME OUT *Westbeach and Its Growing Pains*

In 1979 Chip Wilson founded Westbeach, a surf and skateboard shop in Calgary, Alberta. For seven years it was the largest skateboard distributor in Canada, but in the late 1980s, Wilson decided to focus on his own product line once it started drawing attention at European and North American trade shows. The company then focused its attention on snowboarding. Within the space of a couple of years, its sales went from 80 percent summer to 80 percent winter products. The $40 pair of beach shorts became the $260 waterproof, insulated mountain parka.

Snowboarding grew exponentially in the late 1980s and early 1990s, and Westbeach went along for the ride. Growth has not been painless, however. Westbeach first spent its marketing budget trying to persuade middle-age retailers to carry its youth clothing. Only when Westbeach poured money into advertising—and teens started demanding the products—did stores begin to bite. In 1994 Westbeach signed on snowboard champion Ross Rebagliati, to increase awareness of its products. Rebagliati would go on to win an Olympic gold medal in 1998.

Despite the marketing push, Westbeach lost money on its first foray into Europe because of a bad business venture. The company had budgeted its production costs around a $4 million order from a German distributor, but failed to secure a letter of credit. The German distributor had imitation products made in Turkey sporting counterfeit Westbeach labels, but before these products could flood Europe they were blocked by a last-minute court injunction. It was a costly delay in a promising market. Westbeach finally managed to capitalize on the burgeoning European market in 1995 when it opened a European office in Innsbruck, Austria.

There were also banking headaches. Westbeach was forced to ship its wares at the end of each month because its bank lends twice as much against receivables as against inventory. Another factor was the bonuses the Westbeach partners took out of the company in the early 1990s, a move that ran down its equity. These financial mistakes caused the Hong Kong Bank of Canada to refuse a working line of credit. It cost Westbeach $32,000 to have B.C. Trade Development Corporation guarantee letters of credit so the company could meet export orders.

The once young and inexperienced partners have learned along the way and outgrown their laid-back approach to finances. "They're a classic case of a company that got so far merely on quality product and image," says Mr. Guyle Tippe, a senior manager with Peat Marwick Thorne. Tippe helped Westbeach to set goals, and identify strengths and weaknesses. He helped deemphasize short-term profits to establish a structure that can respond to changing markets. Employees became involved in planning for life after snowboards. "You have to create an environment where almost everybody is an entrepreneur," Tippe says. "It's not easy." For Wilson and his partners, it means sniffing the winds of fashion while wrestling with the discipline of a business strategy that ensures long-range survival. Since then, Westbeach has continued its success in the snowboarding industry. While snowboarding is as popular as ever, growth has leveled off.

Adapted with permission of The Globe & Mail.

strategic alliances will be discussed further in chapter 7.

Internal growth can also occur when a sport organization is able to expand its market share. This growth may be achieved by saturating existing markets with current products or services. Alternatively, a company may take an existing product or service that has been successful in one market into a new market.

Stability Strategies

Hodge and Anthony (1991) suggest that an organization may engage in two types of stability strategies. A *neutral strategy* means that the organization continues to do what it has done in the past with no intent to grow. A **harvesting** or **milking strategy** is used when a product is becoming obsolete or if a business unit lacks potential and there is little chance to turn the situation around.

This type of strategy involves management in an attempt to increase its cash flow from the product or business unit by severely reducing or eliminating the capital it puts into areas such as facility maintenance, advertising, and research (Harrigan & Porter, 1983). There are two possible consequences of a harvesting strategy. First, the product or business unit may justify its existence by continuing to be successful enough, with little or no investiture, to generate cash flow that can

be diverted to other units. Alternately, it may lose market share but generate an initial, albeit short-term increase in capital that can be directed elsewhere. When the cash flow from the product or business unit starts to decline, liquidation usually follows.

Defensive Strategies

Defensive strategies, or what are sometimes termed decline strategies, are used when the demand for a sport organization's product or service starts to decrease. Defensive strategies try to reverse this situation or overcome a particular problem. There are three principle types of defensive strategy: turnaround, divestiture, and liquidation.

Turnaround strategies are used to counter increased costs and falling revenues, and to increase cash flow and liquidity. They involve actions such as reducing or changing the products or markets served, laying off workers, replacing senior management, and cutting costs (Schendel, Patton, & Riggs, 1976). Nike, in an attempt to compete with Reebok's success in the aerobics shoe business, moved into the women's casual shoe market in the early 1980s. As Strasser and Becklund (1991, p. 506) point out, they "struggled to compete in an area in which [they] had no experience, no reputation, poor styling, and no price

---

TIME OUT   *Canadian Broadcasting Consortium Wins 2010 and 2012 Olympic Games Broadcasting Rights*

On February 7, 2005, Jacques Rogge, president of the IOC, announced that the Canadian broadcasting rights to the 2010 and 2012 Olympic Games were won by a consortium composed of Bell Globemedia, CTV, and Rodgers, and their associated television, radio, print, Internet, and cellular divisions for the price of U.S.$153 million ($90 million for the 2010 Winter Games in Vancouver and $63 million for the 2012 Summer Games (location undetermined at the time of bidding). It would be the first time that the Winter Olympic Games cost more than the Summer Games; although that probably had to do with the fact that the 2010 Olympics would be held in Canada.

The Canadian bid won out over CBC's because it had three strong areas (in addition to the financial offer):

1. Enhancement of the Olympic brand

2. Support for national sport organizations and athletes in Canada

3. Use of all possible media sources for transmitting the Olympic Games

Not only was the consortium innovative, but it also stated a strong desire to partner with the various stakeholders in the Canadian sport system to strengthen both sides of the partnership.

Based on information from CBC Sports (2005a).

advantage." As their fortunes continued to decline, founder Philip Knight adopted the elements of a turnaround strategy. He stepped back into the presidency of Nike, a position he had relinquished little more than a year earlier, and told his staff he wanted to lower factory costs, control inventories, improve time lines, and increase profit margins. He also laid off 400 employees, about 10 percent of his workforce.

If a turnaround is not possible a company has the option of divestiture or liquidation. **Divestiture** involves selling off a business or some portion of the ownership of a business. For example, in 1987 Bally Manufacturing tried to divest itself of Health & Tennis Corporation of America, the nation's largest chain of health clubs. As McCarthy (1987, p. 14) noted, divesting itself of Health & Tennis "would help Bally concentrate on its growing hotel and casino businesses, and allay persistent Wall Street concerns that Bally's long-term earnings could be hurt if the fitness boom fizzle[d]."

Liquidation involves closing down a business and selling off its assets. For example, John McCaw's Orca Bay group who had bought an NBA franchise for Vancouver (the Grizzlies) was forced to sell the team because it was incurring too much

cost and was not successful on the court. As it happens, new owner Michael Heisley promptly moved the team to Memphis.

Combination Strategies

The fourth type of corporate strategy involves a diversified sport organization using the different strategies outlined above in combination. **Combination strategy** is the most popular strategy besides growth strategies (Hodge and Anthony, 1991). Rarely will a diversified sport organization have only one strategy; it may seek to expand certain parts of its operation while at the same time reduce or eliminate its involvement in other areas. Global Golf Holdings, a publicly held company involved in the golf industry, exemplifies the use of a combination strategy. In 2002, having incurred losses, the company divested itself of its forestry-related holdings to concentrate on the highly competitive $36.3 billion golf industry. To this end, the company acquired GolfLogix Systems Canada. It also planned to close some of its larger golf course management companies in western Canada while attempting to increase exposure of its various products (Global Golf Holdings Inc., 2003).

TIME OUT   *Sheffield's Sport Event Strategy*

Sheffield, England, used to be know as the "city of steel" because that was the main industry in the city. Through the late 1970s and early 1980s, the steel industry declined—bad news for the city and residents who worked in the industry. At the same time, a new trend was emerging, that of globalization, which offered international recognition for cities and corporations.

In 1987, the municipal government partnered with the local Chamber of Commerce and the Sheffield Economic Regeneration Committee. The goal was to promote the city, stimulate investments, and make the city "world class." A sport and leisure strategy was formulated to reach this goal and to create a new image for the city, revolving around sports. Ultimately the partnership hoped to build infrastructure, bring in tourists, and new capital. This was also being done in Calgary

and Edmonton, Alberta, Canada, with some success. The central element of this strategy was to obtain the chance to host the 1991 World Student Games, which it did. Although the games were financially unsuccessful, they were successful in leaving Sheffield with a sport facility, knowledge, and new infrastructure. More important, the games jump-started Sheffield's image makeover toward a more youthful, energetic, and innovative "city of sports."

On the heels of Sheffield's successful new image, other cities have started using the same strategy. For example, Manchester bid for and won the rights to host the 2002 Commonwealth Games but has so far failed in its attempts to host the Olympic Games.

Based on information in Henry (1999), Whitson and Macintosh (1993).

Portfolio Analysis

In diversified companies that use combination strategies, one popular technique for analyzing the relative merits and cash flow requirements of their product or service offerings is that developed by the Boston Consulting Group (BCG). The BCG approach requires that a company identify **strategic business units** (SBUs) for each of the business areas in which it competes. The SBUs are then assessed along two dimensions: relative market share and growth rate. In assessing the first dimension, the ratio of the SBU's market share to that of its nearest competitor is used. For example, an SBU with a market share of 20 percent in an industry whose largest rival has 30 percent would have a relative market share of 20/30 (.66). A relative market share score over 1 (i.e., it is an industry leader) is seen as high; a score below 1 is low. Growth rate is determined according to whether the SBU's industry is growing faster than the economy as a whole. Growth rates above average are high; those below are low (Hill & Jones, 1989). Using the dimensions of market share and growth rate, a 2 × 2 matrix can be constructed as shown in figure 6.3. Each SBU can then be placed into one of the four cells. The SBUs in cell 1 are referred to as **stars**; they have high growth rates and high market share. Whether or not they are self-sufficient depends on whether they can generate enough cash flow to support their rapid growth. Established stars are likely to be able to support themselves, while emergent stars will need cash support. Stars offer long-term profit potential when the growth rate of their market decreases; that is, they become **cash cows**. The SBUs in cell 2 are **question marks**, sometimes referred to as "problem children." They are weak in that they have a low market share, but because they are in high-growth industries they could become stars. To transform question marks into stars often requires a large infusion of cash. Strategists have to weigh the relative benefits of an increase in capital expenditure against the benefits of selling off this type of unit.

Cash cows, in cell 3, have a high market share and low growth rate; as such, they generate more profit than they need investment. Cash cows are

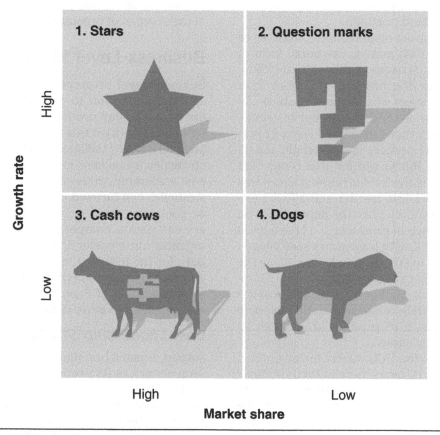

Figure 6.3 *The BCG matrix.*

to be "milked" and the profits they generate used for other corporate functions such as research and development and debt reduction. They can also be used to finance other SBUs such as those classified as question marks or emergent stars. In cell 4 we find **dogs**. Dogs, in low-growth industries with low market share, do not generate large amounts of cash, nor do they require large amounts. Some companies may keep these SBUs active to offer customers an entire product line; others choose to divest themselves of dogs, which offer little potential for growth.

The strategic implications of the BCG portfolio analysis involve maximizing the profitability and growth potential of an organization. The BCG recommends that managers financially support selected question marks and emerging stars, often with capital extracted from cash cows. Managers must also make decisions about selling off those question marks they don't think have potential, to avoid excessive demands on company cash. They must also consider the relative merits of retaining dogs. The manager aims to obtain a suitable balance of cash cows, stars, and question marks. If this balance is not present, the company must look at acquisitions or divestments as a means of producing a balanced portfolio.

All diversified sport organizations, whether or not they use the BCG matrix, use some form of portfolio analysis. Strasser and Becklund (1991), for example, describe how in 1979 more than half of Nike's business was in running shoes, 22 percent in basketball, and 16 percent in tennis. Its market share in those areas had risen 22 percent in running, 77 percent in basketball, and 37 percent in tennis. But Knight felt that tennis had already peaked, the market for running shoes was approaching saturation, and basketball was getting expensive. He "didn't like the dependence on such a narrow range of products. . . . Like a good portfolio manager, Knight was always searching to minimize risk and maximize gain by balancing the sources of revenue" (Strasser & Becklund, 1991, p. 398). Knight made a number of financial decisions to consolidate cash flow and eventually diversify more than before, into product areas such as apparel and soccer shoes.

The strength of the BCG matrix for diversified companies is that it forces them to focus on their cash flow requirements and plan their corporate strategy accordingly. It alerts managers to the need for acquisitions and divestitures. There are, however, as Hill and Jones (1989) point out, several problems with the BCG approach (Seeger, 1984). While the simplicity of the matrix is appealing, market share and growth are not the only two factors to consider when assessing portfolios. A company may have a low market share but establish a strong market position through differentiating its product line to serve the needs of a particular section of the market. Berrett, Burton, and Slack (1993) suggest that a number of entrepreneurs in the sport industry have established such a position by focusing on quality products and service. Hill and Jones (1989) also suggest that the relationship between market share and cost saving is not as straightforward as presented in the BCG matrix, and that a high market share in a low-growth industry does not always produce a high cash yield.

Given the BCG's focus on large diversified companies, it may appear to be of limited use to some sport organizations, particularly those such as collegiate athletic departments or campus intramural departments. However, in an interesting adaptation of portfolio analysis Graham (1983) uses criteria such as cost-per-participation unit, user and community support, or level of participation compared with maximum capacity, as opposed to market share, to show how the BCG matrix could be used by sport managers to develop strategies in these types of organizations.

Business-Level Strategies

Business-level strategies are those used by a sport organization to gain a competitive edge for its particular product or service. The most influential work on this topic is that of Harvard's Michael Porter (1980a) who identifies three basic strategies a business-level manager can choose: cost leadership, differentiation, and focus. These strategies can be used in manufacturing, service, or voluntary sport organizations. Sport managers can gain a competitive advantage for their organization by selecting a strategy appropriate both for the industry in which they are involved and the type of competitive position they seek to establish. Each of Porter's three strategic types are explained in more detail here.

Cost Leadership Strategy

A sport organization that adopts a **cost leadership** strategy prices its product or service lower than that of its competition by using cheaper labor (often developing countries), efficient manufacturing processes, economies of scale, technological innovation, and low levels of product differentiation. Sport organizations that follow a cost leadership strategy do not spend large amounts on new product or service development; rather, they follow market trends and provide the product feature or service when there is an established demand. The idea is that, by providing goods or services at a lower cost, a sport organization can capture a large share of the market or maintain higher profit margins.

Gore-Tex imitators such as Sympatex and Helly Hansen follow a cost leadership strategy. Dan Hansen, marketing coordinator at Helly Hansen said of his company's product, "Our best seller was a basic warm-up suit that retailed at about $120; a Gore product would cost $150 or more. By eliminating the middlemen, we can offer a comparable product at a more competitive price" ("Give them stormy weather," 1986). Many public-sector providers of sport services also follow a cost leadership strategy, in large part because of their mandate of catering to a broad client base.

The main strength of this type of strategy is that a cost advantage protects a sport organization from the fluctuations of the marketplace caused by such factors as changing input costs and imitators. Problems do arise, however, when a competitor finds a way to produce the same product at a lower cost. Cost leaders have to strive constantly to maintain their cost advantage.

There are several structural implications to using this type of strategy. Miller (1988) notes how cost leadership can be linked to control use with tighter control meaning lower costs. This control, combined with the need for economies of scale and efficient manufacturing processes, means that sport organizations that adopt a cost leadership strategy are likely to be centralized, high in complexity, and high in formalization.

Differentiation Strategy

Sport organizations that pursue a **differentiation strategy** attempt to gain a competitive advantage by presenting an image of their product or service as unique. Because the product or service is seen as unique, the sport organization is able to charge a premium price. Reebok followed a differentiation strategy in the athletic footwear industry with The Pump. Golf complexes, such as the Broadmoor did it with luxury and prestige in their service provision. L.L. Bean, the mail-order house specializing in outdoor sport equipment, does it in customer service with its unconditional guarantee: "You can send back a Bean product for any reason at any time, and get a replacement or your money back. Wear it a year, decide that it is not holding up, and send it back; the guarantee still holds" (Skow, 1985, p. 92). The main strength of a differentia-

tion strategy is that it develops product or service loyalty, a relatively enduring phenomenon. The weaknesses of this approach are maintaining the aura of uniqueness for the product or service in a changing market, and ensuring that pricing is in accordance with what the market will bear.

Because it requires creativity to produce unique products or services, sport organizations that adopt a differentiation strategy employ "technocrats—well trained experts such as scientists and engineers—to design innovations" (Miller, 1988, p. 282). Because these people work most efficiently in flexible structures, a sport organization that adopts a differentiation strategy will most likely exhibit low levels of complexity, low levels of formalization, and decentralized decision making.

Focus Strategy

Focus strategy is directed toward serving the needs of a particular market, one defined by such criteria as geographic area, age, sex, or segment of a product or service line. Once the particular market has been chosen, the sport organization decides on a cost leadership or differentiation strategy within that market. L.A. Gear, for example, entered the athletic footwear industry by initially focusing on "the Valley girl" set, 12- to 25-year-olds who wanted fashionable athletic shoes (L.A. Gear, 1988). Concentrating on this market, the company differentiated itself from other manufacturers by producing shoes with fringes, colored cutouts, brightly colored laces, and rhinestones. Human Kinetics has adopted a focus strategy: Although some publishers produce books on a range of subject areas, Human Kinetics specializes in physical education and exercise and sport science publications. Another example is Sumac Ridge Golf Club's decision to offer a women-only club (Kelowna Golf Club, 1994). In the public sector, the decision made by federal government officials to place the efforts of Sport Canada solely on elite sports could also be seen as a focus strategy.

The strengths of a focus strategy are that the company develops the ability to provide products and services that others cannot and, because of a focused market, the company can stay closer to its customers and more easily respond to their changing needs. The main disadvantage is that costs may be higher because of a generally smaller product volume. Also, there is the possibility that the market niche the company occupies, for example L.A. Gear's fashion footwear focus, may disappear or experience a decline in popularity. The type of structure adopted by a sport organization that follows a focus strategy will depend on whether or

TIME OUT   *Bill Nelson, Focusing on Pins*

Bill Nelson, a former marketing professor and entrepreneur, first became aware of the growing interest in decorative and collectible lapel pins during the 1984 Los Angeles Olympic Games. Seeing an opportunity to capitalize on the interest being generated, Nelson and his wife set up business in their home in Tucson, Arizona. While some retailers sell pins as one item in a wide array of sporting goods and memorabilia, Nelson focuses exclusively on pins. In 1988 he was described as the largest U.S. distributor of Olympic pins. He held the exclusive marketing rights to the Olympic pins of Time, Visa, Adidas, Maxwell House, Federal Express, and Blue Cross/Blue Shield. Nelson's strategy for his business involved not only the distribution of pins but also the creation of an eight-page publication titled *The Bill Nelson Newsletter*, which provided information about pins and pin buying, and served as a marketing tool for Nelson's business. The first

newsletter was distributed locally to about 200 "pinheads." By 1988 the newsletter, termed "the pinhead's bible," was mailed to more than 100,000 collectors.

Nelson's rapid success was helped by his decision to focus on a particular market. To cater to the needs of this market he provided information through his newsletter, which also promoted his business. His strategy also involved staying in close contact with his clients. He personalized all correspondence and developed camaraderie with these people. He responded immediately to collectors who answered ads he placed in consumer and trade sport publications. To facilitate the ordering of pins Nelson now makes extensive use of the fax machine and the Internet (www.billnelsonnewsletter.com) to reach as many people as possible.

Based on information in Going for gold (1988).

not it decides to focus either through differentiation or through a low-cost approach.

Stuck in the Middle

Not all sport organizations are able to gain a competitive advantage; some don't make the right choices about their product or service and the markets in which they wish to operate. Porter (1980a) describes these organizations as "**stuck in the middle.**"

Sport organizations get stuck in the middle for a variety of reasons. The low-cost company may decide to use some of its profits to diversify into product markets in which it has less experience, or to invest in research and development that management thinks may bolster the prestige of the organization. Such actions are expensive and have no guarantee of success. "Consequently, bad strategic decisions can quickly erode the cost leader's above-average profitability" (Hill & Jones, 1989, p. 137).

Differentiators may get undercut by imitators, who produce a cheaper or more specialized product. Those who adopt a focus strategy may not keep abreast of market trends and thus lose their market niche. Retaining a competitive advantage requires constant managerial action and attention

to possible tactics: monitoring the environment for changing trends, filing patents to prevent imitations, lobbying to restrict foreign competition, establishing contracts with suppliers to limit their ability to supply competitors, and even acquiring competitors.

Strategy Formulation and Implementation

Formulating and implementing a strategic plan involves a series of interrelated steps. These steps include formulating a mission statement for the sport organization, conducting an analysis of the organization's external environment and internal operations (sometimes called a SWOT analysis—Strengths, Weaknesses, Opportunities, and Threats), making choices about appropriate corporate- and business-level strategies, and selecting the correct organizational structure and integration and control systems to ensure that the strategy is effective. The first three steps are primarily about strategy formulation; the fourth step is the implementation stage. The process is shown graphically in figure 6.4

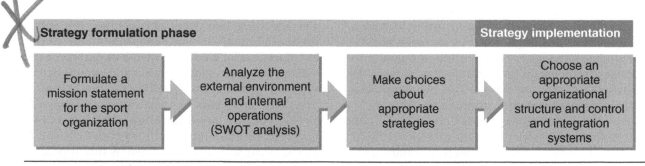

Figure 6.4 *Steps in the formulation and implementation of strategy.*

Although the process of formulating and implementing strategy is shown as a linear progression, it was noted earlier in this chapter that strategy formulation could be either deliberate or emergent. The traditional point of view has been to see strategy formulation as a deliberate process following a series of sequential steps. Emergent strategies are less likely to follow this clearly defined sequence. Sport managers must evaluate the merits of emergent strategies against the organization's mission, its operating strengths, its environmental opportunities, and so on. Only by undertaking this type of comparison is a manager able to determine the "fit" of that strategy for the sport organization. Each of the stages of strategy formulation and implementation are outlined in more detail here.

Defining a Mission Statement

The senior managers' first step in the formulation of a strategic plan involves defining a **mission statement** for the sport organization. They may invite representatives from other subunits, for example, unions, support staff, or students, to be involved in the process. The mission statement or official goal (see chapter 3) defines the purpose of the sport organization, what businesses it is in, and who its principal customers, users, or clients are. The mission statement serves as a foundation for the strategic planning process by prescribing direction for the future. As Hill and Jones (1989, p. 9) point out, it provides "the context within which intended strategies are formulated and the criteria against which emergent strategies are evaluated."

Internal and External Analysis

Once the sport organization's strategic planning group has established a mission statement, the next step in the process of strategy formulation is an analysis of the organization's external environment and internal operations. This step involves what is commonly called a SWOT analysis—an examination of opportunities and threats in the external environment of the organization, and the determination of its internal strengths and weaknesses. When analyzing the external environment, strategic planners must consider the industry or industries within which they are competing. This means looking at current and potential competitors, cost structures and margins, product differentiation levels, existing brand loyalties, and so on. Strategic planners must also consider the broader socioeconomic and political environment, including political issues, economic trends, globalization, and demographic shifts. All have the potential to affect a sport organization and hence must be considered. From an analysis of these environments, strategic planners can identify opportunities and threats facing the sport organization.

The internal analysis assesses strengths and weaknesses in the sport organization's operations by evaluating the available expertise and resources in areas such as research and development, manufacturing, marketing, human resources management, and new product development. In a sport organization that operates in more than one industry, the internal analysis should include an evaluation of the company's business portfolio using a technique such as the BCG matrix.

Selecting an Appropriate Strategy

The final stage in the strategy formulation phase involves making choices about the appropriate strategy or strategies for the sport organization. The choice of strategy will depend on the sport organization's mission and the match between its internal strengths/weaknesses and the external threats/opportunities. As Hill and Jones (1989, p. 12) point out, "For the single business organization, the objective is to match a company's strength to environmental opportunities in order to gain a competitive advantage and thus increase profits. For the multibusiness organization, the goal is to choose strategies for its portfolio of business that align the strengths and weaknesses of the portfolio with environmental opportunities and threats."

For example, for many years Converse was one of the strongest companies in the athletic footwear market; their black high-tops were standard wear on the basketball court. But the athletic footwear boom that started in the 1970s caught Converse off guard. Their black high-tops were not as appealing as the colorful and high-tech Nikes and Reeboks. Seeing the opportunities in athletic footwear, Converse president J.P. O'Neil and chief executive R.B. Loynd decided to focus on this market. "Our strategy," said O'Neil, "was to continue to gain in basketball while introducing strong performance shoes in all product categories." The company decided to change its internal operations by consolidating its strengths; it dumped such product lines as hockey pucks and fishing boots to concentrate on athletic footwear. To promote its athletic footwear a strong marketing campaign was developed that included purchasing the title of "Official Athletic Shoe of the 1984 Olympics." Although their popularity dipped during the 1990s, the recent retro fashion fad has made Converse popular again.

Mintzberg's Three Modes of Strategy Formulation

In each stage of the process of formulating strategy, sport organizations make a number of important decisions. What we have described so far would fit within Mintzberg's (1973b) planning mode of strategy formulation because of its highly rational approach prepared by an analyst or planner working with senior management. The highly structured process subjects all decision choices to systematic cost benefit analysis. In the **planning mode** the "organization's strategy is designed at essentially one point in time in a comprehensive process (all major decisions are interrelated). Because of this, planning forces the organization to think of global strategies and to develop an explicit sense of strategic direction" (Mintzberg, 1973b, p. 48). The planning mode of strategy formulation is most frequently used in large established sport organizations looking for both efficiency and growth.

Although the planning mode has been the most popular method of strategy formulation, Mintzberg

also identifies two other approaches: the entrepreneurial mode and the adaptive mode. In the **entrepreneurial mode**, the owner or entrepreneur makes decisions using intuition and experience to seek out growth opportunities for the organization. The early years of sport organizations such as Nike (cf. Strasser & Becklund, 1991) and Coleman, the outdoor sport outfitters (cf. Coleman & Jones, 1976), were characterized by this approach to strategy formulation. The entrepreneur makes bold decisions about "where his organization can make dramatic gains" (Mintzberg, 1973b, p. 45). This mode of strategy formulation is most frequently found in small and relatively new sport organizations. The process of strategy formulation involves only the owner or entrepreneur (and perhaps some close associates); it is informal in operation, and decisions are rarely committed to paper.

The main characteristic of the **adaptive mode** of strategy formulation is, as its name implies, a continual adjustment of organizational goals and the means by which they are to be achieved. The process of formulating strategy is a reactive one instead of a proactive searching for new opportunities (Mintzberg, 1973b). Decisions are made in an incremental and relatively disjointed manner. This approach to strategy formulation is used in established sport organizations where power is dispersed and there is no simple organizational goal. For example, we may find this approach to strategy formulation in a faculty of health, physical education and recreation where power is dispersed among faculty and where research, teaching, and service are all seen as important goals. Mintzberg suggests that Lindblom's (1959) term "the science of muddling through" is a good description of the adaptive approach to strategy formulation. Certain organizational conditions such as size, leadership, and the degree of competition and stability within the environment favor one mode of strategy formulation over another. It is, however, quite possible that an organization will operate with some combination of these three modes that reflects its particular needs.

Designing an Appropriate Organizational Structure and Selecting Control and Integration Systems

To implement the selected strategy or strategies, an appropriate organizational structure and the necessary control and integration systems need to be put into place. As we saw in chapters 4 and 5, a sport organization can be structured in a number of different ways. An appropriate structure is selected, based on decisions about how to distribute authority within a sport organization and what subunits are required to carry out its functions. Systems must be developed to integrate and control the actions of these various subunits. We discuss the relationship between strategy and structure next.

Strategy and Structure

As we saw in the preceding section of this chapter, an important aspect of implementing a strategic plan is the selection of an appropriate organizational structure along with the necessary integration and control systems. Different types of structures and systems "provide strategic planners with alternative means of pursuing different strategies because they lead the company and the people within it to act in different ways" (Hill & Jones, 1989, p. 222). In this section we look in more detail at the strategy-structure relationship. We start by focusing on the landmark contribution of Alfred Chandler that has influenced much subsequent work on this relationship. We then look at the best known of the contemporary work on this issue, the writings of Miles and Snow. Finally, we conclude the section by looking at the question, "Could structure determine strategy?"

Chandler's Work on the Strategy–Structure Relationship

Published in 1962 Chandler's book *Strategy and Structure*, the first substantive work to examine the relationship of strategy and structure, was based on a study of large American companies such as General Motors, Du Pont, and Sears. Chandler looked at changes in these organizations over a period of approximately 50 years. The companies began by offering a limited number of product lines and exhibited a centralized structure. As they grew they followed a diversification strategy; consequently, if they were to continue to function effectively, they needed a different type of structure. The new structure was more complex because units were added and, over time, decisions were decentralized. Chandler's (1962, p. 15) main conclusion was that a new organizational strategy "required a new or at least refash-

ioned structure if the enlarged enterprise was to be operated efficiently." That is, structure had to follow strategy.

Chandler's research suffered from his limited conceptualization of strategy and structure. In his study, strategy was limited to growth through diversification, and structure was limited to divisionalization. Also, his results cannot be generalized because the organizations in his study were large corporations; there was no attempt to include other types and sizes of organizations. Nevertheless, despite its shortcomings, Chandler's work has been replicated by a number of other scholars (cf. Channon, 1973; Rumelt, 1974), who have all used similar types of organizations to confirm his general findings. It would appear, at least in certain cases, strategy does indeed influence structure. However, the concept of strategy is very broad, and recent work has extended and elaborated ideas about the strategy–structure relationship.

Miles and Snow's Strategic Typology

The best known of the more recent work on strategy and structure is Miles and Snow's four-part classification of organizations as Defenders, Prospectors, Analyzers, and Reactors.

Defenders

Organizations that adopt this type of strategy attempt to limit themselves to a narrow range of products or services offered to only "a limited segment of the total potential market, and the segment chosen is frequently one of the healthiest of the entire market" (Miles & Snow, 1978, p. 37). Organizations operating with this type of strategy carve out a niche for themselves and then work very hard to protect it. They strive for internal efficiencies while at the same time seek to improve the quality and price of their product or service. Because they are inwardly focused, Defenders tend not to pay a lot of attention to changes outside of their immediate domain. The type of structure associated with a Defender strategy is centralized, with a high level of task specialization and a relatively high level of formalization. The centralized structure means control is in the hands of senior managers; integration is achieved through formalized policies and procedures.

An example of a sport organization that has successfully adopted a Defender strategy is the Running Room, a specialty store for running equipment, founded in Edmonton in 1984, with branches in Canada and the United States. The owner of the store quickly carved out a niche in local markets by providing quality running equipment and knowledgeable staff. Although the company experimented with aerobics gear, it found it was more successful just focusing on running. The owner felt that in trying to service a wider market, the company sacrificed focus. He noted (as quoted in a course paper by Liz Zahary at the University of Alberta), "the more we do [stick to our core market] the more successful we've been; then at least you're known for something." In a similar vein, a college or university athletic department that traditionally offers (and is successful in) a limited number of intercollegiate sports, instead of offering a wide range of activities, could be seen as operating with a Defender strategy.

Prospectors

In contrast to Defenders, who stick to established products and markets, Prospectors actively seek new products and new market opportunities. These companies establish their reputation by being the first on the market with new products. Because their success depends on innovation, Prospectors must scan their environments constantly for new trends and opportunities. The need for Prospectors to respond rapidly to environmental changes means they must adopt a flexible structure. Employees require the type of skills that enable them to be moved from one project to another; consequently, task specialization is low, as is formalization; decision making is decentralized but there are complex integration systems. Control is achieved largely through the professional status of the Prospector's employees. W.L. Gore & Associates is an example of a company operating with a Prospector strategy. Constantly looking for new applications for its products—used in running suits, skiwear, and camping equipment—the company has adopted a very informal operating structure referred to as a "lattice" organization (cf. Rhodes, 1982).

Analyzers

Analyzers lie somewhere between Defenders and Prospectors. "A true Analyzer is an organization that minimizes risk while maximizing the opportunity for profit . . . [it] combines the strength of both the Prospector and the Defender into a single system" (Miles & Snow, 1978, p. 68). The Analyzer operates with a mix of products and markets, some of which will exhibit stability while others will be more dynamic. In the stable product market areas Analyzers operate as routinely and efficiently as they possibly can. In the changing environment Analyzers watch their competitors for new, popular products and then move quickly to copy the idea so that their product arrives on the market on the heels of the developer. The idea is to maintain a base of traditional products while at the same time locate and exploit the opportunities available in new markets and products.

The sport organization adopting an Analyzer strategy will have to develop a structure that allows them to exercise tight controls over the stable product and market areas, and looser controls over the areas in which new products are being developed. The organization adopts a more formalized and centralized structure in the former product/market areas and a more decentralized and flexible structure in the latter. Because of the presence of different types of subunits, control involves a delicate balance between systems that are "centralized and budget-oriented to encourage cost-efficient production of standard products [and systems that are] . . . decentralized and results-oriented so as to enhance the effectiveness with which new products can be adapted" (Miles & Snow, 1978, p. 77). The Analyzer label has been ascribed to companies that mass-produce imitations of popular brands, such as the major athletic footwear companies (cf. "U.S. dollar decline," 1988). However, it has also been attached to larger and better-known companies such as Digital Equipment Corporation and IBM (cf. Robbins, 1990), both tangentially involved in the sport industry, the former through its involvement as the official computer vendor of the NFL ("Digital scores with the NFL," 1986) and the latter through its sponsorship of the Olympic Games.

Reactors

Reactors are organizations that do not respond appropriately to their environment. Organizations find themselves operating with a Reactor strategy when "(1) management fails to articulate a viable organizational strategy; (2) a strategy is articulated but technology, structure, and process are not linked to it in an appropriate manner; or (3) management adheres to a particular strategy–structure relationship even though it is no longer relevant to environmental conditions" (Miles & Snow, 1978, p. 82). Because a Reactor strategy is an inappropriate strategy, there are no clear linkages between this type of strategy and structure.

Strategies: According to Environment and Structure

The first three of these strategic positions are each appropriate under different environmental conditions and each requires a different type of structure. It is, of course, possible that two managers in different sport organizations within the same industry may scan their environment and respond with a different strategy. In the 1980s, Paul Fireman of Reebok saw a changing environment for the athletic footwear industry because of the aerobics boom. Consequently, he adopted a Prospector strategy and his company aggressively pursued the aerobics market. Philip Knight and the people at Nike saw aerobics as a passing fad and so adopted a Defender strategy, concentrating on its already successful running shoe business.

Managers who pursue a Prospector strategy need to adopt an organizational structure that can respond quickly to changing environmental conditions. Consequently, they cannot be encumbered by highly formalized procedures and hierarchies that have centralized control through senior managers. Defenders can function with this type of structure because their environment is stable, or changing very slowly, and the highly formalized and bureaucratic structure allows them to capitalize on the efficiencies it provides. Sport organizations that choose an Analyzer strategy must balance the quest for efficiency with the need to be able to respond rapidly to change.

Could Structure Determine Strategy?

Much of the literature on the strategy–structure relationship has followed Chandler and worked from the premise that the selection of an appropriate structure comes after the selection of a strategy. However, a number of writers (cf. Bourgeois & Astley, 1979; Burgelman, 1983; Fahey, 1981) suggest that it is quite possible that structure determines the choice of strategy, or that they evolve simultaneously.

One way to think about the strategy–structure relationship is that decisions on what to do next should be based, at least in part, on the organization's structure and on its capabilities. Fredereckson (1986) looked at the effect that structural dimensions of centralization, formalization, and complexity could have on strategic choice. His ideas are summarized in figure 6.5.

On the other hand, proponents of the Austrian School (e.g., Schumpeter, 1950; Kirzner, 1973; Jacobson, 1992) and authors such as Mintzberg (1990, p. 183) view the structure–strategy relationship as a coordinated one:

> No organization ever wipes the slate clean when it changes its strategy. The past counts, just as the environment does, and the structure is a significant part of that past. . . . We conclude, therefore,

---

TIME OUT   *Coke and Pepsi Follow an Analyzer Strategy in the Sport Beverage Market*

Since it first purchased Gatorade in the mid-1980s, Quaker Oats has turned the sport beverage into an operation with sales of approximately $1 billion. Quaker's success has not gone unnoticed by soft-drink industry giants Coca-Cola and PepsiCo. After some years of watching Gatorade grow, Coke introduced PowerAde and Pepsi brought out All Sport to challenge the Quaker company's preeminent position. In addition to using the force of their distribution operation to promote their new sport drinks, Coke and Pepsi started using their marketing departments to lure away Gatorade drinkers. Basketball star Shaquille O'Neal was recruited by Pepsi; Coke signed football and baseball player Deion Sanders. Both companies also started promoting their new drink through sponsorship of sporting events. These actions started hurting Gatorade's market. The 86.5 percent share held by Gatorade at the beginning of March 1983 was down by 3.6 points in March 1994. To fight back, Quaker Oats expanded its distribution channels beyond grocery stores into vending machines and other outlets, and doubled its advertising spending to over $50 million. To this day, Coke and Pepsi are still battling each other for drink supremacy.

Based on information in Gatorade is starting to pant (1994).

Centralization

As the level of centralization increases, so does the probability that

- the strategic decision process will be initiated only by the dominant few, and that it will be the result of proactive, opportunity-seeking behavior;
- the decision process will be oriented toward achieving "positive" goals (i.e., intended future domains) that will persist in spite of significant changes in means;
- strategic action will be the result of intendedly rational "strategic choice," and moves will be major departures from the existing strategy; and
- top management's cognitive limitations will be the primary constraint on the comprehensiveness of the strategic process; the integration of decisions will be relatively high.

Formalization

As the level of formalization increases, so does the probability that

- the strategic decision process will be initiated only in response to problems or crises that appear in variables that are monitored by the formal system;
- decisions will be made to achieve precise, yet remedial goals, and that means will displace ends (goals);
- strategic action will be the result of standardized organizational processes, and moves will be incremental; and
- the level of detail that is achieved in the standardized organizational processes will be the primary constraint on the comprehensiveness of the strategic decision process; the integration of decisions will be intermediate.

Complexity

As the level of complexity increases, so does the probability that

- members initially exposed to the decision stimulus will not recognize it as being strategic, or will ignore it because of parochial preferences;
- a decision must satisfy a large constraint set, which decreases the likelihood that decisions will be made to achieve organization-level goals;
- strategic action will be the result of an internal process of political bargaining, and moves will be incremental;
- biases induced by members' parochial perceptions will be the primary constraint on the comprehensiveness of the strategic decision process; in general, the integration of decisions will be low.

Figure 6.5 *Propositions regarding the effects of three dimensions of structure.*

ACADEMY OF MANAGEMENT REVIEW by J.W. FREDERECKSON. Copyright 1986 by ACAD OF MGMT. Reproduced with permission of ACAD OF MGMT in the format Textbook via Copyright Clearance Center.

that structure follows strategy as the left foot follows the right in walking. In effect strategy and structure both support the organization. None takes precedence: each always precedes the other and follows it.

This coordinated view has started to dominate the management literature. However some questions still remain. For example, what is the impact of the organization's development stage? In newer organizations managerial choice is likely to be far less constrained than in older organizations, in which structures and modes of operation are well established and hence more likely to constrain choice on strategy issues. Or, how much lag time is there between a strategic decision and its impact on structure? Does this lag time vary within or between industries?

Researchers are also looking at other factors that can influence the strategy–structure relationship. For example, what types of changes in the environment have an impact on strategy and structure and how? How do internal and external innovations affect the strategy–structure relationship within an organization?

The point here is that many questions still need to be answered about the strategy–structure relationship and strategy in general. Strategy is now a popular area of study in organization-management theory; most business schools offer specific courses on business strategy (or "policy" as it is called when related to public-sector organizations). However, few studies focus specifically on strategy in sport organizations. Since sport organizations, like all other organizations, implicitly or explicitly formulate strategy, which in turn influences many other aspects of management, more work needs to be undertaken on this topic in sport management.

Strategy in Voluntary Sport Organizations

Of the small amount of research carried out on the strategies employed by sport organizations, much has focused on the voluntary sector. In a study of Canadian national sport organizations Thibault, Slack, and Hinings (1993) developed a theoreti-cal framework to identify four types of strategies that could be pursued by these organizations. Using work by MacMillan (1983) on nonprofit organizations, Thibault et al. (1993) identified six strategic imperatives that must be considered when developing strategies: fundability, the ability of the sport organization to secure financial resources from external sources; size of client base, the number of clients the sport organization serves; volunteer appeal, the organization's ability to attract human resources; support group appeal, the extent to which the sport organization's programs are visible and appealing to those groups capable of providing current or future support; equipment costs, the amount of money required for equipment at the introductory levels of the sport; and affiliation fees, the costs associated with participating in a sport.

The first four of these imperatives were seen to constitute the organization's level of program attractiveness, that is, its ability to provide services and programs to its members while at the same time securing the necessary resources for these programs. The last two imperatives made up the sport organization's competitive position, that is, its potential to attract and retain members. By dividing the dimensions of program attractiveness and competitive position into high and low components, Thibault et al. (1993) were able to construct a 2 × 2 matrix as shown in figure 6.6. The four quadrants within the matrix represent the

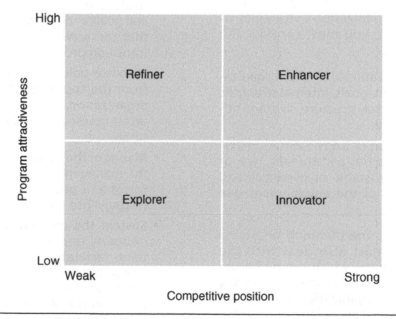

Figure 6.6 *National sport organization strategic types.*

Reprinted, by permission, from L. Thibault, T. Slack, and C.R. Hinings, 1993, "A framework for the analysis of strategy in non-profit sport organizations," *Journal of Sport Management* 7: 1.

types of strategy that national sport organizations can pursue.

Enhancers were those national sport organizations that scored high on both dimensions, such as badminton and soccer. These sport organizations already had well-developed strategies in place and an existing network through which to operationalize new initiatives. The sports in this category were generally popular and inexpensive to pursue; this position gave them the opportunity to experiment with new programs at little risk, thereby enhancing their already well-established strategic position. **Innovators**, such as diving and lacrosse, had a strong competitive position but low program attractiveness. That is, they were relatively cheap to pursue but had little in the way of existing programs and members, so the strategic focus of these organizations was a need to adopt innovative initiatives to get people involved. The strong competitive position of innovators helped these organizations because there were few cost barriers to participation in their sport. **Refiners**, such as hockey or Canadian football, already had well-established strategies but their weak competitive position, that is, the high costs associated with their sport, made expanding these programs difficult. These sport organizations were expected to follow a strategy of refining existing programs. **Explorers**, such as alpine skiing and equestrian, were in the worst strategic position, since they had low levels of program attractiveness and their sport was costly. It was expected that these organizations would explore a number of strategies to create programs to enhance their sport's position. Later, Thibault, Slack, and Hinings (1994) empirically verified the dimensions of their framework and located a sample of national sport organizations according to the type of strategy they were following.

KEY ISSUES FOR MANAGERS

As a manager, you will have to formulate and implement strategies to help your organization become successful. Your hierarchical level will, however, determine whether you will be dealing more with corporate- or business-level strategies. Remember that strategies may not be clear from the outset; they may emerge over time. With this in mind, if you want to determine your organization's strategies or develop a strategy, you must consider the following elements.

- Your organization's nature: organizational mission, goals, internal strengths and weaknesses, structure, size, and tolerance for risk.
- Your organization's environment: external opportunities and threats, type of environment (stable or dynamic), and composition of the environment (see chapter 8).

These points cover the planning phase. As a manager, you must also deal with the implementation phase, which can be harder to do than the planning phase because any change within an organization can lead to resistance. To encourage implementation you must do the following:

- **Motivate.** Establish an environment in which organizational members accept the need for the strategic change and are physically and psychologically committed to the transition.
- **Create and communicate the vision of the desired future state.** Relate the new strategy to the organization's mission and goals and set up intermediate goals that can serve as benchmarks for the transition process.
- **Mobilize political support for change from the top levels of power in the organization.** Reinforce legitimacy and access to resources to facilitate the transition.
- **Manage the transition.** Implement the management structures (e.g., task force) and processes that will set the strategy into motion.
- **Sustain the momentum.** Provide the necessary resources, build support systems, facilitate skills and competency development, and back up desired behavior through a rewards system (Cummings & Worley, 1993). For more information on the change process, see chapter 12.

SUMMARY AND CONCLUSIONS

Organizational strategy is concerned with the long-term goals and objectives of a sport organization. Strategy, one of the major determinants of organizational structure, can be deliberate or emergent. Strategy can be formulated at two levels, the corporate level and the business level. Corporate-level strategies may focus on growth, stability, or decline (defensive strategies); companies may also adopt these strategies in combination. One technique used to determine the strategic needs of a corporation is portfolio analysis. Business-level strategies are used by individual business units to gain a competitive advantage. The most commonly used business-level strategies are cost leadership, product differentiation, and focus.

Strategy formulation and implementation involve a series of steps, including formulating a mission statement, conducting an assessment of external threats and opportunities and internal strengths and weaknesses, selecting the appropriate strategy or strategies, and designing the necessary organizational structure, control, and integration systems. Mintzberg suggests three modes of strategy formulation: the planning mode, the entrepreneurial mode, and the adaptive mode.

The relationship between strategy and structure has been a topic of considerable debate. Alfred Chandler, one of the first writers in this area, suggested that structure follows strategy; a number of other researchers replicated Chandler's work and produced similar results. Recent research, however, has suggested that strategy and structure evolve simultaneously. Work by Miles and Snow identified four strategic types: Defenders, Prospectors, Analyzers, and Reactors. Each strategic type is associated with a particular set of structural arrangements.

KEY CONCEPTS

acquisition (p. 113)

adaptive mode (p. 122)

business-level strategy (p. 112)

cash cows (p. 117)

combination strategy (p. 116)

corporate-level strategy (p. 112)

cost leadership (p. 118)

deliberate strategy (p. 111)

differentiation strategy (p. 119)

diversification (p. 112)

divestiture (p. 116)

dogs (p. 118)

emergent strategy (p. 111)

enhancers (p. 128)

entrepreneurial mode (p. 122)

explorers (p. 128)

focus strategy (p. 119)

harvesting strategy (milking) (p. 115)

horizontal integration (p. 113)

innovators (p. 128)

joint venture (p. 114)

liquidation (p. 116)

merger (p. 113)

mission statement (p. 121)

planning mode (p. 122)

portfolio analysis (p. 112)

question marks (p. 117)

refiners (p. 128)

stars (p. 117)

strategic business unit (p. 117)

stuck in the middle (p. 120)

SWOT analysis (p. 120)

takeover (p. 113)

turnaround (p. 115)

vertical integration (p. 113)

REVIEW QUESTIONS

1. Strategy is more than just setting goals and objectives. What else does it involve?

2. What is the difference between a sport organization with a deliberate strategy and one with an emergent strategy?

3. How does the concept of corporate strategy apply to a university athletic department?

4. Why would a sport organization engage in (a) forward integration, (b) backward integration? Give examples.

5. When would a company within the sport industry use a harvesting strategy? What are its benefits?

6. What are the benefits of a liquidation strategy to a sport organization?

7. A strategic business unit that moves from "a question mark" to "a star" to "a cash cow" has followed a success sequence. Why? What type of movement might be labeled a disaster sequence?

8. What type of structure do you associate with each of Porter's strategic types?

9. If you were formulating a strategy for a university athletic department, what factors do you think you would have to consider in your external analysis?

10. What type of sport organization would you expect to find using the planning mode of strategy formulation? The entrepreneurial mode? The adaptive mode?

11. Why did Chandler conclude that structure followed strategy? Do you think his conclusions would have been different had he used a different sample of organizations?

12. In what type of business-level strategies would you expect a Prospector sport organization to engage?

13. What type of structure would you expect to find associated with each of Miles and Snow's strategic types?

14. Develop an argument that strategy follows structure.

15. How might the stage of a sport organization's development affect the choice of a strategy?

SUGGESTIONS FOR FURTHER READING

A fairly large body of literature within the broader field of management focuses on the topic of organizational strategy. In fact, a major publication, the *Strategic Management Journal*, deals exclusively with research on organizational strategy. Of the available literature, probably the best-known work on strategy is the Porter trilogy *Competitive Strategy: Techniques for Analyzing Industries and Competitors* (1980a), *Competitive Advantage: Creating and Sustaining Superior Performance* (1985), and *The Competitive Advantage of Nations and Their Firms* (1989). Of less popular appeal but equally substantive is the work of Danny Miller. Examples of his work on strategy include his (1986) "Configurations of Strategy and Structure" and (1987b) "The Structural and Environmental Correlates of Business Strategy," both in *Strategic Management Journal;* "Strategy Making and Structure: Analysis and Implications for Performance" (1987a) and "Relating Porter's Business Strategies to Environment and Structure: Analysis and Performance Implications" (1988) appear in the *Academy of Management Journal*. You may also wish to read Miller's (1990) book *The Icarus Paradox*.

You are also recommended to read Miles and Snow's (1978) book *Organizational Strategy, Structure, and Process*; and Quinn, Mintzberg, and James' *The Strategy Process: Concepts, Contexts, and Cases* (1988), a large collection of readings about various aspects of organizational strategy.

There are theories in strategy literature that are increasing in popularity that deal less with the structure aspect and more with determining what will help the organization gain a sustained competitive advantage. For example, the Austrian School believes this is done through entrepreneurial discovery (see Jacobson, 1992). The resource-based view focuses on the importance of the organization's resources, especially intangible resources (see Barney, 1991a; 1991b; Amis, Pant, & Slack, 1997). The knowledge-based view focuses its attention on one intangible resource, knowledge, believing that this resource is the key to success (see Winter, 1987; Kogut & Zander, 1992).

Within the sport management literature there is a large void when it comes to strategy. Chalip and Leyns (2002) are one of the few with a study on business leveraging as a strategy in the context of sporting events. However, some indication of the types of strategies pursued by sport organizations can be gained from books such as Strasser and Becklund's (1991) *Swoosh: The Story of Nike and the Men Who Played There*, and from the articles on sport organizations found in business magazines such as *Fortune*, *Forbes*, and *Business Week*.

CASE FOR ANALYSIS

Roman Abramovich

Described as a "Russian oligarch," Roman Abramovich was born in Saratov, Russia, on October 24, 1966. By the age of four he was an orphan—his mother was killed when he was 18 months old and his father later died in a construction accident. He then went on to be adopted by his paternal uncle and raised by his Jewish family in Komi, northwest Russia. Abramovich attended the Industrial Institute in Ukhta but his academic

Roman Abramovich, a Russian oil tycoon, diversified his business interests by purchasing the British soccer club, Chelsea.

© Associated Press, AP

career was interrupted when he was drafted into the Soviet Red Army. He eventually returned to school and earned a law degree from Moscow State Law Academy in 2000.

Abramovich's early business ventures ranged from selling plastic ducks from an apartment in Moscow to owning pig farms and ultimately to his interest in oil. His first break came in 1992 when he was befriended by Boris Berezovsky, who brought him into the inner circle of former Russian president Boris Yeltsin. Berezovsky advised him to buy shares in Sibneft (Russia's fifth-largest oil company), which had recently become privatized after the fall of communism. Later in 2001 Berezovsky moved to Britain after a falling out with new president Vladimir Putin and ongoing criminal investigations into fraud. This move opened the way for Abramovich. His business successes included the accumulation of 80 percent of Sibneft, 50 percent of Rusal (the Russian aluminum oil monopoly) and 26 percent of Aeroflot (Russia's national airline). The eventual sale of Aeroflot is said to have funded Abramovich's buyout of Chelsea Football Club.

In addition to his business ventures Abramovich entered into politics. In 2000 he became governor of a small northeastern province of Chukotka, Russia, with a population of only 73,000. Some of Abramovich's critics say that this move was merely a ploy to secure higher political office. Abramovich poured over U.S.$200 million into the region, building everything from hotels to supermarkets and cinemas. He even brought in some of his staff from Sibneft to help run the province.

Not only did Abramovich have interests in Russian business and politics, but he also invested in the sport and entertainment industry, buying a television station and ice hockey team. But he loved soccer, and sought to diversify his business ventures outside of Russia by purchasing a leading British soccer team, Chelsea. This move also capitalized on his links with Britain (i.e., Berezovsky and Millhouse Capital, the company that controlled Abramovich's assets). His purchase of Chelsea (or *Chelski* as it is now referred to by the British tabloids) was celebrated by the fans and staff, who saw a new infusion of money into the club. The choice of Chelsea was not random; several other clubs had been considered. Abramovich was looking for a club that was already good and had the potential to go to the top of the game. He wiped out the club's debts and spent close to £24 million (approximately U.S.$44 million) to secure star players like Damien Duff and Wayne Bridge. Chelsea saw almost immediate success.

Based on information from BBC News (2004), Frost (2004), Tran (2003), Wikipedia (2005).

Questions

1. How would you describe the strategy that Abramovich has followed to date?

2. Do a SWOT analysis of Chelsea before and after being bought by Abramovich.

3. Why are Abramovich and Chelsea a good fit?

4. What strategy should Abramovich use in the future?

Chapter **7**

Strategic Alliances

LEARNING OBJECTIVES

When you have read this chapter you should be able to

1. explain what a strategic alliance is,
2. explain the different forms of alliances,
3. describe the key issues in establishing an alliance, and
4. describe the key issues in managing an alliance.

A TRACK AND FIELD CLUB AND LOCAL HIGH SCHOOL FORM AN ALLIANCE

In November 2003, an Ottawa, Ontario, Canada, high school, the École Secondaire Publique Louis-Riel, announced it was partnering with the local track and field club, the Ottawa Lions, to build an indoor multisport facility. The high school wanted its students and the local community to have a place to practice a variety of sports all year round.

Searching for ways to improve its current facilities, the high school came up with the idea of an inflatable building the size of 12 regulation-size gymnasiums that could be set up on its grounds. A 400-meter track proposed in the plan would be the only national competition-standard indoor track in Canada. There were obstacles—the high school's administra-tion and financing. As a government-funded institution facing years of financial cutbacks, the school had neither the resources (financial and human) nor the time to build and maintain such a facility.

To circumvent the problems, Louis-Riel high school entered into an alliance with the Ottawa Lions Track and Field Club, a nonprofit organization. The partnership would provide the club with a year-round training and competition facility. In turn, the club would finance the project and manage the facility, which would be available to the public for use and rental. Any profit would go back into Louis-Riel, making this a win–win situation for both organizations.

Based on information from Ottawa Lions Track and Field Club (2003).

The indoor facility would not have been possible without the alliance that was formed. This approach, called **strategic alliances**, is a strategy that organizations are discovering and implementing in a variety of ways. It has helped groups defend themselves against stronger competitors, go on the offensive to secure a stronger position, and create new opportunities for first-mover advantage, just to name several advantages. An organization that is proactive in entering strategic alliances is found to have superior market-based performance, especially if the organization is small or is in an unstable environment (Sarkar, Echambadi, & Harrison, 2001). The number of strategic alliances has, on average, grown by 25 percent from 1987 to 2000. However, between 50 percent and 70 percent of alliances fail (Barringer & Harrison, 2000). What defines one of these strategic alliances? How do you, as a manager, establish a strategic alliance? Once they are established, how do you manage them so that they are successful? These are the main issues that we will deal with in this chapter.

What Are Strategic Alliances?

Strategic alliances have alternatively been called interfirm cooperation, interorganizational relationships, and joint ventures. However, a joint venture is only one type of strategic alliance. Generally, a strategic alliance is a partnership between two organizations formed in response to an essential opportunity or a threat in the environment (Child & Faulkner, 1998). What makes them different from partnerships is that strategic alliances are based on organizational learning, as in the case of **joint ventures**, **collaborations**, and **consortia**. For example, Disney Corporation could be considered a very large consortium because it includes alliances with media organizations (ESPN, ABC, Web sites, and radio stations), sport teams (e.g., Mighty Ducks hockey team), and entertainment organizations (movie studios, publications, a cruise line, and theme parks). These organizations within the Disney Corporation work together to, for example,

The Anaheim Mighty Ducks, a National Hockey League team, is only one of many organizations that have strategic alliances with Disney Corporation.

promote each other's products and decrease business costs. Partnerships based on skill-substitution arrangements, such as networks or virtual corporations, are not "pure" strategic alliances. However, all are possible forms of cooperative strategies, in contrast to purely competitive strategies. More precisely, joint ventures, networks, and other cooperative strategies allow organizations to compete more effectively through alliances between two organizations within or across industries. This allows organizations to go beyond simply focusing on how the organization can gain a competitive advantage within an industry or for a specific product market.

Before discussing the types of strategic alliances and how to manage them, we need to establish the key characteristics of successful strategic alliances and why an organization would want to form a strategic alliance. Successful strategic alliances are based on *organizational learning* and on *trust*. There cannot be mutual organizational learning without trust. Also, trust must be present because cooperative strategies create mutual dependence between the two organizations (Child & Faulkner, 1998).

Organizational Learning

Organizational learning is the key characteristic that differentiates strategic alliances from other cooperative strategies. Child and Faulkner (1998) describe three levels of organizational learning. The lowest level is technical learning. It focuses on organizational routines. This type of learning emphasizes an organization's acquisition of new and more efficient ways, techniques, or procedures in relation to management or production. For example, Disney may form an alliance with a top retail chain (e.g., Wal-Mart) to learn how to distribute its clothing line more efficiently.

The middle level involves systemic learning. It focuses on how an organization "reeducates" itself to find new ways to integrate its various activities. For example, Disney has partnerships with media and entertainment organizations in order to handle its movie production component, produce movies (e.g., *The Mighty Ducks* movie series), promote the movies, and distribute those movies to the general public.

The highest level is strategic learning. It is purely about the "reeducating" process. This type of learning emphasizes changes in management mind set, especially in how to determine the conditions for organizational success. For example,

Disney forms an alliance with the International Olympic Committee (IOC) to promote the "goodness" of playing sports in Third World countries. It is then seen as a benevolent corporate citizen, a necessary condition for a company to be successful worldwide.

Within alliances, there are two possible learning situations: an underlying collaborative atmosphere and an underlying competitive atmosphere. Collaborative learning can be done in two ways: An organization can learn from its partner or with its partner. The former would be done if the organization has access to the partner's skills and knowledge (e.g., Disney managers learn media management techniques from ABC). The latter would occur if neither partner has a particular knowledge or skill needed as a result of the alliance (especially seen for the development of new technologies). Also, after becoming an alliance, the resulting organization will have to learn how to manage itself. In other words, it will learn what works for it, what doesn't, what should be done, and what can be done. Competitive learning occurs if an organization wants to learn as much as possible about its partner but provide the least amount of information possible to the partner, instead of approaching the alliance as a mutual learning opportunity (Child & Faulkner, 1998). This form of learning may be increasingly popular. For example, large companies such as Nike and Reebok enter emerging economies through alliances with local companies to learn as much as possible about the new market, but they do not have to share their secrets. Over time, collaborative learning is seen as the more productive learning situation (Child & Faulkner, 1998).

For learning to take place, three conditions must be met. They seem obvious when stated, but are not as easy to achieve in practice. First, the organization must have the intention of learning. Value must be placed on the learning opportunities that arise during the alliance. Second, the organization must have the capacity for learning to occur. This means that knowledge must be transferable: Members must be receptive to new information, have the abilities to understand and apply it in the new organization, and must be able to learn from previous experiences and transfer that knowledge to future experiences. Third, the organization must be able to convert the new knowledge into a usable resource that can be disseminated to key individuals throughout the organization (Child & Faulkner, 1998). This can be done through socialization (sharing experiences so that tacit knowledge is transferred from one member to the next), externalization (transforming tacit knowledge into explicit knowledge through different concepts, policies), combination (combining different explicit knowledge elements), and internalization (incorporating explicit knowledge with tacit knowledge; learning by doing) (Nonaka & Takeuchi, 1995).

Learning within alliances can take different forms.

- **Forced:** pressure to learn from the other partner
- **Imitation or experimentation:** desire to copy or try new things
- **Blocked:** lack of opportunity to share knowledge
- **Received:** knowledge willingly received from a partner
- **Integrative:** knowledge shared between partners
- **Segmented:** trust insufficient for easy exchange of knowledge
- **Nonlearning:** insufficient exchange of knowledge; partners operate separately (Child & Markoczy, 1993).

Trust

Organizational trust is the key characteristic of successful strategic alliances because alliances create interdependencies between the partners. Admittedly, if two competitors want to enter into a strategic alliance, it is hard for each to trust the other when they have been rivals for many years. To be more precise, the trust must be between the individuals who work for the organizations forming the alliance. Child and Faulkner (1998) suggest that trust evolves in three stages. In the beginning, there is calculative trust. Here, trust is about expectations between partners, about the willingness to work with each other after weighing the costs and benefits of the alliance. Calculative trust is often based on institutional protection and on the other's reputation. For example, NBC may have determined that it would be cost effective to use a local Chinese broadcaster as a partner to televise the 2008 Olympics through an existing cable network. Once sharing occurs and the alliance is implemented, calculative trust can become mutual understanding. Here, trust is about getting to know more about each other, about sharing ways of thinking. It is knowledge-based. The NBC–Chi-

nese-broadcaster alliance may be mutually beneficial in the sense that the Chinese broadcaster may learn new ways of broadcasting sporting events while NBC learns how to do business in China. As the strategic alliance continues to evolve, mutual understanding can become bonding. Here, trust becomes identity-based. You share common values and moral obligations. The partners start to share an identity in a way. It is akin to a friendship in which each member can place himself in the hands of the other, voluntarily. Over the years, for example, the NBC–Chinese-broadcaster alliance may become so strong that both partners decide to enter into a new venture together, thereby putting the success of each company in the other's hands. As the alliance evolves, so too should trust, if each partner recognizes the positive benefits gained, the mutual investments of each partner, and the increasing potential costs of breaking the alliance (Lewicki & Bunker, 1996; Child & Faulkner, 1998). However, Hamel, Doz, and Prahalad (2002) warn that collaboration is still competition, only in a different form. An organization must be careful about competitive compromise; cooperation does have limits.

Motives for Establishing a Strategic Alliance

Why would an organization risk sharing its precious knowledge and skills with another organization? There are three main interrelated reasons for entering a strategic alliance. The first reason is cost or risk reduction. More precisely, organizations may enter into an alliance because it is the best option to reduce transaction costs, because they want to spread the risk of the venture, or because they want to achieve economies of scale. The second reason is to improve the organization's strategic position. This can include co-opting or blocking competitors, overcoming government or other stakeholder trade and investment barriers, facilitating expansion (especially internationally), and taking advantage of vertical quasi-integration of a supplier or buyer represented by the partner. The third reason is the opportunity for organizational learning. This can include technology exchanges or management techniques (cf. Contractor & Lorange, 1988; Kogut, 1988; Child & Faulkner, 1998). These three reasons are especially seen when, for example, a media organization wants to enter a new market. With today's globalization trend and the Olympics going to Beijing, China, in 2008, you can imagine that media organizations are very interested in entering the huge Chinese market. Without any knowledge of the media setup in China or of Chinese laws and procedures, and lacking any reputation in this new context, it is very hard to enter the market. It then makes sense for a media network such as NBC to enter into a strategic alliance with a Chinese broadcaster. The foreign partner learns how to do business in that country, uses existing infrastructure, and relies on the other organization's reputation to increase its market. In turn, the local organization can increase its technological knowledge and resources.

The preceding reasons are mainly economic in nature. These reasons are not always sufficient for managers. There is usually a political reason underlying the final decision to form a strategic alliance (e.g., the desire to enter the world's largest potential consumer markets, such as China). This is apparent in the argument that the alliance is the best strategy when organizations face a specific environmental threat or opportunity, or an internal strength or weakness. These catalysts need not be the same for both partners, but they must be complementary; the objectives of the alliance must fit each organization's corporate and business goals. The decision to enter into an alliance is, of course, done with incomplete information—the manager does not know the exact transaction cost or potential benefit, and cannot precisely predict the future—so senior management politics (read power) enter the scene (Child & Faulkner, 1998).

Establishing Strategic Alliances

As manager of an organization, you may have decided that you need to form a strategic alliance with another organization. You now face two decisions: who will be your partner and what form the alliance should take. After a review of the literature, Child and Faulkner (1998) argue that there are two basic qualities that should be present in a potential alliance partner: strategic fit and cultural fit. **Strategic fit** between your organization and the potential partner refers to how complementary the organizations are in terms of assets and capabilities (think SWOT analysis; see chapter 6). You are not looking for identical assets and capabilities, but instead those that are compatible or complementary. If the assets and capabilities are identical, then your organization would not gain anything by entering into a strategic alliance with that particular partner. If there is a high level

of complementarity, then strategic fit will be high and there is the potential for a sustained competitive advantage. In the example from our vignette at the beginning of the chapter, Louis-Riel high school had a facility but no human or financial resources to maintain it, while the Lions track and field club had financial and human resources but no indoor track. Both wanted a place for their members (students and athletes) to train and play sports. As such, their needs were complementary and they had strategic fit.

It is possible to establish a strategic alliance with only strategic fit between partners. In fact, a strategic alliance cannot hope to succeed, even in the short term, without strategic fit. However, the strength and durability of the alliance will depend on **cultural fit**. Cultures do not need to be similar—by its nature culture similarity between two organizations is rare. Instead, cultural fit means wanting to understand the cultural differences that exist between the partners as well as being willing to compromise when cultural problems arise (Child & Faulkner, 1998). While culture will be described more fully in chapter 14, suffice to say that many elements form an organization's culture: stories, symbols, rituals, routines, paradigms, power systems, structures, control mechanisms, employee orientation, environmental orientation, international orientation, customer orientation, quality orientation, technology orientation, cost orientation, and innovation orientation (Bronder & Pritzl, 1992; Johnson & Scholes, 1993; Child & Faulkner, 1998). All of these elements must be considered when determining the fit between potential partners' cultures. For example, Mountain Equipment Co-Op (MEC) and the Canadian Avalanche Association have formed an alliance, partly based on a strong cultural fit: MEC is Canada's largest outdoor equipment and clothing supplier with a strong culture based on social and environmental responsibility, and the Canadian Avalanche Association focuses most of its energy on avalanche safety and environmental respect (Mountain Equipment Co-Op, 2004).

Choosing a partner can be based on the amount of information available about that potential partner. Information can come from freely available sources (e.g., Internet, newspapers) or be accumulated through previous alliances with that partner (Gulati, 1999). Information can pertain to different forms of capital (i.e., resources, assets, knowledge) that potential partners may have. In fact, organizations that have a combination of technical, commercial and social capital (i.e.,

TIME OUT *Global Sports Goes on An Alliance Spree*

Alliances are the new trend with corporations. One example is Global Sports, Inc. (www.gsicommerce.com). Global Sports develops and operates the e-commerce sporting goods businesses for specialty retailers, general merchandisers, Internet companies, and media companies. Examples of the company's operations related to the sport industry include buy.com, dunhamssports.com, store.foxsports.com, mcsports.com, qvc.com, sportchalet.com, sportsrus.com, theathletesfoot.com, and thesportsauthority.com.

In the space of four months, Global Sports formed a string of alliances. For example, on July 26, 2000, it formed a strategic alliance with foxsports.com to develop and operate a flagship store on foxsports.com and its regional Web sites. Five days later, Global Sports signed an agreement with toysrus.com to develop a new youth sporting goods Web site,

sportsrus.com. Global Sports also announced an alliance with buy.com to operate its new online sporting goods store. On September 13, the company announced an alliance with iQVC to develop and operate its online sporting goods store. On October 19, Global Sports announced that it would develop and operate the sporting goods Web sites for the MSN eShop. A day later it announced an alliance with America Online for placements within the Sports and Outdoors areas of the Shop@AOL online shopping destinations. On October 24, the company announced that it had bought the outstanding shares of Fog Dog, so that its Web site (fogdog.com) and brand would be integrated into Global Sports' existing infrastructure. Finally, a week later, Global Sports signed an agreement with Excite@Home so that the sporting goods retailers who are part of Global Sports' operations became featured in the Sports and Fitness areas of Excite.com.

Based on information in e-sports! PR sportswire (2000).

knowledge, previous experience, social and network structure) will be more attractive potential partners than organizations that have only one or none of these forms of capital (Ahuja, 2000).

Using previous alliance partners for new alliances can become a routine for the organization. Li and Rowley (2002) term this routinization inertia. Along with inertia, they state that potential partners' prior performance, experience, and reciprocity will influence partner selection.

Alliance Forms

Once potential partners are evaluated in terms of strategic and cultural fit with the organization, an appropriate alliance form must be determined. As mentioned before, true strategic alliances are learning-based relationships. These include joint ventures, collaborations, and consortia. An example of a joint venture would be NBC and a Chinese media organization entering into an agreement to broadcast in Asia. A collaboration example could be the Canadian, Swedish, and Italian ski federations collaborating to share knowledge about

coaching and sport sciences, as well as training facilities. An example of a consortium would be Disney or Time Warner.

Faulkner (1995) suggests that alliances have three distinct dimensions: their scope, their legal nature, and the number of partners. An alliance's *scope* has either focused or complex objectives, for example, the desire to create one product such as a new running shoe versus the desire to create a global mega-event management organization. An alliance's *legal form* involves either the creation of a legally separate organization known as a joint venture, or collaboration with the organizations remaining separate entities. The collaboration is the more flexible form with the least amount of formal bounded initial commitment. Finally, the *number of alliance partners* refers to the size of the alliance. The two-partner alliance is the most common form, as in the Louis-Riel high school and Lions track and field club. However, there also is a consortium when more than two partners are involved, such as in the Disney example. Consortia are usually established for large-scale activities through the pooling of resources for specific purposes (Child & Faulkner,

Table 7.1   Different Forms of Strategic Alliances and Appropriate Alliance Conditions

Alliance form	Conditions
Joint venture	Distinct business required Perception of a need to formally tie partners together Joint management of partner-specific assets needed but need for a predetermined allocation of resource level by each partner Alliance objectives measured through asset use Legal formalization of alliance needed for venture to take place Venture's scope not tied to core business of each partner or to geographic location (e.g., entering new international market)
Collaboration	High uncertainty exists in relation to specific tasks needed for enterprise Need for flexibility between partners Formal (visible) commitment by each partner not required Boundary of enterprise is not a distinct business area
Consortium	Size of enterprise too large and skills needed too wide for only two partners Large size important for credibility of enterprise in the eyes of certain stakeholders (e.g., governments) Wide geographic coverage needed for strong market presence Need to spread or limit each partner's financial risk

From D.O. Faulkner, 1995, *International strategic alliances: Cooperating to compete* (New York: McGraw-Hill Companies). Adapted with permission of The McGraw-Hill Companies.

1998). Table 7.1 provides an overview of the appropriate conditions for each alliance form.

Networks Instead of Strategic Alliances?

If none of the conditions described in table 7.1 seem appropriate for your organization's desired alliance, then perhaps a network is more appropriate. The main difference between strategic alliances and networks is that the alliance is learning-based, while the network is purely skills-based and necessarily involves more than two partners (Child & Faulkner, 1998). However, in practice, it may very well be that you have a network that includes skills-based partnerships as well as learning-based partnerships (alliances).

Reasons for entering into a network include reducing uncertainty, providing flexibility, providing capacity, providing speed, providing access to skills or resources not owned by the organization itself (think outsourcing), and providing information on others with greater ease (Child & Faulkner, 1998). Also, networks, more so than strategic alliances, must establish legitimacy in the eyes of a wide range of stakeholders. Establishing legitimacy includes the use of the network as a preferred form, the network as an entity in itself, and the network as a set of interactions (Human & Provan, 2000).

An example of a network could be the Pepsi Corporation. This organization will create a network, more often of the dominated type, to promote its products. Therefore, the company may partner with a particular grocery store chain to have its products prominently displayed, with sport teams to promote its brand through a sponsorship deal, and with other types of drinks in order to expand its product line and allow those other drinks to use its distribution network.

Negotiating Alliances and Their Valuation

The **negotiation process** generally follows seven main steps, as Fisher and Ury (1981) explain.

1. Information gathering (SWOT; see chapter 6) on prospective partners, including your organization

2. Needs assessment from all potential partners' viewpoints

3. Agenda setting on all issues that must be negotiated, with minimum values for each issue

4. Proposal presentations from each potential partner with question-and-answer follow-ups instead of counterproposal presentations (the actual negotiation stage)

5. Flexibility allows for alternative or repackaged proposals

6. Exchange concessions with values

7. Formal deal closure

Your main goal as a negotiator for a potential strategic alliance is "to achieve a relationship between partners that can enable them together to achieve business success, without either partner needing to accept loss of identity or ultimate independence" (Child & Faulkner, 1998, p. 144). Your goal is to find a win-win solution—a positive-sum game, not a zero-sum game. There are, however, some key elements that are important across all alliances, recognizing that, to a certain extent, all negotiations are context specific and unique. You can't have a standardized approach if you want the alliance to result in a sustained competitive advantage. Child and Faulkner (1998) note that, as a negotiator, you will be faced with two main questions. Both questions will be explained below and supplemented by ways to deal with each of them.

First, how do you set up the alliance so that you achieve the highest level of competitive advantage possible? To deal with this question, Child and Faulkner (1998) suggest you

1. analyze the strategic and cultural fit between the partners,

2. identify the level of congruence between each partner's goals,

3. identify the main project for the alliance and the scope of that project,

4. identify the extent and nature of each partner's contribution,

5. reach an agreement on the alliance's structure and the decision-making process, and

6. reach an agreement on the alliance's termination procedure should one or more partners want to leave the alliance.

Second, how do you obtain the best possible deal for your organization? For the alliance to work, all partners must feel as though they are gaining something. It must be a win-win agreement. There is, of course, a certain amount of compromise that is needed in order to reach this win-win agreement.

Also, an **alliance valuation** must be done for each partner's contribution, which helps determine, for example, the level of decision-making power for each alliance partner. Child and Faulkner (1998) suggest some guidelines thought to apply to most alliances. First, benefits as well as costs for the partners must be considered. What will each get out of the alliance (e.g., in terms of potential profits, reputation, knowledge)? What will it cost them (e.g., potential employee changes, infrastructure costs)? These benefits and costs ought to be measured against not forming the alliance and maintaining the status quo. Second, the level of need of each partner can influence valuation negotiations. For example, NBC could say, "The more they need us, the better position we are in" when thinking of a Chinese broadcasting alliance. But that must be compared with the relative need of NBC for the Chinese broadcaster. Third, an asset's uniqueness gives it a higher value. For example, if 3M develops a material that helps swimmers go faster, then that material is considered a unique and valuable asset for 3M if it enters into an alliance with Speedo to make swimsuits for the Canadian national swimming team. Fourth, the valuation range for an asset should be from the current asset's value to the predicted future benefits for the alliance because of the asset's use. In the 3M example, the material may have a certain value, but by putting it in a swimsuit, its popularity and demand may by predicted to increase by at least tenfold, thereby providing an initial valuation range. The position of the asset's value within that range will depend on the relative strength of each partner, the possible alternative courses of action each partner could take, the uniqueness of each asset brought to the alliance, and the negotiation attitude of each partner.

Managing Strategic Alliances

Once the alliance is established, it needs to be managed and controlled. The following section outlines alliance management, control, human resources, and issues to consider as the alliance evolves.

Alliance Management

Managing the new organization is the crucial, most challenging, and often neglected part of an alliance. The **alliance manager** is now running, in effect, two different organizations, or handling expectations at an international level, a perhaps unfamiliar territory. From the beginning, the alliance manager's role must be clearly determined to avoid ambiguity and role conflict with members of either partner. These issues are especially important in alliances—generally other than joint ventures—that have less formalization in the beginning. According to Child and Faulkner (1998), an alliance manager has four different jobs at the same time:

1. **Decision maker:** an innovator, resource distributor, negotiator, disturbance handler
2. **Internal integrator:** a leader, team builder
3. **External integrator:** a figurehead, networker
4. **Information manager:** a monitor of information, disseminator, and spokesperson

A good alliance manager should have a vision (future-focused and globally focused) for the organization and promote that vision in others. The job must focus on organizational learning and promote lower-level initiatives. The manager should inspire trust in all stakeholders related to the alliance, be good at planning as well as opera-

tionalization, and reach across different cultures (Child & Faulkner, 1998).

To help alliance managers do their job effectively, certain organizational arrangements need to be established. First, there must be clear dispute-resolution mechanisms determining who will make decisions when there is a conflict. Second, it must be clear who has authority and under what circumstances. Third, a clear termination formula must be established. Finally, processes, paths, and mechanisms for information dissemination must be established for the alliance and within each partner for proper learning to occur (Child & Faulkner, 1998).

Alliance Control

Managing an alliance also means knowing who controls what or whom. Having monitoring and sanctioning control mechanisms linked to a cycle of positive returns is shown to contribute to a successful strategic alliance (Kogut, 2000). Child and Faulkner (1998, p. 187) describe **alliance control** as "the process by which the partners influence,

---

TIME OUT   *Federazione Italiana Sport Invernali, Svenska Skidforbundet, and Alpine Canada Alpin Sign a Strategic Alliance*

Following Alpine Canada Alpin's (ACA) commitment to effectively and efficiently increase human, technical, and financial resources for its ski racers, the federation announced that it signed a strategic alliance deal with the Italian and Swedish alpine associations on February 4, 2003. The president of ACA, Ken Read, mentioned how the alliance was a key part of the sport federation's strategic plan of having Canada become a world leader in ski racing.

The alliance calls for the three ski federations to combine their elite racer training programs. More specifically, the nations are to use the latest research to develop common speed and technical racing, equipment testing, and sport science support programs. The nations will also look for new ways to share resources and travel costs to reduce expenses, and they

will look for exciting marketing and sponsorship opportunities. Canadian skiers will also be able to regularly measure themselves against a wider range of competitors during training. In addition, the Canadian skiers, who spend most of the competitive season traveling throughout Europe for World Cup events, will now have better access to training facilities and to accommodations at lower costs.

With Italy hosting the 2005 World Championships and 2006 Winter Olympic Games, Sweden hosting the 2007 World Championships, and Canada hosting the 2010 Winter Olympic Games, all three alliance members will have access to preferred accommodation and training opportunities at the venues, to VIP packages, and to preferential treatment at these events.

Based on information from Alpine Canada Alpin (2003).

Photo courtesy of Alpine Canada Alpin.

Ken Read, president of Alpine Canada Alpin, was instrumental in forming a strategic alliance that combines the resources of ACA with the Italian and Swedish alpine associations.

to varying degrees, the behavior and output of the other partners and the managers of the alliance itself." Influence can refer to the level of power, expertise, and reward delivery (cf. French & Raven, 1960; Child & Faulkner, 1998).

Control itself has three dimensions according to Geringer and Hébert (1989): extent, focus, and mechanisms. The *extent of control* is more important for joint ventures. Killing (1983) explains that there are three levels of control within a joint venture: 1. One partner dominates the joint venture; 2. Both partners have equally active roles; and 3. Neither organization is dominant, and the chosen joint venture's manager holds control. Moreover, the extent of control applies to a whole range of alliance activities and decisions. In this way, one partner can have more control in one area such as production and the second partner may have control over another aspect such as marketing. Overall though, partners have relatively equal con-

trol over the alliance, but each partner's extent of control must be assessed because this can change over time. For collaborations, the extent of control will be more flexible than for joint ventures (Child & Faulkner, 1998).

The Leeds United Football Club–BSkyB alliance, formed in 1999, is an example of control issues. When BSkyB bought a stake in Leeds Sporting (parent company of Leeds United), it gained a seat on Leeds' board of directors and became the exclusive agent for all media deals (except those collectively negotiated by the Premier League) for a five-year period (BBC News, 1999). However, BSkyB does not control the on-field activities of Leeds.

It is important to understand that more control does not necessarily mean more success, as evidenced by Leeds' financial problems from 2002 to 2005. What is important is the control of specific aspects deemed essential by a given partner (Child & Faulkner, 1998). That is the *focus of control*. Selective control is also more sensible economically, because one partner may be able to deliver an aspect of the alliance in a more efficient manner than the other partner. Therefore it makes more sense for the former to take control of that aspect. For collaboration, the focus of control limits the unintentional transfer of proprietary information beyond that agreed upon during negotiation (Child & Faulkner, 1998).

The third control dimension is *control mechanisms*. There are many mechanisms. Child and Faulkner (1998) identify the following mechanisms: control over inputs, behaviors (specification of correct way of doing things), and outputs; socialization (definition and creation) of common values and adaptation (familiarity with others' values and practices); personal involvement (signaling of important issues by managers); hierarchical (emphasis on and support of partners' and alliance's goals); and lateral (interaction across formal boundaries) structures.

While the previous may apply more to joint ventures, there are control mechanisms that are more specific to collaborations and consortia. For example, there must be a gatekeeper role established in each partner organization to ensure appropriate and accurate communication between partners and also within each organization. Gatekeepers control and monitor information flow and alliance implementation. Moreover, the collaboration leaders (e.g., alliance manager) must have an equally important (and powerful) role to that of the gatekeeper. In addition, control mechanisms for collaborations refers more to project plan development and evolution, critical path creation, and control of the allocation of resources.

Related to the dimensions of control are the *bases of control*. After reviewing the main theories on this topic, Child and Faulkner (1998) identify three main factors that form the bases of control. The main factors include the presence of majority equity shareholding (mainly for joint ventures and consortia), bargaining power (stemming from the partner's available alternatives, importance of alliance for the partner's main strategy, and the partner's resource allocation commitment), and the ability and willingness of the partner to commit key resources. Of course, these factors can all be related. For example, if an alliance partner is putting in 75 percent of the financial requirements for the joint venture, then its bargaining power may very well increase, especially if the second partner has fewer resources to commit. You may see this happening when the partner organizations vary drastically in size.

Human Resource Issues

Since people are the ones that create the alliance, human resource management (HRM) is central to any alliance discussion. Communication problems and conflicts of loyalty must be avoided through the development of a HRM policy specific to the alliance. More specifically, issues of joint responsibility, of culture awareness promotion, of information exchange mechanisms, of mutual skills training, and of rewards should be included in the HRM policy. Training and information exchanges are essential for a successful strategic alliance. These HRM policies can be integrated into the control mechanisms during alliance negotiation. In fact, this HRM function should be present from the beginning of the alliance formation process. Of course, the choice of alliance manager is a major HRM issue (Child & Faulkner, 1998).

Evolving Alliances

How alliances evolve is still being debated in the literature. Child and Faulkner (1998) show how most researchers seem to follow a life-cycle approach. For example, Murray and Mahon (1993) explain that a strategic alliance starts with a courtship phase, followed by the negotiation phase, then the alliance start-up phase, the maintenance phase, and finally three possible endings (divorce, amicable separation, or extension of the alliance).

However, Ring and Van de Ven (1994) would argue that an **alliance evolution** is actually a repeating cycle of negotiation, commitment, and execution phases, thereby emphasizing the importance of periodically revisiting the goal and structure of the alliance.

In turn, Bleeke and Ernst (1995) would argue that there are actually six different patterns of alliance evolution:

1. Inherently unstable alliances that cause a collision between the partners

2. Stable and long-lasting alliances that show a partnership of complementary equals

3. Two or more weak organizations wishing to join forces in the hopes of improving their market power, but never being able to reach that goal

4. Bootstrap alliances formed when a weak organization wants to ally itself with a strong organization in the hope of increasing its capabilities, but which usually leads to the buying out of the weak organization by the strong organization

5. Short-term alliances between a weak and a strong organization that are or will eventually become competitors, which usually ends the same way as the bootstrap alliance

6. Strong compatible partners that forge a successful alliance but, because of lingering competitive tensions, one partner will usually sell out to the other

On the other hand, Stuart (2000) argues that organizations choosing larger organizations as partners, and organizations that have the potential to be innovative alliance partners perform better than organizations that do not have such partners. He does add that smaller or younger organizations can benefit more from such an arrangement than older or larger organizations.

Regardless of the debate on the evolution pattern of alliances, such alliances are usually created for specific purposes and rarely exist in the same form for a long period of time. Success depends on the alliance partners allowing for periodic adjustments (even if the goal remains the same, the environment will change over time and the partners must respond accordingly), on the alliance partners developing equally (in a balanced manner), on the development of trust, and on organizational learning.

For success, alliance managers must first be able to manage organizational learning. This means overcoming cognitive and emotional barriers (having the intent to learn and develop trust within the alliance), reducing organizational barriers (fighting organizational inertia—the status quo—and establishing learning procedures), and having an open exchange of information (making information accessible, sharing problems and solutions, and accepting the possibility of conflict) (Child & Faulkner, 1998).

As mentioned earlier, the evolution of the alliance and of trust can be likened to a friendship. While it may happen that a strategic alliance will start between organizations that have existing personal relationships, they will more often begin on impersonal terms. It is therefore important to take the time to develop the friendship; trust should then follow and evolve. Forming this bond will help reduce possible integration and control dilemmas. Trust reduces managerial time spent worrying about the "true" intentions of the other partner. High levels of trust also help dissolve barriers between organizations, so as to increase learning and make the alliance more efficient and successful (Child & Faulkner, 1998).

Deciding to enter into a strategic alliance will be done for both economic and political reasons. Knowing why your organization and your potential partner enter into the alliance, as well as the external and internal catalysts for the decision, will help focus the alliance negotiations. Strategic and cultural fit between partners is necessary for a sustained competitive advantage to be gained. Managers must determine the scope, legal form, and size of the alliance to determine the appropriate form of alliance (joint venture, collaboration, or consortium) (Child & Faulkner, 1998).

Kanter (2002) likens good alliances to good marriages. She explains that such alliances usually meet the following criteria.

- **Individual excellence:** Each partner is strong and has something important to bring to the alliance.

- **Importance:** Both partners want to make the alliance work because it fits with each one's organizational strategies.

- **Interdependence:** The partners have complementary skills and assets, and each truly needs the other to accomplish the goal.

- **Investment:** Each partner takes a stake in the other to show that both are committed.

- **Information:** Communication must be free-flowing at all hierarchical levels for the alliance to succeed.

- **Integration:** Strategic (top managers), tactical (middle managers), operational (workers who perform the daily work), and interpersonal linkages must be made to work together efficiently.

- **Institutionalization:** The alliance receives formal status, meaning there's an official structure, a responsibility distribution, and a decision-making process.

- **Integrity:** Both partners must behave in a way that builds mutual trust.

SUMMARY AND CONCLUSIONS

Strategic alliances are learning-based partnerships formed between two organizations in response to strategic opportunities or threats in the environment. Strategic alliance forms include joint ventures, collaborations, and consortia. Reasons for entering into an alliance include cost and risk reduction, internal and external challenges, a desire to improve the organization's strategic position, an opportunity for organizational learning, and for political reasons.

Entering into a strategic alliance depends on the strategic and cultural fit between partners, and on the amount of information available about the potential partner. Alliances vary in scope, legal form, and number of alliance partners. The extent, focus, mechanisms, and bases of control are essential for managing established alliances properly. Equally important is the choice of the right alliance manager who will be able to plan and operationalize the alliance. The success of the alliance will depend on the quality of the relationship (e.g., trust) between the partners, on good organizational arrangements (e.g., dispute-resolution mechanisms), and on mutual learning.

KEY CONCEPTS

alliance control (p. 141)

alliance evolution (p. 143)

alliance manager (p. 140)

alliance valuation (p. 140)

collaborations (p. 134)

consortia (p. 134)

cultural fit (p. 137)

joint ventures (p. 134)

negotiation process (p. 139)

organizational learning (p. 135)

organizational trust (p. 136)

strategic alliance (p. 134)

strategic fit (p. 137)

REVIEW QUESTIONS

1. Describe the different forms of alliances and give an example for each form.

2. What differentiates a strategic alliance from other types of partnerships?

3. Look at a professional sport team and describe the alliances it is involved in with sponsors, apparel, and so on.

4. You are the manager of a local sporting goods store. What types of alliances could you enter into and why would each be desirable?

5. You are a physical education teacher in a local high school. What types of alliances could you enter into and why would each be desirable?

6. You are running a tournament and must deal with a variety of stakeholders. How would alliances with stakeholders such as professional equipment companies, facilities, food companies, hotels, and any other stakeholder be formed and what are the advantages to forming such alliances?

7. You are the CEO of the national triathlon association. Your organization is facing major funding cuts from the federal government. At the same time, there is an increased popularity of your sport. Would strategic alliances be a good strategy for your organization? If so, what alliances could you form and why?

8. How can a consortium help various alliance members in their respective businesses?

9. What makes for a good alliance manager?

10. What are the dimensions of alliance control?

11. What would you suggest to the Ottawa Lions Track and Field Club and the Louis-Riel high school (presented at the beginning of this chapter) to maintain good alliance control and why?

12. Describe how an alliance evolves.

13. What makes for a good alliance? Give an example of a good strategic alliance that you know.

14. Describe the alliance evolution of the Disney Corporation with respect to a sport organization.

15. Should Time Warner form new alliances with sport organizations? Why? Should it disband current alliances with sport organizations? Why?

SUGGESTIONS FOR FURTHER READING

Strategic alliances have become popular with practitioners, but it has been only within the last 10 years or so that researchers have followed suit. If you are interested in this area, you should read Faulkner's (1995) *International Strategic Alliances: Cooperating to Compete*. Child and Faulkner's (1998) *Strategies of Cooperation: Managing Alliances, Networks, and Joint Ventures* provides a very good overview of alliance formation and management from the alliance's creation to its end. More recently, Barringer and Harrison's (2000) "Walking a Tightrope: Creating Value Through Interorganizational Relationships" in the *Journal of Management* provides a good overview of different theoretical approaches to strategic alliances. The *Harvard Business Review on Strategic Alliances* (2002) was also published and includes eight different chapters on different issues related to strategic alliances. In December 2004, the *Academy of Management Journal* also published a full issue on "Building Effective Networks" (Vol. 47, No. 6).

Strategic alliances in the sport world are also popular as illustrated in the Time Out sections. Interesting articles include Thibault and Harvey's (1997) "Fostering Interorganizational Linkages in the Canadian Sport Delivery System" in the *Journal of Sport Management*, Glover's (1999) "Municipal Park and Recreation Agencies Unite! A Single Case Analysis of an Intermunicipal Partnership" in the *Journal of Park and Recreation Administration*; Thibault, Frisby, and Kikulis' (1999) "Interorganizational Linkages in the Delivery of Local Leisure Services in Canada: Responding to Economic, Political and Social Pressures" in *Managing Leisure*, Chadwick's (2000) "A Research Agenda for Strategic Collaboration in European Club Football" in the *European Journal for Sport Management* now the *European Sport Management Quarterly;* Flynn and Gilbert's (2001) "The Analysis of Professional Sports Leagues as Joint Ventures" in *The Economic Journal;* and Frisby, Thibault, and Kikulis' (2004) "The Organizational Dynamics of Under-managed Partnerships in Leisure Service Departments" in *Leisure Studies*. Thibault, Frisby, and Kikulis also have a chapter titled "Partnerships Between Local Government Sport and Leisure Departments and the Commercial Sector: Changes, Complexities, and Consequences" in Slack's (2004) *The Commercialisation of Sport* that is worth reading. You can also look to business references that sometimes mention sport alliance deals such as *Forbes, Fortune,* or *Business Week*. Finally, www.sportbusiness.com is a good link for sport-related business news around the world. Any large sport strategic alliances will be mentioned in their daily news features.

CASE FOR ANALYSIS

Creation of the Canadian National Sport Centers

The Canadian Olympic Committee (COC), the Coaching Association of Canada (CAC), and Sport Canada entered into a strategic alliance in 1994 when they created the series of national sport centers. The COC brings to the table core funding (Can$4 million between 1997 and 2000), high-performance sport programs, and a concern for the center's activities. The CAC offers coaching expertise, education, and employment. Sport Canada's presence is reflective of the Canadian government's desire to develop the Canadian sport system and support its athletes in their endeavors. Sport Canada also provides core funding to the tune of about Can$3.4 million annually. There is also about Can$18 million in a fund stemming from investments and profits related to the 1994 Commonwealth Games.

The objectives of this alliance are to enhance the level and increase the efficiency (i.e., economies of scale) of delivering services to Canada's coaches and elite athletes and by bringing together under one roof key service professionals such as nutritionists, trainers, psychologists, medical staff, and other experts. This also includes creating opportunities for new funding sources with sponsors, national sport organizations, provincial sport organizations, provincial governments, universities, and local governments to help amateur sport in the country. This strategic alliance was established with the expectation that resulting programs will allow the country to bid for and win major games. These games can in turn bring more facilities, knowledge, skills, and infrastructure for sport across the country.

Seven national sport centers provide access and delivery of services to athletes and coaches. They are located in Vancouver, Calgary, Winnipeg, Saskatchewan, Toronto, Montreal, and Atlantic Canada. Smaller centers are planned for the near future.

Based on information from Sport Canada (2003).

Questions

1. Describe the alliance's characteristics (form, dimensions).
2. Why is there strategic fit between the various partners?
3. What are the possible control mechanisms for this alliance, which are best, and why?
4. Could the alliance survive if Sport Canada dropped out of the alliance? If so, how?

Seven national sport centers provide access and delivery of services to athletes and coaches. They are located in Vancouver, Calgary, Winnipeg, Saskatchewan, Toronto, Montreal, and Atlantic Canada. Smaller centers are planned for the near future.

Questions

1. Describe the alliance's characteristics (form, connections).

2. What are the strategies in between the various players?

3. What are the incentives in the situations, and the linkages among them? Why?

4. About the alliance and Sport Canada, the management of the alliance, and its power.

[T]he objectives of this alliance are to enhance the level and increase the efficiency (i.e., economies of scale) of delivering services to Canada's coaches and elite athletes and by bringing together under one roof key service professionals such as nutritionists, trainers, psychologists, medical staff, and other experts. This also includes creating opportunities for new funding sources with sponsors, national sport organizations, provincial sport organizations, provincial governments, universities, and local governments to help improve sport in the country. This strategic alliance was established with the expectation that rivalries and previous conflicts would be resolved and new partnerships formed, which would bring more and better quality and accessible types of sport across the country.

Chapter 8

Sport Organizations and Their Environments

ADIDAS MAKES FRIENDS AND THEN STRIKES DEALS THAT MOVE SNEAKERS

In the small German town of Herzogenaurach the only tourist attraction is the one-room museum devoted to the history of athletic shoes. There, neatly displayed in glass cases are some 200 pairs of the most famous shoes in sport, including those Jessie Owens wore in the 1936 Olympics. But the shoe museum alone doesn't explain the procession of Olympic-class athletes and sport officials from all over the world who used to visit Herzogenaurach. They came to enjoy the hospitality of the Sport Hotel, a cozy 32-room inn with an indoor swimming pool, tennis courts, soccer fields, saunas, coaches, trainers, and a chef who would do any hotel proud. Best of all,

at checkout time there was rarely a bill to be paid by the guest.

The tab was picked up by Sport Hotel's owner, Adidas, the German shoe and sporting goods maker (officially and legally, its name is not capitalized). Through such largesse, its aim was to turn the world's top athletes into walking, running, vaulting, and kicking billboards for its logo. Adidas believed in making friends, then making deals. From the cash it once secretly gave to Olympic athletes to the free plane tickets it passed out to leaders of sport organizations, Adidas made itself the sugar daddy of international amateur sport.

(continued)

(continued)

Marketing through patronage made Adidas the largest sporting goods company in the world and its chairman, Horst Dassler, one of sport's most important power brokers. Many believe it was Dassler who was behind Juan Antonio Samaranch's rise to the presidency of the IOC and Dassler who was the key player in choosing Seoul (not favorite Nagoya) for the 1988 Summer Olympics. "He is the real boss of sport," said Monique Berlioux, former director of the IOC.

Other companies, of course, saw sport as an attractive marketing vehicle but what set Adidas apart was its emphasis on amateur sport. Like its competitors, it paid professional athletes to wear its products but it also went to unusual lengths to associate its three-stripe logo and trefoil insignia with the five interlocking rings of the Olympics. Besides paying more than its competitors to outfit Olympic teams, Adidas mingled in Olympic politics with the diligence of a Washington lobbyist. An Adidas dinner or reception was commonplace at almost any IOC meeting, and an Adidas representative—usually Dassler himself—would spend the day mixing with delegates.

Adidas and its chairman worked themselves into almost every corner of sport politics. Their main vehicles were their contracts with national teams. For example, in 1985 Adidas gave out U.S.$30 million in cash and equipment to these teams. Like the best of politicians, Dassler listened more than he spoke, and asked more questions than he answered. A small army of Adidas representatives, stationed in many of the countries where the company did business, kept Dassler abreast of local sport politics. Dassler also employed operatives like Hassine Hamouda, a Paris-based former Tunisian military colonel, to influence sport leaders in Arab countries and in French-speaking Africa.

Adidas representatives sat on important Olympic advisory committees. Hamouda, for example, sat on the IOC press commission. Thomas Bach, also hired by Adidas, sat as a member of the athletes' advisory committee, and Richard Pound, a Montreal lawyer and former IOC vice president, did legal work for the company. Dassler acknowledged that his hospitality and other acts of friendship toward national Olympic committee and federation officials directly benefited Adidas as it competed to sponsor teams. "A lot of federations get higher offers than ours but refuse them because of what we have done over the last 10 years," Dassler said.

Dassler's Olympic connections came in handy at the IOC congress in Baden-Baden, Germany, in 1985, when the marketing rights to the 1988 Olympic Games were awarded to ISL Marketing AG, a Swiss company run by former Adidas executives. Dassler and his four sisters owned 51 percent of the shares of ISL. Although sport marketing companies in the United States and Europe were more experienced, ISL—then only two years old—was assigned by the IOC in 1983 to develop a marketing plan for the 1988 games. Other bidders weren't invited, thus making a virtual certainty of the final approval in May 1985 of ISL's contract. Despite initial opposition by the U.S. Olympic Committee, the contract was approved by the majority of the Olympic committees of about 160 nations (including the United States).

A dominant theme in the study of organizations is that the environment in which an organization operates influences its structure and processes. To be effective, an organization must adapt to the demands of its environment. One way is to monitor changes in the environment and then take the necessary steps to respond to or control these changes. Horst Dassler did this better than anyone in sport. By creating links with many of the key figures in the world of amateur sport Dassler was able to keep informed of changes that could influence Adidas. By using his contacts to capitalize on opportunities in the environment, he developed Adidas into the number one sporting goods company in the world at the time.

In this chapter we look at what we mean when we talk about the "environment" of a sport organization. We examine the main research findings on the environment of organizations and the methods that can be used to manage the environment. We also look at some of the major theoretical approaches that take an environmental perspective. Finally, we look at the relationship between a sport organization's environment and its structure.

The Nature of the Organizational Environment

What exactly do we mean when we talk about the environment of an organization? Certainly the term has been used in a wide variety of ways (cf. Starbuck, 1976). In one sense everything outside of the organization being studied is a part of the environment, but such a broad definition has little practical or theoretical use. Most researchers use a more focused approach to understanding the concept, and suggest, as shown in figure 8.1, that organizations have two types of environment: a general environment and a task environment.

General Environment

The **general environment** of an organization includes those **sectors** that, although they may not have a direct impact on the operations of a sport organization, can influence the industry in general ways that ultimately have an impact on the organization (Daft, 2004). The general environment of a sport organization can be divided up into a number of different sectors. Here we look briefly at the impact of each.

Economic

The general economic conditions in which a sport organization operates (whether publicly or privately owned), the system of banking in

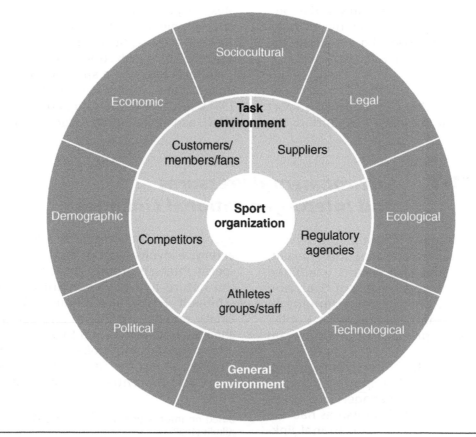

Figure 8.1 *The sport organization's general and task environment.*

the country in which the organization operates, fiscal policies, and patterns of consumption are all components of the economic sector of a sport organization's general environment. Pugh (1989), for example, describes how austere economic conditions influenced the development of the Belfry golf complex. Economics is also the main reason for the NHL's cancellation of the 2004-2005 season.

Political

The prevailing political situation, the extent to which political power is concentrated, and the ideology of the party in power are all factors that can influence a sport organization. Geehern (1991), for example, describes how the dropping of trade barriers as part of the 1992 European Community reforms and the opening up of the former Soviet Bloc, created considerable market potential for golf ball manufacturers such as Spalding and Acushnet. In a somewhat similar vein, bicycle manufacturers benefited considerably from the Mideast crisis of the early 1970s, when the fear of an oil embargo pushed bike sales to record levels (Charm, 1986). The political climate has also had a considerable effect on a number of Olympic Games organizing committees, most notably in 1980 and 1984 when, because of politically motivated rationales, a number of countries did not attend the Summer Olympic Games (cf. Hill, 1992).

Sociocultural

Sociocultural factors that can influence a sport organization include the class structure of the social system, the culture in which the sport organization exists, trends in consumer tastes, and the sporting traditions of the area in which the organization is situated. We see the impact of sociocultural conditions in the attempts to set up professional soccer leagues in North America. Despite soccer's popularity around the world, the sporting culture of the United States and Canada has mitigated against the survival of leagues such as the North American Soccer League, while the Major Soccer League is barely surviving. Manchester United even tried to open up the market more by playing games in the United States in 2003 without, unfortunately, any major impact. It is also well established (cf. Beamish, 1985; Macintosh & Whitson, 1990) that the administrative structures of many sport organizations reflect the inequalities of social life in terms of their class, race, and gender composition.

Legal

The legal conditions surrounding the environment are an important part of an organization's general environment that is often overlooked (Hall, 1982). The type of legal system within the country in which the sport organization operates, the jurisdictions overseen by various levels of government, and the existence of laws covering such areas as taxation, unionization, and the regulation of organizations, all constitute the legal conditions affecting a sport organization. In the United States, antitrust legislations (Freedman, 1987), in Canada, the Competition Act (Barnes, 1988), and in the United Kingdom, the Local Gov-

TIME OUT — *Environmental Pressures and Interorganizational Linkages*

In their study on government leisure services senior managers, researchers Lucie Thibault, Wendy Frisby, and Lisa Kikulis examined the influence of economic, political, and social pressures on the development of interorganizational linkages with public, nonprofit, and private or commercial organizations.

The trio found that interorganizational linkages are increasingly important for government leisure services managers. Moreover, they found that economic pressures had the largest impact on interorganizational link-

age growth. Their research also found "an extensive involvement of local politicians and special interests groups in decisions affecting the nature and development of linkages" (Thibault, Frisby, and Kikulis 1999, p. 133). Finally population growth and demographic changes were also found to affect the use of interorganizational linkages as a preferred strategy, as did the fit between the department and (potential) partner's values and ethics.

Based on information in L. Thibault, W. Frisby, and L. Kikulis (1999).

ernment Act of 1988 (Houlihan, 1991) all provide evidence of the ways legal conditions affect sport organizations.

Demographic

The type of people to whom a sport organization directs its products or services, changes in population distributions, and the age, gender, racial, ethnic, and class composition of the population, can all influence the organization. Sparks (1992) shows, for example, how directing its programming to a primarily male audience affects TSN's (The Sports Network's) operations. Richards (1986) demonstrates the influence of changing population cohorts. He suggests that Brunswick's purchase of Ray Industries, makers of Sea Ray boats, was in part inspired by the company's market research indications that the baby boomers were taking an increased interest in pleasure boats.

Ecological

Because a number of sport organizations depend on their physical surroundings for success, ecological factors are an important part of their general environment. Weather conditions can affect the staging of sport events and the operation of facilities such as ski hills. Hisrich and Peters (1992), for example, describe how in 1980 and 1981 poor snow conditions severely reduced the number of skiers, with a corresponding drop in ski equipment sales. Growing concerns about the total ecological system have encouraged sport organizations to pay attention to how their activities influence the natural environment. For example, companies like Mountain Equipment Co-op (MEC), a Vancouver-based retailer of outdoor gear and clothing, have created a number of environmental conservation programs. It is also this type of thinking that led the organizing committee of the 2000 Sydney Summer Games to include Greenpeace, an environmental group, as part of its preparations for the games.

Technological

All sport organizations are affected by technological developments that may improve production or service. They must monitor constantly any technological developments that could change the nature of the industry in which the sport organization is involved. Technological developments may also lead the sport organization to engage in new activities or approach existing activities in different ways. An example of the impact of technology on the operations of a sport organization is Huffy's decision to use robotics and computer-integrated manufacturing techniques in producing bicycles. This initiative meant Huffy was able to reduce its workforce and increase its daily output of bicycles (Slakter, 1988).

Task Environment

A sport organization's **task environment** is made up of those aspects of its general environment that can influence its ability to achieve its goals. Typically included in a sport organization's task environment are such groups as customers-members-fans, staff, suppliers, competitors, and regulatory agencies (cf. Thompson, 1967). Zeigler's (1985) study of physical education departments similarly describes the task environment, or immediate environment as he calls it, which includes clients, suppliers, controllers, advisers, adversaries and "publics with opinions." In contrast to the general environment, which is more removed from the sport organization, the task environment is of more immediate concern to the sport manager, because it contains those constituents that can strongly affect the success of the organization. Each sport organization's task environment is unique and the constituents making up this environment may change over time.

Although they are conceptually distinct, a sport organization's general environment and its task environment are related. Consider for example, the effect of the increasing societal awareness of the inequalities of gender that exist in all types of managerial positions, including those in sport organizations—an aspect of the general environment. Legislative changes are made as more people become aware of and are actively involved in trying to eliminate such inequalities. These changes influence hiring practices in sport organizations and, consequently, on its human resources practices—aspects of the sport organization's task environment.

Domain

A sport organization's task environment will vary according to the domain in which it chooses to operate. **Domain** refers to the territory that a sport organization stakes out for itself, in regard to the services or products it delivers and the markets in which it operates. Different sport organizations even within the same sector of the sport industry can have different domains and therefore different task environments. MEC and The Running

Room are both sporting goods stores but they have identified different domains in which to operate: MEC focuses on outdoor gear for hiking and mountaineering; The Running Room focuses on gear specifically for runners (and walkers with the Walking Room). Consequently, they come into contact with different suppliers, customers, and competitors.

Perceived Environment

In discussing the concept of environment it is important to distinguish between actual environment and **perceived environment**. The actual environmental conditions surrounding a sport organization may be perceived differently by different managers at the same level (Leifer & Huber, 1977). For example, the same environmental conditions may be perceived as dynamic (providing opportunities for growth) by one sport manager and in a quite different way by the manager of another sport organization operating within the same sector of the industry. Take, for example, the situation of Reebok and Nike in the early 1980s. Reebok's senior managers, watching the aerobics boom, saw a rapidly changing environment for the athletic footwear industry. Nike's managers, however, did not perceive the aerobics boom as any sort of enduring change in their environment; they did not respond immediately to this opportunity and as a result their market share declined. The point here is that, while the actual environment affects the sport organization, it is the perceived environment to which managers respond. As Starbuck (1976) suggests, based on managerial perceptions organizations select those aspects of their environment to which they are going to respond.

Research on Organizational Environments

Many research studies that have contributed to our understanding of organizational environments can be applied to organizations in the sport industry. Here we focus on three of the most important of these contributions: the work of Burns and Stalker, Lawrence and Lorsch, and Duncan.

Burns and Stalker

Burns and Stalker's (1961) study of 20 British manufacturing firms was the first research to try to identify the types of organizational structures and managerial processes most appropriate under different types of environmental conditions. Burns and Stalker examined changes in scientific technology and product markets—changes in the organization's task environment. Their research identified two types of structure and managerial practices, each occurring under different environmental conditions. These were labeled **organic** and **mechanistic**. Organic structures work best in rapidly changing environments; mechanistic structures work best in stable environments.

In the sport industry we would expect to find mechanistic structures in companies like Victoriaville, producers of hockey sticks, and in government agencies such as the Saskatchewan Department of Culture, Youth and Recreation or Sport Manitoba. These sport organizations have relatively stable environments and hence use designs such as the machine bureaucracy. These structures are what Burns and Stalker refer to as mechanistic. In contrast, organic structures are more like Mintzberg's professional bureaucracies or adhocracies, and are found in rapidly changing environments. The structure used by NBC to televise the Olympic Games (see chapter 5) was an organic structure. We would also find organic structures in sport physiology research labs, and when short-term groups are formed to stage a particular sporting event such as a basketball tournament or a road race. Table 8.1 shows the environmental, structural, and managerial characteristics associated with mechanistic and organic sport organizations.

In the most effective sport organizations there is "a fit" between the demands of the environment and the type of structure and managerial practice employed. Burns and Stalker recognized that organic and mechanistic structures are ideal types representing the ends of a continuum. Few if any sport organizations would be purely organic or purely mechanistic; rather, the majority show varying characteristics of each type. Burns and Stalker also did not see one type of structure as superior to the other; the environmental conditions determined which was most appropriate.

Lawrence and Lorsch

Extending the work of Burns and Stalker (1961), Lawrence and Lorsch (1967) examined companies in three industries—plastics, packaged food, and standardized containers—that were seen as having considerably different degrees of environ-

Table 8.1   Comparison of Mechanistic and Organic Systems of Organization

Mechanistic	Organic
1. Tasks are highly fractionated and specialized; little regard paid to clarifying relationship between tasks and organizational objectives.	1. Tasks are more independent; emphasis on relevance of tasks and organizational objectives.
2. Tasks tend to remain rigidly defined unless altered formally by top management.	2. Tasks are continually adjusted and redefined through interaction of organizational members.
3. Specific role definition (rights, obligations, and technical methods prescribed for each member).	3. Generalized role definition (members accept general responsibility for task accomplishment beyond individual role definition).
4. Hierarchic structure of control, authority, and communication; sanctions derive from employment contract between employee and organization.	4. Network structure of control, authority, and communication; sanctions derive more from community of interest than from contractual relationship.
5. Information relevant to situation and operations of the organization formally assumed to rest with chief executive.	5. Leader not assumed to be omniscient; knowledge centers identified were located throughout organization.
6. Communication is primarily vertical between superior and subordinate.	6. Communication is both vertical and horizontal depending upon where needed information resides.
7. Communications primarily take form of instructions and decisions issued by superiors; information and requests for decisions supplied by inferiors.	7. Communications primarily take form of information and advice.
8. Insistence on loyalty to organization and obedience to superiors.	8. Commitment to organization's tasks and goals more highly valued than loyalty or obedience.
9. Importance and prestige attached to identification with organization and its members.	9. Importance and prestige attached to affiliations and expertise in external environment.

Reprinted, by permission, from R. Steers, 1977, *Organizational effectiveness: A behavioral view* (Santa Monica, CA: Goodyear Publishing Company).

mental diversity and uncertainty. The plastics industry was chosen because its environment was uncertain and characterized by rapid changes in technology and customer needs. In contrast, the environment of the container industry was seen as stable and predictable; growth was steady and product innovation was low. The environment of organizations in the food industry was seen as somewhere in between plastics and containers.

Essentially, Lawrence and Lorsch (1967) argued that the more complex and uncertain an organization's task environment, the more differentiated the organization would have to be to handle the uncertainty, that is, the more subunits there would be, each dealing with a particular aspect of the environment. However, to meet the demands of their environment successfully, each subunit would require specialists with different attitudes and behaviors to meet their particular subunit's

goals. As a result, "differentiation" referred not only to the existence of structural differences in functionally specialized subunits within the organization but also to "differences in ways of thinking and working that develop among managers in these . . . units" (Lawrence and Lorsch, 1967, p. 9). These differences manifest themselves in variations in managerial goals, time orientation, and interpersonal orientation among the subunits. For example, applying Lawrence and Lorsch's ideas to an athletic footwear company, the goals of managers in the sales department would be different from those of production managers: Sales managers would be concerned with increasing volume and customer satisfaction; production managers would be concerned with reducing manufacturing costs and time. Similarly, production managers would more likely be concerned with the immediate problems of production, whereas the time orientation of the designers in the research-and-development department would focus on longer-term issues. Table 8.2 shows the type of variation that Lawrence and Lorsch found in the production, research and development, and sales departments of the organizations in their study. The greater this variation among the different organizational subunits, the more complex the organization and thus the greater need for integration through such mechanisms as rules and regulations, policies, and plans.

Lawrence and Lorsch's work was different from previous studies because they did not see the organization's environment as a unitary entity. They suggested that there were parts to the environment, just like there were parts (departments or other similar subunits) to an organization. Essentially, they believed that the ways different departments of an organization varied would reflect the variation in the subenvironment with which they interacted. Consequently, if the external environment of an organization was complex and diverse (i.e., there were a lot of parts to deal with), to be effective the internal structure of the organization would also have to be highly differentiated, leading in turn to the need for sophisticated integration mechanisms to coordinate the differentiated subunits. If an organization's environment was simple and stable, it would be less differentiated and consequently require fewer integrating mechanisms. Lawrence and Lorsch (1967) found that the production, sales, and research-and-development subunits showed higher levels of differentiation in those organizations that had the most diverse and uncertain environments. That is, those organizations in the plastics industry were the most

differentiated, followed by organizations in the food industry, and finally those in the container industry.

However, not only did Lawrence and Lorsch look at levels of differentiation, but they also looked at a number of effectiveness criteria and the use of integration mechanisms in these organizations. They found that, with one exception, the most effective organizations had a higher level of integration. It was not enough for an organization simply to have an appropriate level of internal differentiation to deal with the diversity and complexity of its environment; it also had to have the necessary integrating mechanisms if it was to ensure optimal performance.

What lessons, then, can the sport manager learn from Lawrence and Lorsch's (1967) work? First, it is important to understand that sport organizations, like other organizations, have a number of parts to their environment, each of which presents a varying level of uncertainty. For example, a collegiate football organization has, as part of its environment, the local and national media. While there may be a number of media organizations with which the football program has to interact, there is a level of certainty about this aspect of the environment. The number of media organizations covering the team will not usually change rapidly from one year to the next and their demands are fairly consistent—they want information on players, coaches, future opponents, and so on. This **subenvironment,** or organizational subunit, because of its relative stability, can probably be handled by one or two people. On the other hand, in addition to the media, a college football organization also has, as a part of its environment, a number of high

Table 8.2 Differences in Formality of Structure and Orientation Between Departments

Characteristic	Production	Research and development	Sales
Formality of structure	High	Low	Medium to high
Goal orientation	Cost reduction	Development of new knowledge	Customer problems
	Process efficiency	Technological improvements	Competitive activities
Time orientation	Short	Long	Short
Interpersonal orientation	Task oriented	Varied, depending on type of research	Social oriented

Based on information in P.R. Lawrence and I.W. Lorsch 1967.

school football programs, a source of input in that they provide the players for the college program. Because the football program is likely to deal with far more high schools than media agencies, and because there is a higher level of uncertainty here ("blue chip" players come from different programs each year and are also recruited by other colleges), there is more diversity and uncertainty within this subenvironment, and a higher level of differentiation within the organization is needed to deal with it. That is in general why the football organization will have more staff to deal with high school liaisons, scouting, and recruiting than it will have to deal with the media. This illustration highlights the second lesson sport managers can learn from Lawrence and Lorsch's work: A sport organization must have an appropriate level of internal differentiation to meet the demands of its various subenvironments.

However, a third point that Lawrence and Lorsch's work should alert sport managers to is that it is not enough merely to have appropriately differentiated subunits to deal with its subenvironments. Because different managerial goals, time orientations, and interpersonal orientations exist in these subunits, there must also be the necessary level of integration to ensure that these subunits are working toward a common goal. More complex sport organizations (those in the more diverse and uncertain environments) will accomplish integration through formal means such as policies, cross-functional teams, and systematic planning. In sport organizations operating in simpler environments, integration will be accomplished through more informal mechanisms such as direct supervision by managers.

Duncan

Concerned, like Lawrence and Lorsch, about **environmental uncertainty** and its impact on organizations, Duncan (1972) saw that the uncertainty of an organization's environment was influenced by two factors: the extent to which the environment was simple–complex, and the extent to which it was stable–dynamic (cf. also Dess & Beard, 1984; Tung, 1979).

The complexity of a sport organization's environment is determined by the number and heterogeneity of external elements influencing the organization's operations. **Environmental complexity** is characterized by a large number of diverse elements interacting with or influencing the sport organization. In contrast, a simple environment has only a small number of elements, mostly homogeneous, influencing the organization. The Toronto Raptors, the USOC, the athletic department at Ohio State University, and SMG, a facility management group based in Philadelphia, all have complex environments. For example, a sport organization like the Toronto Raptors must deal with dozens of external elements: the media agencies that cover games, the NBA, the players' union, individual player's agents, companies that merchandise the team's logo, food and beverage companies that supply the concessions, equipment manufacturers, the airline companies that transport the team, and the hotels where the team stays while on the road. In contrast, a small sporting goods store, a local bowling alley, and a recreational soccer team all have, for the most part, a relatively simple environment. They do not interact with a large number of external elements and those they do interact with will be quite similar.

The extent to which a sport organization's environment is stable–dynamic refers to the amount of change in those elements constituting its environment. A sport organization will be seen as having **environmental stability** if (1) its demands on the organization are relatively consistent and dependable (e.g., same types of products and services) and (2) these demands constantly come from very similar clients. A faculty of kinesiology, a publicly owned golf course, and a state high school athletic association, for example, all face relatively stable environments. That is, each faces very similar demands and provides the same service to similar client groups on a year-to-year basis. Dynamic environments, on the other hand, are characterized by rapid change, caused by any number of factors, such as competitors' developing a new product line, increased imports, or a declining market. Athletic clothing manufacturers, such as Body Glove and Speedo, operate in dynamic environments, constantly facing new demands because they continually have to come up with product innovations and try to capture new market segments.

Duncan (1972) used the simple–complex, stable–dynamic dimensions to construct a 2 × 2 matrix as shown in figure 8.2. Each of the cells in the matrix represents a different level of environmental uncertainty. Sport organizations in cell 1, showing the lowest levels of uncertainty, have few elements in their environment, which basically remain the same over time. In contrast, sport organizations in cell 4 have to deal with a large number of highly unpredictable environmental elements.

Complexity of environment		
	Simple	**Complex**
Stable	Low perceived uncertainty. Small number of factors and components in the environment. Factors and components are somewhat similar to one another. Factors and components remain basically the same and are not changing. *Example*: A local sporting goods store	Moderately low perceived uncertainty. Large number of factors and components in the environment. Factors and components remain basically the same. Factors and components are not similar to one another. *Example*: A faculty of physical and health education.
Dynamic	Moderately high perceived uncertainty. Small number of factors and components in the environment. Factors and components are somewhat similar to one another. Factors and components of the environment are in a continual process of change. *Example*: A producer of athletic footwear.	High perceived uncertainty. Large number of factors and components in the environment. Factors and components are not similar to one another. Factors and components of the environment are in a continual process of change. *Example:* The organizing committee of a major sport event such as the Olympic Games

(Left axis label: Amount of change in the environment)

Figure 8.2 *Characteristics of environmental states.*

Reprinted from Characteristics of organizational environments and perceived environmental uncertainty, by R.B. Duncan, published in Administrative Science Quarterly 17(3):320, 1972. ©Johnson Graduate School of Management, Cornell University.

The degree of uncertainty facing a sport organization strongly influences its structure and processes. We now discuss the ways sport managers can control the environmental uncertainty facing their organizations.

Controlling Environmental Uncertainty

All sport organizations face some degree of environmental uncertainty. Uncertainty is therefore a contingency for organizational structure and behaviors (Daft, 2004). To control these uncertainties, sport organizations can either respond to the demands of their external environment (by making changes to their internal structure, processes, and behaviors), or they can attempt to change the nature of the external environment. We look now at some of the techniques sport organizations commonly use to respond to environmental pressure, focusing first on internal changes and then on actions that are externally directed. It is important to note that internal and external initiatives are not mutually exclusive; often several different actions are used at one time. Some techniques are, however, more appropriate to production companies, others to service organizations.

Internally Directed Actions

A sport organization can take internally directed actions to control environmental uncertainty by making changes to the structure and processes of the organization. Details of some of the more popular actions employed by sport organizations are outlined below.

Buffering

The idea of **buffering** emanates from the work of J.D. Thompson (1967). The term essentially refers to attempts to protect the technical core—the part of the organization primarily responsible for production—from fluctuations in the environment. Buffering can occur on the input side by stockpiling raw materials and supplies so the organization is not affected by sudden market shortages, and on the output side by warehousing sufficient amounts of its product to allow its distribution department to meet unexpected increases in demand. Maintenance departments help buffer the technical core by ensuring that machinery is regularly serviced; personnel departments do it by ensuring the required amount of trained labor is available. Some buffering activities, such as stockpiling raw materials and warehousing inventory, involve tying up large amounts of capital and may not be cost effective for some smaller sport organi-

zations. Also, these techniques are not applicable to service-oriented sport organizations, since services cannot be kept in warehouses for use when needed. Buffering may occur, however, in service-orientated sport organizations, through ensuring the ready availability of trained personnel to provide appropriate services when needed.

Boundary Spanners

Boundary spanners are established to obtain information about environmental changes that can affect a sport organization and to disseminate favorable information about the organization to other agencies in its environment (cf. Aldrich & Herker, 1977; Jemison, 1984; Tushman & Scanlan, 1981a; Tushman & Scanlan, 1981b). Boundary spanners can be thought of as links between the sport organization and its environment. The more diverse the environment, the more boundary-spanning roles or units the sport organization is likely to have. Public relations, sales, market research, advertising, and personnel departments can all serve a boundary-spanning role. Staff in these departments scan the environment for information important to the company (cf. Lenz & Engledow, 1986).

In the mid-1980s, when walking was becoming a popular fitness activity for people of many ages, the market research departments of a number of athletic footwear companies saw a potential demand for walking shoes. As a result, Nike, Converse, and Reebok all entered the walking-

---

TIME OUT   *Meeting the Demands of the Athletic Footwear Market*

When the athletic footwear business started to boom, industry leader Reebok could not make shoes fast enough. Over a three-year period sales jumped from $13 million to $60 million to $308 million. Orders were being shipped from six separate warehouses within a 30-mile radius of each other. Basketball shoes went from one warehouse, tennis shoes from another, and running shoes from another. "Each order was shipped from a different location, at a different time, all on separate bills," said Peter McQuaid, Reebok's maintenance engineering manager. "The customer was lucky if he got all of the parts

of his order within three months of each other. Often a customer received a back-order notice, not because we didn't have the product, but because we just could not find it."

To reduce its problems Reebok acquired a new 308,000-square-foot facility and consolidated its distribution. The new facility used bar codes and computers to help with shipping and billing. As a result, fluctuations in customer demand were more easily handled and environmental uncertainty was reduced.

Based on information in Witt (1989), Better customer service justifies new center (1989).

shoe market. By scanning their environment the market research units of these companies, acting as boundary spanners, were able to keep management informed about important new trends.

Smoothing

Smoothing is very much like buffering but it takes place only on the demand side of an organization. Smoothing attempts to reduce fluctuations in the demand for a product or service (Thompson, 1967). Sport managers who operate a facility such as a swimming pool or a hockey rink often offer lower rental or admission prices at off-peak times to encourage people to use their facilities at these times. Another example of smoothing, from Berrett et al.'s (1993) study of entrepreneurs, involves the managers of two retail sporting goods stores, primarily retailers of hockey equipment. They found that, not surprisingly, their sales dropped off in the summer months. Consequently, they expanded their product line to include summer sport equipment, to help reduce seasonal fluctuations in the amount of product they were able to sell.

Rationing

If buffering, boundary spanning, or smoothing does not work, a sport organization can try **rationing**, the practice of allocating resources on the basis of some preestablished criteria. Doctors at a university sport medicine clinic, for example, may ration their services by establishing a priority system for nonvarsity athletes. In a similar vein, many university sport studies departments ration certain classes by allowing only students with necessary prerequisites to enroll, or accepting only those from certain faculties. Rationing, however, as Thompson (1967) notes, is not limited only to service organizations; when supplies are scarce many manufacturers ration allotments of their product to wholesalers or dealers. Rationing in any form is, nevertheless, an unsatisfactory technique because, while this practice may protect the technical core of the sport organization, there are customers in the task environment whose needs are not being met—a problem resulting in lost revenue and the customers' loss of faith in the organization.

Planning and Forecasting

All organizations, including those in the sport industry, control environmental uncertainties by developing plans and attempting to forecast future trends (Boulton, Franklin, Lindsay, & Rue, 1982). The more turbulent the sport organization's environment, the more difficult **planning and fore-**casting become, but the more important it is for sport organizations to engage in these activities to identify future directions. Slack, Bentz, and Wood (1985) describe a planning process that can be used by amateur sport organizations, and Macintosh and Whitson (1990) discuss some of the problems of the rational planning program in which all Canadian sport organizations were required to participate in preparation for the 1988 Olympic Games. Slack, Berrett, and Mistry (1994) also show that, in some cases, planning can actually bring about conflict in a sport organization.

Forecasting is related to planning and involves trying to predict future environmental trends. There are a variety of forecasting techniques, such as surveys, decision-tree analysis, and stochastic modeling. Matthew Levine, president of the Levine Management Group, a San Francisco-based sport and entertainment marketing firm, used in-depth fan surveys (one forecasting technique) to help the Golden State Warriors' organization increase attendance ("Improving your marketing game," 1987).

Externally Directed Actions

To obtain resources from other organizations, gain legitimacy, and sell its product or service, a sport organization must depend on certain elements within its general environment. This dependence creates uncertainty for the sport organization. To reduce this uncertainty an organization can use a number of techniques. The following are the most common.

Contractual Agreements

Sport organizations can reduce environmental uncertainty by entering into long-term **contractual agreements** with firms that supply their input or those involved with the distribution and sale of their outputs. These contracts come in two forms. The first type involves one organization contracting to sell its product to another. For example, in 1984, when L.L. Bean was concerned about falling sales and losing its image as a sporting goods dealer, it entered into a contract with Cannondale, which agreed to supply it with private-label bikes (Charm, 1986; Skow, 1985).

A second form of contractual relationship, termed a licensing agreement, involves one organization buying the rights to use an asset owned by another organization. The most common form of licensing agreement found in the sport industry involves a company buying the right to use a logo, such as the Olympic rings or a professional sport team's emblem, on its product. Between the mid-80s and early 90s, retail sales of licensed sport merchandise rose considerably as a result of this type of contractual agreement. However, these sales hit harder times during the mid-90s and are only now starting to increase again as figure 8.3 shows. The benefits of contracts and licensing agreements are that they reduce environmental uncertainty for a sport organization because they establish formalized links between suppliers and their customers. These links serve as a protection against any change in the relationship between the two organizations for a specified time period.

Joint Ventures

By entering into a **joint venture** (two or more companies forming a separate corporate entity), the organizations involved can achieve objectives they could not attain on their own. For example, a joint venture might be used by a sport equipment manufacturer wanting to do business in a foreign country. By getting involved with a distributor in that country the manufacturer is more easily able to deal with local regulations and modes of operation, reducing environmental uncertainty. Refer to chapter 7 for more information on such strategic alliances.

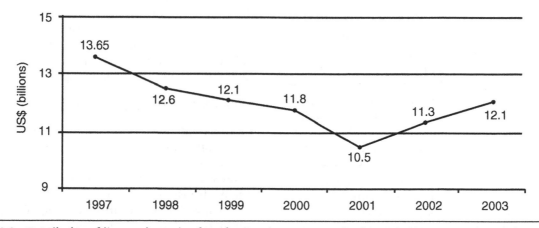

Figure 8.3 *Retail sales of licensed goods of professional sport teams in the United States and Canada.*
Based on information in SGMA International (1999, 2000, 2001, 2004).

TIME OUT   *Joint Venturing: The Medical Fitness Center*

The Los Angeles Athletic Club was already established as an elite sport and fitness club in the middle of downtown, but it was finding difficulty in reaching the potentially lucrative market for executive physicals and fitness evaluations. A solution was found in a joint venture partnership with the California Hospital Medical Center to co-finance and operate the Medical Fitness Center, which functions independently of its parent organizations. The combination of a topflight athletic club and a well-respected medical institution seemed to appeal to both parties as a natural draw for corporate executives in the downtown area.

"The relationship has worked very well," says David L. Geyer, marketing director of the Athletic Club and executive director of the Fitness Center. "We're very blessed to have

the partner we do, a respected medical institution with a strong marketing orientation." The Medical Fitness Center venture came together fairly easily, says Geyer, because the corporate presidents—Charles Hathaway of the Athletic Club and Richard Norling of the Medical Center—served together on the Central City Association, a coalition of downtown business people. Still, says Geyer, the real key to a successful relationship is not how well the partners know each other but how they complement each other's needs. "What someone entering a relationship like this needs to think about is not who would be the best psychological partner for me, but who would be the most attractive to the market I'm interested in."

Reprinted, by permission, copyright 1986, *Athletic Business* magazine.

Cooptation

Cooptation occurs when a sport organization recruits influential people from important parts of its environment to be involved in the organization. Macintosh and Whitson (1990), for example, note how many national sport organizations in Canada have boards made up of business people so they could "open corporate doors" and thus increase the sport organizations' chances of acquiring sponsorships.

Interlocking Directorates

An **interlocking directorate** involves an individual from one company sitting on the board of directors of another. The interlock allows the individual to act as a communication channel between the two companies and to essentially represent one company on the other's board. Such representation means that policy and financial decisions can be influenced. Gruneau (1983) provides evidence of these types of links occurring between Canadian professional sport teams and organizations in both the television and food and beverage industries. Mizruchi and Stearns (1988) suggest that such interlocks are more likely when companies are facing financial uncertainty. Links between professional sport teams and television companies will likely help the team secure a television contract, and greater financial stability and less environmental uncertainty should follow. Stern (1979) also provides evidence of the utility of interorganizational linkages in understanding the evolution of the NCAA.

Executive Recruitment

Several studies have examined the effect that replacing a coach or manager has on a professional sport team's performance (cf. Allen, Panian, & Lotz, 1979; Brown, 1982; Eitzen & Yetman, 1972; Gamson & Scotch, 1964; Grusky, 1963; Pfeffer & Davis-Blake, 1986). Although the general idea behind recruiting a new executive into the senior ranks of a sport organization is that the individual brings new contacts and ideas that can reduce environmental uncertainty and improve performance, the actual results of these studies yield mixed results. Essentially, one theory suggests that the recruitment of a new executive can improve performance, a second suggests it disrupts performance, and a third maintains that it has no effect (Allen, Panian, & Lotz, 1979). Despite these mixed findings, professional sport organizations in particular, and sport organizations in general, still continue to use **executive recruit-** ment as one means of controlling environmental uncertainty.

Public Relations and Advertising

Sport organizations try to influence key individuals and organizations through **public relations** programs and **advertising**. Such programs are especially important in highly competitive markets and in industrial sectors that have a variation in the demand for product. The athletic footwear industry is a case in point: Reebok's decision to underwrite Amnesty International's Human Rights Now concert tour in 1988 is an example of the type of public relations program that both enhanced the company's image and helped it sell shoes. As Graham (1988) points out, the program helped Reebok deal with its competition, because the publicity surrounding the tour helped upstage rival Nike's "Just Do It" campaign.

Mergers and Acquisitions

If a sport organization is unable to reduce environmental uncertainty by techniques such as contractual agreements, establishing interlocking directorates, and developing public relations programs, it may choose to purchase controlling interest in an organization or acquire ownership. While, as we outlined in chapter 6, **mergers and acquisitions** can be a type of growth strategy, they can also be a means of reducing environmental uncertainty by helping the sport organization obtain control over necessary resources or counteract competition. Disney's buying of media organizations (Internet, radio, television, print, and movie) and sport teams (Mighty Ducks hockey team) allows them to have control over content and distribution at the same time.

Changing Domains

Sport organizations, through their senior managers or owners, select the domain in which they wish to operate. Many factors, such as government regulations, a highly competitive marketplace, the increasing cost of supplies, or a declining consumer demand, can create enough uncertainty for a sport organization that it may choose to change or modify its domain. Acquiring new businesses or divesting parts of its existing business are the most frequent ways a sport organization will change its domain; another way is by adding new products or services. For example, Herman's World of Sporting Goods, a chain of sporting goods stores, expanded its offering in the area of water sports in the 1980s. H. George Walker, a vice president of the company, noted that "the water sport category is growing. More people do things at the water. No matter where you are, you find a river, a lake, or a pond. We've expanded the line to give it better presence" (Adams, 1987, p. 28). While Herman's and other sporting goods stores were moving into the water sports domain, the increased competition led to some mass merchandisers divesting themselves of any involvement in this area and focusing on their more traditional markets (Adams, 1987).

Trade and Professional Associations

Some sport organizations will attempt to influence their environment by joining together to form **trade** or **professional associations**. By acting collectively these associations can influence environmental issues such as government policy issues or trade regulations. The British organization the Institute of Leisure and Amenity Management (ILAM) is an example of this type of organization; it is "the professional body for the leisure industry and represents the interests of leisure managers across all sectors and specialisms of leisure" and has at its objective "to develop the profession and promote the value of investment in leisure services" (ILAM, 2005, p. 1). Examples of similar associations operating in North America include the American Society of Golf Course Architects, the International Association of Auditorium Managers, the National Sporting Goods Association, and the United Ski Industries Association. All have either a direct or indirect mandate to work to control environmental uncertainty for their members.

Political Lobbying

Many sport organizations lobby various levels of government in order to influence decisions about issues such as tax regulations, grant programs, and labor questions. **Political lobbying** may occur through a trade or professional association such as those discussed above, or a sport organization may engage in lobbying or other forms of political activity on its own behalf. Macintosh, Bedecki, and Franks (1987) illustrate how a number of Canadian sport organizations, such as the Canadian Sports Advisory Council, the Canadian Association for Health, Physical Education and Recreation (CAHPER), and the Sports Federation of Canada have lobbied the Canadian government at different times for support in reaching program objectives. Burbank, Andranovich, and Heying (2001) provides many examples of the political activity that took place to ensure the smooth operation of the 1984 Los Angeles Olympics, the 1996 Atlanta Olympics, and the 2002 Salt Lake City Olympics.

Illegal Activities

In some cases sport organizations will engage in unethical or **illegal activities** in order to control environmental uncertainty. These activities may include price fixing, monopoly, franchise violation, and illegal mergers and acquisitions (Staw & Szwajkowski, 1975). Also particularly relevant for university sport organizations are recruiting violations, which are becoming almost commonplace in U.S. collegiate athletics. By engaging in illegal recruiting activity the sport team is able to secure the services of a top-quality player; the team performs better, gate receipts go up, and alumni funds and television coverage increases. The net effect of these changes is that the level of environmental uncertainty facing the team is reduced (see Sack & Staurowsky, 1998).

Other Perspectives on the Organization-Environment Relationship

In addition to the work of researchers like Burns and Stalker, Lawrence and Lorsch, and Duncan, there are other ways of examining the relationship between a sport organization and its environment. Here we look briefly at the approaches of stakeholder theory, institutional theory, the resource-dependence perspective, and population ecology.

Stakeholder Theory

Earlier in the chapter, we discussed an organization's general and task environment. The groups that were mentioned, such as clients or suppliers, can be termed stakeholders. Stakeholders are groups, organizations, and individuals who can influence or be affected by an organization's actions (Freeman, 1984). They are typically classified according to their role: governments, clients, media, and so on. Stakeholder theorists are concerned with studying the relationship between an organization and its stakeholders. This involves not only acknowledging stakeholders' interests but also understanding and formulating strategies to respond to these interests.

Stakeholder theory provides an easy way to classify stakeholders: those who must truly be satisfied, those who should be satisfied, and those who don't need to be satisfied in order for the organization to be successful. Mitchell, Agle and Wood (1997) suggest that an organization's managers will want to satisfy salient stakeholders, because they possess power, legitimacy, and urgency.

Harrison and St. John (1996) argue that there is a justification for appropriate stakeholder management activities. Following stakeholder theory can ultimately increase the ability to predict and control the external (stakeholder) environment, enhance product or service success, raise efficiency and flexibility, bring in contracts, and increase media power because of more (positive) interest in the corporation. It can also lead to a decrease in potential conflicts and damaging moves by the external environment. Post, Preston, and Sachs (2002) stated that both managers and scholars recognize the critical interdependencies between a firm and its stakeholders, and managing them correctly is key to the survival, competitive advantage, and wealth of an organization.

Included as a stakeholder are the organization's employees. While often forgotten in stakeholder analysis, they are a critical part of the organization's success. A whole field is dedicated to them in human resource management (HRM). HRM puts a spotlight on employee-related issues such as recruitment, selection, training, and performance appraisal. Planning for human resources means doing an environmental audit, a job analysis, projecting the supply of and demand for human resources, and matching supply and demand. In the sport management literature, there have been a number of studies related to HRM. We have already talked about executive recruitment, but there are also studies on training sport facility staff to deal with the employee–customer interface (Martin, 1990) and on the causes of stress in physical education faculty members (Danylchuk, 1993).

Institutional Theory

The utility of institutional approaches to understanding the organization-environment relationship was first articulated by John Meyer and Brian Rowan in their 1977 article "Institutionalized organizations: Formal structure as myth and ceremony." Following Meyer and Rowan's article a number of researchers have examined the impact of the institutional environment on an organization's structure (cf. DiMaggio & Powell, 1983; Oliver, 1988, 1991; Tolbert, 1985; Tolbert & Zucker, 1983; Zucker, 1983, 1987). The institutional environment of an organization "is conceptualized in terms of understandings and expectations of appropriate organizational form and behavior that are shared by members of society" (Tolbert, 1985,

p. 1). By changing its structure to conform to the expectations of the institutional environment, "an organization demonstrates that it is acting on a collectively valued purpose in a proper and adequate manner" (Meyer & Rowan, 1977, p. 349). This conformity helps to establish the organization as a legitimate entity and in turn to ensure its long-term effectiveness.

Organizations subjected to the same institutional pressures exhibit isomorphism, that is, they tend to become structurally alike. Kikulis (2000) for example, showed how different stages and levels of institutionalization can explain continuity and change in governance and decision making in volunteer boards in national sport organizations. Silk, Slack, and Amis (2000) showed how **institutional theory** can be used to analyze televised sport production.

Resource Dependence

No sport organization exists in isolation from the other organizations in its environment, the source of the material and financial resources a sport organization needs to survive. To obtain these resources a sport organization engages in transactions with the appropriate organizations in its environment. This is called **resource dependence.** Pfeffer and Salancik (1978), in their book *The External Control of Organizations: A Resource-Dependence Perspective,* discuss the nature of these transactions. They focus specifically on the ways organizations depend on their environment for resources, the resulting uncertainty, and the techniques managers use to reduce this uncertainty.

When a sport organization engages in a resource transaction with another organization, it reduces its vulnerability to environmental fluctuations, but at the same time increases its dependence on the organization supplying the resource, thus reducing its own autonomy and ability to act independently. The extent to which a sport organization depends on another organization for resources is determined by three factors: (1) the importance of the resource (i.e., the extent to which the sport organization requires the resource for its continued operation and survival), (2) the extent to which the organization providing the resource has discretion over its allocation and use, and (3) the extent to which there are alternative sources from which the dependent organization can obtain the resource. Slack and Hinings (1992) have shown how national sport organizations in Canada are dependent for their financial resources on the federal government, and how this dependence has allowed the government to control many of the actions of these organizations, in particular the emphasis they were required to place on high-performance sport. Armstrong-Doherty (1996) uses a resource-dependence perspective to show how an athletic department is dependent on different sources, especially central administration, for survival. However, she does not go into details on this topic.

However, while the organization supplying the resource can wield considerable control over the dependent organization, it is not the dependence per se that creates problems but the uncertainty surrounding the availability of resources because the organization's environment is not reliable. The organization then has a choice: not change and possibly not survive or change to respond to the changing environment (Pfeffer & Salancik, 1978).

In order to control the uncertainties created by resource supplies, dependent organizations attempt to "enact" their environment. That is, managers use techniques such as interlocking directorates, joint ventures, and executive succession to reduce the uncertainty surrounding their supply of resources. The resource-dependence perspective has considerable potential for understanding the impact of the environment on the structure and processes of different types of sport organizations, yet there has been virtually no published work in sport management employing this theoretical perspective.

Population Ecology

Originating with the work of Michael Hannan and John Freeman (1977b), the **population ecology,** or natural selection, approach to organization-environment relations is heavily influenced by the biological literature, in particular the notion of the survival of the fittest (cf. Ulrich, 1987a; Ulrich & Barney, 1984; Wholey & Brittain, 1986). The idea is that organizations, like living things, survive if they are able to exploit their environment for resources. Those that are unable to do so adequately, perish. Unlike other environmental approaches, the focus of population ecology is not on individual organizations but on populations of organizations; a population ecologist would not focus on individual sporting goods stores but on the population of these types of stores that exists in a particular community, for example, the state of California. In addition, the environment is limited to the task environment and is focused on resources, so environmental change is largely

defined as fundamental changes in the resource pool.

Researchers who adopt this theoretical position look closely at the birth and death rates of particular types of organizations. New organizations attempt to establish a **niche** for themselves, that is, an area of the market from which they can obtain the resources necessary to survive. The idea is that, like living creatures, organizations must make use of the resources in their niche. If the niche is narrow, a specialist organization such as Peconic Paddler, a canoe rental and sales organization, is most likely to survive. If the niche is wider, a generalist organization is more likely. For example, narrow niches are represented by competitive cyclists' support of custom bike manufacturers such as Terry Precision Bikes for Women, whereas broad-based recreational cyclists who require a wider range of goods and services support the more general cycle manufacturers such as Huffy. Specialists are often more efficient than generalists but, because of their specialization, are more likely to suffer if the environment changes. Generalists, on the other hand, are buffered from environmental changes by the breadth of their operations. If an organization cannot locate itself in a niche, it will ultimately perish.

Each niche has a certain carrying capacity. Just as a forest can only support so many deer or similar animals, so a community can only support so many sport equipment stores or aerobics studios. The competition among these similar organizations for the limited resources means that some will be successful but others will fail (Aldrich, McKelvey, & Ulrich, 1984). In the language of population ecology, they will be selected out, just like weak animals are destined to perish. As well as niches, population ecologists are also interested in the concept of **population density** (Hannan & Freeman, 1988), the extent to which the population of organizations within a niche is able to exploit the resources available.

By using concepts like niche width, carrying capacity, and population density, scholars using the population ecology approach have been able to study the possibilities of success for new organizations entering a specific market, and why entry into the niche becomes less attractive as the number of organizations in a niche grows (i.e., as population density increases). They have also been able to show how organizations pursuing "a leader strategy" (Miles and Snow's Prospectors) may be successful if they are the first to establish themselves in a niche, but how, as population density increases, organizations pursuing "a follow-the-leader strategy," (Miles and Snow's Analyzers) are likely to be more successful. These findings have had a significant impact on our understanding of the way organizations operate.

Despite its utility in helping us understand many issues about organization-environment relation, population ecology has a number of limitations (cf. Hawley, 1981). First, it is highly deterministic, in that the environment is seen as the sole factor in organizational effectiveness. Second (and related to the first limitation), population ecology takes no account of managerial action. For example, population ecologists believe that if you are the owner or manager of an aerobics studio and interest in aerobics as a form of exercise booms, then you will be successful, but if interest wanes you will not survive, regardless of what action you take; the environment has determined success or failure, not the manager. Third, survival is the only measure of organizational effectiveness. If an organization survives, it is effective; if it perishes, it is not effective. Fourth, population ecology is not well suited to the study of certain types of sport organizations, because agencies like the USOC, the IAAF, and Skate Canada are unlikely to be put out of existence; no other organization can challenge what they do because they operate under monopoly conditions. Finally, population ecologists look at changes in organizational populations over relatively long periods of time. Short-term changes are seen as aberrations, which are inconsequential to understanding change in any significant way.

Notwithstanding its limitations, the population ecology approach has considerable potential to increase our understanding of the structure and processes of sport organizations. However, to date, a limited number of studies within the field of sport management have employed the theoretical ideas contained within this approach. Cunningham (2002) is one of the very few to use population ecology, in combination with institutional theory, resource dependence, and strategic choice, to develop a model of organizational change.

The Relationship Between an Organization's Environment and Its Structure

As we have seen, all sport organizations are to some extent dependent on their environment. The more dependent an organization is on its environment the more vulnerable it is to changes in the environment. Here we look briefly at the effect of the environment on the structural attributes of complexity, formalization, and centralization.

Environmental Conditions and Complexity

Under conditions of environmental uncertainty, a successful sport organization will exhibit a relatively high level of complexity. To respond to uncertainty, the organization has "to employ specialist staff in boundary or interface roles—in positions where they form a link with the outside world, securing and evaluating relevant information" (Child, 1984, p. 219). Consequently, an uncertain environment will require an increase in both the number of departments and in the specialist personnel required to buffer the sport organization from environmental fluctuation. Also, there may be an increase in the level of vertical differentiation within an organization (thus increasing complexity) because, under conditions of environmental uncertainty, there is a need to delegate decision making to people who understand the local conditions and can make quick decisions.

Environmental Conditions and Formalization

The increased levels of organizational complexity found under conditions of environmental uncertainty require an appropriate means of integration. Successful organizations are more likely to use "flexible rather than highly formalized or hierarchical methods of coordination and information sharing . . ." (Child, 1984, p. 219), including face-to-face communication, the use of project teams, and the appointment of staff to liaison and negotiating roles. Under stable environmental conditions, sport organizations will tend to adopt formalized operating procedures; there is little need for rapid changes within the organization, so it can capitalize on the economies that result from the use of these formalized procedures.

Environmental Conditions and Centralization

Mintzberg (1979) suggests that the more complex an organization's environment is, the more likely it is to have a decentralized structure. The complexity of the environment means that one person cannot comprehend all the information needed to make appropriate decisions; consequently, the decisions are decentralized to specialists who make the decisions concerning the particular aspect of the environment for which they are responsible. There is, however, evidence (cf. Mintzberg, 1979) to suggest that under conditions of extreme hostility in the environment (i.e.,

a threat to an organization such as the advent of a new competitor), an organization will move to centralize its structure temporarily. While this temporary centralization may pose a dilemma for those organizations that operate in complex environments, given the choice the senior managers tend to opt for a centralized structure in which everyone knows who is in control and decisions can be made quickly.

KEY ISSUES FOR MANAGERS

As you have seen in this chapter, there are different ways of looking at a sport organization's environment. As a manager, you should determine which approach seems appropriate for you and your organization, and use that approach to strategically analyze the environment.

In addition, when determining the composition of the environment (e.g., types of stakeholders) and its nature (i.e., stable–dynamic), your organization should have different structures and processes to respond appropriately to the environment. A stable environment is more accepting of low complexity, high formalization, and high centralization. An

unstable or uncertain environment requires more flexibility and, most likely, organizations with high complexity, low formalization, and high decentralization. Because environmental uncertainty is undesirable for organizations, we have provided methods to help reduce uncertainty: internal actions of buffering, boundary spanning, smoothing, rationing, and planning or forecasting; external actions of contracts, joint ventures, cooptation, interlocking directorates, executive recruitment, public relations and advertising, mergers and acquisitions, domain changes, trade and professional associations, political lobbying, and illegal activities.

SUMMARY AND CONCLUSIONS

The environment, a source of uncertainty for the organization, has a major impact on the structure and processes of a sport organization. Managers must attempt to eliminate or minimize the impact of this uncertainty. While the environment can be broadly conceptualized as anything outside the organization, people managing sport organizations have to be concerned with those sectors of the general environment that can influence their operations and their organization's task environment. The task environment is composed of groups such as customers, suppliers, competitors, and related regulatory agencies. Also important for our understanding of the sport organization-environment relationship are the domain, the area to which the sport organization directs its products or services, and the perceived environment, the manager's perception of the environment, which may be different from the actual environment.

We looked at three of the classic studies on the organization-environment relationship and what they mean for the managers of sport organizations. Burns and Stalker's work suggests that under conditions of environmental uncertainty an organic type of structure is most effective; when the environment is stable a more mechanistic type of structure works best. Lawrence and Lorsch conceptualized an organization's environment as made up of various subenvironments. Organizational subunits are required to meet the demands of these subenvironments if the organization is to be successful. Duncan saw environmental uncertainty as influenced by the complexity of the environment and the extent to which elements within the environment are stable–dynamic. To control environmental uncertainty managers of sport organizations can use a number of techniques, some involving changes to the organization's internal structure and processes, others are directed toward changing the external environment.

We also looked at four of the more recent approaches to understanding the organization-environment relationship: stakeholder theory, resource-dependence theory, institutional theory, and population ecology. The latter two in particular have generated a considerable amount of literature that has contributed considerably to our understanding of the organization-environment relationship.

KEY CONCEPTS

boundary spanners (p. 159)

buffering (p. 159)

contractual agreements (p. 160)

cooptation (p. 162)

domain (p. 153)

environmental complexity (p. 157)

environmental stability (p. 157)

environmental uncertainty (p. 157)

executive recruitment (p. 162)

general environment (p. 151)

illegal activities (p. 163)

institutional theory (p. 164)

interlocking directorates (p. 162)

joint ventures (p. 161)

mechanistic (p. 154)

mergers and acquisitions (p. 162)

niche (p. 165)

organic (p. 154)

perceived environment (p. 154)

planning and forecasting (p. 160)

political lobbying (p. 163)

population density (p. 165)

population ecology (p. 165)

public relations and advertising (p. 162)

rationing (p. 160)

resource dependence (p. 164)

sectors (p. 151)

smoothing (p. 160)

stakeholder theory (p. 163)

subenvironments (p. 156)

task environment (p. 153)

trade and professional associations (p. 163)

REVIEW QUESTIONS

1. Pick a familiar sport organization. How do the different sectors of the general environment influence this organization?

2. What elements would make up the task environment of a private tennis club? Explain how these various elements influence club operations.

3. In understanding managerial action, is it the actual environment or the perceived environment that is most important? Why?

4. Why are organic structures more appropriate for a sport organization operating in a dynamic environment?

5. Pick a familiar sport organization. What can Lawrence and Lorsch's work tell us about the relationship of this organization to its environment?

6. What is the relationship between differentiation and integration? How do sport organizations achieve integration?

7. How do the simple–complex and stable–dynamic environment continuums influence a sport organization?

8. For what type of reasons would an athletic footwear manufacturer engage in political lobbying?

9. Who acts as boundary spanners for your university's athletic department?

10. What would be the advantage of a joint venture with a local distributor for a sport equipment manufacturer trying to enter a new Eastern European market?

11. There have been mixed findings about the relative merits of hiring a new manager or

coach in professional sport. What do you think are the advantages and disadvantages of this means of controlling environmental uncertainty?

12. Describe the stakeholders that have a possible relationship with a high school athletics department. Order them in terms of importance and explain your reasoning.

13. Institutional theory suggests that understandings and expectations about appropriate organizational form and behavior are shared by members of society. What are these understandings and expectations? Do they differ for the various types of sport organizations? How do managers deal with them?

14. How do amateur sport organizations and clubs control resource uncertainty?

15. How could population ecology help our understanding of the rapid growth of fitness clubs?

SUGGESTIONS FOR FURTHER READING

If you are interested in finding out more about the relationship between organizations and their environment begin by looking at the work of Burns and Stalker (1961), Lawrence and Lorsch (1967), and Duncan (1972) because, as we noted earlier in the chapter, these studies outline some of the more important findings on the organization-environment relationship and provide the basis for much of the subsequent work in this area. For those who find the resource-dependence theory an appealing approach, Pfeffer and Salancik's (1978) book *The External Control of Organizations: A Resource-Dependence Perspective* is a must. However, one of the shortcomings of the resource-dependence approach is that, despite its inherent appeal, there has been little in the way of any extension of Pfeffer and Salancik's original ideas.

Anyone interested in institutional theory should start off with Meyer and Rowan's (1977) article "Institutionalized Organizations: Formal Structure as Myth and Ceremony." Also useful and interesting is Lynne Zucker's (1988) book *Institutional Patterns and Organizations,* a collection of papers by scholars who employ the institutional perspective. For an understanding of population ecology it is useful to start with Hannan and Freeman's (1977b) "The Population Ecology of Organizations." A number of books have extended this earlier work. Howard Aldrich's (1979) *Organizations and Environments* is probably the most comprehensive treatment of the organization-environment relationship using the population ecology approach. Also useful is Jitendra Singh's (1990) edited book *Organizational Evolution: New Directions,* a collection of papers written by many of the leading population ecologists. Further work on all these perspectives can be found by looking through any of the major organization or sociology journals *(Academy of Management Journal, Academy of Management Review, Administrative Science Quarterly, American Journal of Sociology, American Sociological Review, Journal of Management Studies,* and *Organization Studies).* Managers may also be interested in arguably the most popular tool for analyzing an organization's environment, Porter's Five Forces Model, which is described in his 1980(b) book *Competitive Strategy.*

If we look specifically at research on sport organizations, there has been little theoretical or empirical work on the organization-environment relationship. Slack and Hinings, in their (1992) article "Understanding Change in National Sport Organizations: An Integration of Theoretical Perspectives," use resource-dependence theory and institutional theory to explain different aspects of the change process. Also their (1994) "Organization Studies" article, based on the arguments of institutional theory, empirically demonstrates the impact of institutional pressures on national sport organizations. Silk, Slack, and Amis in their (2000) "Bread, Butter and Gravy: An Institutional Approach to Televised Sport Production" also use institutional pressures. Finally, Thibault, Frisby, and Kikulis (1999) examine different environmental pressures in relation to interorganizational linkages in their "Interorganizational Linkages in the Delivery of Local Leisure Services in Canada: Responding to Economic, Political and Social Pressures."

CASE FOR ANALYSIS

China as an Emerging Market: Changes in the Environment of the Chinese Sport Landscape

Following long years of state control, the Chinese sport system has undergone major changes thanks to various forces in the environment. In 1978, China came under new leadership with Deng Xiaoping. He moved the governance system away from centralized control toward a more market-led economy in order to increase profits. Foreigners were again allowed to enter China. This had considerable impact on Chinese organizations, particularly those involved in sport.

Large transnational corporations saw a golden opportunity to reach the world's largest consumer market. Corporations like Nike and IMG started finding ways to tap that market. IMG teamed up with FIFA to establish a Chinese soccer league system, as well as operate various seminars to teach Chinese sport managers the "best practices" in terms of soccer's daily operations and logistics. However, this created tension between China's traditional culture and the new capitalist approach to sport, to the extent that sponsorships and investments dropped, causing 11 of the 12 original professional soccer clubs to declare bankruptcy.

In their bid to develop the Asian market, Western teams are creating opportunities to increase their fan base. Manchester United was the first major Western professional team to come to China, playing matches in Shanghai stadium in 1999. Since then other teams such as Real Madrid and Stockport have followed suit.

One of the biggest factors expected to influence the Chinese sport market is the upcoming 2008 Summer Olympic Games to be held in Beijing. China had previously bid for these games but had been repeatedly criticized for its human rights record. It finally won the right to host an Olympics, with rumors of strong commercial interest from the likes of Nike, GM, Xerox, Coke, Heineken, NBC, and Fuji Film influencing the vote. The Chinese government vowed to make the 2008 games the best ever and has been on schedule—even ahead of schedule—in its preparations.

The 2008 Olympic Games, to be held in Beijing, are expected to open the door for Western sport organizations eager to enter the Chinese sport market.

Holding the Olympics in China is expected to facilitate business ventures. Nike, for example, has tried to penetrate the Chinese market since the early 1980s and finally succeeded through a joint venture. Luo (2000, p. 233) noted that "Nike tried to deal directly with state enterprises, but state-owned factories could not comprehend what Nike wanted in terms of price, quality, and delivery. . . . Its American managers faced problems in dealing with China's public sector." In effect, it was a business culture clash. Chen (2001, p. 161) added that there is still a strong socialist force in China with the Communist Party exerting a strong conservative influence, and "foreign businesses forget this at their peril."

There is an exponential increase in the number of Western sport organizations looking to tap the Chinese and broader Asian markets. For example, the Formula One international car racing fed- eration is interested in holding a race in China. MotoGP (the motorcycle racing federation) is also examining opportunities. Most likely other professional sports, such as hockey and baseball, will follow suit. The NBA already has 7-foot, 6-inch Yao Ming on the Houston Rockets.

Based on information from T. Slack, M.L. Silk, & H. Fan (2005).

Questions

1. How has the Chinese sport market been affected by changes in the environment?
2. What factors do Western organizations need to consider when doing business in China?
3. What type of changes in the Chinese sport landscape do you think will occur in the future?
4. What are the drawbacks to Western companies doing business in China?

Holding the Olympics in China is expected to facilitate business ventures. Nike, for example, has tried to penetrate the Chinese market since the early 1980s and finally succeeded through a joint venture. Luo (2000, p. 235) noted that "Nike tried to deal directly with state enterprises, but state-owned factories could not comprehend what Nike wanted in terms of price, quality, and delivery. . . . its American managers faced problems in dealing with China's public sector." In effect, it was a business culture clash. Chen (2001, p. 181) added that there is still a strong socialist force in China, with the Communist Party exerting a strong influence, and "foreign business was a major part of this . . ."

Then, Nike, Reebok, and other businesses began providing businesses looking to tap the Chinese sport market. For example, the Formula One International car racing fed-

eration is interested in holding a race in China. MotoGP (the motorcycle racing federation) is also examining opportunities. Most likely other professional sports, such as hockey and baseball, will follow suit. The NBA already has 7-foot, 6-inch Yao Ming on the Houston Rockets.

Based on Information in "Nike, Adidas, and China" (2004).

Questions

1. How has the Chinese sport market been affected by changes in the environment?
2. What are some Western organizations that are either doing business in China?
3. What types of changes in the Chinese sport market can you think will occur in the future?
4. What are the drawbacks to Western companies doing business in China?

Chapter 9

Sport Organizations and Technology

LEARNING OBJECTIVES

When you have read this chapter you should be able to

1. explain what we mean by technology,

2. describe how the work of Woodward, Perrow, and Thompson has contributed to our understanding of technology,

3. discuss the major critiques of the technology imperative and the important factors to consider when studying technology,

4. explain the principal types of technology being used in sport organizations, and

5. describe how technology influences the structure of a sport organization.

THE CHANGING NATURE OF TECHNOLOGY: MANUFACTURING GOLF BALLS

Maxfli Golf is one of the leading manufacturers of golf equipment. In the 1920s when the company first started making golf balls much of the work was done by hand. A former worker recalls:

In those days after the two halves of the golf balls were joined together and the core inserted they were put into very hot water for about 30 minutes. Then they were put into cold water to cool off for 10 minutes. Next the balls were taken out and the girls used "trimmers"—a little instrument with a wedge—to take off the thin rubber [where the two halves were joined]. After that the paint went

on. Girls put the paint in the palms of their hands [they never touched the ball with their fingers] and rolled the ball around, finally dropping it on the tray. They trimmed and painted all day. After the ball had been hardened other girls stenciled.

Back then, the only machines that were used were for core winding. Forty years later, production methods had altered drastically, practically everything was mechanized. Now refrigeration played an important part in the manufacture of a golf ball. The core of rubber-covered paste on which the ball started was frozen solid for the first winding—5 feet of

(continued)

(continued)

rubber tape. For the second winding, 21 yards of rubber thread were wound on at full tension by an ingenious machine. It held the ball between two oscillating rollers subjected to a jet of compressed air, the combination of forces turning the ball in all directions ensured even winding. The gutta-percha shells were fitted around the core, followed by a molding process that left a seam, and then more freezing took place, rendering it brittle and easier to cut off. A brushing machine brushed the ball clean of dust (no more hands!). Next came a full-scale examination for all types of defects. Then came painting (automatic, of course) and a further series of five tests for resilience, weight, and so on.

Today the production of golf balls is a meta-science. A requirement of any good golf ball surface pattern is to provide uniform aerodynamics. The ball must fly accurately and consistently no matter how it is aligned to the clubface. The surface pattern of Maxfli Golf's DDH (dodecahedron) ball has been designed for greater accuracy, but the unique use of four different computer-established dimple sizes has produced a ball that has been shown in tests to go further than any other leading ball. The 12-pentagon format allows the manufacturer to get more seams on the ball. If you can construct a ball with a lot of seams on it, you will decrease its movement in the air. Some golf balls have only one seam but the dimple formation of the DDH gives it 10 seams; intensive testing has proved that this feature makes the ball the most accurate ever produced.

Adapted, by permission, from J. McMillan, 1989, *The Dunlop story* (London: Weidenfeld and Nicolson Publishers), 116-117.

As the Maxfli example illustrates, the manufacturing process involved in making golf balls has changed considerably over the past 70 years. Originally the balls were made by hand, the process was then mechanized, and today computer technology is used extensively in both the design and manufacturing of golf balls. These changes in the manufacturing process are largely a result of technological advances and their application to the sporting goods industry. Technology has changed the way virtually all sport organizations operate. The Olympic motto of "Faster, Higher, Stronger" could be used for technology's use within sport organizations. Technology is embedded in sport: shark suits for swimmers, computer chip timers for races, synthetic grass for football, gold shoes for Michael Johnson (a U.S. track star), figure skaters' plastic composite skates, electronic form submissions for competitions, electronic file transfers, and live Internet broadcasts of sport events are just a few examples. Companies like Huffy use robotics in their manufacturing process, Adidas uses computer-assisted design technology to develop its sportswear, and coaches everywhere make extensive use of video analysis. Even the local sport club probably has a computer and a fax machine.

Technology is a major imperative that affects the structure and processes of a sport organization. In this chapter we look at what is meant when we talk about technology. We review some of the major research studies that have examined the impact of technology on organizational structure. We then look at some of the critiques of these studies and of the technology imperative. We briefly discuss the impact that the new microelectronic technologies like computer-aided design (CAD) can have on a sport organization. Finally we draw some conclusions about the relationship between technology and the structure of a sport organization.

What Is Technology?

While there has been considerable variation in the way researchers have defined technology it is generally seen as being concerned with the means by which an organization transforms inputs into outputs. More specifically, it includes the materials, knowledge, equipment, and processes required to produce a desired good or service (cf. Perrow, 1967). All sport organizations, whether involved in manufacturing tennis rackets, designing swimming

TIME OUT   *Multiple Technologies in a Single Sport*

Most any sport these days relies on a multitude of technologies. Take figure skating for example. An elite skater will have custom-made skates, train on and off the ice with the latest biomechanical technologies (weight training programs, endurance training techniques, health monitoring, video training). Her coach will use a computer to plan the skater's training and competitive season and keep track of results along the way. When on the road, the skater will use a computer and the Internet to stay in touch with her family and friends through e-mail or Instant Messages, and to do homework if she is still in school. For her competitions, the figure skater will have digitally mastered music programs burned onto a CD and will wear a dress that has been designed and created using computers. Judges' marks will be determined with the help of a computer and video replay. Finally, results will be automatically tabulated and displayed on large digital screens for the audience to see.

© Human Kinetics

When technology and organizations work flawlessly, they can make the athlete. An elite figure skater, for example, relies on a number of biomechanical and computer technologies to present a seemingly effortless performance.

pools, or staging sport events for young children, use some type of technology.

The technology employed in a sport organization can be examined at three different levels. First, we can look at what is commonly referred to as **organizational-level technology**. Second, we can look at the **work-group**, or **department-level, technology**. Finally, we can look at **individual-level technologies**. Organizational-level technology uses the total organization as its unit of analysis and focuses primarily on the technology required to produce the particular product or service. In a sport organization like Hillerich and Bradsby, a manufacturer of baseball bats, the primary type of organizational technology used is referred to as "mass production."

Studies of work-group, or department-level, technology recognize that different units making up an organization employ different types of technologies (Grimes & Klein, 1973; Van de Ven & Delbecq, 1974). For example, Karsten Manufacturing, the makers of Ping golf clubs, will employ a different technologies in its research-and-development department from that used in marketing. Studies of individual-level technology are primarily concerned with the nature of individual jobs and, in particular, job design (Hrebiniak, 1974).

Research on Technology and Organizations

Concern over the impact of technology on organizational structure and processes can be traced back to the work of Adam Smith in the 18th century. However, the 1950s and 1960s saw a heightened interest in the concept and since this time it has been an important variable in the study of organizations. In this section we review the work of three authors whose research has had a major influence on our understanding of the relationship between technology and organizational structure, and provided the basis for much of the subsequent work in this area. We focus specifically on the work of Woodward, Perrow, and Thompson. We then examine some of the criticisms leveled at this work, and also look at some of the related issues to be considered when studying organizational technology.

Woodward: Technological Complexity

In the 1950s Joan Woodward and her research team in the Human Relations Research Unit at South East Essex Technical College studied 100 manufacturing organizations operating in the south of England. The organizations ranged in size from 100 employees to more than a 1,000. Woodward was interested in finding out which of their managers followed classical management principles, and whether they were more effective than those who didn't. Her research team collected data and established measures for a number of different aspects of an organization, including span of control, levels of management, extent of formalization, economic performance, and technology.

Woodward's initial findings (1958; 1965) were that classical management principles were not consistently used in the organizations she studied and that, when they were, the application of these principles did not relate to effectiveness as measured by economic performance. However, Woodward questioned her own findings and started to look for other factors that might be influencing performance. Using the criterion "type of production technology employed," she classified the organizations into 10 groups. Based on their level of technical complexity, these groups were further reduced into three major categories: **unit** or **small-batch** production, **mass** or **large-batch production**, and **continuous-process production**. Unit production was seen as exhibiting the least amount of **technological complexity**, and continuous-process production the most. When they were grouped according to the level of technological complexity, Woodward found that she could identify a typical type of organizational structure for the group, in essence a "correct" way to organize (see table 9.1). The organizations that came closest to this structure were the most effective in terms of economic performance. Those organizations involved in unit production were less structured than those involved in mass production or continuous-process production. They tended to

Table 9.1   Relationship Between Technical Complexity and Structural Characteristics of Effective Organizations

Structural characteristics	Technology		
	Unit production	Mass production	Continuous-process production
Number of levels of management	Low	Low to medium	High
Number of skilled workers	High	Low	High
Supervisor's span of control	Low to medium	High	Low
Manager or supervisor to total personnel ratio	Low	Medium	High
Centralization of decision making	Low	High	Low
Amount of formalization	Low	High	Low
Type of communication			
Verbal	High	Low	High
Written	Low	High	Low

Based on information in J. Woodward (1965).

have a small number of managerial levels in their hierarchy, they were relatively low in formalization, and decision making was decentralized. The focus in these organizations was essentially on custom manufacturing. An example of an organization within the sport industry that employs unit production would be Faulkner Brown, a British architectural company that designed Ponds Forge International and Community Sport Centre, the aquatic facility for the 1991 World University Games.

Companies that manufacture large quantities of the same product often use mass-production assembly lines. The processes employed are repetitive and routine, the span of control is high, the number of skilled workers is low, and formalization is relatively high. Examples of organizations within the sport industry involved in mass production would include Huffy, which can make 16,000 bikes a day, and Fleer, a baseball card manufacturer.

Organizations that use continuous-process production are highly mechanized and their production process does not stop. This type of production is not found within the sport industry; it is generally used by organizations such as oil refineries, chemical plants, and breweries.

Woodward's work demonstrated that, within each of these three categories, those organizations whose scores came closest to the typical structure for the type of technology they exhibited were the most effective. She concluded that technology was the primary determinant of organizational structure. More recently, proponents of structuration theory (a theory that looks at the agent-structure relationships) have supported Woodward's work (cf. Barley, 1986; Orlikowski, 1992).

Perrow: Task Variability and Analyzability

While Woodward's approach to understanding the impact of technology on organizations was limited to manufacturing firms, Perrow's work (1967; 1968) is more generalizable and can be applied to both manufacturing and service firms. It is also more applicable than Woodward's schema to understanding departmental or work-group technology (Daft, 1992). For Perrow (1967, p. 195) technology can be described as "the actions that an individual performs upon an object, with or without the aid of tools or mechanical devices, in order to make some changes in that object. The object or 'raw material' may be a living being, human or otherwise, a symbol, or an inanimate object."

To classify technology Perrow uses two dimensions. The first of these concerns the amount of variation in the tasks being performed, and refers specifically to the number of exceptions encountered in the work situation. When the work being performed is routine, there will be few exceptions. For example, people assembling bikes or running shoes in factories will experience few exceptions

---

TIME OUT *Adidas Gains Market Advantage Through Technology*

When Adidas restructured, it began by defining its three consumer groups and the apparel needs of each (Sport performance, Sport heritage, and Sport style). Adidas' next step was to choose the latest technology to meet these product demands. Of course, Adidas had access to media-related technology (television, print, Internet) for marketing, but it also decided to use the latest technology in innovation, design, and performance.

Adidas updated its running shoes with ClimaCool, a system designed to ventilate, and a3, an energy management technology for footwear. The company has also recently launched the a3 UltraRide (a midsole that offers mechanical cushioning), as well as the Ground Control System, codeveloped with Salomon, to be the first example of ground-leveling technology. The innovations are all meant to save the runner's energy to make running easier.

Adidas also continues to improve its other product lines. It recently launched the T-MAC 4, a laceless basketball shoe. In soccer, Adidas has updated its Predator shoe line with the new Predator Pulse and developed the Roteiro, the first officially approved soccer ball constructed with a thermal-bonding technique.

Based on information in Adidas-Salomon (2004a).

in their work. Their jobs involve considerable repetition and few requirements for creativity. In contrast, people working in sport physiology research labs, or individuals working as player agents, will find a number of exceptions in their day-to-day jobs. They frequently encounter new situations and face problems they have not dealt with before.

Perrow's second dimension concerns the degree to which the exceptions encountered are analyzable. For example, if a problem occurs in some jobs, it is possible to follow a logical sequence of mechanical steps to seek a solution to the problem. The work of a sport lawyer is much like this. Although the problems sport lawyers face are complex, there is usually a fairly well-established body of literature, in the form of previous court rulings and legal precedents, that the lawyer can call on to solve the problems. In contrast, a group of architects commissioned to design a new aquatic facility with both recreational and competitive pools, along with a water-slide facility, will probably not have encountered this situation before and will find little in the way of related literature to help solve the problems. Withey, Daft, and Cooper (1983) have developed a series of questions to determine the extent of **task variability** and **problem analyzability** in a department or work group (see figure 9.1).

Using the two dimensions of task variability and problem analyzability, Perrow was able to construct a 2 × 2 matrix (see figure 9.2). The four types of technology found in this matrix are explained below. Perrow also suggests a simplification of the construction: Because task variability and problem analyzability are often highly correlated (if a task is low in variety it is usually easily analyzable, and if a task is high in variety it is not easily analyzable), it may be possible to have a single dimension of technology. This simplification is also shown in figure 9.2 as the routine–nonroutine continuum.

Perrow's **routine technology** has few exceptions, and those that do occur are easily analyzable. A salesclerk working in a sporting goods store and a person on the assembly line making golf carts are both engaged in routine technology. Craft technologies have very few exceptions, but those that do occur are not easily analyzable; skill and experience are needed to deal with them. Someone making custom bikes, a dance instructor, or a figure-skating choreographer would be involved with a **craft technology**.

Engineering technologies have a high number of exceptions but they are usually handled with relative ease because of established procedures. Sport lawyers usually find a number of exceptions in their work but, as noted, because they can call

---

Task Variability

- How many of these tasks are the same from day to day?
- To what extent would you say your work is routine?
- Do people in this unit do about the same job in the same way most of the time?
- Basically, do unit members perform repetitive activities in doing their jobs?
- How repetitive are your duties?

Problem Analyzability

- To what extent is there a clearly known way to do the major types of work you normally encounter?

- To what extent is there a clearly defined body of knowledge which can guide you in doing your work?
- To what extent is there an understandable sequence of steps that can be followed in doing your work?
- To do your work, to what extent can you actually rely on established procedures and practices?
- To what extent is there an understandable sequence of steps that can be followed in carrying out your work?

Figure 9.1 *Questions to determine the extent of task variability and problem analyzability in a department or work group.*

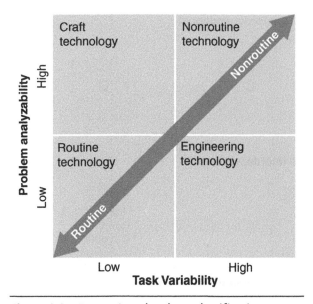

Figure 9.2 *Perrow's technology classification.*
Based on C. Perrow (1967).

on previous decisions for indications of how to proceed, these problems can be handled fairly easily. Architects who design and build traditional swimming pools and running tracks would also employ routine **engineering technology**. However, those who design more custom-built facilities will use **nonroutine technology**. Here the problems in design and construction are likely to be many, and systematic ways of solving these problems will be hard to find; the architect must count on experience and intuition. Researchers in a department of sport studies, and sport administrators who do management consulting also exhibit nonroutine technologies.

Each of the four main technologies identified by Perrow is associated with a different type of organizational structure. Routine technology is found in bureaucratic organizations; control is achieved through high levels of formalization and centralized decision making. Workers engaged in this type of technology are generally unskilled. Craft technologies require a more organic structure; consequently, there is less formalization and centralization. Coordination is achieved through mutual adjustment and the past experience of the staff. Engineering technologies require a structure somewhat like Mintzberg's professional bureaucracy; there is a moderate level of formalization and centralization, but the people in the operating core are often professionally trained and have a certain amount of discretion in the decisions that are made. Nonroutine technology requires a very

flexible structure; formalization is low, and decisions are made collectively by mutual adjustment. The staff members in these organizations are usually professionally trained. Finally, an important point is that quite possibly more than one type of technology will exist in an organization. For example, Reebok's production department has a routine technology but its research-and-development unit use nonroutine technology. When a structure is used that does not fit with the technology employed, the unit tends to be less effective (Gresov, 1989).

Thompson: Task Interdependence

Thompson's (1967) approach to understanding the different types of technology used in organizations is based on the concept of interdependence, a term referring to the extent to which different units or departments within an organization depend on each other for the materials or resources they need to perform their particular tasks. When departments operate independently of each other, interdependence is low; when there is a need for substantive levels of communication and a frequent exchange of materials or resources among departments, interdependence is high. Thompson suggests that different types of interdependence require different technologies. These technologies are associated with different types of organizational uncertainty, and this uncertainty is managed using different types of strategies. We outline here the types of interdependence Thompson identified and the technologies associated with each. We also briefly discuss the structural implications of each type of technology and the way managers cope with the associated environmental uncertainty.

Sequential Interdependence

Sequential interdependence involves a series of steps in which task A must be performed before task B, which in turn must be performed before task C, and so on (see figure 9.3).

In essence the output from one worker or department becomes the input for the next. The steps involved are relatively routine but must be performed in the correct sequence. This type of interdependence, which requires what Thompson (1967) calls long-linked technology, is most frequently found in assembly-line production. Within the sport industry we find **long-linked technology** in companies producing sport equipment such as baseball bats or hockey sticks.

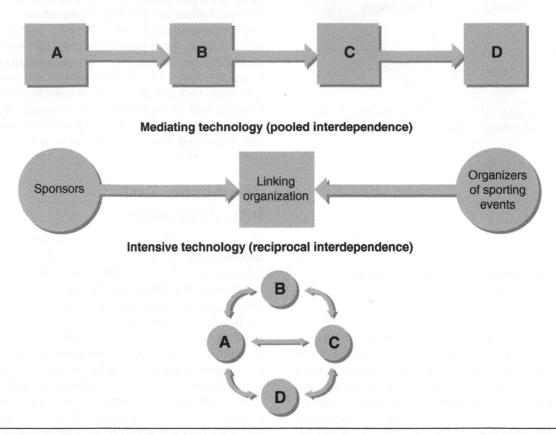

Long-linked technology (sequential interdependence)

Mediating technology (pooled interdependence)

Intensive technology (reciprocal interdependence)

Figure 9.3 *Thompson's categories of technology.*

Sequential interdependence requires high levels of coordination. There is a need to coordinate the various units involved in the different stages of the production process. The requirement that the product flow from one stage to the next necessitates that the organization emphasize planning and scheduling.

Structurally, organizations that employ long-linked technology to mass-produce large quantities of a product show relatively high levels of complexity, high levels of formalization, and a centralized decision-making structure. Uncertainty is usually controlled through a process of vertical integration, either forward, backward, or both. In this way, sources of input and the means of dealing with output are controlled by the manufacturing organization. Nike's purchase of Tetra Plastics (see chapter 6) demonstrates vertical integration.

Pooled Interdependence

As shown in figure 9.3, **pooled interdependence** involves linking two independent customers or cli-

ents, using **mediating technology**. This process involves the organization acting as a go-between for customers and clients. Mediating technology is found mainly in service organizations. Within the sport industry, sport marketing companies like Britain's APA use a mediating technology to link sponsors with the promoters of sport events. We also see a mediating technology used in chains of retail sporting goods stores such as Sport Experts and Mountain Equipment Co-op, which link companies that manufacture sport equipment with those who want to buy it.

Structurally, mediating technology involves low levels of complexity because few units are involved. Coordination is achieved through rules and procedures. Retail stores, for example, use rules and procedures to lay out how business should be conducted; sport marketing companies use contracts to ensure that each party understands its rights and obligations. Given this type of coordinating mechanism, formalization is relatively high. To control uncertainty, sport organizations that use a mediating technology try to increase the number of customers or clients served.

Reciprocal Interdependence

Reciprocal interdependence, the highest form of interdependence, is associated with what Thompson (1967) calls an **intensive technology**. This form of interdependence is found when people or units within an organization influence each other in a reciprocal manner (see figure 9.3). For example, the University of Alberta's Glen Sather Sports Medicine Clinic employs physicians, orthopedic surgeons, X-ray technicians, massage therapists, and physical therapists. A patient who comes to the clinic will first visit a physician, who may then refer the patient for an X-ray. The technician gives the X-ray to the physician and, based on the results of the X-ray, the physician may refer the patient to a surgeon and then physical therapist for treatment. After the treatment the patient returns to the physician, who may consult with the physical therapist and possibly instruct the patient to be X-rayed again or to return for more physical therapy. This is reciprocal interdependence: physicians, surgeons, X-ray technicians, massage therapists, and physical therapists work together; the actions of one influence the behavior of the others. There is no predetermined sequence of events as in long-linked technology; the mix and order in which the skills are used to produce the product or service are in large part a result of feedback from the person or object on which work is being performed. We would also find reciprocal interdependence and an intensive technology in some sport physiology research labs and in some types of health spas, where dietitians, fitness appraisers, and masseurs may work together with a client. Voluntary sport organizations also often exhibit reciprocal interdependence when a group of people work together cooperatively to stage a sport event.

Structurally, sport organizations that employ intensive technology are relatively organic. Coordination is achieved through frequent communication among the parties involved and by mutual adjustment on their part. Teamwork is an important aspect of this technology; decisions are often made collectively. Uncertainty arises out of the nature of the problem itself; while planning can help managers, it cannot possibly cover all the situations that arise in this type of organization. The people who work with this kind of technology are usually highly skilled, and hence able to call on their training and experience to make situations more predictable.

Critiques of the Technology Imperative

The contributions of Woodward, Perrow, and Thompson, as significant as they are, have generated considerable debate within the organizational literature about technology and its impact on organizational structure. In this section we look at some of the research that has sought to critique and extend these initial studies. We then look briefly at some general problems and issues relating to work in organizational technology.

The most notable critique and extension of Woodward's work is that of the Aston group members Hickson, Pugh, and Pheysey (1969). Essentially, what Hickson et al. (1969) suggested was that there were three types of technology: operations technology, materials technology, and work-flow technology. However, their work focused only on operations technology, which they define as "the techniques that [an organization] uses in its workflow activities" (1969, p. 380). Operations technology was assessed using a measure called work-flow integration, a composite measure applicable to both manufacturing and service organizations, examining such factors as the extent to which work-flow equipment was automated, the rigidity of the workflow, the level of interdependence in the workflow, and the specificity of quality evaluation of operations. Organizations scoring high on **work-flow integration** were seen to have a complex technology, a low score meant a simple technology. Using the work-flow integration measure, Hickson et al. (1969) found only a weak relationship between technology and various measures of organizational structure. What their results did show, however, was that size could explain far more variation in structure than technology. Technology did, nevertheless, have an influence on structure in smaller organizations.

One of the first to criticize the Aston findings was Aldrich (1972) (see also Kmetz, 1977, 1978; Starbuck, 1981). Aldrich reexamined the Aston data using path analysis and suggested a different causal sequence, with technology influencing size. He (1972, p. 40) suggested the Aston group's rejection of the technological imperative "to be ill-advised and premature."

At the same time that Aldrich was critiquing the Aston data, Child was replicating their work in what is known as the national study (see chapter 4). Child and Mansfield (1972) reexamined the technology, size, and structure relationship

TIME OUT   *Sport Teams: Variations in Levels of Interdependence*

Robert Keidel suggests that business managers can learn from the way sport is organized. One of his articles on this topic focuses on the different types of interdependence exhibited by teams in three U.S. sports: baseball, football, and basketball. Although Keidel acknowledges that to some extent each sport can exhibit every form of interdependence, each has a dominant form.

He suggests that, of the three sports, professional baseball exhibits the greatest degree of pooled interdependence. Team-member contributions are made relatively independent of each other. Where interaction does occur, it is usually between no more than two or three players (on the same team), for example, pitcher and catcher, batter and base runner, fielder and fielder. Rarely are more than a few of the players on the field involved directly in making a play, outside of making adjustments in fielding positions in anticipation of a play (or to back up a play). The basic unit in baseball is the individual. More than in football or basketball, overall performance approximates the sum of a team member's performances. This idea is vividly demonstrated by the way offense works: Players come up to bat one at a time. Of course, scoring typically requires a sequence of actions such as walks, hits, and sacrifices; but individual contributions remain rather discrete.

Professional football exhibits sequential interdependence in two ways. First, on offense, the line leads the backfield by providing the blocking necessary for running and passing. Second, in a more fundamental sense, the flow of plays usually required to score—a linear series of "first downs" across a "grid-iron"—could not be more sequential. The basic units in football are the large group or platoon (offense, defense, and special teams) and to a lesser degree, the small group (linemen, linebackers, backfield, and so forth). Overall performance is basically the sum of the platoon's performances. Each platoon's challenge is to be as machine-like as possible—a metaphor that is especially apt for this sport. It is instructive to picture the football field as a factory with the moving line of scrimmage representing product flow through the factory.

Professional basketball exhibits a high degree of reciprocal interdependence, as demonstrated by the back-and-forth flow of the ball among players. The reciprocal character of the sport is also shown in the often frenetic movement up and down the court—a far cry from the deliberate, measured advance of a football scoring drive. If offense and defense are "linked" in football, they are overlapping or "intersecting" in basketball. Offense and defense turn into each other instantaneously. The transition game is not a separate piece with separate players as it is in football, it is a continuous part of the flow. The basic unit in basketball is the team. With only five players on the court, an intermediate grouping between the team and the individual is unrealistic. Unit performance, therefore, is a function of player interaction, where each player may be involved with every other player on the court.

Reprinted from *Organizational Dynamics,* Vol 12, R.W. Keidel, Baseball, football, and basketball: Models for business, pgs. 5-18, Copyright 1984, with permission from Elsevier.

using the Aston work-flow integration measure of technology. Their work essentially confirms the Aston findings (see also Child, 1973a, 1973b, 1975b). Although role specialization, functional specialization, and standardization showed a reasonable correlation with technology, the correlation with size was higher, leading Child and Mansfield (1972) to reject the technological imperative in favor of the size-structure relationship. However, a more recent study by Reimann (1980) used a measure of technology based on Woodward's work and found significant correlations with several structural variables.

Like Woodward's work, Perrow's ideas have also been critiqued and extended. A number of studies have tested Perrow's conceptualization of technology; some have been concerned with the routine–nonroutine continuum emanating from his model, while others have focused on his fourfold classification scheme.

Van de Ven and Delbecq (1974) used measures of task difficulty, a concept similar to Perrow's problem analyzability, and task variability to examine structural variability within work units. Their results also support Perrow's predictions: Those organizations involved with routine type work were more highly formalized than those involved with nonroutine activities.

Grimes and Klein (1973) used a slight variant of Perrow's four-cell matrix to examine the relationship of technology to the autonomy of management, something Perrow (1967) had alluded to in his original article. They found (1973, p. 596) "a direct although modest relationship" between technology and managerial autonomy. The influence of technology as a determinant of managerial autonomy was greatest at the work-group level; its influence became more diffuse as one moved further from this level.

Although Thompson's (1967) typology of technology is generally considered to be conceptually the richest of the three seminal works (cf. Bedeian & Zammuto, 1991; Das, 1990), it has probably led to the least amount of subsequent research. Mahoney and Frost (1974) examined the relationship of Thompson's three types of technology to measures of organizational effectiveness. Their results support Thompson's ideas; they found that, in organizations that used long-linked technology, the predominant criteria of effectiveness were smoothness of operations, output performance, and reliability of performance. In organizations using mediating technology, flexibility, smoothness of operations, output performance, supervisory control, and staff development were all cited as indicators of effectiveness. For those using intensive technologies, performance was once again important but so too were cooperation and staff quality; planning was not seen to be as important. Van de Ven, Delbecq, and Koenig (1976) used both task uncertainty (the difficulty and variability of the work undertaken), a concept from Perrow's framework, and Thompson's notion of work-flow interdependence, to look at the modes of coordination at the work-unit level. They added to Thompson's types of interdependence a fourth category, "a team arrangement." As figure 9.4 shows, their results generally support Thompson's idea that the use of coordinat-

ing devices would increase as interdependence increased. They also show the relative use of the different coordinating mechanisms for the different types of technology.

In addition to the findings of studies that have sought to critique and extend the work of Woodward, Perrow, and Thompson, a number of other important issues should be mentioned in any consideration of technology as a structural imperative. The first concerns the definition of what exactly we mean when we talk about "technology." As we have seen, different studies have used the term in different ways. As Rousseau (1983, p. 230) notes, researchers have used the term "to refer to anything from job routineness to the hardness of raw materials." She goes on to suggest that "there is disagreement as to whether technology is an object, such as an assembly line or a computer, or a process, such as the flow of throughput within an organization." Even recently, Scott (2000) referred to technology simply as the work that is performed by an organization. This lack of agreement as to exactly what technology is may well be a major reason for the different findings about its impact on organizational structure.

Another issue relates to the focus of the studies carried out on the technological imperative. Again, as Rousseau (1983) points out, the vast majority of work in this area has been conducted at the organizational level, and considerably less work at the work-group, department, and individual levels. Studies carried out at the work-group level have generally produced stronger support for the technological imperative than research conducted at the organizational level, possibly because technology is more directly related to the work group. As Robbins (1990, p. 193) notes, when we look at the overall impact of technology we must consider the size of the organization because "the smaller the organization the more likely it is that the whole organization will be impinged upon by the production workflow or operating core."

Another point raised by Robbins (1990), which indirectly relates to the size issue, is the fact that the industry and the niche within that industry will affect its technology. For example, SP-Teri (figure skating) and Bauer (hockey) both make skates but the technology they employ is very different. In Perrow's terms, Bauer's technology is routine, while SP-Teri uses a craft technology, a difference in technology determined in large part by the niche these sport organizations have selected for their operations. It would not be efficient for a large

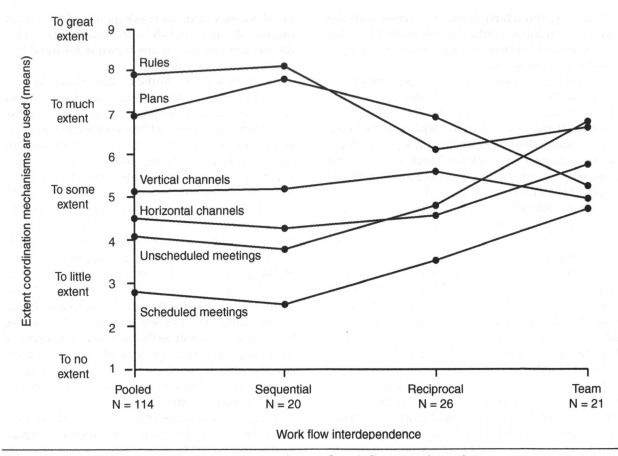

Figure 9.4 *Profile of coordination mechanisms on types of work-flow interdependence.*

Reprinted, by permission, from A. H. Van de Ven, A.L. Delbecq, and R. Koenig Jr., 1976, "Determinants of coordination modes within organizations," *American Sociological Review* 41: 322-338.

mass-production company like Bauer to have its customers send their specific foot casts to the production plant for modifications to their skates, as they do at SP-Teri for their custom figure skates.

A final concern about technology is the issue of manufacturing versus service technologies. The bulk of the research on organizational technology has been carried out on manufacturing organizations, but many of the organizations in the sport industry are service oriented. Consequently, in any study of a service organization, sport related or otherwise, it becomes important to take account of differences in the two types of organizations (see figure 9.5) and to employ a framework that takes account of these differences.

What then is the relevance, for people involved in sport management, of the studies that have sought to critique and extend the work of Woodward, Perrow, and Thompson and the related issues they have raised? Given the importance of technology and the paucity of work on technology and sport organizations, the studies reviewed here

should provide an initial basis for some thoughts and subsequent studies of the impact of technology on the organizations within our field. Regardless of the diversity of findings, technology is an important factor that influences the structure and operation of all organizations.

It should also be apparent, notwithstanding some conflicting results, that technology can influence the structuring of an organization, particularly at the work-group or department level. Consequently, it becomes important for managers in sport organizations to understand the impact of technology, in particular the changing technology, of their organization. Understanding the "fit" between structure and variables such as technology and size is also important, because it can influence the effectiveness of an organization. Finally, it is important that sport managers, if they are to create effective organizations, understand the difference between manufacturing and service technologies, and the relationship between these technologies and factors such as the size of a sport

Service organizations

- Intangible output
- Customized output
- Customer participation
- Simultaneous production and consumption
- Labor intensive

Examples of service organizations within the sport industry

- Department of sport studies
- Sport medicine clinics
- Sport marketing companies
- Municipal government sport departments
- Fitness clubs

Manufacturing organizations

- Tangible output
- Standardized output
- Technical core buffered from the customer
- Goods consumed at a later point in time
- Capital intensive

Examples of manufacturing organizations within the sport industry

- Athletic footwear companies
- Baseball card companies
- Golf club manufacturers
- Sportswear companies
- Tennis racket manufacturers

Figure 9.5 *A comparison of the characteristics of service and manufacturing organizations within the sport industry.*

Based on information in D.E. Bowen, C. Siehl, and B. Schneider (1989).

organization and the industrial niche in which it operates.

Microelectronic Technologies

In the past 15 years or so, many traditional manufacturing and service technologies have been replaced or augmented with microelectronic technologies, most of which are computer related. Athletic footwear manufacturers like Nike and Reebok, for example, use advanced computer technologies to help design their shoes, and sales reps at Spalding Sports World use laptop computers to check the availability of goods and to place orders (Radding, 1989). Computers are now a major factor to be considered by organizational designers (Child, 1984). In fact, it is practically impossible today to think of sport organizations not using one form of technology or another. In this section we look briefly at the types of microelectronic technology that may be used in a sport organization, the rationale for using these technologies, and the impact they can have on organizational structure and operations.

Types of Microelectronic Technology

Two major facets of microelectronic technology are influencing the structure and operations of sport organizations: computer-integrated manufacturing (CIM) and advanced information technologies (AIT).

Computer-Integrated Manufacturing

Computer-integrated manufacturing (CIM) is the term used to refer to the linking by computers of the different parts of the manufacturing process: the ordering and inventory of raw materials; the sequencing and control of the production process; and the warehousing, shipping, and servicing of the finished product (Pennings, 1987). The different components of computer-integrated manufacturing may include an automated materials-handling system, computer-assisted engineering, and (the two most common elements of CIM) **computer-assisted design** (CAD) and **computer-aided manufacturing** (CAM). Computer-assisted design, used to help in the design and drafting of new products, speeds up these processes by allowing designers to easily make modifications to products using the available computer technology. In this way alternative designs can be developed and tested to meet changing customer needs. Because of the ease with which changes are made, CAD is more cost effective than traditional methods of product design.

Computer-aided design is used within the sport industry to produce a wide variety of sport equipment, from running shoes to tennis rackets. Heery International, one of the leading builders of sport facilities, uses CAD in its design process. It is also a leader in the development of computer-aided design drafting software and the utilization of this software to produce construction documents.

Computer-assisted manufacturing (CAM) utilizes machines controlled by a computer to fabricate and assemble a product. This technology, because it requires fewer people to operate, can save a manufacturer money; it is also much quicker than conventional manufacturing technology. Using CAM, a manufacturer can easily change from one product to another by merely changing software. This flexibility enables the manufacturer to respond more quickly to changing customer orders and the changing demands of the marketplace. When Huffy, the bicycle manufacturer, switched to computer-assisted manufacturing, it enabled the company to undersell Taiwanese imports and keep its manufacturing plant in Ohio. "Computer-aided manufacturing means creating a factory of the future," according to Huffy's chairman Harry A. Shaw (Sator, n.d.).

Advanced Information Technology

Advanced information technology (AIT) is a result of the merging of computer and telecommunications technology. By linking computers together via telephone systems, AIT allows anyone with a computer to send and receive information.

This type of technology can be used to manage geographically dispersed operations, to place orders and control inventory, to facilitate group decision making through conference calls, and simply to enhance communications. Quicker than traditional methods of sending and receiving information, it allows for better identification of problems and facilitates broader participation in decision making. Many sport organizations make use of AIT. The 1999 Pan American Games Host Society was one of the first large-scale sport organizations to use e-mails to communicate. Mountain Equipment Co-op and other sport equipment manufacturers and distributors allow you to order from them online. University departments of sport studies use local area network (LAN) systems so interdepartmental memos and announcements

---

TIME OUT *Snowboard Technology*

Jake Burton Carpenter has been riding snowboards since the late 1970s. Back then, the boards were made of wood, in fact Carpenter's first snowboard was a modified surfboard. As snowboarding popularity grew, technology was developed to help snowboarders go higher, faster, and farther.

Carpenter took his love of the sport and turned it into a business, Burton Snowboards. It is a rider-based company, meaning the owner and engineers practice what they preach. As snowboarders themselves, they take risks, put in long hours, build and destroy boards, all in the name of producing a better experience for the snowboarder. From wooden boards with fins and rope to boards with edges and bindings, Carpenter has tested thousands of boards. The key was to make boards that are light, flexible, and maneuverable but also sturdy. The company used a technology called Engineered Grain Direction (EGD), which refers to how the wood grain of the core is placed at different angles and directions within the core to provide the right combination of edge grip and durability.

In 2003, the company engineered a lighter core of aluminum honeycomb called the Alumafly core (the same material found on F-16 fighter jets). The new board combined the Alumafly core with some wood, again laminated through EGD. In its quest to make lighter and better snowboards, Burton Snowboards is preparing the next generation of boards called the Vapor, to be ready in 2006. Burton Snowboards now controls 30 percent of the global market.

Based on information in Burton Snowboards (2005), and Connacher (2005).

Photo courtesy of Burton Snowboards

Jake Burton Carpenter rides a 1982 Backhill Burton snowboard in 1981. Carpenter is the founder of Burton Snowboards, a rider-based company that incorporates input from their professional snowboarders at each step in the development process.

are no longer typed, photocopied, and placed in mail boxes—they are sent via e-mail. They are also able to instantly send and receive messages from colleagues in different parts of the world.

Benefits of Advanced Technologies

We have already briefly alluded to some of the benefits of advanced technologies. Here we elaborate on the reason sport organizations are utilizing these types of manufacturing and information systems. We focus specifically on four reasons identified by Child (1984): reduced operating costs, increased flexibility, better quality products and services, and increased control and integration.

Reduced Operating Costs

The introduction of advanced technologies like CAD and CAM is often accompanied by a reduction in the size of the organization's workforce. Huffy, for example, was able to reduce overtime by 65 percent as a result of the changes to its manufacturing process (Smith Barney, 1989). While there are obviously significant social consequences of laying off employees or reducing their workload,

there is little doubt that, despite the fact that an initial large outlay of capital may be required, switching to CIM can ultimately reduce workforce costs. Such a move can also lower costs through "the reduction of wasted material and time [which is] made possible by the greater precision and lack of fatigue of programmed electronic devices" (Child, 1984, p. 249). Huffy's waste was reduced 45 percent when CAM was introduced (Smith Barney, 1989). Costs are reduced because inventory information is easy to access and orders can be quickly filled, reducing wasted search time and the costs of back-ordering products not in stock. Reebok's director of distribution, Don Petersen, estimated that when they installed computers to operate their distribution center, output per hour doubled, thus generating a large saving for the company.

Increased Flexibility

Using microelectronic technologies like CAM allows a manufacturer to produce a range of different products with the same equipment. Different software systems can be used to reprogram design and manufacturing equipment so modifications are easily made. With traditional methods these changes were often difficult, time-consuming, and costly. The 1989 Annual Report of Sun Ice (p. 7), a golf and snow sports apparel company, for example, notes that with a computer-aided design system "designers can change styles, colors, and coordinates in minutes, [resulting in] efficient turnaround time, greater accuracy, and increased production readiness." Advanced information technologies also provide increased flexibility; equipment such as cellular phones, fax machines, laptop computers, handheld electronic organizers, and modems mean that people do not have to be in a fixed location to send or receive information. They can also send or receive information worldwide with one click of the mouse.

Better-Quality Products and Services

Microelectronic technologies also improve the quality of products and services produced. The quality of manufactured products is improved with CIM because more design options can be considered, human errors in production are eliminated, and the completed product is more easily and rigorously tested. Sport organizations in the service sector are able to improve the quality of their service because, with AIT, more comprehensive information is more readily available than with traditional methods. Consider, for example, a fitness center that uses a computer to store information about client exercise programs, changes in levels of cardiovascular fitness, weight changes, and so on—all of this information is available at the push of a button, and so the fitness consultant is able to provide a more informed assessment of a client's future needs.

Increased Control and Integration

Control and integration are important aspects of the management process and as a result "management will therefore look to new technology to assist in meeting these requirements in ways that are more effective and less costly" (Child, 1984, p. 251). Computer-integrated manufacturing increases managerial control by allowing managers to monitor the work-flow process of the sequenced jobs. The central computer controlling the manufacturing process becomes the source of information for managers whereas, when traditional manufacturing methods are used, information about the process would have to be obtained from the supervisors of the different parts of the process. Integration is enhanced because, by definition, CIM integrates the different aspects of the manufacturing process.

Information technologies improve control because they provide readily available information, which is more easily monitored and less subject to error than information supplied using traditional methods. Integration is also improved because AIT brings information from several people or units together into one place. It is also possible to link people in different places, through teleconferencing or computer networks. The Minnesota Twins baseball team, for example, uses a computer system to merge its own scouting reports with statistics supplied by the Howe News Bureau and other sources (Darrow, 1990). They also equip their scouts with laptop computers so they can enter their own reports and communicate instantly with headquarters instead of sending reports through "snail mail."

Impact of Microelectronic Technologies on Organizational Structure

Interest in the relationship between technology and organizational structure is not restricted to a concern about traditional technologies. With the increased use of microelectronic technologies researchers have started to examine the impact of new forms of technology on organizational structure. Table 9.2 compares the kind of structural attributes typically found in a mass-production technology organization with those found in an organization that uses CIM.

As can be seen, organizations with a CIM system are more organic than the traditional mass-production company, with a narrower span of control and a smaller number of vertical levels in their hierarchy. The work to be carried out requires a higher level of skill than that needed when mass-production technology is used. Employees often work in teams that are required to be innovative in their work processes, decentralizing decision making. This type of team approach requires an emphasis on horizontal rather than vertical communication, so managers need the skills to integrate work groups. As Skinner (1983, p. 112) notes about these managers:

> Their skills feature the abilities to form up and lead effective teams for problem solving, systems design, and experimental manufacturing systems. . . . They seem to thrive on change, uncertainty, and ambiguity and indeed become easily bored with routine production. They delegate easily

Table 9.2   A Comparison of the Structural Characteristics of Sport Organizations

Structural characteristics	Organizations using mass-production technology	Organizations using CIM technology
Span of control	Wide	Narrow
Number of vertical levels	High	Low
Tasks	Routine or repetitive	Responsive or craftlike
Specialization	High	Low
Decision making	Centralized	Decentralized
Information flow	Vertical	Horizontal
Basis of power	Position	Knowledge
Overall design type	Machine bureaucracy	Adhocracy

Based on information in P.L. Nemetz and L.W. Fry (1988).

and in fact rather loosely, relying more on trust and less on formal controls and reports.

Mintzberg's (1979) adhocracy is the type of organizational structure most suitable for a company using a CIM system.

Relationship Between Technology and Organizational Structure

While the debate over whether or not technology determines the structure of an organization has produced conflicting results, some important points can be made about the relationship between technology and the different elements of structure. In this section we briefly review some findings on the relationship of technology to complexity, formalization, and centralization.

Technology and Complexity

Findings about the relationship between technology and complexity yield a mixed message. Technologies such as Woodward's mass-production technology, Perrow's routine technology, and Thompson's long-linked technology are generally associated with bureaucratic structures. Therefore, we can expect this type of technology to be related to relatively high levels of task specialization and vertical differentiation. However, specialization as measured by the amount of professional

training of the workforce is likely to be low (cf. Hage & Aiken, 1969). When technology is nonroutine, as in Perrow's classification or Woodward's unit production technology, we are likely to find a more organic structure. Here task specialization and the number of vertical levels in the organization will be low, but complexity as measured by the amount of professional training of staff is likely to be high. These mixed results should not be construed as a product of weak or inadequate research. Rather, they serve to underscore a point made by Hrebiniak (1974, p. 408), that both structure and technology are multidimensional concepts and "that when dealing only with general categories of either concept [such as the notion of complexity] it might be unreasonable to assume clear relationships or empirical trends."

Technology and Formalization

Notwithstanding Hrebiniak's caution about the problems of trying to relate technology to broadly based concepts of organizational structure, we do find, at least at one level, a clearer pattern in regard to technology and formalization. Gerwin (1979) reviewed five studies (Blau & Schoenherr, 1971; Child & Mansfield, 1972; Hickson, Pugh, & Pheysey, 1969; Hinings & Lee, 1971; Khandwalla, 1974) that showed technology to be positively related to formalization. However, when he controlled for size the relationship disappeared. What Gerwin's review suggests is that the smaller the organization, the greater the impact of technology on formalization.

Technology and Centralization

While there are exceptions (cf. Hinings & Lee, 1971) the majority of studies (cf. Blau & Schoenherr, 1971; Child & Mansfield, 1972; Hage & Aiken, 1969; Hickson, Pugh, & Pheysey, 1969; Khandwalla, 1974) have shown a relationship, albeit often small and not statistically significant, between the level of technology within an organization and the extent to which decision making is decentralized. Generally speaking, organizations that employ routine technology will be more centralized; those with nonroutine technology are likely to be decentralized.

KEY ISSUES FOR MANAGERS

One form of technology, the Internet—or World Wide Web—is now fundamentally important for successful organizations. Computer access to the Internet has become the most obvious technological consideration for managers. It is a source of information for the organization and also about the organization. For example, the Internet allows a sport organization to reach more clients from all around the world quickly and relatively cheaply. It is also faster to conduct business by communicating through e-mail. The Internet also affects organizational design and size. For example, the internet has created an increased need for IT support, thus creating more divisions within an organization. Finally, it provides an additional way to get information about other organizations in the same environment. Because of this it becomes essential that managers consider the Internet when developing or modifying strategies, organizational design and size, and when scanning the environment.

The popularity of the Internet has created a unique type of commerce—the e-business—that has changed all the traditional elements of space, structure, and time. Such businesses can operate with almost no tangible resources and little overhead except for a computer, printer, and Internet connection. This means that intangible resources, such as product or service quality and organizational reputation, become very important for gaining a competitive advantage (Haberberg and Rieple, 2001). For these reasons, e-businesses must be acutely aware of the technological environment for potential opportunities and threats (e.g., new forms of technologies, competitive e-businesses, or obsolete technologies).

SUMMARY AND CONCLUSIONS

The relationship between technology and organizational structure is one of the most controversial and hotly debated issues in the study of organizations. In this chapter we looked first at what we mean when we talk about technology. At the general level technology is the process by which an organization turns inputs into outputs. However, as we noted later in the chapter, researchers have used many different definitions of technology, and in part this may be the cause of some of the conflicting results coming from studies examining the relationship of technology to organizational structure.

Much of the work conducted on technology has been based on the studies of Woodward, Perrow, or Thompson. We looked at the principle arguments put forward in these studies and how the major concepts outlined in each related to sport organizations. We also looked at some of the critiques and extensions of this work and we raised questions as to whether or not there is a technological imperative, that is, whether technology determines structure. It was suggested that there was stronger support for the technological imperative where studies had been conducted at the work-group, or department, level. Studies conducted at the organizational level have produced mixed results. The issue of organizational level versus work-group, or department, level studies raised the issue of organizational size; we also saw evidence that size may influence the technology-structure relationship. We briefly touched on the issue of how the industry or niche within a sport industry may influence its technology, and we highlighted the differences between manufacturing and service technologies.

After considering traditional technologies and the debates conducted about their relationship to organizational structure, we moved on to consider microelectronic technologies, and suggested that CIM and AIT have had and will continue to have a significant impact on sport organizations. We looked at some of the benefits of these technologies for sport organizations, and the impact they could have on organizational structure. In the final part of the chapter we looked at some general rela-

tionships between technology and the structural elements of complexity, formalization, and centralization. We conclude that, regardless of some of the mixed findings that research studies have produced, technology is an important variable in the study of sport organizations.

Yet, as we have seen, little theoretical or empirical work within the field of sport management has looked at the influence of technology on any type of sport organization. We need to begin to address this important omission from the sport management literature, given the rapid changes occurring in technology and the impact these changes can have on sport organizations.

KEY CONCEPTS

advanced information technology (p. 186)

computer-aided manufacturing (p. 185)

computer-assisted design (p. 185)

computer-integrated manufacturing (p. 185)

continuous-process production (p. 176)

craft technology (p. 178)

engineering technology (p. 179)

individual-level technology (p. 175)

intensive technology (p. 181)

long-linked technology (p. 179)

mass or large-batch production (p. 176)

mediating technology (p. 180)

nonroutine technology (p. 179)

organizational-level technology (p. 175)

pooled interdependence (p. 180)

problem analyzability (p. 178)

reciprocal interdependence (p. 181)

routine technology (p. 178)

sequential interdependence (p. 179)

task variability (p. 178)

technological complexity (p. 176)

unit or small-batch production (p. 176)

work-flow integration (p. 181)

work-group or department-level technology (p. 175)

REVIEW QUESTIONS

1. Explain the different ways in which technology has been defined and why it is difficult to arrive at a single definition.

2. What type of organizational structure would you expect to find associated with Woodward's unit and mass-production technologies? Relate them to familiar sport organizations.

3. What kinds of sport organizations would you expect to find using the types of technology proposed by Perrow?

4. Within a single sport organization could you find an example of a department that uses routine technology and one that uses nonrou-

tine technology? How would their structures differ?

5. What commonalties can you find among the classifications of technology proposed by Woodward, Perrow, and Thompson?

6. In the Time Out that focused on Burton Snowboards it was implied that improving on past boards is ongoing if the rider wants to go farther, faster, and higher. If this is the case, what can sport management professors teach students about technology?

7. Explain the different types of sport organizations you would expect to find using long-linked, mediating, and intensive technology.

8. What is the difference between organizational-level and work-group-level technology? At what level does technology have the greatest impact on structure?

9. From what you have read, discuss what you think is the best way to explain the technology, size, and structure relationship.

10. What are the differences between manufacturing and service technologies?

11. Could a sport organization use both manufacturing and service technologies?

12. What type of structural changes can a sport organization expect to undergo if it moves from a mass-production technology to one that uses CIM?

13. Why do sport organizations adopt technologies like CAD and CAM?

14. Think of a familiar sport organization. How does it use AIT?

15. Think of a familiar sport organization. How can the Internet affect it?

SUGGESTIONS FOR FURTHER READING

If you want to understand more about the technology-structure relationship, you should begin by looking at the original work by Woodward, Perrow, and Thompson. It would also be useful to look at the work by scholars who have sought to critique and extend these original studies; a number of these are mentioned in this chapter. Excellent overviews of studies on the technology-structure relationship and details of some of the important issues to be considered in work of this nature can be found in Fry's (1982) article "Technology-Structure Research: Three Critical Issues" in the *Academy of Management Journal;* Reimann and Inzerilli's (1979) "A Comparative Analysis of Empirical Research on Technology and Structure" in the *Journal of Management;* and Rousseau's chapter "Technology in Organizations:

A Constructive Review and Analytic Framework," which is in Seashore and colleagues' (1983) book *Assessing Organizational Change.*

The only work that focuses on sport is Keidel's (1984) "Baseball, Football, and Basketball: Models for Business" in *Organizational Dynamics* (see Time Out in this chapter) and his extension of the ideas (1987) contained in "Team Sports Models as a Generic Organizational Framework," in *Human Relations.* You may, however, gain some ideas about the impact of technology on sport organizations by looking for articles about companies such as Nike, Reebok, and Huffy, which sometimes appear in periodicals such as *Forbes, Fortune, Business Week, Sports Illustrated* and at sportbusiness.com.

CASE FOR ANALYSIS

SBC Ballpark in San Francisco Goes Wireless

When the San Francisco Giants' opened their fifth season at SBC Park, fans discovered many technological enhancements to their ballpark experience.

The Giants franchise, along with their partners SBC and Nortel Networks, set up 121 wireless stations throughout the ballpark's concourses and seating areas for continuous and universal coverage. This makes the ballpark one of the largest wireless locations in the world. Fans bringing their PDAs (Personal Digital Assistants), tablet PCs, laptops, or other wireless devices can now access the Internet through SBC's FreedomLink network free of charge.

Intel's contribution to the partnership is its premier mobile computing technology and its knowledge related to improving the consumer's wireless experience. The compatibility of the FreedomLink service is enhanced with Intel's best wireless mobile computing technology, Centrino.

The Giants also partnered with Kosmo Studios to create the Giants Digital Dugout, an in-park entertainment system running over the wireless network. Through the Digital Dugout, fans can play electronic games, receive game-day statistics in real time, retrieve up-to-date scores and other news from around the league, make purchases, and access local information. In addition, all the ballpark suites are equipped with HP computers, flat-panel screens, and wireless accessories. This new setup provides access to the Internet and to more exclusive content from the Digital Dugout, such as in-suite food ordering and archived team video footage.

Larry Baer, the executive vice president and COO of the Giants, explained, "Whether fans take advantage of our technological capabilities at the ballpark, at home, in the office, or on the road, we strive to employ the latest and greatest technology to maximize convenience and to provide a unique entertainment experience for our fans."

For their part, SBC believes, "Our vision is to extend the broadband world beyond the home and the office, and SBC Park is a perfect fit. It is a grand slam that complements the hotels, airports, convention centers and other locations that SBC is turning into broadband hot spots." Don Macdonald, vice president for the Intel Sales and Marketing Group, added, that "Wi-Fi (wireless system) has given people more freedom and flexibility to connect to the Internet wirelessly in hotels, airports, cafés, and now even ballparks."

But the Giants did not stop there. Other innovations designed to enhance fans' experience at the ballpark were added. They include

- a Giants' 24-hour box office. For 24-hours, seven-days a week automated ticketing kiosks operate outside the ballpark's gates. These kiosks also provide express game-day ticket pickup, which facilitates fans' entry into the ballpark.

- a ticket relay. An electronic ticket transfer system sends tickets to purchasers through e-mail. Fans can also electronically donate their unused tickets to Bay Area nonprofit and charitable organizations of their choice.

- a double play ticket window. An Internet-based protected system allows season-ticket holders to sell some of their tickets on www.sfgiants.com. Conversely, individuals wishing to buy prime seats at the ballpark can access this system. Portions of the sale of these tickets can be donated to the Giants Community Fund to buy tickets for kids involved in the Junior Giants Baseball Program.

- Xtreme rewards. An exclusive online program is designed so fans can sign up for membership packages ($25 to $45) that offer priority access to game tickets and team memorabilia.

Based on information from San Francisco Giants (2004).

Questions

1. What types of technology (stated and unstated) would be present in such a stadium?

2. What impact is wireless technology likely to have on the structure and operations of organizations that own sport facilities?

3. How could this type of technology change the business of a team with a wireless stadium?

4. If you were the manager of a sport facility like SBC Park, how would you deal with this new technology?

Chapter 10

Power and Politics in Sport Organizations

LEARNING OBJECTIVES

When you have read this chapter, you should be able to

1. explain what we mean when we talk about strategic choice,

2. distinguish between power and authority,

3. explain the sources of power that individuals within a sport organization can use,

4. explain how subunits come to acquire power in a sport organization, and

5. describe the types of political activity that we might find taking place in a sport organization.

POWER AND POLITICS IN THE FIGURE-SKATING WORLD

There's no politics like skating politics. Most figure-skating insiders would probably agree with this statement, especially in recent years with the International Skating Union (ISU) being plagued by accusations of judging corruption. The ISU was created in 1892. Since then, it has been the international governing body of both figure skating and speed skating. However, it is the figure-skating arm of the ISU that has received much attention lately.

First, there is the judging problem plaguing the sport. While the ice dancing judging has been under scrutiny for some time, figure skating—and the ISU—lost considerable credibility during the 2002 Salt Lake City Olympics. The judging scandal surrounding two pairs of teams (a Russian team and a Canadian team)

brought to the surface problems long seen in the ice dancing competition: judges' accountability and objectivity in judging performance, not reputation. While the ISU did not want to change the pairs' scoring results, stating that judges' results are final, it took considerable pressure from the international media and especially the International Olympic Committee (IOC) for the president of the ISU, Ottavio Cinquanta, to acknowledge that the 6.0 system may be inadequate. A new system was being tested in selected competitions during the 2003-2004 year, but some of the more powerful national skating federations (e.g., Russia and United States) believed the new system pushed by Cinquanta did not do enough to increase judges' accountability while protecting them

(continued)

(continued)

Associated Press, AP

The International Skating Union—led by its president, Ottavio Cinquanta—used its power as the international governing body of figure skating to withstand recent challenges that centered around judging.

ated in 2003 by former figure-skating champions, top referees, and skating administrators from countries such as the United States, Britain, and Canada. The WSF is trying to become the IOC-recognized international governing body for figure skating. The WSF even filed an antitrust lawsuit on December 12, 2003, against the ISU and its president. The acting president of the WSF and an ISU Olympic and championship official, Ronald Pfenning, stated the following in a press release (World Skating Federation, 2003, p. 1):

> In this lawsuit, we allege that Ottavio Cinquanta, fearing a new democratic organization and fighting to protect his autocratic control of the sport and its lucrative television contracts, responded by threatening to "blacklist" or banish anyone connected with the WSF. By filing this lawsuit, we seek to subject the ISU's anticompetitive conduct to judicial review. I am confident that justice will be done, and that those who subscribe to the WSF's principles will be allowed to freely express their views in the near future.

from possible corruption. Yet, Cinquanta managed to get the system approved at the end of the 2003-2004 season for use at all internationally sanctioned competitions. This may be partly due to the IOC's pressuring the ISU to clean up its act or risk having figure skating dropped from future Olympics.

Second, there is the challenge by the new athlete-centered nonprofit World Skating Federation (WSF), partly in reaction to the perceived unresponsiveness of the ISU to the problems plaguing the sport. The WSF was cre-

While the WSF is supported by former figure skaters and certain administrators, the national skating associations who dictate actions for the amateur figure skaters have, for the most part, stayed with the ISU after the ISU made eligibility threats. It is able to do so because it is the IOC-recognized international skating body. The WSF lawsuit went to court and, on February 15, 2005, it was dismissed thereby showing the supremacy of the ISU in the figure-skating world.

Based on information in World Skating Federation (2003, 2005).

The vignette about the world of figure skating introduces us to the concepts of power and politics. In chapters 8 and 9 we looked at how environment and technology influenced the structure of a sport organization. Although each of these imperatives (or contingencies, as they are sometimes called) can help us explain how a sport organization should be structured, none

provides a total explanation. For each imperative there are questions about its explanatory power. Ford and Slocum (1977) suggested that more explanatory power might be obtained by combining variables. They noted that few studies of organizational structure consider more than one contingency at the same time, besides size and technology. However, Child (1972b) suggests that even if this approach is employed it can still leave up to 40 percent of the structural variance in an organization as unaccounted.

Some researchers have questioned the rational approach to understanding organizations that is the basis of contingency theory. They suggest that a focus on power and politics in organizations may be a better approach and one that would help us understand much of the unexplained variance in organizational structure. Essentially, the argument made by those who subscribe to a political model of organization is that those who hold the power in the organization will choose a set of structural arrangements that will maintain or increase their power: They will engage in politically motivated behavior. Followers of this school of thought see organizations differently from those who view them as rational entities. In the rational model, organizations are seen as entities in which members share common goals, make decisions in an orderly and logical manner, and see conflict as dysfunctional to their central purpose. In the political model it is accepted that people and groups within organizations have different goals, make decisions in their own best interests, and engage in conflictual behavior.

In this chapter we look at the issues of organizational power and politics. We look first at the concept of **strategic choice**. This "typically includes not only the establishment of structural forms but also the manipulation of environmental features and the choice of relevant performance standards" (Child, 1972b, p. 1). We then look at the issue of power and how it differs from another common concept in the study of organizations, authority. We examine how power is obtained, and we look at both individual and organizational sources of power. Next, we look at political activity in sport organizations and the types of political tactics that can be employed to acquire, develop, and use power.

Strategic Choice

The notion of strategic choice was first put forward by John Child in 1972 as an argument against the emphasis that was being placed on structural imperatives. Essentially, what Child suggested was that although imperatives such as environment and technology constrain managers in the decisions they make, these people still have the power to exercise choice in regard to these contingency factors and consequently they have the power to determine the type of organizational structure

they adopt. For example, Child argued that the decision makers in an organization had far more power to choose their environment, technology, and size than was commonly inferred by those who argued for the importance of these imperatives in explaining organizational structure.

In terms of environment, he suggested (1972b, p. 4) that "organizational decision makers may have certain opportunities to select the type of environment in which they will operate." For example, the senior managers at Nike exercised their power of choice in 1979, when they decided to enter the sport apparel market; so, too, would the chair of a sport management department who chose to direct her department's efforts toward teaching and executive development rather than toward research. In deciding to enter a particular environmental domain, the senior managers of a sport organization are at the same time deciding the types of organizations with which they will have to interact, the type of regulations to which they will be subject, and who their competitors will be. These decisions in turn will influence their choice of structure. In short, senior managers influence structure by the choices they make about environmental domain rather than the environment itself.

Child (1972b, p. 6) also maintains that technology and its relationship to structure should be "viewed as a derivative of decisions made by those in control of the organization regarding the tasks to be carried out in relation to the resources available to perform them." So, for example, when Bill Holland chose to make custom bike frames in his small workshop in Spring Valley, California, with a group of five or six employees, he was at the same time electing to use a craft technology. It would have been very difficult for him to enter into mass production. Managers, therefore, dictate structure by their choice of domain, which in turn influences the choice of technology.

Size, too, is subject to the choices made by managers. Although having to manage many organizational members and their activities may constrain certain structural choices, there are still numerous important choices (Child, 1972b). For example, managers may choose to break down large units into smaller ones that can act independently; alternatively, they may choose to limit the size of a unit. Berrett, Burton, and Slack (1993) describe how some entrepreneurs within the sport industry made a choice to limit the size of their business in order to maintain centralized control.

TIME OUT · *Power Play: The Firing of Madame Monique Berlioux*

Monique Berlioux's first connection with the Olympic Games movement was in 1948 when she represented France in swimming. Nearly 20 years later she was employed by the IOC to handle press relations, but in 1968 when IOC secretary Johan Westerhoff resigned, it was Berlioux who assumed his duties. During her time with the IOC the organization changed considerably. When she first joined the IOC staff, the organization hardly had the money to pay her salary. The increased revenue from television contracts changed the IOC's financial position and, as the organization became more powerful, so, too, did Berlioux. She is described as an authoritarian figure who kept tight control of her staff at the IOC headquarters in the Chateau de Vidy in Lausanne.

Like Avery Brundage and then Lord Killanin, the first two presidents she served, Berlioux was strongly committed to amateurism and opposed to any commercialization of the games. Both Brundage and Killanin conducted their duties of IOC president from their homes, and the day-to-day operation of the organization was left to Berlioux. However, in 1980 Juan Antonio Samaranch took over the presidency of the IOC from Lord Killanin. Shortly after his appointment Samaranch moved into residence in Lausanne. His staff quickly grew to rival that of Berlioux's and the two groups became suspicious of each other. It is rumored that Berlioux even told Samaranch she didn't think there was room in the city for both of them; prophetically, she was right.

Samaranch was firmly committed to the commercialization of the games. In the early 1980s he talked to Horst Dassler of Adidas who, along with Patrick Nally, had formed International Sport and Leisure (ISL). ISL had experience marketing the rights of the Federation Internationale de Football Associations (FIFA) and the World Cup of Soccer. Dassler offered ISL's services to the IOC and in 1983 a report was presented to the IOC's Commission for New Sources of Finance. Although Berlioux was not opposed in principle to using ISL to increase the standing and influence of the IOC, her critics believed that she was concerned that ISL involvement would reduce her own power and prestige. As a result, she was reluctant to sanction ISL as anything more than consultants to the IOC. It soon became clear that Madame Berlioux's ideas of ISL's role and the future structure of the IOC were different from that of President Samaranch.

Samaranch seemed to also be finding other ways to decrease Madame Berlioux's power. In 1983, Samaranch named Canadian IOC member Dick Pound, not Madame Berlioux, to head the negotiations for television broadcasting rights of the 1988 Summer and Winter Olympic Games. As Pound was moving up in the power ranks, Madame Berlioux was moving down.

Finally, at the IOC's 1985 session in East Berlin, Samaranch asked Dick Pound to inform Madame Berlioux that she was "to resign." Her 17-year "reign" (as many saw her time at the IOC) was now over.

Based on information in Barney, Wenn, and Martyn (2004), Killanin (1983), and Hill (1992).

In addition to making choices about their organization's environment, technology, and size, Child (1972b, p. 4) suggests that in some cases managers "may command sufficient power to influence the conditions prevailing within environments where they are already operating." Organizations are not always influenced by their environment; some can "enact" it (Weick, 1969). In large companies in particular, managers can create a demand for a product and take steps to limit the amount of competition within their environment. The Cana-

dian Football League's (CFL) lobbying of Canada's federal government to prevent the World Football League from placing a franchise in Toronto, and the 1979 merger of the NHL with the World Hockey Association, are both examples of the ways managers of sport organizations (in this case the CFL and the NHL) have worked to enact their environment by limiting competition.

A third argument that Child (1972b) makes for strategic choice concerns the difference between the actual environment of an organization and the way it is perceived by its managers. As we saw in chapter 8 managers make choices based on the way they perceive their environment to be, not necessarily the way it actually is. As such it is managerial choice rather than the actual nature of a sport organization's environment that is most likely to influence structural design. For example, a sportswear manufacturer may see Eastern Europe as a dynamic, growing environment with new market opportunities. To meet this demand new product lines may be developed, staff increased, and new manufacturing facilities acquired. Eastern Europe may or may not be a dynamic environment, but managerial perception and the choices managers make based on this perception lead to structural change, not the actual nature of the environment.

A final area where Child (1972b) suggests the influence of strategic choice can be felt is the area of organizational effectiveness. Most studies of organizational effectiveness treat performance as a dependent variable. Child (1972b) suggests that, in contrast, a theory concerned with organizational structure should propose structural variables as being dependent on the decisions made in reference to certain performance standards. Structure is therefore the dependent variable. Managers do not always make decisions to utilize a structure that will produce the highest level of performance, because this decision may reduce their power or destabilize the organization. Rather, they select a structure that will achieve an optimal level of performance, allowing the decision group to use structural arrangements that match their preferences, which in turn allows them to increase or maintain their level of power and autonomy. An example of this type of situation is once again found in Berrett, Burton, and Slack's (1993) study of entrepreneurs in the sport and leisure industry. One of the entrepreneurs was quite willing to forego the increased profits (one of the most common measures of effectiveness) that could be achieved by expansion, in order to retain the type of structural arrangements that allowed him to maintain control of his operation.

Power and Authority

Power is one of the most widespread yet more problematic concepts in the organizational theory literature. While some scholars have suggested that there is an overabundance of writing on power (Clark, 1967), others have indicated that the concept has not received much attention

(Kotter, 1977). Martin (1971, p. 240) suggested that "theorizing about power has often been confusing, obscurantist, and banal"; he adds, "it is not surprising that March (1966) concluded that 'on the whole power is a disappointing concept.'"

Power is not something we can see within a sport organization, but its effects can be clearly felt. While there are numerous definitions within the organizational literature (cf. Astley & Sachdeva, 1984; Pfeffer, 1992), the most commonly accepted conceptualization suggests that power is the ability to get someone to do something they would not have otherwise done or "the probability that one actor in a social relationship will be in a position to carry out his own will despite resistance, regardless of the basis on which this probability rests" (Weber, 1947, p. 152).

Notwithstanding the widespread use of this definition, these kinds of explanations of the concept of power are not without problems. Martin (1971, p. 243), for example, suggests that this type of definition implies that power involves conflict or antagonism and ignores "the possibility that power relations may be relations of mutual convenience: [and] power may be a resource facilitating the achievement of the goals of both A and B." Martin also saw as problematic the fact that the Weberian definition of power (and others like it) view power as being personalized instead of the product of the social relationships between actors. In this regard Emerson (1962) points out that these types of relationships are not one-sided and often include mutual interdependence.

Also important to note about the use of the term "power" is that some writers use it interchangeably with, or to encompass, concepts such as coercion, influence, manipulation, and authority (cf. Bachrach & Baratz, 1962; Styskal, 1980). **Authority** is in fact one form of power; it is the power that is formally sanctioned by a sport organization, the power that accrues to a person because of his or her role within the organization (cf. Weber, 1947). Authority is only legitimate within the sport organization that grants the authority. The power by which managers exercise strategic choice is, in essence, authority—the power they derive from the position they hold in the organization. This is not to say that people who don't have authority can't influence these choices. Authority must be accepted by the role-holder's subordinates, and it is exercised down the organizational hierarchy. In contrast, power can be exercised vertically up or down the organizational hierarchy, and horizontally. The examples in figure 10.1 illustrate acts that

Actions based on authority

- A quarterback calling the plays in a football game
- A sport management professor giving a student an extension to complete a term paper
- The chief executive officer of a sporting goods company signing a contract to sponsor a sport event
- The president of a university suspending a coach for recruiting violations

Actions based on other forms of power

- The president of a national sport organization calling a friend who holds a government position to enlist help in securing grant funding
- An athletic director having the university's athletic therapist treat her 14-year-old son's sprained ankle
- The president of a sport consulting company asking his secretary to buy a birthday gift for his wife
- A college basketball coach hiring a high school player to work at the college's summer basketball camp in order to encourage her to attend the college

Figure 10.1 *Actions based on authority and other forms of power.*

involve authority and those that entail the use of other forms of power.

Sources of Power

While we often think of people as being powerful, the way a sport organization is structured can lead to some subunits becoming powerful, regardless of the people within them. In this section we look first at the ways individuals acquire power. We then focus on organizational sources of power.

Sources of Individual Power

One of the most widely cited accounts of the sources of individual power is French and Raven's (1959) five-part typology: legitimate power, reward power, coercive power, referent power, and expert power. A description of each of these types is presented below. It is important to note that the types of power cited are not discrete and in fact may overlap. Shetty (1978, p. 177) notes, for example, that the "possession of one type of power can affect the extent and effectiveness of other types.

TIME OUT *Power in the Hands of One Man*

Mario Vásquez-Raña is a Mexican furniture-store millionaire and media mogul. For over 20 years now, he has been the head of the Pan American Sports Organization (PASO), as well as the Association of National Olympic Committees (ANOC). In fact, Vásquez-Raña is the single power figure in PASO; he is the king of kings of sport in the Americas. Anything you do in relation to the Pan American Games must be approved by Vásquez-Raña. If he doesn't like you, good luck getting anything done. If you want to achieve your objectives, you must get along with Vásquez-Raña because there is no one else to turn to.

His personal wealth and power has allowed him to stay in charge of PASO and ANOC over the years, and has granted him a position on the International Olympic Committee—an unpopular appointment but one that was pushed by then-president Juan Antonio Samaranch, himself the ultimate power in amateur sports.

Based on information in Manson (1999), Pound (2004).

The judicious use of reward power and coercive power can increase the effectiveness of legitimate power; inappropriate use, however, will decrease legitimate power."

Legitimate Power

Legitimate power is the same as authority. People acquire it by virtue of their position within a sport organization. Managers, athletic directors, deans, members of the board of directors of a voluntary sport organization, and coaches are all examples of people who, because of the positions they hold in their respective sport organizations, can expect compliance from their subordinates when they request that things be done. They have legitimate power. This type of power comes from a person's position and not because of any other special qualities she or he may possess. This does not mean, however, that people who occupy the same position will use the power of their office in the same way. Hill (1992), for example, describes the differing ways in which Lord Killanin and his successor Juan Antonio Samaranch utilized the power of the IOC presidency. Killanin left much of the day-to-day running of the IOC to his staff; Samaranch was a "hands-on" president who was seen as less consultative in the way he operated.

Reward Power

The power that comes from one person's control of another person's rewards is termed **reward power**. The larger the reward and the greater the importance of the reward to the recipient, the more power the person who gives the reward is able to exercise. The owner of a professional sport team may offer rewards to players who perform well. Coaches can give rewards in the form of more playing time or a starting position. The volunteer president of a national sport organization can reward other volunteers by lobbying for them to be appointed to international committees or by giving them perks like naming them to honorary positions with teams traveling to major sport events.

Coercive Power

Coercive power is the power derived from the ability that one person has to punish another. The fear of punishment can be a strong motivator and in some ways coercive power can be seen as the counterpart of reward power. Although many people see coercive power as dysfunctional because it alienates people and builds up resentment, it is not uncommon to see this type of power used in sport organizations. For example, the ISU's threat of banishment for individuals supporting the WSF described in the vignette at the beginning of the chapter would be considered coercive power.

Referent Power

Referent power is based on an individual's charisma and another person's identification with this

---

TIME OUT   *Marketing Charisma*

To the corporate mind, sporting success is only one ingredient in the marketing mix. Far more important is the star's image and personality, and Real Madrid soccer superstar (formerly of Manchester United) David Beckham has tons of it.

For Manchester United, Beckham, nicknamed Becks, was a cash cow. He may be able to bend the ball like no other with his right foot but that's not why he is a cash cow; he can sell more jerseys than any other athlete in the world, plain and simple. As financial executive Alvin Tan noted, "What David Beckham has is not just football skills, but the name recognition. Name and face is synonymous with football these days."

Real Madrid does not need another football star on its roster, it already has plenty. What Real Madrid wanted—and was willing to pay handsomely for it (€40 million [approximately U.S.$48 million] over four years)—was to see its merchandise sales figures go up and to open the Asian fan base, where Becks (through Adidas and Manchester United) was already popular.

Today, soccer negotiations no longer revolve only around the player's abilities; lengthy discussions occur between players and clubs around image rights.

Based on information in J. Chen (2003).

quality. In many ways referent power is very much like the Weberian notion of **charismatic authority**. Referent power can occur when the members of a sport organization identify very strongly with the values espoused by their leader. Coaches like Dean Smith, formerly of the University of North Carolina, and Bobby Knight from Texas Tech are strong personalities, seen by many people as charismatic; as such they have referent power. People with referent power are often used to promote sport teams, events, and equipment.

Expert Power

Expert power accrues because of a person's special knowledge or skill. That person does not have to be particularly high up in the sport organization's hierarchy to have expert power. For example, a computer technician in a sport organization that uses computer-aided design may wield considerable power if she is the only person in the company who knows how to operate the computers. Coaches, product designers, researchers, and player's agents may all be seen to have expert power because of their credibility in their specialized area. One of the ways individuals can acquire expert power is through the information they possess.

Organizational Sources of Power

As we saw in the last section, some sources of individual power are a result of holding positions of authority in a sport organization; others reflect personal qualities that are unrelated to the organization. In this section we look at the power that accrues to organizational subunits as a result of the way in which the sport organization is designed. We focus specifically on five organization-based sources of power: the acquisition and control of resources, the ability to cope with uncertainty, centrality, nonsubstitutability, and control over the decision-making process.

Acquisition and Control of Resources

One of the primary ways a subunit within a sport organization can obtain power is through its ability to acquire resources and the **control of resources**. As Pfeffer (1981, p. 101) points out, because organizations require a continuous supply of resources those subunits within the organization "that can provide the most critical and difficult-to-obtain resources come to have power in the organization." The important point to draw from Pfeffer's statement is that it is not just the ability to acquire

and control resources that gives an organizational subunit power, but the fact that it can secure resources critical to the organization's operations and difficult to obtain. Resources may come in a variety of forms and can include money, people, information, and legitimacy. Burbank, Andranovich, and Heying examined the 1984 Los Angeles Olympics, the 1996 Atlanta Olympics, and the 2002 Salt Lake City Olympics in their 2001 book and found that business people dominated organizing committees because they have access to desired resources.

Money is a particularly important resource to any organization because it can be used to acquire other resources, and "it can be stored and is relatively divisible in terms of its use" (Pfeffer, 1981, p. 101). In universities, those departments that are able to generate large amounts of external funding are often regarded as powerful. On many U.S. campuses the athletic department, which is often able to generate funds through its sport programs, is seen as a powerful subunit (cf. Sack & Staurowsky, 1998). People are also a valuable resource; nowhere is this more apparent than in the competition among professional and collegiate sport teams for highly skilled players. The teams that are able to secure the most talented group of players become the most powerful subunit within their respective league.

The Ability to Cope With Uncertainty

Sport organizations of all types are constantly coping with **uncertainty**, arising out of changes in the task environment of the sport organization—suppliers, competitors, fans, regulatory agencies, and the like. Uncertainty can also arise as a result of the technological interdependence we discussed in chapter 9. Because uncertainty creates problems for an organization, those subunits that can reduce or control uncertainty gain increased power (Hinings, Hickson, Pennings, & Schneck, 1974). Hickson, Hinings, Lee, Schneck, and Pennings (1971) suggest three methods to help organizations cope with uncertainty. The first is by acquiring information about future trends. Market research units within sport organizations are designed exactly for this purpose. If they are successful in predicting trends such as product demand they can become a very powerful entity within the organization. Studies of fan attendance at various sporting events (cf. Gauthier & Hansen, 1993; Hansen & Gauthier, 1989; Schofield, 1983) are in essence designed to identify those factors that affect attendance. Subunits that can utilize this information to maintain or increase attendance can help reduce uncertainty and thus are able to increase their own power within the organization.

The second method of coping with uncertainty is absorption. Absorption involves taking action after an event has occurred (Hickson et al., 1971). For example, if a sporting goods store that encounters a sharp drop in sales can counter with some novel selling methods, it has coped via absorption. Exercycle, for instance, is one of the oldest manufacturers of exercise bicycles. In 1959 the company sold 10,000 Exercycles, a company record. However, since fitness and lifestyle products have become more popular, the company's fortunes have declined. In the mid-1980s the company was selling only 2,000 to 3,000 machines per year in what was a $2 billion-per-year fitness industry. In 1987 President Richard Baird started to take steps to turn this situation around. Using a new marketing strategy the company targeted its marketing efforts on three groups, "aging consumers who want the ease of home use; executives who don't have time for racquetball or other physical activities; and the medical therapy community" (Bottorff, 1987, p. 54).

Acquiring information and absorption are methods used to cope with uncertainty after it occurs. It is also possible to cope with uncertainty by preventing its occurrence, the third method suggested by Hickson and colleagues (1971). For example, in 1975 the running boom had taken off in America, and Nike (or Blue Ribbon Sports, as it was then called) was a rapidly growing company. However, sales manager Jim Moodhe and his staff could see that Blue Ribbon was going to have problems meeting the demand for its product. Its credit lines were stretched and it didn't have the money to produce the shoes that were going to be needed. To solve this problem and prevent the potential uncertainty of not being able to meet the demand for the product, Moodhe developed a program he called "Futures." "The idea behind Futures was to offer major customers an opportunity to place large orders six months in advance and have them commit to that noncancellable order in writing. In exchange, customers would get a 5 to 7 percent discount and guaranteed delivery on 90 percent of their order within a two-week window of time" (Strasser & Becklund, 1991, p. 200). The plan was a success; Moodhe and his sales department were able to cope with the uncertainty facing Blue Ribbon Sports by preventing it from happening.

Centrality

A subunit's position in the work or information flow of a sport organization helps determine the amount of power that the subunit possesses. Subunits that are more central to the work or information flow will be more powerful than those on the periphery. In large part, **centrality** is determined by the sport organization's strategy and the problems it is facing at a particular time. Slack, Berrett, and Mistry (1994) show how the strategic emphasis on high-performance sport adopted by a Canadian national sport organization increased the power of a group of coaches employed by the organization. In an organization strategically oriented to the marketplace, for example, a sport equipment manufacturer, the marketing department is likely to be one of the most important functional units. If a sport organization adopts a strategy of increased efficiency and fiscal control, the finance department is likely to gain increased power merely because its activities are central to the strategic approach adopted by the organization.

Financial people are also likely to become more powerful if the sport organization faces a financial crisis. Similarly, when sales fall, the marketing and sales departments become a primary focus for the sport organization, and thus their power increases. It has even been suggested that in some organizations, subunits central to the organization's operations may sometimes create problems that they have to solve. In this way the members of the subunit are able to remind others in the organization of their importance (cf. Pfeffer, 1977b).

Nonsubstitutability

Nonsubstitutability (that is, being irreplaceable) is an important means of gaining power for both subunits and individuals. In their strategic contingencies theory of power, Hickson and colleagues (1971) suggest that the less a subunit's activities can be substituted, the more organizational power it has. However, to retain their power base subunits and individuals have to ensure that the particular knowledge or skills they possess are not easily replaced. As Pfeffer (1981, p. 113) points out, "if others can obtain access to the expert's information" then their power base is quickly destroyed. Consequently, those with power will use strategies to maintain their status. These strategies may include "using specialized language and symbols that make the[ir] expertise look even more arcane and difficult to comprehend" (Pfeffer, 1981, p. 114), or preventing individuals with a similar expertise from being a part of the organization. In sport organizations coaches often use specialized language. Swimming coaches, for example, talk about tapering, shaving down, and bilateral breathing. This use of specialized language makes it difficult for others involved peripherally in swimming (particularly the parents of swimmers) to comprehend; thus the power of the coaching subunit is maintained.

Control Over the Decision-Making Process

Another way that subunits and individual members of a sport organization can gain power is to have **control over decision making**. Power is gained not only by having input in the decision process but also through control of the process itself. Those subunits and individuals who can influence when decisions are made, who are involved in the decision process, and what alternatives are presented become very powerful. Macintosh and Whitson (1990) suggest that we have seen this type of control exercised in Canada's national sport organizations. The growing number of professional administrators in these organizations, because of their location in the sport organization's structure, have been able to limit volunteer involvement in the decision-making process. As Macintosh and Whitson point out, participation in the decision process "is restricted to those who agree on ends and [those] who are unlikely to persist in raising

issues that complicate the pursuit of those ends" (p. 131). As a result, the professional administrators within these sport organizations have become very powerful.

Organizational Politics

The study of organizational politics has not received a lot of attention within the sport management literature. Yet, like power, **politics** pervades all sport organizations, although it is somewhat intangible and hard to measure. Political skills are not easily taught to students or would-be managers. Politics is related to the use of power; political skills involve "the ability to use the bases of power effectively—to convince those to whom one has access; to use one's resources, information, and technical skills to their fullest in bargaining; to exercise formal power with a sensitivity to the feelings of others; to know where to concentrate one's energies; to sense what is possible; to organize the necessary alliances" (Mintzberg, 1983, p. 26).

As table 10.1 shows, a study of chief executives, staff managers, and supervisors found that organizational politics is seen to be both helpful and harmful to the individual members of an organization and to the operation of the organization itself.

Some people see politics as involving coercion, dishonesty, and manipulative behavior by individuals seeking to further their own self-interests. Others see politics as an integral feature of organizations and a way in which differences

Table 10.1 Helpful and Harmful Features of Organizational Politics

To the individual	Percentage of response by group			
	Combined	CEO	Staff	Supervisor
Helpful				
Advance career	60.9	56.7	53.6	72.4
Recognition, status	21.8	13.3	25.0	27.6
Enhance power, position	19.5	20.0	25.0	13.8
Accomplish personal goals	14.9	26.7	10.7	6.9
Get the job done	11.5	13.3	14.3	6.9
Sell ideas, projects, programs	10.3	10.0	7.1	13.8
Feelings (achievement, ego, control, success)	8.1	6.7	10.7	6.9
Survival	4.7	3.3	0.0	10.3

Harmful

Loss of power, strategic position, credibility	39.1	33.3	39.3	44.8
Loss of job, demotion, and so on	31.0	30.0	32.1	31.0
Negative feelings of others	21.8	33.3	14.3	17.2
Passive loss of promotion, transfers, and so on.	19.5	6.7	32.1	20.7
Internal feelings, guilt	12.6	6.7	14.3	17.2
Promotion to level of incompetence	9.2	6.7	0.0	20.7
Job performance hampered	3.5	0.0	0.0	10.3

	Percentage of response by group			
To the organization	**Combined**	**CEO**	**Staff**	**Supervisor**
Helpful				
Organization goals achieved, get job done	26.4	30.0	28.6	20.7
Organization survival, health, processes	26.4	26.7	25.0	27.6
Visibility of ideas, people	19.5	16.7	21.4	20.7
Coordination, communication	18.4	23.3	17.9	13.8
Develop teams, group functioning	11.5	16.7	7.1	10.3
Esprit de corps, channel energy	10.3	10.0	10.7	10.3
Decision making, analysis	6.9	3.3	14.3	3.5
No response (unable to mention helpful result)	14.9	10.0	10.7	24.1
Harmful				
Distract from organization goals	44.8	43.3	35.7	55.2
Misuse of resources	32.3	36.7	32.1	27.6
Divisiveness, splits, fights	21.8	20.0	21.4	24.1
Climate: tension, frustration	19.5	16.7	21.4	20.7
Incompetents advanced	14.9	3.3	21.4	20.7
Lower coordination, communication	10.3	3.3	10.7	17.2
Damage organization image, reputation	10.3	6.7	10.7	13.8
No response (no harm mentioned)	3.5	3.3	7.1	0.0

Reprinted by permission of Sage Publications Ltd from D.W. Madison et al., "Organizational politics: An exploration of manager's perceptions," *Human Relations* 33: 92. Copyright © 1965 by Sage Publications.

among interest groups are resolved and tasks are accomplished. A study by Gandz and Murray (1980) (see table 10.2) found that people felt politics was a common feature of organizations, that political activity occurred more frequently at the higher levels of an organization, and that to be successful in an organization one had to be good at politics. However, like the study by Madison, Allen, Porter, Renwick, and Mayes (1980), Gandz and Murray's work also found that respondents felt there were problems and drawbacks to organizational politics.

We now examine some of the different types of political tactics used in sport organizations. While we focus specifically on four activities—building coalitions, using outside experts, building a network of contacts, and controlling information—there are, as table 10.3 shows, a number of other political tactics used in organizations.

Building Coalitions

One of the main ways people in sport organizations can increase their political power is by building coalitions with others (cf. Pfeffer, 1981). Coalitions are built when people spend time communicating their views to others, establishing trust relationships, and building mutual respect. While these activities can occur within the formal confines of the sport organization, they often occur over dinner, in the bar, or on the golf course. Coalitions are only effective when they are tightly united around a particular issue. Sometimes political activity is directed at weakening coalitions by

Table 10.2 Characteristics of Workplace Politics

Statement	Percentage of agreement
(a) The existence of workplace politics is common to most organizations,	93.2
(b) Successful executives must be good politicians.	89.0
(c) The higher you go in organizations, the more political the climate becomes.	76.2
(d) Only organizationally weak people play politics.	68.5
(e) Organizations free of politics are happier than those with a lot of politics.	59.1
(f) You have to be political to get ahead in organizations.	69.8
(g) Politics in organizations are detrimental to efficiency.	55.1
(h) Top management should try to get rid of politics within the organization.	48.6
(i) Politics help organizations function effectively.	42.1
(j) Powerful executives don't act politically.	15.7

Table 10.3 Managerial Perception of Organizational Politics Tactics

Tactic	Percentage of respondents who mentioned tactic			
	Combined groups	Chief executive officers	Staff managers	Supervisors
Attacking or blaming others	54.0	60.0	50.0	51.7
Use of information	54.0	56.7	57.1	48.3
Image building or impression management	52.9	43.3	46.4	69.0
Support building for ideas	36.8	46.7	39.3	24.1
Praising others, ingratiation	25.3	16.7	25.0	34.5
Power coalition, strong allies	25.3	26.7	17.9	31.0
Association with the influential	24.1	16.7	35.7	20.7
Creating obligations or reciprocity	12.6	3.3	14.3	30.7

using a "divide-and-conquer" tactic. Coalitions can occur within sport organizations; for example, the coming together of the players in an organization such as the National Hockey League Players Association (NHLPA) is a form of coalition. Coalitions can also occur among sport organizations. For example, in Canada in 1993 a large number of national sport organizations came together as a coalition for a series of "Sport Forums" designed to lobby the federal government on a number of issues relating to the funding of sport.

The Use of Outside Experts

Another common method of exercising political power used in a number of sport organizations is to hire outside **experts** to support or legitimize one's position. While government agencies and large companies in the sport industry often have their own in-house experts, these people often "carry baggage"; that is, they are seen to represent a particular constituency within the organization and favor that group's position. Hiring outside experts, perhaps a consulting company, is seen as a means of gaining an "objective view." However, despite an aura of objectivity it is often possible for those people hiring the experts to manipulate the outcome of any reports. For example, government departments such as those responsible for sport in Canada have often commissioned reports by outside experts to look at a number of different aspects of the sport delivery system; these reports are usually tabled with the minister, the elected official responsible for overseeing the department. If the minister likes the report and it fits with the department's stance, it can be made public, thus supporting and legitimizing the department's position. If the report is not to the minister's liking and contrary to the department's position, it can be merely received as information, in which case its contents will not be released to the public by the minister's office. Similar tactics may be used by the CEO of a large corporation within the sport industry. The organizing committee for the 2000 Sydney Olympic Games hired individuals from Greenpeace to legitimize their position as the "Green Games."

In addition to offering support and legitimacy, outside experts can be used for other political purposes. One vivid example in sport is the Canadian government's use of a commission headed by the Associate Chief Justice of the Province of Ontario to investigate the events surrounding Ben Johnson's positive drug test in the 1988 Olympic Games 100-meters race. Although ostensibly set up to examine the use of performance-enhancing drugs by Canadian athletes, the Dubin Inquiry (1990), as it was known, served a number of political purposes for the Canadian government in regard to its involvement in sport, particularly track and field. As Beauchesne (cited by Hall, Slack, Smith, & Whitson, 1991, p. 224) notes, its primary purpose was "(1) to dissociate the government or government bodies from scandal; (2) to convey the impression of taking action to remedy the problem; and (3) implicit in the trial format itself, to expose the guilty and to affirm the power of sanction as the best means to deter the situation."

Building a Network of Contacts

To be politically effective in a sport organization, it is necessary to gain the support of other people. Creating a network of contacts may involve building links with people inside and outside of the organization. **Networks** are established through the formal mechanisms of the sport organization but also through informal means. Kanter (1977) suggests that within an organization three types of people are important in building a network of contacts: sponsors, peers, and subordinates.

Sponsors are those individuals at a higher level of the organization. Kanter (1977) suggests these people fulfill three important networking functions. First, they can fight for their contacts at the upper levels of the organization. Second, they can often help bypass the organizational hierarchy or at least help guide someone through it. Third, sponsors can be "an important signal to other people, a form of reflected power" (Kanter, 1977, p. 181). Peers are sometimes overlooked in the process of building contacts. However, acceptance by one's peers is often a necessary step in obtaining the favors and recognition required to acquire political power and build the type of coalition discussed above. Subordinates are also important contacts:

> The accumulation of power through alliances [is] not always upward oriented. For one thing, differential rates of hierarchical progress could mean that juniors or peers one day could become a person's boss the next. So it would be to a person's advantage to make alliances downward in the hierarchy with people who looked like they may be on the way up (Kanter, 1977, pp. 185-186).

It is also advantageous to build alliances with subordinates because they carry out the tasks necessary to acquire political power. A lack of compliance by subordinates makes the power holder powerless.

A network of contacts can often be enhanced by hiring, promoting, transferring, or firing selected individuals. Sometimes it may even be beneficial to coopt into one's network someone with a dissenting view. For example, an academic member of staff who feels the athletic teams are getting too much money from the university's central administration may, if appointed to the department's budget committee, see the athletic director's point of view and realize that athletic teams are not overfunded. Such cooptation brings the dissenting member into the athletic department's network.

In addition to building a network of contacts within the sport organization, it is also important to build outside contacts. Frank King, chairman of the 1988 Olympic Games organizing committee, in his book *It's How You Play the Game: The Inside Story of the Calgary Olympics,* describes how he and his committee spent large amounts of time, both prior to getting the games and in the time leading up to the games, networking with IOC members, government bureaucrats, international sport personnel, and corporate officials. This is not an isolated incident—both McGeoch (1994) for the 2000 Sydney Olympics and Yarbrough (2000) for the 1996 Atlanta Olympics describe the same thing.

Controlling Information

Controlling information is a form of political activity that can be used by sport managers to influence the outcomes of the decision-making process within their organization or a decision concerning their organization. By emphasizing facts that support their position, or by hiding, limiting, or ignoring other relevant information, managers can promote their own position or discredit the points of view put forward by others. It has been argued that this type of tactic is frequently used by those bidding to host major sport events like the Olympic Games (cf. Auf de Maur, 1976; McGeoch, 1994; Pound, 2004; Reasons, 1984). Essentially what happens is that those in favor of the games emphasize the positive aspects of staging these events—the creation of new facilities, the infusion of tourist dollars into the community, and the creation of jobs. Advocates of the games choose not to discuss that their cost will be borne by local taxpayers, the facilities are often used by privately owned professional sport teams after the games, low-income residents are often displaced, public funds from ethnic and cultural programs are transferred to the games, and any long-term economic benefits to hosting them are relatively minimal (cf. Lenskyj, 2000). By controlling information, supporters of a games bid hope to influence the decision process positively.

Power in Sport Management Research

In the past, power has been a neglected area of study in sport management. Recently, however, researchers have begun to consider power in their studies. Henry (2001) argued that the moral dimensions of power must be addressed when analyzing aspects of contemporary urban sport and leisure policy. Fink, Pastore, and Riemer (2001) considered power as one issue that may explain diversity in Division IA intercollegiate athletic organizations. Wolfe, Meenaghan, and O'Sullivan (2002) developed a model that can demonstrate power relationships within a sport network context. Finally, Crompton, Howard, and Var (2003) used community power structure as one source of momentum explaining increased public investment in major league facilities.

SUMMARY AND CONCLUSIONS

Power and politics are two of the most neglected topics of study in sport management, yet they are present in every sport organization. Much of the research conducted in the area of sport management adopts a rational view of organizations, which assumes that sport organizations have specific goals, that everyone agrees on these goals, and the organization's structure is a product of rational responses to changes in contingency variables such as size, technology, and environment. In contrast, a political perspective on organizations assumes diverse goals, individuals and groups acting in their own self-interest, and organizational structure as the product of managers or the organization's

KEY ISSUES FOR MANAGERS

There are two types of elements when looking at an organization: the basic formal elements, such as its organizational structure, and the informal elements such as power and political structures. Both are equally important in understanding sport organizations. As a manager, you must be able to recognize the types of power and political activities found within your organization and promote the positive aspects of power and politics.

While managing power may be simpler under certain circumstances (e.g., a small local sporting goods store), it may be more difficult under others. For example, large publicly held sport organizations such as Nike not only have to deal with power issues within the organiza-

tion, but they also have to deal with the outside stakeholders. The larger the organization the harder it can be to manage this because of the increasing numbers of stakeholders. So the question becomes, in this case, who actually controls the organization? Interestingly, Fligstein and Brantley (1992) found that it doesn't matter who controls the organization. Rather, organizational factors such as the CEO's background, the industry's growth, and its product or service strategies are aspects that have a greater effect on performance. Shen and Cannella (2002) cautioned that the power dynamics among the senior executives influences how a CEO is dismissed and whether the result is an internal or external succession.

dominant coalition making decisions to preserve their own privileged position.

In this chapter on power and politics in sport organizations we looked first of all at Child's challenge to the rational ideas of contingency theory, expressed in his notion of strategic choice. Child argued that the structure of an organization was less dependent on determinants such as size, technology, and environment, and more a product of decisions made by managers about these areas. The reconciliation of these two viewpoints is one of the major issues in the study of organizations.

The concept of strategic choice is built upon the idea that managers or the members of the dominant coalition have the power to make choices about their organization's domain of operations.

Consequently, we looked at the concept of power and some of the issues that surround the concept. We specifically highlighted the difference between power and authority. We then focused on the different sources of power. Using French and Raven's five-part typology, we discussed sources of individual power. We also looked at the way in which different subunits or groups within an organization could acquire power.

Power is intimately related to politics and we looked at the advantages and disadvantages of the use of political activity in a sport organization. We examined some activities that people engage in to acquire political power—building coalitions, using outside experts, building a network of contacts, and controlling information.

KEY CONCEPTS

authority (p. 199)

centrality (p. 203)

charismatic authority (p. 202)

coalitions (p. 206)

coercive power (p. 201)

control of resources (p. 202)

control over decision making (p. 204)

controlling information (p. 208)

experts (p. 207)

expert power (p. 202)

legitimate power (p. 201)

networks (p. 207)

nonsubstitutability (p. 203)

politics (p. 204)

power (p. 199)

referent power (p. 201)

reward power (p. 201)

strategic choice (p. 197)

uncertainty (p. 202)

REVIEW QUESTIONS

1. Pick a familiar sport organization. Who are the powerful individuals within the organization? Why?

2. How can we reconcile the arguments made by contingency theorists with Child's arguments about strategic choice?

3. Compare and contrast the concepts of power and authority.

4. Pick a sport organization that you know well. What type of strategic choices have the managers in this organization made and how have they affected their organization's structure?

5. How do the use of reward power and the use of coercive power relate to the use of authority?

6. Could someone at a lower level of sport organization be powerful? If so, how?

7. Regrettably there are very few women who hold senior-level positions in sport organizations. Given what you have read about sources of individual power, how are women constrained in moving to senior-level management positions?

8. If you think about a sport organization that you know well, what subunits within this organization are powerful? Why?

9. You are a recent graduate of a sport management program and you have just accepted a position as a marketing assistant in a professional sport franchise. What can you do to acquire power?

10. How is the use of power likely to differ in a mechanistic, as opposed to an organic, organizational structure?

11. How does control over where decisions are made confer power on someone?

12. You are the head administrator of a high school athletic department. What types of power and political activity could have an impact on you? Give examples.

13. How does a sport organization's strategy influence the power structure of the organization?

14. How do the rational and political views of organizations differ? Relate these views to Morgan's metaphorical view of organizations outlined in chapter 1.

15. Can you think of any sport organizations that are not influenced by the political activity of its members?

SUGGESTIONS FOR FURTHER READING

The best two books on power are by Jeff Pfeffer, specifically his 1981 text *Power in Organizations* and his more recent (1992) and more applied work *Managing with Power.* You are advised to read both if you are interested in this topic. Henry Mintzberg's (1983) *Power in and Around Organizations* is also good reading and, although more sociologically than managerially oriented, you could benefit from Steven Lukes, (1974) classic *Power: A Radical View.*

There is somewhat of a dearth of writing on power in the sport management literature. Hill's (1992) book *Olympic Politics* (especially chapter 3) provides useful material on issues of power and authority in the Olympic movement. Also, many popular-press books give an idea of the type of

power wielded by some of the major figures in sport. Auf De Maur's (1976) *The Billion Dollar Games* shows the type of power exercised by Montreal mayor Jean Drapeau in obtaining and running the 1976 Olympic Games. Other popular books about the Olympics include Alfred Senn's (1999) book *Power, Politics, and the Olympic Games;* Helen Lenskyj's (2000) book *Inside the Olympic Industry: Power, Politics, and Activism;* Burbank, Andranovich, and Heying's (2001) book *Olympic Dreams: The Impact of Mega-Events on Local Politics;* and Dick Pound's (2004) book *Inside the Olympics: A Behind-the-Scenes Look at the Politics, the Scandals, and the Glory of the Games.* The power of Malcolm Edwards, the former owner of Manchester United soccer team, is discussed by

Crick and Smith (1989) in their book *Manchester United: The Betrayal of a Legend* and both Stephen Aris (1990) and Neil Wilson (1988), in their respective books *Sportsbiz* and *The Sports Business*, provide accounts of the power plays inherent in the sport industry. Finally David Prouty's (1998) book, *In Spite of Us: My Education in the Big and Little Games of Amateur and Olympic Sport in the U.S.,* talk about the cycling world.

CASE FOR ANALYSIS

Anatomy of the NFL-AFL Merger

Until the late 1950s, major league baseball was the number one sport in the United States. During the off-season, American sport fans watched college football. Professional football came in a distant second to baseball in the hearts of most sport fans.

However, the tide was beginning to turn. The media started covering some NFL games. At about this same time the American Football League (AFL) formed. The NFL viewed this new league as inferior, yet this upstart league started stealing college athletes from the NFL, grabbing headlines, and gaining credibility. The AFL even managed to sign on NFL players. In 1963, when a Chargers scout tried to sign University of Nebraska lineman John Kirby to an AFL contract, right on the field, Minnesota Vikings scout Joe Thomas, who had been tailing the player for weeks to recruit him to the NFL, reportedly leaped from the stands and punched Kirby.

Things had gotten serious, so serious in fact that all-out war exploded between the NFL and AFL over the players, especially the collegians. In response to the AFL's actions the NFL created "Operation Baby-Sit," a program set up for scouts to tail and guard potential college drafts and keep them away from AFL recruiters. NFL headquarters even had a protected room dedicated to airline tickets for emergency trips anywhere in the United States. Scouts could hop on planes at a moment's notice to whisk away players to keep them from the AFL.

Baby-sitters resorted to whatever was needed to keep their recruits: "blackmail, bribes, crap-shooting, drinking, finagling of every magnitude, flashy cars and flashy women, kidnappings as necessary, a multitude of lying, and plenty of spying" (Weiss & Day, 2003 p. 23). Players were so well guarded they couldn't even call their mothers.

Operation Baby-Sit became so big that there weren't enough scouts to go around. So NFL commissioner Pete Rozelle enlisted the help of New York advertising agencies to keep a constant guard over draft choices. Enlisting the help of these agencies was just one example of Rozelle's ability to establish ties with powerful people from different spheres of influence to help the NFL achieve its goals. He also turned to United Airlines for help. It responded by providing Gold League passes to baby-sitters. When flashed, this pass assured seats immediately to the holder and those with him, no questions asked.

Despite these efforts, the AFL kept luring players. It even signed a lucrative television deal in 1964 with NBC worth $36 million.

Needless to say, the NFL and AFL hated each other. But this hate was getting expensive. In 1965, both leagues reportedly spent $25 million just for signing college players. With $400,000 starting salaries, established players felt they were worth more. Frank Ryan, the Browns champion quarterback, who incidentally was about to receive his PhD in mathematics from Rice University, reasoned that if Joe Namath was worth $400,000 as a new player, then he had to be worth $1,000,000.

The situation was getting out of hand. Owners were increasingly concerned about the future of professional football and about their financial bottom line. Something had to change but the anger on both sides was still a major issue.

Rumors started surfacing of clandestine meetings between sides, but to no avail. This wasn't helped by the fact that the AFL had a pending antitrust suit against the NFL. The AFL had even suggested on many occasions a championship play-off game with the NFL, which was crisply rebuffed every time—there was no way the NFL was going to be on the same field as the AFL to let it gain credibility.

Still, the NFL and AFL commissioners managed to strike a gentlemen's agreement not to raid each other's rosters, which helped a little for professional players but not for the war over collegians. The agreement was to end in April 1966 with the AFL naming a new commissioner, Al Davis, who wanted capitulation, not merger. Rozelle had never been enthusiastic about a merger possibility anyway.

Meanwhile, known to few, six weeks before, serious discussions had started between Dallas Cowboys owner Tex Schramm and Los Angeles Rams owner Dan Reeves about a merger idea. Schramm presented the idea to Rozelle. It was agreed that discussions would be limited to the owners who would be directly involved (i.e., Giants, 49ers, Jets, and Raiders). The idea was therefore discussed in March with Wellington Mara (New York Giants owner) and Lou Spadia (San Francisco 49ers president). While the reactions weren't very enthusiastic, they weren't negative either. A strategy was formulated: Assemble a plan that NFL owners could support, then present the plan to AFL owners.

By early April, NFL attorneys had been consulted. On April 4, Schramm then approached Kansas City Chiefs owner Lamar Hunt, one of the AFL's principal founders. He was well respected by his peers, tired of the war, and didn't have any personal vendettas. Schramm talked confidentially to Hunt and a plan was hatched. Secretly Schramm, Hunt, and Rozelle started logging hundreds of hours and traveling thousands of miles to convince owners of their plan.

While the situation looked promising, the process was suddenly hindered by the naming of Al Davis and the announcement that several teams would be going on the market. Schramm and Hunt met again, and reassurances were made that the process was not derailed. However, Hunt explained to Schramm that the merger could be costly to AFL owners, especially in California and New York.

Schramm and his fellow conspirators were getting tired. The plan was to be publicly discussed at the mid-May meeting of NFL owners but that was tabled in favor of confidential talks with different owners to gain their support.

As it turned out, the secrecy was moot. On the second day of meetings, Mara had a press conference announcing the signing of free agent placekicker Pete Gogolak from the Buffalo Bills, an AFL team. It was like a bomb had gone off! Had Mara, an NFL patriarch, considered signing someone from the "other" league, at considerable price no doubt? Had Rozelle approved the deal?

Heated discussions ensued between what were thought to be old friends. But instead of retiring to their rooms to cool down, a number of influential team representatives met: Schramm, Mara, Spadia, St. Louis's Stormy Bidwill, Green Bay's Vince Lombardi, Cleveland's Art Modell, and Baltimore's Carroll Rosenbloom. It seemed attitudes had changed:

NFL teams were being financially eroded and the Gogolak affair was the last straw.

For his part, Rozelle now thought the NFL was going to win the war, and he hadn't truly been supporting the merger idea after all. Despite this, Schramm was sent on behalf of the other owners to tell Rozelle that the merger was going to happen with or without him. Rozelle thought about it for a short time, finally agreeing that the merger was going to happen.

Rozelle started conferring with the other owners, and by Memorial Day, they were all onboard. He next went to Dallas to meet with Schramm and put the finishing touches on the proposal before presenting it to Hunt. The deal hinged on the New York and San Francisco situations.

On May 31, Schramm presented the deal to Hunt who then flew to New York to confer with AFL Boston and Buffalo owners. Unbeknownst to the NFL and Schramm, these two owners had apparently been acting as an "unofficial" committee to help Hunt. The committee drafted 26 changes and additions. With Rozelle's help, Schramm decided a third of the changes were acceptable, a third of the changes were not, and a third of the changes required some negotiation. On Sunday June 5, Hunt sat down with Schramm in Dallas to discuss the sticking points, and by midnight most were resolved. Early Monday morning, Hunt flew to New York to finish the tentative agreement, communicating with Schramm by phone. On Tuesday June 7, Rozelle was told of the final agreement and he contacted all owners to get their assent that morning.

The lawyers urged Rozelle to announce the merger as soon as possible to halt the rampant rumors. Before doing that, though, two key congressional leaders had to be informed: Senator Philip Hart from Michigan and Representative Emanuel Celler from New York in order to gain their support and avoid costly and lengthy government delays, as the merger would mean a monopoly in professional football in the U.S.

Rozelle flew to Washington that day to meet with Hart, then with Schramm and Hunt to iron out the finishing touches. They finished at 3 a.m. on June 8. Later that morning, Rozelle spoke to Celler, then flew back to New York for the official announcement. On the evening of June 8, 1966, sanity was restored to professional football with the merger of the NFL and AFL.

AFL commissioner Al Davis knew nothing of it!

Based on information in D. Weiss and C. Day (2003).

Questions

1. What were the sources of power in this case?

2. How did power issues affect the NFL-AFL merger process?

3. Provide examples of how personal and organizational power can assist or hurt goal achievement, in this case the NFL-AFL merger.

4. Why did the merger's conspirators choose to talk to Lamar Hunt instead of the AFL commissioner?

Chapter 11

Managing Organizational Conflict

LEARNING OBJECTIVES

When you have read this chapter, you should be able to

1. explain the essential elements found in definitions of conflict,

2. discuss whether conflict is functional or dysfunctional to the operation of a sport organization,

3. explain why conflict should be viewed as a process and not a single incident,

4. outline the major sources of conflict in a sport organization,

5. describe the various strategies that can be used to manage conflict, and

6. identify techniques that can be used to stimulate conflict in a sport organization.

THE CANCELLED 2004-2005 NHL SEASON

In 2003-2004, the National Hockey League (NHL) was a $2.1 billion industry. Despite its healthy income, the NHL is the poorest of the four North American professional sport leagues. Small-market teams are especially struggling to survive.

For example, in the mid-1990s, the Ottawa Senators owner threatened to sell the team to U.S. buyers. The Calgary Flames and Edmonton Oilers were also in financial straits. The Quebec Nordiques moved to the United States, as did the Winnipeg Jets. A Canadian federal government commission, headed by member of Parliament Dennis Mills, was established initially to examine professional sports in Canada, but changed its focus to examine the Canadian sport system. During the same time frame, the minister of industry proposed to support the Canadian professional hockey teams, but a huge backlash occurred to stop this initiative; Canadians did not see why they should spend money on those millionaires. The average Canadian preferred to see their tax dollars go to improvements in health care or education (c.f. Whitson, Harvey, & Lavoie, 2004).

Meanwhile, players' salaries increased. To balance the books, owners raised ticket prices and sought more sponsorships. Some team owners, such as the Edmonton Oilers, even imposed salary caps on themselves because they simply could not afford the high player salaries. Yet other teams, like the New York Rangers, kept paying more and more to obtain and retain players.

(continued)

215

(continued)

Organizational conflict in the world of professional hockey led to the cancellation of the 2004-2005 National Hockey League season.

© Brian Drake/SportsChrome

Salary caps are maximum dollar amounts that each team can spend on player salaries. Caps in professional sports can be hard (no possibility of exceeding stated amount without severe penalties) or soft (a specific dollar value exists but there are exceptions, such as for disabled or rookie players, for example). The NFL (National Football League) has a hard salary cap while the NBA (National Basketball Association) has a soft salary cap. For its part, the NHL had different salary cap options available to it: A league-wide salary cap of no less than $32 million and no more than $42 million (equivalent to a 53- to 55-percent league-wide cap), or individual player-based salary caps with minimum and maximum dollar values for salaries.

When the current collective agreement ended with the 2003-2004 season, talks between NHL owners, represented by Commissioner Gary Bettman, and the National Hockey League Players Association's (NHLPA) executive director and general counsel Bob Goodenow, ensued over the summer. The owners wanted to fix the whole system so that the teams could be profitable. They argued that teams lost $273 million in the 2002-2003 season and $224 million in 2003-2004, with player salaries making up 75 percent of the budget. The owners proposed that the only way to make the system profitable again and

keep all 30 teams is by enforcing a salary cap attached to revenues. For their part, the players did not think the management difficulties were their problem; it was the owners, after all, who technically were increasing salary offers. They conceded to having luxury taxes on salaries. The owners rejected the idea.

Instead of the 2004-2005 season beginning in September, the owners locked out the players because the economic problems of the league had not been reconciled. Both sides settled in for a battle. There was some talk between the two sides and even rumors of bad blood between Bettman and Goodenow, which was dismissed by them. Final offers would be proposed, only to be rejected by the other side, and the process would start again. The salary cap issue was still the major problem. At one time, Goodenow offered a 24 percent salary rollback for the following year. But that wasn't enough for the owners, they wanted cost certainty. Hockey is a business after all.

Surveys of fans in Canada showed support was behind the owners, not the players. In the United States, little attention was paid to the lockout.

More than 150 days from the beginning of the lockout, the owners put their final offer on the table with a $40 million team salary cap, take it or leave it. Goodenow countered with, for the first time, a salary cap of $49 million—this major change in position was a surprise to the actual players. The owners countered with a $42.5 million salary cap. This was their final offer. Their argument was that currently only four teams (Detroit, New Jersey, Philadelphia, and Toronto) were above that amount, before factoring in free agents, and two more (Dallas and Colorado) were very close to that amount.

The NHLPA had until 11 a.m. the next morning, Wednesday February 16, 2005, to accept. Having not heard from the players by that time, Gary Bettman convened a press confer-ence at 1 p.m. to announce that the 2004-2005 season was officially cancelled, a first for any professional North American sport leagues. It would be the first time since the Spanish flu of 1919 that there would be no Stanley Cup playoffs.

Both sides deeply apologized to the fans. But most fans had already moved on.

The lockout officially ended July 22, 2005 with league and player approval of a collective bargaining agreement featuring a 24 percent salary rollback on all existing contracts and a salary cap of $34 million (US) per team (with a minimum salary total of $21.5 million).

Based on information in canada.com (2005), CBC Sports (2005b), J. Fitzpatrick (2005), and P. Lebrun (2005).

Anyone who has been involved in any type of sport organization, amateur or profes-sional, national or local, profit or nonprofit, will have experienced the conflict that can occur in these organizations. The vignette above provides an example of the frustration, financial concerns, and bickering that can be found in many sport organizations. A 1976 study by the American Management Association found that mid- and top-level managers reported that they spent approximately 20 percent of their time dealing with conflict (Thomas & Schmidt, 1976). There is no reason to believe things are different in sport organizations. Conflict is endemic to all types of organizations; in the same study, managers rated **conflict management** equally important as topics such as planning, communication, and motivation, which were being taught in American Management Association courses (Thomas & Schmidt, 1976). The "ability to navigate through the small and large conflicts within an organization is critical to success" (Mannix, 2003, p. 543).

In the next three chapters we explore a number of the processes that, like conflict, are common phenomena in sport organizations. In addition to conflict, the focus of this chapter, we look at the process of organizational change and the process of decision making. In this chapter, we look first of all at what we mean by the term "conflict." Next we discuss horizontal and verti-cal forms of conflict, followed by an examination of whether conflict is **functional** or **dysfunctional** to the operation of a sport organization. Because conflict is more than just a single incident, we look at conflict as a process and also examine the sources of conflict in a sport organization. The final two sections look at ways of managing conflict and the seemingly contradictory notion of how to stimulate conflict.

What Is Conflict?

There are many different definitions of conflict within the organizational literature (cf. Schmidt & Kochan, 1972; Thomas, 1992). March and Simon (1958, p. 112) describe it as a "breakdown in the standard mechanisms of decision making so that an individual or group experiences difficulty in selecting an action alternative." Thompson (1960, p. 390) is more succinct: Conflict is "behavior by organization members which is expended in opposition to other members"; Morgan (1986, p. 155) is even more precise, suggesting that "con-flict occurs whenever interests collide." Robbins (1974) suggests that conflict should be viewed as a continuum ranging from "no conflict" at one end to "the total annihilation and destruction of the opposing party" at the other.

Notwithstanding the variety of explanations of what constitutes conflict, some important com-monalties underpin most definitions. First, and of particular importance, the parties involved must perceive a conflict to exist. If no one perceives a conflict as existing then no conflict exists. (This does not mean that all perceived conflict is real; however, perceived conflict that is not real can still result in antagonism and interference.) Second, a conflict situation must involve two or more parties in opposition. Third, one or more of the parties must be involved in preventing one or more of the other parties from achieving its goal(s) by some form of **blocking behavior**. Finally, this blocking behavior must result in frustration, anger, or some other form of emotional response.

Kolb and Putnam's (1992) definition of conflict essentially encompasses these points. They suggest that "conflict may be said to exist when there are real or perceived differences that arise in specific organizational circumstances and that engender emotion as a consequence" (p. 312). These writers, however, caution against an over-reliance on rigid definitions of conflict, since such explanations should always take into account the contextual circumstances in which the conflict takes place "because it is always difficult to draw a line between episodes of 'conflict' and the normal give and take of social interaction."

Horizontal and Vertical Conflict

One method of categorizing the conflicts that can occur in a sport organization is to distinguish conflicts that take place between subunits at the same level of the organization (**horizontal conflict**) from those that take place between different hierarchi-

cal levels (**vertical conflict**). Figure 11.1 shows this type of distinction as it might occur in a university athletic department.

Horizontal Conflict

Horizontal conflict occurs between subunits, or those individuals representing subunits, that are on the same level of the organizational hierarchy. The organizational behavior (OB) literature focuses on this type of conflict. Instead of trying to eliminate this type of conflict, OB researchers currently call for managing it instead (cf. Bendersky, 2003). As figure 11.1 shows, horizontal conflict may occur in an athletic department between those individuals within the intercollegiate athletic program and those involved in the campus recreation program. The campus recreation staff may not agree with the amount of funding given to the athletic program, or conflicts may occur over scheduling or access to facilities. The two groups, because they have different roles to play in providing sport and recreational opportunities for students, tend to develop different goals and priorities. These types of conflicts are not uncommon in athletic departments or sport organizations in general. The job of the athletic director is to resolve conflicts that do occur and prevent future flare-ups by coordinating

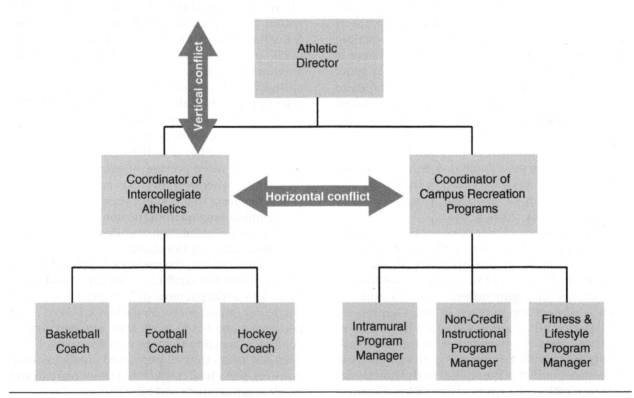

Figure 11.1 *Horizontal and vertical conflict.*

and encouraging collaboration among the units under her direction.

Vertical Conflict

As figure 11.1 shows, vertical conflict arises between different hierarchical levels of a sport organization. Industrial relations (IR) theorists focus on this type of conflict because of the inevitable power differential found in the workplace (Bendersky, 2003). Conflict between an athletic director and a coordinator of intercollegiate athletics may occur over such issues as salary, the amount of authority the coordinator is allowed to exercise, differences over the goals of the athletic department, or the way it should operate. Much of this type of conflict stems from the need for control in a sport organization and an individual's or subunit's need for autonomy. Organizational members have to balance their own needs for personal expression and fulfillment against the demands imposed by the structure of the organization, in particular its hierarchical reporting relationships and formalized procedures.

Vertical conflicts can be avoided by appropriate leadership behavior, or techniques such as management by objectives (MBO), where there is an attempt to establish some degree of congruence between individual and organizational goals. However, none of these methods will completely eliminate vertical conflicts and all generally involve a trade-off between the amount of control that can be exercised and an individual's or subunit's autonomy. A frequent form of vertical conflict involves managers (or owners) and workers. We see this type of conflict in professional sport

organizations in struggles between team owners and players (see Dworkin, 1981).

Is Conflict Dysfunctional to the Operation of a Sport Organization?

For most of us, conflict carries a negative connotation. We are brought up to believe that conflict is bad, something we should avoid. Psychologist Abraham Maslow (1965, p. 185) suggested that within North America there is "a fear of conflict, of disagreement, of hostility, antagonism, enmity" and that we place "much stress on getting along with other people, even if [we] don't like them."

These ideas about conflict are reflected in our view of sport organizations. The common perception of an effective sport organization is one where everybody gets along with each other and works toward a common goal—there is an emphasis on cooperation. Members of organizations where cooperation is high are said to interact more effectively, make better progress on tasks, and strengthen their work relationships (Tjosvold, 1988). It is also claimed that employee satisfaction is higher and the managers of these organizations are held in more esteem. In contrast, conflict is seen as dysfunctional; because it hinders the achievement of organizational goals, it is something we should avoid in our organizations.

This view of conflict as dysfunctional can be found in both the classical approach to organization theory and the human relations school. In the former, with its emphasis on bureaucratic

TIME OUT   *Volunteers' Job Conflicts*

Most sporting events are headed and run by volunteers. While this is an inexpensive way to operate, most volunteers—especially higher up in the hierarchy—find themselves with time conflicts. Typically, these volunteers have full-time day jobs, working at least eight hours per day five days a week, and then that same number of hours on the event, sometimes more. Some volunteers are lucky enough to let their organization run itself, checking in only once in a while, but that is the exception

to the rule. Most volunteers are not presidents of their own companies, and they don't have the luxury of taking a leave of absence.

Working those long hours causes two things: work can suffer or the event loses a future volunteer. After putting so many hours into an event, volunteers will choose to retire from the volunteering world, believing it is time someone else takes over. The problem is, oftentimes, there isn't anyone with the individual's expertise.

rationality, conflict is at best avoided and at worst managed through the imposition of rules and regulations (cf. Taylor, 1911). Human relations theorists (cf. Likert & Likert, 1976) also see conflict as bad. However, for these people, conflict is controlled by providing people with training sessions on how to get along, or using third-party intervention when conflict arises. Both of these perspectives are limited, because they fail to acknowledge the functional benefits of conflict to an organization.

Those who subscribe to the view that an optimal level of conflict can be beneficial to an organization's operation see it as a source of change and creativity. Pondy (1992, p. 259) even goes as far as to suggest that "if conflict isn't happening then the organization has no reason for being." Conflict, because it often arises over dissatisfaction with the way things are, prevents complacency and stimulates new ideas. Sport organizations that are totally free of conflict will have no reason to change and may ultimately flounder. This is not to say that all conflict in sport organizations is beneficial; the emphasis is on an optimal level of conflict. If conflict is too low, sport managers need to stimulate constructive conflict; we deal with ways of stimulating conflict later in this chapter. If conflict is too high, the manager's job is to reduce it. Figure 11.2 shows how levels of conflict that are

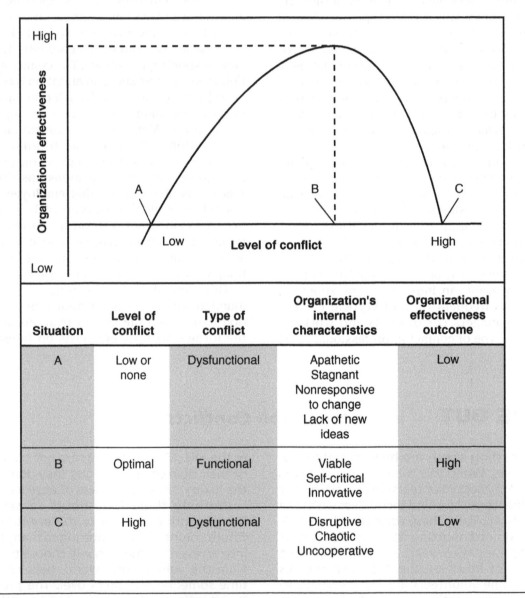

Situation	Level of conflict	Type of conflict	Organization's internal characteristics	Organizational effectiveness outcome
A	Low or none	Dysfunctional	Apathetic Stagnant Nonresponsive to change Lack of new ideas	Low
B	Optimal	Functional	Viable Self-critical Innovative	High
C	High	Dysfunctional	Disruptive Chaotic Uncooperative	Low

Figure 11.2 *Conflict and organizational effectiveness.*

ROBBINS, STEPHEN P., ORGANIZATION THEORY: STRUCTURES, DESIGN, AND APPLICATIONS, 3rd Edition, © 1990. Reprinted by permission of Pearson Education, Inc., Upper Saddle River, NJ.

too high or too low can influence an organization's level of effectiveness adversely.

The job of the sport manager is to recognize the situation within the organization and take the necessary steps to develop an optimal level of conflict. Obviously, managers need to adopt an attitude toward conflict that sees it as a source of innovation rather than a destructive force.

The Conflict Process

Often we tend to think of conflict situations as discrete events: The conflict occurs and then is resolved by some means. However, some organizational theorists (cf. Pondy, 1967; Rahim, 1986) have suggested that a conflict situation is made up of a series of interrelated stages. By being aware of the stages of the **conflict process**, and consequently the conditions that produce conflict and the events that can trigger a conflict situation, those people responsible for the operation of a sport organization can be in a better position to manage the incident. Pondy (1967) developed the most frequently cited of the stage models of conflict. Figure 11.3 shows an adaptation of Pondy's model; each stage in the model is discussed in detail.

Pondy's Five-Stage Model of Conflict

The first stage in Pondy's model is the latent stage of conflict. Essentially what Pondy argues is that certain conditions frequently found in organizations provide the latent potential for conflict to occur. These conditions are condensed into three basic types of **latent conflict**. The first of these involves competition for scarce resources. For example, when two or more groups, such as the teams within an athletic department, are vying for a portion of the organization's financial resources, there is a latent potential for conflict.

The second condition that creates a latent potential for conflict is the drive for autonomy. Individuals and subunits within sport organizations frequently attempt to operate autonomously. However, this ability is limited by the structure of the organization and the existence of similar aspirations in other individuals and subunits. For example, the owner or manager of a franchised sporting goods store may wish to undertake certain marketing activities to respond to the local conditions in his area, but he may be constrained by the company's corporate headquarters, which has a standardized approach to marketing for a consistent image of the company. Finally, latent conflict is a product of the differing goals that subunits within an organization can have. The athletic department at a university, for example, will have goals different from the physical education department, thus creating the potential for conflict.

The second stage of Pondy's model is **perceived conflict**, the stage in which one or more of the parties involved becomes aware, through some type of stimulus or information received, of the potential for a conflict. Pondy suggests that some only mildly threatening conflicts may be suppressed. Also, because organizations are often faced with more conflicts than they can handle, only a few are dealt with, usually those "for which short-run, routine solutions are available" (Pondy, 1967, pp. 301-302).

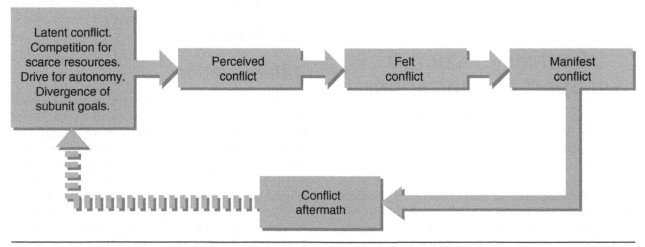

Figure 11.3 *Pondy's five-stage model of conflict.*

TIME OUT   *Creative Tension:*
An Optimal Level of Conflict?

Managing the 1984 Los Angeles Olympic Games was a large and difficult task. Peter Ueberroth, the president of the Los Angeles Olympic Organizing Committee (LAOOC), knew it was not a normal business and didn't run in the customary way. "It was unusual," he noted. "These were not normal practices, not normal business practices. It wasn't a time for kindness, to take time to help people through problems."

"Creative tension" was the phrase some staff members used to describe the regime under which the Olympic committee was directed. Ueberroth said it was not his term. But he readily acknowledged that he intentionally created some tensions in daily operation as a means of testing his staff. He recalled, "It was essential for Harry (Harry L. Usher, Ueberroth's executive vice president), for me, commissioners, for the leaders to set goals, create difficulties, make

people perform against deadlines, against expectations, so that they were in training for some pressure that I didn't know how to measure. And if there weren't some tensions to see how people reacted, we couldn't have run the games."

Examples of tensions include the "Peter test," a test administered by the president himself to all newcomers, with only 24 hours' notice before its administration. Another test of sorts related to each individual being assigned a country and expected to be the resource person for that country. If the president received a delegation, for example, he would call all individuals who were supposed to know about that country and quiz them to get the desired information.

Based on information in McDonald (1991) and Reich (1986).

The third stage of Pondy's model is **felt conflict**. Here emotions such as anger, hostility, and frustration are encountered. The fourth stage is **manifest conflict**. Here some sort of adversarial behavior is exhibited, ranging from apathy and rigid adherence to rules to violence and physical abuse, although thankfully the latter is rare in sport organizations.

The final stage of the model Pondy terms the **conflict aftermath**. Here the conflict is either resolved or becomes the basis for future conflicts, as indicated by the broken line in figure 11.3.

Sources of Conflict in Sport Organizations

Conflict in a sport organization can stem from a number of different sources and take a variety of different forms. Much of the work carried out on conflict in organizations has been micro in orientation (Nelson, 1989), that is, it has tended to be sociopsychology-based and to focus on conflicts at the interpersonal level. In keeping with our emphasis on the structuring of sport organizations, we focus here on structurally derived conflicts, those rooted in the way a sport organization

is structured. This analysis is important to our understanding of sport organizations because, as Hall (1982, pp. 151-152) points out, "conflict in organizations involves more than simple interpersonal conflict (not that interpersonal conflict is necessarily simple) . . . the very nature of organizations themselves contribute to conflict situations." We look specifically at those structural **sources of conflict** most frequently cited in the literature (cf. Corwin, 1969; Walton & Dutton, 1969; Walton, Dutton, & Cafferty, 1969) and the application of this literature to sport organizations (cf. Amis, Slack, & Berrett, 1995).

Differentiation

In most sport organizations work is broken down and allocated to different subunits to achieve the goals of the organization more effectively. However, as we saw in chapter 8 the process of differentiation results in subunits exhibiting different goals, management philosophies, and time orientations (Lawrence & Lorsch, 1967). As Langhorn and Hinings (1987, p. 560) point out, although "organizations differentiate for technical reasons, these boundaries of task and expertise are reinforced by sociopsychological processes that result in technical boundaries becoming social and political boundaries." The more a sport organization differentiates (i.e., breaks down work and allocates it to different subunits), the greater the likelihood of conflict, because the greater the differences created between subunits. Individuals within subunits may think differently, use different work methods, have different priorities, come from different educational backgrounds, and perhaps even use a totally different set of terminology. While these differences are appropriate and necessary aspects of the operation of a sport organization, they do not engender tolerance and empathy for the problems that other subunits may confront.

Macintosh and Whitson (1990) identify how the increasing differentiation of Canadian national sport organizations, which occurred with the hiring of additional professional staff during the 1984-1988 quadrennial planning period, helped precipitate conflict in these organizations. Professional staff brought new and different goals to national sport organizations, goals that emphasized high-performance sport and new ideas about how these organizations should operate, which led to clashes with the volunteers who had traditionally operated these organizations.

Interdependence

Where there are high levels of differentiation and subsequently considerable variations in the value orientation, mode of operation, and power of the subunits within a sport organization, the potential for conflict is high. However, as Pondy (1967) points out, this potential is latent. For conflict to become manifest, some level of interdependence between the subunits is necessary. Interdependence creates the opportunity for the interference and blocking associated with conflict.

As we saw in chapter 9, Thompson (1967) identified three types of interdependence—pooled, sequential, and reciprocal—each progressively more complex and requiring increased levels of coordination. The more complex the interdependence in a sport organization, the greater the likelihood of conflict. For example, conflict is more likely to occur in a sport and fitness center in which subunits are reciprocally interdependent than between franchised sporting goods stores exhibiting pooled interdependence.

Low Formalization

One of the ways to manage the complexity associated with increased differentiation and reciprocal interdependence is through the use of rules, regulations, policies, and procedures. Formalization helps clarify roles, establish standard ways of operating, and reduce ambiguity. Consequently, when formalization is high, the potential for conflict in a sport organization is low; when formalization is low, the potential for conflict is high. It is important to note, however, that some writers disagree with this position and argue that rules and regulations can in fact contribute to conflict in organizations (cf. Corwin, 1969).

A lack of formalized regulatory mechanisms such as rules and regulations means that subunits come to rely more on political tactics and coercion to conduct their operations. As an example, a number of Canadian national sport organizations have formalized their selection criteria for national team athletes and made the criteria known well before the selection process. This formalization reduces the subjective and political nature of the selection process, helping avoid the conflicts that sometimes occur over this issue.

Competition Over Resources

When two or more subunits within a sport organization compete for a share of limited resources, they come into conflict with each other. Because sport organizations only have so much money, space, or equipment, there is conflict over who is going to get what. Also, since these resources often help subunits accomplish their goals more easily and quickly, managers often use such strategies as inflating budgets or political maneuvers to increase their share.

Conflict over resources can occur horizontally in a sport organization, for example, when the sport studies department within a university has to compete with other departments for increased funding. It can also occur vertically, particularly between owner/managers and workers. The NHL's 2004 to 2005 cancelled season featured at the beginning of this chapter is a good example of conflict over resources, in this case, financial resources.

Differences in Reward Systems

The nature of the reward system used within a sport organization will help determine the extent to which subunits cooperate or are in conflict with each other (cf. Walton & Dutton, 1969). The more frequently the managers of the various departments within an organization are rewarded for achieving the overall goals of the organization, as opposed to their own departmental goals, the higher the level of cooperation within the organization (Cliff, 1987). The more rewards are based on the performance of each individual subunit, as opposed to the overall sport organization, the greater the potential for conflict. In a sport organization that produces equipment, for example, if the sales department is rewarded for increased sales volume, it will want to establish as many new accounts as possible. Some may have risky credit ratings and the accounting department, which gets rewarded for minimizing losses, will not want to take them on as new clients. These cross-purposes will lead to conflict between these two departments. In another example, Slack, Berrett, and Mistry (1994) show how, in a national sport organization, the high salary paid to coaches led to conflict with lower-paid administrators, who felt they made an equal contribution to the operation of the organization.

Power Incongruence

As we saw in chapter 10 even though subunits may be on the same level of a sport organization's hierarchy, some are able to wield more power because they are more central to the work-flow or they can acquire and control needed resources. These differences in power can lead to conflict, particularly when the actual day-to-day interactions do not reflect perceived power. For example, in an athletic department the athletic director is higher up the organization hierarchy than the basketball coach. However, due to the importance attributed to the basketball program on many U.S. university campuses, the basketball coach may perceive himself and be perceived by others as having considerable power. If the coach then starts to give "orders" to the athletic director, conflict is likely to ensue.

Communication Problems

One of the most frequent causes of conflict between organizational subunits is a lack of clear and adequate communication. As information moves vertically up and down a sport organization's hierarchy, it may get distorted or misinterpreted and, as a result, conflict may ensue. Communication between subunits on the same horizontal level is also subject to misinterpretation. As we saw earlier, the personnel who staff the various subunits of a sport organization come from different backgrounds and may use a different vocabulary in order to conduct their

work. For example, the terminology used in the research-and-development department of a ski manufacturing company such as Rossignol or Head will be different from that used in sales or marketing. If one of these two departments have to interact with research and development, then communication problems can occur and conflict can result.

Conflict can also occur if one subunit stops communicating with another or withholds information. Slack, Berrett, and Mistry (1994) describe one national-level sport organization that was forced to move its main offices; in the move, files were withheld, contributing to conflict between members who lived in the region where the office was located and the staff hired to run the new office. Jollimore (1992) cites accusations of a "failure to communicate with players" as an important issue in the conflict between factions of the Canadian Women's Field Hockey Association, over the firing and subsequent rehiring of national coach Marina van der Merwe.

Participative Decision Making

Although often promoted as an important means of getting people involved in an organization, "the opening up of organizational decisions to discussion and debate raises, or maintains, the level of conflict in the institution" (Zald, 1962, p. 47). By allowing more people "to have their say," participative decision making facilitates the expression of more diverse opinions, heightening the potential for conflict. The interaction that occurs between members of a sport organization, rather than breaking down barriers, can serve to reinforce differences and thus may entrench people in their position even more.

Does this mean we shouldn't use participative decision making in sport organizations? The answer is obviously no; participative decision making can be a very productive way of operating, even though it has the potential to precipitate conflict. Levels of participation in a sport organization's decision-making processes may range from "consultative participation," in which employees have input into the process but are not responsible for the final decision, to "employee involvement," when employees have input about work procedures and job responsibilities (Cotton, Vollrath, Froggatt, Lengnick-Hall, & Jennings, 1988). A number of national sport organizations in Canada and the United States have successfully adopted what is termed "rep-

TIME OUT   *Role Conflict: The Problems of the Athletic Department's Academic Advisers*

Many of the major U.S. university and college athletic directors employ academic advisers to tutor student athletes. Every day these people face role conflicts: how to keep players eligible for intercollegiate athletics while ensuring that they receive a college education. Coaches demand that players spend an enormous amount of hours per week training, practicing, attending team meetings, viewing game films, traveling, and playing their sports; for most athletes, this regimen precludes spending the time and effort necessary for a decent college education.

If an academic adviser is high-minded and concerned about an athlete's education, the adviser soon disputes the coach's demands on the player's time. Because athletic departments sympathize with their coaches, and also have the self-interest of needing winning teams, they decide most of these conflicts in favor of the coaches. Advisers who want to keep their jobs learn "to go along to get along" and to acquiesce to the coaches' commands.

The adviser's role conflict begins as soon as the athlete arrives on campus. His or her first task is to arrange the athlete's schedule of classes. Immediately, a conflict between eligibility and education arises: Should the athlete be allowed to take the same courses as other first-year students or be placed in the school's "hideaway curriculum" to ensure eligibility?

Based on information in M. Sperber (1990).

resentative participation"; representatives from the countries' different geographic regions, from the officials' organization, and from the ranks of the athletes are involved in the decision-making process. The trade-off for the sport manager in any initiative to increase the number of different viewpoints is: Does the potential for reduced alienation and improved morale outweigh the possible conflicts that could result?

Role Conflict

People often find themselves in a conflict situation if their role responsibilities suddenly change, or if different expectations are placed on them. Changing a person's role in a sport organization, even if it is seen as a desirable move, can cause disruption and stress that can lead to conflict. If the change is viewed as a demotion, the level of stress increases and so does the potential for conflict. Roles also carry certain expectations for the person filling the role. These expectations may relate to the nature of the work, the salary, the opportunity to travel, or a new office. If these expectations are not met or if the person filling the job has different expectations from other powerful people in the organization, then they both may experience a frustration that can manifest itself in conflict. The USOC's restructuring in 2003 stemmed from mul-

tiple examples of role conflict between the board, CEO, head of ethics, and the ethics committee.

Conflict Management Strategies

Because conflict has both positive and negative consequences, it has to be managed. The ideal situation for the sport manager is one where there is an optimal level of conflict within her organization. A number of strategies are outlined below that can be used to manage conflict. Conflict can be managed by either changing behavior or changing attitudes. A **behavioral change** is superficial and does not really get at the root of the conflict; it is a short-term solution. A **attitudinal change** requires a greater commitment and usually takes longer to accomplish, but it is the basis for a more collaborative sport organization. We look at some strategies solely designed to change behavior, and others used to establish more long-term attitudinal changes.

Authority

One of the most common methods of managing conflict is for the senior managers of the sport organization to use their formal authority to resolve or suppress the conflict situation. While the parties involved may not always agree with the manager's decision, they will usually recognize and comply with whatever resolution is made. We see this type of resolution used in professional sport, where the commissioner has certain powers to resolve disputes. In major league baseball, for example, all parties abide by what is called the Major League Agreement and "commit themselves contractually to submit all disputes and controversies among themselves to the commissioner for arbitration, to accept the commissioner's judgment as binding, and to waive any right to recourse in the courts" (Scully, 1989, p. 15). The problem with this conflict resolution is that it is short-term, and addresses only the immediate problem, without bringing about the attitudinal changes required for long-term stability.

Avoidance

Another commonly used technique for dealing with conflict is avoidance: either directing attention away from a conflict or ignoring that it exists. If the dean of a faculty of sport studies is involved in a heated conversation with the athletic director over the resources allocated to their respective areas, he may, for example, change the subject to one less contentious. In a somewhat similar vein, an athletic director may choose to "turn a blind eye" to illegal payments to university athletes, hoping that any conflict that could ensue from such an illegal practice will be avoided. However, like the use of authority, avoidance is a short-term solution.

Separating or Merging Conflicting Units

Because conflict emanates from the interdependence between the subunits of a sport organization, one way to manage such conflict is to remove the interdependence. Where there is no need for the units to work together on organizational tasks, a manager could order the actual physical separation of the two groups, preventing any contact between them. A related but opposite way of handling this type of situation is to reduce the interdependence between two subunits by making them into one, that is, merge them. In part, notwithstanding the economic benefits, the merging of some of the major professional sport leagues has been motivated by the desire to reduce conflict. Harris (1987, p. 16), for example, notes that

after the NFL and AFL merger "peace . . . descended on the football business," a stark contrast to "the war that had preceded it."

Increasing Resources

As we saw earlier, resource scarcity can precipitate conflict. It follows then that one way to manage a conflict over resources is to increase availability. While it is not always possible to give all subunits everything they want, selected resource increases may translate into savings because wasteful conflicts are avoided. For example, in a sport management department conflict could arise between faculty and graduate students who both have to use the same photocopying machine. If use is heavy, faculty members may feel they should have priority. At the same time, graduate students who have research and teaching responsibilities feel their needs are equally important. The simple answer to avoiding or removing any conflict over this situation is to provide each group with a photocopier. However, while it is often a very satisfactory means of resolving or preventing a conflict, all too often resources for this kind of initiative are not readily available.

Integrating Devices

Integrating devices may involve the use of a small group (a committee or a task force) or an individual. Essentially, the role of these groups or individuals is to span the boundaries between subunits. If a group is used, it usually contains representatives from the subunits that are or potentially could be in conflict. Bringing these people together is seen as an effective way of solving problems because they come to see each other's perspective (Blake & Mouton, 1984). Committees are frequently used in many sport organizations to manage or prevent conflict. For example, Cross Country Canada has a high-performance committee with representatives from the coaches, athletes, and sport scientists. By having representatives from these different groups involved in decision making about high-performance sport, the incidences of conflict can be minimized. Individual sport managers themselves may sometimes fill a similar role in a committee or task force; part of every manager's job is to enhance collaboration between the subunits under managerial control. Mid-level sport managers may also act as integrators between senior managers and lower-level workers. Like those strategies that follow, the use of integrating devices is directed toward attitudinal, rather than behavioral, change.

Confrontation and Negotiation

Confrontation means that the parties involved in a conflict come together face-to-face and try to resolve their differences. Those involved recognize that conflict does exist and that it needs to be dealt with. Confrontation as a conflict resolution technique requires a certain amount of maturity; facts have to be faced, and emotions, as much as possible, have to be put aside. Although confrontations are risky, if successful they can provide a basis for continued collaboration. Negotiations occur during the confrontation process; each subunit or their representative(s) work through the situation to try to come to an agreement. It is important to emphasize that in the negotiation process the focus should not solely be on points of difference but also on points of agreement. Owners and players frequently use confrontation and negotiation as a means of resolving disputes over contracts or salaries. Millson (1987) provides an account of the negotiation process that took place between Toronto Blue Jays officials Paul Beeston and Pat Gillick, and players Ernie Whitt and Jim Clancy. Similar accounts of this process can be seen in the many books on professional athletes and professional sport organizations.

Third-Party Interventions

If a conflict is particularly drawn out, a third-party intervention may be used to resolve the dispute. Here a person who is not associated with the conflict is brought in to try to resolve the situation. Although the person brought in will not be associated with either side in the conflict, the principals involved are often given the right to approve or disapprove of the person who will be the third party. The best example of this strategy in sport organizations is the situation where labor arbitrators resolve contract disputes between the owners of professional sport teams and their players. One of the best-known arbitration decisions in sport, referred to as the Seitz decision, resulted in Jim "Catfish" Hunter of the Oakland Athletics becoming baseball's first free agent in 1974 (Scully, 1989).

Resolution of conflict within a sport organization can involve third-party intervention. In 1974, a contract dispute involving pitcher Jim "Catfish" Hunter went to arbitration, with the result that Hunter became baseball's first free agent.

TIME OUT *Alternative Dispute Resolution: A New Form of Resolving Conflicts in Sport*

At the 2000 Sydney Olympic Games, two legal battles challenged an athlete's right to participate: One case involved an equestrian who wanted reinstatement, claiming he was wrongly banned from the sport for drug use, and another was a 50-meter swimmer whose coach supposedly forgot to add him to the list of participants. Cases like these are increasingly frequent or, at least, are seen more often in the media. When an athlete takes an organization to court, it can tie up the courts for weeks. Because these cases are time-sensitive, they take precedence over criminal cases, causing a backlog in the courts. In addition, it is a costly initiative for athletes who, for the most part, have little money to spare.

Canada has created an alternative dispute resolution (ADR) system to help remedy such situations in the Canadian sport system. ADR "has been defined as a series of processes that

are alternatives to litigation . . . [and they include] prevention, negotiation, mediation, facilitation, and arbitration" (Kidd & Ouellet, 2000, p. 4). The general goals of ADR are to decrease time and costs for dispute resolution, "maintain or improve the disputants' relationship, ensure that the outcome of the system is workable, durable and implementable [and] develop a process that people can learn from" (Kidd & Ouellet, 2000, p. 5).

The Canadian government has set up the Sport Dispute Resolution Centre of Canada. National sport organizations are now required to refer to this Centre when conflicts need resolution. The ADR system also uses the International Court of Arbitration for international matters.

Based on information from B. Kidd and J.-G. Ouellet (2000).

Superordinate Goals

As we saw in chapter 3 the subunits within a sport organization develop their own goals. The incompatibility of these goals with those of other subunits can sometimes precipitate conflict. A strategy used to address this type of conflict is the creation of superordinate goals, higher-level goals that require subunits to work together if they are to be achieved. These goals must be seen as more important than the goals subunits possess individually. The creation of superordinate goals can enhance cooperation within an organization; attention is directed away from the individual subunit goals, the basis of the conflict, to the superordinate goals that must be achieved collaboratively.

A very powerful superordinate goal is survival. In good times, when resources are relatively plentiful, vigorous union lobbying for salary increases often leads to conflicts with owners and management. When a sport organization's survival is threatened, a situation that affects everyone's welfare, then groups tend to work together more, to ensure survival. Such was the case in 1975; the WFL, in its second season, was threatened with col-

lapse. Chris Hemmeter, the league commissioner, devised a plan that had as its goal minimizing operating expenses. Owners and players agreed to work together to try to ensure the league's survival. Owners committed to deposit between $600,000 and $1.2 million with the league, and players agreed to work for a percentage of team gross income (Chang & Campo-Flores, 1980). Although Hemmeter's plan is a good example of the type of superordinate goal that can get the factions of a sport organization working together, the league eventually folded—some owners simply could not come up with the money.

Job Rotation

Sometimes conflict can be prevented or managed by engaging in job rotation. Very simply, a person from one subunit works in another subunit, usually on a temporary basis. Through this practice the person who is moved comes to understand the attitudes, issues, and problems in the subunit to which she is moved. The individual who is moved is also in a good position to relate similar information about her own department. Although it often takes considerable time, job rotation can have a significant effect on changing some of the underlying attitudes that precipitate conflict. While some types of job rotation are not feasible, for example, having the tennis coach trade places with the football coach, the concept is applicable to a variety of sport organizations, most notably those involved in the manufacturing of sport equipment.

Issues Management

Conflict can come from internal issues but also from the environment. External issues can have a major impact on the organization's activities. One way to ensure that conflict from external sources is prevented or managed in time is to use the issues management process. According to Nigh and Cochran (1987), an organization would start with these steps:

1. Identify external issues by determining gaps between internal and external needs and expectations as well as perceived trends.
2. Analyze identified issues.
   - Examine the issue's history and forecast how it might develop over time.
   - Determine the probability of the issue's various outcomes.
   - Assess the issue's impact on the sport organization.
   - Prepare the agenda (list or order of issues for management consideration with three categories of issues: (1) high probability of outcomes having an impact on the firm, (2) lower probability but should be tracked periodically, and (3) potential issue).
3. Formulate and implement a response to prevent or manage the issues.

The management process allows the sport organization to be proactive in its conflict resolution by identifying problems before they get out of hand. For example, the director of a high school athletics department may realize a growing discrepancy between the needs of students (physical activity, being healthy), the expectations of parents (a wide range of sports available), and the funding provided by the government (in decline). Having identified this issue, the director will look at what's been done in the past and consider possible solutions for the present. Solutions may be to decrease the number of sports, consult students about their desired sports, lobby the government for more money, or find alternative avenues of funding. Determining that the latter solution may be the most acceptable to all constituencies, given the strong sport program at the school, the director may present a proposal to the school's administration to prevent a possible conflict at budget time. The administration would then take the proposal, along with issues identified by other departments in the school, and prioritize a response according to resources available and the potential impact of the issues left unresolved.

Stimulating Conflict

Earlier in this chapter it was suggested that the effectiveness of a sport organization is influenced by the level of conflict within the organization. Because conflict can often be below an optimally desirable level, Robbins (1978) has suggested a number of questions (see figure 11.4) to determine if the level of conflict in an organization is too low.

Robbins (1978, p. 71) notes that "while there is no definitive method for universally assessing the need for more conflict, affirmative answers to one or more of the . . . questions suggests there may be a need for more conflict stimulation." Using some of the ideas suggested by Robbins, we briefly explore how **conflict stimulation** can be used in a sport organization.

Introducing New Blood

Sometimes people within a sport organization become complacent; one of the ways to "wake them up" is to introduce one or more new people into the organization, individuals who bring new and different ideas to the sport organization, people who challenge existing modes of operation, and make staff think about new ideas. Bringing "new blood" into the organization was exactly what Reebok's Paul Fireman had in mind in 1987 when he hired C. Joseph LaBonté, a former CEO of Twentieth Century Fox Film Corporation, to become president and CEO. Prior to LaBonté's hiring, Reebok was a one-product company. When he arrived at Reebok, LaBonté added new product lines and began a series of acquisitions designed to diversify and strengthen the company. He also cut the size of the apparel group, instituted a series of controls that created a more structured organization, and began a series of cost-cutting measures. LaBonté's initiatives created a series of conflicts:

1. Are you surrounded by "yes people"?
2. Are subordinates afraid to admit ignorance and uncertainties to you?
3. Is there so much concentration by decision makers on reaching a compromise that they may lose sight of values, long-term objectives, or the company welfare?
4. Do managers believe that it is in their best interest to maintain the impression of peace and cooperation in their unit, regardless of the price?
5. Is there an excessive concern by decision makers in not hurting the feelings of others?
6. Do managers believe that popularity is more important for the obtaining of organizational rewards than competence and high performance?
7. Are managers unduly enamored with obtaining consensus for their decisions?
8. Do employees show unusually high resistance to change?
9. Is there a lack of new ideas forthcoming?
10. Is there an unusually low level of employee turnover?

Figure 11.4   *Is there a need to stimulate conflict in your organization?*

Copyright ©1978, by The Regents of the University of California. Reprinted from California Management Review, Vol. 21, No. 2. By permission of The Regents.

While Reebok had gained control over its internal operations, there were indications it had lost control of its external relations. Notwithstanding these problems, Reebok's profits rose 28 percent in 1989, but that same year LaBonté left the company (cf. Jereski, 1990; Van Fleet, 1991).

Manipulating Communications

Robbins (1978) suggests that manipulating communications can help managers stimulate conflict. Ambiguous or threatening information can create situations in which tensions run high. For example, information suggesting that certain intercollegiate athletic programs will be cut because of funding shortages can create the kind of conflict that can reduce complacency and improve the health of an athletic department. Leaving an individual or subunit out of the communication process can have the effect of signaling to them that they are not important. The confrontation resulting from this type of omission, however, can cause the individuals or subunits concerned to reexamine their role in the sport organization and their contribution to its strategic direction. There is, of course, an ethical question to consider when using this type of tactic.

Creating Competition

Creating competition between subunits or individuals is a third way managers can stimulate conflict. Coaches use this technique when they institute competitions between players on their teams. It is also used by sport organizations such as retail stores selling sport equipment, when they create competitions to see who can sell the most in a particular time period. The conflict usually resulting from these ventures is rarely hostile, as invariably everybody wins in some way or other. However, if the competition results in no net gain, or if there is a duplication of effort, such as in a case when two groups of sales people in the same sporting goods company compete for a large contract, the level of conflict is likely to be higher.

Current Research About Conflict

For a half century, researchers have worked to develop the theories outlined previously. It is only in the last decade that researchers began testing those theories. However, the balance has already shifted back to the need for more theorizing. Within sport management, few researchers directly examine organizational conflict. One notable exception is the study by Burke and Collins (2000) which provides issues, approaches, and implications of work conflict for sport managers.

Mannix (2003) suggested avenues of conflict research that apply very well to the sport management field. First, she argued for research on cross-cultural conflict. Next, she proposed conflict situations be followed over a period of time,

KEY ISSUES FOR MANAGERS

The point of this chapter is that successful sport organizations and managers must be able to recognize and deal with conflict. Negative conflict can hurt a sport organization and its employees. Recognizing and dealing with conflict properly and as soon as possible, before it gets out of hand, allows the sport organization to save time, money, and other precious resources. Sport managers must also be able to choose an appropriate conflict management strategy, recognizing that the strategies we presented earlier in the chapter are not mutually exclusive. Sometimes a combination of strategies is best. The ADR example presented in the Time Out "Alternative Dispute Resolution: A New Form of Resolving Conflicts in Sport" is, in effect, a combination of a negotiation and a third-party intervention. In addition, sport managers must look at potential conflict not only within the organization but also across the organization's boundaries. One emerging type of conflict in an increasingly globalized world is the potential differences between cultures. Expectations and needs may be very different between, say, American and Chinese counterparts, which can lead to potential conflict. Being able to recognize this possibility beforehand will save the sport organization much time and effort.

Nugent (2002) proposed four steps for managers to decide the appropriate level of involvement when faced with a conflict situation. First, managers must determine whether an intervention is even necessary. Can the protagonists be made to handle the situation themselves or is a third party needed? Second, if an intervention is required, what is the most appropriate type of intervention: autocratic, arbitration, facilitating, bargaining, or collaborative problem solving? Third, the manager must determine whether she is the best person to intervene. Is someone with more power better? Finally, if the manager is the best person, does she need the assistance of an independent resource person (and how would this person be used)?

Successful sport organizations and managers must also be able to promote positive conflict. This can increase creativity, communication, and preparedness to help the organization gain and sustain a competitive advantage. However, most people do not see conflict as positive. Yet, it could mean the difference between success and failure, as seen in the Peter Ueberroth–LAOOC example presented in an earlier Time Out. As a manager, it is your responsibility to use conflict stimulation when needed and in an appropriate manner so that the exercise does not have a negative effect on employees.

because organizational disputes are not isolated occurrences. Instead, they influence future decisions and actions. Third, she argued for the need to better understand the "links between the types of conflict and performance" (p. 544). Fourth, she argued for a detailed description of negotiation's

underlying mechanisms and processes. Finally, she argued for the need to link specific types of diversity (social diversity, informational diversity, and value diversity) with specific conflict types and conflict resolution processes and outcomes.

SUMMARY AND CONCLUSIONS

Conflict is one of the most neglected issues in the field of sport management. There has been virtually no empirical research on the topic, and most textbooks have chosen to ignore the occurrence of conflict in sport organizations. This omission is problematic because, as the media and many popular books on sport frequently show, conflict in

sport organizations is widespread. In this chapter a number of issues related to conflict in sport organizations were addressed. Definitions of conflict drawn from the literature featured a number of common elements that delineate the occurrence of a conflict situation. However, it was noted that caution should be applied when using definitions of conflict, because it is sometimes difficult to distinguish between conflict situations and the normal daily social interaction that takes place in a sport organization. Conflict was described as existing in both the horizontal and vertical levels of a sport organization. It was then shown that, contrary to what has been presented in the sport management literature, conflict can in fact be functional to the operation of a sport organization. Pondy's conflict model was used to show that conflict is not a single discrete event but rather a series of interrelated stages. The most frequent

sources of structurally based conflict in sport organizations were identified as differentiation, interdependence, low formalization, competition over resources, differences in reward systems, power incongruence, communication problems, participative decision making, and role conflict. Several strategies were presented to manage the conflict arising from these sources. A discussion of the more common ways to stimulate conflict in a sport organization if it drops below an optimally desirable level concluded the chapter.

KEY CONCEPTS

attitudinal change (p. 225)

behavioral change (p. 225)

blocking behavior (p. 218)

conflict aftermath (p. 222)

conflict management (p. 217)

conflict process (p. 221)

conflict stimulation (p. 229)

dysfunctional conflict (p. 217)

felt conflict (p. 222)

functional conflict (p. 217)

horizontal conflict (p. 218)

latent conflict (p. 221)

manifest conflict (p. 222)

perceived conflict (p. 221)

sources of conflict (p. 222)

vertical conflict (p. 218)

REVIEW QUESTIONS

1. Explain how Kolb and Putnam's definition of conflict applies to a conflict situation you have seen occur in a sport organization.

2. What did Kolb and Putnam mean when they suggested it is sometimes difficult to distinguish conflict from the normal give-and-take of social interaction?

3. Do vertical and horizontal conflicts always occur separately or could one influence the other? If you believe they do interact, provide an example.

4. How would people who subscribe to the scientific management school of thought suggest we deal with conflict? How do their ideas differ from human relations theorists?

5. Peter Ueberroth suggested that a state of "creative tension" in the LAOOC was necessary in order for him to run the 1984 Olympic Games effectively. What do you think Ueberroth meant by this remark? Explain the possible problems of this approach to management.

6. What does a sport organization gain from conflict? What does it lose?

7. Using a conflict that has occurred in a sport organization you know, identify the different stages of the conflict using Pondy's model.

8. How is structurally derived conflict different from interpersonal conflict?

9. What do Langhorn and Hinings (1987) mean when they suggest that the boundaries of task and expertise that are created in organizations become social and political boundaries?

10. Why is conflict more likely in a sport organization that exhibits reciprocal interdependence than one that exhibits pooled interdependence?

11. Although it was suggested that low levels of formalization can be a source of conflict, some people have actually argued that high levels of formalization can have just the same effect. Why would they say this?

12. Do you think that computers have added to or reduced the conflict that can occur in sport organizations as a result of poor communication?

13. Pick a situation where you have seen a sport manager use avoidance to handle a conflict situation. Discuss what other ways the conflict could have been handled.

14. You have just been hired to be the managing director of the national governing body of one of your country's major team sports.

When you arrive you find that the board of directors, who are all volunteers, are in conflict with the national coach, who is a paid professional. The conflict essentially revolves around the fact that the board does not agree with the coach's selection of several of the players on the team. How will you go about resolving this conflict?

15. What do you think is the relationship between the structure of a sport organization and the incidence of conflict in that organization?

SUGGESTIONS FOR FURTHER READING

There have been a large number of books within the field of management written about conflict. One of the more comprehensive texts is Afzalur Rahim's (1989) edited book *Managing Conflict: An Interdisciplinary Approach*. Also interesting is Dean Tjosvold's (1991) *The Conflict-Positive Organization*. Tjosvold, unlike many writers, presents a view of conflict as a positive organizational phenomenon. Students who want more information about conflict should also look at the major organizational journals. In particular, Vol. 13, No. 3 (1992) of the *Journal of Organizational Behavior* is a special issue titled "Conflict and Negotiation in Organizations: Historical and Contemporary Perspectives."

In terms of the sport literature, newspapers, magazines, and many popular-press books contain descriptive accounts of the type of conflicts that occur in sport organizations. If you are interested in conflict in professional sport and associated issues

like arbitration, you can look into books such as Gerald Scully's (1989) *The Business of Major League Baseball* and James Dworkin's (1981) *Owners Versus Players*, or the more popular-press–type books such as Jack Sands and Peter Gammons' (1993) *Coming Apart at the Seams*. A number of the articles cited in these books also provide useful insights into the issue of conflict in professional sport organizations. While the academic literature on conflict in other kinds of sport organizations is sparse, Slack, Berrett, and Mistry's (1994) article "Rational Planning Systems as a Source of Organizational Conflict" provides some interesting ideas about how planning, an exercise normally believed to eliminate disputes from organizations, can actually precipitate conflict. Also, the article by Amis, Slack, and Berrett (1995) shows how the structural antecedents of conflict operate in voluntary sport organizations.

CASE FOR ANALYSIS

Bickering at the USOC

The USOC was designated by Congress in 1978 as the principal Olympic group in the United States. The organization, which had previously had its headquarters in a small office in New York City, was moved to a former Air Force base in Colorado Springs. To operate the organization, a 105-member board made up of representatives from the 38 member U.S. sport associations was established. The organization was operated by an executive director, F. Donald Miller, a former colonel in the U.S. Air Force, and well connected in the world of sport. These contacts, along with his

disciplined approach to the operation of the USOC, ensured that the organization ran smoothly.

When the U.S. senior IOC member, Douglas Robey, announced he was retiring, Miller was, to many, the obvious choice to take his place. Members of the USOC were so intent on getting Miller appointed to the IOC that they offered to make a deal with its president, Juan Antonio Samaranch. If Samaranch would nominate Miller, a virtual guarantee of his appointment, the USOC would drop their opposition to TOP (the Olympic sponsorship program) and also allow Horst Dassler's ISL (the organization behind the TOP marketing program) a four-year trial operation in the United States. Samaranch needed the support of the USOC if TOP was to work, and the USOC wanted to see Miller elected. What appeared to be a mutually beneficial plan was scuttled by USOC president Robert Helmick, who went behind the backs of the USOC members supporting Miller. Helmick reportedly sold Samaranch on the idea that as president of the USOC he could be more useful to the IOC than Miller. Helmick was duly appointed.

Nine months after his appointment Helmick informed Samaranch that the IOC would be getting $7 million from the Los Angeles Olympic Games profits. There had been a dispute over the amount of money that should go to the IOC after the 1984 games. F. Donald Miller left the USOC, replaced in 1985 by George Miller, also a former military man, who had been the deputy commander of the U.S. Strategic Air Command. Although George Miller had supported Helmick when he ran for the presidency of the USOC, within months of Miller's taking over as executive director, the two began to fight. Some suggest Helmick saw Miller as a threat to his power.

George Miller's appointment to the USOC's executive director position followed on the heels of the success of the Los Angeles Olympics. As a result of the games' profits, each athletic federation in the USOC received about $1.2 million; sponsorship opportunities were also rife. One of the consequences of this increased availability of funds was that the member federations became less dependent on the USOC, and therefore less subservient. Because of a 1985 policy decision, the remaining $85 million surplus from the games went to a special fund created for the "long-term needs" of athletes, not to the USOC's operating budget. Consequently, when George Miller took over as executive director his principal task was to enhance the organization's financial position. He spent much of his time, however, fighting with the member federations. An attempt to convert the regionally based Olympic Festival Games into a national event that could generate sponsorship money failed, because most federations would not send their top athletes. A move to organize a joint marketing licensing program also received little support from the member federations. Miller was quoted as saying that trying to achieve consensus among these organizations was "nearly impossible." When he warned a number of them against competing in the 1986 Goodwill Games sponsored by Ted Turner, alleging that it would

hurt the USOC, many ignored his warning and competed anyway.

Miller's relationship with Helmick also became increasingly strained. Helmick set up his own office in his hometown of Des Moines, Iowa, something no other president had done. In conducting his business he ran up considerable expenses; he also alienated Miller when he legislated that all major TV and sponsorship contracts would require his signature. Previously this task was the responsibility of the executive director. Miller felt that Helmick wanted to let the member federations make all the decisions. Helmick, for his part, disagreed with Miller's style of operation. Helmick supporters felt Miller wanted to run the USOC like a military unit. The problems between the two came to a head in August 1987 when Helmick wanted to spend $100,000 for a Pan American Games reception. Miller turned down the request and Helmick told him he could either resign or be fired. Miller chose the first option and negotiated a $700,000 buyout.

Despite the struggles between Miller and Helmick, the USOC did make progress. Sponsorships were obtained, which along with a commemorative coin program were expected to generate revenues of up to $200 million for the organization by 1992. This money and more, however, was needed for 8 to 10 new training centers, because only three existed. The plan was to locate these centers closer to inner cities, where a number of the best athletes lived. There was also a need to get more young athletes into Olympic competition and to provide increased financial support for them.

To help with these tasks Harvey W. Schiller was appointed as the next executive director of the USOC. Schiller's plan was to create a leaner and meaner organization, something he received support for from both the membership and Helmick. However, when he took up his position at the USOC, he found he was immediately swamped with complaints and demands from the member federations. On January 15, 1988, just a few weeks prior to the Calgary Olympics, Schiller addressed a group of coaches, administrators, and other federation officials and told them of his love for the U.S. Olympic movement. Schiller spoke with passion and the crowd loved his speech. Three days later he resigned, saying he couldn't stand the infighting at the USOC. He had held the position of executive director for 19 days.

Some felt the infighting that had been going on in the organization spilled over to the competition site; the United States won only six medals in Calgary. Many blamed the weak showing on poor management and lack of support from the USOC. One sport marketing consultant described the USOC as "a national embarrassment." To address the criticism, a task force was established prior to the end of the Calgary Games. George Steinbrenner, owner of the New York Yankees, was to head the group, which was to review all the USOC's programs.

Based on information in *"If there were a gold medal for bickering the U.S. would win"* (1988), Simpson and Jennings (1992).

Questions

1. If you were Steinbrenner, what types of issues would you see the task force addressing?

2. What types of recommendations do you think the task force would be likely to make?

3. How do the concepts of differentiation and interdependence help you understand the conflict that arose in the USOC?

4. What does this case tell you about the relationship between different constituencies in the amateur sport system?

tion site, the United States won only six medals in Calgary. Many blamed the weak showing on poor management and lack of support from the USOC. One sport marketing consultant described the USOC as "a national embarrassment." To address the criticisms, a task force was established prior to the end of the Calgary Games. George Steinbrenner, owner of the *New York Yankees*, was to head the group, which was to review all the USOC's programs.

Questions

1. If you were Steinbrenner, what types of issues would you see the task force addressing?

2. What types of recommendations do you think the task force would be likely to make?

3. How do the concepts of differentiation and interdependence help you understand the conflict that arose in the USOC?

4. What does this case tell you about the relationships between control, the dynamics in the market, right now?

Chapter 12

Organizational Change

LEARNING OBJECTIVES

When you have read this chapter, you should be able to

1. understand what we mean when we talk about organizational change and explain why change is seen as paradoxical,

2. explain the major perspectives that are used to understand change,

3. discuss the factors that cause change,

4. explain the sources of resistance to change and how this resistance can be managed,

5. describe the stages of the change process and the concept of tracks, and

6. explain why sport organizations need to be innovative.

CHANGES IN THE STRUCTURE AND OPERATIONS OF THE NATIONAL COLLEGIATE ATHLETIC ASSOCIATION

In 1906, 38 U.S. schools formed the first national governing body of college and university athletics. The Intercollegiate Athletic Association (IAA), as the organization was then known, was established as a result of public concern over the rampant violence in intercollegiate football. The members of the organization worked together to counter this concern. They established a standard set of rules and introduced the forward pass, which opened up play and made the game safer. In 1910 the IAA changed its name to the National Collegiate Athletic Association (NCAA) and expanded the scope of its mandate to encompass all unethical conduct in college sport. In its early years the NCAA was a loosely structured group of colleges and universities operated by seven representatives of the member institutions. Although the original intent of the organization was to regulate and control intercollegiate sport through the establishment of a set of stringent rules and strict enforcement codes, this idea was dropped in favor of accomplishing its purposes through educational means. The actual control of intercollegiate sport was placed in the hands of each individual member institution, and the NCAA had no power to sanction—its primary role was an advisory one to its membership.

The NCAA grew rapidly. The size of its executive board increased to nine in 1921 and was further expanded in 1928. The first NCAA national championship was held in 1921 in track and field; swimming followed in 1924,

(continued)

237

(continued)

The National Collegiate Athletic Association (NCAA), with headquarters in Indianapolis, Indiana, has experienced changes in purpose, structure, and the scope of its operations since its inception in the early 1900s.

wrestling in 1928, and boxing in 1937. The first NCAA basketball championship was held in 1939. Membership size increased from the initial 38 schools to 148 in 1926; by 1951 there were 368 member schools and 24 conferences. The organization hired its first full-time staff director in 1949.

Despite its considerable growth it was not until 1952 that the NCAA was granted any type of regulatory power over its member institutions. Public disclosures about unethical recruiting, illegally paying student athletes, point-shaving in college basketball, and tampering with student transcripts resulted in mounting pressure to do something about intercollegiate athletics. As a result a group of college and university presidents met as members of the American Council on Education to recommend that athletics be deemphasized as a part of the college and university curriculum. Faced with the threat of someone from outside intervening in their affairs, the NCAA moved quickly to develop a system under which sanctions against member institutions could be invoked. The organization's

role changed, from being a passive observer and consultant on issues related to intercollegiate sport, to exercising the power to penalize member institutions that violated its rules.

Since 1952 the NCAA's power and the scope of its operations have continued to grow. It now controls virtually all aspects of big-time college and university sport in the United States, including the regulation of national championships, the eligibility of student athletes, the administering of financial aid, and the length of the playing and practice seasons. The organization has a budget of $452.5 million and a membership of just over 1,000 four-year colleges and universities. It operates 87 national championships in 22 sports and regulates a number of college football bowl games. Its headquarters are centralized in Indianapolis, Indiana, and it has a paid staff of 254. Along with a 20-person executive council, more than 125 other committees run the affairs of the organization. Its operating policies and procedures are outlined in a manual almost 500 pages in length.

Based on information contained in Sage (1982), Stern (1979), Garrison (1992), National Collegiate Athletic Association (2003a, 2003b, 2004).

Change, such as that exhibited by the NCAA, is one of the most visible features of all sport organizations. As discussed in chapters 6 through 9, to survive and grow, a sport organization must be able to adapt to changes in strategy, size, environment, and technology. As it grew larger the NCAA required a different operating structure from that used in its early years. As the scope of its mandate changed, so did its mode of operation. In the vignette at the start of chapter 1 we saw Nike undergo a similar type of transformation as it evolved from a company operating out of the trunk of Philip Knight's car to one of the biggest athletic footwear manufacturers in the world.

The purpose of this chapter is to explore the multifaceted nature of change in sport organizations. We begin by looking at the concept of change and what we mean when we talk about organizational change; we then explore the paradoxical nature of change. Next, six major theoretical approaches to understanding change are briefly outlined. We then look at what causes the need for change in sport organizations, what are the barriers to change, and how change is managed. Some theorists have suggested that change can be conceptualized as a series of stages; we look briefly at this approach, but then argue that the concept of "tracks" provides a better and more realistic understanding of the change process. Finally, we look at the notion of innovation and why sport organizations need to be innovative.

The Concept of Change

Sport organizations are in a constant state of change; new people enter the organization, some leave, parts of the organization's physical layout are reorganized, and new programs or product lines are developed. In this chapter our focus is not on the day-to-day fluctuations evident in all sport organizations but on planned change, change that a sport organization systematically develops and implements to retain a competitive advantage in whatever market it targets. The pressures for such change may be generated externally in the sport organization's environment or they may originate from within the organization itself. Over the past decade external pressures—the changing economic situation in North America, Asia, and Europe, technological advances in the manufacturing of sport equipment, and increased societal

interest in sport and leisure—have all contributed to changes in organizations within the sport industry. Internal factors such as an emphasis on service quality, a move to self-managed teams, and the demand for flexible operating procedures have also produced pressures for change.

As figure 12.1 shows change can occur in four different areas of a sport organization: technology, products and services, structures and systems, and people (cf. McCann, 1991).

Technological change refers to the changes that occur in an organization's production process, the skills and methods it uses to deliver its services, or its knowledge base. Huffy underwent considerable technological change when it moved to a computer-integrated manufacturing plant (Slakter, 1988). A **change** in the **products** or **services** of a sport organization may involve the addition, deletion, or modification of other areas. For example, in the 1980s and 1990s as snowboarding was increasing in popularity, many sporting good stores increased the amount of store space allocated to these products, and the amount of advertising about the availability of these products. **Structural and systemic changes** involve modifications to areas of a sport organization such as its division of labor, its authority

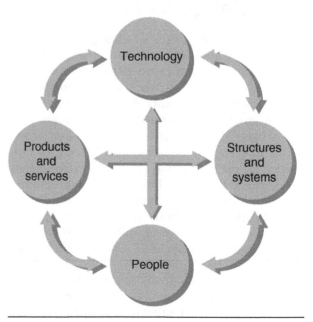

Figure 12.1 Potential areas of change in a sport organization.

structure, or its control systems. Such changes occurred when the NCAA increased the size of its council and added committees and professional staff. **People change** involves modifications to the way people think and act and the way they relate to each other. This type of change is often brought about through techniques such as sensitivity training, team-building exercises, and group planning. While we focus primarily on structural change in this chapter, these four areas are interrelated; a change in one area will often require a change in one or more of the others.

Regardless of the area of change, there are two types of change: radical and convergent. According to Greenwood and Hinings (1996), **radical change** is frame bending, completely changing orientation, while **convergent change** is more about fine-tuning a specific orientation. For example, Bombardier—the original maker of Ski-Doo and Sea-Doo—was created in 1942. Its progressive acquisition since 2000 of divisions related to other modes of transportation besides recreational-based transportation—specifically trains and planes—shows convergent change. However, Bombardier underwent a radical change in its orientation by divesting itself of its entire recreational division—its original core purpose—in 2003 to focus on the train and plane divisions.

Change as Paradox

The **paradoxical nature of change** stems from the fact that a sport organization must change if it wishes to remain competitive (Peters, 1990). However, as we saw earlier, management prefers stability and predictability. A sport organization's output, costs, and workforce must remain relatively fixed if it is going to be successful. At the same time, sport managers need to look for new markets, new technology, and innovative means for service delivery. The sport organization, therefore, must find a balance between change and stability. If a sport organization fails to change it may follow what Miller (1990) refers to as a "trajectory of decline." On the other hand, if it changes too rapidly or just for the sake of change, its operations will be disrupted. If incorrectly managed, the success of previous change can become a sport organization's downfall. As Miller (1990, p. 3-4) notes, "productive attention to detail, for instance, turns into an obsession with minutia; rewarding innovation escalates into gratuitous invention; and measured growth becomes unbridled expansion."

Achieving a balance between stability and change is not an easy task. The sport manager must recognize the need for change and understand how it can be successfully implemented and managed. Changes in environment and technology will impact the amount of change a sport organization will require. Those organizations that operate in stable environments with routine technologies will require less change than those facing dynamic environments with nonroutine technology.

Perspectives on Organizational Change

For many years the dominant models of change were what Chin and Benne (1985) describe as "normative reeducative." Essentially, change was seen as a linear process consisting of a series of steps that involved diagnosing problems in organizations, developing solutions to these problems, identifying resistance to the changes that would be needed to implement these solutions, formulating and implementing a change strategy, and monitoring and reviewing the change process. Particular emphasis was placed on the role of change agents, individuals who used a variety of organizational development techniques to guide the change process. In the last 20 years the political and economic fluctuations that have characterized North American and Western European societies have drawn increased attention to the process and management of change. As a result we have seen new theoretical developments in this area, and hence new ways of looking at change. In this section we briefly examine the most popular of these perspectives. Although these perspectives are dealt with separately, they are not necessarily discrete. Some, such as **institutional theory** and **population ecology**, have been seen as converging with each other (cf. Carroll & Hannan, 1989; Zucker, 1989) and some, for example, population ecology and the contextualist approach are considerably different in their intellectual underpinnings and their method.

Population Ecology

As we saw in chapter 8 the population ecology approach to understanding organizations developed out of the biological literature and particularly the Darwinian notion of survival of the fittest. The focus here is not on change in single organizations but on a population of like organizations in a particular geographic area or niche, for example, all sporting goods stores in the state of New York (cf. Carroll & Hannan, 1989; Delacroix & Carroll, 1983). Population ecologists conceptualize organizational change as a three-stage process (see figure 12.2).

In the first stage of the process, considerable variation in the organizational form is found in a particular population of organizations. This variation occurs because entrepreneurs set up organizations to fill a gap in the market, or as a result of a perceived need. For example, in the last 25 years the number of sporting goods stores in North America increased as consumers demanded a variety of sport and recreational equipment. The stores created to fill this need show variation in their structural form, the products they sell, and the way they service their customers. Some of these variants will be better equipped to meet the demands of their environment. Some will be unable to exploit this environment to obtain the resources necessary to operate or there may be an insufficient demand for their product or services. Those that fail to meet the demands of the environment will be "selected out," that is, they will fail. Those that are positively selected survive and are retained within the market niche. Over time the demands of the environment will change. For instance, in our example of sport stores, over the last few years there has been a greater demand for products such as in-line skates and licensed apparel. Sport organizations have to change their structure, products, and services to meet these types of environmental demands. Those that do will be retained; those that don't will flounder and cease to exist.

Resource Dependence

The essential premise of resource-dependence theory, as we saw earlier, is that organizations are unable to generate internally the different types of resources they need to operate; consequently, they come to depend on their environment for resources critical to their survival. However, as Pfeffer and Salancik (1978, p. 3) point out, "environments can change, new organizations enter and exit, and the supply of resources becomes more or less scarce." Because organizations depend on resources for their operation, this potential for a reduction of resources creates uncertainty for managers. Managers can reduce this uncertainty by changing their activities in response to these environmental factors. Cunningham (2002) argues that **resource dependence** is part of an organization's structural change process. Managers can also act to change the nature of their organization's resource environment. The techniques used include mergers, diversification, and joint ventures. Mergers between two competing organizations help reduce uncertainty by eliminating some of the competition for resources. Diversification can be used to stabilize a sport organization's dependence on its environment by reducing the uncertainty that may result from trends in individual market areas and economic fluctuations. Joint ventures reduce uncertainty by pooling resources such as capital and expertise. All of these initiatives result in changes to an organization's structure and operations; more details of such changes can be found in chapters 6 through 8.

The Life Cycle Approach

Like population ecology, the **life cycle approach** is based on the idea that biology "provides certain concepts and models that . . . appear to have some relevance for understanding organizational cycles" (Kimberly, 1980, p. 6). Unlike population ecology, however, the life cycle approach is concerned with single organizations or small groups of organizations, rather than entire populations. Essentially, the central theme of the life cycle approach is that organizations, like animals or people, change as they go through different life stages. These stages are described variously: creation, transformation, and decline (Kimberly, 1980); birth, growth,

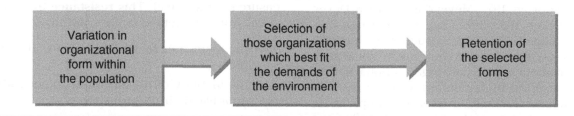

Figure 12.2 *Stages of the change process: the population ecology approach.*

maturity, old age, and death (Adizes, 1979); the entrepreneurial stage, the collectivity stage, the formalization and control stage, the elaboration of structure stage, and the decline stage (Cameron & Whetten, 1983a). These stages are sequential, not random, and as such they are predictable. However, the length of time that individual organizations spend in each stage may vary considerably, and every organization will not necessarily go through every stage. Some, for example, may go straight from the entrepreneurial stage to decline. Each stage has different managerial requirements. Change is seen as a developmental progression through these stages.

Certain key events in the various stages can significantly influence future changes. For example, Kimberly (1980) argues that organizations, like people, are very much influenced by the conditions of their birth. Also, like people, an organization's history will strongly influence any future changes it may make. Although it does not specifically employ the life cycle approach, Slack's (1985) study of the Alberta Section of the Canadian Amateur Swimming Association provides some indication of the stages that a sport organization may pass through. Also, Theodoraki (2001) considers the temporal aspect when examining structural configurations of Olympic Games organizing committees. Many popular press accounts of the growth of sport organizations (cf. Kogan, 1985 [Brunswick]; Geiger, 1987 [The Broadmoor]; Strasser & Becklund, 1991 [Nike]) provide implicit indications of their various life cycle stages.

Although criticized as overly deterministic, the life cycle approach is intuitively appealing as a means of understanding change. In some ways it has also been the forerunner of more recent work by John Kimberly, one of the original proponents of the life cycle approach, in which he adopts what he terms a "biographical" approach to understanding organizational change (cf. Kimberly, 1987; Kimberly & Rottman, 1987).

Institutional Theory

Institutional theorists (DiMaggio & Powell, 1983; Meyer & Rowan, 1977; Meyer & Scott, 1983; Oliver, 1991; Zucker, 1983, 1987) suggest that organizations change their formal structure to conform with expectations within their institutional environment about appropriate organizational design. Usually exerted by regulatory agencies such as the state, professions, or interest groups, these institutional expectations come to define the appropriate and necessary ways to organize. As Slack and Hinings (1992, p. 123) note, "components of the structural design of an organization become widely accepted as both appropriate and necessary. In simple terms a way to organize becomes the way to organize." Organizations change and conform to the expectations of their institutional environment because by doing so they help increase their legitimacy and thus help ensure the continued flow of resources necessary for their operation (Hinings & Greenwood, 1988).

Major changes occurred in Canadian national sport organizations in the period 1984 to 1988 when the Canadian government agency Sport Canada created institutional pressures for these organizations to adopt a more professional and bureaucratic structure (cf. Macintosh & Whitson, 1990; Slack & Hinings, 1992). Ideas about the appropriateness of this particular organizational form were reinforced through government publications, by pressure from Sport Canada consultants, through the rewards and kudos given to conforming organizations, and through the increased employment of professional staff in national sport organizations (Slack & Hinings, 1994). Slack and Hinings (1992) show how, as a result of these pressures, these organizations changed, increasing the number of professional staff they employed and systematizing their operating procedures. National sport organizations even had their headquarters in the same building—the James Naismith building—although since then, they have moved to different locations.

Evolution and Revolution

The evolution and revolution approach to organizational change is best exemplified by the work of Greenwood and Hinings (1988); Miller and Friesen (1980a, 1980b); Nadler and Tushman (1989a); Tushman, Newman, and Romanelli (1986); and Tushman and Romanelli (1985). These authors suggest that organizations resist change. Even when faced with the possibility of failure, organizations will often continue to do what they have been doing in the past and not make the necessary adjustments to ensure their survival. This **resistance to change** stems from a variety of factors, including

- the reluctance to deviate from existing programs,
- the inability of organizations to accurately appraise their performance,
- the costs of facilities or equipment,

- the culture of the organization, and
- the fear by some managers that change will reduce their power.

As a result of this resistance to change the dominant organizational condition is what Miller and Friesen (1980b) refer to as momentum. Momentum is merely the tendency of an organization to stay within its existing structural design (e.g., a simple structure). **Evolutionary change** occurs as organizations make incremental adjustments in their strategy, structure, or processes, while still remaining within this particular design. In contrast, **revolutionary change** takes place in response to a major upheaval or crisis in an organization's environment requiring a "simultaneous and sharp shift in strategy, power, structure, and controls" (Tushman, Newman, & Romanelli, 1986, p. 31). Organizations that make a change from one design type to another, that is, a move from a simple structure to a professional bureaucracy, exhibit revolutionary change. Slack and Hinings (1992) saw this type of change occurring in many of Canada's national sport organizations during the 1984 to 1988 period, and Kikulis, Slack, and Hinings (1992) provide a framework for understanding this type of change.

Contextualist Approach

The contextualist approach to understanding organizational change emanates from the work of Andrew Pettigrew and the staff of the Centre for Corporate Strategy and Change at the University of Warwick Business School. Pettigrew (1985a, p. 15) criticizes much of the existing work on organizational change as being "ahistorical, aprocessual, and acontextual." Much of this work, he claims, focuses on a single change event or a discrete episode of change. There are, he notes, "remarkably few studies of change that actually allow the change process to reveal itself in any kind of substantially temporal or contextual manner" (Pettigrew, 1987, p. 655). Research studies are therefore concerned "with the intricacies of narrow *changes* rather than the holistic and dynamic analysis of *changing*" (emphasis in original).

To address this concern, Pettigrew suggests a multilevel analysis of change over long periods of time (Pettigrew, 1985b, 1987). This work calls for examination of three areas related to change: context (divided into inner and outer context), content, and process. Pettigrew (1987) graphically portrays an interaction among these three

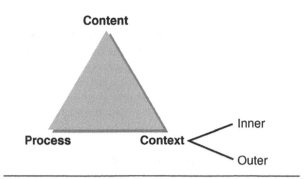

Figure 12.3   *Contextualist approach to change.*

by placing them at the corners of a triangle (see figure 12.3). The outer context "refers to the social, economic, political, and competitive environment in which the [organization] operates" (Pettigrew, 1987, p. 657). The inner context is made up of those organizational elements that influence the change process, such as the organization's structure, culture, and political makeup. Content refers to the aspects of an organization that are being changed, and may include technology, people, products, and services. The term process "refers to the actions, reactions, and interactions from the varied interested parties as they seek to move the [organization] from its present to its future state" (Pettigrew, 1987, pp. 657-658).

This approach to change, unlike several of the others examined here—population ecology, institutional theory, and contingency theory—does not focus solely on environmental pressures as a source of change. Rather, the work of Pettigrew and his colleagues emphasizes the interrelated role over time of environment (context), structure, and human agents, in shaping the change process (Pettigrew, 1985a; Pettigrew & Whipp, 1991). Unlike many studies of change, Pettigrew's methods draw heavily on the detailed construction and analysis of case studies.

Unfortunately, no studies within sport management have used this approach. The richness of data that the contextualist approach can yield makes it a very viable method for enhancing our understanding of sport organizations. Studies on organizations within our field could also be used to extend the theory.

What Causes Organizational Change?

The impetus for change may arise externally in the environment of a sport organization or from inside the organization itself. As we have seen, many theorists, for example, contingency theorists and population ecologists, focus on external sources of change, while others—resource-dependence theorists and those who adopt the contextualist approach—stress the interaction of external and internal factors. Externally a wide variety of factors can cause the need for change in a sport organization. The fall of communism in the former Soviet Union has allowed many countries to be seen as emerging economies with increasing opportunities for sport. The acquisition of new equipment and technology can also cause changes in the way a sport organization operates. For example, scanners and bar codes have changed the way retail sporting goods stores do business. Inventory and warehousing is easier to control, hence ordering can be standardized, pricing changes are easily made, and sales figures can be quickly retrieved from a store's computer.

Changes in government legislation may also initiate changes in the way sport organizations are structured and operated. Title IX, for example, has had a significant effect on many U.S. college and university athletic programs. These organizations are also affected by legislation that deals with such issues as "unrelated business" income tax. Craig and Weisman (1994) have described how certain revenues raised by colleges and university athletic programs may be subject to this tax, a factor that may subsequently cause a change in the way they operate.

Internally, change is often initiated by "change agents," people whose job it is to ensure that a sport organization makes the necessary changes to maintain or increase its effectiveness. CEOs, vice presidents, coaches, human resources development staff, union representatives, and external consultants can all act as change agents. It is important to realize that the changes these people recommend usually reflect their own interests and values. For example, the changes the Player Relations Committee may want to make to the collective bargaining agreement of major league baseball will likely be quite different from changes the Players Association would like to see. The types of changes senior managers want to see are different from those of the union representatives. What may be an acceptable change to some members of a sport organization will not be acceptable to others. As we noted earlier, change is a political process that may require changes not only to the structure of a sport organization but also to the dominant values expressed by its members.

One of the ways people in a sport organization try to bring some objectivity to the change process is to bring in an outside consultant. As Pfeffer (1981, p. 142) points out, these people "can serve to legitimate the decision reached and to provide an aura of rationality to the decision process." They are purportedly hired to look impartially at the problems and issues that confront the sport organization and make suggestions for change. However, it is possible for management or those doing the hiring to manipulate the results that come from this type of process, through hiring the "right" consultant and often through a consultant's realization that, even though he has been hired to be impartial, future business from those who hired him may be contingent on his coming up with the "correct recommendation" (cf. Pfeffer, 1981).

TIME OUT   *Values and Organizational Change*

Amis, Slack, and Hinings have argued that organizational change is dependent not only on external factors but also on the organization's own members. In a 12-year study of Canadian national sport organizations, the authors examined the impact of organizational members' values on the degree of conformance with expected changes. They found that if an organization had members whose values were close to those of the prescribed change, the organization would go through the change process successfully. If, however, an organization had members whose values opposed the change, the organization would only superficially conform—largely in response to coercive pressures—and then it would revert to an organizational form more in line with the members' values.

Based on information in J. Amis, T. Slack, and C.R. Hinings (2002).

Resistance to Change

Although change is a pervasive and constant feature of sport organizations, so, too, is resistance to change. This resistance may come from within the organization itself or from external constituents. Sport managers, if they are to deal effectively with resistance to change, must understand the reasons for this opposition, and realize that resistance is not always dysfunctional. Resistance can force sport managers to reevaluate the appropriateness of their proposed actions. The opposition to change that comes from interest groups inside or outside the organization can bring forward important issues management may not have considered. Resistance is a means of identifying possible problems before they arise and taking action to prevent them. What follows is a brief discussion of four of the major sources of resistance to change.

Self-Interest

As we saw in chapter 10, subunits within a sport organization often act to maximize their own vested self-interests and help them achieve their own goals. In any change process, some groups will benefit while others may lose. As a result, individuals or groups tend to consider proposed changes in terms of their own self-interest. For example, Patti (1974) suggests that if goals relating to power, money, prestige, convenience, job security, or professional competence are threatened as a result of any potential change, the change will be resisted, even in situations where the proposed changes are beneficial to the organization as a whole, as is arguably the case for the NHL's cancelled 2004-2005 season. Another example would be in 1986 when financial problems threatened the very existence of the Canadian Football League (CFL). The CFL Players Association strongly opposed a salary cap and threatened to strike if such a program were put into place.

Lack of Trust and Understanding About the Implications of Change

Change produces a degree of uncertainty for the members of a sport organization. Employees and groups within the organization are unsure of the impact it will have on them, especially where there is a lack of trust between those initiating the change and those it will impact. This lack of trust may produce rumor, innuendo, and distorted information about the nature and consequences of a change, leading to defensive behavior on the part of those affected. To minimize this resistance, management should explain—in advance—to the members of a sport organization why a change is being made and what impact it will have on them.

Differing Assessments of Change Consequences

Change will be resisted when the members of a sport organization or other significant stakeholders have differing opinions of the costs and benefits of the proposed change. This situation frequently occurs when the people affected by the change have inadequate information about the change or when they exhibit fundamentally different values in regard to the proposed change.

The Cost of Change

Some groups or individuals may resist change because it is costly in terms of time, effort, and money, particularly in the short run. They do not see the benefits of the changes as being greater than the costs involved. Changes involving a significant financial investment for new facilities, technology, or machinery are often opposed on the basis of cost. For example, a sport equipment manufacturing company may wish to change to some type of computer-aided manufacturing system, but shareholders may oppose the move because of the large capital costs involved in such a change and the subsequent impact (albeit short-term) on profits.

Dealing With Resistance and Implementing Change

In the previous section we identified four of the major sources of resistance to change. Here we discuss how sport managers can deal with resistance and implement change. The approaches outlined are not independent; frequently they are used in combination to influence those who oppose change. The first six techniques identified are based on Kotter and Schlesinger's (1979) work.

TIME OUT *Scouts Resist Changes to the Drafting of Players*

For as long as baseball existed, there was one way to scout potential players. The baseball player was supposed to look a certain way, act a certain way, catch, pitch, or hit a certain way. However, when Billy Beane became general manager of the Oakland A's, he changed the whole process, starting with the minor league (farm) teams and then the Oakland A's themselves. He devised a system that used a more objective approach to scouting by examining statistics of various kinds such as on-base average, walks, and hits. When Beane's scouts found out he was looking into players who would be 19th-round draft picks or later, they vocalized their displeasure and made it clear that they weren't going to change the way they did their jobs. It was only after the team made up of oddities became successful that the scouts came around and accepted his approach.

Based on information in M. Lewis (2003).

Education and Communication

As we saw in the previous section, resistance to change can stem from a lack of information or inaccurate perceptions about the consequences of the change process. Sport managers responsible for initiating change often have information about the process that is not available to all members of their organization. Educating these people about the necessity for change, and using communication techniques to keep them informed of how the change is progressing—group meetings, workshops, memos, and direct discussions between those initiating the change and those affected by it—can go some way to reducing resistance. This method of dealing with resistance and implementing change works best when the different groups have relatively similar goals and when the resistance to change is based on misinformation or a lack of communication. It requires a high degree of trust between the parties involved if it is to be successful.

Participation and Involvement

One of the most effective ways to deal with resistance to change and aid the implementation process is to involve those groups and individuals most likely to exhibit resistance to the planning and implementation process. The idea is that this involvement creates a commitment to the process, and hence reduces opposition. By involving potential opponents to the change process, it is possible to deal with problems before they escalate and also use the skills, knowledge, and political contacts these people possess to help smooth implementation. The downside of this approach is that it is time-consuming and, as we saw in chapter 11, participative decision making can actually heighten conflict, which hinders the change process. The Canadian government, for example, asked for public input in 2000 and 2001 when it was involved in developing a new policy affecting the way sport was delivered in the country. The meetings, attended by members of the sport community and other stakeholders, were designed to gather reactions from those who were likely to be affected by the new policy and the subsequent changes. A problem with these particular meetings (and the process in general) was that, despite obtaining input, there was no guarantee that the organization making the change (in this case the federal government) would actually take public response into account.

Establishing Change Teams

One of the ways to get the support and cooperation that change requires is to establish change teams. As Kanter (1983, p. 242) points out, energizing people about change "through participation in team problem-solving has indeed produced significant results for many companies." Task forces, new venture groups, and interdepartmental committees are all excellent ways to manage resistance and implement change. These groups can undertake responsibility for training, counseling, and communicating the need for change.

Idea Champions

Daft (1992, p. 273) suggests that idea champions are "one of the most effective weapons in the battle for change." **Idea champions** are intensely interested and committed to the proposed changes (Chakrabarti & Hauschildt, 1989; Maidique, 1980). They play a dominant role in getting other people involved in the change process and in reducing opposition. Chakrabarti (1974) suggests that, to be successful, an idea champion must have technical competence, knowledge about the company, drive, aggressiveness, knowledge of the market, and political astuteness. Wolfe, Slack, and Rose-Hearn (1993), in their study of employee fitness programs, stressed the important role that idea champions played in getting these programs implemented in a number of major corporations.

Facilitation and Support

Some resistance to change arises from the fear and anxiety created by the uncertainty of the process. Providing a supportive atmosphere for those affected by the change can help reduce this resistance. As Zander (1950, p. 9) points out, "resistance will be prevented to the degree that the changer helps the changees to develop their own understanding of the need for change, and an explicit awareness of how they feel about it, and what can be done about those feelings." The facilitation and support provided may take the form of career counseling, job training, and therapy. This method of dealing with resistance and implementing change is particularly useful where the change can create personal problems for members of the sport organization. The biggest disadvantages of this approach are that it is time-consuming, expensive, and not accompanied by a guarantee of success. For example, employees of a large sport equipment manufacturing company that is forced to restructure its operations will be concerned that the restructuring may cost them their jobs. Consequently, some type of support during the change process, while it may not totally remove the employees' fears, may help to reduce them and thus smooth the changes that occur as a result of the restructuring.

Negotiation

Negotiation or bargaining is used when one or more powerful groups involved in a proposed change are offered some sort of incentive to comply. Negotiation is a reflection of the political reality of sport organizations. However, in many ways it is a short-term answer to suppressing resistance. If one group is given concessions, other groups may adjust their positions and begin

to negotiate to get similar considerations. Such interactions are costly in both time and money and can detract from the actual change process. This type of negotiation process took place in 1994 when the owners of the Calgary Flames hockey club threatened to move their team from Calgary. To prevent the change in location the city of Calgary contributed $16 million to the Flames organization. The Calgary Cannons AAA baseball club tried to negotiate a similar concession to upgrade its ballpark, but was unsuccessful.

Manipulation

Manipulation, although considered unethical, is frequently used as a means of bypassing potential resistance to change. Manipulation can involve such practices as distorting information or disseminating false information, splitting groups that may resist change, and influencing power brokers. Zimbalist (1992, p. 139) for example, suggests that although the Civic Center Redevelopment Corporation owned by the City of St. Louis was valued at between $75 million and $90 million, August Busch, owner of the St. Louis Cardinals, was able "to manipulate behind the scenes to eliminate a competitive bidder" and buy the corporation that owned what is now called Busch Stadium for $53 million.

Cooptation

Cooptation, as we saw in chapter 8, involves absorbing key resisters or influential individuals in a sport organization's decision-making structure. King (1991), for example, describes how, as the driving force behind Calgary's bid for the 1988 Winter Olympics, he secured the support of influential individuals from the City of Calgary and the Province of Alberta before officially placing the bid. These people were absorbed into the organization because of their ability to influence key organizations in the bid committee's environment and as such help counter potential opposition to the bid.

Coercion

Coercion is frequently used to deal with resistance and implement change when all other methods fail. It may involve the threat of dismissal, demotion, the loss of a promotion opportunity, and transfer. Coercion is most likely to be used when a crisis situation is being faced and decisions have to be made quickly. It is problematic, in that it can result in alienation and create problems in any future change attempts.

Stages of the Change Process

A number of writers have suggested that change can be conceptualized as a series of stages (Robbins, 1990; Greiner, 1967). In this section we look at one of the best-known and most widely accepted of these models. We then look at the concept of "tracks," a different approach to understanding the way in which organizations change.

Greiner's Patterns of Organizational Change

Greiner (1967), surveying the change literature in an attempt to distinguish successful from unsuccessful change, found that successful change processes were characterized by six stages, each involving a stimulus and a reaction. Figure 12.4 presents a diagrammatic representation of these stages; the following explains each in more detail.

Stage 1: Pressure and Arousal

In this initial stage of the change process, strong pressures are placed on an organization's senior management. These pressures may arise from external environmental factors, such as low sales or an innovative breakthrough by a competitor, but they can also arise internally as a result of events such as a strike or interdepartmental conflict. The pressures for change increase when internal and external forces act simultaneously. These pressures arouse top management to take action.

Stage 2: Intervention and Reorientation

Although strong pressures may arouse top management and cause them to take action, they will not necessarily make the proper responses. Management tends to rationalize the problems they face by blaming another group. For example, in a professional sport team the blame for low attendance may be placed on apathetic

fans. Consequently, for a change to be successful, it requires the intervention of an outsider such as a new senior manager or a consultant. This person enters the organization and is able to bring some degree of objectivity to the problems it faces. The newcomer is able to encourage managers to reevaluate their past practices and current problems; they then undergo a form of reorientation to address the real problems they face.

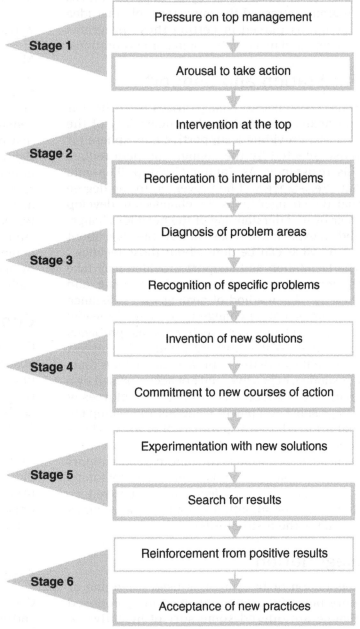

Figure 12.4 Stages of the change process.

Adapted by permission of *Harvard Business Review.* "Patterns of organization change" by L.E. Greiner, May-June 1967. Copyright ©1967 by the Harvard Business School Publishing Corporation; all rights reserved.

Stage 3: Diagnosis and Recognition

In this stage different groups within the organization join together to locate the cause of problem issues. There is a sharing of power among the members of the organization; groups from different hierarchical levels meet to diagnose and recognize problems. Greiner (1967, p. 128) describes this as an important stage because it signals that "(a) top management is willing to change, (b) important problems are being acknowledged and faced up to, (c) ideas from lower levels are being valued by upper levels." Less successful change processes did not include this step, because senior managers felt they knew what the problems were and did not need the help of other members of the organization in correcting them.

Stage 4: Invention and Commitment

Once problems have been identified, new and unique solutions have to be invented and a commitment has to be made to a course of action. Creative solutions must be developed; the newcomer plays a role in this stage by encouraging new and creative practices. Shared power is an important feature in the development of these solutions and in securing commitment to them. Members from the lower levels of the organization show a greater commitment to solutions they helped develop.

Stage 5: Experimentation and Search

Once the solutions to problems have been decided, they are tested. The testing takes the form of a number of small-scale decisions made at different levels of the organization. This type of experimentation serves as a credibility check before the change is introduced on an organization-wide basis.

Stage 6: Reinforcement and Acceptance

In the final stage of the change process, the positive results obtained in stage 5 start to be reinforced and expanded to all parts of the organization. Over time they become accepted as new practice. There is also an acceptance of the use of shared power as a means of introducing and implementing change.

Tracks and the Dynamics of Change

While models such as those proposed by Greiner (1967) and others are intuitively appealing as a means of explaining the change process, they do have a number of shortcomings. For example, change is conceptualized as a linear process in which organizations clearly move from one phase to the next. As such, there is no provision in these models to capture the temporal dynamic of change, or to address the fact that change is rarely a smooth or sequential process. Also, no account is taken within these models for the possibility of incomplete change or change that is only partially completed and then abandoned. An alternative and somewhat more realistic method of explaining change can be found in Greenwood and Hinings, (1988) concept of "tracks."

The approach of Greenwood and Hinings (1988) has its roots in the evolution and revolution theory of change. As such, it is best suited for explaining the dynamics of large-scale revolutionary change. These authors suggest that central to understanding the dynamics of the change process are the two concepts: archetypes and tracks. The concept of **archetypes** is related to Mintzberg's notion of configuration, which was addressed in chapter 5. However, it extends Mintzberg's ideas to include not only a set of structural arrangements (which is the basis of Mintzberg's work) but also the underlying values and beliefs that hold these structures in place. As Greenwood and Hinings (1988) note, design archetypes are to be identified by isolating the distinctive ideas, values, and meanings pervasively reflected in and reproduced by clusters of structures and systems. An organizational archetype in this sense is a particular composition of ideas, beliefs, and values connected with structural and systemic attributes.

In their work on Canadian national sport organizations, Kikulis, Slack, and Hinings (1992) identified three archetypes as being present in this particular institutional sphere. The structure of these archetypes and their associated underlying values are shown in table 12.1. The kitchen table archetype is somewhat akin to Mintzberg's simple structure and the executive office archetype parallels many of the characteristics of the professional bureaucracy. Similar archetypes to these could probably be found in national sport organizations in other countries. Also, different institutional spheres of sport organizations may contain different archetypes.

Tracks help map and explain the incidence and nature of change and the absence of change between archetypes (Greenwood & Hinings, 1988). These researchers suggest that if an organization makes a revolutionary change from one archetype

Table 12.1   Institutionally Specific Design Archetypes for National Sport Organizations

	Kitchen table	Boardroom	Executive office
Organizational values			
Orientation	Private, volunteer, nonprofit (membership and fund-raising)	Private, volunteer, nonprofit (public and private funds)	Private, volunteer, nonprofit (government and corporate funds)
Domain	Broad: mass-high performance sport	Competitive sport opportunities	Narrow: high performance sport
Principles of organizing	Minimal coordination; decision making by volunteer executives	Volunteer hierarchy; professionally assisted	Formal planning; professionally led and volunteer assisted
Criteria of effectiveness	Membership preferences; quality service	Administrative efficiency and effectiveness	International success
Organizational structure			
Specialization	Roles based on interest and loyalty	Specialized roles and committees	Professional, technical, and administrative expertise
Standardization	Few rules, little planning	Formal roles, rules, and programs	Formal roles, rules, and programs
Centralization	Decisions made by a few volunteers	Decisions made by the volunteer boards	Decisions decentralized to the professional staff

Reprinted, by permission, from L. Kikulis, T. Slack, and C.R. Hinnings, 1992, "Institutionally specific design archetypes: A framework for understanding change in national sport organizations," *International Review for the Sociology of Sport* 27: 343-370.

(A) to another archetype (B) there is the potential for three intermediate positions. These positions, however, should be considered indicative rather than definitive, since it is difficult if not impossible to establish empirically the discrete boundaries between positions. These three positions, along with two archetypal positions, are shown at the top of figure 12.5. Archetype coherence reflects a situation where an organization's structure and the underlying values held by members are consistent. For example, any of the three situations described by Kikulis et al. (1992) would reflect such coherence. Embryonic archetype coherence is a situation in which the structure of an organization nearly reflects the values of the members, but some items are discordant, for example, a kitchen-table organization that has started to hire professional staff. In a schizoid state the structure of an organization reflects the tensions between two sets of values. For example, the organization has competing groups, some of whom value the informal operating procedures and volunteer control of a kitchen-table archetype, and others who value the systematization and professional control of the executive office. Structure in these

organizations will reflect the competing values: Certain elements will be like those found in the kitchen-table archetype and others will be more characteristic of the executive office. These design arrangements are incompatible.

The three positions can be used to establish the tracks that organizations follow when they make revolutionary change or when they attempt such a change but fail to complete it. As shown in figure 12.5, Greenwood and Hinings (1988) identify four possible tracks. An inertial track reflects evolutionary change, the type of change that occurs when an organization is in an archetype and the changes it makes are small, reinforcing the archetype. An aborted excursion occurs when an organization starts to change by moving away from its existing archetype, but for some reason returns to its original position. A reorientation track can take the form of a linear progression, an oscillation, or a delay; all represent successful change from one archetype to another. The linear progression is the normal sequential type of change process; the oscillation reflects the fluctuations that can occur as an organization changes; the term delayed is used to describe the situation when

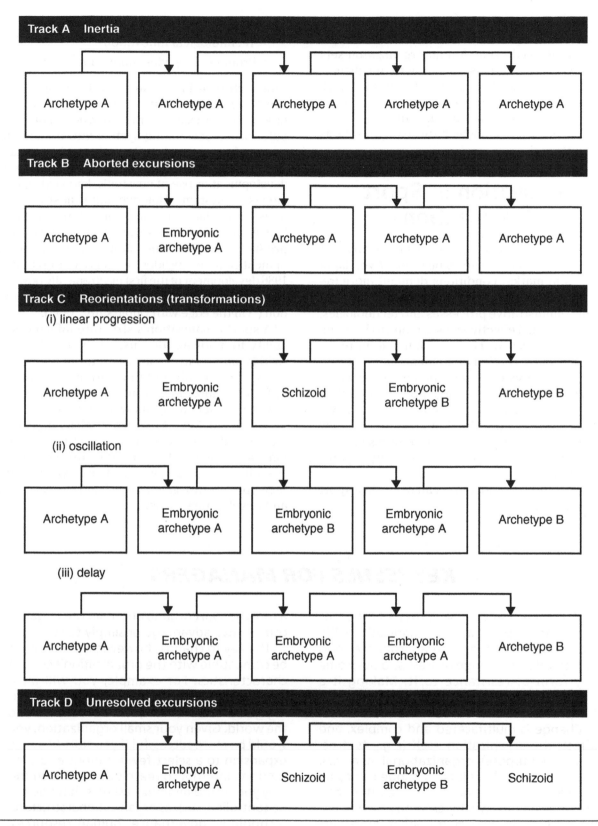

Figure 12.5 *Organizational archetypes and tracks.*

Reprinted, by permission, from R. Greenwood and C.R. Hinings, 1988, "Organizational design types, tracks and dynamics with strategic change," *Organization Studies* 9: 305.

an organization resists change for some time and then makes a rapid transition to a new archetype. In an unresolved excursion an organization sets off on a change but fails to complete the change. Kikulis, Slack, and Hinings (1995b), in their work on Canadian national sport organizations, have empirically verified the existence of these tracks in a change process in which these organizations were involved.

Innovation in Sport Organizations

One of the major challenges confronting all sport organizations is the need to be innovative. Rapid changes in market conditions demand more frequent innovations in product and service delivery, and in administrative processes and technologies, if organizational effectiveness is going to be maintained or increased. The term innovation refers to "the implementation of an idea—whether pertaining to a device, system, policy, program, or service—that is new to the organization at the time of adoption" (Damanpour, 1987, p. 676). Innovation involves the introduction of something new into the organization; as such it requires change. However, change does not necessarily involve innovation.

Three types of innovation can occur in a sport organization:

- Administrative innovation
- Technological innovation
- Product or service innovation

Administrative innovations involve changes to a sport organization's structure or administrative processes. For example, the introduction of a computer-based accounting system into a municipal sport and recreation department is an administrative innovation. A **technological innovation** involves the development or use of new tools, knowledge, techniques, or systems. Hillerich and Bradsby's move to use tracer lathes in the manufacture of baseball bats is an example of a technological innovation. A **product** or **service innovation** involves the development of a new product or service. Dupliskate's 1986 development of the first electronically powered skate sharpener is an example of a product innovation ("On the edge with Dupliskate," 1993).

A sport organization's structure influences its ability to innovate. Because of the emphasis on rigidity and control, bureaucratic organizations are seen as inhibiting innovation. In contrast, organic organizations, which are less structured, are seen as facilitating innovation. This view, however, oversimplifies the situation. Many big companies like Nike, although highly structured, are also innovative; they foster innovation through the use of such techniques as venture teams, small groups of people who are given a free hand to experiment and develop new ideas.

KEY ISSUES FOR MANAGERS

Change will happen, whether planned or not, at some point in the organization's life cycle. Good managers use appropriate tools to facilitate the change process and overcome any form of resistance to it. Making it a positive experience for all involved will ease the process.

Change is multifaceted and complex, and affects the organization itself (e.g., its structure, core purpose), organizational members, and external stakeholders. Change can come from an inside stimulus, but more often than not, the stimulus will be external, such as the presence of an emerging market. Managers then have a choice to act (and start a change process) or not. In this instance, change can be a tool the sport organization can use to gain a competitive advantage or simply to survive.

The key to change, however, is that it must be compatible with the organization's current characteristics. For example, you will most likely fail if you try to expand your local sporting goods stores into 1,000 locations around the world. Given your small organization, you would be more successful if you started a slow expansion to a select few locations and then used the Internet to reach other areas. In this way you would minimize aspects that need to be controlled, such as organizational structure, technology, governance, human resources, and organizational culture.

SUMMARY AND CONCLUSIONS

Change is an inevitable feature of all sport organizations. It can occur in an organization's products and services, its technology, its structures and systems, and its people. Managers prefer stability but the demands of a changing environment require that sport organizations change if they are to remain competitive. The last 20 years have seen considerable environmental uncertainty for organizations and consequently the need to change. As a result of the transformations occurring in organizations, change has become a major area of research in organizational theory. Consequently, a number of new and different approaches to studying change have been developed. Some, such as population ecology, focus on the environment as a major factor influencing change; others, such as the contextualist approach, focus more on the interaction of structure, environment, and agency.

These different foci demand different samples and methods. For example, population ecologists study large groups of organizations and usually use quantitative methods. Contextualists study much smaller groups of organizations, sometimes even a single organization, and rely on detailed case studies. The theoretical diversity in the change literature offers considerable potential for the study of sport organizations.

The pressures for sport organizations to change can come from a number of different sources either internal or external to the organization. Sometimes sport organizations use consultants to help initiate change. Along with pressure for change comes resistance to change—from the self-interest of those affected by the change, from a lack of trust and understanding about the change, from differing perceptions of the consequences of the change, and from the costs associated with change. We identified a number of techniques that sport managers can use to deal with resistance as they implement changes.

A number of researchers have posited different stages in the change process. One of the most common of these models, Greiner's, was outlined. However, the concept of tracks was presented as a more realistic means of explaining patterns of change. In the final section of the chapter we looked at the concept of innovation and how and why sport organizations need to be innovative.

KEY CONCEPTS

administrative innovation (p. 252)

archetypes (p. 249)

change as paradox (p. 240)

evolutionary change (p. 243)

idea champions (p. 247)

institutional theory (p. 240)

life cycle approach (p. 241)

people change (p. 240)

population ecology (p. 240)

product or service change (p. 239)

product/service innovation (p. 252)

radical and convergent change (p. 240)

resistance to change (p. 242)

resource dependence (p. 241)

revolutionary change (p. 243)

structural and systemic change (p. 239)

technological change (p. 239)

technological innovation (p. 252)

tracks (p. 249)

REVIEW QUESTIONS

1. Describe the four areas of a sport organization in which change can occur and explain how a change in one area can lead to change in the other areas.

2. Explain how sport organizations manage the dilemma of requiring both stability and change in order to be successful.

3. Why must sport organizations change if they are to remain competitive?

4. How would population ecologists see change occurring in sport organizations?

5. What are the similarities and differences between the population ecology and the resource-dependence approach to understanding change?

6. Explain what problems you see with the life cycle approach to understanding organizational change.

7. Explain how institutional theorists view change.

8. Discuss the evolution and revolution approach to change and use it to explain how change has occurred in a sport organization with which you are familiar.

9. What external factors could lead to change in a university athletic department?

10. Do population ecologists and institutional theorists see the stimulus for change arising from inside or outside the sport organization? What does this tell you about the shortcomings of these theoretical approaches?

11. What are the major sources of resistance to change? Can you think of other reasons why the members of a sport organization would resist change?

12. Select a familiar sport organization that has recently undergone change. What were the sources of resistance to this change and how were these managed?

13. Describe the archetypes that you might find in a sample of retail stores selling sporting goods.

14. Discuss the relative merits of Greiner's model of change as compared with the notion of archetypes and tracks.

15. How do large bureaucratically structured companies promote innovation?

SUGGESTIONS FOR FURTHER READING

There is a large body of literature on organizational change, so if you are interested in this area consult the major organizational journals. In addition, for those interested in population ecology, Hannan and Freeman's (1989) book *Organizational Ecology* and Singh's (1990) *Organizational Evolution* provide what is probably the most comprehensive account of work in this area. The principal work on resource-dependence theory is Pfeffer and Salancik's (1978) *The External Control of Organizations: A Resource-Dependence View*. Those interested in the life cycle approach should see Kimberly and Miles's (1980) book, *The Organizational Life Cycle*. Institutional theory is best represented by Zucker's (1988) *Institutional Patterns and Organizations* and Powell and DiMaggio's (1991) *The New Institutionalism in Organizational Analysis*. However, anyone interested in this area should also read the articles by DiMaggio and Powell (1983), Meyer and Rowan (1977), Oliver (1991), and Zucker (1983, 1987, 1988, 1989), which can be found in the bibliography. Details of the evolution and revolution approach can be found in Miller and Friesen's (1984) difficult but valuable *Organizations: A Quantum View*. Also useful and more readable is Hinings and Greenwood's (1988) *The Dynamics of Strategic Change*. Pettigrew is the main proponent of the contextualist approach and his (1985a) book *The Awakening Giant* is a good example of this type of work. Also useful is Pettigrew and Whipp's (1991) book, *Managing Change for Competitive Success*.

In the sport literature the primary work on change comes from the University of Alberta. Kikulis, Slack, and Hinings's (1992) article, "Institutionally Specific Design Archetypes: A Framework for Understanding Change in National Sport Organizations," provides a useful account of how the concept of archetype can be applied to our field. An extension of this work can be found in the article by these authors in the *Journal of Management Studies* (1995b), where they empirically explore the notion of tracks. Slack and Hinings's *Journal of Sport Management* (1992) article is a good example of how certain theoretical perspectives of change can be integrated to give a more complete picture of the process. The *Organization Studies* article by Slack and Hinings (1994) shows how institutional theory can be applied to organizations in our field. In addition, the article by Amis, Slack, and Hinings (2002) in *The Journal of Applied Behavioral Science* looks at values in relation to organizational change.

Finally there are a few popular books dealing with changes in sport organizations. Michael Lewis's (2003) *Moneyball: The Art of Winning an Unfair Game* discusses changes within the Oakland A's operations, and Don Weiss and Chuck Day's (2003) book, *The Making of the Super Bowl: The Inside Story of the World's Greatest Sporting Event*, outlines with the evolution of the Super Bowl.

CASE FOR ANALYSIS

The Impact of 9-11

On September 11, 2001, terrorists flew two passenger airliners into the World Trade Center towers. Thousands died and thousands more were injured. Countries around the world put their citizens on high alert. The United States and its allies changed laws to protect their citizens and went to war on terrorism. Since September 11 many more examples of terrorist activity, from kidnappings to bombings, have been reported in the media. Citizens have altered aspects of their daily lives. The sporting world has also changed its operations.

The 2002 Salt Lake City Olympic Games was the first major sporting event since September 11, 2001.

The organizing committee had to readjust plans and emphasize security concerns. The games prepared for every conceivable attack—even though no credible threat had been received—biological or chemical. Security personnel and technology were strengthened. Crowd-control fencing, X-ray equipment, contraband detection systems, and a no-fly zone were put in place. The country also went on high alert. Thousands of military personnel; 7,000 federal, state, and local law enforcement personnel; and 5,000 security volunteers worked to make the games secure. No terrorist incidents occurred.

In 2002 the World Cup of soccer was held in Japan and South Korea, and again committee

© Frances M. Roberts rlevine@Levineroberts.com

Sport organizations responded to the September 11, 2001, terrorist attacks by increasing security measures at sporting events.

members did not want to chance terrorist activity. The organizers placed 420,000 police on guard. Antiaircraft missiles were set up around the stadiums and fighter jets were deployed to survey the skies. Because soccer is also notorious for its riots, participating countries worked together to ensure that gang ringleaders were identified and blocked at customs. No major incidents occurred.

The Athens Olympic Committee spent over $1.4 billion (U.S.) for security for the 2004 Summer Olympics. More than 45,000 security personnel were called upon from a variety of countries, including: 25,000 police, 7,000 military, 3,000 coast guards, 1,500 firefighters, 3,500 private security contractors, and 5,000 security volunteers. Patriot missiles and other antiaircraft devices were put in place around the city and across the country. Security checkpoints, surveillance cameras, and no-fly zones were established. Police had helicopters and a blimp for air surveillance. Nevertheless, security had to be tightened even more after a Canadian in a tutu and tights managed to get through security and jump into the diving pool. Despite this, on the last day, a spectator broke through the barrier along the route of the men's marathon and pushed the lead runner from Brazil into the sideline, causing him to lose precious time—he managed to win the bronze medal.

After every major sport event since September 11, there's been praise for the lack of problems and criticism for the excessive amount of money spent on security.

Based on information in ABC Online (2002), About.com (2002), BBC News (2004), Brown (2002), CBC.ca (2004).

Questions

1. What changes do you think occurred in the organizing committees' structures after September 11, 2001?

2. Who has benefited from this increase in security and who has been negatively affected?

3. What would you suggest to the next major event's organizing committee in relation to the degree of security planning needed?

4. How does the terrorism threat affect smaller events?

Chapter **13**

Organizational Decision Making

LEARNING OBJECTIVES

When you have read this chapter, you should be able to

1. explain the concept of decision making,
2. discuss the conditions under which decisions are made,
3. understand the difference between the rational approach to decision making

and the concept of bounded rationality, and
4. describe the major models of organizational decision making.

DECIDING ON THE 2010 WINTER OLYMPIC GAMES

On July 2, 2003, the International Olympic Committee (IOC) chose Vancouver-Whistler to host the 2010 Winter Olympics. Getting to that point, however, was a lengthy process composed of many decisions by many people.

In 1998, the Canadian Olympic Committee (COC) chose Vancouver-Whistler over Calgary and Quebec City. The Vancouver-Whistler 2010 Bid Corporation was formed the following year. The corporation had a bid budget of $34 million and was supported by more than 70 public and private organizations.

The COC had until February 4, 2002, to submit Vancouver as its bid for the 2010 Winter Olympics. Seven other cities were in the running: Andorra la Vella, Andorra; Bern, Switzerland; Harbin, China; Jaca, Spain;

Pyeongchang, South Korea; Salzburg, Austria; and Sarajevo, Bosnia-Herzegovina. On May 31 bid cities submitted executive summaries of their bids—in French and English—along with $100,000. Only Bern, Pyeongchang, Salzburg, and Vancouver were short-listed to become candidates. In early September, the IOC met with the candidate cities to discuss the next step of the bid. A couple of weeks later (September 27), Bern dropped out of the running for lack of support. The three remaining candidate cities had to pay the $500,000 bid fee by October 31 to continue the process.

Candidate cities submitted their bid proposals on January 10, 2003, and were able to start marketing their city's bid. At the same time, Vancouver voted in a new mayor, who

(continued)

257

(continued)

had campaigned on the premise of putting the issue up to a vote, because there had been concerns about public support. In the February 22 plebiscite, 64 percent of voters supported the bid. It cost nearly $600,000 to carry out the balloting. Surrounding cities, although not able to vote on it, also strongly supported the bid.

Between February 14 and March 16, the IOC evaluation committee visited the three cities, and on May 2 it reported its decision. Vancouver was rated as being the highest, Salzburg second, and Pyeongchang third.

At the IOC session in July 2003, board members made their decision. To help with the process, they considered that Europe would host the next two Olympics (Athens in 2004 and Turin in 2006). Next the games would go to China in 2008. Five European cities (London, Leipzig, Madrid, Moscow, and Paris) had already submitted their names for the 2012 Summer Games—the marquee event

with more countries participating than in the Winter Olympics. In addition, most IOC members are from a European country. One of the unwritten rules of the IOC is to geographically spread out the Olympic Games, and the members had to decide what country would promote their interests and the interests of the Olympic movement best. Finally, the members weighed which city would be most successful—technically speaking—in hosting the event. Vancouver was rated highest in this aspect by the IOC evaluation committee.

Voting allegiance (members are known to vote in cliques) and current or future Olympic Games locations resulted in Salzburg receiving only 16 votes and being dropped from the voting list. Surprisingly, Pyeongchang had the most votes with 51, barely missing out on winning the actual bid—they needed 50 percent plus one vote to win. Vancouver initially received 40 votes, but won 56 to 53 over Pyeonchang on the following ballot.

Based on information in CBC Sports Online (2002), GamesBids.com (2003).

Not all decisions made in sport organizations are as long and complex as choosing a city for an Olympic Games. Mintzberg (1973a), in his book *The Nature of Managerial Work*, found decision making to be one of the major tasks in which managers were involved; some people see decision making as the single most important process in an organization. The decisions made in a sport organization may range from deciding on the color and style of the company's letterhead to orchestrating a multibillion-dollar takeover bid. Some decisions prove to be successful, such as the one made by Peter Ueberroth when he decided to seek private support for the Los Angeles Olympic Games, or Petro Canada's decision to sponsor the 1988 Olympic Torch Relay. Others, such as Nike's decision to use its name to get into the casual shoe market, have been less than successful (Willigan, 1992).

In this chapter we look first at the term "decision making" and what it means. We then identify the conditions under which decisions are made. Next we examine the different approaches to decision making, focusing first on individual decision

making and then examining models of organizational decision making.

Defining Decision Making

In his book *The Effective Executive* management guru Peter Drucker (1966, p. 143) suggests that "a decision is a judgment . . . a choice between alternatives." Sport managers use their judgment to make decisions about whether to hire or fire employees, to add new programs, to sell off a division that is losing money, or to trade a player. Simon (1960) suggests that the decisions a manager makes can be categorized into two types: programmed and nonprogrammed.

Programmed Decisions

Programmed decisions are repetitive and routine. They are made on the basis of clearly defined policies and procedures and a manager's past experiences. The types of problems that can be solved using programmed decision making are usually well structured, have adequate information available, and present clear alternatives whose viability is relatively easy to assess. Examples of programmed decisions in a sport organization include the decision by the manager of a sporting goods store to exchange a returned purchase, the decision by a pool manager to put more lifeguards on duty when the number of swimmers increases, the decision by a football coach on the next play, and the decision by a university's sport information director about what to include in a media information kit. If faced with a choice managers prefer programmed to nonprogrammed decisions.

Nonprogrammed Decisions

Nonprogrammed decisions are new and unique. There are no established guidelines or procedures to direct the way this type of decision should be handled. Often the sport organization has never faced decisions about this exact situation. There are no clear alternatives from which to select. Decisions such as those made by the board of governors of the NHL to grant franchises to new cities could be considered nonprogrammed; so, too, could the decision by Benoit de Chassey, director of information systems for the Albertville Olympics, to build a client-server information system using "Foundation for Cooperative Processing," an untested computer-aided software engineering (CASE) tool to provide information to officials and media at the 1992 games (Ricciuti, 1991).

Programmed decisions, because they are well structured, are generally made by the sport organization's lower-level managers and operators. Nonprogrammable decisions, because of their novel characteristics, are more likely to be handled by senior managers or highly trained professional staff. Whenever possible, sport managers attempt to program the decision making, because these choices can be handled by less-qualified, cheaper staff.

Conditions Under Which Decisions Are Made

Because sport organizations and the environments in which they exist change constantly, sport managers can never be exactly sure of the consequences of any decision they make. It is generally accepted that decisions are made under three types of conditions, each based on the extent to which the outcome of a decision alternative is predictable. These three conditions are discussed below.

Certainty

A decision is made under a condition of **certainty** when the manager making the decision knows exactly what the available alternatives are, and the costs and benefits of each alternative. In other words, the manager understands completely the available alternatives and the outcomes of each, with 100 percent certainty. One example often used to illustrate decision making under certainty conditions is an investment in a bond or some other security with a guaranteed rate of return. For example, a voluntary sport group that finds itself with surplus cash on hand may choose to invest it in government bonds or treasury bills. The bonds may pay 6 percent but require a minimum investment time of five years; the treasury bills may pay only 4 percent but have a minimum investment time of one year. Here the decision maker knows the alternatives and the benefits of each. It is simply a matter of making the most appropriate choice.

Risk

Unfortunately, very few decisions in sport organizations are made under conditions of certainty. Under a condition of **risk** (a far more common condition for decision making in sport organizations), a decision maker has a basic understanding of the available alternatives, but the potential cost and benefits associated with each are uncertain. For example, a professional sport franchise owner wants to relocate her team. Three cities have offered their facilities, all fairly similar. One will charge a rental fee of $2 million per year, give the owner the rights to concessions and parking, and guarantee no change to this arrangement for the next 10 years. Another city wants only $1 million per year, will also grant the rights to concessions and parking, but will only give a 5-year guarantee. The third city will rent at a nominal $1 per year, will guarantee this rent for 5 years, but wants to retain all revenues from parking and concessions. In this situation the owner must assign probabilities to outcomes and work out the best decision, a process sometimes done objectively with available data, but often a subjective process based on past experiences.

TIME OUT — *Phil Knight on Risky Decisions About Advertising*

In a 1992 interview with a *Harvard Business Review* writer, Nike CEO Phil Knight explained one of the strategies his company uses to maintain its preeminent position in the athletic footwear industry is innovative advertising. However, Knight also pointed out that the decision to run innovative commercials was a risky one. He cited the Hare Jordan–Air Jordan commercial that was shown during the 1992 Super Bowl. The commercial, which cost millions of dollars to produce, featured Chicago Bulls star Michael Jordan on the basketball court with cartoon character Bugs Bunny. Knight felt there was considerable risk in showing a basketball superstar, Nike's key advertising resource, with a cartoon character. Knight was afraid people would think the commercial was silly. However, it was well received and *USA Today* rated it the best Super Bowl commercial that year.

Knight also found out humorous commercials can be risky. Citing a 1987 campaign directed toward females, he noted that what he and his advertising team found funny, some women saw as insulting. As a result Nike received numerous complaints and spent more than three years meeting with women to find out their views on sport and fitness.

Based on information from G.E. Willigan (1992).

Uncertainty

Under conditions of **uncertainty** the decision alternatives and their potential outcomes are both relatively unknown. Here there is no historical data or past experience on which to base a decision. These decisions are the most difficult to make, the kind that can make or break a manager's career. The manager of a sporting goods equipment manufacturing company entering the Eastern European market would face conditions of uncertainty; while this part of the world holds considerable potential for sporting goods, the political and economic situation is very uncertain.

Approaches to Understanding Decision Making

A large number of different models of the decision-making process can be found in the management literature, some are more applicable to the decisions made by individual sport managers, others pertain more to organizational-level decisions. In this section we look at both individual and organizational decision making.

Individual Decision Making

The two basic models of individual decision making are discussed here. The first is the rational model; the second, the administrative model, is sometimes referred to as the bounded-rationality model.

The Rational Model

The rational model of decision making is more a description of how decisions should be made than an account of how they actually are made. This approach focuses on a linear step-by-step analysis of the problem situation and the identification of solutions. Managers define problems and then systematically look for solutions to them; each alternative is carefully weighed as to its outcomes and the single best alternative is selected. The basic premise of this approach is that managers act in an economically rational way. In addition managers are assumed to have the relevant information about each of the decision alternatives, and to act in a nonpolitical, nonemotional manner. The rational model of decision making is usually depicted as a series of steps (see Archer, 1980; Blai, 1986). Figure 13.1 depicts these steps, and an explanation of each follows.

- **Monitor the decision environment:** In the first stage of the decision-making process a manager scans the sport organization's internal and external environment to determine deviations from expected norms. The technique includes such activities as analyzing financial statements or sales figures, observing competitors, or talking to employees. For example, a manager of a retail sporting goods store who wants to remain com-

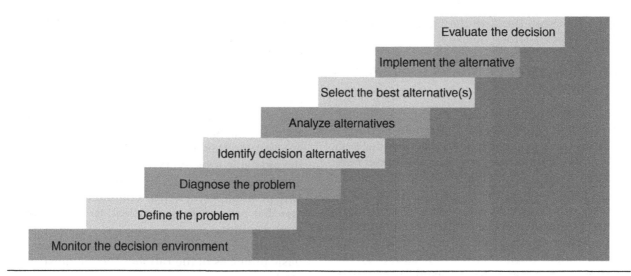

Evaluate the decision

Implement the alternative

Select the best alternative(s)

Analyze alternatives

Identify decision alternatives

Diagnose the problem

Define the problem

Monitor the decision environment

Figure 13.1 *Steps in the decision-making process.*

petitive must monitor other stores, check what items are popular, keep up with new product availability, and so forth.

• **Define the problem about which a decision has to be made:** If a manager detects a deviation from the expected norms, then a problem exists: a discrepancy between the existing state of affairs and the desired state. In our example of the sporting goods retail store, the manager may define her problem as "low profits."

• **Diagnose the problem:** Here the manager must get at the root cause of the problem so that appropriate action can be developed. In this stage it may be necessary to gather additional data. The sporting goods store may survey a number of competitors, for example, and determine that they seem to be doing a better trade because they offer a wider range of products.

• **Identify decision alternatives:** Here all the possible solutions to the problem are identified. The manager may sometimes seek the advice of others at this stage of the decision process. For the sporting goods store manager, one decision alternative may be to increase the amount of stock she carries; another may be to focus on a narrower area; another may be to cut margins on existing stock to make it more saleable.

• **Analyze alternatives:** When the possible alternatives have been identified the manager has to analyze each one critically, based on statistical data or on personal preference and past experiences. The merits of each alternative and its possible outcomes are assessed; for example, our sporting goods store manager will have to consider the costs of increasing her available

stock and the probability that this decision will increase trade. This alternative has to be weighed against a choice such as focusing on a narrower market niche, which could be strongly influenced by fluctuations in this particular market.

• **Select the best alternatives:** Here the manager picks the best alternative from all of the possibilities not eliminated in the analysis phase. Sometimes it is impossible to select just one solution. At other times two or three possible best alternatives may emerge from the analysis and more data will need to be collected before a choice can be made. In some sport organizations it may even be possible to implement more than one of the alternatives, to see which performs the best.

• **Implement the alternative:** The chosen alternative must then be implemented. Sometimes this may be easy to do; in other cases the manager will have to use her administrative skills, coercion, authority, and so forth, to get the decision implemented. The implementation process may be long and involved. In our example, if the manager chooses to increase stock she may need to secure a line of credit with a bank, contact suppliers, refurbish displays, and advertise her new products. All of these can present barriers to the actual implementation of a decision.

• **Evaluate the decision:** The final step in the **rational decision-making** process, a step that some sport managers often neglect is to evaluate the outcome of the decision to see if the original problem has been rectified. In our sporting goods store example, the manager will have to monitor sales and cash flow to see if increasing stock is actually helping raise profits. Managers sometimes neglect this step because they don't like to find out they made a wrong decision.

The Administrative Model (Bounded Rationality)

Despite the inherent logic of the systematic approach outlined in the rational model, managers are rarely this thorough or precise in their decision making. The limitations of the rational model were first identified by Nobel laureate Herbert Simon in his (1945) book *Administrative Behavior*. Simon drew a distinction between economic reality and what happens in everyday life. Rather than being a completely rational process, he suggested that organizational decisions were bounded by the emotions of the managers involved, by their limited cognitive ability to process information, and by factors such as time constraints and imperfect information. Hence, managers operate with what is referred to as **bounded rationality**: In any decision situation a manager has a limited perception; he cannot possibly understand all of the available alternatives, and even if he does, the limits of the human mind would not allow all of that information to be processed. In addition, any attempt at rationality is constrained by the manager's emotions and experience.

As a result of these limitations, Simon argued, decision makers construct simplified models of complex decision processes. The models contain only that information that the manager feels best able to handle; consequently, only a limited number of decision alternatives and outcomes are considered. This means that managers satisfice rather than strive for the optimum solution to a decision. When this solution is found the search for other potentially better solutions stops; not all decision alternatives are considered.

An example of satisficing that is often used and can be applied to our field concerns a student who has recently graduated from a sport management program and is looking for a job. To make a rational decision this person would have to look at all the available jobs everywhere. This is obviously impossible; as a result he takes the first acceptable position, rather than continuing to look for one that pays more or may lead to better career opportunities.

Table 13.1 summarizes and compares the basic premises of the rational and administrative models.

Organizational Decision Making

While individual managers may make decisions using both the rational and administrative models, most decisions in organizations are made by groups. The information, resources, and authority needed to make most of the decisions in complex organizations are rarely the domain of a single individual. Some decisions will require the participation of not only different managers but also sometimes representatives of different divisions, perhaps even different organizations. Studies of organizational decision making have identified five major approaches: the management science approach, the Carnegie model, the structuring of unstructured processes approach, the garbage can model, and the Bradford studies.

Table 13.1   Comparison of the Rational and Administrative Models of Decision Making

Rational model	Administrative model
The decision maker is the person who knows and understands all decision alternatives and their outcomes. This individual is unaffected by time constraints, emotions, and so on.	The decision makers are limited by their mental capacity to evaluate all alternatives and their outcomes, and must respond to time constraints, emotions, and so on.
All criteria affecting a decision are considered and evaluated according to the sport organization's goals.	A limited number of criteria are identified and these form a simple model to evaluate the problem being faced.
All possible decision alternatives are considered.	A limited number of decision alternatives that reflect the decision maker's personal preference are identified.
After careful analysis of all alternatives, the most economically viable alternative is selected.	Alternatives are considered until one that is suitable is found.

Management Science

The **management science** approach to decision making, which involves the use of complex mathematics and statistics to develop a solution to a problem (Markland, 1983), was developed during World War II to solve military problems (Leavitt, Dill, & Eyring, 1973). If, for example, allied planes wanted to fire on enemy warships, they had to make decisions based on information about trajectories, the distance between the plane and its target, the speed at which the plane was traveling, wind speed, the altitude of the plane, and so forth. Each of these variables was modeled using mathematical equations to provide details of the best conditions under which to attack.

After the war the principles of management science were applied to industry, and then further improved. Military people such as Robert McNamara, who would later become the U.S. secretary of defense, joined companies like Ford and began using management science techniques to improve the quality of decision making. Today a number of companies use these techniques; their popularity and utility being enhanced by the advent of computers.

Linear programming, queuing theory, Monte Carlo techniques, and decision trees are all examples of management science techniques that can be used to make decisions about a problem. The management science approach works best when data relevant to the decision are easily identified and quantifiable, and problems are structured and logical. The shortcoming of management science is that it does not consider the more qualitative aspects of decision making, such as the political climate or ethical issues.

A considerable number of management science studies have looked at decisions in sport organizations (Andreu & Corominas, 1989; Farina, Kochenberger, & Obremski, 1989). Topics include such diverse issues as scheduling major league baseball games, determining batting lineups, deciding whether or not to go for the two-point conversion, assigning swimming order in a relay race, simulating road race finishes, and deciding when to pull the goalie in hockey.

The Carnegie Model

Richard Cyert and James March were both associated with what is now Carnegie Mellon University and their approach to decision making is often referred to as the Carnegie model. Their ideas are best illustrated in their 1963 book *A Behavioral*

Theory of the Firm. Cyert and March's approach to decision making, which in some ways extends Simon's ideas of bounded rationality (Simon was also at Carnegie Mellon), challenges the notion that an organization makes decisions rationally as a single entity. Rather, what Cyert and March show is that organizations are made up of a number of subunits, each with diverse interests. Decision making has to allow for this diversity.

Organizational-level decisions are made by **coalitions** of managers, who do not all have the time or cognitive ability to deal with all aspects of a problem. Consequently, decisions are split into subproblems. For example, in a sport equipment manufacturing company the research-and-design department deals with design problems, the production department handles manufacturing, and so forth. This process of splitting problems leads to coalition building, where managers try to find out other managers' points of view and enlist their support for a particular decision. There is a continuous process of bargaining among the various groups in the organization, each trying to influence the decision outcome. As a result, Cyert and March suggest, managers spend more time on managing coalitions than they do on managing the problems confronting the organization itself.

Managers need to resolve the internal conflicts that result from coalition building. While they may agree with each other on organizational goals, there is often little consensus on how to achieve these goals. Decisions are therefore broken down into subproblems and allocated to subunits. But the danger is that these subunits address and solve these problems based on their own rationality and their own interests, not on what is best for the organization as a whole. Also, managers become concerned with short-term solutions rather than long-term strategies. They may involve themselves in what are called **problemistic searches**: When a problem occurs managers quickly search around for a way to handle or resolve it; as soon as one is found, the search stops. Managers tend to rely more on past experiences and procedures when problems are somewhat familiar than when they are unfamiliar, because relying on the past requires less time spent on politics and bargaining.

Cyert and March's work tells us that decision makers need to build coalitions because decision making is a political process. One of the great coalition builders in sport was Horst Dassler, the late head of Adidas. Dassler employed key figures in the world of sport on every continent, who kept him in touch with what was happening in sport in

---

TIME OUT   *Using a Computer Simulation Model to Make Decisions About Golf Course Backup Problems*

In order to maximize profits, golf course managers have to make decisions to ensure that their playing facility is used to capacity. The ability of the golfers who play the course, the speed at which they play, the need to use the course for play while still performing maintenance, the dawn-to-dusk playing hours, and the seasonal nature of the game are all factors that influence these decisions. Frequently, golfers experience backups (times when players have to wait for the party ahead of them) at certain points on the course. These delays in continuous play are a problem for golf course managers because they limit capacity: They increase the number of players on the course at any one time (and hence the number of expensive golf carts the club must buy), they decrease the number of players who can play the course in any day, they frustrate players, who may then never return to the course, and who (some studies show) are less likely to use clubhouse food and beverage services. All of these factors affect profits.

In order to make decisions about tee-off intervals that can reduce waiting and maxi-mize capacity, Haywood-Farmer, Sharman, and Weinbrecht (1988) suggest the use of a simple simulation model using the Lotus 1-2-3 microcomputer spreadsheet program. Essentially, in this model each hole was broken down into segments, one for par-3s, two for par-4s, and three for par-5s. Using a standard time of nine minutes between tee-off intervals, and calculating variables that measured the different times that players were involved in waiting, starting, and finishing each segment, Haywood-Farmer and his colleagues constructed a model of the way a group moves around the course. The model was able to predict cumulative waits on certain tees. By adjusting the time between tee-offs the model could be used to estimate how lines at various points could be affected and the influence the lines would have on capacity. With this knowledge the manager of the golf course could then make a decision about the appropriate interval between start times.

Based on information contained in J. Haywood-Farmer, T. Sharman, and M.S. Weinbrecht (1988).

---

their respective areas. In this way Dassler was able to make decisions that worked in the best interest of his company.

We see the principles of the Carnegie model in action if we look at the way in which the decision is made about the host city for the Olympic Games. Ostensibly the IOC has as its goal to award the bid to the city that will stage the best games. However, what happens in actuality is that various individuals within the IOC form coalitions. Evaluation committee members visit the bid sites to evaluate facilities, financing, security, and so forth. Each individual forms his or her preference as to what would be the best site. Coalitions are formed based on what the evaluation committee has seen or on geopolitical lines, and these groups engage in lobbying in an effort to try to make sure the committee makes the decision most favorable to them. King (1991), for example, describes how Canadian IOC member Dick Pound traveled to a number of places with the Calgary Games organizers to lobby other IOC delegates to support the Calgary bid.

The Structuring of Unstructured Processes

In their research on decision making Mintzberg, Raisinghani, and Théorêt (1976) focus on decisions made at the senior levels of an organization. They argue that much of the management science approach to decision making has focused on routine operating decisions, but it is really at the top levels where an organization must make better decisions. In contrast to the concern with political factors evident in Cyert and March's (1963) work, Mintzberg and colleagues (1976) focus on identifying a structure to describe the unstructured process of strategic decision making. Data were obtained on 25 decision processes that were tracked from the initial identification of a problem to the acceptance of a decision solution. Over two thirds of the decision processes took longer than a year to complete; the majority of the decisions were nonprogrammed, that is, unique.

Essentially, Mintzberg and colleagues (1976) suggest that major decisions in an organization are broken down into smaller decisions that collectively contribute to the major decision. Their research identified three major phases to the decision process. Each phase contains different **routines**, seven in total. The decision process is also characterized by what are called **interrupts**, events that result in a change in the pace or direction of the decision process. Interrupts cause delays because they force an organization to go back and modify its solution, find another one, or engage in political activity to remove an obstacle. Each of these three phases, the routines they contain, and the notion of interrupts are explained more fully in the section that follows.

The first phase in the decision process is the identification phase. There are two routines involved in this phase. The decision recognition routine occurs when a manager recognizes a problem about which a decision must be made. A decision is required when there is "a difference between information on some actual situation and some expected standard" (Mintzberg et al., 1976, p. 253). Stimuli that signal the beginning of the need for a decision may originate both within and outside the organization. After the decision recognition routine comes the diagnosis routine; here issues around the problem are clarified and defined. Diagnosis can be explicit and formal or informal and implicit. The more crisislike the problem to be addressed, the less likely there is to be formal diagnosis.

Following the identification phase is the development phase. Mintzberg and colleagues (1976, p. 255) describe this phase as "the heart of the decision-making process . . . the set of activities that leads to one or more solutions to a problem." There are two routines within this phase. First, in the search routine, managers look for solutions to the problem situation. Initial searches are carried out by considering past experiences. If these searches fail, a more active search is carried out, involving looking in "more remote and less familiar areas."

If this search procedure is not successful, a custom-made solution is developed in the design routine. Mintzberg and colleagues (1976, p. 256) point out that this "is a complex, iterative procedure . . . designers grope along building their solution brick by brick without really knowing what it will look like until it is completed."

The final phase of the decision process is the selection phase. Here, a choice is made about a solution. The first routine in the selection phase is the screening routine, used when there are too many ready-made alternatives and a custom design is not required. During screening, certain alternatives are rejected so that a usable number can be handled. The second routine is the evaluation-choice routine. Evaluation and choice can be determined either by judgment, bargaining, or analysis: "In judgment, one individual makes a choice in his own mind with procedures that he does not, perhaps cannot explain; in bargaining, selection is made by a group of decision makers with conflicting goal systems, each exercising judgment; and in analysis . . . factual evaluation is carried out, generally by technocrats, followed by managerial choice by judgment or by bargaining" (Mintzberg et al., 1976, p. 258).

The authorization routine is the final routine in the decision-making process. Authorization occurs when the person or group making the decision does not have the necessary power to commit the organization to the particular solution. Consequently, the decision is passed up the hierarchy; in some cases it may even have to receive the support of external bodies who could block the decision solution. Sometimes decisions are rejected when passed up to higher levels.

Figure 13.2 shows the stages of Mintzberg and colleagues' (1976) decision process and the various routines. The figure also shows the most common interrupts. At the identification phase there may be internal interrupts or political interrupts because organizational members can't agree about the need for a strategic decision. New option interrupts occur late in the development phase or in the evaluation-choice routine, and may result in going back to the design routine, to changes in the new option, or simply to evaluation and choice, where the new option is accepted or rejected. External interrupts occur in the final phase and involve attempts by external agents to block the solution. The zigzag lines in the figure signal the possible delays from scheduling, timing, and feedback that occur at each stage of the decision process.

Although there have been no analyses using the approach outlined by Mintzberg and colleagues (1976) of the major decisions made in sport organizations, it is quite applicable to situations in our field. Decisions such as Canstar's move into the Canadian in-line skate market, the NBA's decision to hold annual tournaments against foreign teams

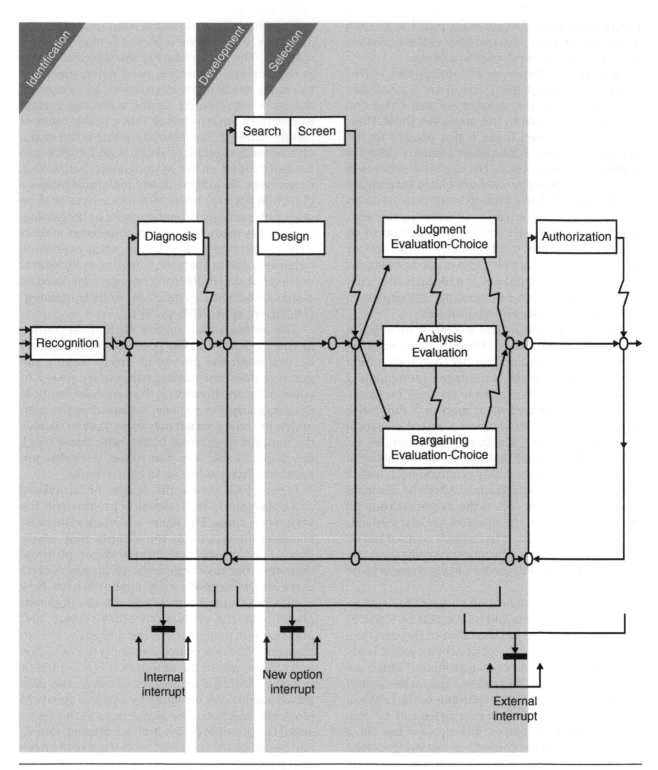

Figure 13.2 *General model of the strategic decision process.*

Reprinted from The structure of "Unstructured" decision processes, by H. Mintzerg, D. Raisinghani, and A. Theoret published in Administrative Science Quarterly 21, no. 2, 1976 by permission of Administrative Science Quarterly. ©Johnson Graduate School of Management, Cornell University.

and broadcast games in Europe, and the CFL's decision to establish franchises in the United States, could all be analyzed using the "structuring of unstructured processes" approach.

The Garbage Can Model

Much of the work on decision making assumes that the various activities making up the process can be ordered into some logical sequence. Cohen, March, and Olsen (1972) suggest that in reality the situation is much more confusing (see also Cohen & March, 1974; March & Olsen, 1976); in the decision process of an organization many different things are going on at one time. "Technologies are changing and poorly understood; alliances, preferences, and perceptions are changing; problems, solutions, opportunities, ideas, people, and outcomes are mixed together in a way that makes their interpretation uncertain and their connections unclear" (March, 1982, p. 36). Cohen, March, and Olsen refer to this situation as **organized anarchy**. It is found in organizations that are highly organic in their structure and are required to change rapidly. Decision making in these organizations is an outcome of four independent streams of events.

• **A stream of problems.** Problems result from dissatisfaction with current performance. Examples include not winning enough games, declining sales, low graduation rates, or a lack of adequately trained staff.

• **A stream of choice opportunities.** This refers to the occasions when a decision is usually made in an organization. Included could be when someone is hired or fired, a budget is finalized, a new service is added, or a team is selected.

• **A stream of participants.** These are the people who make choices in an organization. They come and go as a result of hirings, firings, transfers, retirements, and so forth. Participants come from different backgrounds and have different ideas about problems and solutions.

• **A stream of solutions.** Many participants have ideas to which they are deeply committed; as a result they may try to sell their ideas to the other members of the organization. In some organizations, people such as planners and systems analysts are actually hired to come up with solutions for situations where problems do not exist. Solutions can then exist without problems being present.

The existence of these four streams means that the process of decision making is somewhat random. The organization is described as a garbage can into which problems, choices, participants, and solutions are all placed. Managers have to act with the resultant disorder; as a result decisions are rarely systematic and logical. Choices are made when problems come together with the right participants and solutions. As a consequence, some problems are never solved, solutions are put forward even when a problem has yet to be identified, and choices are made before problems are understood.

The strength of the **garbage can model** is that it draws our attention to the role that chance and timing play in the decision-making process. Also, unlike other approaches, which tend to focus on single decisions, the garbage can approach is concerned with multiple decisions.

Bradford Studies

The Bradford studies, so named because they were conducted by Professor David Hickson and his research team at the University of Bradford in England, were carried out over approximately 15 years from the early 1970s to the mid-1980s (see Butler, Astley, Hickson, Mallory, & Wilson, 1979/1980; Cray, Mallory, Butler, Hickson, & Wilson, 1988, 1991; Hickson, Butler, Cray, Mallory, & Wilson, 1985, 1986; Mallory, Butler, Cray, Hickson, & Wilson, 1983; Wilson, Butler, Cray, Hickson, & Mallory, 1986). Using data from 150 decisions, Hickson and colleagues (1985) focus on the process of decision making as opposed to the outcome and implementation of a decision. His research team identified five dimensions of process, encompassing 12 variables.

The first of these dimensions, scrutiny, concerns the information sources available to the decision maker(s). Four variables were identified as making up this particular dimension. Expertise, the first variable, was assessed by the number of internal and external sources from which information about the decision was obtained. Disparity refers to the extent to which the decision makers had confidence in the different sources from which information was obtained. Externality was "measured as the ratio of the confidence in external information to that placed in all information" (Cray et al., 1988, p. 16). Effort refers to the way in which the information was acquired—was it merely the result of recalling personal experiences or did it involve the use of working groups or other similar mechanisms to generate and analyze information?

The second dimension, interaction, had three variables. Informal interaction was a measure of the extent to which the decision to be made was discussed informally, such as in hallways or over coffee. Formal interaction concerns the extent to which the decision process was structured through meetings, work groups, and so forth. Scope of negotiation, the final variable, assessed the extent to which the decision was made by one individual or was subject to negotiation before a choice was made.

The third dimension, flow, relates to the delays, reconsiderations, and disruptions found in the decision process. Two variables made up this dimension. Disruptions, the first variable, concerned the length and occurrence of disruptions that took place in the decision process. Impedance concerned the extent to which the cause of delays could be controlled.

The fourth dimension, duration, was made up of two variables. Gestation time was the length of the period from the initial mention of the decision issue until specific action was taken toward making a decision. Process time was the time from the start of the specific action to when the decision was authorized. Finally, the last dimension, authority, was a single measure of the level in the organization at which the decision was authorized.

Compiling data on each of these variables, Hickson and his colleagues analyzed 136 of the decisions they studied, using cluster analysis. There were incomplete data on 14 of the decisions, so they could not be used in the cluster program. Three distinct ways of making decisions were identified: sporadic processes, fluid processes, and constricted processes. The characteristics of these decisions are shown in figure 13.3 and explained in more detail in the following discussion.

Sporadic decision processes are made in a manner characterized by disruption and delay. Short periods of activity are followed by delays, during which information is gathered and the various constituents in the process argue over the relative merits of what has been uncovered. The scope of negotiation is fairly wide, indicating the number of individuals and groups involved in the process but, because much of the negotiation takes place in informal settings, decision making takes longer than average. There is some tendency for the decision process to require authorization by the most senior level of the organization. In short, the actual process of decision making is fairly wide-ranging and uneven, but ultimately the decision must be approved through the organization's highest level.

In contrast to sporadic decisions, **fluid decision** processes have fewer and less serious interruptions; fewer experts are involved and the whole process is quicker. The information base used to make the decision is more homogeneous and much of the interaction during the actual making of the decision takes place in a formal setting. The search for a decision, while encompassing considerable scope for negotiation, is narrowed quickly and

Sporadic process	Fluid process	Constricted process
Higher level of disruption - impedance - expertise - confidence disparity - informal interaction - process time Some negotiation scope High level of authorization	Higher level of formal interaction Lower level of disruption - impedance - expertise - confidence disparity - process time Some negotiation scope High level of authorization	Higher level of expertise Lower level of authorization - negotiation scope - informal interaction - effort

Figure 13.3   *Characteristics of three types of strategic decision making.*
Based on information in D. Cray, G.R. Mallory, R.J. Butler, D.J. Hickson, and D.C. Wilson (1988).

ultimately approved at the highest level of the organization.

Constricted decision processes are made with the use of expert information but there is little effort to seek data not readily obtainable. Most of the interaction around this type of decision process is informal, because the relatively few people involved are in frequent contact. There is little scope for negotiation here; decisions emanate from the lower levels of senior management and will probably be ratified by the CEO (unlike sporadic and fluid decisions, which usually require board approval). Much of this process is focused on a single decision maker, in most cases the organization's CEO.

As with Mintzberg and colleagues (1976), no work within the sport management literature has attempted to use the Bradford approach to understand the decision-making process in sport organizations. However, the considerable

KEY ISSUES FOR MANAGERS

Nutt (2004) argued that decisions fail because judgment is rushed, time and resources are unwisely allocated, and solutions are taken from stakeholder claims or current practices instead of exploring other possibilities.

In this chapter, the decision-making process has been presented as being made under conditions of certainty, but in truth, most decisions have a certain element of uncertainty to them—especially strategic decisions. However, the level of uncertainty can be decreased by doing a SWOT analysis (see chapter 6). Therefore, if you examine the following elements, you will be able to make more-informed decisions:

- Organizational strengths and weaknesses
- Opportunities and threats in the environment
- Types and number of stakeholders in the environment
- Possibly emerging issues:
  - Positive and negative
  - Large and small
  - Those that stakeholders may or may not, should or should not, and could or could not be aware of

Ford and Gioia (2000) mentioned that creativity may be a good way to deal with uncertainty and fear in decision making. However, they explained that "adopting creative choices may increase the odds of resolving the problem(s) at hand, but at the cost of leaving decision makers open to the stones and arrows of the critics should the decision fail" (p. 725). Therefore, the best solution may sometimes be the riskiest for a manager or the organization. Whether or not to go down that route is a decision each manager must make after weighing the pros and cons. Still, Nutt (2004) argued that a successful decision-making process should use multiple perspectives to find innovative possibilities once objectives are clearly defined.

The decision-making process, when put into practice is rarely linear in nature, going from one clear phase to the next, as the rational model would suggest. Instead, decision making is a complex process. It involves going back and forth between phases, it is discontinuous, recursive, and relies on incomplete information, and it even incorporates an aspect of educated guesswork, also referred to as luck, gut feeling, or intuition (cf. Sadler-Smith & Shefy, 2004).

There are also factors that can make a decision more complex or more difficult. As a manager, you must be aware of potential ethical issues (such as Nike's use of sweatshops to decrease production costs but to the detriment of the workers). Another concern is the power and political dynamics—issues discussed in chapter 10—that can influence whether a decision is made, how the decision-making process occurs (who's involved, which choices are examined), what decision is made, how the decision is implemented, and, ultimately, whether the result is successful. However, as Bakan (2004) would argue, managers can only be acting morally when they act in the best interest of the shareholders and no one else.

number of published works emanating from this research project is one measure of its acceptance in the general field of management. The dimensions and variables identified by Hickson and colleagues are quite applicable to a variety of sport organizations. Replications and extensions of this work using sport organizations could not only enhance our understanding of the decision-making process in the organizations in our field but also extend existing theory on this topic and thus contribute to management studies in general.

SUMMARY AND CONCLUSIONS

All sport managers make decisions, and an understanding of how the decision-making process works can increase the effectiveness and efficiency of these decisions. In this chapter we began by explaining the concept of decision making, distinguishing between programmed and nonprogrammed decisions. We noted that managers prefer programmed decisions because they are more predictable and, because of their predictability, are most frequently found at lower levels of a sport organization. Nonprogrammed decisions are found at higher levels. We looked at the three conditions under which decisions can be made: certainty, risk, and uncertainty. Most decisions in sport organizations are made under conditions of risk and uncertainty.

In the biggest section of this chapter we looked at the major theoretical approaches to understanding decision making. We focused on individual decision making—the rational approach and the more realistic notion of bounded rationality—and compared and contrasted the two approaches. We then examined organizational decision making. Five major approaches to organizational decision making were identified: the management science approach, the Carnegie model, the structuring of unstructured processes, the garbage can approach, and the Bradford studies. We noted that no work in the sport management literature had made use of any of these approaches. Examples were provided of the type of sport organizations' decisions that these theoretical models could be used to understand. By understanding the decision process and hence the factors that influence decision making, sport managers can make better decisions and become better managers.

KEY CONCEPTS

bounded rationality (p. 262)

certainty (p. 259)

coalitions (p. 263)

constricted decisions (p. 269)

fluid decisions (p. 268)

garbage can model (p. 267)

interrupts (p. 265)

management science (p. 263)

nonprogrammed decisions (p. 259)

organized anarchy (p. 267)

problemistic search (p. 263)

programmed decisions (p. 258)

rational decision making (p. 261)

risk (p. 259)

routines (p. 265)

sporadic decisions (p. 268)

uncertainty (p. 260)

REVIEW QUESTIONS

1. What type of programmed decisions would you expect to find being made in a local non-profit track and field club?

2. In what type of sport organization would you expect to find a large number of non-programmed decisions?

3. Think of a familiar sport organization; under what type of conditions are most of the decisions made in this organization?

4. In what way do athletic directors try to eliminate the risk involved in hiring a new basketball coach?

5. What criticism would you make about the rational approach to decision making?

6. What techniques would you use to evaluate the effectiveness of the decisions made in a sport organization?

7. What factors did Simon see as limiting the ability of managers to make rational decisions?

8. How do sport managers satisfice when they make decisions? Give examples.

9. What are the strengths and weaknesses of the management science approach to decision making?

10. How would you use the Carnegie approach to explain the decision making that takes place about an athletic department's budget?

11. What similarities can you see in Simon's idea of bounded rationality and Cyert and March's Carnegie model?

12. Select a major decision that you have seen made in a sport organization and analyze it using Mintzberg, Raisinghani, and Théorêt's approach.

13. "Managers don't make large decisions; they only make small ones." Do you agree or disagree with this statement? Why?

14. Explain the four streams of events proposed in the garbage can model. How do they occur independently?

15. Using the variables employed in the Bradford studies, how would you describe the IOC members' decision process (outlined at the start of this chapter) regarding candidate city choice?

SUGGESTIONS FOR FURTHER READING

As we have noted at several places in this chapter, little research in the sport management literature has looked at the process of managerial decision making in sport organizations. While some accounts of the problems confronted by decision makers can be found in the popular press, they contain little in the way of any scholarly analysis. If you are looking for more information on this topic, you are advised to consult the general organizational literature. For work on bounded rationality, begin with Simon's (1945) text *Administrative Behavior*. While this is quite an old book, it does form the basis for much of the future work conducted on this concept. Examples of work that builds on Simon's ideas can be found in all of the major organizational journals. For example, see Simon's (1987) article "Making Management Decisions: The Role of Intuition and Emotion" in *Academy of Management Executive*; Lyles' (1987) article "Defining Strategic Problems: Subjective Criteria of Executives" in *Organization Studies*; and Jackson and Dutton's (1988) "Discerning Threats and Opportunities" in *Administrative Science Quarterly*.

For those interested in the management science approach to decision making, we recommend the journal *Interfaces*, which sometimes contains research on sport organizations. In terms of the Carnegie model, you are advised (as with work on bounded rationality) to read the original research and then see the major management journals for extensions of this approach. Stevenson, Pearce, and Porter's (1985) "The Concept of 'Coalition' in Organization Theory and Research," in the *Academy of Management Review*, is one example of how Cyert and March's original ideas can be extended. In terms of the unstructured processes approach, the garbage can model, and the Bradford approach, you are likewise advised to read the references cited in the chapter and look through the management and organizational journals for extensions of this work. All of these approaches have good potential for being applied to sport organizations. Finally, the *Academy of Management Executive* published a special issue in 2004 on decision making and firm success (Vol. 18, No. 4).

CASE FOR ANALYSIS

Manchester United Goes Global

When David Beckham signed a deal with Adidas and his popularity soared in Asia, his team, Manchester United, saw a golden opportunity. Asian consumers, known for player loyalty, loved Beckham, but not Manchester United. Though it was at the top of the European soccer world, the club lacked notoriety elsewhere, but as a publicly traded organization it had a primary duty to its shareholders to make money. Manchester United saw a chance to capitalize on Beckham's fan base in Asia, an emerging market, particularly because China is to host the 2008 Summer Olympics. So the club set a plan into motion: It would globalize into the many untapped commercial markets worldwide.

In 1999, Manchester United went to Asia to promote itself as a brand. The club played games, built megastores, and Manchester United–themed cafés. The plan began to work, as loyalty and merchandise sales grew. By 2003, the club had the highest sales of any team. Manchester United's value was also climbing, although it lagged behind at least one league team. Manchester and Beckham seemed intrinsically linked—David Beckham was a cash cow for the club that basically owned his image.

In 2002, Manchester United signed a 13-year deal with Nike for $430 million that conflicted with Beckham's Adidas sponsorship. In 2003, Beckham was transferred to Real Madrid—an Adidas sponsored team—and with him went the fans.

When other teams, such as Real Madrid, tried to grab a piece of the Asian market, Manchester United entered another untapped soccer market,

Manchester United used the popularity of its star soccer player, David Beckham, to promote itself in Asia. Even after Beckham's trade to another club, Manchester United continued its global efforts by entering the untapped soccer market in the United States.

the United States. The club teamed up with the New York Yankees in a joint venture to help each sport penetrate the other's respective markets. Manchester United played games in the United States for two summers (2003 and 2004), increasing their popularity every time.

In 2004, Manchester United became the world's most valuable team at $1.1 billion. It was now the most popular sport team in Europe, Asia, and North America, even without Beckham.

By 2005, China surpassed the United States as the largest consumer. To keep the Asian loyalty fires burning, Manchester returned to Asia in 2005. The club also has plans to work with Nike to build its brand in other untapped markets, namely Australia and New Zealand.

Based on information in Connolly (2003), Forbes.com (2004).

Questions

1. Describe the conditions under which Manchester United chose to globalize and go to Asia first.

2. How would you use Cyert and March's work (the Carnegie model) to understand the decision-making process outlined in this case?

3. Do you think Manchester United is regretting transferring David Beckham to Real Madrid? Why?

4. Using Mintzberg, Raisinghani, and Théorêt's approach to understanding decision making, identify the different "routines" and "interrupts" that apply to Manchester United's globalization attempt.

Managing Organizational Culture

ORGANIZATIONAL CULTURE AT MOUNTAIN EQUIPMENT CO-OP

In 1971 in the midst of a savage mountain storm, a small group of students huddled together in a tent and discussed the need for a place to buy sophisticated mountaineering gear. The high-end gear they spoke of was unavailable at regular sporting goods stores. They decided to create a cooperative called Mountain Equipment Co-op (MEC) that asked the customers—and therefore gear users—how the company should operate. The organization grew to its current size of two million members from 192 countries.

The founders took their love of the outdoors and turned it into the organization's culture. MEC's core purpose is "to support people in achieving the benefits of self-propelled wilderness-oriented recreation." MEC strives to be "an innovative, thriving cooperative that inspires excellence in products and services, passion for wilderness experiences, leadership for a just world, and action for a healthy planet." They value ethics, integrity, respect for others and the environment, protection of the environment, community spirit and cooperation, personal growth, continual learning, and adventure.

Those statements are not just words. They are found in every action MEC takes, from its choice of environmentally friendly material for its products to the programs it creates. For

(continued)

(continued)

Photo courtesy of Mountain Equipment Co-Op

Mountain Equipment Co-Op designed and built its retail outlet in Ottawa to have the least possible impact on the environment, an action that reflects the organization's culture.

example, in 1987 MEC started an environment fund, and each year, 0.4 percent of MEC's sales and all interest made from the fund go to Canadian-based organizations working toward environmental conservation or education, and recreational projects. Aside from the external steps it has taken, MEC has made internal changes over the last decade as it has been "greening" its buildings to make them more efficient in their use of energy, water, and materials.

Based on information in Mountain Equipment Co-op (2005a, 2005b, 2005c, 2005d).

The description of MEC and the activities the company is involved in tell us about the culture of the organization. Culture, as we will see, is concerned with characteristics such as the type of values and beliefs found in an organization and the accepted modes of operation. At MEC the important values about protecting the environment are a central part of the organization's culture. Helping with national and local environmental projects is an accepted part of the mode of operation of the company. Everybody—employees and customers (members)—at MEC is expected to work to this end. Individuals are hired because they believe in and will work to promote this ideal. The culture of the company is reflected and reinforced by the fact that employees are encouraged to pursue outdoor activities.

In the final chapters of the book we explore two of the topics seen as crucial in bringing an organization together as an integrated whole: **organizational culture** and leadership. First we examine the concept of organizational culture. To begin we look at what we mean when we talk about the culture of an organization. We then look at how culture manifests itself in sport organizations. We discuss the idea of thick and thin cultures, examine whether or not a sport organization has just one culture, and explore the relationship of culture to effectiveness in sport organizations. Finally, we look at how cultures are created, managed, and changed in sport organizations.

What Is Organizational Culture?

Organizational culture is one of the most recent introductions into the field of organization theory.

In part, the concern with culture has grown out of the success of Japanese industry, which began in the 1970s. Increasingly, organizational theorists began to see that Japanese organizations operated in a different way from most North American and Western European organizations. While obviously Japanese culture was different from the culture of countries in these geographic areas, it was not so much the cultural context in which Japanese organizations existed that caught and held the attention of organization theorists, but something that has been termed their "corporate culture." Japanese organizations operated using different values and beliefs, different norms of interaction, and a different set of understandings from their counterparts in North America and Western Europe.

The increased interest in organizational (or what is sometimes referred to as corporate) culture led several organizational theorists to attempt to define what the concept actually means. While no definition can do complete justice to the meaning of any term, looking at some of the more common definitions can give us a good understanding of what these people are talking about when they refer to organizational culture.

Pettigrew (1979, p. 572), for example, describes organizational culture as an "amalgam of beliefs, ideology, language, ritual, and myth." Schein (1985, p. 9) sees it as "a pattern of basic assumptions—invented, discovered, or developed by a given group as it learns to cope with its problems of external adaptation and internal integration—that has worked well enough to be considered valid and therefore, to be taught to new members as the correct way to perceive, think, and feel in relation to those problems." For Sathe (1983, p. 6) culture is "the set of important understandings (often unstated) that members of a community share in common." For Wilkins (1983a, p. 25) it is "the taken-for-granted and shared meanings that people assign to their social surroundings."

There are some general themes within these different definitions, including a concern with the **values, beliefs, basic assumptions, shared understandings**, and taken-for-granted meanings on which a set of individuals base the construction of their organization, group, or subgroup. These characteristics, commonly accepted as forming the basis for an organization's culture, provide stability to an organization and convey to new members the understanding that enables them to make sense of organizational activities.

The increased popularity of the concept of culture among managers and organizational theorists,

Robey (1986, pp. 426-427) insightfully suggested, can be attributed to two main qualities found in this approach: "First, for many macro organization theorists, culture provides a way to bring *people* back into their analyses without using psychological models of human behavior. . . . Second, culture is widely accepted by managers, because the concept describes organizational realities that are hard to define but very relevant to running an organization" (emphasis in original).

These are important points to consider as we think about organizational culture. While they are relevant to all types of organizations they are particularly important to the study of sport organizations. Work in sport management had traditionally employed sociopsychological approaches to explain the qualities and actions of sport managers. A focus on organizational culture provides a different approach to understanding patterns of action in sport organizations. This approach, if combined with traditional macroorganizational theory, could provide for richer insights into the organizations we study. An approach that focuses on organizational culture should also have considerable appeal to those of us interested in sport, because the organizations in our field are rife with such characteristics as **stories**, **myths**, **symbols**, and **rituals**. These characteristics are some of the principle manifestations of an organization's culture, as we will see in the next section of this chapter. A focus on these characteristics would help shed new light on the way sport organizations operate.

Manifestations of a Sport Organization's Culture

Because an organization's culture is based on values, beliefs, accepted patterns of meaning, and so on, and because these features are hard to pin down, researchers who study culture have tended to focus on the way it manifests itself in organizations. To fully focus they often find it necessary to immerse themselves in the organizations they are studying. Consequently, studies of organizational culture have tended to be qualitative in nature—it is difficult to develop an understanding of an organization's culture using questionnaire-based studies. Trice and Beyer (1984) suggest a number of cultural manifestations that researchers can observe (see figure 14.1). In this section of the chapter we look at some of the most important of these manifestations.

rite—Relatively elaborate, dramatic, planned sets of activities that consolidate various forms of cultural expressions into one event, which is carried out through social interactions, usually for the benefit of an audience.

ceremony—A system of several rites connected with a single occasion or event.

ritual—A standardized, detailed set of techniques and behaviors that manage anxieties, but seldom produce intended, technical consequences of practical importance.

myth—A dramatic narrative of imagined events, usually used to explain origins or transformations of something; also, an unquestioned belief about the practical benefits of certain techniques and behaviors that is not supported by demonstrated facts.

saga—An historical narrative describing the unique accomplishments of a group and its leaders, usually in heroic terms.

legend—A handed-down narrative of some wonderful event that is based in history but has been embellished with fictional details.

story—A narrative based on true events; often a combination of truth and fiction.

folktale—A completely fictional narrative.

symbol—Any object, act, event, quality, or relation that serves as a vehicle for conveying meaning, usually by representing another thing.

language—A particular form or manner in which members of a group use vocal sounds and written signs to conveys meanings to each other.

gesture—Movements of parts of the body used to express meanings.

physical setting—Those things that surround people physically and provide them with immediate sensory stimuli as they carry out culturally expressive activities.

artifact—Material objects manufactured by people to facilitate culturally expressive activities.

Figure 14.1 *Manifestations of organizational culture.*

Stories and Myths

Stories are narratives recounted among employees and told to new employees. Myths are stories, often about the origins and transformations of a company, that are not supported by fact (Trice & Beyer, 1984). Both stories and myths convey a number of important messages about a sport organization. First, they present a sense of its history. As Pettigrew (1979, p. 576) notes about myths, they "anchor the present in the past, offer explanations and, therefore legitimacy for social practices, and contain levels of meaning that deal simultaneously with the socially and psychologically significant in any culture." Stories and myths, because they help establish the organization as an enduring entity, can reduce uncertainty for employees (cf. Martin, Feldman, Hatch, & Sitkin, 1983). If the stories are about hard times, as they sometimes are, the employees sense the ability of the organization to overcome problems. Stories also help transmit messages about organizational goals and the way employees should act. They are, as Wilkins (1983b, p. 82) notes, "important indicators of the values participants share, the social prescriptions concerning how things are done, and the consequences of compliance or deviance. The stories may also indicate the social categories and statuses which are legitimate in the organization and thus are important guides for what kinds of people can do what." Wilkins goes on to suggest that this information is important for the successful participation of people in the organization.

At Nike, for example, a story is told about the company's early days when, during a particularly heated meeting in which sales reps were criticizing corporate officials for their supply mechanisms, a rep from Minnesota stood up and said to his colleagues, "Listen, these guys are at least 51 percent right so far in everything they're doing. And that's enough. You only have to be right 51

TIME OUT *John Wooden and the Pyramid of Success*

John Wooden is one of the most successful basketball coaches ever. While at UCLA his teams won numerous conference and NCAA titles. Wooden built his program around his Pyramid of Success (see figure 14.2). The pyramid outlines those values and beliefs that

Wooden saw as important to a successful team. Although he never used the term, the values and beliefs outlined in the pyramid were the basis for the organizational culture of the UCLA basketball teams.

percent of the time." As Strasser and Becklund (1991) point out, long after the person making the comment was forgotten, this story became a part of Nike's culture; it was seen as an indication of what reps should and shouldn't do. The idea was "don't be afraid to make mistakes. If you take a fall, it's because you're learning and that's better than playing it safe; the name of the game is not to be right all the time . . . the name of the game is to win; there's a difference" (Strasser & Becklund, 1991, p. 195).

Symbols

Symbols are used to convey meaning about a sport organization to its members and to the public at large. The symbol of the falcon, for example, was chosen for the Atlanta-based NFL team because "the falcon is proud and dignified with great courage and fight; it never drops its prey; it is deadly and has a great sporting tradition" (Falcons, 1989, p. 13). Nike's "swoosh" conveys speed; it is also no coincidence that Nike is the Greek goddess of victory. Other examples of symbols that serve to convey meaning about sport organizations can be found in corporate documents like organizational charts. The ski resort Nakiska has inverted its organizational chart so that the employees in direct contact with customers are at the top of the chart and the general manager, president, and board of directors are at the bottom. The organization thus conveys to its first-level staff their importance to the company's success. Symbolism can also be found in something as seemingly mundane as letterhead. The Broadmoor Golf Resort uses gold-embossed letterhead, a symbolic representation of the type of luxury it provides.

Closely allied to the use of symbols is the use of **slogans**. Clichés such as "When the going gets tough, the tough get going" and "No pain, no gain" are frequently used by athletic coaches to convey

expectations about appropriate modes of behavior in their organizations. In a somewhat similar vein, Nike's "Just do it" slogan has taken on particular significance for the company; it conveys meaning about success in sport and about success in the Nike organization.

It has also become somewhat fashionable for company owners or chief executive officers to develop sayings or sets of sayings that convey the organization's culture to employees. MEC has a corporate philosophy that contains such items as "We conduct ourselves ethically and with integrity. We show respect for others in our words and actions. We act in the spirit of community and co-operation. We respect and protect our natural environment. We strive for personal growth, continual learning, and adventure" (MEC, 2005b, p. 1). At W.L. Gore, Bill Gore was frequently heard to ask employees "Have you had fun today? Did you make any money?" (Blank, 1986, p. 23).

Language

Different sport organizations develop their own specialized **language** or jargon to communicate with each other. Through language, members "acquire the structured 'ways' of [the] group, and along with the language, the value implications of those ways" (Pettigrew, 1979, p. 575). Basketball coaches and players talk about their 2-1-2 full court press, working the ball into the paint, or screening away from the ball. While to most people these terms mean little, to the coaches and players on the team they are part of everyday communication, and as such represent one aspect of the team's culture. They serve to strengthen the team as an organization by providing commonality, and to separate the team from others who do not communicate in this way. They highlight boundaries as to who is and who isn't part of the organization (Wilkins, 1983b).

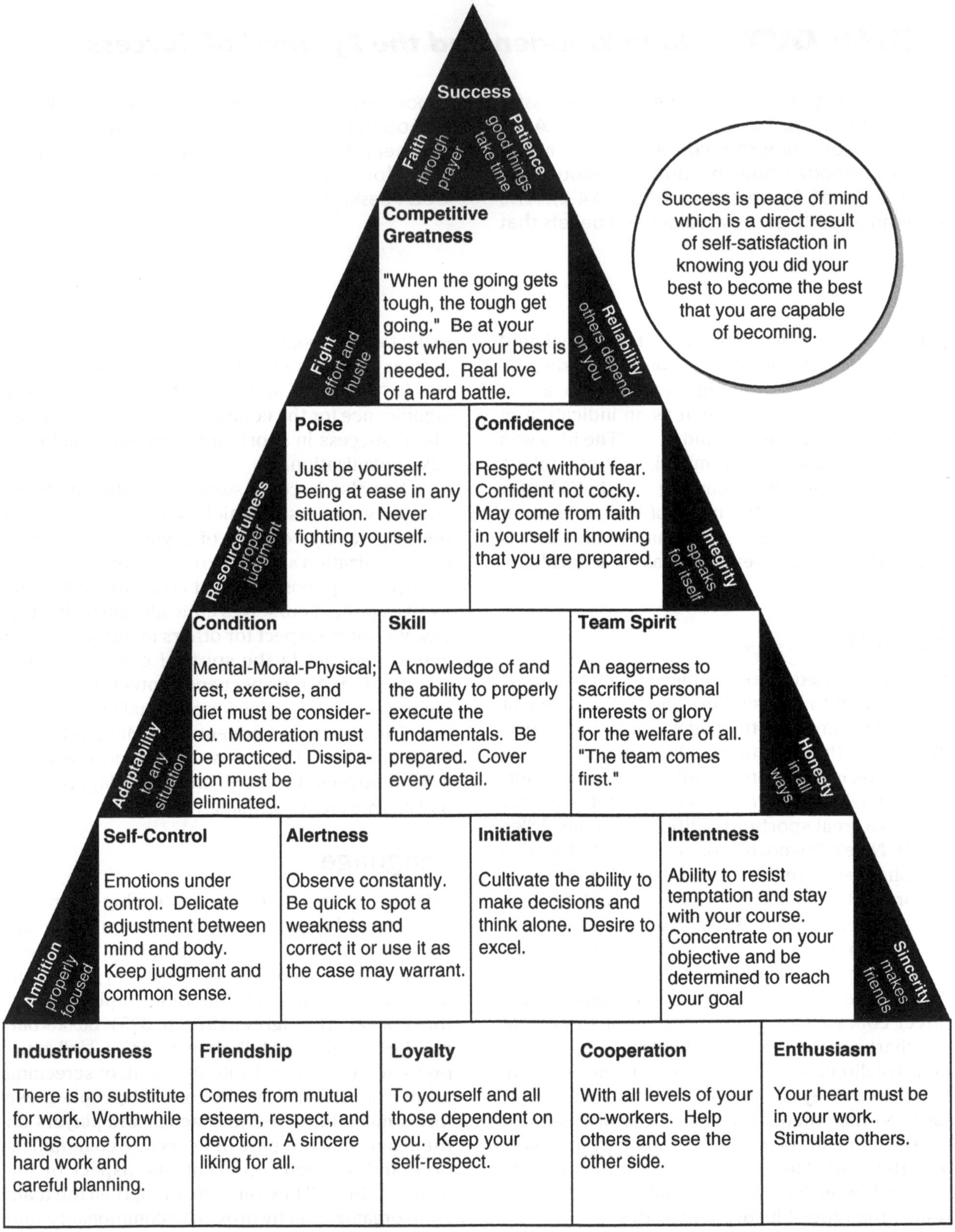

Success

Faith — through prayer

Patience — good things take time

Competitive Greatness

"When the going gets tough, the tough get going." Be at your best when your best is needed. Real love of a hard battle.

Fight — effort and hustle

Reliability — others depend on you

Success is peace of mind which is a direct result of self-satisfaction in knowing you did your best to become the best that you are capable of becoming.

Resourcefulness — proper judgment

Poise

Just be yourself. Being at ease in any situation. Never fighting yourself.

Confidence

Respect without fear. Confident not cocky. May come from faith in yourself in knowing that you are prepared.

Integrity — speaks for itself

Adaptability — to any situation

Condition

Mental-Moral-Physical; rest, exercise, and diet must be considered. Moderation must be practiced. Dissipation must be eliminated.

Skill

A knowledge of and the ability to properly execute the fundamentals. Be prepared. Cover every detail.

Team Spirit

An eagerness to sacrifice personal interests or glory for the welfare of all. "The team comes first."

Honesty — in all ways

Ambition — properly focused

Self-Control

Emotions under control. Delicate adjustment between mind and body. Keep judgment and common sense.

Alertness

Observe constantly. Be quick to spot a weakness and correct it or use it as the case may warrant.

Initiative

Cultivate the ability to make decisions and think alone. Desire to excel.

Intentness

Ability to resist temptation and stay with your course. Concentrate on your objective and be determined to reach your goal

Sincerity — makes friends

Industriousness

There is no substitute for work. Worthwhile things come from hard work and careful planning.

Friendship

Comes from mutual esteem, respect, and devotion. A sincere liking for all.

Loyalty

To yourself and all those dependent on you. Keep your self-respect.

Cooperation

With all levels of your co-workers. Help others and see the other side.

Enthusiasm

Your heart must be in your work. Stimulate others.

Figure 14.2 *Pyramid of Success.*

From J. Wooden, *They call me coach* (1973). Word Books.

Ceremonies or Rites

All sport organizations, in fact all organizations, develop certain types of traditions that we usually refer to as **ceremonies** or **rites**. Rookie initiations, team awards nights, pregame meals, an annual Christmas party, and a pep rally are all examples of the types of ceremonies we find in sport organizations. In each, certain shared values within the organization are reinforced. These events also provide evidence of what the organization values; they are symbolic representations of the type of beliefs and activities important in the organization. Trice and Beyer (1984) identify different types of rites. A rite of passage marks a change in the role and status of the person or persons involved. For example, rookie night ceremonies are designed to initiate new members and make them part of the team. A rite of degradation dissolves the social identity and associated power of the person involved by pointing out problems with his or her work performance. The firing of coaches and general managers, a common occurrence in professional sport organizations, is a rite of degradation. Smith and Shilbury (2004) have identified 12 dimensions (and 68 subdimensions) of Australian National Sport Organization, among them rituals, symbols, size, and history or tradition.

Physical Setting

The **physical setting** in which a sport organization operates can convey meaning about the nature of its culture. Davis (1984) suggests three important parts of the physical setting useful in understanding an organization's culture: the physical structure, physical stimuli, and symbolic artifacts.

The **physical structure** can be defined as "the architect's design and physical placement of furnishings in a building that influence or regulate social interaction" (Davis, 1984, p. 272). Having an open floor plan instead of closed-door offices, round tables instead of rectangular ones in meeting rooms, and simply the physical location of a facility can all convey messages about a sport organization. For example, in April 1985 shortly after Doug Mitchell took over as commissioner of the CFL, he moved the league's headquarters from cramped surroundings in downtown Toronto to plush offices in the center of the city's trendy Bloor Street shopping district, an "indication he want[ed] to upgrade the league's crusty image" (Barr, 1985, p. 1). In a similar vein, the CEO of the Canadian Sport and Fitness Administration Centre, Wilf Wedmann, moved his offices from the top floor of the building to the ground floor, because being at the top of the building gave the

---

TIME OUT *A Huffy Rep Cycles to Glory*

Soft light filters down from multicolored windows as the crowd far below eagerly awaits the awards ceremony. Then a hush falls as a spotlight sweeps across the ornate old movie palace and comes to rest on a distinguished executive in a tuxedo on stage. Nearby, the trophy gleams as the speaker lists the accomplishments of the person to be honored, gradually building the suspense.

Finally, he mentions the winner's name and amid thunderous applause, the winner rises from his seat and walks toward the stage grinning. The spotlight follows him as the crowd, now standing, continues the ovation, their faces displaying a mixture of admiration, envy, and joy. It is almost like the Academy Awards. Every detail is painstakingly arranged to create and build the excitement for Steve Magers, Huffy Bicycle's sales representative of the year.

The Sales Representative of the Year award is presented at Huffy's annual sales meeting in August. In attendance are the 70 salespeople from the five independent rep firms that represent the company nationwide, plus Huffy's staff and top management. The purpose of the award is to set the rep of the year up as an example to new reps. "We are in essence saying this is the person we think, particularly this year, put all the pieces together and ran their business as Huffy would like it to be run," said Steve Goubeaux, Huffy Bicycle's national sales manager and administrator of the recognition program. "Young people in the organization model themselves after what appears to be a winning style, and that is what we are trying to set up."

Reprinted permission of Sales and Marketing Management June 1986.

TIME OUT — *Designing a Municipal Identity*

Building and maintaining an identity is not only an organizational necessity but also a municipal necessity. The city of Edmonton in Alberta, Canada, has the slogan "City of Champions" to exemplify its identity, but words are not enough. You have to back up the statement with actions. To this end, the city has actively sought and hosted major events, such as the Commonwealth Games, the Universiade Games, the World Track and Field Championships, and the World Masters Games. It actively supports its professional sport teams, the Edmonton Eskimos and the Edmonton Oilers, as well as myriad minor league teams. Athletes continue to comment

on the great fans in Edmonton and how they support their teams. But Edmonton also carries the "champions" concept outside the arena of sport. Its citizens actively volunteer and turn out in droves to support causes to combine sport and other areas. In February 2005, Brent Saik built his own makeshift hockey rink and hosted the world's longest hockey game—as a fund-raiser and record-breaking activity—along with 39 other hockey players. The men played continuously for 240 hours to raise money for cancer research. This is just one example of the meaning of "City of Champions."

wrong impression about the role of the center's administration.

In turn, **physical stimuli** include such activities as coffee breaks and mail delivery. These events can become rituals. They often determine who talks to whom and when. They establish patterns of interaction in a sport organization and, as such, how information is channeled.

Finally, **symbolic artifacts** individually or collectively provide clues about a sport organization's culture. Banners in hockey or basketball arenas, trophies and pictures of past teams and successful individual players, and the like are artifacts that convey a message about the team as a successful organization.

Thick and Thin Cultures

The strength of a sport organization's culture will vary from one company to another. Peters and Waterman (1982, p. 75) suggest that in the organizations they studied, "the dominance and coherence of culture proved to be an essential quality of the excellent companies." Most sport organizations strive to develop strong, or what are usually referred to as thick, cultures. A **thick culture** is one in which the members of the sport organization agree about the importance of certain values and employ them in their daily routines. A thick culture helps hold an organization together by making frequent use of stories, rituals, slogans, and so on. Also, employees will be recruited into

the organization because they are seen to fit with the culture that exists. This fit is further developed through the use of indoctrination ceremonies, training programs, and orientations in which new employees are expected to be involved.

Joe Montgomery built a thick culture at Cannondale with his 11-point corporate philosophy as a base. But Cannondale's culture, like any thick culture, is more than just words on paper—the words are put into practice. The company practices its credo about caring for employees by promoting from within. Ted Kutrumbos started at Cannondale loading trucks; he rose through the ranks and became company president. Cannondale also demonstrates its concern for employees by sharing profits with them. Flexibility in working conditions is encouraged by having no formal job descriptions and moving people to jobs they enjoy ("A Freewheeler," 1989).

In a **thin culture** we don't see common values or the type of activities that Cannondale uses to build its culture. While thin cultures can be found in all types of sport organizations, one example could be a university faculty that encompasses both a department of sport studies and an athletic department. The dominant values among the staff involved in the athletic program will be ones concerned with producing the best teams, recruiting "blue chip" players, and catering to alumni. The sport studies staff will be more concerned with publishing and generating research grants. While these values are not mutually exclusive, their very presence can serve to produce a thin culture. A

TIME OUT   *Sport as a Component of Our Media Culture*

Sporting contests have always captivated the human imagination. From the spectacle of competition in Rome's Coliseum to Boston's Fenway Park, sport events have been and continue to be popular. As further evidence, sport has infiltrated all parts of the media beyond the radio or television broadcasting of live contests. A variety of movies, such as *Bend It Like Beckham, Friday Night Lights, Girlfight, Million Dollar Baby, Remember the Titans, Rocky, Breaking Away,* and *When We Were Kings,* all have a sport as the central theme. The recent popularity of reality television also incorporates sport into shows such as *Survivor* (physical activities required), *The Amazing Race* (a footrace around the world), *Making the Cut* (hockey), and *The Contender* (boxing).

Sport is more accessible than ever in our culture. Outlets, from the traditional print media, television, and radio to the more high-tech satellite transmissions and the Internet, allow sport fans to stay up to date with their favorite sport 24 hours a day.

	No				Yes
1. Existence of specific slogans?	0	0	0	0	0
2. Existence of some dominating stories in the company?	0	0	0	0	0
3. Existence of well-known heroes in or at least for the company?	0	0	0	0	0
4. Existence of symbolic actions or symbols?	0	0	0	0	0
5. Overlapping social rituals and social norms?	0	0	0	0	0
6. Existence of a specific language in the firm?	0	0	0	0	0
7. Does the company have a history which is considered long?	0	0	0	0	0
8. Does membership last for many years?	0	0	0	0	0
9. Lack of acceptable cultural alternatives for members of the company?	0	0	0	0	0

Figure 14.3 *Assessing the strength of corporate culture.*

Reprinted from *Long Range Planning*, volume 20, C. Scholz, Corporate culture and strategy: The problem of strategic fit, page 82, Copyright 1987, with kind permission from Elsevier Science Ltd, The Boulevard, Langford Lane, Kindlington OX5 1GB, UK.

thin culture will also be found in sport organizations where the membership is constantly changing or has only been a part of the organization for a short period of time (cf. Schein, 1984).

Scholz (1987) has produced a simple set of questions to help determine how strong (thick) or how weak (thin) an organization's culture is (see figure 14.3). If the answers to the questions are mainly toward the "no" end of the continuum the organization's culture can be considered thin. More "yes" answers indicate a thick culture.

One or More Cultures

Implicit in our discussion so far has been the idea that sport organizations have one single culture. This notion is implied in many of the definitions of organizational culture when they talk about shared understandings and common values. It is, however, somewhat idealistic to suggest that all members of a sport organization will think alike. The reality, that different people in different parts of the organization actually have different values and employ different norms of behavior, does not deny the possibility of "an organizational culture"; rather, it highlights the fact that sport organizations actually have a dominant culture, which reflects the core values of the majority of people in the organization (or at worst those with the most power), and a series of subcultures. Gregory (1983), for example, argues that organizations should be seen as **multicultural**. Meyerson and Martin (1987, p. 630) extend this line of thought to suggest that, because "organizations reflect broader societal cultures and contain elements of occupational, hierarchical, class, racial, ethnic, and gender-based identifications [they] . . . create overlapping, nested subcultures." Slack and Hinings' (1992) work on change in Canadian national sport organizations showed how a culture built around values for volunteer control and governance clashed with a new developing culture based on more professionally and bureaucratically oriented values. Subcultures may also develop in different departments of a sport organization. For example, the research and development department of a company producing sport equipment will most likely exhibit a somewhat different culture from the sales department. While sport managers should strive to develop unified values in the organizations they manage, it is also important for them to realize that such a goal is unlikely to be fully achieved. In actuality, as Meyerson and Martin (1987, p. 631) point out, organizations are composed of a "diverse set of subcultures that share some integrating elements of a dominant culture." It is this diversity and these common elements of culture that have to be managed.

Organizational Culture and Effectiveness

Many of the popular writers on organizational culture have stressed the links between a strong (thick) culture and an effective organization (cf. Deal & Kennedy, 1982; Peters & Waterman, 1982). Arogyaswamy and Byles (1987, p. 648) suggest, however, that it is erroneous to infer from these popular works "that there is one best culture,

---

TIME OUT *Club Corporation of America: Building a Thick Culture*

Club Corporation of America (CCA) is the leading North American company in the golf and country-club business. One of the keys to CCA's success has been its commitment to building a culture that emphasizes service for its members. CCA has developed a slogan to install a service mentality among staff members: It's an acronym for PRIDE—personal recognition is desirable every day. The same slogan applies to the special attention and treatment the CCA affords its staff.

CCA's hiring philosophy emphasizes attitude more than aptitude. The formal screening process includes a battery of psychological tests. "We want people who really feel that it is noble to turn someone else on," says Bob Dedman, chairman of the board of CCA. Every employee is continually involved in some aspect of the company's extensive training program, the Educational Series for Club Operations, or ESCO. New employees recruited from hospitality programs or other segments of the industry are taught ("brainwashed," as Dedman puts it) the CCA way, and seasoned employees attend seminars regularly to broaden and update their skills. In addition, the company has several hundred people in their management training program. CCA likes to promote from within and its management classes are filled with a mix of MBAs and maître d's. Typically, trainees spend a year or two as assistant managers in a club near the corporate headquarters before an appropriate manager's job opens up.

The success of the training program is measured continuously. In addition to frequent tests on such subjects as etiquette, wine regions, and labor law, the clubs are scrutinized closely by the regional office. Each club uses a standardized bookkeeping system and club managers get a call from regional managers if the numbers show any significant deviation from the established norms. There is also a formal—and often unannounced—inspection of every club at least once a year.

In keeping with CCA's priorities, however, the ultimate evaluators are the members. CCA has a set of quality standards but it is up to each club manager to go beyond those standards, depending on the needs of that club's membership. The company hires independent research firms to do annual in-depth surveys of every club's membership and staff, and to compare the results with a substantial data base.

Reprinted by permission of Club Industry.

which if established in firms, would lead to success." Rather, they suggest that certain types of cultural characteristics are appropriate in certain types of organizations. To understand culture and its relationship to performance in sport organizations, it is necessary to look at the various contingencies that influence the organization. To be effective there must be a fit between such variables as strategy, environment, technology, and culture.

Porter (1980a), for example, emphasized that to be successful an organization that adopts a cost-leadership strategy (see chapter 6) will be required to develop a culture that emphasizes financial efficiency and close attention to reducing costs. Skinner, Stewart and Edwards (2004) illustrated how the changes in the Queensland Rugby Union were meant to lead to professionalism by generating and implementing policies through a governmentlike technology; such structural and cultural changes resulted in a managerialist culture. A company like W.L. Gore, which follows what Miles and Snow (1978) refer to as a prospector strategy, requires a culture that emphasizes creativity, high levels of horizontal communication, and some degree of risk taking.

Sport organizations that operate in stable environments should seek to develop thick cultures. However, if its environment is rapidly changing, a thick culture may actually be detrimental to the performance of a sport organization. Thick cultures by their very nature are hard to change, but dynamic environments demand that if organizations are to be successful they must change as their environment changes.

The use of different technologies also requires a different culture. In a company like Victoriaville or Sherwood-Drolet, which mass-produces hockey sticks, we would expect to find a culture where little emphasis is placed on individual initiative but where control and conformity to hierarchical communications are emphasized. In contrast, in a company like Heery, which designs custom sport facilities, we would expect to find a culture that supports creativity, group work, and a high level of horizontal communication.

Creating, Managing, and Changing a Sport Organization's Culture

A sport organization's culture doesn't just happen; it is created and developed over a period of time.

Some sport managers will work hard to maintain an existing culture if they feel it is benefiting their organization. Others will want to change their organization's culture. Here, we look at the tasks of creating, maintaining, and changing a sport organization's culture, important issues for the people who manage these organizations.

Creating a Culture Within a Sport Organization

While there are several differing opinions about how culture is created within an organization (cf. Louis, 1985; Scholz, 1987), most researchers agree that the founders of an organization have a fairly significant impact on establishing its culture. There is also general agreement that the original ideas of the founder will continue to influence the organization for a long time, sometimes even after the founder is no longer with the organization (cf. Schein, 1983). Strasser and Becklund's (1991) book shows, for example, how the informal operating codes and freewheeling atmosphere created by Philip Knight and the University of Oregon track colleagues who joined him in Nike's early years continued to influence the organization, well after it was established as a major company in the athletic footwear industry.

Peters and Waterman (1982) describe two important ways of developing culture for those who lead organizations. The first method, they suggest, operates at a high level of abstraction and involves the setting of a vision. The founder or leader of a sport organization must generate excitement and enthusiasm about the fundamental values and purpose of the organization. For Philip Knight the purpose of Nike was clear: to produce good quality shoes at a reasonable price for U.S. athletes and to push Adidas into the number two spot in the industry. For Sheri Poe, head of Ryka, a small but rapidly growing athletic footwear company, her vision is to produce aerobic shoes designed especially for women and to work on behalf of women.

The second of Peters and Waterman's (1982, p. 287) suggestions is that founders or leaders can help develop culture by their attention to detail. They are to directly instill "values through deeds rather than words: No opportunity is too small." John Stanton ran to get fit and then opened a store called the "Running Room." Stanton continues to promote health and exercise by hosting clinics and running with his clients. Sheri Poe has attempted to instill as part of Ryka's culture a belief that the organization should work on behalf of women. To this end, Poe has done more than just establish this belief as a part of the company's mission; she enforces it by putting 7 percent of her company's profits into a fund called Ryka ROSE (Regaining One's Self-Esteem Foundation), employing a predominantly female workforce (70 percent), and speaking out on women's issues (Stodghill, 1993).

Managing a Sport Organization's Culture

Once a sport organization's culture has developed, it has to be managed. Assuming the culture is one that the company wishes to maintain, the manager of a sport organization can do a number of things to sustain and reinforce the organization's culture.

Schein (1985, pp. 224-225) suggests five primary mechanisms:

1. What leaders pay attention to, measure, and control
2. Leader reaction to critical incidents and organizational crises
3. Deliberate role modeling, teaching, and coaching by leaders
4. Criteria for allocation of rewards and status
5. Criteria for recruitment, selection, promotion, retirement, and excommunication

We look briefly at these mechanisms now. It should be noted that Schein uses the term "leaders" instead of "managers." While there is some debate about whether or not the terms can be used synonymously in this book, we follow Yukl's (1998) suggestion that the two are interchangeable. For consistency the term "managers" is used in the subheadings.

What Managers Pay Attention to, Measure, and Control

Managers can reinforce the important aspects of a sport organization's culture by paying particular attention to these areas. As Schein (1985, p. 225) notes, paying attention may mean "anything from what is noticed and commented on, to what is measured, controlled, rewarded, and in other ways systematically dealt with." At L.L. Bean, the outdoor equipment supplier, great stress is placed on building a culture that emphasizes customer

service, a culture reinforced when Bean's own employees are treated well by their managers. Van Fleet (1991, p. 352) points out this practice:

> Employees are paid reasonable wages, are treated with dignity, and have ample opportunity for advancement. They are also given considerable freedom in how they do their job—as long as they do it well. Employees know that they can always put the needs and opinions of customers first, without fear of reprisal or rebuke from a supervisor who worries too much about the cost of something.

This attention to feelings and the dignity they are afforded by supervisors communicate to employees what the company believes in and how in turn they should treat customers. Hoeber and Frisby (2001) noted that managers can fail to see a mismatch of organizational values (gender equity in their case) and practices if they simply rely on the dominant narrative.

Managers' Reaction to Critical Incidents and Organizational Crises

If a sport organization faces a crisis or critical incident, the way the senior managers deal with the crisis can help reinforce an organization's culture. Schein (1985, p. 230) suggests that crises aid the transmission of culture because "the heightened emotional involvement during such periods increases the intensity of learning [and] if people share intense emotional experiences . . . they are more likely to remember what they have learned." Such learning may occur, for example, in an athletic department that has built a culture based on values of fair play and an ethical approach to running an intercollegiate program. If the athletic director dismisses a coach for violating some minor recruiting regulations, it may create a crisis situation for the organization, but it provides a signal to the remaining coaches that this type of behavior is inappropriate to this organization and thus serves to reinforce the culture within which they operate. Likewise, if a sport equipment manufacturer faces declining sales, the way this crisis is dealt with may strengthen its culture. For instance, if the company had previously tried to develop a culture stressing the importance of every employee, and all staff members, including senior managers, take a salary cut to prevent layoffs of production staff, the fairness of the gesture serves to heighten this cultural dimension. Often after these crises we hear managers say things like, "we are all better for what happened" or "we are stronger because of it." The implication is that organizational learning has taken place and certain values that underpin the sport organization's culture have been reinforced.

Deliberate Role Modeling, Teaching, and Coaching

Managers can stress the type of culture they are seeking to build in a sport organization through their own actions and by directly teaching and coaching staff. Bill Gore, who has been referred to several times in this book, is an excellent example of someone who used this approach to build the culture of his company. Gore would frequently wander through his production plants, meeting, talking to, and helping associates (as employees are called). He stressed that experienced associates should sponsor new associates and teach them the ways of the organization; ultimately these associates would become sponsors. In that way, the traditions and habits of cooperation and working together are managed and maintained, the essence of W.L. Gore's culture.

Criteria for Allocation of Rewards and Status

The members of a sport organization learn about the organization's culture by looking at what is rewarded, and likewise what is punished, or not rewarded, in their organization. As Schein (1985, p. 234) points out, "an organization's leaders can quickly get across their own priorities, values, and assumptions by consistently linking rewards and punishments to the behavior they are concerned with." For example, the chair of a department of sport management with a culture supporting research and scholarly writing can strengthen this culture by rewarding those faculty members who engage in this type of work. A sporting goods store trying to develop a culture based on customer service would reward sales clerks on the quality of service they provide, not on sales volume.

Criteria for Recruitment, Selection, Promotion, Retirement, and Excommunication

Schein (1985) suggests that one of the most subtle yet potent ways of reinforcing an organization's culture is through the selection of new members (cf. Schneider, 1987). These selection decisions, when coupled with the criteria used to promote,

pressure into retirement, or fire, are a very powerful means of strengthening and maintaining a sport organization's culture. There is, however, a problematic dimension to this type of approach, in that "organizations tend to find attractive those candidates who resemble present members in style, assumptions, values, and beliefs" (Schein, 1985, p. 235). Hall, Cullen, and Slack (1989) suggest it is one of the major reasons for the virtual exclusion of women from senior management positions in Canadian national sport organizations. Consequently, while a homogeneous group of people may strengthen a sport organization's culture (and certainly decisions about employee selection, promotion, and so on can reinforce a culture), managers must be sensitive to the fact that what Kanter (1977) calls "the homosocial reproduction of managers" can exclude certain groups from the upper levels of management.

Changing a Sport Organization's Culture

Change can involve increasing or decreasing the number of employees in a sport organization, expanding markets or product lines, and other kinds of structural modifications. However, "in a more subtle but equally important way [it also] requires a basic rethinking of the beliefs by which the company defines and carries out its business" (Lorsch, 1986, p. 97). Kanter (1984) calls this rethinking "culture change." Changing the culture of a sport organization is a long and often difficult process, because it involves changing values and beliefs that have been established over a period of years.

Changes in staff behavior do not necessarily signal that cultural change has taken place. The staff of a sport organization may comply with and exhibit the newly prescribed behavioral expectations while at the same time cling to the values and beliefs that underpinned the organization's previous structure and mode of operations. When this superficial compliance occurs, change is likely to be short-lived, and the sport organization involved is quite likely to revert to its former situation (cf. Kikulis, Slack, & Hinings, 1995b).

Lorsch (1986) suggests that when faced with the need for change, managers will first attempt to fix the problem with minor modifications. At times these incremental changes may be successful; however, the basic nature of the organization's culture remains the same. When environmental pressures are more severe, more substantive change is needed, calling for change in the culture of an organization.

Lorsch goes on to suggest that there are four basic stages to this change. The first of these stages he labels awareness. Top management gradually becomes aware that in order to ensure its survival, substantive change is needed in their organization, necessitating changes in the underlying pattern of values and beliefs within the organization. This awareness is followed by a period of confusion. Here, managers agree that existing beliefs are not working but cannot agree about the new direction. This confusion often results in the appointment of a new leader to guide the organization. When appointed, the new manager starts to develop a strategic vision for the organization and tries to commit other top managers to this vision. The vision that is created, while it involves fundamentally new ideas, is also meshed with aspects of the company's old culture. This interlocking is one way of helping minimize resistance to this type of change. The final stage of the change process Lorsch (1986) labeled experimentation. Here, companies experiment with new products, new markets, and new people until they arrive at a suitable situation. If in this stage the managers come to realize that their vision is not realistic, they may reformulate their strategic direction.

Slack and Hinings (1992) describe a similar process to that laid out by Lorsch (1986), occurring in Canadian national sport organizations (NSOs). Throughout much of the 1970s these organizations, faced with pressures from their major funding source (the Canadian government) to establish more businesslike operations, made incremental changes to their structure and operations. In the 1983-1984 period, when increased amounts of government funding escalated these pressures,

---

KEY ISSUES FOR MANAGERS

There are various features that make up a sport organization's culture, and it is a way for it to distinguish itself from other organizations in the same market. Kent and Weese (2000) showed there is a link between effective provincial sport organizations and their culture-building activities. It is the job of managers to make sure these activities are the correct fit for the company's goals and project the right image, because the organization's culture can have an impact on its competitive advantage—be it financial or otherwise (e.g., best company to work for). Also, having too many thin cultures within the organization can hinder this advantage. However, the central point here is that while culture is an important variable in determining the effectiveness of an organization, it is not (as many popular writers have implied) the only variable. A sport organization's culture must still *fit* with contingency variables such as strategy, environment, and technology.

While many managers may not often think about their organization's culture, they ultimately may have to adopt it. This is especially the case when the sport organization partners with another organization, as happens with strategic alliances. In such cases, it is very important to examine the corporate culture of both organizations to determine the fit between partners. The better the fit, the easier to set up and manage the alliance. If the two have completely different cultures, it could be a sign that the search should continue for a more compatible arrangement.

While we have presented ways to create and manage culture, what happens if a change in organizational culture is required? How do you determine if, in fact, change is occurring in the culture of an organization? Sathe (1985) suggests three tests. First, is there evidence of intrinsically motivated behavior: Are employees engaging in the expected behaviors without expectation of material gain? Second, is there evidence that employees "automatically do what seems to be appropriate in light of the desired culture without waiting for directions from the organization's leadership or prodding from the organization's systems?" (Sathe, 1985, p. 400). Finally, do people operate in a way that is counter to the old culture norms but in line with the new expectations? While Sathe (1985) notes that these tests are not foolproof, they can provide a reasonable indication of cultural change.

national sport organization members became confused. Should they continue to operate with the volunteer-based culture that had guided their operation for many years, or should they adopt the more professional bureaucratic and implicitly businesslike culture being advocated by government officials? As Slack and Hinings (1992, p. 127)

note, to deal with these pressures for cultural change, "some NSOs made fairly radical changes in their management structure." In several cases they appointed a new CEO, and often the first task in the transformation of the culture of these organizations was to create a vision for the organization.

SUMMARY AND CONCLUSIONS

Culture, one of the newest concepts in the study of organizations, has great potential to enhance our understanding of the structure and processes of sport organizations. A focus on organizational culture forces us to question some of the rational notions of the contingency perspective and start to consider sport organizations as complex patterns of human interaction. By studying a sport organization's culture, we are forced to pay attention to the somewhat intangible, but no less important, aspects of organizational life, such as the values and beliefs, the accepted modes of operation, and the shared assumptions that guide behavior within an organization. Culture is in fact often defined using these terms. Because it is somewhat difficult to see, researchers often study culture by looking at the stories, myths, symbols, language, ceremonies, and rites that are integral to life in an organization. The physical setting in which an organization exists, including its physical structure, physical stimuli, and the

symbolic artifacts it exhibits, are also important indicators of its culture.

Some sport organizations will try to develop strong or thick cultures to enhance behavioral consistency. However, if change is required this type of culture can be constraining. In contrast, thin cultures are easily changed.

While culture is often presented as a unitary entity, most sport organizations have a dominant culture and one or more subcultures. These competing cultures can lead to organizational conflict if they are not managed. Culture can contribute considerably to the effectiveness of a sport organization but it must align with the organization's strategy, technology, and environment.

The creation of a sport organization's culture is influenced greatly by the organization's founder. Culture can nevertheless be managed and, if necessary, changed; we outlined a number of ways that change can be managed.

KEY CONCEPTS

basic assumptions (p. 275)

beliefs (p. 275)

ceremonies (p. 279)

language (p. 277)

multicultural (p. 281)

myths (p. 275)

organizational culture (p. 274)

physical setting (p. 279)

physical stimuli (p. 280)

physical structure (p. 279)

rites (p. 279)

rituals (p. 275)

shared understandings (p. 275)

slogans (p. 277)

stories (p. 275)

symbolic artifacts (p. 280)

symbols (p. 275)

thick culture (p. 280)

thin culture (p. 280)

values (p. 275)

REVIEW QUESTIONS

1. What factors have contributed to the recent emergence of culture as a key variable in understanding organizational structure and processes?

2. What are the key characteristics used to define organizational culture?

3. How does the cultural context in which a sport organization operates vary from its corporate culture?

4. Select a familiar sport organization. Describe its culture.

5. What type of symbols do we find in a professional sport organization and how do they relate to the culture of the organization?

6. What role do stories and ceremonies play in developing and maintaining a sport organization's culture?

7. Some organizational theorists have suggested that a strong organizational culture is a substitute for high levels of formalization. Why would they suggest this connection?

8. When would it be beneficial for a sport organization to have a thick culture? When would a thin culture be beneficial?

9. Some researchers have argued that organizations are multicultural. Can you think of sport organizations that have competing cultures?

10. How would you expect the culture of a sport organization with a routine technology to vary from one that uses a less-routine technology?

11. What type of culture do you think would fit best with each of the four strategic types proposed by Miles and Snow?

12. How does the founder of a sport organization influence its culture?

13. If you were the athletic director at a small junior college, what type of action could you take to strengthen the culture of the athletic department?

14. How could the manager of a sport organization go about implementing a change in the organization's culture?

15. Under what conditions is changing a sport organization's culture most likely to be accepted?

SUGGESTIONS FOR FURTHER READING

A number of popular management texts deal to differing degrees with the issue of organizational culture. The most notable is Peters and Waterman's (1982) *In Search of Excellence*. However, despite the popularity of these books their academic content is limited. Better coverage of the major issues related to organizational culture can be found in Schein's (1985) *Organizational Culture and Leadership*; Deal and Kennedy's (1982) *Corporate Cultures: The Rites and Rituals of Corporate Life;* and Sathe's (1985) *Culture and Related Corporate Realities*. Also useful, albeit somewhat more challenging, material can be found in two collections of essays on organizational culture. The first of these, *Organizational Culture,* edited by Frost, Moore, Louis, Lundberg, and Martin (1985), contains work by some of the leading writers on culture who address such issues as whether organizational culture can be managed, how organizational culture should be studied, and how culture and the wider cultural context are linked. The second collection, edited by Pondy, Frost, Morgan, and Dandridge (1982), is titled *Organizational Symbolism*. It focuses on the symbolic capacity of organizations and its relationship to organizational culture. Essays are titled "Managing Organizational Symbols," "Making Sense of Organizational Symbols," and "Shaping Organizational Reality Through Language." Paul Bates' (1995) book *Strategies for Cultural Change* presents a somewhat different and more critical view of organizational culture. In addition to these texts, the editors of *Administrative Science Quarterly* produced a special issue on the topic of organizational culture (Vol. 28, No. 3, 1983) and the editors of *Organization Studies* produced a special issue on organizational symbolism (Vol. 7, No. 2, 1986).

Despite the great potential that sport organizations offer for the study of organizational culture, there has been little scholarly writing in this area of sport management. However, there are some exceptions. There is, notably, Weese's

(1995a, 1995b, 1996) work, which looks at leadership and organizational culture, Westerbeek's (1999) modeling of organizational culture in sport organizations, Doherty and Chelladurai's (1999) examination of cultural diversity in sport organizations, Kent and Weese's (2000) study of organizational effectiveness and culture, and Colyer's (2000) article "Organizational Culture in Selected Western Australian Sport Organizations."

CASE FOR ANALYSIS

Developing Organizational Culture in the Los Angeles Olympic Organizing Committee

Like all organizing committees for major sporting events, the Los Angeles Olympic Organizing Committee (LAOOC) had a fixed life span. Founded on March 26, 1979, the organization ceased to exist shortly after the games ended on August 12, 1984. Originally staffed by only a handful of employees, the LAOOC mushroomed to 2,500 in early 1984, and by the time the games began there were some 20,000 paid employees along with 50,000 volunteers. One of the problems faced by the LAOOC, like any group founded very quickly and lasting only a short time, was to get everyone to feel "a part of the organization." Specific plans were made to help people fit in, to remind them of the importance of the games, and to make them feel like they were a part of history.

The orientation program was fairly brief; there wasn't much time to train staff. The orientation meetings were held in the LAOOC headquarters. A drab building that had once been a helicopter plant, it had the wide-open floor plan typical of a manufacturing facility. The interior had been decorated with brightly colored banners and mobiles. Large colorful pillars had been added to the building, and the scaffolding that would be used to decorate the competition sites brightened up the place. The presence of these colorful decorations constantly reminded employees of why they were involved. Even getting into the headquarters was an exercise designed to reinforce the nature of the games. Security was a major concern to the organizers and each visitor to the headquarters had to pass through four security checks, ranging from verbal questioning to X-ray machines and frisking.

The actual orientation was conducted by senior staff members who talked about the organization's purpose and philosophy. They stressed that the athlete was the center of the games. They also underscored the financial conditions under which the games operated: Taxpayers were not to be burdened and new building was to be kept to a minimum. These were the "Spartan" games; there would be no excess costs. Stress was also placed on the long-term benefits to the community and the decentralization of services, some contracted out to private operators.

At the orientation each new staff member was provided with a policies and procedures manual. Four policies became frequent topics of conversation among staff: the dress code, the number of signatures needed on any transaction, the "Peter" [Ueberroth] tests, and the allocation of parking passes. The dress code was a conservative one. Women had to wear dresses (not shorts), stockings, and "proper undergarments." Men were expected to wear ties, and beards were not allowed. Some employees were offended by the code, although no one could ever remember anybody being fired for breaking the rules. One story was told of a woman wearing long shorts one day (because she was going to be moving boxes) being reprimanded by an older woman in "a gross polyester floral muumuu." The requirement of numerous signatures on any transaction was a reminder of the tight fiscal constraints under which the games were being run.

To develop an understanding of the games, several "Peter" tests were developed. One allegedly involved each new staff member being assigned a participating country. They were told that at any time the president of the LAOOC could call them into his office and quiz them about this country. The idea was that if a delegation from this country showed up, there was a source of current information available. It also helped the staff feel they held an important role in the operations, by being one of the few experts in this area. Another "Peter" test apparently involved staff being required to take a test on the history of the Olympics, details of the local community, and the LAOOC. A number of horror stories rapidly spread about the tests and although no one was known to have been fired as a result, Peter Ueberroth was said to have personally come down to acknowledge the only person ever to receive a perfect score.

The fourth policy area frequently discussed was parking. The limited spaces at the headquarters were allocated by department heads, by rank within the department, by seniority, or by favoritism. Who had passes and who had to park in the additional spots (20 minutes away) and catch the shuttle was a hot hallway topic.

Stories also grew up around other activities at the LAOOC. One concerned a staff member who was fired for not walking fast enough. Many of these stories were exchanged in the "Café de Coubertin," where staff was encouraged to eat by offering workers a $2.00 subsidy per day. The idea was to reduce downtime and to build camaraderie. A "Days to Go" calendar was updated, showing the progress of the Olympics torch relay. Inspirational Olympics news was shown at lunch, uniforms were modeled, and sports were demonstrated. All served to build excitement toward the games.

Jokes developed about official suppliers. There were questions about who was the "official toilet paper" supplier. Staff members were required to use IBM computers, Xerox copiers, and Brothers typewriters. They were given free M&Ms, Snickers, Coca-Cola, and Perrier. Delivery people from unofficial suppliers had to turn their company shirts inside out when they visited the headquarters. Distinguished guests visited frequently, each stressing the magnitude of the games and the important role the staff played in making the games a success.

Based on information in P. McDonald (1991).

Questions

1. What were the problems of building culture in an organization like the LAOOC, which was only in existence for a relatively short while?

2. How was culture built at the LAOOC?

3. What manifestations of culture can you see in this case? What others do you think there might have been?

4. What purpose did culture serve for this sport organization?

Chapter 15

Leadership and Sport Organizations

LEARNING OBJECTIVES

When you have read this chapter, you should be able to

1. explain the basic principles of the trait approach to understanding leadership and the types of studies emanating from this research,

2. explain the principles of the behavioral theories of leadership and the way this approach has been used in sport management studies,

3. explain the major research studies that have used the contingency approach to understanding leader effectiveness,

4. discuss the basic concepts that underpin theories of charismatic and transformational leadership, and

5. describe the types of leadership studies that could be conducted in the field of sport management.

LEADERS IN THE FIELD OF SPORT MANAGEMENT

Sheri Poe

In 1972 Sheri Poe, a first-year student at Southern Illinois University, was raped at gunpoint. Although she reported the crime to the authorities, Poe got little support because police, doctors, and even a therapist placed much of the blame for the attack on the fact that she was hitchhiking. Emotionally scarred by the rape, Poe dropped out of school and went through several years of psychological trauma, medical difficulties, and financial problems. She eventually moved to California where she met and married Martin

Birrittella, a marketing executive for a giftware company. As her recovery progressed, Poe began a walking program and then got into aerobics. When she suffered back pains from her exercise regime, Poe began looking at the design of aerobics shoes and noticed that they did little to accommodate the higher arch and narrower heel of most women. With Birrittella, Poe managed to scrape up enough money to start a small company to produce a workout shoe specifically designed for women. The company, called Ryka, was founded in 1987. With the help of a banker who was also an

(continued)

(continued)

Dr. Earle F. Zeigler, professor emeritus at the University of Western Ontario, is regarded as the founder of the academic field of sport management.

Dr. Donna Lopiano serves as the executive director of the Women's Sport Foundation.

become leaders in NASSM and other areas of physical education and sport studies. Dr. Zeigler has received many awards for his contributions to our field. Each year members of NASSM select an individual to give the Earle F. Zeigler lecture at a banquet held at the organization's annual conference. The award is given in honor of Dr. Zeigler's work as a leader in the field of sport management.

aerobics fanatic, the company went public in 1988. In 1993 Ryka had revenues of about $15 million. Poe has promoted the company as the only manufacturer of women's athletic shoes that is actually run by women; 70 percent of its workforce is female. She has also developed the Ryka ROSE (Regaining One's Self Esteem) Foundation as a part of her company. Ryka channels 7 percent of pretax profits to the foundation. Along with moneys raised through fund-raising ventures and special events, the profits are used to help women who have been the victims of violent crimes.

Dr. Earle F. Zeigler

Earle Zeigler is in many ways the founding father of the academic field of sport management. Educated at Yale, Dr. Zeigler taught in a number of Canadian and American universities. His numerous books and articles, many of which were written well before the founding of the North American Society for Sport Management (NASSM), were among the first academic works in the area. His ideas have influenced many people in the field, and his former graduate students have gone on to

Dr. Donna Lopiano

Dr. Donna Lopiano graduated from Southern Connecticut State College in 1968. She holds an MA degree and a PhD from the University of Southern California. Dr. Lopiano coached both men's and women's college volleyball and women's college basketball, field hockey, and softball. She was an outstanding athlete, participating in 26 national championships in four different sports. She was a nine-time All-American at four different positions in softball. Between 1975 and 1992 Dr. Lopiano served as the director of Intercollegiate Athletics for Women at the University of Texas in Austin. She is a highly respected leader in athletic administration, having served as the president of the Association of Intercollegiate Athletics for Women (1981); she was a member of the United States Olympic Development Committee (1984 to 1988), and chair of the NCAA Legislative Review Committee. Since 1992 she has been executive director of the Women's Sport Foundation, an organization committed to improving opportunities for women's involvement in sport. Dr. Lopiano was a keynote speaker at the 1993 conference of the North American Society for Sport Management.

Information on Sheri Poe was obtained from Commentary (1993) and Stodghill (1993).

Few people would argue that Sheri Poe, Earle Zeigler, and Donna Lopiano are leaders in the field of sport management. But what is it that makes them leaders? They all come from different backgrounds, they have all had different accomplishments, and each works in a different sector of the field of sport management. Leadership is in many ways one of the great mysteries in the field of management. While Bass and Stogdill's *Handbook of Leadership* (Bass, 1990a) contains over 7,500 citations (Weese, 1994), Bennis and Nanus (1985, p. 4) commented on the state of leadership research that "never have so many labored so long to say so little."

The popularity of leadership research in the broader field of management is also reflected in the sport management literature. Paton (1987), after a thorough review of research in the field, concluded that leadership was the topic most frequently studied by sport management scholars. However, despite the proliferation of leadership studies in sport management, most of the work has been descriptive and atheoretical, and rarely uses in any meaningful or substantive way the leadership literature that exists in the broader field of management. (Work by Chelladurai and his colleagues [1978, 1980, 1983, 1987b] and research by Weese [1995a, 1995b, 1996] are the exceptions to this general trend.) There has also been little attempt to tie this work on leadership to other organizational phenomena, and because of this it has contributed little to our understanding of the structure and processes of sport organizations.

In this chapter we look at the topic of leadership, although any comprehensive review of all the literature in this area is beyond the scope of a textbook. We look at the major theoretical approaches to the study of leadership, specifically the trait approach, the style (or behavioral) approach, and the contingency (or situational) approach (Bryman, 1992). In addition, we look at the currently popular notions of charismatic and transformational leadership. After reviewing the theoretical literature and the way it has been used in the field of sport management, we examine some of the problems with work on leadership, and make some suggestions regarding the type of leadership research that should be undertaken in our field.

Trait Approach

The trait approach was one of the earliest approaches to leadership research. Its basic premise is that good leaders are born, not made. That is, leaders possess certain personal qualities that distinguish them from other members of an organization. Early researchers used psychological tests to try to identify these traits, but within this research little attention was paid to how effective these leaders were. The type of traits most frequently examined by researchers can be classified into three categories: the individual's physical characteristics (height, physical appearance, age); intellectual qualities such as intelligence, speaking ability, and insight; and such personality features as emotional stability, dominance, and sensitivity.

In a comprehensive review of 124 studies based on the trait approach carried out between 1904 and 1948, Stogdill (1948) found some support for a difference in the traits exhibited by leaders and those exhibited by nonleaders. Despite this supportive evidence, Stogdill's results showed considerable variance from one situation to the next, causing him to conclude that "the qualities, characteristics, and skills required in a leader are determined to a large extent by the demands of the situation in which he is to function as a leader" (Bass, 1981, p. 65).

While some suggested that Stogdill's 1948 review had brought an end to trait research, he conducted another review of such research in 1974 and uncovered that 163 studies of this type were conducted between 1949 and 1970. Figure 15.1 shows some of the **leadership traits** identified by Stogdill (1974) in his 1974 review. The studies included in the 1974 review were more methodologically sophisticated than the earlier research studies, leading, arguably, to more consistent results than those found in the 1948 review (Yukl, 1998). Following the 1974 review Stogdill retreated somewhat from his earlier position and suggested that this work and similar reviews by others had placed too much emphasis on situational factors and downplayed the universal traits that certain leaders seemed to possess. He concluded:

"The leader is characterized by a strong drive for responsibility and task completion, vigor and persistence in the pursuit of goals, venturesomeness and originality in problem-solving, drive to exercise initiative in social situations, self-confidence and a sense of personal identity, willingness to accept the consequences of his or her decisions and actions, readiness to absorb interpersonal stress, willingness to tolerate frustration and delay, ability to influence other people's behavior, and the capacity to structure social interaction systems to the purpose at hand" (Bass, 1990a, p. 87).

Active and energetic

High socioeconomic background

Superior judgment

Aggressive and assertive

Objective

Enthusiastic

Self-confident

Responsible

Cooperative

Being above average height

Well educated

Speaks well

Independent

Resourceful

High personal integrity

High achiever

Interacts easily

Good interpersonal skills

Figure 15.1 *Leadership traits.*
Based on Stogdill's 1974 review and B.M. Bass (1981).

Stogdill's position should not be accepted as some sort of claim for the absoluteness of trait research. Rather, it reflects a belief that the possession of certain traits can increase the chances of a leader being successful in certain situations.

Research on leadership traits has given rise to other more substantive lines of inquiry. However, even as recently as 1991 Kirkpatrick and Locke suggested that traits such as drive, the desire to lead, honesty and integrity, self-confidence, cognitive ability, and knowledge of business were important leadership qualities. The popular press also still continues to describe the leadership abilities of such individuals as coaches and team managers in terms of the traits they exhibit.

One of the research themes to develop from earlier work on leadership traits has been concerned with the processes of managerial selection and recruitment. Commonly referred to as the **assessment center approach**, the focus of this research is to use various tests, some of which are job related, to identify traits that can predict management potential and the ability to progress to the higher levels of an organization (Gaugler, Rosenthal, Thornton, & Bentson, 1987). The assessment center approach uses projective

and situational tests. One such test is the in-basket exercise, a hypothetical situation in which a candidate has a certain amount of time to act on the directives that accumulated in the "in basket," to determine if the candidate has management traits and skills. These tests may often be accompanied by exercises to assess such skills as writing and oral communication. Many organizations, including some in the sport industry, use these kinds of tests to improve their managerial selection and promotion processes. The traits that best predict advancement can include such qualities as resistance to stress, the tolerance of uncertainty, and the candidate's level of activity (Bray, Campbell, & Grant, 1974). The assessment center approach, and much of the other work that has emanated from trait research, has one major limitation for our understanding of leadership: While it has been designed to identify those traits that predict managerial effectiveness or advancement, it does not necessarily follow that these are useful predictors of good leadership, although as Bryman (1986, p. 34) notes, "writers such as Yukl (1981) and Bass (1981) appear, at least by inference, to take assessment center studies . . . to be relevant to the study of leadership." The assessment center approach has also been criticized because results may be influenced by the gender of the assessor and the assessee (Walsh, Weinberg, & Fairfield, 1987).

Another area of research emanating from the trait studies of leadership seeks to identify **managerial competencies,** or skills. Several researchers in our field have attempted to utilize this approach to determine the competencies required by sport managers. Zeigler and Bowie (1983), for example, argued that sport managers need the types of skills identified by Katz (1955): technical skills (knowledge about the manner in which certain specialized activities are carried out and the expertise to use the equipment related to that activity), human skills (knowledge about interpersonal relationships, the ability to communicate effectively, and establish working relationships), and conceptual skills (the ability to think logically about one's work situation, to formulate complex ideas, and solve problems). Zeigler and Bowie (1983) add that sport managers should also have personal skills (the ability to improve in areas such as perception, assertiveness, and negotiation) and conjoined skills (the ability to balance technical, human, and conceptual skills and employ them in combination to achieve a goal).

More recently Jamieson (1987) also argued for a competency-based approach to sport

TIME OUT   *Hockey and Business: The Traits of Success*

Wayne Gretzky is a leader in the sport of hockey. Most people, even those who aren't hockey fans know some of Gretzky's accomplishments. During his career he's broken records for number of goals, assists, and points and won trophies for sportsmanship, highest scorer, and most valuable player. While in the NHL he led his team to the Stanley Cup championship. The hockey legend's influence didn't stop there. Gretzky was instrumental in the management of Team Canada (Canada's hockey team) at the 2002 Winter Olympic Games and the 2004 World Cup of Hockey, where the teams won gold medals each time. Off the ice, he participates in countless charity functions and is now co-owner of the Phoenix Coyotes hockey team. He's reached a level of renown that prompted Andy Warhol to paint his portrait along the way.

Mark McCormack, who passed away on May 16, 2003, was a leader in the business of sport. He started his business, International Management Group (IMG), by shaking the hand of a young golfer named Arnold Palmer in 1960. Since then IMG has grown to become the world's top sport and lifestyle marketing and management company. With a staff of more than 2,200 in 70 offices in 30 countries, IMG represents hundreds of athletes, artists, celebrities, entertainers, writers, musicians, television properties, and prestigious organizations from around the world, including Olympic Games organizing committees.

Based on information in CBC.ca (2004), and IMG (2005).

management. She suggested that sport managers need competence in such areas as business procedures, resource management, personnel management, planning and evaluation, and programming techniques. Unfortunately, most studies on competencies are often seriously flawed; they are often either too general, and produce patently obvious findings (e.g., sport managers need good decision-making skills), or they fail to recognize that different competencies are required, to a greater or lesser extent, in the various sectors of the sport industry. For example, the skills needed by the CEO of a professional basketball franchise will be quite different from those required by the volunteer president of a community sport club. McLennan (1967) has shown that the skill requirements of managers vary depending on such factors as the nature of the organization, its size, and the extent to which decisions are centralized or decentralized. The impact of such contingencies has not been addressed in the sport management literature.

Style or Behavioral Approach

As Stogdill's (1974) review showed, trait research was alive and well through much of the 1950s and 1960s. Leadership research during this time, however, moved increasingly toward what are called studies of leadership style or leadership behavior. The focus of this research is to identify the style of leadership or leader behaviors most likely to increase the effectiveness of subordinates. This concern with how leaders or managers treat employees paralleled the growth of the human relations school of management. Conducted primarily by psychologists, the two research programs that best exemplify the **style approach** are what are referred to as the Ohio State Studies and the Michigan Studies. We look briefly at the major concepts employed in both approaches and, where possible, the work conducted in sport management using the ideas they contain.

The Ohio State Studies

The Ohio State researchers (Fleishman & Harris, 1962; Fleishman, Harris, & Burtt, 1955; Halpin, 1957; Halpin & Winer, 1957; Hemphill & Coons, 1957) used questionnaires to identify the types of behaviors in which leaders engaged, that is, their leadership style. From a list of about 1,800 possible leader behaviors these researchers developed a list of 130 questions. The instrument, known as the Leader Behavior Description Questionnaire (**LBDQ**), was administered to 300 individuals, mainly people involved in the military. The resulting factor analysis of the completed questionnaires showed that subordinates conceptualized their leader's behavior as occurring primarily along two dimensions: the extent to which the leaders exhibit consideration, and what is referred to as initiating structure. **Consideration** is "the extent to which leaders promote camaraderie, mutual trust, liking, and respect in the relationship between themselves and their subordinates" (Bryman, 1992, p. 5). The term **initiating structure** concerns the degree to which leaders structure their own work and that of their subordinates to obtain the organization's goals. Examples of actions under initiating structure include creating job descriptions, establishing performance standards, ensuring subordinates work to maximum performance levels, and establishing deadlines.

The initial conception of these two dimensions was that one was in some ways the antithesis of the other. That is, leaders who scored high on consideration were likely to score low on initiating structure and vice versa, and initiating structure was the primary correlate of effective performance. Research by Halpin (1957), however, showed that leaders who scored high on both dimensions were seen as effective by their superiors, while at the same time having subordinates who were satisfied in their jobs.

Over the years the LBDQ has been modified (the latest version is termed the LBDQ-Form XII) and has been used in some capacity in many leadership studies (cf. Katerberg & Hom, 1981; Larson, Hunt, & Osborn, 1976; Schriesheim, 1980). Bryman (1992), nevertheless, suggests that despite its popularity, the Ohio research and much of the other research characteristics of the style approach are open to a number of criticisms. First, the findings from LBDQ studies have produced inconsistent and, in some cases, statistically insignificant results (cf. Fisher & Edwards, 1988). Second, the studies using this approach rarely take into account situational factors; when they have, most notably in the path-goal approach (House, 1971; House & Mitchell, 1974), there has been "a tendency for atheoretical investigations of particular moderating variables" (Bryman, 1992, p. 7). A third problem Bryman (1992) identifies is that, because most LBDQ-type studies are cross-sectional, the direction of causality is rarely established; hence, it is wrong to conclude that leadership style influences factors such as group performance or satisfaction—quite possibly group performance and job satisfaction could influence leadership style. A fourth concern is the tendency of studies in the Ohio State tradition to focus on group-level or averaged responses,

a situation by which the leader's relationship to individual organization members is masked. This tendency is problematic because we know leaders treat individual subordinates differently. There is also a failure in LBDQ studies to address the question of informal leadership, a relevant practice in many organizations. Finally, there are concerns about the validity of LBDQ measures (cf. Rush, Thomas, & Lord, 1977).

Despite these shortcomings LBDQ-type studies have been used by researchers in the sport management field. Olafson and Hastings (1988) used the LBDQ-Form XII to assess administrative behavior, relating it to what they term personal style. Their results suggest that personal style is important in understanding a leader's decision-making behavior. Snyder (1990) used the LBDQ to examine the effect of leader behavior on intercollegiate coaches' job satisfaction. His work showed that the degree of consideration exhibited by leaders (athletic directors) was significantly correlated with coaches' satisfaction with their work and their supervision. Initiating structure did not correlate with either work satisfaction or supervision. In another study using the LBDQ, Branch (1990) looked specifically at athletic directors and the effect of their behavior on the effectiveness of intercollegiate athletic organizations. Using athletic directors' self-perceptions of their level of consideration and initiating structure, Branch concluded that "effective athletic organizations have leaders who are more predisposed to goal and task accomplishment than to developing good interpersonal relationships with their subordinates" (p. 161). The seemingly contradictory findings of Snyder's (1990) and Branch's (1990) research draws attention to the theoretical and methodological problems of work that has used the LBDQ in sport management. Both these pieces of work exhibit many of the problems identified by Bryman (1986).

The Michigan Studies

At approximately the same time as the Ohio State research was being conducted researchers at the University of Michigan were also involved in an extensive program of leadership studies. The first group of these studies (Katz, Maccoby, Gurin, & Floor, 1951; Katz, Maccoby, & Morse, 1950) were directed toward determining the behaviors of effective leaders. Results showed that leaders in high-performing organizational units were more likely to

- clearly differentiate their role by spending less time doing the things that subordinates did and more time planning and supervising,

- be oriented toward their work group by being **"employee centered"** as opposed to **"production centered,"**

- not engage in close supervision of their subordinates and thus allow them more latitude in what they did,

- develop a sense of cohesiveness within their work group, and

- receive general rather than close supervision from their supervisors.

The results from the Michigan studies, along with information from the Ohio State research, were summarized by Bowers and Seashore (1966). These two researchers identified four dimensions of leadership emerging from the two sets of studies:

1. Support
2. Interaction facilitation
3. Goal emphasis
4. Work facilitation

The first two concepts focus on relationship-oriented behaviors, the second two on task-oriented behaviors. Bowers and Seashore (1966) argued that the practices they identified could be carried out by formal leaders or members of the particular work group. Hence they coined the terms **managerial leadership** and **peer leadership**. Taylor and Bowers (1972) developed a set of questions to assess the role played by peer and managerial leadership in contributing to the four dimensions identified by Bowers and Seashore (1966). The identification of the concept "peer leadership" drew attention to the role of informal leaders, something that had not been addressed in earlier leadership studies. It also laid the foundation for a whole series of subsequent studies that have looked at participative leadership (Miller & Monge, 1986; Strauss, 1977; Vroom & Yetton, 1973).

Summary of Behavioral Approaches to Leadership

The Ohio State and Michigan studies have a number of similarities. Both focus on the behavior of leaders or their style, not the personal qualities leaders possess. Both identify two dimensions of style, one focusing on organizational tasks and the other on employee relations. Much of the leadership research conducted in the 1970s and 1980s has its basis in the concepts that emanated from these two research programs (cf. Lord, Binning, Rush, & Thomas, 1978; Misumi & Peterson, 1985; Schriesheim, 1980; Stinson & Johnson, 1975). The Ohio State and Michigan studies are not without problems, and many of the criticisms of the Ohio State studies identified previously also apply to the Michigan studies.

Researchers in sport management (Branch, 1990; Olafson & Hastings, 1988; Snyder, 1990) have used the LBDQ developed by the Ohio researchers to conduct work on sport organizations. However, rarely if ever have any of the concerns identified about this approach been addressed in the sport management literature. In addition, although not specifically dealt with here, several studies have used the LBDQ to assess the leadership qualities of coaches as opposed to managers (Case, 1987; Chelladurai & Carron, 1983; Danielson, Zelhart, & Drake, 1975). When managers have been studied they are invariably athletic directors (Branch, 1990; Snyder, 1990); only Olafson and Hastings (1988) studied managers in other sectors of the sport industry.

Contingency or Situational Approach

One of the shortcomings of the Ohio State and Michigan studies, and indeed much of the work in this tradition, is its failure to take account of how contingency or situational variables moderate the relationship between the behavior of a leader and different outcomes. While it is an intuitively appealing notion that different types of leader behavior will be more appropriate than others in particular situations, not until the 1970s did we see the emergence of a significant body of research focusing in any systematic way on the impact of contingency variables—task structure, the characteristics of the environment, or subordinate's characteristics—on leadership effectiveness. Contingency theories of leadership "draw attention to the notion that there are no universally appropriate styles of leadership, [but that] particular styles have an impact on various outcomes in some situations but not in others" (Bryman, 1992, p. 11). In this section we focus on those theories of leadership that have placed contingency factors as the central focus of their analysis. We look specifically at three of the best-known **contingency approaches**: the path-goal theory of leadership, Hersey and Blanchard's situational theory, and Fiedler's LPC approach. The main ideas behind each of these approaches are outlined and when it exists, work in the field of sport management that used these approaches is discussed.

The Path-Goal Theory of Leadership

Developed primarily by House (1971) and his colleagues (House & Dessler, 1974; House & Mitchell, 1974) the **path-goal theory** of leadership is concerned with understanding how a leader's behavior influences the satisfaction and efforts of subordinates. Essentially the theory proposes that the influence of the leader's behavior on subordinate satisfaction and effort is contingent on situational variables such as the nature of the task being undertaken and the characteristics of the subordinates. These contingency variables "determine both the potential for increased subordinate motivation and the manner in which the leader must act to improve motivation" (Yukl, 1998, p. 266). They also influence the preferences that subordinates have for a particular type of leader behavior. House and Mitchell (1974) and Filley, House, and Kerr (1976) identify four types of leader behavior, shown in figure 15.2.

The path-goal model seeks to explain what effect different types of leader behavior will have under various situational conditions. When work is stressful, frustrating, tedious, or low in autonomy, **supportive leadership** will increase the satisfaction and effort of subordinates (House, 1971; House & Dessler, 1974; Schuler, 1976; Stinson & Johnson, 1975). This style of leadership is seen to enhance the intrinsic value of the task and, by increasing subordinate self-confidence and lowering anxiety, it raises the expectancy level that tasks will be successfully completed. When tasks are not stressful, frustrating, tedious, or dissatisfying supportive leadership does not have a major impact on the satisfaction level of subordinates or the amount of effort they put into their work. When tasks are unstructured and complex in nature, when subordinates have little experience in doing the tasks and no formalized procedures to help them complete their work, **instrumental leadership** (sometimes called directive leadership) will enhance the satisfaction and effort of subordinates. Indik (1986; cited by Yukl, 1989), in a meta-analysis, provided general support for the

Supportive leadership. The leader exhibits concern about the welfare of subordinates, considers their needs, and attempts to create a work environment that is pleasant and caring.

Instrumental (or directive) leadership. The leader places a great deal of emphasis on planning, coordinating, directing, and controlling the activities of subordinates.

Participative leadership. Leaders treat subordinates almost as equals. Subordinates are encouraged to let their views be known; there is a sharing of power with subordinates.

Achievement leadership. Leaders have confidence in their subordinates. Challenging goals are set for subordinates, and they are expected to assume responsibility for meeting these goals.

Figure 15.2 *Four types of leader behavior*

Based on information in A.C. Filley, R.J. House, and S. Kerr (1976). *Managerial process and organizational behavior,* 253. Scott, Foresman.

impact of instrumental leadership on employee satisfaction and motivation under conditions of low task structure.

While ideas about **participative leadership** are not as well developed as those about supportive or instrumental leadership, it is hypothesized that participation increases subordinate satisfaction and effort when tasks are relatively unstructured. Participative leadership, it is felt, can increase subordinates' understanding of the relationship between their efforts and goal attainment; it helps them select goals in which they are personally interested and hence toward which they are more likely to be motivated. It can also increase subordinates' control over their own work, thus increasing satisfaction. Indik's (1986) meta-analysis found support for the fact that participative leadership can in fact increase employee satisfaction when tasks are relatively unstructured.

Like participative leadership, work on **achievement leadership** has not been extensively developed. It is generally felt that achievement leadership "will cause subordinates to strive for higher standards of performance and to have more confidence in their ability to meet challenging goals" (House & Mitchell, 1974, p. 91) when tasks are unstructured. When tasks are straightforward, achievement leadership has little effect.

While there are questions about the conceptual underpinnings of the path-goal theory of leadership (Schriesheim & Kerr, 1977) and concerns over the direction of causality in some of the findings attributed to this approach (Greene, 1979), it has made a significant contribution to leadership research by helping researchers identify relevant situational variables. It has also given rise to a substantial body of research.

In the field of sport management Chelladurai and Saleh's (1978) work has its basis in the path-goal model. Building on House's (1971) ideas, Chelladurai and Saleh (1978) identify five types of leader behavior in the sport setting: training behavior, autocratic behavior, democratic behavior, social support, and rewarding behavior. It was shown that athletes in interdependent sports (essentially team sports) preferred coaches to emphasize training behavior (actions akin to the Ohio State concept of initiating structure) more than did athletes in independent sports (individual sports). Athletes in what are termed "closed" sports (there is low task variability, such as golf or swimming) preferred coaches to emphasize more training behavior than did those in what are termed "open" sports. Male athletes preferred more autocratic behavior and social support than females. Unfortunately, Chelladurai and Saleh's (1978) work focused only on athletes and coaches, not managers. No published work in sport management has used the path-goal approach to look at the contingencies influencing the leadership behaviors of sport managers.

Hersey and Blanchard's Situational Leadership Theory

Hersey and Blanchard's (1984) **situational leadership theory** is based on two types of leader behavior. **Task behavior**, very similar to the Ohio State concept of initiating structure, involves the leader in structuring how work is to be done. **Relationship behavior**, similar to the concept of consideration, involves providing support to employees and openly communicating with them. The mediating situational variable between task or relationship behavior and leader effectiveness is called **subordinate maturity**. Two dimensions make up this concept. The term job maturity describes the subordinate's technical ability; psychological maturity is the level of self-confidence and self-respect they bring to the task. Sub-

ordinates with high levels of maturity score high on both job maturity and psychological maturity. They possess the skills to do the task, will assume responsibility, and establish high aims for themselves. Subordinates with low maturity have little ability and low self-confidence. Although maturity is actually a continuum, Hersey and Blanchard divide the continuum up into four segments (see figure 15.3).

When subordinates show low levels of maturity in regard to the tasks to be performed, leaders who exhibit high task behavior are most effective; the leader provides direction by establishing clear ways of operating and standards of task accomplishment. At the medium levels of maturity (quadrants 2 and 3) leaders need to focus more on relationship behavior and gradually reduce the amount of direction they provide the subordinates as they exhibit more maturity relative to the task. At the highest level of maturity the leader offers little direction and allows the subordinate to make decisions about how tasks are carried out.

A leader can influence the maturity level of a subordinate by using what are termed **developmental interventions**, which may involve techniques such as reducing the amount of direction given a subordinate and allowing them to take responsibility for a task. If the subordinate does well, praise and support are used to strengthen the behavior. A more complex intervention, termed contingency contracting, involves negotiating

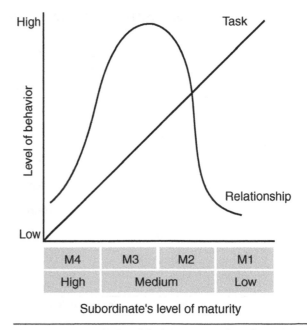
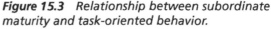

Figure 15.3 *Relationship between subordinate maturity and task-oriented behavior.*

the subordinate's tasks and responsibilities. The length of time may vary to "mature" to do the task well, depending on the nature of the task.

Hersey and Blanchard's work draws attention to the need for leaders to treat different subordinates in different ways as they progress in their work. It also draws attention to ways leaders can work with subordinates to build up their abilities and confidence level. There have been very few attempts, however, to empirically test the concepts and relationships outlined in Hersey and Blanchard's work, even in the general field of management and organization studies. No published work in the field of sport management has used this approach.

Fiedler's LPC Approach

Fiedler's (1967) approach is the oldest of the contingency theories of leadership. Unlike the path-goal approach and Hersey and Blanchard's work, both of which focus on leader behavior, Fiedler focuses on how situational variables moderate the relationship between leader traits and organizational effectiveness. The cornerstone of Fiedler's work is a measure called the **Least Preferred Coworker** (LPC) score. This score, an indicator of a leader's motivational traits, is developed using an instrument that asks leaders to think of the person with whom they can work least well, and to assess that person on a series of bipolar

descriptors. The 16 pairs of descriptors include adjectives such as pleasant–unpleasant, helpful–frustrating, cold–warm, supportive–hostile, and gloomy–cheerful. A leader who obtains a low LPC score is motivated by task accomplishment and will only be concerned with relationships with subordinates if the work unit is seen to be performing well. A leader who gets a high LPC score will, in contrast, be motivated to develop close interpersonal relations with subordinates; task-directed behavior is of a lesser concern, becoming important only when sound interpersonal relations have been established with subordinates and peers.

Mediating the relationship between the leader's motivational traits and group performance is a situation variable called situational favorability. Favorability is made up of three situational components:

1. **Leader–member relations:** the leader's personal relationship with the other members who make up the work group
2. **Position power of the leader:** the degree of formal authority the leader obtains from his or her position
3. **Task structure:** the extent to which the tasks the group have been assigned to perform are structured

The three components of situational favorability can give eight possible conditions (see table 15.1).

Table 15.1 Fiedler's Situational Favorability Factors and Leadership Effectiveness

Condition	Situational favorability			Effective leadership
	Leader–member relations	Task structure	Position power	
1	Good	High	Strong	Low LPC
2	Good	High	Weak	Low LPC
3	Good	Weak	Strong	Low LPC
4	Good	Weak	Weak	High LPC
5	Poor	High	Strong	High LPC
6	Poor	High	Weak	High LPC
7	Poor	Weak	Strong	High LPC
8	Poor	Weak	Weak	Low LPC

Adapted from F.E. Fiedler, 1967, *A theory of leadership* (New York: McGraw-Hill Companies), 34. By permission of author.

TIME OUT   *Effects of Culture as a Situational Variable Influencing Leadership Effectiveness*

Chelladurai, Malloy, Imamura, and Yamaguchi (1987) suggested that one of the situational variables that could influence leadership effectiveness is culture. They defined culture as the attitudes, beliefs, and values of a society. Using a sample of 106 male Japanese students and 156 male Canadian students, Chelladurai and colleagues used an instrument they had developed some years earlier with Saleh (Chelladurai & Saleh, 1980), the Leadership Scale for Sports, to assess the preferred leadership of the two samples. Their results showed that Japanese students preferred more supportive leadership than Canadian students. It was also found that Japanese students in modern sports (track and field, rugby, volleyball, and so on) preferred a more participative leadership structure than Canadian students. Japanese students in traditional sports (judo, kendo, and kyuto) preferred a more authoritarian (i.e., directive) style of leadership. The researchers concluded that both the cultural background of subordinates (athletes) and the type of sport in which they were involved were situational variables that could influence leadership effectiveness.

Based on information in P. Chelladurai, D. Malloy, H. Imamura, and Y. Yamaguchi (1987).

Fiedler suggests that task-oriented leader behavior (i.e., a low LPC leader) is most effective in situations of high situational favorability (conditions 1, 2, or 3) or unfavorable situations (condition 8). In situations that are moderately favorable or moderately unfavorable (conditions 4 to 7), someone who is more attentive to subordinate relations (a high LPC leader) will be more effective.

There have been a number of criticisms of Fiedler's model (Kennedy, 1982; Schriesheim & Kerr, 1977) and it has fallen out of favor within the general field of management and organizational studies. However, reviews of the large number of studies conducted using this approach (Peters, Hartke, & Pohlmann, 1985; Strube & Garcia, 1981) provide general support for the model.

Within the field of sport management, a number of doctoral dissertations have used the LPC instrument to examine leadership (cf. Soucie, 1994). However, in terms of published work there is very little research. Bagley (1975) used Fiedler's work to look at graduate departments of physical education. She found little support for Fiedler's model and suggested that these types of organizational subunits require relationship-oriented leaders. Chelladurai and Quek (1995) also used Fiedler's work to examine decision-making styles in high school basketball coaches. The LPC approach did not correlate to coaches' decision style choices.

Charismatic and Transformational Leadership

In the last 20 years or so leadership researchers have become increasingly interested in charismatic and transformational leadership. As Yukl (1989, p. 204) points out, the terms **transformational leadership** and **charismatic leadership** refer to the process of "influencing major change in the attitudes and assumptions of organization members and building commitment for the organization's mission or objectives. Transformational leadership is usually defined more broadly than charismatic leadership but there is considerable overlap between the two conceptions." This overlap is compounded by research that uses related terms such as "visionary leadership" (Sashkin, 1986, 1988; Westley & Mintzberg, 1989), "magic leadership" (Nadler & Tushman, 1989b), and "transferential leadership" (Pauchant, 1991). Bryman (1992, pp. 104-113) provides a good overview of the difference between transformational and charismatic leadership. In this section we first look at some of the major writings on charismatic leadership and then work at examining transformational leadership.

Charismatic Leadership

The notion of charisma has been around for a long time but it is Weber, in his book *Economy and Society* (1968), who is most often credited with first using the term to describe leadership in an organizational setting. Focusing primarily on religious groups and primitive tribes Weber saw leaders as gaining authority from their charisma. Charisma for Weber was "a certain quality of an individual personality by virtue of which he is considered extraordinary and treated as endowed with supernatural, superhuman, or at least specifically exceptional powers or qualities. These are such as not to be accessible to the ordinary person, but are regarded as of divine origin or as exemplary and on the basis of them the individual concerned is treated as a leader" (1968, p. 241).

Despite Weber's early writings on charisma and its links to leadership it was not until the late 1970s and early 1980s that organizational or management researchers started to embrace the concept and examine it in any systematic way (Etzioni, 1961 and Oberg, 1972 are two notable exceptions).

House's Research on Charismatic Leadership

House's (1977) work represents one of the first and in many ways most substantive attempts to understand charismatic leadership. His theory seeks to explain the characteristics of charismatic leaders and their behaviors. It is suggested that charismatic leaders can be distinguished from other leaders in that they are able to establish "follower trust in the correctness of the leader's beliefs, similarity of follower's beliefs to those of the leader, unquestioning acceptance of the leader, affection for the leader, willing obedience to the leader, identification with and emulation of the leader, emotional involvement of the follower in the mission, heightened goals of the follower, and the feeling on the part of followers that they will be able to accomplish, or contribute to the accomplishment of, the mission" (p. 191). House also stresses that charismatic leaders are likely to have self-confidence, a strong conviction about their own ideals and beliefs, and a desire for the power to be able to influence others.

A charismatic leader acts as a role model for followers, so that they will identify with the leader's values and beliefs. Leaders also engage in image-building to look competent and successful in the eyes of their followers. They present ideological goals that represent the types of values and beliefs they would like followers to share. There are high expectations set for followers to aspire to and charismatic leaders support and show confidence in their followers. Finally, charismatic leaders try to arouse motives relevant to the group's mission—the need to overcome a common foe, the need for excellence, affiliation, power, and the like. Phil Knight's desire to overcome Adidas and push it into second place in the athletic footwear market is an example of this type of motive.

Conger's Theory of Charismatic Leadership

Conger's initial work on charismatic leadership was conducted with Kanungo (Conger & Kanungo, 1987; 1988). Their approach is based on the idea that charisma is an attributional phenomenon. Leaders are attributed certain charismatic qualities by their followers. The focus of their research was to identify the types of leader behavior that result in these attributions.

Central to the attributional process is the creation, by the leader, of an "idealized goal" or vision that deviates sufficiently from the existing condition of the organization. Leaders are also seen as charismatic if they involve themselves in activities that call for self-sacrifice and high personal risk to achieve the vision they have created. They use unconventional means to achieve their vision and are able to assess environmental opportunities and threats realistically. Using this information they have to time the strategies they employ appropriately to help realize their vision. This type of leader is most likely to come to the fore when an organization is in a crisis, although crisis is not necessarily a precondition for their emergence. These people are confident in their ability to lead; they make great use of their personal power, for example, their expert knowledge, rather than their positional power, to commit others to their vision.

The concepts put forward by Conger and Kanungo (1987, 1988) were extended by Conger in his 1989 book *The Charismatic Leader: Behind the Mystique of Exceptional Leadership*. Conger essentially viewed the process of attribution that resulted in some individuals being seen as charismatic leaders as a series of stages. In the first stage, the leader senses opportunity and formulates a vision. The vision is designed to bring people in the organization together; it may be a result of dissatisfaction with the existing situation and can be a vehicle to challenge the status quo. The second stage involves the leader articulating the vision. The third stage requires the charismatic leader to build trust in the vision; he or she must be seen as having the ability to lead the organization toward achieving the vision. An emphasis on previous accomplishments and shared values with subordinates can help in building this trust. The final stage involves achieving the vision. Subordinates are empowered so that they feel they can help achieve the lofty goals that have been set. Achieving success along the way is an important factor at this stage.

Transformational Leadership

In part research on charismatic leadership in organizations has been a result of the growing interest in transformational leadership. In this section we look at the work of three of the best-known writers on transformational leadership.

Burns

The central focus of Burns' work is to contrast transformational leadership with what he refers to as transactional leadership. **Transactional leadership** involves the leader in some form of transaction with subordinates. Appealing to their self-interest, transactional leaders exchange pay or prestige for a subordinate's compliance with their orders. However, there is no enduring bond between the two parties. A relationship exists between leader and followers, but it does not unite the "leaders and followers together in a mutual and continuing pursuit of a higher purpose" (Burns, 1978, p. 20).

In contrast, transformational leadership involves "leaders and followers rais[ing] one another to higher levels of motivation and morality" (Burns, 1978, p. 20). Transformational leaders work by appealing to the ideals and values of subordinates. They seek to unite subordinates as they work toward a common purpose. Transformational leaders pay attention to and are sensitive to the needs of their subordinates as well as their own needs. They must appeal to the whole person and their total range of higher-level needs such as justice and equality. Lower-level emotions such as fear and greed have no place in transformational leadership. The bulk of the early work on leadership focused on transactional leaders.

Bass

Much of the research conducted on Burns' notion of transformational leadership has been carried out by Bass and his associates (Avolio & Gibbons,

1988; Avolio & Yammarino, 1990; Bass, 1985, 1990b; Bass & Avolio, 1989, 1990a, 1990b, 1990c; Hater & Bass, 1988; Yammarino & Bass, 1990). Unlike Burns, who saw transformational and transactional leadership as being ends of a continuum, Bass sees them as separate; a leader can be both transformational and transactional (Bryman, 1992). Bass would classify leaders like Adolph Hitler and David Koresh as transformational.

Bass suggests that transformational leaders enhance their subordinates' confidence and increase awareness of selected goals and how they may be obtained. They also inspire subordinates to look beyond their own self-interests and seek to satisfy such higher-level needs as self-actualization. For Bass, transformational leaders may be charismatic; they provide personal attention to the needs of subordinates, they seek to empower them, and they provide them with a constant flow of new ideas about ways to operate.

To determine the extent to which leaders exhibit the characteristics of transformational and transactional leadership, Bass and his associates developed the Multifactor Leadership Questionnaire (MLQ). The most common version of this instrument contains 70 items asking respondents to describe the behavior of a leader in seven areas of leadership (Bass & Avolio, 1990b):

- **Charismatic leadership:** the degree to which the leader is seen as charismatic
- **Inspirational leadership:** the extent to which a leader inspires subordinates
- **Individual consideration:** how much a leader gives personal attention to subordinates
- **Intellectual stimulation:** the way in which the leader promotes new ideas and challenges old ways of operating
- **Contingent rewards:** the way in which a leader rewards subordinates for following specific directions
- **Management by exception:** how leaders take action when irregularities occur
- **Laissez-faire:** the extent to which the leader abdicates his leadership role

The first four of these measurements assess transformational leadership behaviors; contingent rewards and management by exception assess transactional leadership, and laissez-faire is a type of nonleadership assessment. The scores from the MLQ are related to organizational outcome measures such as leader effectiveness, subordinate satisfaction, and subordinate motivation. The four transformational qualities, along with contingent rewards, are more likely to be associated with positive outcomes than management by expectation and laissez-faire.

Tichy and Devanna

In their 1986 book *The Transformational Leader*, Tichy and Devanna carried out a study of 12 CEOs. The focus of the study was to try to determine how those leaders went about transforming their organizations to meet the demands of a changing marketplace. With one exception, data were collected through interviews with the CEO and sometimes other members of the organization. Based on these interviews, Tichy and Devanna identified a three-stage process that takes place when leaders transform organizations.

First, the transformational leader must recognize a need to revitalize and change the organization. This recognition can be difficult, particularly when environmental changes are occurring gradually. The leader needs to convince other important people in the organization of the need for change. Tichy and Devanna suggest a number of strategies to help key organizational members recognize the need for change: encouraging people to look objectively at the organization and challenge the status quo, encouraging people from the organization to visit other organizations to see how they are managed and operated, evaluating organizational performance against that of competitors (not indicators from previous years), and creating an external network of contacts who can provide an objective assessment of the organization's performance. Once people recognize the need for change, the leader needs to establish what changes are necessary, and manage the transition process. Members of the organization will have to let go of existing values and beliefs and accept new ones, and there may be a change in the authority structure of the organization. The leader's job is to help people feel positive and confident about the transition.

One way of helping people feel better about the future is to create a vision of the way they want things to be. Vision is Tichy and Devanna's (1986) second stage. The vision cannot be one individual's ideas but must be the product of a diverse group of organization members. It must paint a picture of the organization sufficiently attractive to make people comfortable with the change process. The vision must provide a central purpose and a source of self-esteem for organizational members. The central component of the vision is the mission statement, which provides direction for organization members and reflects the values found in the vision. Following the establishment of a vision and a mission statement, more specific decisions have to be made: the allocation of rewards, the authority structure of the organization, and how senior members of the organization will be selected. Members of the organization must be informed about the benefits the vision will have for them and they must be made to feel a part of the implementation process.

The final stage of the transformational process involves what Tichy and Devanna (1986) refer to as institutionalizing the vision. A new group of people committed to the vision may be brought on board, and new structures, strategies, and policies put in place. These changes can be facilitated through such activities as planning workshops, conducting team-building exercises, establishing new positions, changing the reward structure of the organization, and redesigning appraisal systems.

In looking at each of the three phases, Tichy and Devanna (1986) identified a number of characteristics that distinguish transformational leaders from transactional leaders. Transformational leaders are visionaries who see themselves as change agents; they take risks, they believe in the people in the organizations, they articulate the core values that direct the organization, they learn from experience, and they handle the complexity and uncertainty that change brings.

Ulrich (1987b) extends Tichy and Devanna's (1986) work and applies it to the field of sport management. He suggests a six-stage process that sport managers need to adopt if they are to function as transformational leaders: creating and communicating the need for change, overcoming resistance to change, making personal commitment and sacrifices for change, articulating a vision, generating commitment to the vision, and institutionalizing the vision. Ulrich makes a number of suggestions as to how sport managers can operationalize these functions.

The Critique of Leadership and Some Suggestions for Leadership Research in Sport Management

As noted at the beginning of this chapter, it is impossible to conduct a comprehensive review of all the literature on the subject of leadership in a textbook of this nature. However, in this section, a brief overview of some of the strengths and weaknesses of leadership research is presented. Some suggestions are then made about the direction future leadership studies in the field of sport management could take.

The Critique of Leadership

As Pettigrew (1987) points out, for those scholars interested in the study of leadership, reviews of the field conducted throughout the past 20 years do not make comfortable reading. Stogdill (1974, p. vii) noted that "the endless accumulation of empirical data has not produced an integrated understanding of leadership." Miner (1975) even suggested that the concept of leadership should be abandoned, and Bass (1985) bemoaned the narrow and repetitive focus of leadership research focusing on such limited concepts as directive versus participative leadership and initiation versus consideration. Bryman (1986) describes past research as disappointing and suggests that future leadership researchers may be "clutching at straws." More recently Leavy and Wilson (1994) have criticized leadership research for being overly voluntaristic, that is, focusing too much on the actions of a single individual, and failing to consider the contextual pressures that shape leaders' actions. However, it is perhaps Kets de Vries (1994, p. 73) who sums up these concerns the best: "When we plunge into the organizational literature on leadership we quickly become lost in a labyrinth: There are endless definitions, countless articles, and never-ending polemics. As far as leadership studies go, it seems that more and more has been studied about less and less, to end up ironically with a group of researchers studying everything about nothing."

What, then, are the problems with leadership research and what types of studies should we in sport management be undertaking? One of the first problems is the failure of leadership research to produce conclusive findings; many of the complaints just cited refer to this shortcoming. While to a certain extent researchers have been able to describe the traits and behaviors that leaders possess, rarely have they been able to explain where these qualities come from, how they are developed, and why some leaders are successful when others fail. The literature has made no attempt to explain why leaders are described as effective at certain times and ineffective at others—a situation that

could obviously be applied to the myriad coaches and general managers who are "visionaries" when they win and buffoons when they lose!

Writing about leadership and organizational performance, Pfeffer (1977a) has suggested that leadership has become a repository for much of the unexplained variance. Lieberson and O'Conner (1972) found little support for the ability of leaders to influence performance; to be sure, studies of executive succession, many of which have been conducted on sport organizations, have produced inconclusive results.

Another major critique of leadership research is its failure to study leaders actually doing their jobs. Pettigrew (1987, p. 652) suggests some improvements:

> Approaches to leadership should be less short-range and atomistic—less reductionist. Leaders should be studied in natural settings using observational and other qualitative methodologies. Leadership should be examined through the holistic study of actual behavior rather than breaking down the activities of leaders and the responses of followers into categories of independent and dependent variables.

Certainly much of the leadership research in the field of sport management has been bivariate in nature. There has been no systematic attempt to study what it is leaders in sport organizations actually do and how they operate.

Leadership research should also become less reductionist in nature. Both Leavy and Wilson (1994) and Whittington (1993a) have criticized the leadership literature for focusing too much on individuals and not paying enough attention to the history and context of the organizations in which leaders operate. Similarly, Lieberson and O'Conner (1972, p. 29) suggest that "in emphasizing the effect of leadership [on organizational performance] we may be overlooking far more powerful environmental influences." Tied to this criticism is the tendency, particularly in the more recent work on charismatic and transformational leadership, to view leaders as men (and as Whittington, 1993b, p. 45 notes "men they almost always are"), heroes who ride in on white horses to rescue the organization in distress. Bennis and Nanus' (1985, p. 218) effusive statement exemplifies this deification of leaders:

> Leadership is "causative," meaning that leadership can invent and create

institutions that can empower employees to satisfy their needs. Leadership is morally purposeful and elevating, which means, if nothing else, that leaders can, through deploying their talents, choose purposes and visions that are based on the key values of the work force and create the social architecture that supports them. Finally, leadership can move followers to higher degrees of consciousness, such as liberty, freedom, justice, and self-actualization.

As Pettigrew (1987, p. 653) cryptically notes, this view is "hard to take." Such attributions of godlike qualities are found in much of the research on this type of leadership.

A final critique of the writing on leadership is the inherent gender bias in this type of research. Women are rarely used as examples of great leaders, either in the general management literature or the sport management literature. This issue is addressed more fully in the suggestions for future research outlined below.

Some Suggestions for Leadership Research in Sport Management

While there is considerable potential for many types of different research on leaders in the field of sport management, here we look briefly at five possible areas of study: shared leadership, leadership and organizational change, leadership and strategy, leadership and gender, and leadership and organizational culture. But first, we provide an alternative approach to leadership research, one through critical management.

Critical Management and Leadership

Wendy Frisby (2005) has argued that sport management research should use a critical perspective. The argument can especially be made for leadership research. Alvesson and Deetz (2000) can be of help here by providing a framework of three overlapping tasks. First, insight refers to examining and questioning taken-for-granted knowledge by focusing on "the complex relationships between local forms of domination and the broader contexts in which they are situated" (Frisby, 2005, p. 7) such as values, rules and policies, culture, and reward systems. Once this is known, the second task, critique, can occur, focusing on understanding how the various forms of domination (e.g., differ-

ences in power, information, and communication) benefit one group over another. Finally, the third task, transformative redefinition, is a description of how to change the situation—a task especially appealing to managers because it can provide new skills that can help the manager become a better leader. The leadership literature would greatly benefit from a using a critical perspective.

Shared Leadership

The previous quotes, such as the one by Bennis and Nanus, tend to suggest that research in leadership would have us believe that leadership can be held only by one "heroic leader" (Yukl, 1998, p. 504). However, because of the information overload managers and top executives must deal with in today's high-tech society, asking these people to also be leaders becomes an enormous demand. It is appealing therefore to think of a shared leadership when responsibility is parceled out and followers are empowered. "The extent to which leadership can be shared, the conditions facilitating success of shared leadership, and the implications for design of organizations" (Yukl, 1998, p. 504) therefore become interesting but also important questions to be answered.

Research by Inglis (1997) provides a start in this direction. In a study of the structure of an amateur sport organization (volunteers versus paid staff) she states that "shared leadership is at least partly shaped by the expertise of the volunteers and paid staff" (p. 14).

Leadership and Organizational Change

Linking leadership and organizational change is in many ways an obvious area for study. Leaders, after all, are supposed to direct and manage change in organizations. They mediate between the internal forces that promote stability and the external pressures that demand change if the organization is going to remain competitive. Despite these obvious linkages there has been little attempt to look at the relationship between leadership and change within the broader field of organization studies, and even less in the field of sport management. The exception is the work of Tushman and his colleagues (Nadler & Tushman, 1990; Tushman & Romanelli, 1985; Tushman, Virany, & Romanelli, 1986). In their 1985 and 1986 articles Tushman and his colleagues argue that organizations change by going through convergent periods or by experiencing what are called strategic reorientations or re-creations. Convergent periods are times when the organization exhibits incremental change, or what Miller and Friesen (1984) call evolutionary change. During these relatively long periods, organizations elaborate on their strategic focus. In contrast, strategic reorientations, or re-creations, may involve changes in strategy, power, and structure, and are triggered by contextual pressures (Tushman & Romanelli, 1985). Different types of leadership are required in convergent periods from those required in re-creations: "During convergent periods executive leadership emphasizes symbolic activities and incremental change, while during recreations, executive leadership engages in major substantive as well as symbolic activities. Beyond these substantive and symbolic behaviors, executive leadership must also choose to initiate recreations" (Tushman & Romanelli, 1985, p. 214). The paradox for leaders, as Tushman and Romanelli go on to argue is to "encourage inertial forces during convergent periods" and, when necessary, to "initiate and implement reorientations" (p. 214).

In their later work Nadler and Tushman (1990) extend these ideas to deal with the notion of charismatic leadership. They suggest that in large-scale changes, leaders in the senior management team must drive the change process. While charismatic leadership is important in these kinds of changes, it is not enough on its own. "Charismatic leadership must be bolstered by instrumental leadership; [leaders must] build strong teams, systems, and management processes to leverage and add substance to [their] vision and energy" (Nadler & Tushman, 1990, p. 94). They must also work to institutionalize change at all levels of the management system.

In the field of sport management, Slack and Hinings (1992) and Macintosh and Whitson (1990) have stressed the importance of transformational leaders in the change process in national-level sport organizations. As Slack and Hinings (1992, p. 128) point out, "As well as creating a vision, transformational leaders must mobilize commitment to change. The creation of management teams, the setting of goals, and volunteer involvement through committees . . . were all indications of steps transformational leaders were taking in [national sport organizations] to generate commitment to change." If carried out across different sectors of the sport industry, further research extending some of these ideas about the intersection of leadership and change would help broaden our knowledge about leadership and the important roles leaders play in the change process.

Leadership and Strategy

While strategy and leadership are two central topics in the study of organizations, little consideration has been given to how these concepts are related. For some, leadership is merely the personification of an organization's strategy. However, as Leavy and Wilson (1994, p. 2) note, "the leader is just one important element in . . . strategy formulation. History and context are the other two." The interactions of these three factors in shaping an organization's strategy and growth are important considerations to pursue in sport management; researchers in our field have never empirically examined these interactions when trying to understand sport organizations. Detailed case studies that examined sport managers as leaders would help show how contextual features have influenced their actions. In addition to helping bring social, political, and economic factors into an understanding of leadership choices, work of this nature would also make clear the symbolic nature of leadership, because it would direct our attention to whether the role of the leader is in fact substantive or merely symbolic. Finally, as Leavy and Wilson (1994, p. 186) point out, research that incorporated history and context with the study of leadership would "avoid the danger of developing an overly heroic and somewhat mythological view of these rare and important individuals."

The actions of sport leaders like Peter Ueberroth, Marvin Miller, Sylvia Rempel, and David Stern could all be studied by linking their actions to the historical conditions of their respective organizations and the contexts in which they operate. This type of research would help show how strategy formulation is at times shaped by the autonomous choices made by individual leaders, but in other instances is more a product of opportunities and threats in an organization's context. Such studies would also demonstrate how leaders respond to contextual pressures and, as such, why sometimes they are effective and at other times they fail.

Leadership and Gender

Czarniawska-Joerges and Wolff (1991) suggest that the concept of leader has become culturally defined as an inherently masculine role. Calas and Smircich (1991, p. 567) suggest the leadership literature "functions as a seductive game" and is overtly sexually biased. Both sets of researchers draw attention to the gender biases that exist in much of the research and writing about leadership. Studies of leadership have in fact shown that men emerge as leaders more frequently than women (Carbonell, 1984). This is certainly true in the field of sport management where women are very much underrepresented in leadership positions (Bryson, 1987; Fasting, 1987; Hall, Cullen, & Slack, 1989; White & Brackenridge, 1985). Women's underrepresentation in leadership positions has been attributed in the general field of organizational studies to the internal and external barriers that women face in progressing to the senior levels of an organization (Cockburn, 1991; Powell, 1993; Terborg, 1977; Wentworth & Anderson, 1984). Hall, Cullen, and Slack (1989) and Hovden (2000) have identified the presence of similar barriers in sport organizations.

Despite the obvious lack of women in leadership positions in sport organizations, there has been little attempt within our field to look at the gendered nature of leadership in sport. Studies that have taken account of gender are restricted to examining the competencies and characteristics of female leaders, usually coaches (Klonsky, 1991; Weiss, Barber, Sisley, & Ebbeck, 1991), looking at the relative distribution of male and female coaches (Lovett & Lowry, 1988), or leader selection descriptions according to gender (Hovden, 2000). There is considerable potential for work relating gender to leadership in sport management.

Qualitative studies of the careers of women who are leaders in sport organizations could help shed light on the barriers these people have faced as they have risen to the senior levels of their organizations. Although research (Brenner, Tomkiewicz, & Schein, 1989) shows that the barriers to the emergence of female leaders are gradually being lowered, women who aspire to these positions still experience considerable constraints (Alimo-Metcalfe, 1994). Studies helping to identify these barriers would provide a basis for removing these limitations on women's career progress in our field. Useful and interesting work could also be carried out on the comparative leadership styles of women and men. While some studies have shown there are few if any differences between the sexes (Bartol, 1978; Ferber, Huber, & Spitze, 1979; Reif, Newstrom, & Monczka, 1975), others (Denmark, 1977; Muldrow & Bayton, 1979) have found differences. There has been no work within sport management that has looked at this issue.

Another possible area for work on gender and leadership in sport organizations is suggested by Hall, Cullen, and Slack (1989), who point out that in order to understand the gender structuring of sport organizations we need to look at issues of power and sexuality. Sexuality has, in recent years, become an increased focus of attention for organizational researchers. Given Calas and Smircich's (1991) assertion that the leadership literature is overtly sexually biased studies of sexuality and leadership in sport organizations could produce useful insights into an area that lacks research in our field.

Shaw and Slack (2002) have started examining this area. They found that in traditional organizations, the masculine form of management is preferred, and women—and their feminine styles—were undermined, thereby reinforcing traditional practices. However, in younger organizations, some resistance to this type of practice was found. Gender relations were therefore somewhat more equitable.

Leadership and Organizational Culture

As we saw in chapter 14, over the past 20 years, the concept of organizational culture has received increased attention from organizational theorists. Leaders play an important role in creating and transmitting an organization's culture. Founders, as leaders, are important in shaping culture because, as Schein (1992, p. 211) points out, they "not only choose the basic mission and the environmental context in which the new group will operate, but they choose the group members and bias the original responses that the group makes in its efforts to succeed in its environment and to integrate itself."

Leaders also play a role in embedding and transmitting the culture of an organization. As we saw in chapter 14, what leaders pay attention to, measure, and control; how they react to critical incidents and crises; how they allocate resources; how they distribute rewards; and the criteria they use for recruitment and promotion are all actions that serve to communicate an organization's culture to its employees.

At different stages of an organization's life cycle, the leader's role in managing culture takes on different forms. In its early years culture is a force for growth; it needs to be developed and clearly articulated. Later on, as diverse subcultures form within an organization, the leader is faced with managing these subcultures by using the techniques outlined previously. When an organization reaches maturity, its culture can keep it operating smoothly, but if it is not appropriate for the situation in which the organization finds itself, it can become dysfunctional. To counter this, a major internal upheaval or external crisis may be needed to change the culture to a more appropriate one. The leader plays an important role in managing this process.

The significant links between organizational culture and leadership, as can be seen, present considerable potential for work in this area. However, even within the general field of management there has been relatively little research on this subject. In the field of sport management only Weese's (1995a) study has examined this interre-lationship. Using a sample made up of managers from Big Ten and Mid-American athletic conference campus recreation programs, Weese's work showed that managers who scored high as transformational leaders directed programs with stronger organizational cultures and were more involved in culture-building activities. Other studies could be conducted that look at how leaders construct organizational culture, how the roles of leadership and culture change over time, and how leaders help transmit culture to new members of an organization.

KEY ISSUES FOR MANAGERS

While we are wary of recipes for leadership success as seen on bookstore shelves (if they actually worked, there wouldn't be so many of these types of books), Yukl (1998) came up with six qualities he believes are at the center of an effective leader after his close examination of the leadership issue. A leader should:

1. Agree on objectives and priorities,

2. Show commitment and persistence when faced with obstacles and setbacks,

3. Foster cooperation and mutual trust between group and organizational members,

4. Coordinate all activities for complex tasks to efficiently use people and resources,

5. Build acceptance and support from stakeholders, and

6. Define and maintain boundaries for the task by establishing a clear identity.

There are also many issues that leaders must consider beyond bringing a group together to achieve a common goal. Some areas leaders should be aware of are: gender issues that may influence the appropriate leadership style, possible racist behavior, the latest technological advances, political issues in this era of globalization, and the appearance of unethical behavior and practices. In addition to these general management issues, sport leaders must also consider the types of employees (volunteers versus professionals) they are leading and the source of financial support of the organization, which can affect the vision a leader is trying to project and how successful the leader is in accomplishing the vision.

SUMMARY AND CONCLUSIONS

Some researchers have suggested that leadership is a major factor in producing an effective organization (Peters & Waterman, 1982); others have been less optimistic (Pfeffer, 1977a). While there has certainly been extensive study of the topic of leadership within the organizational literature, the question remains, does it tell us anything? McCall and Lombardo (1978, p. 3) suggest about the leadership literature that "the number of unintegrated models, theories, prescriptions, and conceptual schemes . . . is mind boggling [but] much of [it] is fragmentary, trivial, unrealistic, or dull."

In many ways the same could be said of the leadership literature in sport management. While Paton (1987) was probably correct in his assessment of the area—that it is the most researched topic in our field—the majority of these studies have been doctoral dissertations or master's theses. Only a few have ever been published and many of those have used coaches, not managers, as their sample. There is very little work on the leadership of sport managers.

In this chapter we have reviewed the major theoretical perspectives on leadership. Where possible, examples from sport management have been used to show the type of studies conducted in our field. Some of the criticisms of leadership research were also examined and five potentially fruitful areas for future research were briefly outlined. While not the only areas for possible study, work on the topics suggested would help link leadership to other organizational phenomena and, given the often "abstracted" nature of leadership studies, would be a welcome addition to the literature. Also, studies of the type outlined would challenge the highly voluntaristic and overly rational conceptions of leadership that pervade the field. While we should retain a healthy skepticism about the ability of leaders as sole creators of an organization's structure and processes, we cannot ignore the role that these senior members of an organization play in integrating and directing a sport organization.

KEY CONCEPTS

achievement leadership (p. 298)

assessment center approach (p. 294)

charismatic leadership (p. 301)

consideration (p. 296)

contingency (situational) approach (p. 298)

developmental interventions (p. 299)

employee centered (p. 297)

initiating structure (p. 296)

instrumental leadership (p. 298)

LBDQ (p. 295)

leadership traits (p. 293)

least preferred coworker (p. 300)

managerial competencies (p. 294)

managerial leadership (p. 297)

participative leadership (p. 298)

path-goal theory (p. 298)

peer leadership (p. 297)

production centered (p. 297)

relationship behavior (p. 299)

situational leadership theory (p. 299)

style (behavioral) approach (p. 295)

subordinate maturity (p. 299)

supportive leadership (p. 298)

task behavior (p. 299)

transactional leadership (p. 303)

transformational leadership (p. 301)

REVIEW QUESTIONS

1. Think of the leaders of familiar sport organizations. Can you identify traits they possess that distinguish them from nonleaders?

2. Discuss how useful you think tests such as those used in the assessment center approach are for identifying the leadership abilities of managers.

3. Do you think it is possible for leaders who score high on consideration to also score high on initiating structure?

4. How could factors such as group performance and employee satisfaction influence a manager's leadership style?

5. How would situational variables influence leadership practices in a sport medicine clinic? In a sport equipment company?

6. Pick a situation from a sport organization that you think work would be tedious and low in autonomy. How would supportive leadership influence subordinates?

7. Discuss how subordinate maturity would influence the amount of task behavior and relationship behavior a leader would have to exhibit.

8. What are the similarities and differences between the path-goal approach to leadership, Hersey and Blanchard's situational leadership theory, and Fiedler's work?

9. What are the major differences between charismatic and transformational leadership?

10. Some researchers have talked about "the dark side of charisma." What do you think

...

this is and how is it relevant to studies of leadership?

11. Those who subscribe to the charismatic and transformational theories of leadership put great emphasis on the creation of a vision as a means of focusing organizational members on a common goal. However, the process of creating and implementing a vision can actually bring members into conflict. Discuss how you think this occurs.

12. Discuss the criticisms that have been made about leadership research. Do you think these criticisms are valid?

13. What types of studies could you design to examine the role that leadership plays in the process of organizational change?

14. What steps could be taken in a sport organization to place more women in leadership positions?

15. Leaders are often attributed as being a major factor in creating an organization's culture. Given what you have read about culture do you think this is an accurate statement?

SUGGESTIONS FOR FURTHER READING

If you are interested in furthering your knowledge in the area of leadership, you are advised to look at the original writings of the key theorists whose works are outlined in this chapter. However, of these, Burns' (1978) book *Leadership*, and Bryman's two texts *Leadership and Organizations* (1986) and *Charisma and Leadership in Organizations* (1992) offer the most substantive analysis of the subject. McCall and Lombardo's (1978) *Leadership: Where Else Can We Go?* is a collection of essays by leading organizational theorists, people who have not necessarily focused on the topic of leadership, who attempt to answer the question in the book's title.

For more about the suggested research areas outlined at the end of the chapter, Leavy and Wilson's (1994) *Strategy and Leadership* is a good start for the first topic area. In terms of work on leadership and change, Pettigrew's (1987) *Journal of Management Studies* article, "Context and Action in the Transformation of the Firm," would be helpful. So, too, would Hendry and Johnson's (1993) book *Strategic Thinking: Leadership and the Management of Change*. In terms of leadership and gender, Calas and Smircich's (1991) article "Voicing Seduction to Silence Leadership" is a difficult but interesting read. Alimo-Metcalfe's (1994) strangely titled "Waiting for Fish to Grow Feet!" is also helpful, as is Rosener's (1990) more practical *Harvard Business Review* article, "Ways Women Lead." For those interested in culture and leadership, Schein's (1985) *Organizational Culture and Leadership* is a must. Also interesting is Bass and Avolio's (1990b) article "Transformational Leadership and Organizational Culture."

The most substantive body of work on leadership in the field of sport management has been produced by Chelladurai and colleagues (Chelladurai & Carron, 1983; Chelladurai & Saleh, 1978, 1980; Chelladurai et al., 1987b). However, much of this work focuses on coaches, not on people in managerial positions in sport organizations. Inglis (1997) and Kent and Weese (2000) are the only ones to focus on executive leadership within sport management.

CASE FOR ANALYSIS

Bringing the IOC Into the New Millennium

In July 1980, Juan Antonio Samaranch became the president of the International Olympic Committee (IOC) on the first round of votes. Besides this almost unheard-of accomplishment, he managed to have his chosen executive committee members elected—and in a predetermined order—even though it was a secret ballot.

Before becoming president of the IOC, Samaranch had been the president of the Spanish Olympic Committee and a *chef de mission* for Spain's Olympic team. He had served as a minor governmental official under the Franco regime and then became Spain's ambassador to the Soviet Union.

His predecessor, Ireland's Lord Killanin, had been a softer and agreeable man who used a kitchen-table approach to his part-time presidency of the IOC. However, the complex international issues that faced the IOC in the 1970s (e.g., the Munich Olympic hostage crisis, Olympic boycotts) required a tougher hand at the helm. Enter Samaranch.

He is a man of excellent organizational skills and work ethic coupled with a lot of ambition. He worked behind the scenes of the IOC, never making waves or being involved in problematic issues. He built alliances (attending all major Olympic gatherings of the various committees and "working the room") and studiously avoided offending anyone while steadily building support for his potential candidacy as president.

Juan Antonio Samaranch served as the president of the International Olympic Committee from 1980 to 2001. A powerful leader, Samaranch shaped the IOC according to his vision.

© Bongarts/SportsChrome

money was power. To do this, he surrounded himself with "yes-men" but hired a few key individuals he knew would think for themselves. Decisions were by consensus—in other words, do what the president wanted. When dissention occurred, Samaranch tabled the decision until a later, more favorable time for him. He also developed the ability to have very short meetings with individuals or organizations who wanted their case heard by the president. These constituents left with the feeling that they had been treated fairly, even though results were, for the most part, not what they initially desired.

Samaranch understood politics and understood his organization's current and potential upper and lower limits. With his self-discipline and strong ethical approach, he believed he could shape the IOC into the leading sport organization that it is today, but he needed to be a more involved president. The IOC—an organization of volunteer members—meets only once a year and the executive committee only four or five times a year, an unwieldy situation. Samaranch believed the IOC needed full-time direction, and his first step was to move from Spain to a room in a hotel in Lausanne, Switzerland, the location of the IOC's headquarters. He had an intense schedule, attending as many major sporting events as possible to show that the IOC was everywhere—and that he was the IOC.

Samaranch created numerous commissions to study issues related to the IOC, all the while amassing more power to make the IOC into his vision. He wanted a united Olympic movement, a universal Olympic movement, and a financially healthy Olympic movement. He was keenly aware that

But Samaranch was not without fault. He had a fixation on the supposed power of the international federations, a power that he thought ought to be the IOC's. He had little time for the National Olympic Committees, and he changed IOC rules to suit his ambitions, such as raising the age limit for members so he could seek a third term as president. Samaranch believed the media's role was to promote the IOC and ignore anything negative, and he was always wary of others' motives.

Despite his manipulative style and the scandals that plagued the IOC near the end of Samaranch's turn as president, when he stepped down in 2001, he had achieved his vision for the IOC.

Based on information in R.W. Pound (2004).

Questions

1. How would you describe Samaranch's leadership style given what you've read in this chapter?

2. Was Samaranch a good leader? Why or why not?

3. How are power and leadership linked?

4. Do you need power to be a good leader? Why or why not?

Bibliography

ABC Online. (2002, May 31). World Cup opens with a plea for peace. Retrieved February 28, 2005, from http://abc.net.au/worldcup2002/items/s570405.htm.

About.com. (2002). Salt Lake City safe, says Ridge. Retrieved February 28, 2005, from http://usgovinfo.about.com/library/weekly/aa011102a.htm.

Abrams, B. (1986, January 23). Sports boss: Adidas makes friends, then strikes deals that move sneakers. *Wall Street Journal, 1,* 15.

Academy of Management (2004). Special research forum on building effective networks. *Academy of Management Journal, 47(6),* 795-963.

Adams, M.J. (1987, July). A welcome wave hits. *Stores,* 27-35.

Adidas-Salomon. (2004a). Adidas. Retrieved February 15, 2005, from www.adidas-salomon.com/en/investor/strategy/adidas/default.asp.

Adidas-Salomon. (2004b, September 8). Adidas by Stella McCartney: Introducing the first true sport performance design collection for women. Retrieved February 15, 2005, from www.adidas-salomon.com/en/news/_downloads/pdfs/press_release_stella_corporate.pdf.

Adizes, I. (1979). Organizational passages: Diagnosing and treating life cycle problems of organizations. *Organizational Dynamics, 8,* 3-25.

Ahuja, G. (2000). The duality of collaboration: Inducements and opportunities in the formation of inter-firm linkages. *Strategic Management Journal, 21,* 317-343.

Aiken, L.S., & West, S.G. (1991). Multiple regression: Testing and interpreting interactions. Thousand Oaks, CA: Sage Publications.

Aldrich, H.E. (1972). Technology and organization structure: A re-examination of the findings of the Aston group. *Administrative Science Quarterly, 17,* 26-43.

Aldrich, H.E. (1975). Reaction to Donaldson's note. *Administrative Science Quarterly, 20,* 457-460.

Aldrich, H.E. (1979). *Organizations and environments.* Englewood Cliffs, NJ: Prentice Hall.

Aldrich, H.E., & Herker, D. (1977). Boundary spanning roles and organization structure. *Academy of Management Review, 2,* 217-230.

Aldrich, H.E., McKelvey, B., & Ulrich, D. (1984). Design strategy from the population perspective. *Journal of Management, 10,* 67-86.

Alexandris, K., Dimitriadis, N., & Kasiara, A. (2001). The behavioral consequences of perceived service quality: An exploratory study in the context of private fitness clubs in Greece. *European Sport Management Quarterly, 1,* 280-299.

Alimo-Metcalfe, B. (1994). Waiting for fish to grow feet!: Removing organizational barriers to women's entry into leadership positions. In M. Tanton (Ed.), *Women in management,* 27-45. London, UK: Routledge & Kegan Paul.

Allen, M.P., Panian, S.K., & Lotz, R.E. (1979). Managerial succession and organizational performance: A recalcitrant problem revisited. *Administrative Science Quarterly, 24,* 167-180.

Alpine Canada Alpin. (2003, February 4). Italy and Sweden sign strategic alliance with Alpine Canada Alpin. Retrieved March 4, 2004, from www.canski.org/e/html/news/e_newsdetail.asp?articleID=797&article TypeID=2.

Alvesson, M., & Deetz, S. (2000). *Doing critical management research.* London, UK: Sage.

Alvesson, M., & Willmot, H. (2003). *Studying management critically.* London, UK: Sage.

Amis, J., Pant, N., & Slack, T. (1997). Achieving a sustainable competitive advantage: A resource-based view of sport sponsorship. *Journal of Sport Management, 11,* 80-96

Amis, J., & Slack, T. (1996). The size-structure relationship in voluntary sport organizations. *Journal of Sport Management, 10,* 76-86.

Amis, J., Slack, T., & Berrett, T. (1995). The structural antecedents of conflict in national sport organizations. *Leisure Studies, 14,* 1-16.

Amis, J. Slack, T., & Hinings, C.R. (2002). Values and organizational change. *The Journal of Applied Behavioral Science Behavior, 38,* 436-465.

Andreu, R., & Corominas, A. (1989). SUCCCES92: A DSS for scheduling the Olympic Games. *Interfaces, 19,* 1-12.

Archer, E.A. (1980). How to make a business decision: An analysis of theory and practice. *Management Review, 69,* 54-61.

Argyris, C. (1964). *Integrating the individual and the organization.* New York: Wiley.

Aris, S. (1990). *Sportsbiz: Inside the sports business.* London, UK: Hutchinson.

Armstrong-Doherty, A.J. (1996). Resource dependence-based perceived control: An examination of Canadian interuniversity athletics. *Journal of Sport Management, 10,* 49-64.

Arogyaswamy, B., & Byles, C.M. (1987). Organizational culture: Internal and external fits. *Journal of Management, 13,* 647-659.

Associated Press. (2004, March 23). Roof falls in on swim body's Olympic hopes. *The Ottawa Sun*, p. 57.

Astley, W.G., & Sachdeva, P.S. (1984). Structural sources of interorganizational power: A theoretical synthesis. *Academy of Management Review, 9*, 104-113.

Athens2004. (2004, August 10). *The Globe and Mail*, 2-3.

Athens2004. (2004). Sponsors. Retrieved March 22, 2004, from www.athens2004.com/athens2004/page/legacy?lang=en&cid=fc08470429149f00VgnVCMServer28130b0aRCRD

Auf de Maur, N. (1976). *The billion-dollar game*. Toronto: James Lorimer.

Avolio, B.J., & Gibbons, T.C. (1988). Developing transformational leaders: A life span approach. In J.A. Conger & R.N. Kanungo (Eds.), *Charismatic leadership: The elusive factor in organizational effectiveness*, 276-308. San Francisco: Jossey-Bass.

Avolio, B.J., & Yammarino, F.J. (1990). Operationalizing charismatic leadership using a levels of analysis framework. *Leadership Quarterly, 1*, 193-208.

Babbie, E. (1999). *The basics of social research*. Belmont, CA: Wadsworth.

Babiak, K.M. (2003). *Examining partnerships in amateur sport: The case of a Canadian national sport centre*. Unpublished doctoral dissertation. Vancouver: University of British Columbia.

Bachrach, P., & Baratz, M.S. (1962). The two faces of power. *American Political Science Review, 56*, 947-952.

Bagley, M. (1975). Leadership effectiveness contingency model: Implications. In E.F. Zeigler & M.J. Spaeth (Eds.), *Administrative theory and practice in physical education and athletics*, 98-112. Englewood Cliffs, NJ: Prentice Hall.

Bakan, J. (2004). *The Corporation: The pathological pursuit of profit and power*. Toronto: Penguin Group.

Ballard, S. (1989, February 20). A show that has all the goods. *Sports Illustrated*, 37-40.

Ballinger, J. (1993). The new free-trade heel: Nike jumps on the backs of Asian workers. In R.M. Jackson (Ed.), *Global issues 93/94* (9th ed.), 130-131. Guilford, CT: Dushkin.

Barley, S. (1986). Technology as an occasion for structuring: Evidence from observation of CT scanners and the social order of radiology departments. *Administrative Science Quarterly, 31*, 78-109.

Barnes, J. (1988). *Sport and the law in Canada*. Toronto: Butterworth.

Barney, J. (1991a). Special theory forum. The resource-based model of the firm: Origins, implications, and prospects. *Journal of Management, 17*, 97-98.

Barney, J. (1991b). Firm resources and sustained competitive advantage. *Journal of Management, 17*, 99-120.

Barney, R.K., Wenn, S.R., & Martyn, S.G. (2004). *Selling the five rings: The International Olympic Committee and the rise of Olympic commercialism* (rev. ed.). Salt Lake City: The University of Utah Press.

Barr, G. (1985, July 1). The daunting challenge of selling the CFL. *Financial Times, 1*, 18.

Barringer, B.R., & Harrison, J.S. (2000). Walking a tightrope: Creating value through interorganizational relationships, *Journal of Management, 26*, 367-403.

Barthes, R. (1957). *Mythologies* (trans., A. Lavers, 1973). London, UK: Paladin.

Bartol, K.M. (1978). The sex structuring of organizations: A search for possible causes. *Academy of Management Review, 3*, 805-815.

Bass, B.M. (1981). *Stogdill's handbook of leadership*. New York: Free Press.

Bass, B.M. (1985). *Leadership and performance beyond expectations*. New York: Free Press.

Bass, B.M. (1990a). *Bass and Stogdill's handbook of leadership: Theory, research, and managerial application* (3rd ed.). New York: Free Press.

Bass, B.M. (1990b). From transactional to transformational leadership: Learning to share the vision. *Organizational Dynamics, 18*, 19-31.

Bass, B.M., & Avolio, B.J. (1989). Potential biases in leadership measures: How prototypes, leniency, and general satisfaction relate to ratings and rankings of transformational and transactional leadership constructs. *Educational and Psychological Measurements, 49*, 509-527.

Bass, B.M., & Avolio, B.J. (1990a). Developing transformational leadership: 1992 and beyond. *Journal of European Industrial Training, 14*, 21-27.

Bass, B.M., & Avolio, B.J. (1990b). The implications of transactional and transformational leadership, team, and organizational development. *Research in Organizational Change and Development, 4*, 231-272.

Bass, B.M., & Avolio, B.J. (1990c). Transformational leadership and organizational culture. *International Journal of Public Administration, 17*, 541-554.

Bate, P. (1995). *Strategies for cultural change*. Oxford, UK: Butterworth.

Bates, D.L., & Eldredge, D.L. (1984). *Strategy and policy: Analysis, formulation, and implementation* (2nd ed.). Dubuque, IA: Brown.

Bauer, M.W. (2000). Classical content analysis: A review. In M.W. Bauer & G. Gaskell (Eds.), *Qualitative researching with text, image and sound*. London, UK: Sage.

Bauer, M.W., & Aarts, B. (2000). Corpus construction: A principle for qualitative data collection. In M.W. Bauer & G. Gaskell (Eds.), *Qualitative researching with text, image and sound*. London, UK: Sage.

Bauer, M.W., & Gaskell, G. (Eds.) (2000). *Qualitative researching with text, image and sound*. London, UK: Sage.

BBC News. (1999, August 31). Business: The company file. BSkyB buys stake in Leeds. Retrieved April 6, 2004, from http://news.bbc.co.uk/1/hi/business/the_company_file/434233.stm.

BBC News. (2004, April 17). The oil tycoon tempted by Chelsea. Retrieved February 17, 2005, from http://news.bbc.co.uk/1/hi/business/3036996.stm.

BBC News. (2004, July 27). Athens Installs Patriot Missiles. Retrieved February 28, 2005, from www.worldpress.org/Europe/1908.cfm.

Beamish, R. (1985). Sport executives and voluntary associations: A review of the literature and introduction to some theoretical issues. *Sociology of Sport Journal*, *2*, 218-232.

Bedeian, A.G., & Zammuto, R.F. (1991). *Organizations: Theory and design*. Chicago: Dryden Press.

Bendersky, C. (2003). Organizational dispute resolution systems: A complementarities model. *Academy of Management Review*, *28*, 643-656.

Bennis, W.G., & Nanus, B. (1985). *Leaders: The strategies for taking charge*. New York: Harper & Row.

Benson, J.K. (1977). Innovation and crisis in organizational analysis. *Sociological Quarterly*, *18*, 3-16.

Berrett, T., Burton, T.L., & Slack, T. (1993). Quality products, quality service: Factors leading to entrepreneurial success in the sport and leisure industry. *Leisure Studies*, *12*, 93-106.

Better customer service justifies new center. (1989, March). *Modern Material Handling*, 14-15.

Bettner, J. (1988, September 12). Bowling for dollars. *Forbes*, 138.

Bhaskar, R. (1989). *Reclaiming reality: A critical introduction to contemporary philosophy*. London, UK: Verso.

Blai, B. (1986, January). Eight steps to successful problem solving. *Supervisory Management*, 7-9.

Blake, R.B., & Mouton, J.S. (1984). Overcoming group warfare. *Harvard Business Review*, *62*, 98-108.

Blank, S. (1986). The future workplace. *Management Review*, *75*, 22-25.

Blau, P.M., & Schoenherr, R.A. (1971). *The structure of organizations*. New York: Basic Books.

Blau, P.M., & Scott, W.R. (1962). *Formal organizations*. San Francisco: Chandler.

Bleeke, J., & Ernst, D. (1995 January/February). Is your strategic alliance really a sale? *Harvard Business Review*, 97-105.

Boronico, J.S., & Newbert, S.L. (2001). An empirically driven mathematical modeling analysis for play calling strategy in American Football. *European Sport Management Quarterly*, *1*, 21-38.

Borzilleri, M.-J. (2003, March 12). USOC sponsor asks for accounting. *The Gazette*. Retrieved on February 14, 2005, from http://usoc.gazette.com/fullstory.php?id=147.

Borzilleri, M.-J. (2003, March 19). Olympian Gardner joins fray. *The Gazette*. Retrieved February 14, 2005, from http://usoc.gazette.com/fullstory.php?id=144.

Bottorff, D. (1987, June 15). Exercycle takes detour in hot pursuit of buyers who can pay steep prices. *New England Business*, 54-55.

Boulton, W.R., Franklin, S.G., Lindsay, W.M., & Rue, L.W. (1982). How are companies planning now?: A survey. *Long Range Planning*, *15*, 82-86.

Bourgeois, L.J., and Astley, W.G. (1979). A strategic model of organizational conduct and performance. *International Studies of Management and Organization*, *6*, 40-66.

Bowen, D.E., Siehl, C., & Schneider, B. (1989). A framework for analyzing customer service orientations in manufacturing. *Academy of Management Review*, *14*, 75-95.

Bowers, D.G., & Seashore, S.E. (1966). Predicting organizational effectiveness with a four-factor theory of leadership. *Administrative Science Quarterly*, *11*, 238-263.

Branch, D. (1990). Athletic director leader behavior as a predictor of intercollegiate athletic organizational effectiveness. *Journal of Sport Management*, *4*, 161-173.

Brannigan, G.G. (Ed.) (1999). *The sport scientist: Research adventures*. New York: Addison Wesley Longmen.

Braverman, H. (1974). *Labor and monopoly capital*. New York: Monthly Review Press.

Bray, D.W., Campbell, R.J., & Grant, D.L. (1974). *Formative years in business: A long-term AT&T study of managerial lives*. New York: Wiley.

Brenner, O.C., Tomkiewicz, J., & Schein, V. (1989). The relationship between sex-role stereotypes and requisite management characteristics revisited. *Academy of Management Journal*, *32*, 662-669.

Bronder, C., & Pritzl, R. (1992). Developing strategic alliances: A conceptual framework for successful co-operation. *European Management Journal*, *10*, 412-420.

Brooke, M.Z. (1984). *Centralization and autonomy*. London, UK: Holt, Rinehart & Winston.

Brown, G. (2002, April 21). 2002 World Cup preview. Retrieved February 28, 2005, from www.infoplease.com/spot/02worldcup1.html.

Brown, M.C. (1982). Administrative succession and organizational performance: The succession effect. *Administrative Science Quarterly*, *27*, 1-16.

Brown, R.J. (1990). The management of human resources in the leisure industry. In I.P. Henry (Ed.), *Management & planning in the leisure industries*, 70-96. Basingstoke, Hants, UK: Macmillan Educational.

Bruce, P. (1985, October 14). Two Bavarian companies battle for citizens soles. *The Toronto Globe and Mail*, B4.

Bruni, F., & Carassava, A. (2002, December 13). Le sprint olympique d'Athènes [Athens' Olympic sprint]. *La Presse*, S10-S11.

Brunswick. (2003). 2003 Annual report. Retrieved February 12, 2005, from http://phx.corporate-ir.net/phoenix.zhtml?c=97828&p=irol-reportsannual.

Brunswick's dramatic turnaround. (1988, January/February). *Journal of Business Strategy, 9*, 4-7.

Bryman, A. (1986). *Leadership and organizations.* London, UK: Routledge & Kegan Paul.

Bryman, A. (1992). *Charisma and leadership in organizations.* London, UK: Sage.

Bryson, L. (1987). Sport and the maintenance of masculine hegemony. *Women's Studies International Forum, 10*, 349-360.

Burbank, M.J., Andranovich, G.D., & Heying, C.H. (2001). *Olympic dreams: The impact of mega-events on local politics.* Boulder, CO: Lynne Rienner.

Burden, J. (2000). Community building, volunteering, and action research. *Society and Leisure, 23*, 353-370.

Burgelman, R.A. (1983). A model of the interaction of strategic behaviour, corporate context, and the concept of strategy. *Academy of Management Review, 8*, 61-70.

Burke, V., & Collins, D. (2000). Dealing with work conflict: Issues, approaches and implications for sport managers. *European Journal for Sport Management, 7*, 44-64.

Burns, J.M. (1978). *Leadership.* New York: Harper & Row.

Burns, T., & Stalker, G.M. (1961). *The management of innovation.* London, UK: Tavistock.

Burrell, G. (1984). Sex and organizational analysis. *Organization Studies, 5*, 97-118.

Burrell, G., & Morgan, G. (1979). *Sociological paradigms and organizational analysis: Elements of the sociology of corporate life.* London, UK: Heinemann Educational.

Burton Snowboards. (2005). The company. Retrieved February 22, 2005, from www.burton.com/company/default.asp.

Butler, R.J., Astley, W.G., Hickson, D.J., Mallory, G.R., & Wilson, D.C. (1979-80). Strategic decision making: Concepts of content and process. *International Studies of Management and Organization, 9*, 5-36.

Calas, M.B., & Smircich, L. (1991). Voicing seduction to silence leadership. *Organization Studies, 12*, 567-602.

California State Racquetball Association. (2003). General talking points on the US Congress/USOC restructuring effort. Retrieved February 15, 2005, from www.californiaracquetball.org/2_bullet_points.doc.

Cameron, K.S. (1980). Critical questions in assessing organizational effectiveness. *Organizational Dynamics, 9*, 66-80.

Cameron, K.S. (1984). The effectiveness of ineffectiveness. In B.M. Staw and L.L. Cummings (Eds.), *Research in organizational behavior,* Vol. 6, 235-285. Greenwich, CT: JAI Press.

Cameron, K.S. (1986). Effectiveness as paradox: Consensus and conflict in conceptions of organizational effectiveness. *Management Science, 32*, 539-553.

Cameron, K.S., & Whetten, D.A. (1981). Perceptions of organizational effectiveness over organizational life cycles. *Administrative Science Quarterly, 26*, 525-544.

Cameron, K.S., & Whetten, D.A. (1983a). Models of the organizational life cycle: Application to higher education. *Review of Higher Education, 6*, 269-299.

Cameron, K.S., & Whetten, D.A. (1983b). *Organizational effectiveness: A comparison of multiple models.* New York: Academic Press.

Campbell, J.P. (1977). On the nature of organizational effectiveness. In P.S. Goodman, J.M. Pennings, and Associates (Eds.), *New perspectives on organizational effectiveness,* 36-41. San Francisco: Jossey-Bass.

Can Nike just do it? (1994, April 18). *Business Week,* 86-90.

Canada.com (2005). Ice breaker: NHL, NHLPA finally come to an agreement. Retrieved September 06, 2005, from http://www.canada.com/sports/hockey/labourdispute/index.html.

Canadian Olympic Committee. (2003, May 13). Canadian Olympic Committee: General by-law. Retrieved March 24, 2004, from www.olympic.ca/EN/organization/governance/files/By-Law%20iv03-e.pdf.

Carbonell, J.L. (1984). Sex roles and leadership revisited. *Journal of Applied Psychology, 69*, 44-49.

Carlisle, H.M. (1974). A contingency approach to decentralization. *S.A.M. Advanced Management Journal, 39*, 9-18.

Carper, W.B., & Snizek, W.E. (1980). The nature and types of organizational taxonomies: An overview. *Academy of Management Review, 5*, 65-75.

Carroll, G.R., & Hannan, M.T. (1989). Density dependence in the evolution of populations of newspaper organizations. *American Sociological Review, 54*, 524-541.

Carter, D. (2003, February 3). USOC's problems endanger financial support—Commentary—United States Olympic Committee—Editorial. Retrieved February 14, 2005, from www.findarticles.com/p/articles/mi_m5072/is5_25/ai_97729.

Case, B. (1987). Leadership behavior in sport: A field test of the situational leadership theory. *International Journal of Sport Psychology, 18*, 256-268.

Cashmore, E. (2000). *Making sense of sport* (3rd ed.). London, UK: Routledge & Kegan Paul.

Castaing, M. (1970, March 7). *Le Monde* (n.p.). Cited by Brohm, J. (1978) *Sport: A prison of measured time.* London, UK: Inks Links.

CBC.ca. (2004). 2004 Athens. Retrieved February 28, 2005, from www.cbc.ca/olympics/.

CBC.ca. (2004). Top ten greatest Canadians: Wayne Gretzky. Retrieved February 28, 2005, from www.cbc.ca/greatest/top_ten/nominee/gretzky-wayne.html.

CBC Sports. (2005a, February 7). CTV wins 2010 and 2012 Olympic broadcasting rights. Retrieved May 16, 2005 from http://www.cbc.ca/story/sports/national/2005/02/07/Sports/ctv050207.html.

CBC Sports. (2005b). Lingo of the hockey biz: Defining common terms in hockey negotiations. Retrieved May 18, 2005 from http://www.cbc.ca/sports/indepth/cba/glossary/.

CBC Sports Online. (2002, August 28). Vancouver bid makes 2010 Olympic short list. Retrieved February 28, 2005, from www.cbc.ca/pcgi-bin/templates/sportsView.cgi?/news/2002/08/27/Sports/olybid020827.

Chadwick, S. (2000). A research agenda for strategic collaboration in European club football. *European Journal for Sport Management, 7*, 6-29.

Chakrabarti, A.K., & Hauschildt, J. (1989). The division of labour in innovation management. *R & D Management (UK), 19*, 161-171.

Chalip, L., Costa, C., Gibson, H., Inglis, S., Rascher, D., & Wolfe, R. (2003). Report of the NASSM strategic planning team. Retrieved February 11, 2005, from www.nassm.com/strategic%20plan/2003(Nov).rtf.

Chalip, L., Green, B.C., & Hill, B. (2003). Effects of sport event media on destination image and intention to visit. *Journal of Sport Management, 17*, 214-234.

Chalip, L., & Leyns, A. (2002). Local business leveraging of a sport event: Managing an event for economic benefit. *Journal of Sport Management, 16*, 132-158.

Chandler, A.D., Jr. (1962). *Strategy and structure: Chapters in the history of the industrial enterprise.* Cambridge, MA: MIT Press.

Chang, K., & Chelladurai, P. (2003). Comparison of part-time workers and full-time workers: Commitment and citizenship behaviors in Korean Sport Organizations. *Journal of Sport Management, 17*, 394-416.

Chang, Y.N., & Campo-Flores, F. (1980). *Business policy and strategy.* Santa Monica, CA: Goodyear.

Channon, D. (1973). *Strategy and structure in British enterprise.* Boston: Harvard Graduate School of Business Administration.

Charm, R.E. (1986, November 3). Like the company's sales, aluminum bikes of Cannondale stand out from the pack. *New England Business*, 41-43.

Chelladurai, P. (1985). *Sport management: Macro perspectives.* London, ON: Sports Dynamics.

Chelladurai, P. (1987). Multidimensionality and multiple perspectives of organizational effectiveness. *Journal of Sport Management, 1*, 37-47.

Chelladurai, P. (1992). A classification of sport and physical activity services: Implications for sport management. *Journal of Sport Management, 6*, 38-51.

Chelladurai, P., & Carron, A.V. (1983). Athletic maturity and preferred leadership. *Journal of Sports Psychology, 5*, 371-380.

Chelladurai, P., & Haggerty, T.R. (1991). Measures of organizational effectiveness in Canadian national sport organizations. *Canadian Journal of Sport Science, 16*, 126-133.

Chelladurai, P., Haggerty, T.R., Campbell, L., & Wall, S. (1981). A factor analytic study of effectiveness criteria in intercollegiate athletics. *Canadian Journal of Applied Sport Science, 6*, 81-86.

Chelladurai, P., Malloy, D., Imamura, H., & Yamaguchi, Y. (1987). A cross-cultural study of preferred leadership in sports. *Canadian Journal of Sport Sciences, 12*, 106-110.

Chelladurai, P., & Quek, C.B. (1995). Decision style choices of high school basketball coaches: The effects of situational and coach characteristics. *Journal of Sport Behavior, 18*, 91-108.

Chelladurai, P., & Saleh, S.D. (1978). Preferred leadership in sports. *Canadian Journal of Applied Sport Sciences, 3*, 85-92.

Chelladurai, P., & Saleh, S.D. (1980). Dimensions of leader behavior in sports: Development of a leadership scale. *Journal of Sport Psychology, 2*, 43-45.

Chelladurai, P., Szyszlo, M., & Haggerty, T.R. (1987). Systems-based dimensions of effectiveness: The case of national sport organizations. *Canadian Journal of Sport Science, 12*, 111-119.

Chen, J. (2003, July). The cents and sensibility of Beckham's real deal. Retrieved February 15, 2005, from http://theurbanwire.com/jul03/sports/beckham.html.

Chen, M.-J. (2001). Inside Chinese business. Boston: Harvard Business School Press.

Child, J. (1972a). Organization structure and strategies of control: A replication of the Aston study. *Administrative Science Quarterly, 17*, 163-177.

Child, J. (1972b). Organizational structure, environment and performance: The role of strategic choice. *Sociology, 6*, 1-22.

Child, J. (1973a). Parkinson's progress: Accounting for the number of specialists in organizations. *Administrative Science Quarterly, 18*, 328-348.

Child, J. (1973b). Predicting and understanding organization structure. *Administrative Science Quarterly, 18*, 168-185.

Child, J. (1975a). Comments on Donaldson's note. *Administrative Science Quarterly, 20*, 456.

Child, J. (1975b). Managerial and organizational factors associated with company performance (Part II): A contingency analysis. *Journal of Management Studies, 12*, 12-27.

Child, J. (1984). *Organization: A guide to problems and practice* (2nd ed.). London, UK: Chapman.

Child, J., & Faulkner, D. (1998). *Strategies of cooperation: Managing alliances, networks, and joint ventures.* New York: Oxford University Press.

Child, J., & Mansfield, R. (1972). Technology, size, and organization structure. *Sociology, 6,* 369-393.

Child, J., & Markoczy, L. (1993). Host-country managerial behaviour and learning in Chinese and Hungarian joint ventures. *Journal of Management Studies, 30,* 611-631.

Chin, R., & Benne, K.D. (1985). General strategies for effecting change in human systems. In W.G. Bennis, K.D. Benne, & R. Chin (Eds.), *The planning of change,* 22-45. New York: Holt, Rinehart & Winston.

City of Winnipeg. (1990). *Sports services policy.* Winnipeg, Manitoba: Author.

Clark, T.N. (1967). The concept of power: Some overemphasized and underrecognized dimensions. *The Southwestern Social Science Quarterly, 48,* 271-286.

Cleary, M. (2002, April 26). Envoy vows Greece will be ready for 2004 games. *The Ottawa Citizen,* A13.

Clegg, S. (1989). *Frameworks of power.* London, UK: Sage.

Clegg, S., & Dunkerley, D. (1980). *Organization, class, and control.* London, UK: Routledge & Kegan Paul.

Cliff, G. (1987, May). Managing organizational conflict. *Management Review, 76,* 51-53.

Clifford, M. (1992, November 5). The China connection: Nike is making the most of all that cheap labour. *Far Eastern Economic Review, 60.*

CNN.com. (2003, February 13). Congress asked to fix problems at USOC. Retrieved February 14, 2005, from www.cnn.com/2003/ALLPOLITICS/02/13/usoc.ap.

COC.ca. (2005, February 8). Manager, media relations. Retrieved February 12, 2005, from www.olympic.ca/EN/organization/employment/02_08_05.shtml.

Cockburn, C. (1991). *In the way of women: Men's resistance to sex equality in organizations.* Houndmills, UK: Macmillan.

Coffey, A., & Atkinson, P. (1996). *Making sense of qualitative data.* Thousand Oaks, CA: Sage.

Cohen, M.D., & March, J.G. (1974). *Leadership and ambiguity: The American college president.* New York: McGraw-Hill.

Cohen, M.D., March, J.G., & Olsen, J.P. (1972). A garbage can model of organizational choice. *Administrative Science Quarterly, 17,* 1-25.

Cole, W. (1989, July). Tee time for baby boomers. *Venture,* 69-73.

Coleman, S., & Jones, L.M. (1976). *The Coleman story.* New York: Newcomen Society in North America.

Colyer, S. (2000). Organizational culture in selected western Australian sport organizations. *Journal of Sport Management, 14,* 321-341.

Comité Organisateur des Jeux de la Francophonie (COJF). (2001). *Manuel d'événement rédigé à l'intention des délégations* [Delegations' event manual]. Ottawa-Hull, Canada: Comité Organisateur des Jeux de la Francophonie.

Commentary. (July-August 1993). *Sports Business,* 98.

Conger, J.A. (1989). *The charismatic leader: Beyond the mystique of exceptional leadership.* San Francisco: Jossey-Bass.

Conger, J.A., & Kanungo, R.N. (1987). Towards a behavioral theory of charismatic leadership in organizational settings. *Academy of Management Review, 12,* 637-647.

Conger, J.A., & Kanungo, R.N. (1988). Behavioral dimensions of charismatic leadership. In J.A. Conger & R.N. Kanungo (Eds.), *Charismatic leadership: The elusive factor in organizational effectiveness,* 78-97. San Francisco: Jossey-Bass.

Connacher, I. (2005). Snowboard madness [television series episode]. In I. Connacher, *Daily Planet.* Toronto: Discovery Channel Canada.

Connolly, M. (2003, August). *The world's team: Just as they have done in Asia and Europe, Manchester United are aggressively aiming to capture the hearts of American soccer fans—and money.* Retrieved February 28, 2005, from www.findarticles.com/p/articles/mi_m0FCN/is_3_26/ai_106143238.

Connolly, T., Conlon, E.M., & Deutsch, S.J. (1980). Organizational effectiveness: A multiple constituency approach. *Academy of Management Review, 5,* 211-218.

Contractor, F.J., & Lorange, P. (1988). Why should firms cooperate? The strategy and economic basis for cooperative ventures. In F.J. Contractor, & P. Lorange (Eds.), *Cooperative strategies in international business,* 3-28. New York, NY: Lexington Books.

Cooper 'natural fit' for Canstar. (1990, March 13). *Globe and Mail,* B15.

Corwin, R. (1969). Patterns of organizational conflict. *Administrative Science Quarterly, 14,* 507-520.

Cotton, J.L., Vollrath, D.A., Froggatt, K.L., Lengnick-Hall, M.L., & Jennings, K.R. (1988). Employee participation: Diverse forms and different outcomes. *Academy of Management Review, 13,* 8-22.

Cousens, L., & Slack, T. (1996). Using sport sponsorship to penetrate local markets: The case of the fast food industry. *Journal of Sport Management, 10,* 169-187.

Craig, C.K., & Weisman, K. (1994). Collegiate athletics and unrelated business income tax. *Journal of Sport Management, 8,* 36-48.

Cray, D., Mallory, G.R., Butler, R.J., Hickson, D.J., & Wilson, D.C. (1988). Sporadic, constricted, and fluid processes: Three types of strategic decision making in organizations. *Journal of Management Studies, 25,* 13-39.

Cray, D., Mallory, G.R., Butler, R.J., Hickson, D.J., & Wilson, D.C. (1991). Explaining decision processes. *Journal of Management Studies, 28,* 227-251.

Creamer, R.W. (1973, April 16). Scorecard: More basketball business. *Sports Illustrated,* 21.

Creswell, J.W. (2003). *Research design: Qualitative, quantitative and mixed methods approaches.* London, UK: Sage.

Crick, M., & Smith, D. (1989). *Manchester United: The betrayal of a legend.* London, UK: Pan Books.

Crocker, O., Chiu, J., & Charney, C. (1984). *Quality circles.* New York: Metheun.

Crompton, J.L., & Howard, D.R. (2003). Financing major league facilities: Status, evolution and conflicting forces. *Journal of Sport Management, 17,* 156-184.

Crossley, J., & Ellis, T. (1988, October). Systematic innovation. *JOPERD, 59,* 35-38.

Crotty, M. (1998). *The foundations of social research: Meaning and perspective in the research process.* Thousand Oaks, CA: Sage.

Culture and Sport Secretariat. (2004, August 31). Mandate of divisions, branches, sections and other offices. Retrieved February 14, 2005, from http://app.infoaa.7700.gnb.ca/gnb/pub/ListOrgMandate 1.asp?DeptID2=22.

Cummings, L.L., & Berger, C.J. (1976). Organization structure: How does it influence attitudes and performance? *Organizational Dynamics, 5,* 34-49.

Cummings, T.G., & Worley, C.G. (1993). *Organization development and change.* St. Paul: West.

Cunningham, G.B. (2002). Removing the blinders: Toward and integrative model of organizational change in sport and physical activity. *Quest, 54,* 276-291.

Cyert, R.M., & March, J.G. (1963). *A behavioral theory of the firm.* Englewood Cliffs, NJ: Prentice Hall.

Czarniawska-Joerges, B., & Wolff, R. (1991). Leaders, managers, entrepreneurs on and off the organizational stage. *Organization Studies, 12,* 529-546.

Daft, R.L. (1989). *Organization theory and design* (3rd ed.). St. Paul: West.

Daft, R.L. (1992). *Organization theory and design* (4th ed.). St. Paul: West.

Daft, R.L. (2004). *Organization theory and design* (8th ed.). Mason, OH: Thomson/South-Western.

Damanpour, F. (1987). The adoption of technological, administrative, and ancillary innovations: Impact of organizational factors. *Journal of Management, 13,* 675-688.

Danielson, R.R., Zelhart, P.F., & Drake, C.J. (1975). Multidimensional scaling and factor analysis of coaching behavior as perceived by high school hockey players. *Research Quarterly, 46,* 323-334.

Danylchuk, K.E. (1993). Occupational stressors in physical education faculties. *Journal of Sport Management, 7,* 7-24.

Darrow, B. (1990, April 2). PCs break into the lineup. *Infoworld,* 42-43.

Das, H. (1990). *Organization theory with Canadian applications.* Toronto: Gage Educational.

Davies, P. (1990, May). Hot shoes. *Report on Business Magazine,* 91-95.

Davis, T.R.V. (1984). The influence of the physical environment in offices. *Academy of Management Review, 9,* 271-283.

Deal, T.E., & Kennedy, A.A. (1982). *Corporate cultures: The rites and rituals of corporate life.* Reading, MA: Addison-Wesley.

Delacroix, J., & Carroll, G.R. (1983). Organizational foundings: An ecological study of the newspaper industries in Argentina and Ireland. *Administrative Science Quarterly, 28,* 274-291.

Denmark, F.L. (1977). Styles of leadership. *Psychology of Women Quarterly, 2,* 99-113.

Denscombe, M. (1998). *The good research guide for small-scale social research projects.* Buckingham, UK: Open University Press.

Denzin, N.K., & Lincoln, Y.S. (2000). *Handbook of qualitative research* (2nd ed.). Thousand Oaks, CA: Sage.

Dess, G.G., & Beard, D.W. (1984). Dimensions of organizational task environments. *Administrative Science Quarterly, 29,* 52-73.

Digital scores with the NFL. (1986, March 22). *Financial Post,* C16.

Dillman, D.A., Sinclair, M.D., & Clark, J.R. (1993). Effects of questionnaire length, respondent-friendly design, and a difficult question on response rates for occupant-addressed census mail surveys. *Public Opinion Quarterly, 57,* 289-304.

DiMaggio, P.J., & Powell, W.W. (1983). The iron cage revisited: Institutional isomorphism and collective rationality in organizational field. *American Sociological Review, 35,* 147-160.

Doherty, A.J., & Chelladurai, P. (1999). Managing cultural diversity in sport organizations: A theoretical perspective. *Journal of Sport Management, 13,* 280-297.

Donaldson, L. (1975). Organizational status and the measurement of centralization. *Administrative Science Quarterly, 20,* 453-456.

Donaldson, L., & Warner, M. (1974). Structure of organizations in occupational interest associations. *Human Relations, 27,* 721-738.

Drucker, P. (1954). *The practice of management.* New York: Harper & Row.

Drucker, P. (1966). *The effective executive.* New York: Harper & Row.

Dubin, C.L. (1990). *Commission of inquiry into the use of drugs and banned practices intended to increase athletic performance.* Ottawa: Canadian Government Publishing Centre.

Duncan, R.B. (1972). Characteristics of organizational environments and perceived environmental uncertainty. *Administrative Science Quarterly, 17,* 313-327.

Durkheim, E. (1933). *The division of labor in society* (trans., G. Simpson). London, UK: Free Press. (Original work published in 1893.)

Dworkin, J.B. (1981). *Owners versus players: Baseball and collective bargaining.* Boston: Auburn House.

Eales, R. (1986). Is Nike a long distance runner? *Multinational Business, 1,* 9-14.

Economic Intelligence Unit. (1990). *The sports market overview.* (Research Rep. No. 84). London, UK: Author.

Ehrlich, E. (1985, August 12). Behind the AMF takeover: From highflier to sitting duck. *Business Week,* 50-51.

Eisenhardt, K.M. (1989). Building theories from case study research. *Academy of Management Review, 14,* 532-550.

Eitzen, S.D., & Yetman, N.R. (1972). Managerial change, longevity, and organizational effectiveness. *Administrative Science Quarterly, 17,* 110-116.

Elvin, I. (1990). *Sport and Physical Recreation.* Harlow, UK: Longman.

Emerson, R.E. (1962). Power-dependence relations. *American Sociological Review, 27,* 31-41.

ESPN.com. (2001, March 8). Knightline: The firing of Bob Knight. Retrieved February 14, 2005, from http://espn.go.com/ncb/s/bobknightindex.html.

e-sports! PR sportswire. (2000, November 4). Global Sports reports third quarter results. Retrieved March 22, 2004, from www.buzzle.com/editorials/text11-4-2000-1285.asp.

Etzioni, A. (1961). *A comparative analysis of complex organizations.* New York: Free Press.

Evan, W.M. (1976). Organizational theory and organizational effectiveness: An exploratory analysis. In S.L. Spray (Ed.), *Organizational effectiveness: Theory, research, utilization,* 15-28. Kent, OH: Kent State University Press.

Evans, A.N. (1998). *Using basic statistics in the social sciences* (3rd ed.). Scarborough, ON: Prentice Hall Allyn and Bacon Canada.

Fahey, L. (1981). On strategic management decision processes. *Strategic Management Journal, 2,* 43-60.

Fairley, S. (2003). In search of relived social experience: Group-based nostalgia sport tourism. *Journal of Sport Management, 17,* 284-304.

Farina, R., Kochenberger, G.A., & Obremski, T. (1989). The computer runs the Bolder Boulder: A simulation of a major running race. *Interfaces, 19,* 48-55.

Fasting, K. (1987). Sport and women's culture. *Women's Studies International Forum, 10,* 361-368.

Faulkner, D.O. (1995). *International strategic alliances: Cooperating to compete.* Maidenhead: McGraw-Hill.

Feinstein, J. (1986). *A season on the brink.* New York: Macmillan.

Ferber, M., Huber, J., & Spitze, G. (1979). Preferences for men as bosses and professionals. *Social Forces, 58,* 466-476.

Ferguson, A. (1988, August). Wide tyre boys. *Management Today,* 58-60.

Fiedler, F.E. (1967). *A theory of leadership effectiveness.* New York: McGraw-Hill.

Fielding, L.W., Miller, L.K., & Brown, J.R. (1999). Harlem Globetrotters International, Inc. *Journal of Sport Management, 13,* 45-77.

Filley, A.C., House, R.J., & Kerr, S. (1976). *Managerial process and organizational behavior* (2nd ed.). Glenview, IL: Scott Foresman.

Fine, G.A. (1987). *With the boys: Little league baseball and preadolescent culture.* Chicago: University of Chicago Press.

Fink, J.S., Pastore, D.L., & Riemer, H.A. (2001). Do differences make a difference? Managing diversity in Division IA intercollegiate athletics. *Journal of Sport Management, 15,* 10-50.

Fisher, B.M., & Edwards, J.E. (1988). Consideration and initiating structure and their relationships with leaders' effectiveness: A meta-analysis. Best paper proceedings, Academy of Management. Anaheim, CA: Academy of Management. (Cited by Bass, 1990a.)

Fisher, R., & Ury, W. (1981). *Getting to yes.* London, UK: Hutchinson.

Fitzpatrick, J. (2005). Q. What do the NHL owners want from a new collective bargaining agreement? Retrieved May 18, 2005 from http://proicehockey.about.com/od/collectivebargainingfaq/f/owners_positions.htm.

Fleishman, E.A., & Harris, E.F. (1962). Patterns of leader behavior related to employee grievances and turnover. *Personnel Psychology, 15,* 43-56.

Fleishman, E.A., Harris, E.F., & Burtt, H.E. (1955). *Leadership and supervision in industry.* Columbus: Ohio State University, Bureau of Educational Research.

Fligstein, N., & Brantley, P. (1992). Bank control, owner control, or organizational dynamics: Who controls the large modern corporation? *American Journal of Sociology, 98,* 280-307.

Flynn, M.A, & Gilbert, R.J. (2001). The analysis of professional sports leagues as joint ventures. *The Economic Journal, 111,* 27-46.

Forbes.com. (2003). Forbes 500s. Retrieved March 22, 2004, from www.forbes.com/finance/lists/38/2003/LIR.jhtml?passListId=38&passYear=2003&passListType=Company&uniqueId=DGXN&datatype=Company.

Forbes.com. (2004, February 26). *The world's richest people.* Retrieved March 22, 2004, from www.forbes.com/maserati/billionaires2004/bill04land.html.

Forbes.com. (2004, April 4). Champions of wealth. Retrieved February 28, 2005, from www.forbes.com/free_forbes/2004/0412/126tab.html.

Ford, C.M., & Gioia, D. (2000). Factors influencing creativity in the domain of managerial decision making. *Journal of Management, 26,* 705-732.

Ford, J.D., & Slocum, J.W., Jr. (1977). Size, technology, and environment and the structure of organizations. *Academy of Management Review, 2,* 561-575.

Fourre, C. (2001, November). The sporting metaphor in professional training: The example of "outdoor" courses organized for business managers. *Revue Européenne de management du sport,* 251-254.

Fredreckson, J.W. (1986). The strategic decision process and organizational structure. *Academy of Management Journal, 11,* 280-297.

Freedman, W. (1987). *Professional sports and antitrust.* New York: Quorum Books.

Freeman, R.E. (1984). *Strategic management: A stakeholder approach.* Boston: Pitman.

Freewheeler on firm ground, A. (1989, March 22). *New England Business,* 34-39, 80-81.

French, J.R.P., Jr., & Raven, B. (1959). The bases of social power. In D. Cartwright (Ed.), *Studies in social power,* 150-167. Ann Arbor: University of Michigan Press.

French, J.R.P. Jr., & Raven, B. (1960). The bases of social power. In D. Cartwright and A. Zander (Eds.), *Group dynamics: Research and theory* (2nd ed.), 607-623. New York: Harper & Row.

Frisby, W. (1985). A conceptual framework for measuring the organizational structure and context of voluntary leisure service organizations. *Society and Leisure, 8,* 605-613.

Frisby, W. (1986a). Measuring the organizational effectiveness of national sport governing bodies. *Canadian Journal of Applied Sport Science, 11,* 94-99.

Frisby, W. (1986b). The organizational structure and effectiveness of voluntary organizations: The case of Canadian national sport governing bodies. *Journal of Park and Recreation Administration, 4,* 61-74.

Frisby, W. (2005). The good, the bad, and the ugly: Critical sport management research. *Journal of Sport Management, 19,* 1-12.

Frisby, W., Crawford, S., & Dorer, T. (1997). Reflections on participatory action research: The case of low-income women accessing local physical activity services. *Journal of Sport Management, 11,* 8-28.

Frisby, W., Thibault, L., & Kikulis, L. (2004). The organizational dynamics of under-managed partnerships in leisure service departments. *Leisure Studies, 23,* 109-126.

Frost, C. (2004, December 28). Roman Abramovich: Profile. Retrieved February 16, 2005, from www.bbc.co.uk/bbcfour/documentaries/profile/abramovich.shtml.

Frost, P.J., Moore, L.F., Louis, M.R., Lundberg, C.C., & Martin, J. (Eds.) (1985). *Organizational culture.* Beverly Hills, CA: Sage.

Frost, P.J., Moore, L.F., Louis, M.R., Lundberg, C.C., & Martin, J. (Eds.) (1991). *Reframing organizational culture.* Thousand Oaks, CA: Sage.

Fry, L.W. (1982). Technology-structure research: Three critical issues. *Academy of Management Journal, 25,* 532-552.

Funk, D.C., Ridinger, L.L., & Moorman, A.M. (2003). Understanding consumer support: Extending the Sport Interest Inventory (SII) to examine individual differences among women's professional sport consumers. *Sport Management Review, 6,* 1-31.

Galbraith, J.R. (1974). Organization design: An information processing view. *Interfaces, 4,* 28-36.

Galbraith, J.R. (1977). *Organization design.* Reading, MA: Addison-Wesley.

GamesBids.com. (2003, July 4). Bid city profile and fact sheet: Vancouver, Canada. Retrieved February 28, 2005, from www.gamesbids.com/english/bids/vancouver.shtml.

GamesBids.com. (2003, July 23). Bid profile and fact sheet—2010 Winter Olympic bids. Retrieved February 28, 2005, from www.gamesbids.com/english/bids/2010.shtml.

Gamson, W.A. (1966). Reputation and resources in community politics. *American Journal of Sociology, 72,* 121-131.

Gamson, W.A., & Scotch, N.A. (1964). Scapegoating in baseball. *American Journal of Sociology, 70,* 69-72.

Gandz, J., & Murray, V.V. (1980). The experience of workplace politics. *Academy of Management Journal, 23,* 237-251.

Garrison, L. (1992, December). The centennial celebration: Intersectional play. *Athletic Administration,* 10-13.

Gaskell, G. (2000). Individual and group interviewing. In M.W. Bauer & G. Gaskell (Eds.), *Qualitative researching with text, image and sound.* London, UK: Sage.

Gaskell, G., & Bauer, M.W. (Eds.) (2000). Towards public accountability: Beyond sampling, validity and reliability. In M.W. Bauer & G. Gaskell (Eds.), *Qualitative researching with text, image and sound.* London, UK: Sage.

Gatorade is starting to pant. (1994, April 18). *Business Week,* 98.

Gaugler, B.B., Rosenthal, D.B., Thornton, G.C., & Bentson, C. (1987). Meta-analysis of assessment center validity. *Journal of Applied Psychology, 72,* 493-511.

Gauthier, R., & Hansen, H. (1993). Female spectators: Marketing implications for professional golf events. *Sport Marketing Quarterly, 2,* 21-28.

Geehern, C. (1991, August 8). Balls. *New England Business,* 40-45, 63.

Geiger, H.M. (1987). *The Broadmoor story* (rev. ed.). Denver: Hirschfeld Press.

Geringer, J.M., & Hébert, L. (1989). Control and performance of international joint ventures. *Journal of International Business Studies, 20,* 235-254.

Gerth, H.H., & Mills, C.W. (1946). *From Max Weber.* New York: Oxford University Press.

Gerwin, D. (1979). Relationships between structure and technology at the organizational and job levels. *Journal of Management, 16,* 70-79.

Gill, P. (1987, July). Winning pace for footwear. *Stores*, 36-38, 40, 44-49.

Give them stormy weather. (1986, March 24). *Forbes*, 174.

Gladden, J.M., & Funk, D.C. (2002). Developing an understanding of brand associations in team sport: Empirical evidence from consumers of professional sport. *Journal of Sport Management, 16*, 54-81.

Gladwell, N.J., Anderson, D.M., & Sellers, J.R. (2003). An examination of fiscal trends in public parks and recreation from 1986 to 2001: A case study of North Carolina. *Journal of Park and Recreation Administration, 21*, 104-116.

Glaser, B.G., & Strauss, A.L. (1967). The discovery of grounded theory: Strategies for qualitative research. Chicago: Aldine.

Global Golf Holdings. (2003, October 28). Form 10-K/A for Global Golf Holdings Inc. /DE/ Annual Report. Retrieved March 31, 2004, from Yahoo! Finance at http://biz.yahoo.com/e/031028/gglfe.ob10-k_a.html.

Glover, T.D. (1999). Municipal park and recreation agencies unite! A single case analysis of an intermunicipal partnership. *Journal of Park and Recreation Administration, 17*, 73-90.

Going for gold. (1988, October). *Target Marketing, 72*, 74.

Goodman, P.S., Atkin, R.S., & Schoorman, F.D. (1983). On the demise of organizational effectiveness studies. In K.S. Cameron & D.A. Whetten (Eds.), *Organizational effectiveness: A comparison of multiple models*, 163-183. New York: Academic Press.

Goodman, P.S., & Pennings, J.M. (1977). Perspectives and issues: An introduction. In P.S. Goodman, J.M. Pennings, and Associates (Eds.), *New perspectives on organizational effectiveness*, 1-12. San Francisco: Jossey-Bass.

Goodman, P.S., Pennings, J.M., and Associates (Eds.) (1977). *New perspectives on organizational effectiveness*. San Francisco: Jossey-Bass.

Gordon, W.C., & Babchuk, N. (1959). A typology of voluntary organizations. *American Sociological Review, 24*, 22-29.

Gore, W.L. (1985). The lattice organization: A philosophy of enterprise. Internal Document. W.L. Gore & Associates. Newark, DE.

Gould, A. (1989). *The new entrepreneurs*. Toronto: Seal Books.

Gouldner, A.W. (1954). *Patterns of industrial bureaucracy*. New York: Free Press.

Graham, J. (1988, July 18). Reebok scores with "Boss." *Advertising Age*, 22.

Graham, P. (1983). Strategic planning management concepts applied to team sports. In *Proceedings of the International Congress: Teaching Team Sports*, 17-182. Rome: CONI-Scuola dello Sport.

Green, B.C. (1997). Action research in youth soccer: Assessing the acceptability of an alternative program. *Journal of Sport Management, 11*, 29-44.

Green, L.W., George, M.A., Daniel, M., Frankish, C.J., Herbert, C.J., Bowie, W.R., & O'Neill, M. (1995). *Study of participatory research in health promotion: Review and recommendations for the development of participatory research in health promotion in Canada*. University of British Columbia: Institute of Health Promotion.

Greene, C.N. (1979). Questions of causality in the path-goal theory of leadership. *Academy of Management Journal, 22*, 22-41.

Greenwood, R., & Hinings, C.R. (1976). Centralization revisited. *Administrative Science Quarterly, 21*, 151-155.

Greenwood, R., & Hinings, C.R. (1988). Organizational design types, tracks, and the dynamics of strategic change. *Organization Studies, 9*, 293-316.

Greenwood, R., & Hinings, C.R. (1996). Understanding radical organizational change: Bringing together the old and the new institutionalism. *Academy of Management Review, 21*, 1022-1054.

Gregory, K.L. (1983). Native-view paradigms: Multiple cultures and culture conflicts in organizations. *Administrative Science Quarterly, 28*, 359-376.

Greiner, L.E. (1967). Patterns of organizational change. *Harvard Business Review, 45*, 119-130.

Gresov, C. (1989). Exploring fit and misfit with multiple contingencies. *Administrative Science Quarterly, 34*, 431-453.

Grimes, A.J., & Klein, S.M. (1973). The technological imperative: The relative impact of task unit, modal technology, and hierarchy on structure. *Academy of Management Journal, 16*, 583-597.

Grinyer, P.H., & Yasai-Ardekani, M. (1980). Dimensions of organizational structure: A critical replication. *Academy of Management Journal, 23*, 405-421.

Gruneau, R. (1983). *Class, sports and social development*. Amherst: University of Massachusetts Press.

Grusky, O. (1963). Managerial succession and organizational effectiveness. *American Journal of Sociology, 69*, 21-31.

Guba, E.C. (Ed.) (1990). *The paradigm dialog*. Newbury Park, CA: Sage.

Gulati, R. (1999). Network location and learning: The influence of network resources and firm capabilities on alliance formation. *Strategic Management Journal, 20*, 397-420.

Guttmann, A. (1978). *From ritual to record*. New York: Columbia University Press.

Haas, J.E., Hall, R.H., & Johnson, N.J. (1966). Towards an empirically derived taxonomy of organizations. In R.V. Bowers (Ed.), *Studies on behavior in organizations*, 157-180 Athens: University of Georgia Press.

Haberberg, A., and Rieple, A. (2001), *The strategic management of organizations*. Harlow: Prentice Hall.

Hage, J. (1965). An axiomatic theory of organizations. *Administrative Science Quarterly, 10*, 289-320.

Hage, J. (1980). *Theories of organizations*. New York: Wiley.

Hage, J., & Aiken, M. (1967a). Program change and organizational properties: A comparative analysis. *American Journal of Sociology, 72*, 503-519.

Hage, J., & Aiken, M. (1967b) Relationship of centralization to other structural properties. *Administrative Science Quarterly, 12*, 72-91.

Hage, J., & Aiken, M. (1969). Routine technology, social structure, and organizational goals. *Administrative Science Quarterly, 14*, 366-376.

Hage, J., & Aiken, M. (1970). *Social change in complex organizations*. New York: Random House.

Haggerty, T.R. (1988). Designing control and information systems in sport organizations: A cybernetic perspective. *Journal of Sport Management, 2*, 53-63.

Haig, M. (2004). Brand royalty: How the world's top 100 brands thrive & survive. Retrieved February 15, 2005, from www.buildingbrands.com/reviews/BrandRoyaltyChapter1.pdf.

Hall, M.A., Cullen, D., & Slack, T. (1989). Organizational elites recreating themselves: The gender structure of national sport organizations. *Quest, 41*, 28-45.

Hall, M.A., Slack, T., Smith, G., & Whitson, D. (1991). *Sport in Canadian society*. Toronto: McClelland & Stewart.

Hall, R.H. (1963). The concept of bureaucracy. *American Sociological Review, 69*, 32-40.

Hall, R.H. (1968). Professionalization and bureaucratization. *American Sociological Review, 33*, 92-104.

Hall, R.H. (1982). *Organizations: Structure and process* (3rd. ed.). Englewood Cliffs, NJ: Prentice Hall.

Hall, R.H., & Clark, J.P. (1980). An ineffective effectiveness study and some suggestions for future research. *Sociological Quarterly, 21*, 119-134.

Hall, R.H., Haas, J.E., & Johnson, N.J. (1967). Organizational size, complexity, and formalization. *American Sociological Review, 32*, 903-912.

Hall, R.H., & Tittle, C.R. (1966). Bureaucracy and its correlates. *American Journal of Sociology, 72*, 267-272.

Halpin, A.W. (1957). The observed behavior and ideal leaders behavior of aircraft commanders and school superintendents. In R.M. Stogdill & A.E. Coons (Eds.), *Leader behaviors: Its description and measurement*, 65-68. Columbus: Ohio State University, Bureau of Business Research.

Halpin, A.W., & Winer, B.J. (1957). A factorial study of the leader behavior descriptions. In R.M. Stogdill & A.E. Coons (Eds.), *Leader behaviors: It's description and measurement*, 39-51. Columbus: Ohio State University, Bureau of Business Research.

Hamel, G., Doz, Y.L., & Prahalad, C.K. (2002). Collaborate with your competitors—and win. In *Harvard Business Review on strategic alliances*, 1-21. Boston: Harvard Business School Press.

Hampton, J. (1984, October). Q. and A. One-on-one with H.R. "Bum" Bright. *Dallas*, 23-25, 86.

Hannan, M.T., & Freeman, J. (1977a). Obstacles to comparative studies. In P.S. Goodman & J.M. Pennings, and Associates (Eds.), *New perspectives on organizational effectiveness*, 106-131. San Francisco: Jossey-Bass.

Hannan, M.T., & Freeman, J. (1977b). The population ecology of organizations. *American Journal of Sociology, 82*, 929-964.

Hannan, M.T., & Freeman, J. (1988). Density dependence in the growth of organizational populations. In G.R. Carroll (Ed.), *Ecological models of organizations*, 7-32. Cambridge, MA: Ballinger.

Hannan, M.T., & Freeman, J. (1989). Organizational ecology. Cambridge, MA: Harvard University Press.

Hansen, H., & Gauthier, R. (1989). Factors affecting attendance at professional sport events. *Journal of Sport Management, 3*, 15-32.

Harrigan, K.R., & Porter, M. (1983). End-game strategies for declining industries. *Harvard Business Review, 61*, 111-120.

Harris, D. (1987). *The league, the rise and decline of the NFL*. Toronto: Bantam Books.

Harrison, J.S., & St. John, C.H. (1996). Managing and partnering with external stakeholders. *Academy of Management Executive, 10*, 46-60.

Hartley, R.F. (1989). *Marketing mistakes* (4th ed.). New York: Wiley.

Harvard Business Review (2002). *Harvard Business Review on strategic alliances*. Boston: Harvard Business School Press.

Harvard Business School. (1984). *Nike* (B). (Case No. 9-385-027). Boston: HBS Case Services.

Harvey, J., & Proulx, R. (1988). Sport and the state in Canada. In J. Harvey & H. Cantelon (Eds.), *Not just a game: Essays in Canadian sport sociology*, 93-119. Ottawa: University of Ottawa Press.

Hater, J.J., & Bass, B.M. (1988). Superiors' evaluations and subordinates' perceptions of transformational and transactional leadership. *Journal of Applied Psychology, 73*, 695-702.

Hawley, A.H. (1981). Human ecology: Persistence and change. *American Behavioral Scientist, 24*, 423-444.

Haywood-Farmer, J., Sharman, T., & Weinbrecht, M.S. (1988). Using simple simulation models to manage sports services. *Journal of Sport Management, 2*, 118-128.

Hearn, J., & Parkin, P.W. (1983). Gender and organizations: A selective review and a critique of a neglected area. *Organization Studies, 4*, 219-242.

Hearn, J., & Parkin, P.W. (1987). *"Sex" at work: The power and paradox of organisational sexuality*. Brighton, UK: Wheatsheaf.

Hearn, J., Sheppard, D.L., Tancred-Sheriff, P., & Burrell, G. (1989). *The sexuality of organization*. London, UK: Sage.

Hemphill, J.K., & Coons, A.E. (1957). Development of the leaders behavior description questionnaire. In R.M. Stogdill & A.E. Coons (Eds.), *Leader behaviors: Its description and measurement*, 6-38. Columbus: Ohio State University, Bureau of Business Research.

Hendry, J., and Johnson, G., with Newton, J. (Eds.). (1993), *Strategic thinking: Leadership and the management of change*. Chichester, UK: Wiley.

Henry, I. (2001). Postmodernism and power in urban policy: Implications for sport and cultural policy in the city. *European Sport Management Quarterly, 1*, 5-20.

Hersey, P., & Blanchard, K.H. (1984). *Management of organizational behavior* (4th ed.). Englewood Cliffs, NJ: Prentice Hall.

Herzberg, F., Mausner, B., & Snyderman, B. (1959). *The motivation to work*. New York: Wiley.

Hickson, D.J., Butler, R.J., Cray, D., Mallory, G.R., & Wilson, D.C. (1985). Comparing one hundred fifty decision processes. In J.M. Pennings (Ed.), *Organizational strategy and change*, 114-142. San Francisco: Jossey-Bass.

Hickson, D.J., Butler, R.J., Cray, D., Mallory, G.R., & Wilson, D.C. (1986). *Top decisions: Strategic decision making in organizations*. San Francisco: Jossey-Bass.

Hickson, D.J., Hinings, C.R., Lee, C.A., Schneck, R.E., & Pennings, J.M. (1971). A "strategic" contingencies theory of interorganizational power. *Administrative Science Quarterly, 14*, 378-397.

Hickson, D.J., Pugh, D.S., & Pheysey, D.C. (1969). Operations, technology and organization structure: An empirical reappraisal. *Administrative Science Quarterly, 14*, 378-397.

Higgs, C.T., & Weiller, K.H. (1994). Gender bias and the 1992 Summer Olympic Games: An analysis of television coverage. *Journal of Sport and Social Issues, 18*, 234-246.

Higham, J.E.S., & Hinch, T.D. (2003). Sport, space, and time: Effects of the Otago Highlanders franchise on tourism. *Journal of Sport Management, 17*, 235-257.

Hill, C.R. (1992). *Olympic politics*. Manchester, UK: Manchester University Press.

Hill, C.W.L., & Jones, G.R. (1989). Strategic management: An integrated approach. Boston: Houghton Mifflin.

Hinings, C.R., & Greenwood, R. (1988). *The dynamics of strategic change*. Oxford, UK: Basil Blackwell.

Hinings, C.R., Hickson, D.J., Pennings, J.M., & Schneck, R.E. (1974). Structural conditions of interorganizational power. *Administrative Science Quarterly, 17*, 22-44.

Hinings, C.R., & Lee, G.L. (1971). Dimensions of organization structure and their context: A replication. *Sociology, 5*, 83-93.

Hinings, C.R., & Slack, T. (1987). The dynamics of quadrennial plan implementation in national sport organizations. In T. Slack & C.R. Hinings, (Eds.), *The organization and administration of sport*. London, ON: Sport Dynamics.

Hisrich, R.D., & Peters, M.P. (1992). *Entrepreneurship*. Homewood, IL: Irwin.

Hodge, B.J., & Anthony, W.P. (1991). *Organization theory: A strategic approach*. Boston: Allyn & Bacon.

Hoeber, L., & Frisby, W. (2001). Gender equity for athletes: Rewriting the narrative for this organizational value. *European Sport Management Quarterly, 1*, 179-209.

Holdaway, E.A., Newberry, J.F., Hickson, D.J., & Heron, R.P. (1975). Dimensions of organizations in complex societies: The educational sector. *Administrative Science Quarterly, 20*, 37-58.

Horine, L. (1985). *Administration of physical education and sport programs*. Philadelphia: Saunders.

Horwich, A. (1989, August). REI: Where good citizenship makes good business sense. *Outside Business*, 30-35, 68-69.

Houlihan, B. (1991). *The government and politics of sport*. London, UK: Routledge & Kegan Paul.

House, R.J. (1971). A path-goal theory of leader effectiveness. *Administrative Science Quarterly, 16*, 321-339.

House, R.J. (1977). A 1976 theory of charismatic leadership. In J.G. Hunt and L.L. Larson (Eds.), *Leadership: The cutting edge*, 189-207. Carbondale: Southern Illinois University Press.

House, R.J., & Dessler, G. (1974). The path-goal theory of leadership: Some post hoc and a priori tests. In J. Hunt and L. Larson (Eds.), *Contingency approaches to leadership*, 29-55. Carbondale: Southern Illinois Press.

House, R.J., & Mitchell, T.R. (1974). Path-goal theory of leadership. *Contemporary Business, 3*, 81-98.

Hovden, J. (2000). Gender and leadership selection processes in Norwegian sporting organizations. *International Review for the Sociology of Sport, 35*, 75-82.

Howden, D. (2004, March 22). Torch set for odyssey to Olympics. *The Ottawa Citizen*, S2.

Hrebiniak, L.G. (1974). Job technology, supervision, and work group structure. *Administrative Science Quarterly, 19*, 395-410.

Hrebiniak, L.G., & Joyce, W.F. (1985). Organizational adaptation: Strategic choice and environmental determinism. *Administrative Science Quarterly, 30*, 336-349.

Huffy Corporation. (2004). Overview. Retrieved February 11, 2005, from www.huffy.com/overview.shtml.

Huizenga, R. (1994). *You're OK. It's just a bruise*. New York: St. Martin's Press.

Hult, J.S. (1989). Women's struggle for governance in U.S. amateur athletics. *International Review for the Sociology of Sport, 24*, 249-263.

Human, S.E., & Provan, K.G. (2000). Legitimacy building in the evolution of small-firm multilateral networks: A comparative study of success and demise. *Administrative Science Quarterly, 45,* 327-365.

Hunnicutt, D. (1988). Integrating quality circles into college athletic departments. *Journal of Sport Management, 2,* 140-145.

If there were a gold medal for bickering the U.S. would win. (1988, March 21). *Business Week,* 106, 108.

ILAM. (2005). About us. Retrieved February 21, 2005, from www.ilam.co.uk/aboutus.asp.

IMG. (2005). History. Retrieved February 28, 2005, from www.imgworld.com/history/default.sps?itype=5415& icustompageid=8811.

Improving your marketing game. (1987, November). *Athletic Business,* 16.

India Sports Forum. (2005, January 26). Adidas is official sportswear partner for Beijing Olympic Games. Retrieved February 15, 2005, from http://sport.dcealumni.com/archives/286/adidas-beijing-olympic-games.

Indik, J. (1986). Path-goal theory of leadership: A meta-analysis. Best paper proceedings, Academy of Management. Anaheim, CA: Academy of Management. (Cited by Yukl, 1989.)

Inglis, S. (1997). Shared leadership in the governance of amateur sport: Perceptions of executive directors and volunteer board members. *Avante, 3,* 14-33.

International Olympic Committee. (2004). Global Broadcast Revenues. Retrieved on March 22, 2004 from www.olympic.org/uk/organisation/facts/revenue/broadcoast_uk.asp.

International Olympic Committee. (2005a). Evolution of Olympic marketing during the 20th century: 2002 Salt Lake City (Winter). Retrieved May 14, 2005 from http://www.olympic.org/uk/organisation/facts/introduction/100years_uk.asp.

International Olympic Committee (2005b). Athens 2004: Games of the XXVIII Olympiad. Retrieved February 27, 2005, from www.olympic.org/uk/games/past/index_uk.asp?OLGT=1&OLGY=2004.

Jackson, E.L., & Burton, T.L. (Eds.) (1998). *Leisure studies: Prospects for the 21st century,* 119-133. State College, PA: Venture.

Jackson, S.E., & Dutton, J.E. (1988). Discerning threats and opportunities. *Administrative Science Quarterly, 33,* 370-387.

Jacobson, R. (1992). The "Austrian" School of strategy. *Academy of Management Review, 17,* 782-807.

Jacoby, A. (1965). Some correlates of instrumental and expressive orientations to associational membership. *Sociological Inquiry, 35,* 163-175.

Jamieson, L.J. (1987). Competency-based approaches to sport management. *Journal of Sport Management, 1,* 48-56.

Jemison, D.B. (1984). The importance of boundary spanning roles in strategic decision making. *Journal of Management Studies, 21,* 131-152.

Jensen, C.R. (1983). Administrative management of physical education and athletic programs. Philadelphia: Lea & Febiger.

Jereski, L. (1990, June 18). Can Paul Fireman put the bounce back in Reebok? *Business Week,* 181-182.

Johnson, G., & Scholes, K. (1993). *Exploring corporate strategy* (3rd ed.). Hemel Hempstead: Prentice Hall.

Johnson, R. (1986, November 4). Brunswick Corp. agrees to buy Bayliner Marine. *Wall Street Journal,* 10.

Johnson, T.J. (1972). *Professions and power.* Basingstoke, UK: Macmillan Education.

Joint ventures: Creating opportunities in the fitness business. (1986, January). *Athletic Business,* 26, 28, 30, 32.

Jollimore, M. (1992, June 27). Women show hockey might in Canada. *Globe and Mail,* A20.

Jones, R. (2002). Partnerships in action: Strategies for the development of voluntary community groups in urban parks. *Leisure Studies, 21,* 305-325.

Kang, J.-H. (2002). A structural model of image-based and utilitarian decision-making processes for participant sport consumption. *Journal of Sport Management, 16,* 173-189.

Kanter, R.M. (1977). *Men and women of the corporation.* New York: Basic Books.

Kanter, R.M. (1983). *The change masters.* New York: Simon & Schuster.

Kanter, R.M. (1984). Managing transitions in organizational culture: The case of participative management at Honeywell. In J.R. Kimberly & R.E. Quinn (Eds.), *Managing organizational transitions,* 195-217. Homewood, IL: Irwin.

Kanter, R.M. (2002). Collaborative advantages: The art of alliances. In *Harvard Business Review on strategic alliances,* 97-128. Boston: Harvard Business School Press.

Kanter, R.M., & Brinkerhoff, D. (1981). Organizational performance: Recent developments in measurement. In R.H. Turner & J.F. Short (Eds.), *Annual review of sociology,* Vol. 7, 321-349. Palo Alto, CA: Annual Reviews.

Katerberg, R., & Hom, P.W. (1981). Effects of within-group and between-groups variations in leadership. *Journal of Applied Psychology, 66,* 218-222.

Katz, D., & Kahn, R.L. (1978). *The social psychology of organizations* (rev. ed.). New York: Wiley.

Katz, D., Maccoby, N., Gurin, G., & Floor, L. (1951). *Productivity, supervision, and morale among railroad workers.* Ann Arbor: Survey Research Center, University of Michigan.

Katz, D., Maccoby, N., & Morse, N. (1950). *Productivity, supervision, and morale in an office situation.* Ann

Arbor: Institute for Social Research, University of Michigan.

Katz, R.L. (1955). Skills of an effective administrator. *Harvard Business Review, 33,* 33-42.

Keeley, M. (1978). A social-justice approach to organizational evaluation. *Administrative Science Quarterly, 23,* 272-292.

Keidel, R.W. (1984). Baseball, football, and basketball: Models for business. *Organizational Dynamics, 12,* 5-18.

Kelle, U. (2000). Computer-assisted analysis: Coding and indexing. In M.W. Bauer & G. Gaskell (Eds.), *Qualitative researching with text, image and sound.* London, UK: Sage.

Kelly, T.W. (1991). Performance evaluation. In R.L. Boucher & W.J. Weese (Eds.), *Management of recreational sports in higher education,* 153-165. Carmel, IN: Benchmark Press.

Kennedy, J.K. (1982). Middle LPC leaders and the contingency model of leadership effectiveness. *Organizational Behavior and Human Performance, 30,* 1-14.

Kent, A., & Chelladurai, P. (2001). Perceived transformational leadership, organizational commitment and citizenship behavior: A case study in intercollegiate athletics. *Journal of Sport Management, 15,* 135-159.

Kent, A., & Weese, W.J. (2000). Do effective organizations have better executive leaders and/or organizational cultures? A study of selected sport organizations in Canada. *European Journal for Sport Management, 7,* 4-21.

Kets de Vries, M.F.R. (1994). The leadership mystique. *Academy of Management Executive, 8,* 73-89.

Khandwalla, P.N. (1974). Mass output orientation of operations technology and organizational structure. *Administrative Science Quarterly, 19,* 74-97.

Kidd, B. (1988). The elite athlete. In J. Harvey & H. Cantelon (Eds.), *Not just a game: Essays in Canadian sport sociology,* 287-307. Ottawa: University of Ottawa Press.

Kidd, B., & Donnelly, P. (2000). Human rights in sport. *International Review for the Sociology of Sport, 35,* 131-148.

Kidd, B., & Ouellet, J.-G. (2000, May). A win-win solution: Creating a national alternate dispute resolution system for amateur sport in Canada. Retrieved December 1, 2000, from www.pch.gc.ca/coderre/report-rapport/ADR-2000.pdf.

Kikulis, L.M. (2000). Continuity and change in governance and decision making in national sport organizations: Institutional explanations. *Journal of Sport Management, 14,* 293-320.

Kikulis, L., Slack, T., & Hinings, C.R. (1992). Institutionally specific design archetypes: A framework for understanding change in national sport organizations. *International Review for the Sociology of Sport, 27,* 343-370.

Kikulis, L., Slack, T., & Hinings, C.R. (1995a). Does decision making make a difference: Patterns of change within Canadian national sport organizations. *Journal of Sport Management, 9,* 273-299.

Kikulis, L., Slack, T., & Hinings, C.R. (1995b). Sector specific patterns of organizational design change. *Journal of Management Studies, 32,* 67-100.

Kikulis, L., Slack, T., Hinings, C.R., & Zimmermann, A. (1989). A structural taxonomy of amateur sport organizations. *Journal of Sport Management, 3,* 129-150.

Killanin, Lord. (1983). *My Olympic years.* London, UK: Secker & Warburg.

Killing, J.P. (1983). *Strategies for joint venture success.* New York: Praeger.

Kimberly, J.R. (1976). Organizational size and the structuralist perspective: A review critique, and proposal. *Administrative Science Quarterly, 21,* 571-597.

Kimberly, J.R. (1980). The life cycle analogy and the study of organizations: Introduction. In J.R. Kimberly, & R.H. Miles (Eds.), *The organizational life cycle,* 1-14. San Francisco: Jossey-Bass.

Kimberly, J.R. (1987). The study of organizations: Toward a biographical perspective. In J.W. Lorsch (Ed.), *Handbook of organizational behavior,* 223-237. Englewood Cliffs, NJ: Prentice Hall.

Kimberly, J.R., & Miles, R.H. (1980). *The organizational life cycle.* San Francisco: Jossey-Bass.

Kimberly, J.R., & Rottman, D.B. (1987). Environment, organization and effectiveness: A biographical approach. *Journal of Management Studies, 24,* 595-622.

King, F.W. (1991). *It's how you play the game: The inside story of the Calgary Olympics.* Calgary, AB: Writers' Group.

Kirkpatrick, S.A., & Locke, E.A. (1991). Leadership: Do traits matter? *Academy of Management Executive, 5,* 48-60.

Kirzner, I. (1973). *Competition and entrepreneurship.* Chicago: University of Chicago Press.

Klonsky, B.G. (1991). Leader's characteristics in same-sex sport groups: A study of interscholastic baseball and softball teams. *Perceptual and Motor Skills, 72,* 943-964.

Kmetz, J.L. (1977-78). A critique of the Aston studies and results with a new measure of technology. *Organization and Administrative Sciences, 8,* 123-144.

Kogan, R. (1985). *Brunswick: The story of an American company from 1845 to 1985.* Skokie, IL: Brunswick Corporation.

Kogut, B. (1988). Joint ventures: Theoretical and empirical perspectives. *Strategic Management Journal, 9,* 319-332.

Kogut, B. (2000). The network as knowledge: Generative rules and the emergence of structure. *Strategic Management Journal, 21,* 405-425.

Kogut, B., & Zander, U. (1992). Knowledge of the firm, combinative capabilities, and the replication of technology. *Organization Science, 3,* 383-397.

Kolb, D.M., & Putnam, L.L. (1992). The multiple faces of conflict in organizations. *Journal of Organizational Behavior, 13,* 311-324.

Kotter, J.P. (1977). Power, dependence and effective management. *Harvard Business Review, 55,* 125-136.

Kotter, J.P., & Schlesinger, L.A. (1979). Choosing strategies for change. *Harvard Business Review, 57,* 106-124.

Kronberger, N., & Wagner, W. (2000). Keywords in context: Statistical analysis of text features. In M.W. Bauer & G. Gaskell (Eds.), *Qualitative researching with text, image and sound.* London, UK: Sage.

Kyle, G.T., Kerstetter, D.L., & Guadagnolo, F.B. (2003). Manipulating consumer price expectations for a 10K road race. *Journal of Sport Management, 17,* 142-155.

Langhorn, K., & Hinings, C.R. (1987). Integrated planning and organizational conflict. *Canadian Public Administration, 30,* 550-565.

Larson, L.L., Hunt, J.G., & Osborn, R.N. (1976). The great hi-hi leader behavior myth: A lesson from Occam's razor. *Academy of Management Journal, 19,* 628-641.

Larson, M. (1977). *The rise of professionalism: A sociological analysis.* Berkeley: University of California Press.

Lawler, E., & Mohrman, S. (1985). Quality circles: After the fad. *Harvard Business Review, 63,* 64-71.

Lawrence, P.R., and Lorsch, J. (1967). *Organization and environment.* Boston: Harvard Graduate School of Business Administration.

Lawson, H.A. (1984). *Invitation to physical education.* Champaign, IL: Human Kinetics.

Leavitt, H.J., Dill, W.R., & Eyring, H.B. (1973). *The organizational world.* New York: Harcourt Brace Jovanovich.

Leavy, B., & Wilson, D.C. (1994). *Strategy and leadership.* London, UK: Routledge & Kegan Paul.

Lebrun, P. (2005, February 16). NHL commissioner Bettman says its lights out on the 2004-05 NHL season. Retrieved Februaru 24, 2005 from http://www.canada.com/sports.hockey/oilersstory.html?id=7180be25-9314-418f-aabl-34f30cee2346.

Leifer, R., & Huber, G.P. (1977). Relations among perceived environmental uncertainty, organizational structure, and boundary spanning behavior. *Administrative Science Quarterly, 22,* 235-247.

Lenskyj, H.J. (2000). *Inside the Olympic industry: Power, politics, and activism.* Albany: State University of New York Press.

Lenz, R.T., & Engledow, J.L. (1986). Environmental analysis units and strategic decision making: A field study of selected "leading edge" corporations. *Strategic Management Journal, 7,* 69-89.

Lesley, E. (1992, November 30). What next, Raider's deodorant? *Business Week,* 65.

Lewicki, R.J., & Bunker, B.B. (1996). Developing and maintaining trust in work relationships. In R.M. Kramer, & T.R. Tyler (Eds.), *Trust in organizations: frontiers of theory and research,* 114-139. Thousand Oaks, CA: Sage.

Lewis, M. (2003). *Moneyball: The art of winning an unfair game.* New York: Norton.

Li, S.X., & Rowley, T.J. (2002). Inertia and evaluation mechanisms in interorganizational partner selection: Syndicate formations among U.S. investment banks. *Academy of Management Journal, 45,* 1104-1119.

Lieberson, S., & O'Conner, J.F. (1972). Leadership and organizational performance: A study of large corporations. *American Sociological Review, 37,* 117-130.

Likert, R. (1967). *The human organization.* New York: McGraw-Hill.

Likert, R., & Likert, J.G. (1976). *New ways of managing conflict.* New York: McGraw-Hill.

Lincoln, J., & Zeitz, G. (1980). Organizational properties from aggregate data. *American Sociological Review, 45,* 391-405.

Lindblom, C.E. (1959). The science of muddling through. *Public Administration Review, 19,* 79-88.

Lord, R.G., Binning, J.F., Rush, M.C., & Thomas, J.C. (1978). The effects of performance cues and leader behavior on questionnaire rating of leader behavior. *Organizational Behavior and Human Performance, 21,* 27-39.

Lorsch, J. (1986). Managing culture: The invisible barrier to strategic change. *California Management Review, 28,* 95-109.

Louis, M.R. (1985). An investigator's guide to workplace culture. In P.J. Frost, L.F. Moore, M.R. Louis, C.C. Lundberg, & J. Martin (Eds.), *Organizational culture,* 73-93. Beverly Hills, CA: Sage.

Lovett, D.J., & Lowry, C.D. (1988). The role of gender in leadership positions in female sport programs in Texas colleges. *Journal of Sport Management, 2,* 106-117.

Lovett, D.J., & Lowry, C.D. (1994). "Good old boys" and "good old girls" clubs: Myth or reality. *Journal of Sport Management, 8,* 27-35.

Lukes, S. (1974). *Power: A radical view.* London, UK: Macmillan.

Luo, Y. (2000). *How to enter China: Choices and lessons.* Ann Arbor: University of Michigan Press.

Lyles, M. (1987). Defining strategic problems: Subjective criteria of executives. *Organization Studies, 8,* 263-280.

Macintosh, D., Bedecki, T., & Franks, C.E.S. (1987). *Sport and politics in Canada.* Kingston, ON: McGill-Queen's University Press.

Macintosh, D., & Whitson, D.J. (1990). *The game planners: Transforming Canada's sport system.* Montreal & Kingston, ON: McGill-Queen's University Press.

MacKinnon, M. (2004, March 22). Dogs of Athens had their day. *The Ottawa Citizen*, A1, A12.

MacMillan, I.C. (1983). Competitive strategies for nonprofit agencies. In R.B. Lamb (Ed.), *Advances in strategic management*, Vol. 1, 61-82. Greenwich, CT: JAI Press.

Macnow, G. (1985, July 17). Eastern Michigan's plan to tie coaches' pay to performance derided on other campuses. *Chronicle of Higher Education*, 27-28.

Madison, D.L., Allen, R.W., Porter, L.W., Renwick, P.A., & Mayes, B.T. (1980). Organizational politics: An exploration of managers' perceptions. *Human Relations, 33*, 79-100.

Magnet, M. (1982, November 1). Nike starts on the second mile. *Fortune*, 159-162.

Mahoney, T.A., & Frost, P.J. (1974). The role of technology in models of organizational effectiveness. *Organizational Behavior and Human Performance, 11*, 122-138.

Maidique, M.A. (1980). Entrepreneurs, champions, and technological innovation. *Sloan Management Review, 21*, 59-76.

Mallory, G.R., Butler, R.J., Cray, D., Hickson, D.J., & Wilson, D.C. (1983). Implanted decision making: American owned firms in Britain. *Journal of Management Studies, 20*, 192-211.

Manley, D., & Friend, T. (1992). *Educating Dexter*. Nashville: Rutledge Hill Press.

Manning-Schaffel, V. (2002, May 27). Adidas: Contender. Retrieved February 15, 2005, from www.brandchannel.com/features_profile.asp?pr_id=71.

Mannix, E. (2003). Editor's comments: Conflict and conflict resolution—a return to theorizing. *Academy of Management Review, 28*, 543-546.

Manson, B. (1999, July 8). Shaking the trees in Tijuana. Retrieved February 23, 2005, from www.sdreader.com/php/cityshow.php?id=C070899.

March, J.G. (1966). The power of power. In D. Easton (Ed.), *Varieties of political theory*, 39-70. Englewood Cliffs, NJ: Prentice Hall.

March, J.G. (1982). Theories of choice and making decisions. *Society, 20*, 29-39.

March, J.G., & Olsen, J.P. (Eds.) (1976). *Ambiguity and choice in organizations*. Bergen, Norway: Universitetsforlaget.

March, J.G., & Simon, H. (1958). *Organizations*. New York: Wiley.

Markland, R.E. (1983). *Topics in management science* (1st ed.). New York: Wiley.

Marshall, J. (2003, October 18). US Olympic panel OKs restructuring plan. Retrieved February 14, 2005, from www.deaftoday.com/news/archives/003245.html.

Martin, C.L. (1990). The employee/customer interface: An empirical investigation of employee behaviors and customer perceptions. *Journal of Sport Management, 4*, 1-20.

Martin, J. (2002). *Organizational culture: Mapping the terrain*. Thousand Oaks, CA: Sage.

Martin, J., Feldman, M.S., Hatch, M.J., & Sitkin, S.B. (1983). The uniqueness paradox in organizational stories. *Administrative Science Quarterly, 28*, 438-453.

Martin, R. (1971). The concept of power: A critical defense. *British Journal of Sociology, 22*, 240-256.

Martindell, J. (1962). *The scientific appraisal of management*. New York: Harper & Row.

Maslow, A.H. (1943). A human theory of motivation. *Psychological Review, 50*, 370-396.

Maslow, A.H. (1965). *Eupsychian management*. Homewood, IL: Irwin.

Mason, D.S., & Slack, T. (2003). Understanding principal-agent relationships: Evidence from professional hockey. *Journal of Sport Management, 17*, 37-61.

McCall, M.W. Jr., & Lombardo, M.M. (1978). *Leadership: Where else can we go?* Durham, NC: Duke University Press.

McCann, J.E. (1991). Design principles for an innovating company. *Academy of Management Executive, 5*, 76-93.

McCarthy, M.J. (1987, October 19). Bally plans sale of health clubs for $500 million. *Wall Street Journal*, 34.

McDonald, P. (1991). The Los Angeles Olympic Organizing Committee: Developing organizational culture in the short run. In P.J. Frost, L.F. Moore, M.L. Reis, C.C. Lundberg, and J. Martin (Eds.), *Reframing organizational culture*, 26-38. Newbury Park, CA: Sage.

McGehee, N.G., Yoon, Y., & Cárdenas, D. (2003). Involvement and travel for recreational runners in North Carolina. *Journal of Sport Management, 17*, 305-324.

McGeoch, R. (1994). *The bid: How Australia won the 2000 Games*. Port Melbourne, Victoria, Australia: William Heinemann Australia.

McGregor, D. (1960). *The human side of enterprise*. New York: Van Nostrand.

McKelvey, B. (1975). Guidelines for the empirical classification of organizations. *Administrative Science Quarterly, 20*, 509-525.

McKelvey, B. (1978). Organizational systematics: Taxonomic lessons from biology. *Management Science, 24*, 1428-1440.

McKelvey, B. (1982). *Organizational systematics*. Los Angeles: University of California Press.

McLennan, K. (1967). The manager and his job skills. *Academy of Management Journal, 3*, 235-245.

McMillan, J. (1989). *The Dunlop story*. London, UK: Weidenfeld and Nicolson.

McShane, L. (2004, August 10). Phevos and Athena—mascots from hell. *The Ottawa Citizen*, A7.

Merton, R.K. (1957). *Social theory and social structure.* London, UK: Free Press of Glencoe.

Meyer, J.W., & Rowan, B. (1977). Institutionalized organizations: Formal structure as myth and ceremony. *American Journal of Sociology, 83,* 340-363.

Meyer, J.W., & Scott, R. (1983) *Organizational environments: Rituals and rationality.* Beverly Hills, CA: Sage.

Meyerson, D., & Martin, J. (1987). Cultural change: An integration of three different views. *Journal of Management Studies, 24,* 623-647.

Michael, D.N. (1973). *On learning to plan—and planning to learn.* San Francisco: Jossey-Bass.

Michaelis, V. (2003, October 19). USOC moves toward restructuring. *USA Today.* Retrieved February 14, 2005, from www.usatoday.com/sports/olympics/2003-10-19-usoc-restructuring.htm.

Miles, M.B., & Huberman, A.M. (1994). *Qualitative data analysis* (2nd ed.*).* Thousand Oaks, CA: Sage.

Miles, R.E., & Snow, C.C. (1978). Organizational strategy, structure, and process. New York: McGraw-Hill.

Miles, R.E., Snow, C.C., Meyer, A.D., & Coleman, H.J. (1978). Organizational strategy, structure and process. *Academy of Management Review, 3,* 546-562.

Miller, D. (1981). Toward a new contingency approach: The search for organizational gestalts. *Journal of Management Studies, 18,* 1-26.

Miller, D. (1986). Configurations of strategy and structure: Towards a synthesis. *Strategic Management Journal, 7,* 217-231.

Miller, D. (1987a). Strategy making and structure: Analysis and implications for performance. *Academy of Management Journal, 30,* 7-32.

Miller, D. (1987b). The structural and environmental correlates of business strategy. *Strategic Management Journal, 8,* 55-76.

Miller, D. (1988). Relating Porter's business strategies to environment and structure: Analysis and performance implications. *Academy of Management Journal, 31,* 280-308.

Miller, D. (1990). *The Icarus paradox: How exceptional companies bring about their own downfall.* New York: HarperCollins.

Miller, D., & Dröge, C. (1986). Psychological and traditional determinants of structure. *Administrative Science Quarterly, 31,* 539-560.

Miller, D., & Friesen, P. (1980a). Archetypes of organizational transition. *Administrative Science Quarterly, 25,* 268-292.

Miller, D., & Friesen, P. (1980b). Momentum and revolution in organizational adaptation. *Academy of Management Journal, 23,* 591-614.

Miller, D., & Friesen, P. (1984). *Organizations: A quantum view.* Englewood Cliffs, NJ: Prentice Hall.

Miller, G.A. (1987). Meta-analysis and the culture free hypothesis. *Organization Studies, 4,* 309-325.

Miller, K.I., & Monge, P.R. (1986). Participation, satisfaction, and productivity: A meta-analytic review. *Academy of Management Journal, 29,* 727-753.

Mills, A.J., & Tancred, P. (1992). *Gendering organizational analysis.* London, UK: Sage.

Mills, D. (1991). The battle of Alberta: Entrepreneurs and the business of hockey in Edmonton and Calgary, AB. *Alberta: Studies in the Arts and Sciences, 2,* 1-25.

Mills, P.K., & Margulies, N. (1980). Toward a core typology of service organizations. *Academy of Management Review, 5,* 255-265.

Millson, L. (1987). *Ballpark figures: The Blue Jays and the business of baseball.* Toronto: McClelland and Stewart.

Miner, J.B. (1975). The uncertain future of the leadership concept: An overview. In J.G. Hunt and L.C. Larson (Eds.), *Leadership frontiers,* 197-208. Kent, OH: Kent State University Press.

Mintzberg, H. (1973a). *The nature of managerial work.* New York: Harper & Row.

Mintzberg, H. (1973b). Strategy making in three modes. *California Management Review, 16,* 44-53.

Mintzberg, H. (1978). Patterns in strategy formulation. *Management Science, 24,* 934-948.

Mintzberg, H. (1979). *The structuring of organizations.* Englewood Cliffs, NJ: Prentice Hall.

Mintzberg, H. (1982). A note on that dirty word "efficiency." *Interfaces, 12,* 101-105.

Mintzberg, H. (1983). *Power in and around organizations.* Englewood Cliffs, NJ: Prentice Hall.

Mintzberg, H. (1984). A typology of organizational structure. In D. Miller & P. Friesen, *Organizations: A quantum view,* 68-86. Englewood Cliffs, NJ: Prentice Hall.

Mintzberg, H. (1987). The strategy concept—I: Five Ps for strategy. *California Management Review, 30,* 11-24.

Mintzberg, H. (1990). The design school: Reconsidering the basic premises of strategic management. *Strategic Management Journal, 11,* 171-195.

Mintzberg, H., Raisinghani, D., & Théorêt, A. (1976). The structure of "unstructured" decision processes. *Administrative Science Quarterly, 21,* 246-275.

Misumi, J., & Peterson, M. (1985). The performance-maintenance (PM) theory of leadership: Review of a Japanese research program. *Administrative Science Quarterly, 30,* 198-223.

Mitchell, R.K., Agle, B.R., & Wood, D.J. (1997). Toward a theory of stakeholder identification and salience: Defining the principle of who and what really counts. *Academy of Management Review, 22,* 853-886.

Mizruchi, M.S., & Stearns, L.B. (1988). A longitudinal study of the formation of interlocking directorates. *Administrative Science Quarterly, 33,* 194-210.

Molnar, J.J., & Rogers, D.L. (1976). Organizational effectiveness: An empirical comparison of the goal and system resource approaches. *Sociological Quarterly, 17,* 401-413.

Morgan, G. (Ed.) (1983). *Beyond method: Strategies for social research.* Beverly Hills, CA: Sage.

Morgan, G. (1986). *Images of organization.* Beverly Hills, CA: Sage.

Morrow, W.W., & Chelladurai, P. (1992). The structure and processes of Synchro Canada. *Journal of Sport Management, 6,* 133-152.

Mountain Equipment Co-op. (2004). Social & environmental responsibility: Canadian Avalanche Association. Retrieved April 6, 2004, from www.mec.ca/Main/content_text.jsp?CONTENT%3C%3Ecnt_id=363217&FOLDER%3C%3Efolder_id=619117&bmUID=1081283758223.

Mountain Equipment Co-op. (2005). Mission and values. Retrieved February 25, 2005, from www.mec.ca/Main/content_text.jsp;jsessionid=Cf7PahPf7EHWCv5aYKajsvA1YMT4Lq34XrSnSuXReO49vjmG2kKt!1026745886!170918943!2003!7002?FOLDER%3C%3Efolder_id=619263&bmUID=1109392143851.

Mountain Equipment Co-op. (2005a). About our co-op: About Mountain Equipment Co-op. Retrieved February 28, 2005, from www.mec.ca/Main/content_text.jsp?CONTENT%3C%3Ecnt_id=8987&FOLDER%3C%3Efolder_id=619263&bmUID=1109650617041.

Mountain Equipment Co-op. (2005b). About our Co-op: Mission and values. Retrieved February 28, 2005, from www.mec.ca/Main/content_text.jsp?CONTENT%3C%3Ecnt_id=8987&FOLDER%3C%3Efolder_id=619263&bmUID=1109650617041.

Mountain Equipment Co-op. (2005c). MEC environment fund. Retrieved February 28, 2005, from www.mec.ca/Main/content_text.jsp?FOLDER%3C%3Efolder_id=619063&bmUID=1109650617043.

Mountain Equipment Co-op (2005d). MEC's green building program. Retrieved February 28, 2005, from www.mec.ca/Main/content_text.jsp?FOLDER%3C%3Efolder_id=618971&bmUID=1109650617044.

Muldrow, T.W., & Bayton, J.A. (1979). Men and women executives and processes related to decision accuracy. *Journal of Applied Psychology, 64,* 99-106.

Murray, E.A., & Mahon, J.F. (1993). Strategic alliances: Gateway to the new Europe? *Long Range Planning, 26,* 102-111.

Nadler, D.A., & Tushman, M.L. (1989a). Organizational frame bending: Principles for managing reorientation. *The Academy of Management Executive, 3,* 194-204.

Nadler, D.A., & Tushman, M.L. (1989b). What makes for magic leadership? In W.E. Rosenbach & R.L. Taylor (Eds.), *Contemporary issues in leadership,* 135-138. Boulder, CO: Westview.

Nadler, D.A., & Tushman, M.L. (1990). Beyond the charismatic leader: Leadership and organizational change. *California Management Review, 32,* 77-97.

National Collegiate Athletic Association. (2003a, July 2). The National Collegiate Athletic Association revised budget for fiscal year ended August 31, 2004. Retrieved April 14, 2004, from www.ncaa.org/financial/2003-04_budget.pdf.

National Collegiate Athletic Association. (2003b) 2003 NCAA membership report. Retrieved April 14, 2004, from www.ncaa.org/library/membership/members_report/2003/2003ncaamembershipreport.pdf.

National Collegiate Athletic Association. (2004). NCAA governance at a glance. Retrieved April 14, 2004, from www1.ncaa.org/membership/governance/org_chart.html.

National Sporting Goods Association. (2002). *2002 Consumer purchases by category.* Retrieved March 22, 2004 from www.nsga.org/public/pages/index.cfm?pageid=161.

Nelson, R.E. (1989). The strength of strong ties: Social networks and intergroup conflict in organizations. *Academy of Management Journal, 32,* 377-401.

Nemetz, P.L., & Fry, L.W. (1988). Flexible manufacturing organizations: Implications for strategy formulation and organizational design. *Academy of Management Review, 13,* 627-638.

Newstrom, J.W. (1980, January). Evaluating the effectiveness of training methods. *Personnel Administrator,* 55-60.

Nigh, D., & Cochran, P.L. (1987). Issues management and the multinational enterprise. *Management International Review, 27,* 4-12.

Nonaka, I., & Takeuchi, H. (1995). *The knowledge-creating company.* New York: Oxford University Press.

Nord, W.R. (1983). A political-economic perspective on organizational effectiveness. In K.S. Cameron & D.A. Whetten (Eds.), *Organizational effectiveness: A comparison of multiple models,* 95-131. New York: Academic Press.

Nugent, P.S. (2002). Managing conflict: Third-party interventions for managers. *Academy of Management Executive, 16,* 139-155.

Nutt, P.C. (2004). Expanding the search for alternatives during strategic decision-making. *Academy of Management Executive, 18,* 13-28.

Oberg, W. (1972). Charisma, commitment, and contemporary organization theory. *MSU Business Topics, 20,* 18-32.

O'Brien, D., & Slack, T. (2003). An analysis of change in an organizational field: The professionalization of English Rugby Union. *Journal of Sport Management, 17,* 417-448.

Olafson, G.A. (1990). Research design in sport management: What's missing, what's needed? *Journal of Sport Management, 4,* 103-120.

Olafson, G.A., & Hastings, D.W. (1988). Personal style and administrative behavior in amateur sport organizations. *Journal of Sport Management, 2,* 26-39.

Oliver, C. (1988). The collective strategy framework: An application to competing predictions of isomorphism. *Administrative Science Quarterly, 33,* 543-561.

Oliver, C. (1991). Strategic responses to institutional processes. *Academy of Management Review, 16,* 145-179.

On the edge with Dupliskate. (1993, January-February). *Sports Business,* 44.

Orkin, L. (2002, March 6). Athens running out of time for 2004 Games: Plagued by delays, local organizers dealt yet another setback. *Edmonton Journal,* D8.

Orlikowski, W.J. (1992). The duality of technology: Rethinking the concept of technology in the organization. *Organization Science, 3,* 398-427.

Ottawa Lions Track & Field Club. (2003, November 5). New inflatable multisport structure at Louis-Riel Public Secondary School. Retrieved January 15, 2004, from www.ottawalions.com/news/2003/111003-LouisRiel_Track.htm

Ozanian, M.K. (2003, September 15). Showing you the money. Retrieved March 21, 2004 from http://www.forbes.com/free_forbes/2003/0915/081tab.html.

PAGS. (1999). *XIII Pan American Games: PASO report.* Winnipeg, MB: PAGS.

Parsons, T. (1956). Suggestions for a sociological approach to the theory of organizations. *Administrative Science Quarterly, 1,* 63-85.

Paterno, J. (1991). *Paterno: By the book.* New York: Berkley.

Paton, G. (1987). Sport management research: What progress has been made? *Journal of Sport Management, 1,* 25-31.

Patti, R.J. (1974). Organizational resistance and change: The view from below. *Social Service Review, 48,* 367-383.

Pauchant, T.C. (1991). Transferential leadership. Towards a more complex understanding of charisma in organizations. *Organization Studies, 12,* 507-527.

Pedersen, P.M., Whisenant, W.A., & Schneider, R.G. (2003). Using a content analysis to examine the gendering of sports newspaper personnel and their coverage. *Journal of Sport Management, 17,* 376-393.

Peek, L. (2004, August 7). Athens' Olympic preparation not a gold-medal performance. *The Ottawa Citizen,* A14.

Penn, G. (2000). Semiotic analysis of still images. In M.W. Bauer, & G. Gaskell (Eds.), *Qualitative researching with text, image and sound.* London, UK: Sage.

Pennings, J.M. (1973). Measures of organizational structure: A methodological note. *American Journal of Sociology, 79,* 686-704.

Pennings, J.M. (1987). Technological innovations in manufacturing. In J.M. Pennings & A. Buitendam (Eds.), *New Technology as organizational innovation,* 197-216. Cambridge, MA: Ballinger.

Pennings, J.M., & Goodman, P.S. (1977). Toward a workable framework. In P.S. Goodman, J.M. Pennings, & Associates (Eds.), *New perspectives on organizational effectiveness,* 146-184. San Francisco: Jossey-Bass.

Perrow, C. (1961). The analysis of goals in complex organizations. *American Sociological Review, 26,* 854-866.

Perrow, C. (1967). A framework for the comparative analysis of organizations. *American Sociological Review, 32,* 194-208.

Perrow, C. (1968). The effect of technology on the structure of business firms. In B.C. Roberts (Ed.), *Industrial relations: Contemporary issues,* 205-219. London, UK: St. Martin's Press.

Perrow, C. (1970). *Organizational analysis: A sociological view.* Belmont, CA: Brooks/Cole.

Perrow, C. (1972). *Complex organizations: A critical essay.* Glenview, IL: Scott Foresman.

Peters, L.H., Hartke, D.D., & Pohlmann, J.T. (1985). Fiedler's contingency theory of leadership: An application of the meta-analytic procedures of Schmidt and Hunter. *Psychological Bulletin, 97,* 274-285.

Peters, T. (1990). Get innovative or get dead. *California Management Review, 33,* 9-26.

Peters, T.J., & Waterman, R.H. (1982). *In search of excellence.* New York: Harper & Row.

Pettigrew, A.M. (1979). On studying organizational cultures. *Administrative Science Quarterly, 24,* 570-581.

Pettigrew, A.M. (1985a). *The awakening giant.* Oxford, UK: Basil Blackwell.

Pettigrew, A.M. (1985b). Contextualist research: A natural way to link theory and practice. In E. Lawler (Ed.), *Doing research that is useful in theory and practice,* 222-248. San Francisco: Jossey-Bass.

Pettigrew, A.M. (1987). Context and action in the transformation of the firm. *Journal of Management Studies, 24,* 649-670.

Pettigrew, A.M., & Whipp, R. (1991). *Managing change for competitive success.* Oxford, UK: Basil Blackwell.

Pfeffer, J. (1977a). The ambiguity of leadership. *Academy of Management Review, 2,* 104-112.

Pfeffer, J. (1977b). Power and resource allocation in organizations. In B.M. Staw & G.R. Salancik (Eds.), *New directions in organizational behavior,* 235-265. Chicago: St. Clair Press.

Pfeffer, J. (1981). *Power in organizations.* Marshfield, MA: Pitman.

Pfeffer, J. (1992). *Managing with power: Politics and influence in organizations.* Boston: Harvard Business School Press.

Pfeffer, J., & Davis-Blake, A. (1986). Administrative succession and organizational performance: How administrator experience mediates the succession effect. *Academy of Management Journal, 29,* 72-83.

Pfeffer, J., & Salancik, G. (1978). *The external control of organizations: A resource-dependence perspective.* New York: Harper & Row.

Poe, G.S, Seeman, I., McLaughlin, J., Mehl, E., & Dietz, M. (1988). "Don't know" boxes in factual questions in a mail questionnaire: Effects on level and quality of response. *Public Opinion Quarterly, 52,* 212-222.

Pondy, L.R. (1967). Organizational conflict: Concepts and models. *Administrative Science Quarterly, 12,* 296-320.

Pondy, L.R. (1992). Reflections on organizational conflict. *Journal of Organizational Behavior, 13,* 257-261.

Pondy, L.R., Frost, P.J., Morgan, G., & Dandridge, T.C. (Eds.) (1982). *Organizational symbolism.* Greenwich, CT: JAI Press.

Porter, M.E. (1980a). *Competitive strategies: Techniques for analyzing industries and competitors.* New York: Free Press.

Porter, M.E. (1980b). *Competitive strategy.* New York: Free Press.

Porter, M.E. (1985). *Competitive advantage: Creating and sustaining superior performance.* New York: Free Press.

Porter, M.E. (1989). *The competitive advantage of nations and their firms.* New York: Free Press.

Post, J.E., Preston, L.E., & Sachs, S. (2002). Managing the extended enterprise. The new stakeholder view. *California Management Review, 45,* 6-28.

Pound, R.W. (2004). *Inside the Olympics: A behind-the-scenes look at the politics, the scandals, and the glory of the games.* Mississauga, ON: Wiley Canada.

Powell, G.N. (1993). *Women and men in management* (2nd ed.). Newbury Park, CA: Sage.

Powell, W.W., & DiMaggio, P.J. (1991). *The new institutionalism in organizational analysis.* Chicago: University of Chicago Press.

Price, J.L. (1972). The study of organizational effectiveness. *Sociological Quarterly, 13,* 3-15.

Prouty, D.F. (1988). *In spite of us: My education in the big and little games of amateur and Olympic sport in the U.S.* Brattleboro,VT: Vitesse Press.

Pugh, D.S., Hickson, D.J., & Hinings, C.R. (1969). An empirical taxonomy of work organizations. *Administrative Science Quarterly, 14,* 115-126.

Pugh, D.S., Hickson, D.J., Hinings, C.R., & Turner, C. (1968). Dimensions of organizational structure. *Administrative Science Quarterly, 13,* 65-105.

Pugh, P. (1989). *The Belfry: The making of a dream.* Trowbridge, Wilts, UK: Cambridge Business.

Quinn, J.B., Mintzberg, H., & James, R.M. (1988). *The strategy process: Concepts, context, and cases.* Englewood Cliffs, NJ: Prentice Hall.

Quinn, P. (2004, April 10). "What we need is lots of work," Greek deputy minister says. *The Ottawa Citizen,* S4.

Quinn, R.E. (1988). *Beyond rational management.* San Francisco: Jossey-Bass.

Quinn, R.E., & Cameron, K.S. (1983). Organizational life cycles and shifting criteria of effectiveness: Some preliminary evidence. *Management Science, 9,* 33-51.

Quinn, R.E., & Rohrbaugh, J. (1981). A competing values approach to organizational effectiveness. *Public Productivity Review, 5,* 122-140.

Quinn, R.E., & Rohrbaugh, J. (1983). A spatial model of effectiveness criteria: Towards a competing values approach to organizational analysis. *Management Science, 29,* 363-377.

Radding, A. (1989, April 10). Spalding Sports moves cautiously in pitching laptops to sales reps. *Computerworld,* SR9-SR10.

Rahim, M.A. (1986). *Managing conflict in organizations.* New York: Praeger.

Rahim, M.A. (Ed.) (1989). *Managing conflict: An interdisciplinary approach.* New York: Praeger.

Rednova.com. (2004, June 14). Ueberroth named new USOC board chairman. Retrieved February 14, 2005, from www.rednova.com/news/display/?id=64644.

Reich, K. (1986). *Making it happen: Peter Ueberroth and the 1984 Olympics.* Santa Barbara, CA: Capra Press.

Reichert, J. (1988, January). Reichert bowls a perfect game: Keeping up with the Joneses. *Management Review, 77,* 15-17.

Reif, W.E., Newstrom, J.W., & Monczka, R.M. (1975). Exploding some myths about women managers. *California Management Review, 17,* 72-79.

Reimann, B.C. (1980). Organizational structure and technology in manufacturing: System versus workflow level perspectives. *Academy of Management Journal, 23,* 61-77.

Reimann, B.C., & Inzerilli, G. (1979). A comparative analysis of empirical research on technology and structure. *Journal of Management, 5,* 167-192.

Rhodes, L. (1982, August). The un-manager. *Inc.,* 34-43.

Ricciuti, M. (1991, September). A CASE for Client/Server. *Datamation,* 28-30.

Richards, B. (1986, December 1). Brunswick Corp. plans to acquire Ray Industries. *Wall Street Journal,* 15.

Richards, M.E., & Edberg-Olson, G. (1987, August). A manual for all seasons. *Athletic Business,* 38-40.

Ring, P.S., &Van de Ven, A.H. (1994). Developmental processes of cooperative interorganizational relationships. *Academy of Management Review, 19,* 90-118.

Robbins, S.P. (1974). *Managing organizational conflict: A nontraditional approach.* Englewood Cliffs, NJ: Prentice Hall.

Robbins, S.P. (1978). Conflict management and "conflict resolution" are not synonymous terms. *California Management Review, 21,* 67-75.

Robbins, S.P. (1990). *Organization theory: Structure, design and applications* (3rd ed.). Englewood Cliffs, NJ: Prentice Hall.

Robey, D. (1986). *Designing organizations* (2nd ed.). Homewood, IL: Irwin.

Roche, M. (1994). Mega-events and urban policy. *Annals of Tourism Research, 21,* 1-19.

Rohrbaugh, J. (1981). Operationalizing the competing values approach. *Public Productivity Review, 2,* 141-159.

Rose, D. (2000). Analysis of moving images. In M.W. Bauer & G. Gaskell (Eds.), *Qualitative researching with text, image and sound.* London, UK: Sage.

Rosener, J. (1990). Ways women lead. *Harvard Business Review, 68,* 119-125.

Rosentraub, M.S., & Swindell, D. (2002). Negotiating games: Cities, sports, and the winner's curse. *Journal of Sport Management, 16,* 18-35.

Ross, I. (1985, July 1). Irwin Jacobs lands a big one—finally. *Fortune,* 130-136.

Roth, T. (1987, February 6). Puma hopes superstar will help end U.S. slump, narrow gap with Adidas. *Wall Street Journal,* 24.

Rousseau, D.M. (1983). Technology in organizations: A constructive review and analytic framework. In S.E. Seashore, E.E. Lawler III, P.H. Mirvis, & C. Cammann (Eds.), *Assessing organizational change,* 229-255. New York: Wiley.

Rumelt, R.P. (1974). *Strategy, structure, and economic performance.* Boston: Harvard Graduate School of Business Administration.

Running Room Ltd. (2003). About us: History of the Running Room. Retrieved February 15, 2005, from www.runningroom.com/content/?id=124.

Rush, M.C., Thomas, J.C., & Lord, R.G. (1977). Implicit leadership theory: A potential threat to the internal validity of leaders' behavior questionnaires. *Organizational Behavior and Human Performance, 20,* 93-110.

Rushing, W.A. (1980). Organizational size, rules and surveillance. In J.A. Litterer (Ed.), *Organizations: Structure and behavior* (3rd ed.), 396-405. New York: Wiley.

Sack, A.L., & Kidd, B. (1985). The amateur athlete as employee. In A.T. Johnson & J.H. Frey (Eds.), *Government and sport: The public policy issues,* 41-61. Totowa, NJ: Rowman & Allenheld.

Sack, A.L., & Staurowsky, E.J. (1998). *College athletes for hire: The evolution and legacy of the NCAA's amateur myth.* Westport, CT: Praeger.

Sadler-Smith, E., & Shefy, E. (2004). The intuitive executive: Understanding and applying "gut feel" in decision-making. *Academy of Management Executive, 18,* 76-91.

Sage, G.H. (1982). The intercollegiate sport cartel and its consequences for athletes. In J. Frey (Ed.), *The governance of intercollegiate athletics,* 131-143. West Point, NY: Leisure Press.

Sandefur, G.D. (1983). Efficiency in social service organizations. *Administration & Society, 14,* 449-468.

Sands, J., & Gammons, P. (1993). *Coming apart at the seams.* New York: Macmillan.

San Francisco Giants. (2004, March 30). Press release: Ballpark becomes the first professional sports facility to provide universal Wi-Fi connectivity. Retrieved April 12, 2004, from http://sanfrancisco.giants.mlb.com/NASApp/mlb/sf/news/sf_press_release.jsp?ymd=20040330&content_id=674289&vkey=pr_sf&fext=.jsp.

Sarkar, M., Echambadi, R., & Harrison, J.S. (2001). Alliance entrepreneurship and firm market performance. *Strategic Management Journal, 22,* 701-711.

Sashkin, M. (1986). True vision in leadership. *Training and Development Journal, 40,* 58-61.

Sashkin, M. (1988). The visionary leader. In J.A. Conger & R.N. Kanungo (Eds.), *Charismatic leadership: The elusive factor in organizational effectiveness,* 122-160. San Francisco: Jossey-Bass.

Sathe, V. (1983). Implications of a corporate culture: A manager's guide to action. *Organizational Dynamics, 12,* 5-23.

Sathe, V. (1985). *Culture and related corporate realities.* Homewood, IL: Irwin.

Sator, D. (n.d.). Huffy bikes will remain Ohio-built. *Dayton Daily News and Journal Herald,* 1.

Schein, E.H. (1983). The role of the founder in creating organizational culture. *Organizational Dynamics, 12,* 13-28.

Schein, E.H. (1984). Coming to a new awareness of organizational culture. *Sloan Management Review, 25,* 3-16.

Schein, E.H. (1985). *Organizational culture and leadership.* San Francisco: Jossey-Bass.

Schein, E.H. (1992). *Organizational culture and leadership* (2nd ed.). San Francisco: Jossey-Bass.

Schendel, D.G., Patton, R., & Riggs, J. (1976). Corporate turnaround strategies: A study of profit decline and recovery. *Journal of General Management, 3,* 3-11.

Schinke, R.J., & da Costa, J.L. (2001). Understanding the development of major-games competitors' explanations and behaviors from a contextual viewpoint. *Athletic Insight: The Online Journal of Sport Psychology, 3(3):*1.

Schmidt, S.M., & Kochan, T.A. (1972). Conflict: Towards conceptual clarity. *Administrative Science Quarterly, 17,* 359-370.

Schneider, B. (1987). The people make the place. *Personnel Psychology, 40,* 437-453.

Schofield, J.A. (1983). Performance and attendance at professional team sports. *Journal of Sport Behavior, 6,* 196-206.

Scholz, C. (1987). Corporate culture and strategy: The problem of strategic fit. *Long Range Planning, 20,* 78-87.

Schriesheim, J.F. (1980). The social context of leader-subordinate relations: An investigation of the effects of group cohesiveness. *Journal of Applied Psychology, 65,* 183-194.

Schriesheim, J.F., & Kerr, S. (1977). Theories and measures of leadership: A critical appraisal. In J.G. Hunt and L.L. Larson (Eds.), *Leadership: The cutting edge,* 9-45. Carbondale: Southern Illinois University Press.

Schriesheim, J.F., Von Glinow, M.A., & Kerr, S. (1977). Professionals in bureaucracies: A structural alternative. In P.C. Nystrom & W.H. Starbuck (Eds.), *Prescriptive models of organizations,* 55-69. Amsterdam, Netherlands: North-Holland.

Schuler, R.S. (1976). Participation with supervisor and subordinate authoritarianism: A path-goal reconciliation. *Administrative Science Quarterly, 21,* 320-325.

Schumpeter, J. (1950). *Capitalism, socialism, and democracy.* New York: Harper & Row.

Schweitzer, M.E., Ordóñez, L., & Douma, B. (2004). Goal setting as a motivator of unethical behaviour. *Academy of Management Journal, 47,* 422-432.

Scott, W.R. (2000). *Organizations: Rational, natural and open systems* (5th ed.). Englewood Cliffs, NJ: Prentice Hall.

Scully, G.W. (1989). *The business of major league baseball.* Chicago: University of Chicago Press.

Seashore, S.E., Lawler, E.E., III, Mirvis, P.H, & Cammann, C. (Eds.) (1983). *Assessing organizational change.* New York: Wiley.

Seeger, J.A. (1984). Reversing the images of the BCG's growth share matrix. *Strategic Management Journal, 5,* 93-97.

Seijts, G.H., Latham, G.P., Tasa, K., & Latham, B.W. (2004). Goal setting and goal orientation: An integration of two different yet related literatures. *Academy of Management Journal, 47,* 227-239.

Senn, A.E. (1999). *Power, politics and the Olympic Games.* Champaign, IL: Human Kinetics.

Shaw, S., & Slack, T. (2002). "It's been like that for donkey's years": The construction of gender relations and the cultures of sports organizations. *Culture, Sport, Society, 5,* 86-106.

Shen, W., & Cannella, A.A., Jr. (2002). Power dynamics within top management and their impacts on CEO dismissal followed by inside succession. *Academy of Management Journal, 45,* 1195-1206.

Shetty, Y.K. (1978). Managerial power and organizational effectiveness: A contingency analysis. *Journal of Management Studies, 15,* 176-186.

Silk, M. (2001). Together we're one? The "place" of the nation in media representations of the 1998 Kuala Lumpur Commonwealth Games. *Sociology of Sport Journal, 18,* 277-301.

Silk, M.L., & Amis, J. (2000). Institutional pressures and the production of televised sport. *Journal of Sport Management, 4,* 267-292.

Silk, M.L., Slack, T., & Amis, J. (2000). Bread, butter and gravy: An institutional approach to televised sport production. *Culture, Sport, Society, 3,* 1-21.

Simmons, J. (1987). People managing themselves. *Journal for Quality and Participation, 10,* 14-19.

Simpson, V., & Jennings, A. (1992). *The lords of the rings.* Toronto: Stoddart.

Simon, H.A. (1945). *Administrative behavior.* New York: Macmillan.

Simon, H.A. (1960). *The new science of management decision.* Englewood Cliffs, NJ: Prentice Hall.

Simon, H.A. (1987). Making management decisions: The role of intuition and emotion. *Academy of Management Executive, 1,* 57-64.

Singer, A.W. (2004, September-October). An ethics officer of Olympian proportions: Pat Rodgers and the USOC scandal. Retrieved February 14, 2005, from www.singerpubs.com/ethikos/html/olympics.html.

Singh, J. (Ed.) (1990). *Organizational evolution: New directions.* Beverly Hills, CA: Sage.

Sinofile.net. (2004, November 8). David Beckham presents first ever Adidas lifestyle range. Retrieved February 15, 2005, from www.saiweng.net/Saiweng/swsite.nsf/Pr?readform&3146.

Skate Canada (2004). About Skate Canada: Who we are. Retrieved March 22, 2004, from www.skatecanada.ca/en/about_skate_canada/who_we_are/.

Skinner, J., Stewart, B., & Edwards, A. (2004). Governmentality and organizational change. *International Journal of Sport Management, 5,* 72-89.

Skinner, W. (1983). Wanted: Managers for the factory of the future. *Annals of the American Academy of Political and Social Science, 470,* 102-114.

Skow, J. (1985, December 2). Using the old Bean. *Sports Illustrated,* 84-88, 91-96.

Slack, T. (1985). The bureaucratization of a voluntary sport organization. *International Review for the Sociology of Sport, 20,* 145-166.

Slack, T. (1991a). Sport management: Some thoughts on future directions. *Journal of Sport Management, 5,* 95-99.

Slack, T. (1991b). The training of leisure managers. *Proceedings of the CESU Conference,* 63-83). Sheffield, UK: FISU.

Slack, T. (1993). Morgan and the metaphors: Implication for sport management. *Journal of Sport Management, 7,* 189-193.

Slack, T. (Ed.) (2004). *The commercialization of sport.* London: Routledge.

Slack, T., & Amis, J. (2004). "Money for nothing and your cheques for free?" A critical perspective on sport sponsorship. In T. Slack (Ed.), *The commercialisation of sport,* 269-286. London, UK: Frank Cass.

Slack, T., Bentz, L., & Wood, D. (1985). Planning for your organization's future. *CAHPER Journal, 51,* 13-17.

Slack, T., Berrett, T., & Mistry, K. (1994). Rational planning systems as a source of organizational conflict. *International Review for the Sociology of Sport, 29,* 317-328.

Slack, T., & Hinings, C.R. (Eds.) (1987a). *The organization and administration of sport.* London, ON: Sport Dynamics.

Slack, T., & Hinings, C.R. (1987b). Planning and organizational change: A conceptual framework for the analysis of amateur sport organizations. *Canadian Journal of Sport Sciences, 12,* 185-193.

Slack, T., & Hinings, C.R. (1992). Understanding change in national sport organizations: An integration of theoretical perspectives. *Journal of Sport Management, 6,* 114-132.

Slack, T., & Hinings, C.R. (1994). Institutional pressures and isomorphic change: An empirical test. *Organization Studies, 15,* 803-827.

Slack, T., Silk, M.L. & Fan, H. (2005). Cultural contradictions/contradicting culture: Transnational corporations and the penetration of the Chinese market? In M.L. Silk, D.L. Andrews, & C.L. Cole, (Eds.), *Sport and Corporate Nationalisms,* 253-274. Oxford, UK: Berg.

Slakter, A. (1988, Winter). Productive plant puts Huffy in the lead. *Mid America Outlook,* 8-9.

A slimmed-down Brunswick is proving Wall Street wrong (1984, May 28). *Business Week,* 90, 94, 98.

Smith, A. (1937). *An inquiry into the nature and causes of the wealth of nations.* New York: Modern Library. (Original work published in 1776.)

Smith, A.C.T., & Shilbury, D. (2004). Mapping cultural dimensions in Australian sporting organizations. *Sport Management Review, 7,* 133-165.

Smith Barney (1989, September 15). Consumer products research: Huffy Corporation (investment report).

Snow Valley Ski Club. (1992). *Snow Valley Ski Club.* Edmonton, Alberta: Author.

Snyder, C.J. (1990). The effects of leader behavior and organizational climate on intercollegiate coaches' job satisfaction. *Journal of Sport Management, 4,* 59-70.

Soucie, D. (1994). Effective managerial leadership in sport organizations. *Journal of Sport Management, 8,* 1-13.

Sparks, R. (1992). "Delivering the male": Sports, Canadian television, and the making of TSN. *Canadian Journal of Communication, 17,* 319-342.

Sperber, M. (1990). *College sports inc.* New York: Holt.

Sport Canada. (2002). The Canadian sport policy. The Policy development process. Retrieved April 9, 2004, from www.pch.gc.ca/progs/sc/pol/pcs-csp/2003/2_e.cfm.

Sport Canada. (2003, December 9). Canadian sport centres. Retrieved March 4, 2004, from www.pch.gc.ca/progs/sc/prog/cns-nsc/index_e.cfm.

Starbuck, W.H. (1976). Organizations and their environments. In M.D. Dunnette (Ed.), *Handbook of industrial and organizational psychology,* 1069-1123. Chicago: Rand McNally.

Starbuck, W.H. (1981). A trip to view the elephants and rattlesnakes in the garden of Aston. In A.H. Van de Ven & W.J. Joyce (Eds.), *Perspectives on organization design,* 167-198. New York: Wiley.

Statistics Canada CANSIM table 203-0001. (2004, January 27). Average household expenditures, provinces and territories. Retrieved March 22, 2004 from www.statcan.ca/english/Pgdb/famil16a.htm.

Staw, B.M., & Szwajkowski, E. (1975). The scarcity-munificence component of organizational environments and the commission of illegal acts. *Administrative Science Quarterly, 20,* 345-354.

Steers, R.M. (1975). Problems in the measurement of organizational effectiveness. *Administrative Science Quarterly, 20,* 546-558.

Steers, R.M. (1977). *Organizational effectiveness: A behavioral view.* Santa Monica, CA: Goodyear.

Stern, R.N. (1979). The development of an interorganizational control network: The case of intercollegiate athletics. *Administrative Science Quarterly, 24,* 242-266.

Stevenson, W.B., Pearce, J.L., & Porter, L.W. (1985). The concept of "coalition" in organization theory and research. *Academy of Management Review, 10,* 256-268.

Stinson, J.E., & Johnson, T.W. (1975). The path goal theory of leadership: A partial test and suggested refinement. *Academy of Management Journal, 18,* 242-252.

Stodghill, R. (1993, June 14). What makes Ryka run? Sheri Poe and her story. *Business Week,* 82, 84.

Stogdill, R.M. (1948). Personal factors associated with leadership: A survey of the literature. *Journal of Applied Psychology, 25,* 35-71.

Stogdill, R.M. (1974). *Handbook of leadership: A survey of theory and research.* New York: Free Press.

Stotlar, D.K. (2000). Vertical integration in sport. *Journal of Sport Management, 14,* 1-7.

Strasser, J.B., & Becklund, L. (1991). *Swoosh: The unauthorized story of Nike and the men who played there.* New York: Harcourt Brace Jovanovich.

Strauss, A.L. (1987). *Qualitative analysis for social scientists.* Cambridge, UK: Cambridge University Press.

Strauss, G. (1977). Managerial practices. In J.R. Hackman and J.L. Suttle (Eds.), *Improving life at work,* 279-363. Santa Monica, CA: Goodyear.

Strube, M.J., & Garcia, J.E. (1981). A meta-analytic investigation of Fiedler's contingency model of leadership effectiveness. *Psychological Bulletin, 90,* 307-321.

Stuart, T.E. (2000). Interorganizational alliances and the performance of firms: A study of growth and innovation rates in a high-technology industry. *Strategic Management Journal, 21,* 791-811.

Stubbs, D. (1989). Swimming Canada charts a new course for the future. *Champion, 13,* 20-23.

Stupak, B. (2004). House committee approves Stearns/Stupak Olympics bill. Retrieved May 15, 2005 from http://www.house.gov/stupak/press2003-2004/022504olympics.html.

Styskal, R.A. (1980). Power and commitment in organizations: A test of the participation thesis. *Social Forces, 58,* 925-943.

Swearingen, T.C., & Johnson, D.R. (1995). Visitors' responses to uniformed park employees. *Journal of Park and Recreation Administration, 13,* 73-85.

Symonds, W.G. (1989, June 19). Driving to become the IBM of golf. *Business Week,* 100-101.

Tarrant, M.A. (1996). Attending to past outdoor recreation experiences: Symptom reporting and changes in affect. *Journal of Leisure Research, 28,* 1-17.

Taylor, F.W. (1911). *The principles of scientific management.* New York: Harper & Row.

Taylor, J., & Bowers, D.G. (1972). *The survey of organizations: A machine scored standardized questionnaire instrument.* Ann Arbor: Institute for Social Research, University of Michigan.

Taylor, T. (2003). Diversity management in a multi-cultural society: An exploratory study of cultural diversity and team sport in Australia. *Annals of Leisure Research, 6,* 168-188.

Telander, R. (1989). *The hundred yard lie: The corruption of college football and what we can do about it.* New York: Fireside Press.

Terborg, J.R. (1977). Women in management: A research review. *Journal of Applied Psychology, 62,* 647-664.

Terkel, S. (1972). *Working.* New York: Avon.

Theodoraki, E.I. (2001). A conceptual framework for the study of structural configurations of organizing committees for the Olympic Games (OCOGs). *European Journal for Sport Management, 8,* 106-124.

Theodoraki, E., & Henry, I.P. (1994). Organizational structures and context in British national governing bodies of sport. *International Review for the Sociology of Sport, 29,* 243-263.

Thibault, L., Frisby, W., & Kikulis, L. (1999). Interorganizational linkages in the delivery of local leisure services in Canada: Responding to economic, political and social pressures. *Managing Leisure, 4,* 125-141.

Thibault, L., Frisby, W., & Kikulis, L.M. (2004). Partnerships between local government sport and leisure departments and the commercial sector: Changes, complexities, and consequences. In T. Slack (Ed.), *The commercialisation of sport,* 119-140. London, UK: Frank Cass.

Thibault, L., & Harvey, J. (1997). Fostering interorganizational linkages in the Canadian sport delivery system, *Journal of Sport Management, 11,* 45-68.

Thibault, L., Slack, T., & Hinings, C.R. (1991). Professionalism, structures and systems: The impact of professional staff on voluntary sport organizations. *International Review for the Sociology of Sport, 26,* 83-99.

Thibault, L., Slack, T., & Hinings, C.R. (1993). A framework for the analysis of strategy in nonprofit sport organizations. *Journal of Sport Management, 7,* 25-43.

Thibault, L., Slack, T., & Hinings, C.R. (1994). Strategic planning for nonprofit sport organizations: Empirical verification of a framework. *Journal of Sport Management, 8,* 218-233.

Thomas, K.W. (1992). Conflict and conflict management: Reflections and update. *Journal of Organizational Behavior, 13,* 265-274.

Thomas, K.W., & Schmidt, W.H. (1976). A survey of managerial interests with respect to conflict. *Academy of Management Journal, 19,* 315-318.

Thompson, J.D. (1960). Organizational management of conflict. *Administrative Science Quarterly, 4,* 389-409.

Thompson, J.D. (1967). *Organizations in action.* New York: McGraw-Hill.

Thompson, P., & McHugh, D. (1990). *Work organizations.* London, UK: Macmillan.

Thompson, V.A. (1961). *Modern organization.* New York: Knopf.

Tichy, N.M., & Devanna, M.A. (1986). *The transformational leader.* New York: Wiley.

Timelines. (mimeographed) distributed by Nike.

Tjosvold, D. (1988). Cooperative and competitive interdependence: Collaboration between departments to serve customers. *Group and Organization Studies, 13,* 274-289.

Tjosvold, D. (1991). *The conflict-positive organization.* Reading, MA: Addison-Wesley.

Tobin, D. (1989, March). Selling by serving. *Club Industry,* (n.p.).

Tolbert, P.S. (1985). Institutional environments and resource dependence: Sources of administrative structure in institutions of higher education. *Administrative Science Quarterly, 30,* 1-13.

Tolbert, P.S., & Zucker, L.G. (1983). Institutional sources of change in the formal structure of organizations: The diffusion of civil service reforms, 1880-1935. *Administrative Science Quarterly, 23,* 22-39.

Trail, G., & Chelladurai, P. (2002). Perceptions of intercollegiate athletic goals and processes: The influence of personal values. *Journal of Sport Management, 16,* 289-310.

Tran, M. (2003, July 2). Roman Abramovich. Retrieved February 16, 2005, from www.guardian.co.uk/russia/article/0,2763,989568,00.html.

Trice, H.M., & Beyer, J.M. (1984). Studying organizational cultures through rites and ceremonials. *Academy of Management Review, 9,* 653-669.

Trochim, W.M.K. (2001). *The research methods knowledge base* (2nd ed.). Cincinnati: Atomic Dog.

Tsang, T. (2000). Let me tell you a story: A narrative exploration of identity in high-performance sport. *Sociology of Sport Journal, 17,* 44-59.

Tung, R.L. (1979). Dimensions of organizational environments: An exploratory study of their impact on organization structure. *Academy of Management Journal, 22,* 672-693.

Tushman, M.L., Newman, W.H., & Romanelli, E. (1986). Convergence and upheaval: Managing the unsteady pace of organizational evolution. *California Management Review, 29,* 29-44.

Tushman, M.L., & Romanelli, E. (1985). Organizational evolution: A metamorphosis model of convergence and reorientation. In L.L. Cummings & B.M. Staw (Eds.), *Research in organizational behavior,* Vol. 7, 171-222. Greenwich, CT: JAI Press.

Tushman, M.L., & Scanlan, T.J. (1981a). Characteristics and external orientations of boundary spanning individuals: Part I. *Academy of Management Journal, 24,* 83-98.

Tushman, M.L., & Scanlan, T.J. (1981b). Boundary spanning individuals: Their role in information transfer and their antecedents: Part II. *Academy of Management Journal, 24,* 289-305.

Tushman, M.L., Virany, B., & Romanelli, E. (1986). Executive succession, strategic reorientations, and organizational evolution: The microcomputer industry as a case in point. *Technology in Society, 7,* 297-313.

Ulrich, D.R. (1987a). The population perspective: Review, critique, and relevance. *Human Relations, 40,* 137-152.

Ulrich, D.R. (1987b). The role of transformational leaders in changing sport arenas. In T. Slack & C.R. Hinings (Eds.), *The organization and administration of sport.* London, ON: Sport Dynamics.

Ulrich, D.R., & Barney, J. (1984). Perspectives in organizations: Resource dependence, efficiency, and population. *Academy of Management Review, 3,* 471-481.

Urwick, L.F. (1938). *Scientific principles and organization.* New York: American Management Association.

Van de Ven, A.H. (1976). A framework for organizational assessment. *Academy of Management Review, 1,* 64-78.

Van de Ven, A.H., & Delbecq, A.L. (1974). A task contingent model of work unit structure. *Administrative Science Quarterly, 19,* 183-197.

Van de Ven, A.H., Delbecq, A.L., & Koenig, R. (1976). Determinants of coordination modes within organizations. *American Sociological Review, 41,* 322-338.

Van de Ven, A.H., & Ferry, D. (1980). *Measuring and assessing organizations.* New York: Wiley.

VanderZwaag, H.J. (1984). *Sport management in schools and colleges.* New York: Wiley.

Van Fleet, D.D. (1991). *Contemporary management* (2nd ed.). Boston: Houghton Mifflin.

von Bertalanffy, L. (1950). The theory of open systems in physics and biology. *Science, 3,* 23-29.

von Bertalanffy, L. (1968). *General systems theory: Foundations, development, applications.* New York: Braziller.

Vroom, V.H., & Yetton, P.W. (1973). *Leadership and decision making.* Pittsburgh: University of Pittsburgh Press.

Waldrop, H. (1986, June). A Huffy rep cycles to glory. *Sales & Marketing Management,* 116-122.

Walsh, J.P., Weinberg, R.M., & Fairfield, M.L. (1987). The effects of gender on assessment center evaluations. *Journal of Occupational Psychology, 60,* 305-309.

Walton, E.J. (1981). The comparison of measures of organization structure. *Academy of Management Review, 6,* 155-160.

Walton, R.E., & Dutton, J.M. (1969). The management of interdepartmental conflict: A model and review. *Administrative Science Quarterly, 14,* 73-84.

Walton, R.E., Dutton, J.M., & Cafferty, T.P. (1969). Organizational context and interdepartmental conflict. *Administrative Science Quarterly, 14,* 522-542.

Walvin, J. (1975). *The people's game.* Newton Abbot, Devon, UK: Readers Union.

Warriner, C.K. (1965). The problems of organizational purpose. *Sociological Quarterly, 6,* 139-146.

Watman, M. (Ed.) (1979). *The ghost runner.* Kent, UK: Athletics Weekly.

Weber, M. (1947). *The theory of social and economic organizations* (trans., T. Parsons). New York: Free Press.

Weber, M. (1968). *Economy and society* (Vol. 1) (trans., G. Roth & C. Wittich). Berkeley: University of California Press. (Original work published in 1925.)

Weese, W.J. (1994). A leadership discussion with Dr. Bernard Bass. *Journal of Sport Management, 8,* 179-189.

Weese, W.J. (1995a). Leadership and organizational culture: An investigation of Big-Ten and Mid-American Conference campus recreation administrators. *Journal of Sport Management, 9,* 119-134.

Weese, W.J. (1995b). Leadership, organizational culture, and job satisfaction in Canadian YMCA organizations. *Journal of Sport Management, 9,* 182-193.

Weese, W.J. (1996). Do leadership and organizational culture really matter? *Journal of Sport Management, 10,* 197-206.

Weick, K.E. (1969). *The social psychology of organizing.* Reading, MA: Addison-Wesley.

Weiss, D., & Day, C. (2003). *The making of the Super Bowl: The inside story of the world's greatest sporting event.* New York: Contemporary Books.

Weiss, M.R., Barber, H., Sisley, B.L., & Ebbeck, V. (1991). Developing competence and confidence in novice female coaches: Perceptions of ability and affective experiences following a season-long coaching internship. *Journal of Sport and Exercise Psychology, 13,* 336-363.

Wentworth, D.K., & Anderson, L.R. (1984). Emergent leadership as a function of sex and task type. *Sex Roles, 11,* 513-523.

Westbeach Sports. (2003). Company: History. Retrieved April 1, 2004, from www.westbeach.com.

Westerbeek, H.M. (1999). A research classification model and some (marketing oriented) reasons for studying the culture of sport organizations. *European Journal for Sport Management, 6,* 69-87.

Westley, F.R., & Mintzberg, H. (1989). Profiles of strategic vision: Levesque and Iacocca. In J.A. Conger & R.N. Kanungo (Eds.), *Charismatic leadership: The elusive factor in organizational effectiveness,* 161-212. San Francisco: Jossey-Bass.

White, A., & Brackenridge, C. (1985). Who rules sport? Gender divisions in the power structure of British sport organizations from 1960. *International Review for the Sociology of Sport, 20,* 95-107.

Whitson, D., Harvey, J., & Lavoie, M. (2004). Government subsidisation of Canadian professional sport franchises: A risky business. In T. Slack (Ed.) *The commercialisation of sport.* 75-100. New York: Routledge.

Whitson, D.J., & Macintosh, D. (1989). Gender and power: Explanations of gender inequalities in Canadian national sport organizations. *International Review for the Sociology of Sport, 24,* 137-150.

Whitson, D., & Macintosh, D. (1993). Becoming a world-class city: Hallmark events and sport franchises in the growth strategies of western Canadian cities. *Sociology of Sport Journal, 10,* 221-240.

Whittington, R. (1993a). Social structures and strategic leadership. In J. Hendry and G. Johnson with J. Newton (Eds.), *Strategic thinking: Leadership and the management of change,* 181-197. Chichester, Sussex, UK: Wiley.

Whittington, R. (1993b). *What is strategy and does it matter?* London, UK: Routledge & Kegan Paul.

Wholey, D.R., & Brittain, J.W. (1986). Organizational ecology: Findings and implications. *Academy of Management Review, 11,* 513-533.

Wikipedia. (2005, February 15). Roman Abramovich. Retrieved February 17, 2005, from http://en.wikipedia.org/wiki/Roman_Abramovich.

Wilkins, A.L. (1983a). The culture audit: A tool for understanding organizations. *Organizational Dynamics, 12,* 24-38.

Wilkins, A.L. (1983b). Organizational stories as symbols which control the organization. In L.R. Pondy, P.J. Frost, G. Morgan, & T.C. Dandridge (Eds.), *Organizational symbolism,* 81-92. Greenwich, CT: JAI Press.

Williams, P. (1995). *Cardsharks: How Upper Deck turned a child's hobby into a high stakes, billion dollar business.* New York: Macmillan.

Williamson, R. (1993, December 6). Chairman of the boards. *Globe and Mail,* B6.

Willigan, G.E. (1992, July-August). High performance marketing: An interview with Nike's Phil Knight. *Harvard Business Review, 70,* 91-101.

Wilson, D.C., Butler, R.J., Cray, D., Hickson, D.J., & Mallory, G.R. (1986). Breaking the bounds of organization in strategic decision making. *Human Relations, 39,* 309-332.

Wilson, N. (1988). *The sports business.* London, UK: Piatkus.

Winter, S.G. (1987). Knowledge and competence as strategic assets. In D.J. Teece (Ed.), *The competitive challenge.* Cambridge, MA: Ballinger.

Withey, M., Daft, R.L., & Cooper, W.H. (1983). Measures of Perrow's work unit technology: An empirical assessment and a new scale. *Academy of Management Journal, 26,* 45-63.

Witt, C.E. (1989, March). Reebok's distribution on fast track. *Material Handling Engineering,* 43-45, 48.

Wolfe, R., Meenaghan, T., & O'Sullivan, P. (2002). The sports network: Insights into the shifting balance of power. *Journal of Business Research, 55,* 611-622.

Wolfe, R., Slack, T., & Rose-Hearn, T. (1993). Factors influencing the adoption and maintenance of Canadian, facility based worksite health promotion programs. *American Journal of Health Promotion, 7,* 189-198.

Wooden, J. (1972). *They call me coach.* Waco, TX: Word Books.

Woodward, J. (1958). *Management and technology.* London, UK: Her Majesty's Printing Office.

Woodward, J. (1965). *Industrial organization: Theory and practice.* London, UK: Oxford University Press.

World Skating Federation. (2003). Press Release: World Skating Federation files antitrust lawsuit against the International Skating Union and its president. Retrieved April 13, 2004 from http://www.worldskating.org/news/isu-complaint-12dec-2003.shtml.

World Skating Federation. (2005). Welcome! Retrieved May 17, 2005 from http://www.worldskating.org/.

Yarbrough, C.R. (2000). *And they call them games: An inside view of the 1996 Olympics.* Macon, GA: Mercer University Press.

Yammarino, F.J., & Bass, B.M. (1990). Transformational leadership and multiple levels of analysis. *Human Relations, 43,* 975-995.

Yavitz, B., & Newman, W.H. (1982). *Strategy in action: The execution, politics, and payoff of business planning.* New York: Free Press.

Yin, R.K. (2003). *Case study research: Design and methods* (3rd ed.). Thousand Oaks, CA: Sage.

Yuchtman, E., & Seashore, S.E. (1967). A systems resource approach to organizational effectiveness. *American Sociological Review, 32,* 891-903.

Yukl, G.A. (1981). *Leadership in organizations.* Englewood Cliffs, NJ: Prentice Hall.

Yukl, G.A. (1989). *Leadership in organizations* (2nd ed.). Englewood Cliffs, NJ: Prentice Hall.

Yukl, G.A. (1998). *Leadership in organizations* (4th ed.). Englewood Cliffs, NJ: Prentice Hall.

Zahary, L. (1991). *An analysis of the Running Room.* A paper submitted for the course PESS 350. Edmonton: University of Alberta.

Zald, M. (1962). Power balance and staff conflict in correctional institutions. *Administrative Science Quarterly, 7,* 22-49.

Zander, A. (1950, January). Resistance to change: Its analysis and prevention. *Advanced Management,* 9-10.

Zeigler, E.F. (1985). Understanding the immediate managerial environment in sport and physical education. *Quest, 37,* 166-175.

Zeigler, E.F. (1987). Sport management: Past, present and future. *Journal of Sport Management, 1,* 4-24.

Zeigler, E.F. (1989). Proposed creed and code of professional ethics for the North American Society for Sport Management. *Journal of Sport Management, 3,* 2-4.

Zeigler, E.F., & Bowie, G.W. (1983). *Management competency development in sport and physical education.* Philadelphia: Lea & Febiger.

Zimbalist, A. (1992). *Baseball and billions.* New York: Basic Books.

Zucker, L.G. (1983). Organizations as institutions. In S.B. Bacharach (Ed.), *Advances in organizational theory and research,* Vol. 2, 1-43. Greenwich, CT: JAI Press.

Zucker, L.G. (1987). Institutional theories of organization. *Annual Review of Sociology, 13,* 443-464.

Zucker, L.G. (1988). *Institutional patterns and organizations.* Cambridge, MA: Ballinger.

Zucker, L.G. (1989). Combining institutional theory and population ecology: No legitimacy, no history. *American Sociological Review, 54,* 542-545.

Ziegler, E.F. (1987). Sport management: Past, present and future. Journal of Sport Management, 1, 4-24.

Ziegler, E.F. (1989). Proposed creed and code of professional ethics for the North American Society for Sport Management. Journal of Sport Management, 3, 2-4.

Ziegler, E.F., & Bowie, G.W. (1983). Management competency development in sport and physical education. Philadelphia: Lea & Febiger.

Zimbalist, A. (1992). Baseball and billions. New York: Basic Books.

Zucker, L.G. (1987). Organizations as institutions. In S.B. Bacharach & N. DiTomaso (Eds.), Research in the sociology of organizations. Vol. 2. Greenwich, CT: JAI Press.

Yukhman, E., & Seashore, S.E. (1967). A systems resource approach to organizational effectiveness. American Sociological Review, 32, 891-903.

Yukl, G.A. (1981). Leadership in organizations. Englewood Cliffs, NJ: Prentice Hall.

Yukl, G.A. (1989). Leadership in organizations (2nd ed.). Englewood Cliffs, NJ: Prentice Hall.

Yukl, G.A. (1998). Leadership in organizations (4th ed.). Englewood Cliffs, NJ: Prentice Hall.

Zakrajsek, D. (1991). An analysis of the Running Room: A paper submitted for the course PEDS 550. Edmonton: University of Alberta.

Index

Note: The italicized *f* and *t* following page numbers refer to figures and tables, respectively.

About the Authors

Trevor Slack, PhD, is Canada research chair of the International Institute for the Study of Sport Management at the University of Alberta in Edmonton, Alberta. Slack is widely published in major sport and organization journals and has presented as a keynote speaker at conferences on sport organizations around the world. He has been editor of the *Journal of Sport Management* and the *European Journal of Sport Management,* and he has been on the editorial board of several journals related to sport management. Slack has been awarded numerous grants for social science and humanities research projects. In 1995 he presented the Zeigler Lecture, the leading lecture in sport management, and in 2001 he was awarded the Canada Research Chair for his work in sport management.

Milena M. Parent, PhD, is an assistant professor in the School of Human Kinetics at the University of Ottawa. Parent completed her PhD in the International Institute for the Study of Sport Management at the University of Alberta. She has experience as a national-level figure skater, a coach, and an administrator. Her doctoral research in sport management is on organizational theory and strategic management of large-scale sporting events. Parent is a coach for Skate Canada and a member of the Administrative Sciences Association of Canada, the Academy of Management, and the North American Society of Sport Management. She also serves as a reviewer for *European Sport Management Quarterly* and for the Administrative Sciences Association of Canada conference.